On the Translation of Native American Literatures

Edited by Brian Swann

Smithsonian Institution Press
Washington and London

Grateful acknowledgment is made for permission to reprint excerpts from the following copyrighted works: Larry Evers's and Felipe S. Molina's translation of "Deer Person" from *Yaqui Deer Songs/Maaso Bwikam: A Native American Poetry,* reprinted by permission of the University of Arizona Press, copyright © 1986 by the University of Arizona. W. S. Merwin's translation of "The Creation of the Moon," reprinted by permission of Georges Borchardt Inc. for the author, copyright © 1956, 1957, 1958, 1959, 1960, 1961, 1962, 1965, 1966, 1967, 1968 by W. S. Merwin. Jerome Rothenberg's "Gift Event II," reprinted by permission of Sterling Lord Literistic, Inc., copyright © 1972 by Jerome Rothenberg.

Editor: Gregory McNamee
Production Editor: Duke Johns
Designer: Janice Wheeler

Library of Congress Cataloging-in-Publication Data
On the translation of native American literatures / edited by Brian Swann.
 p. cm.
 Includes bibliographical references and index.
 ISBN 1-56098-074-5 (alk. paper).—ISBN 1-56098-099-0 (pbk. : alk. paper)
 1. Indian literature—Translations into English. 2. Indians—Languages—Translating into English.
I. Swann, Brian.
PM159.05 1992
428'.0297—dc20   91-10625

British Library Cataloguing-in-Publication Data is available

Manufactured in the United States of America
99 98 97 96 95 94 93 92   5 4 3 2 1
∞ The paper used in this publication meets the minimum requirements of the American National Standard for Permanence of Paper for Printed Library Materials Z39.48-1984

The turtle figure accompanying the title page and part titles is adapted from a birchbark transparency made by a Woodlands tribe member in the Historic Period, perhaps as a pattern for beading designs. The bird figure accompanying the chapter titles is carrying a speech symbol; this image is from eastern Missouri. The cover image is the interior decoration on a Tusayan food bowl.

Contents

Part Three:
Central and
South America

Contributors

Donald Bahr is professor of anthropology at Arizona State University. He has studied the Pima-Papago since the 1960s. Since publishing *Piman Shamanism and Staying Sickness* in 1974, he has concentrated on original studies of this people's mythology, songs, and oratory, and on comparing them with equivalent genres from neighboring tribes.

Judith Berman is Keeper of the American Section of the University Museum of Archaeology and Anthropology at the University of Pennsylvania. She is now completing her doctoral dissertation, "The Seals' Sleeping Place: Method and Theory in the Interpretation of Boas's Kwakw'ala Texts."

John Bierhorst is the translator of *Cantares Mexicanos* and the author of a Nahuatl-English dictionary. Among his most recent books are *The Mythology of North America*, *The Mythology of South America*, and *The Mythology of Mexico and Central America*. His bilingual edition of the sixteenth-century Nahuatl manuscript *Codex Chimalpopoca* was published in 1992.

Louise M. Burkhart is assistant professor of anthropology at the State University of New York at Albany. Her book *The Slippery Earth: Nahua-Christian Moral Dialogue in Sixteenth-Century Mexico* was issued in 1989. She has also published several articles on colonial Nahuatl catechistic and devotional literature. She is now translating and analyzing the earliest known extant dramatic script from the Americas, a Nahuatl interpretation of a Spanish Passion play.

Allan F. Burns is associate professor of anthropology, linguistics, and Latin American studies at the University of Florida. He began working on the translation of Yucatec Maya oral literature in 1970. Today he continues to spend several months of the year in the Yucatán conducting his research. In addition, he has been working with Guatemalan Maya refugees who have settled in Florida, and has produced documentary videos on the subject.

William M. Clements teaches in the Department of English, Philosophy, and Languages at Arkansas State University. His publications on Native American literature include *Native American Folklore, 1879–1979: An Annotated Bibliography* (with Frances M. Malpezzi) and *Native American Folklore in Nineteenth-Century Periodicals,* as well as essays in the *Journal of American Folklore, MELUS,* and *Western American Literature.*

Willard Gingerich is associate dean of the Graduate School of Arts and Sciences at St. John's University. He teaches American literature and has published critical studies and translations of Aztec and other Native American literatures.

Nancy H. Hornberger is associate professor in the Graduate School of Education at the University of Pennsylvania. Her work has focused on Quechua linguistics and sociolinguistics. She is the author of *Trilingual Dictionary: Quechua of Cusco, Spanish, English* (with Esteban Hornberger), *Bilingual Education and Language Maintenance: A Southern Peruvian Quechua Case* and a special issue of the *International Journal of the Sociology of Language* called "Bilingual Education and Language Planning in Indigenous Latin America."

Dell Hymes is professor of anthropology and English at the University of Virginia and a fellow (1990–1992) of the Commonwealth Center for Literary and Cultural Change. Among the most recent of his many books are *"In Vain I Tried to Tell You": Essays in Native American Ethnopoetics, Essays in the History of Linguistic Anthropology,* and *Vers la compétence de communication.* He is a regular contributor of translations of Native American materials to the literary journal *Calapooya Collage.*

M. Dale Kinkade is professor of linguistics at the University of British Columbia. He has published numerous articles on Salishan narratives and languages, and he is currently working on comparative Salishan studies, dictionaries of Upper Chehalis and Cowlitz, grammatical studies of various Salishan languages, and analyses of Upper Chehalis and Columbian Salish texts.

Arnold Krupat has coedited (with Brian Swann) *Recovering the Word: Essays on Native American Literature* and *I Tell You Now: Autobiographical Essays by Native American Writers,* and he is currently editing a volume called *Indian Lives: An Anthology of Native American Autobiographies*. He is the author of *For Those Who Come After: A Study of Native American Autobiography, The Voice in the Margin: Native American Literature and the Canon,* and the forthcoming *Ethnocriticism: Ethnography, History, Literature.* He teaches at Sarah Lawrence College.

Toby C. S. Langen, a medievalist whose interest in Lushootseed oral narrative arose from a need to understand the orality of medieval literature, has published articles on Old English saints' lives, Old Icelandic family sagas, and contemporary Native American literature. She is currently working on a study of the repertoire of the Tulalip narrative artist Martha Lamont. She teaches in the Department of English at Western Washington University.

Miguel León-Portilla, historian and cultural anthropologist, is professor emeritus at the National University of Mexico. His publications include *The Broken Spears: An Aztec Account of the Conquest of Mexico, Aztec Thought and Culture, Native Mesoamerican Spirituality,* and *Time and Reality in the Thought of the Maya,* as well as many articles in Mexican, European, and American scholarly journals. Since 1987 he has represented Mexico as ambassador to UNESCO.

William K. Powers is professor of anthropology and director of the Graduate Certificate Program in North American Indian Studies at Rutgers University. He has conducted research among the Oglala at Pine Ridge, South Dakota, and other American Indian communities since 1948. His publications include *Oglala Religion, Yuwipi: Vision and Experience in Oglala Ritual, Sacred Language: The Nature of Supernatural Discourse in Lakota, Beyond the Vision: Essays in American Indian Culture,* and *War Dance: Essays on Plains Indian Musical Performance.*

Julian Rice is professor of English at Florida Atlantic University. He has published many articles on the Lakota oral tradition and is the author of *Lakota Storytelling: Black Elk, Ella Deloria, and Frank Fools Crow* and *Black Elk's Story: Distinguishing Its Lakota Purpose.*

Jerome Rothenberg is the author of over forty books of poetry and editor of seven anthologies of experimental and traditional poetry and performance, among them *Technicians of the Sacred, Shaking the Pumpkin, America a Prophecy,* and *Symposium of the Whole.* A principal founder and promoter of ethnopoetics, he was awarded the 1982

American Book Award of the Before Columbus Foundation for his book of selected essays, *Pre-Faces*. He is professor of visual arts and literature at the University of California at San Diego.

Kay Sammons is a graduate student of linguistic anthropology at the University of Texas at Austin. She has worked with Sierra Populuca speakers in Veracruz, Mexico, since 1987, producing a master's thesis, "The Sierra Populuca Story of Homshuk: Functions of Performance." Her current research involves sociolinguistic and ethnobotanical aspects of Native healing techniques.

David Leedom Shaul is on the faculty of Indiana University, Fort Wayne, and is associated with the Bureau of Applied Research in Anthropology at the University of Arizona. He has worked with Hopi linguistics and literature for several years, and is currently preparing a reference grammar of Hopi, a study of Hopi narrative art, and an anthology of early Hopi music.

Joel Sherzer is professor of anthropology and linguistics at the University of Texas at Austin. Most of his research has dealt with the language and culture of the Kuna Indians of Panama. His books include *An Areal-Typological Study of American Indian Languages North of Mexico, Kuna Ways of Speaking: An Ethnographic Perspective,* and *Verbal Art in San Blas: Kuna Culture Through Its Discourse.* He has edited, with Greg Urban, *Native South American Discourse* and, with Anthony Woodbury, *Native American Discourse: Poetics and Rhetoric.*

Brian Swann is professor of English at The Cooper Union in New York. He is the author of a number of books of poetry and fiction as well as the translator of collections of poetry. His most recent publications are *The Collected Poems of Primo Levi* (with Ruth Feldman), *The Plot of the Mice* (fiction), and *The Middle of the Journey* (poetry). He also edited *Smoothing the Ground: Essays on Native American Oral Literature* and, with Arnold Krupat, *I Tell You Now: Autobiographical Essays by Native American Writers* and *Recovering the Word: Essays on Native American Literature.*

Dennis Tedlock is James H. McNulty Professor of English at the State University of New York at Buffalo. His books are *Finding the Center: Narrative Poetry of the Zuni Indians, Teachings from the American Earth: Indian Religion and Philosophy* (with Barbara Tedlock), *The Spoken Word and the Work of Interpretation, Popol Vuh: The Mayan Book of the Dawn of Life,* and *Days from a Dream Almanac.* He received the PEN Translation Prize in Poetry for *Popol Vuh.*

Nile Robert Thompson is a specialist on Salishan language, culture, and society. He has published numerous articles on Coast Salish art, with particular attention to basketry. He has also done extensive research on Coast Salish ethnobiology and reservation settlement in the nineteenth century. In 1988–89 he helped the Steilacoom Tribe establish its own museum. He is currently the executive director of the Puget Sound Railways Historical Association in Snoqualmie, Washington.

Peter Whiteley teaches anthropology at Sarah Lawrence College. He has conducted field research at Hopi since 1980, beginning with a fourteen-month residence at the village of Bacavi. His books *Deliberate Acts: Changing Hopi Culture Through the Oraibi Split* and *Bacavi: Journey to Reed Springs* appeared in 1988.

Paul G. Zolbrod is the author of *Dine bahane': The Navajo Creation Story* and has written numerous essays on the poetry of Athabascan, Uto-Aztecan, and Algonquin peoples. He has also written extensively about classical, medieval, and Renaissance literature. He is Frederick F. Seeley Professor of English at Allegheny College.

Introduction

Brian Swann

The fact that Indians were human took some time to sink in. The fact that their languages had value took longer. For every Abbé Clavigero who remarked that it was not easy to find a language "so fit for metaphysical subjects, and so abounding in abstract terms, as the Mexican," or a Du Ponceau who professed "astonishment at the copiousness and admirable structure of the American languages," there was more than one De Forest, ignorant of any native language, who came to the opposite conclusion, and for whom the idea of a literature was inherently ludicrous since the languages themselves were primitive: "It is evident from the enormous length of many of the words, sometimes occupying a whole line, that there was something about the structure of these languages which made them cumbersome and difficult to manage" (De Forest 1851:42–43).

The fact that Indians had a literature of great significance took longest to be acknowledged. Indian songs were regarded as the howls of wild beasts and the stories as, at best, curiosities. Some of the great books of the Toltec and Mayans were sent to Europe. The rest, the vast majority, were burnt since they challenged the true faith. It is sobering to learn that the unique copy of the *Popol Vuh* was made by the Dominican friar Francisco

Ximénez in the seventeenth century. It was not until well into the nineteenth century that the languages and literature of the Americas began to be taken seriously by the conquerors, and not until this century that their complexity and richness began to be fully realized.

If statements made by seventeenth-century informants are reliable, the "Hymn of Teotihuacan" is the oldest surviving poetic text of the Americas. It appears twice in the Manuscripts of Sahagún, both times attributed to the ancient Teotihuacans whose city dominated northern Mesoamerica between A.D. 400 and 750. As Willard Gingerich has pointed out (1978:80), the poem is as old or older than Caedmon's Hymn, the oldest known poem in English, which Bede dates before A.D. 680. The earliest transcription of a full native language text is *Unos anales históricos de la nación mexicana* (also known as *Anales de Tlatelolco*), a Nahuatl manuscript from Mexico City, and probably written by a native. It is largely history, with a few song texts.

The oldest attempt to record songs that I have been able to find in North America was made by Marc Lescarbot in New France (Acadia) between 1606 and 1607. He noted down some Micmac songs ("to the praise of the Devil"), words and music, the latter in a tonic system. Here is one example: "haloet ho ho hé he ha ha haloet ho ho hé," which was repeated several times. "The tune," he says, "is in my . . . table-book in these notes: re fa sol sol re sol sol fa fa re re sol sol fa fa." Unfortunately, he does not provide a translation, which might be just as well since he seems to suspect that what he is hearing is a kind of debased Hebrew. Interestingly, he notes that one "John de Leri" had transcribed some Brazilian songs, and quotes one, with a paraphrase by de Leri himself (1929:175). And this Jean de Léri's *Histoire d'un Voyage Fait en la Terre du Brésil* (1578) is behind the songs Montaigne paraphrased in his essay "On Cannibals," published in 1580, where he gives us "a song made by a prisoner," and then tells us, in Florio's translation, "I have another amorous canzonet, which beginneth in this sence: Adder stay, stay good adder, that my sister may by the patterne of thy partie-coloured coat drawe the fashion and worke of a rich lace, for me to give unto my love; so maye thy beautie, thy nimbleness or disposition be ever preferred before all other serpents." Montaigne points out that "the first couplet is the burthen of the song," and that it has "no barbarisms," being "altogether Anacreontike" (1923:228).[1]

The oldest text surviving from what is now the United States is in William Strachey's *The History of Travaile into Virginia Britannia,* published in 1612. Strachey collected the song during his stay as the Virginia colony's first secretary, from May 23, 1610, to October 1611. He outlines a vigorous literary tradition among the Powhatans: "They have their *errotica carmina,* which they will sing tunable enough." They also made "a kind of angry song" in "homely rhymes, which concludeth with a king of petition onto their okeus [god or gods], and to all the host of their idols, to plague the Tassantasses (for so they call us) and their posterities." Unfortunately, Strachey gives no examples of love or curse poems. He does, however, give an example (78–79) of a "scornful song," commemorating the time when the Powhatans killed and captured some of the English. "That song goeth thus":

1. Matanerew shashashewaw erawango pechecoma
   Whe Tassantassa inoshashawyehockan pocosack.
   Whe whe, yah haha nehe wittowa, wittowa.

2. Matanerew shashashewaw erawango pechecoma
   Capt. Newport inoshashaw neir mhoc natian matassan
   Whe whe, etc.

3. Matanerew shashashewaw erawango pechecoma
   Tom. Newport inoshashaw neir inhoc natian moncock:
   Whe whe, etc.

4. Matanerew shashashewaw erawango pechecoma
   Pochin Simon moshashaw ningon natian monahack,
   Whe whe, etc.

Strachey provides a paraphrase of the meaning in English, but he doesn't seem too sure of himself since he eschews the indicative. The song, he says, "Maye signified how they killed us for all our poccasacks, that is our guns," and so on.

As transcribed, the song falls into four "verses." The first line of each verse is a refrain (which, conveniently ignoring the fact that we do not know where the stresses fell, one is tempted to read as curiously trochaic dimeter-like, anticipating *Hiawatha!*). There is another "true" refrain in the lines "Whe, whe" etc., and there seems to be something like rhyme (Strachey noted that the "angry songs" had "homely rhymes") with "pocosack"/"moncock"/"monahack," as well as repetition with variation, as in the second lines. But it would be dangerous to push this analysis too far. For one thing, while Strachey is invaluable for us—his Powhatan material is the earliest recorded in quantity of any that has survived in any Algonquian language—his handwriting presents all sorts of problems, and there are, as Frank T. Siebert notes, many mistranslations in his work "from minor deviations to unequivocal howlers" (1975:292).

The earliest "translation" of an Indian song is from the Cherokee. It occurs in *The Memoirs of Lieut. Henry Timberlake,* published in London in 1765, a book which Robert Southey made extensive use of in the preparation of his epic poem *Madoc,* (1805). Timberlake came to know the Cherokees quite well, and he includes the following translation of a war song in his book (1927:81–82). He chose the war song as an example of the Cherokee "sort of loose poetry" rather than a love song because many of the latter "contain no more than the young man loves the young woman, and will be uneasy, according to their own expression, if he does not obtain her." The war song, he notes, will be given without "the expletive syllables, merely introduced for their music, and not the sense, just like the toldederols of many old English songs."

A Translation of the War-Song

Caw waw noo dee, & C.

Where'er the earth's enlighten'd by the sun,
Moon shines by night, grass grows, or waters run,

Be't known that we are going like men, afar,
In hostile fields to wage destructive war;
Like men we go, to meet our country's foes,
Who, woman-like, shall fly our dreaded blows;
Yes, as a woman, who beholds a snake,
In gaudy horror, glisten thro' the brake,
Starts trembling back, and stares with wild surprize,
Or pale thro' fear, unconscious, panting, flies.
Just so these foes, more tim'rous than the hind,
Shall leave their arms and only cloaths behind;
Pinch'd by east blast, by ev'ry thicket torn,
Run back to their own nation, now its scorn:
Or in the winter, when the barren wood
Denies their gnawing entrails nature's food,
Let them sit down, from friends and country far,
And wish, with tears, they ne'er had come to war.

We'll leave our clubs, dew'd with their country show'rs,
And, if they dare to bring them back to our's,
Their painted scalps shall be a step to fame,
And grace our own and glorious country's name.
Or if we warriors spare the yielding foe,
Torments at home the wretch must undergo.

But when we go, who knows which shall return,
When growing dangers rise with each new morn;
Farewel, ye little ones, yet tender wives,
For you alone we would conserve our lives!
But cease to mourn, 'tis unavailing pain,
If not fore-doom'd, we soon shall meet again.
But, O ye friends! in case your comrades fall,
Think that on you our deaths for vengeance call;
With uprais'd tommahawkes pursue our blood,
And stain, with hostile streams, the conscious wood,
That pointing enemies may never tell
The boasted place where we, their victims, fell.

Samuel Cole Williams, editor of the 1927 edition, notes that Timberlake, who did not speak Cherokee, could only have learned the substance of the song through an interpreter. Clearly, the translation into heroic couples, the most popular mode of his day, is in the mode of "imitation" rather than close or "literal" translation. We have no indication of the original form and content.

If translation itself is problematic, the translation of Native American literatures is twice so. To questions of paraphrasis and metaphrasis, parataxis and syntactis, to epistemological, aesthetic, and theoretical considerations, are added problems of transcription and recording, as well as moral and political dimensions. In a subversively creative way the question of whether or how we should resist unifying theories and practices is added. The whole study of Native American literature, moreover, is fraught with ironies, lives with ironies, starting with those three words themselves. Students and scholars need constantly to be aware of their own "cultural subjectivity," and of what A. Irving Hallowell has called "categorical abstraction," even when it phrases itself as openness, when it calls for cherishing "otherness"—part of a Western essentializing need (1975:144).

As its best, Native American translation has no desire to ignore such ironies, even if it could, but instead floats itself on them. The desire is not for appropriation but some sort of participation; a touch of an elusive essence. The fact that we no longer believe we can *possess* is what affords value. So, even at its most "definitive," any translation of a Native American text will always partake of the unknowable. Given the history of this hemisphere, to settle for the dignity of mystery is far preferable to any claims of definitiveness. The appropriation can lead to many undesirable results, even to the invention, or reinvention, of Native American tradition, a tradition which is fed back to the native community, and then out again, thus inflicting multiple damage. As William Powers has noted, a good deal "of what passes today for Indian culture and religion has been fabricated by the white man, or the Indians who have been trained in the white man's schools" (1990:52).

Which brings us to the question: Who benefits by translation, or essays such as those collected here? In a session at the American Anthropological Association meetings in December 1989 devoted to Vine Deloria's *Custer Died for Your Sins,* Dell Hymes described the state of native culture in the Northwest, and brought up the question of reparation. Information for those native people who desire to know about their own heritage is seldom available, or if it is available, it is not accessible geographically or is in a form available only to specialists. Hymes noted that we have here "an example of *alienation* in the Marxist sense." A community's labor has become an external alien object.

I would like to think that this collection of essays, at least in part, is a small component of the (ironic) process of returning a community's labor to it.[2] I say "part" because there are many other processes under way, from, in this country, the Federal Cylinder Project program, transcribing Edisonphone wax cylinders and aluminum discs onto tape, to the fine work being done at the Alaska Native Language Center. The work of retrieval and translation—or retranslation; see, in this collection, the two essays on Boas, one by Judith Berman, the other by M. Dale Kinkade, as well as Dennis Tedlock's now classic "On the Translation of Style in Oral Literature" (1983:31–61)—proceeds impressively, from languages very much alive, to those extinct or on the verge of extinction.[3] I hope that we will all benefit from this collection. Important and prophetic voices have been raised in the past, from Henry David Thoreau and Mary Austin to D. H. Lawrence and William Carlos Williams, explaining why knowledge of Native American history and culture is vital. But the word has still not gone out far and wide enough.

A few years ago I expressed a desire for a volume of essays devoted to the question of translation, and hoped someone would undertake the task (Krupat 1989:137). For, no matter how we attempt to finesse the problem, the question of translation remains paramount. All other topics are subsumed in it. After waiting for that someone, impatient, I set about the task myself.

The approaches of the essayists here are varied, but each one has reached out from a specific discipline, whether anthropology, linguistics, folklore, or English, to seek common ground where the humanities and social sciences meet in polyphony. There is something of a family feel to this volume, since there are three scholarly generations present. For instance, Joel Sherzer was Dell Hymes's student, and Kate Sammons was Joel Sherzer's!

I set out to include essays from and on all the Americas, for there is only one native America, one thought, one spirit, from Tahuantisuyo and points south, to Hochelaga and points north, and all points in between. And there is a unity to the literatures, from the "literary" tradition of the Aztec Brotherhood's great court poetry and other Central and South American "high art" to the four-line chants of the Midewiwin or the complex Navajo Chantways.

When it came to arranging this wealth of material, its range and styles and approaches, after various attempts I fell back on my original plan: An introductory section, a largely historical overview of Native American translation; then Section Two, the largest section, devoted to North America, essays grouped by language and geography; and finally Section Three on Central and South America, replicating the arrangement of Section Two. If we count my brief introduction, we come up with a highly desirable grouping into four.

In editing, I constantly had in mind the fact that I intended this volume to be a teaching tool. In the letters I sent out to hundreds of people, organizations, and journals in the Americas and in Europe, I invited essays "on any aspect of the subject [translation] which interests you," and noted that "while the book is not intended primarily for the general reader, I would prefer the essays not to be esoteric or overly 'specialized.' I would be happy if, in addition to scholars in Native American Studies and related fields, college teachers at an upper undergraduate and graduate level were able to use this book." This came as a relief to some. One contributor wrote, "I had somehow lost sight of just how technical some of that material is! It will be a joy to rewrite for a more general audience."

I would like to thank my friend Arnold Krupat for his encouragement, expert help, and generosity, and take this opportunity to note that he and I will be series editors for the semiannual Smithsonian Series of Studies on Native American Literatures, the first volume of which will be edited by Krupat and devoted to "new voices in criticism." I am also grateful to Donald Bahr, Willard Gingerich, Dell Hymes, Julian Rice, Alfonso Ortiz, and Joel Sherzer, and would like to thank the officers and editors of a number of societies and journals, particularly the following: the Society for the Study of Indigenous Languages of Americas; the Latin American Indian Literatures Association; SAIL (Studies in American Indian Literatures); The Journal of Indigenous Studies (Canada); and Canadian Ethnic Studies. Thanks also to the many people who sent me suggestions, and to Daphne Samuel for expert secretarial assistance. Above all, I am grateful to all the contributors to this volume, and to Daniel Goodwin for enthusiastically taking it on.

All royalties from the sale of this book are being donated to the American Indian College Fund.

Notes

1. Jacob Zeitlin has pointed out that Joseph Warton adapted this "amorous canzonet" and published it as "An American Love Ode" in *Poems on Several Occasions,* by Thomas Warton (the Elder) in 1747 (two years before, Dr. Johnson, editing *The Gentleman's Magazine,* had published the first Inuit-language poem with translation, "Greenland Ode," celebrating the birthday of King Christian of Denmark):

> Stay, stay, thou lovely fearful snake,
> Nor hide thee in yon darksome brake:
> But let me oft thy charms review,
> Thy glittering scales, and golden hue;
> From these a chaplet shall be wove,
> To grace the youth I dearest love.
>
> Then ages hence, when thou no more
> Shalt creep along the sunny shore,
> Thy copied beauties shall be seen;
> The red and azure mixed with green,
> In mimic folds shalt thou display—
> Stay, lovely, fearful adder, stay.

See *The Essays of Michel de Montaigne,* translated and edited by Jacob Zeitlin, volume 1 (New York, Alfred A. Knopf, 1934), page 378.

2. I am acutely aware of what Judith Berman, in a letter to me, calls "the very problematic relationship between the academics who study this material and become its interpreters to American society at large, and the people (the Indians) who live it." This is a point she elaborates in a review of *Recovering the Word* in *Journal of American Folklore* and kindly sent to me in advance. "The meanings and uses of Native American literature," she writes, "can be very different to the native Americans who make it than to the scholars who study it," and "the question must be raised whether we really want to confine the privilege of explaining native culture to those who have mastered Western academic discourse. If we are really 'open,' surely other kinds of discourse are also valid?" This is one of the vital issues we hope to face up to more fully in the Smithsonian Series of Studies on Native American Literatures. On a related issue, I regret not having any Native American scholars represented here. I contacted all I knew, but no one had any work appropriate for this volume.

3. Reevaluation of recent translations generally regarded as exemplary also moves forward. See, for example, the critique of Howard Norman's work by John D. Nichols ("*The Wishing Bone Cycle:* A Cree 'Ossian'?"), and by Robert Brightman ("Tricksters and Ethnopoetics"), both in *International Journal of American Linguistics,* vol. 55, no. 2 (April 1989), 155–203. I am grateful to James Ruppert and Arnold Krupat for this reference.

References

De Forest, John W. 1851. *History of the Indians of Connecticut.* Hartford, Conn.: Hamersley.

Gingerich, Willard. 1978. Notes on Translations. *Rapport* 10 (Fall).

Hallowell, A. Irving. 1975. Ojibwa Ontology, Behavior, and World View. In *Teachings from the American Earth*, Dennis and Barbara Tedlock, eds. New York: Liveright.

Krupat, Arnold, and Brian Swann. 1989. Of Anthologies, Translation, and Theories: A Self-Interview. *North Dakota Quarterly* 57 (2): 137–47.

Lescarbot, Marc. 1929. *Nova Francia: A Description*, trans. P. Erondelle. London: Routledge and Sons.

Montaigne, Michel Eyquem de. 1923. *The Essays of Michael, Lord of Montaigne* vol. 1, trans. John Florio. New York: E. P. Dutton.

Powers, William. 1990. When Black Elk Speaks, Everybody Listens. *Social Text* no. 2.

Siebert, Frank T. 1975. Resurrecting Virginian Algonquian from the Dead. In *Studies in Southeastern Indian Languages*, James M. Crawford, ed. Athens: University of Georgia Press.

Strachey, William. 1849. *The History of Travaile into Virginia Britannia*. R. H. Major, ed., for the Hakluyt Society. London.

Tedlock, Dennis. 1983. *The Spoken Word and the Work of Interpretation*. Philadelphia: University of Pennsylvania Press.

Timberlake, Henry. 1927. *The Memoirs of Lieut. Henry Timberlake*, Samuel Cole Williams, ed. Johnson City, Tennessee: The Wantagh Press.

Part One:
General

On the Translation of Native American Song and Story: A Theorized History

Arnold Krupat

Any history of translations from the various Native American languages into English—a history also necessarily of transcription, of the transformation of oral literatures into textual literatures—must have some theoretical principle guiding its selection of examples. The most obvious principle (usually thought of by those who actually seek to apply it as the disinterested avoidance of aprioristic principle) is, of course, the principle of non-selectivity, or total inclusiveness: with world enough and time, one *might* produce the history of translations from Native languages by attempting to collect *every* translation extant. While such an encyclopedic project for most other subjects would, today, painfully recall the deluded efforts of George Eliot's Casaubon or Flaubert's Bouvard and Pecuchet, for our particular subject, it might, in point of fact, be almost manageable, the "facts" of the case, unfortunately, being so many fewer. But even were such a history to be produced—and it would, doubtless, be a valuable resource—it would still leave open the question, What to make of all these examples of various kinds?

My own attempt to sketch the history of translations of Native American literary expression will not even gesture in the direction of exhaustiveness. Instead, as a guiding principle for the examination of translations of Native American literatures from their earliest appearance until the present (and I don't pretend to know all of these), but also, potentially, for the examination as well of translations which do not as yet exist, I will suggest that all translations must situate themselves in relation to the principles of Identity and Difference (Sameness and Otherness, Likeness and Unlikeness, Ours and Theirs)—which principles, in any given translation, manifest themselves in terms of *accessibility* and *authenticity*, as these situate the particular translation in the disciplinary domain of art or of (social) science.

This is to say that Euroamericans, to transcribe and translate Native American verbal expression, must assume that it is in some degree *like* Euroamerican ("Western") literary expression (otherwise it would not be recognizable to "us" *as* literary art) but also that it is in some degree *unlike* Euroamerican ("Western") literary expression (otherwise it would not take the obvious into account, that it is transmitted orally, in non-Indo-European languages, frequently in ritual or ceremonial performances, and so on). Western divisions of disciplinary labor have traditionally been such that the poets and novelists or literary critics are usually in charge of that which is *like* the literature we know, while the anthropologists and linguists have usually been in charge of that which is *unlike* what we know. In every case, it is my claim, all English translations from Native language performances cannot help but place themselves in relation to Western conceptions of art (literature) or of (social) science as they inevitably privilege *either* the Sameness of Native American verbal expression in forms aspiring to what is accessibly recognizable as literary, *or* its Difference, in forms committed to scientific authenticity and accuracy.

As James Clifford has written of museum shows and collections of tribal art and artifacts, the decision to call certain "tribal" productions works of art or to call them artifacts is to place them in the context of esthetics or of ethnography, emphasizing individual "genius" and its presumed capacity to transcend culture-specific determinations, or emphasizing exactly the force of cultural codes. But "Science," Clifford writes, "can be aestheticized, art made anthropological" (203), and something like this process has taken place in the history of translation from Native American literatures. When the literary people estheticize science, accuracy and authenticity are inevitably lost in some degree; when the anthropologists scientize art, its charm, force, beauty are inevitably lost in some degree.

What must be noted, however, is that there is an imbalance here so far as the relation to original performances is concerned. Euroamerican social scientists have regularly been able to operate apart from the concerns of Euroamerican poets or literary critics; but the literary people, whether they were willing to admit it or not, have only rarely been able to work independently of the scientists. Simply put, the social scientists have been able to work directly with Native performers, or at least with Native language transcriptions, without worrying too much about any reductiveness in their procedures, for all that these confront highly complex and subtle esthetic acts. The poets and the literary critics, however, have very little been able to work directly with Native performers, or with Native language transcriptions because they have not, for the most part, developed competence in Native languages—for all that they may appreciate the esthetics of Native expression.

As translators have become increasingly sensitive and sophisticated, they have, to be sure, attempted to see the relation between Identity and Difference, accessibility and authenticity, art and science as more nearly a dialectical than a purely oppositional relation.[1] Efforts to estheticize science and to scientize esthetics in these regards, are, I believe, wholly to be applauded—for all that, as I have tried to show elsewhere, it is unlikely that any fully satisfactory translation strategy—as accurate as it is accessible, as scientifically valid as it is esthetically beautiful, etc.—can be produced.[2] Given the very different structure of Native American languages from Indo-European languages (and from one another as well), and given the different assumptions and possibilities of oral and textual performance, one cannot help but sacrifice, in some measure, closeness to the original for a sense of "literariness," or a sense of "literariness" for a sense of the actual structure and syntax of the original. All of this is to say, as Dennis Tedlock, in his seminal essay "On the Translation of Style in Oral Literature," quoted Herbert Spinden, that translators must work according to "the double standard of fidelity to the original source and artistic quality in the rendering."[3] (Spinden in Tedlock 1983:32).

Let me briefly mention two more matters before proceeding to the theorized history I have promised. First, it should be explicitly acknowledged that what follows is, indeed, an account of Indian to *English* literary translation. The work of francophone persons in the Southeast and Northwest, or of Spanish speakers in Florida and the Southwest, important as these are, is not considered. And the work of even anglophone scholars in what for five hundred years has been the Spanish-speaking world is barely alluded to. Clearly attention to both of these aspects of the subject is needed to supplement what I offer. Second, it will readily be noted that my account is exclusively concerned with the translation of what can generally be catalogued as Native American song and story, so that an important category of Indian discourse, that of oratory, is not considered.

I ask the reader to believe that this is not because I think Indian oratory uninteresting, unimportant, or irrelevant to the history of translation. Indeed, on the contrary, I think oratory raises so many questions of importance that it would extend this paper to unmanageable proportions to try to attend to it here. Donald Bahr's article on the subject and Andrew Wiget's discussion are the best brief overviews I know,[4] and I will offer among the references at the end of this essay work by Bahr, the Dauenhauers, Michael Foster, Miguel León-Portilla, and Joel Sherzer, which—along with the bibliographic references each of these provides—should enable the interested reader to pursue this subject in the detail it deserves.

Although Euroamericans from the seventeenth century forward were quite certain that Indian peoples had need of Western texts—the Bible, most particularly, of course—in their languages, it took rather longer for them to decide that the textualization of Indian performances in English might be of interest and use to themselves. Brian Swann's introduction has already provided some sense of early European encounters with the possibility of an indigenous literature,[5] so I will only repeat a few lines of his quotation from Lieutenant Henry Timberlake's eighteenth-century "Translation of the WAR-SONG, *Caw waw noo dee, &c*" from the Cherokee to save the reader the trouble of turning pages.

> Where'er the earth's enlighten'd by the sun,
> Moon shines by night, grass grows, or waters run,
> Be't known that we are going, like men, afar,
> In hostile fields to wage destructive war;
> Like men we go, to meet our country's foes,
> Who, woman-like, shall fly our dreaded blows.

However absurd Timberlake's couplets may look to us today as a rendering of anything Cherokee warriors might actually have sung—and Timberlake's "*Caw waw noo dee, &c*" indicates the limited extent of his interest in transcribing the Cherokee language original—it should be noted that his translation, in its adoption of the principle of Identity, its determination to present Cherokee song as recognizably literary, accessible to readers of, say, Dryden, is not lightly to be dismissed. If Timberlake is at all correct in his comment that "Both the ideas and verse are very loose in the original, and they are set to as loose a music," which, however, he finds "extremely pretty, and very like the Scotch" (83), his procedure certainly has a coherent logic to it. Still, it is obvious that we will never know, from Timberlake's rendering, what eighteenth-century Cherokee war songs were "really" like; all we can know from him is that they could be taken as sophisticatedly artful—no less so than Western literary art.

    Moving forward to the mid-nineteenth century, I would cite Henry Rowe Schoolcraft's work as showing a certain awareness of the dialectic I have posited as inevitably operative. Schoolcraft's "Chant to the Firefly" offers a transcription of the Chippewa original, followed by what Schoolcraft calls a "literal" translation, and, finally, a "literary" translation. Here, first, is the Indian original, as quoted by Dell Hymes (1981:39):

Chant to the Fire-Fly

Chippewa (Ojibwa) (Schoolcraft's orthography is preserved):

Wau wau tay see!	Wau wau tay see!
Wau wau tay see!	Wau wau tay see!
E mow e shin	Was sa koon ain je gun.
Tahe bwau ne baun-e wee!	Was sa koon ain je gun.
Be eghaun—be eghaun—ewee!	

Schoolcraft's "literal" translation uses a kind of highly exclamatory prose:

Flitting-white-fire-insect! waving-white-fire-bug! give me light before I go to bed! give me light before I go to sleep. Come, little dancing white-fire-bug! Come, little flitting white-fire-beast! Light me with your bright white-flame-instrument—your little candle.

The "literary" translation, however, is versified. Here are the first four lines as reproduced by Hymes (1981:40):

> Fire-fly, fire-fly! bright little thing,
> Light me to bed, and my song I will sing.
> Give me your light, as you fly o'er my head,
> That I may merrily go to my bed.

For an Indian "chant" to appear accessibly "literary," it would still seem that rhyme and meter are required; nonetheless, there is at least some recognition of the potential value of a more "literal" version. As the curious consequence of changing taste, Schoolcraft's "literal" version may, as Hymes has remarked, currently strike us as more "literary" than his "literary" version. That Schoolcraft has, at least, provided a rough transcription of the original is particularly fortunate—if only, as Dell Hymes has acerbically remarked, because "thanks to Schoolcraft's scholarship, we can appreciate in depth how bad his translation is" (1981:40). Schoolcraft's "scholarship" importantly provides the basis for the possibility of "poetic retranslation" such as Hymes himself has offered.[6] Schoolcraft also translated—or, perhaps one should say offered "versions," or reinterpretations—of Native legend and story.[7]

     In the last decades of the nineteenth century we find a substantial body of translations of Native American song and story that is quite remarkable for its solid linguistic data and its detailed ethnographic acquaintance with the cultures in question. For all that this work comes from "amateurs"—lawyers like Horatio Hale or medical men like Washington Matthews—not associated with the universities and only tangentially and irregularly to the government bureaus, it is not, as the conventionally received view would have it, vague and impressionistic. Indeed, this conventional view is badly in need of revision, reflecting as it does the triumph of Boasian standards for "scientific" translation (I shall briefly discuss these below). Horatio Hale's *Iroquois Book of Rites,* published in a volume of Daniel G. Brinton's "Library of Aboriginal American Literature" (1883), and Washington Matthews's translations of the Navajo *Mountain Chant* (1887), and of the *Night Chant* (1902) are two outstanding examples from this period, and there are translations worthy of contemporary attention to be found in the work of Major John Wesley Powell among "the Numic people of Western North America" and the Rev. H. R. Voth among the Hopi.[8]

     I will cite the "First Song of the First Dancers" from Matthews's presentation of the *Mountain Chant.* There is, initially, a transcription of the original in the conventional orthography of the period (456):

**Qaniè qaò yaè, qaniè qaò yaè
Qaniè iè oayè oayè.**

1.	Qadjinäìa qaò yaè,	9.	Qadjinäìa qaò yaè,
2.	Kaç dsil çilhyíli qaò yaè,	10.	Kaç dsil litsòï qaò yaè,
3.	'Çaltsoï tsèë qaò yaè,	11.	Bitselitsòï qaò yaè,

4. Cija cigèlgo qaò yaè.
    Náhi ìni èhi oayè, náhi ìni èhi oöhè.

5. Niqoyastcàdje qaò yaè,
6. Kaç dsil çolíji qaò yaè,
7. Kini bitsëë qaò yaè,
8. Cija cigèlgo qaò yaè.
    Náhi ìni, etc.

12. Cija cigèlgo qaò yaè.
    Náhi ìni, etc.

13. Niqoyastcàdje qaò yaè,
14. Kaç dsil lakàie qaò yaè,
15. A'a'i tsèe qaò yaè,
16. Cija cigèlgo qaò yaè.
    Náhi ìni, etc.

We next have something Matthews denotes simply "Translation." This, as the reader will note, includes not only linguistic but ethnographic information of a particularly important kind:

Translation.—1, 9. Qadjinàï, "Place-where-they-came-up," a locality in the San Juan Mountains where, according to their mythology, the Navajo emerged from the lower world to this. 5, 13. Niqoyastcàdje, another name for Qadjinàï. 2, 6, 10, 14. Kaç, now; dsil, mountain; çilhyíli, black; çolíji, blue; litsòï, yellow; lakàie, white. These verses refer to four mountains surrounding Qadjinàï, which are designated by colors only to indicate their topographical positions. 3, 7, 11, 15. 'Çaltsoïaça litsòï, "yellow wing," a large bird of prey; kini, hen hawk; bitselitsòï, "yellow tail," a bird of undetermined species; a'a'i, magpie; tse, a tail; bitse, its tail. 4, 8, 12, 16. Cija, my treasure; cigèl, my desideratum, my ultimatum, the only thing I will accept. When supposed to be said by a god, as in this song, it means the particular sacrifice which is appropriate to him. In this case probably the feathers spoken of are "cigèl" and the mountains "eija." The refrain, "qaò yaè" is a poetic modification of qaa', it looms up, or sticks up, said of some lofty object visible in the distance, whose base cannot be seen.

Finally, there is a "free translation" (456–57):

Free translation.

Place-whence-they-came-up looms up,
Now the black mountain looms up,
The tail of the "yellow wing" looms up,
My treasure, my sacrifice, loom up.

Land-where-they moved-out looms up,
Now the blue mountain looms up,
The tail of the hen-hawk looms up,
My treasure, my sacrifice, loom up.

Place-whence-they-came-up looms up,
Now the yellow mountain looms up,
The tail that is yellow looms up,
My treasure, my sacrifice, loom up.

Land-where-they-moved out looms up,
Now the white mountain looms up,
The tail of the magpie looms up,
My treasure, my sacrifice, loom up.

I suppose it might be said that in addition to the advances made in linguistic and ethnographic information in the forty-some years separating the work of Schoolcraft and Matthews, the chief advantage the latter enjoys as a translator may be that he is not particularly interested in poetry as such. Matthews clearly is not indifferent to the matter of literary accessibility, and so he offers a loosely versified "free translation." But unlike Schoolcraft, Matthews does not find it necessary to push further toward a "literary" translation.

Matthews's procedure is worth comparing to that of another "amateur," one who is clearly more oriented toward the esthetic/accessible axis of translation than—as in the case of Matthews—toward the scientific/accurate axis: Natalie Curtis Burlin. Burlin seems not to have been competent in any one of the several languages from which she offered translations, and, further, her pronouncements concerning the "primitive charm" of the art of a "child race" and her self-characterization as the "white friend" who "had come to be the pencil in the hand of the Indian[s]" (xxi) who "walked in the sunset hour of their native life . . . [with] the night . . . soon to come," (xxii) are deeply embarrassing to read today. Nonetheless, the translations from many Native languages of story and "legend" in her *Indians Book* of 1907, have much to recommend them, for she includes—albeit in a quite unsystematic manner—rough transcriptions of Native language originals with at least some of her "literal" and "literary" translations. Here is a Pawnee "Spirit-Dance" song as Burlin gives it (116) in Indian and in English in parallel columns:

Kehare Katzaru	**Song of the Spirit-Dance**
Ruwerera, ruwerera,	Star of Evening, Star of Evening,
Operit ruwerera,	Look, where yonder she cometh,
Operit ruwerera.	Look, where yonder she cometh.
Rerawha-a, rerawha-a,	Stars of heaven, stars of heaven,
Operit rerawha-a,	Lo, the many are coming,
Operit rerawha-a.	Lo, the many are coming.
Ruwerera, ruwerera,	Mother-Moon, Mother-Moon,
Atira ruwerera,	Look, where yonder she cometh,
Atira ruwerera.	Look, where yonder she cometh.
Ruwerera, ruwerera,	Star of Morning, Star of Morning,
Operit ruwerera,	Look, where yonder he cometh,
Operit ruwerera.	Look, where yonder he cometh.
Ruwerera, ruwerera,	Father-Sun, Father-Sun,
Atius ruwerera,	Look, where yonder he cometh,
Atius ruwerera.	Look, where yonder he cometh.

There is no literal translation in this instance, and the "literary" translation, for all that it appeared in the twentieth century, takes as its model a pre-Whitmanian or -Dickinsonian esthetic for poetry. For all of that, the juxtaposition of this translation to a (versified) "original" at least allows the general reader to wonder whether or how, for example, *ruwerera* and *rerawha-a* are related: are they singular and plural forms of the verb "to come," and, indeed, do they somehow include an inflection that would legitimate Burlin's shift from "Look" to "Lo"? In an appendix (544), Burlin offers at least some bits of linguistic information that might aid the reader concerned to know about these matters:

Ruwerera	**operit**	**rerawha-a**
it is coming yonder	*star (Evening Star understood in first verse, Morning Star in fourth)*	*they are coming yonder (re, yonder:* ra, *coming:* wha-a, *many)*
Atira	**Atius**	
Mother (Mother-Moon)	*Father (Father-Sun)*	

Even from this little, one can see that, indeed, there is no equivalent for either "look" or "lo" in the original, and that a "literal" translation of the first two stanzas might be something like, "It is coming yonder, Evening Star comes, Evening Star comes. / They are coming yonder, they come," and so forth. Burlin's procedure does not, to be sure, attend to linguistic or for that matter ethnographic data in anything like the detail of Matthews; indeed, her stated desire "that the *real* meaning [might] truthfully flash through the English words, and that the translation should retain the *fragrance* [!?], *the color, and, above all, the spirit* of the original" (xxv, my emphases) is such as to diminish the importance of such data; those translators after the "fragrance" and "spirit" of the original need not trouble overmuch with its actual words and phonemes. Still, it must be said for Burlin that she did take the trouble to consult both Native singers and storytellers as well as accredited linguistic experts.[9]

Further, Burlin's *Indians Book,* as in the example below, often tries to convey the melodic component of Native song, so that one may indeed recall that these particular compositions were sung, rather than recited. Schoolcraft, who offered a Chippewa "chant," and Matthews, who offered a Navajo "song," did not, to my knowledge, provide the reader with any guide to the musical content. Burlin, working with models established around the turn of the century by her contemporaries Alice Fletcher and Frances Densmore,[10] as in the example below, does offer such a guide:

Tawi' Kuruks
Song of the Bear Society
Sung by Letakots-Lesa (Eagle Chief)

(Burlin 1968: 117)

NOTE: Meter signature should properly read $\frac{2}{8}$—Ed.

Another important "artistic" contributor to translation in the first decades of the twentieth century is Mary Austin. To be sure, inasmuch as her work was, so far as I am aware, entirely uninformed by specific linguistic or ethnographic competences of any detail whatever, and explicitly offered not as translation but rather as "versions" or "interpretations" of Native American literary expression oriented toward the esthetic dimension of charm and beauty, it could be argued that her work does not strictly belong in any history of translation practices. I am insufficiently dogmatic, however, to do more than note the logic of such an argument. Austin was quite influential in her time, and, for all the legitimacy of the subsequent criticism (of the 1970s and after) of her highly impressionistic manner, her efforts to bring to general attention the literary expression of Native American people is worthy of note.[11] This is most particularly the case because, in a manner very different from that of Natalie Burlin, attention to Indian poetry for Austin was not an antiquarian occupation but rather a commitment to the present and future. It was Austin's unequivocal view that a relationship was "about to develop between Indian verse and the ultimate literary destiny of America" (1918:xv–xvi). Remarking on the similarities between the imagist and verslibriste manner of many of the poets of her period and the manner of at least some Indian songs, Austin insisted that "American poetry must inevitably take, at some period of its history, the mold of Amerind verse, which is the mold of the American experience shaped by the American environment" (1930:42). Perhaps to aid in this "inevitable" process, Austin, in her *American Rhythm* (1923:116), offered such texts as the following, from the Oglala Sioux:[12]

Personal Song of Daniel Red Eagle

The fierce hawk of death is over me,
The fierce hawk of death.

Now and again
Its wing shadows
Brush my shoulders.

The fierce hawk of death,
When will it strike!

Here, Austin, to borrow a phrase from Michael Castro, "interprets the Indian"[13] in such a way as to align Native American literary expression with the dominant esthetic principles for poetry in her own time. Insofar as she remakes Indian poetry according to the model of the imagists or verslibristes of her time, she is vulnerable to the criticism Karl Kroeber has recently made of Brian Swann's work, and others have made of the work of Jerome Rothenberg (see below).

In varying degrees, then, there are a number of translations in the last decades of the nineteenth century and the first decades of the twentieth century that do indeed attempt to operate within the paradoxical or dialectical bounds of that "double standard of fidelity to the original source and artistic quality in the rendering," remarked by Spinden in the 1930s, with Hale, Matthews, and others more nearly emphasizing the former and Burlin, at least, if not quite Austin, more nearly emphasizing the latter. This dialectic, however, is largely undone by the work of Franz Boas and his students, the "double standard" somewhat crudely reduced to the single standard of anthropological scienticity.

That Boas *was* the founder of a genuinely "scientific" anthropology in this country has been the view militantly and persistently asserted by his students (e.g., Margaret Mead, Ruth Benedict, Alexander Lesser, Irving Goldman, and others). That assertion has been powerfully objected to by, among others, Leslie White and Marvin Harris; and I have myself published an interpretation of this debate.[14] For our present purposes, what needs to be considered is the nature of Boasian preferences in the presentation and translation of Native American literary performance. In what I take to be an oblique reference to Boas and his influence, John Bierhorst (1974:xii, my emphasis) remarks, "The school of literary anthropology D. G. Brinton might have founded in the 1880's failed to materialize in the tide of reaction that swept American Indian studies into the twentieth century (leaving the cult of myth and even *the comparative method,* the lifeblood of literary anthropology, far behind."[15]

In somewhat similar fashion, Dennis Tedlock (1983:31) has claimed that the Boasian advocacy of " 'a faithful rendering of the native tales' " for the most part produced "what professional translators would call a 'crib' or a 'trot'—not a true translation into literate English, but rather a running guide to the original text, written in an English that was decidedly awkward and foreign." This "awkward" English, which Tedlock refers to (38) as "informant English," I believe *might*—as I shall indicate in discussing the work of Anthony Mattina just below—have been exploited for literary rather than strictly literal effect. In this regard, that is, I disagree with both Tedlock and Dell Hymes insofar as they have asserted the necessity of the textual conventions of Western poetry for conveying the artfulness of Indian narrative. Nonetheless, Tedlock convincingly demonstrates that a good many of the literal prose translations of Boas and his students—among them those of Melville Jacobs, who did indeed wish to "enhance [the] enjoyment" (Jacobs in Tedlock 1983:40) of Clackamas narrative—are largely disastrous for perceiving let alone understanding the esthetic strategies and effects of Native American literary expression.

Some sense of Boas's procedure may be gained from the example below, taken from his *Kootenai Tales* (1918:190–91):

64. Coyote and Tree Chief

Ho'ya's hutsqa'łanuxwa'te· k!a'k!łan·aq!o'xᵤmałe·'et.

(a) Coyote Becomes Tree Chief's Friend

Qao˘sa˘qa'ₐne·skɩ'n·ku·ts. nułpałnetɩ't¡ne· ka'qa·ps nɩtsta'-
ha·łs ka'qa·ps nɩtsta'ha·łs ksao˘˙sa'qa·ps. qałwi'yne·: "hułts!-
ɩna'm·i·ł. ktsxa'ł'e·n ka'swu ne¡ nɩtsta'hał pał kqa'kyam
kqasts!o'mqa'qa." ta'xa ne¡ nɩtsta'hał qał'atɩ'łne· k!a'k!ła-
n·aq!o'xᵤmałe'et. ts!ɩna'xe· skɩ'n·ku·ts. qo·s qana'xe·. n'ɩtkɩ'ne·
kᵤwɩ'łqᵤwa't!e·'s. n'u'pste· skɩ'n·ku·ts yu·hanqa'me·k. pał k.łɩt-
q!uxma'saq! tsukᵘa'te· a'ła·s. qanakɩ'n·e· aₐ 'ksa'q!e·s. ta'xas
wɩłkɩ'sqłe·k!a'łne·. qaₐnmɩtu'kse· yaqaₐnet.ła'ₐke· k!a'k!łan·a-
q!o'xᵤmałe·'et. łe'¡ne·s qo·s qa'qałxona'pse· kwɩ'łqᵤwat!s

5

10

12 *Arnold Krupat*

skʊ'n·ku·ts. k!u'pχa ma'e·s k!a`k!łan·aq!o'χ_umałe·'et, qake'_ine·
ne_i tʊłna'mu: "a: kse'_iłso_uk qo ha'mke· łe'ins swu'e·s
kanχa'łe·." nułpałnitʊ't_ine· qo_us ktsχana'me·s skʊ'n·ku·ts.
qayaqana'χe·. ma'te· ne_is χałtsʊ'n'e·s k_uwʊ'łq_uwat!s. łaχa'χe·
ne_is tʊłna'mu·'s. tʊnaχa''mne·. qakʊ'łne·: "ka_a kʊ'nskił'a_aqa'ke·
qo_u ku˘q^ua'ham łe'_ine·." n'u'pχ_ane· ne_i tʊłna'mu ne_is pał
n'ʊ'nse· ne_is nʊtsta'hałs. ma kskʊłyʊłna'_antstaps. qakʊ'łne·
skʊ'n·ku·ts·: "a: ma koq^ua'ke· łe'e·ns swu'e·s kanχa'łe·."
qao'_une· ne_is ke'e·ns skʊ'n·ku·ts·. ta'χas sła˘qa˘qa'pse·
ktso'_uk^uat ktsχa'ł'e·ns swuʊ'se·s χałe''e·s. n'u'pχ_ane· ne_is
χałe''e·s ktsχa'ł'e·ns naso'_ukwe·ns. qao˘sa˘qa'_ane· skʊ'n·ku·ts
a_a˘kʊt.ła.ʊ'se·s swu'e·s.

15

20

64. Coyote and Tree Chief

Well, I will tell you about Tree Chief. |

(a) Coyote Becomes Tree Chief's Friend

There was Coyote. He heard about a youth. | There was a youth.
He thought: "I'll go, | and the youth shall be my friend, because it is
said ‖ that he is clever." The name of this youth was Tree Chief. |
Coyote started. He went along. He met | a mule. Coyote took him
and rode him. Because his legs were lean, | he took moss and stuffed
his legs. Then | he had big calves. Tree Chief's tent was on a river. ‖
Coyote came riding along on the mule | opposite (the tent). When
Tree Chief's mother saw him, the old woman said: | "Oh, I wish the
passer-by would be my son's friend!" | Coyote heard her talking. |
He went past. He left his mule and came ‖ to the old woman. He
entered, and said to her: "What did you say | when I passed there
on the other side?" The old woman saw that | he was a youth.
She was pleased with him. She said | to Coyote: "I said this: 'I
wish you would be my son's friend.'" | She did not know that it
was Coyote. Therefore ‖ she took him to be her son's friend. She
knew that | her son was to be a chief. There was Coyote | in his
friend's tent. |

5

10

15

20

Here, special phonetic symbols are employed to render the sounds of the Indian original as
exactly as possible (but, of course, only for the scientifically trained reader able to decode
those symbols), and the original is printed facing a sentence by sentence translation into
English—a translation which attempts to achieve approximately word for word literality.
It should be fairly apparent, however—and I have not gone out of my way to choose some
particularly dreadful example—that, whatever the gain in literal accuracy, it is purchased
at a fairly considerable price in the loss of literariness, a sense that these tales do indeed
have the beauty and power of sophisticated verbal art. Yet, to repeat, Boas's influence in
this area was enormous for much of this century.

An extreme reaction against the apparently dead hand of this scientific literality
comes from the poet Jerome Rothenberg in the 1960s and '70s in the practice of what he

calls "total translation," a "means of delivery & of bringing to life . . . words, sounds, voice, melody, gesture, event, etc., . . . a full and total experience" (306). This is obviously something very far from Boasian literal translation. The following lines are from Rothenberg's version of a Kwakiutl performance that he calls "Gift Event II" from his collection, *Shaking the Pumpkin* (1972:1988):

Gift Event II

Start by giving away different colored glass bowls.
Have everyone give everyone else a glass bowl.
Give away handkerchiefs & soap & things like that
Give away a sack of clams & a roll of toilet paper.
Give away teddybear candies, apples, suckers & oranges.
Give away pigs & geese & chickens, or pretend to do so.
Pretend to be different things.
Have the women pretend to be crows, have the men pretend to be something else.
Talk Chinese or something.
Make a narrow place at the entrance of a house & put a line at the end of it that you have to
    stoop under to get in.
Hang the line with all sorts of pots & pans to make a big noise.
Give away frying pans while saying things like "Here is this frying pan worth $100 & this
    one worth $200."
Give everyone a new name.
Give a name to a grandchild or think of something & go & get everything.

One does not suppose, of course, that any Kwakiutl performer actually ever said anything like "Talk Chinese or something." But Rothenberg's interest, like Burlin's, or Austin's, is in the esthetic feel of the thing, a rendering of the Indian performance in a manner that we can easily find, whatever its accuracy and authenticity, moving, powerful, and so on. Rothenberg has been extensively criticized for the liberties he takes with Native expression[16]—criticisms which, from a different quarter, have just recently been reiterated for some of the work of Brian Swann.

Swann's more recent attempt to privilege the charm and "literariness" of Native expression is much more sensitive to the sorts of issues just mentioned. What Swann offers in *Song of the Sky* do not claim to be "translations" but are, instead, readily acknowledged as poetic versions, "white man's poetry" (1985:4), but, nonetheless, a poetry based upon linguistically and ethnographically informed—but altogether literal and not very "poetic"—work of earlier anthropologists. I quote a lovely text based on material translated by John Swanton:

You
     where have you
          fallen
             from
                fallen

```
                              You
                          have been
                    falling
                falling
        Have you
                fallen
                    from the top
                        of the salmon-
                                    berry bushes
                        falling
                            falling¹⁷
```

As I have said, Swann is much more careful than his predecessors in the interpretive line ever were to admit that what he puts on the page does not closely conform to what any particular performance was "really" like. What he offers is, once again, an imaginative recreation for a Western audience of the feel or sense of what they said or sang. But, as Karl Kroeber (1989:47) notes, "so far as *Song of the Sky* deserves and repays attention *as* modern [Euroamerican] poetry, its value for those interested in Indian poetry and song is principally in being so unlike the Indian songs it secondhandedly reshapes." ¹⁸

I believe Kroeber is generally correct although insufficiently historical. The "interest," that is, that one may take in the work of Austin, Rothenberg, and Swann, is, to be sure, an interest largely determined by the likeness of their work to what Euroamericans of the 1920s, 1960s, and 1980s have found attractive in (some of) the poetry of those periods. But it does not logically follow that the poetry of those periods—and so the poetic "versions" produced according to the esthetics of those periods—is necessarily "unlike the Indian songs it secondhandedly reshapes." Timberlake's "version," that is to say, conforms to an esthetic that is probably very decidedly "unlike" any Cherokee esthetic; there is almost surely a very bad fit between iambic pentameter couplets and Cherokee war songs. But it may be that the distance between imagist poetics or those of "open" poetry and Indian song is less; it may be, I mean to suggest, that the fit, as I have called it, is indeed somewhat better. (For all that, it remains the case that we will not get any sense of the word-for-word meaning and the ethnographic import of that meaning from these translators' procedures.)

In my terms, the procedures of Austin, Rothenberg, and Swann, as also those of Henry Rowe Schoolcraft and Lt. Henry Timberlake emphatically privilege the Identity of Native performance with that of Western literary art, assuming the likeness not the unlikeness of the two—and, indeed, they thereby mask much of the strangeness and Difference of Indian expression, as the price paid for asserting the esthetic power of Native American work. I am quite sure that Rothenberg and Swann would agree that the danger of such procedures resides in the fact that they might unintentionally seem to suggest that, to cite William Bevis, we might still be able to "get" Indian literature almost as cheaply as we got Manhattan: ¹⁹ to suggest, that is, that the translator need not take the trouble to study the indigenous languages of the Americas (the resources for some of which today—

grammars, dictionaries, textbooks—are considerably more abundant than they were in an earlier time), need not bother to learn very much about traditional cultures and their continuance today.

To convey something of the feel of the thing without so great a loss in formal structure and literal meaning as there was in Rothenberg's work, has been, in different ways, the aim of the transcriptions and translations of the two most influential contemporary mythographers, Dell Hymes and Dennis Tedlock. Hymes, a formidable linguist, has focused predominantly on myth narratives of the Northwest, rearranging and retranslating earlier transcriptions and translations. Emphasizing the dramatic quality of Native storytelling from a linguistic and narratological perspective, Hymes has devised a system involving divisions into acts and scenes and a translation method which offers Indian narratives in "measured verse," [20] determining line breaks according to the recurrence of linguistic particles in the original transcriptions from which he works. Hymes scrupulously includes transcriptions of the Native text with each of his own translations. I will cite the first section of his 1977 translation of a much discussed Clackamas text called "Seal and her younger brother lived there." [21] Hymes first gives the versified translation (1981:310):

Seal and her younger brother lived there

[i. The "wife" comes]

(A)	(1)	They lived there, Seal, her daughter, her younger brother.	1
		After some time, now a woman got to Seal's younger brother	2
(B)	(2)	They lived there.	3
		They would 'go out' outside in the evening.	4
	(3)	The girl would say,	5
		she would tell her mother:	6
		"Mother! Something is different about my uncle's wife.	7
		"It sounds just like a man when she 'goes out.'"	8
	(4)	"Shush! Your uncle's wife!"	9
(C)	(5)	A long long time they lived there like that.	10
		In the evening they would each 'go out.'	11
	(6)	Now she would tell her:	12
		"Mother! Something is different about my uncle's wife.	13
		"When she 'goes out' it sounds just like a man."	14
	(7)	"Shush!"	15

It is followed by a versified original language text (1981:312):

Wálxayu iCámxix gaLxílayt

[i. The "wife" comes]

(A)	(1)	GaLXílayt, Wálxayu, wagáxan, iCámxix.	1
		LHúxwan qánCixbÉt, aGa iLGagílak gaLigúqam Wálxayu iCámxix	2

(B)	(2)	GaLXílayt.	3

(B) (2) GaLXílayt.   3
        ALúya tLáXnix xábixix.   4
    (3) Wak'aSkaS alagíma,   5
        agulxáma wákaq: 6
        "Áqu! Dángi iXlúwidix wiCLm ayágikal.   7
        "TL'á wiLÉkala-díwi alubáya."   8
    (4) "Ak'waSka! IwímiLm ayágikal!"   9
(C) (5) I yatLqdix k'wátLqi gaLXílayt.   10
        Xábixix aLubáywa.   11
    (6) AGa agulxáma: 12
        "Áqu! Dáng(i) iXlúwida wiCLm ayágikal.   13
        "Alubáya tL'á wiLÉkala díwi."   14
    (7) "Ák'waSka!"   15

Hymes's interest in "performance," is predominantly discursive (e.g., 1981:79–86, 200–259, and passim) and concerned with such things as the "presentational" strategies (1981:317 ff) of narrative: working predominantly from texts, he does not much discuss the dynamics of actual performances.

These dynamics, however, are exactly what interests Tedlock, who, unlike Hymes, works from his own tape recordings, which he then transcribes and translates. His practice, initiated with Zuni materials in the 1970s, has for the most part been to break lines according to pauses on the part of the narrator, and to print each line according to a typographical scheme which attempts to indicate such things as the tempo of the narration, the performer's pronunciation of phonemes, his volume, and, indeed, even the audience's (generally rule-governed, but occasionally spontaneous) reaction and response. Tedlock's techniques are oriented toward the production of what he has called a "performable translation" (1983:13), its performability being aided by Tedlock's provision of a "Guide to Reading Aloud" (1983:20–22). I offer a brief excerpt from near the end of the long story from the Zuni Tedlock calls "The Girl and the Protector" (1983:104):

> When he reached the top he made this
> Old Lady stand up, (*softly*) he tried it there
> he tried it
> and it was working. When it was working
> HE STARTED OFF, and when he'd gone a way the Protector began
>   to call out (*as if from a distance, very high*):
> "Grandmaaaaaaaaaaaaaaaaaaaaaaaa come help me, some one
>   is cha sing meeeeeeeeeeeeeeeeeeeeeeeee."
> His grandmother was making porridge.
> AFTER A MOMENT HE CALLED AGAIN and his grandmother
>   heard him.
>
> When she looked outside he called again:
> "Grandma come help me, some one is chasing meeeeeeeeeeeeeee," he
>   said.
> "Dearie me! grandson, you big fool," she said.

There is no versified Zuni original provided; Tedlock, to my knowledge has only printed one Zuni versified original, for the story translated as "Coyote and Junco."

I suspect that the enormous influence of Hymes and Tedlock[22] derives from the fact that they have been foremost among those committed to mediating the distance between Identity and Difference in transcription and translation. Competent in the languages from which they translate, and committed to high degrees of linguistic accuracy, both are also thoroughly sophisticated in their esthetic awareness (they have, for example, written and published their own poetry). For all their (salutary) influence, however, their methods have not exhausted the possibilities of contemporary translation. And, moreover, their insistence on the presentation of Native performance, regardless of whether these are sung, chanted, or narrated, in lines and stanzas, as "poetry" on the page, that is, rather than in the sentences and paragraphs of a prose page format, has increasingly been called into question for making a necessity of what is perhaps better considered an option.

Thus, Anthony Mattina, a Salishan linguist, has opted for prose in his translation of a folktale narrated by the late Peter Seymour, one of the last Colville speakers of Western Montana. Resisting all claims that versified format is necessary for conveying the literariness of Indian narrations, Mattina forcefully insists (1987: 142–43) that

Mythography is the work of collecting and transcribing once-oral texts. Narratives on the printed page are museum artifacts, just as arrowheads in a museum case are spent projectiles. A transcript of a narrative has no more sound than a musical score. The understanding which readers gain from the script is in direct proportion to what they know about the tradition and the context of the text. . . . Let the texts come forth, in whatever typographic arrangement the editor deems appropriate.

Mattina's prose, it should be said, is not standard English, but, rather, that pan-Indian phenomenon he calls "Red English," the English actually spoken by many contemporary Native American persons—in this particular case, the "informant English" of his collaborator in the translation project, Peter Seymour's cousin Mary Madeline de Sautel. I will not attempt to summarize Mattina's persuasive defense of "Red English" translations as literarily valuable[23] except to note his claim that they are indeed capable of conveying all the expressive elements one could ask of any literature. As the examples cited below indicate, along with his easily readable Red English translations, Mattina offers (1985:92) a "continuous" translation, a transcription of the tape-recorded Colville original, and an "interlinear" translation:

They all have night caps on, that's their mark, what they go by. She matches them together, the oldest one with your oldest brother, he'll get her to go to bed with; and the next one with the next woman, he'll sleep with her; and the middle one, he'll have the middle woman; and you two youngest, you'll go to bed with her (1985:25).

72. yə-yʕà-t   c-qʷəc-qʷác-qn-əlx,   c-s-ən-qáp-qən,
72. They all   have caps on,   night caps,

    c-s-ɫq̓-əlx-áyaʔ-qən,   uɫ   aɫìʔ   ixìʔ   iʔ
    caps,   that's   what

    k-ťək-mín-s,   uɫ   axàʔ   cəm̓   ʔíck-st-əm-s;   cəm̓
    they go by,   and   they play with them;

    axàʔ   anwìʔ   waẙ   ilìʔ   nixʷ
    (with) you   also

    a-s-ənk̓ʷ-əs-tʔíw-t-x.
    (will play) the youngest one.

72. They all have caps on, night caps, caps, that's what they go by, and they play with them; the youngest one will play with you.

To bring this theorized history to a close, let me mention the contributions to Native American song sets of the Southwest in the work of Donald Bahr with Pima and Papago materials, Larry Evers and Felipe Molina with Yaqui Deer and Coyote songs, and Leanne Hinton with Havasupai songs. In 1983, Bahr published an essay on four Papago "Butterfly songs" in which he offered (1983:180)

a format and a method [for translation]. The format consists of certain writing procedures: the use of plain language words, of song language syllable transcription, of slashes to show a theoretically important zone within song lines, etc. . . . The method gives primacy to textual analysis and assumes in effect that song is a special way of telling stories. . . . [But] versification is also present and is controlled for . . . through the method of defining and rendering lines.

Bahr notes (1983:181) that Leanne Hinton's work with Havasupai materials in a number of ways parallels his own: [24]

The key similarity between our formats is the inclusion of native ordinary language interpretations. These are often lacking in publications of American Indian songs, and we [Bahr and Hinton] feel that they should not be. We differ in where the process goes from there. Hinton moves next into English words and morpheme glosses and free translation, I [Bahr] into plain English equivalents and Papagoized literal translation. We differ also on whether to include a separate musical transcription: she would include one, while I would not.

I give, below, Bahr's "Song language and literal translation" (1983:176) and his "Ordinary language version" (1983:177) of the first song of the set he considers.

Song 1

Row A
ga	ge	si	CU	CU	ke	HO	KI	MA	LI
a	bi	ig	BLA	A	ack	BU	U	TIER	FLIES

Row B
iya	ñei	yo	pa	ge	GA	MU	YA	HA	jo	WA	WA ÑE
toi	ju	ump	out	and	A	A	NA	A	rrow	STREEA	EATCH
herewill											

Row C
mai	hyo	si	me	ko	na	SU	DA	YA KI
a	a	way	fa	a	a	WA	A	STREE
	a way						gi	ME EAM
							ter	

Row D
WU	WI	WI	HI HI	ME
TO	OW	mo	GO O	O
		ards	HI O	

Row E
da	ma	no	da	dai	wa	GA	MU	WI PI	MU NO
o o	o o	on	si	i	it	A	A	WA A	A ASH
	on					and	wa	way	

Ordinary language version

Song 1

<table>
<tr><td>ge si</td><td>/s-cúk ho</td><td>/hókimal</td></tr>
<tr><td>Big</td><td>/black but</td><td>/terflies:</td></tr>
</table>

<table>
<tr><td>í:ya at o wa ñéiyopak</td><td>/gám hu wa á/j wáwañ</td></tr>
<tr><td>Here will jump out and</td><td>/away nar /row stretch</td></tr>
</table>

<table>
<tr><td>gámai hu si mé:kdam</td><td>/ṣú:dagi á</td><td>/kimel</td></tr>
<tr><td>Away far</td><td>/water stre</td><td>/am:</td></tr>
</table>

<table>
<tr><td>/wúi am hí</td><td>/him</td></tr>
<tr><td>/Towards g</td><td>/o,</td></tr>
</table>

<table>
<tr><td>dá:m dádiwak</td><td>/gn hú wa wí/pino</td></tr>
<tr><td>On sit and</td><td>/away wa /sh.</td></tr>
</table>

Although Bahr refers to what he calls "free translation" as the sort of thing that would probably approximate to what our historical overview of the subject has called "literary" translation, he does not care to provide such a translation (as Washington Matthews, who, although he did offer a "free translation," still did not go very much beyond the literal). By 1987, in a paper on Pima "Heaven Songs," Bahr does provide "free translations," along with what he here calls "Pima Language and English Syllable Matching Translation" (1987:210, 223). I will cite both translations for the first song of the set:

Song 1 (1)

ku	ña	si	ya	hu	nu	ki	me
and	I	he	ere	de	e	e	scend

ku	ña	si	ya	hu	nu	ki	me
and	I	he	ere	de	e	e	scend

i	ne	pi	a	pe	ka	me	ñe	we	na	ma	ne	hu	nu	ki	me
he	ere	ba	s	a	a	ad	ea	earth u	po	on	de	e	e	scend

soi	ga	le	ñi	boi	nag
po	o	or	my	y	heart

wa	ñi		pi	ma	ma	ce
that	I		don'	tkno	o	ow

1 (1). Jesus descends to bad earth.

Here I descend.
Here I descend,

On this bad earth descend.
My poor heart,
I don't know.[25]

In his current work in progress on Pima "Oriole" songs, Bahr continues his willingness—albeit still with some reluctance—to accommodate the literary reader's interest in the English language esthetics of Native American songs, while resisting accommodation in any degree that might obscure the formal, word-for-word syntactic as well as semantic integrity of the songs he has tape-recorded. With Bahr's permission, I next cite some examples from this latest work (n.d.: 148):

Nee, k i:d hab hahawa ep kaij mas g tas mu:. O hob kaij i:da mat am ha-wi'in. Eda g u'uhig pi mai mat has e-a:ngew, may has masma wo da:, "flai awai." Ne:, k i:d hab ep hi kaij mas g tas mu:. "Tas mu:, tas mu:. Eda g we:s ha'icu u'uhig e-kukui dagito," b hen kaij, b hen ha'icu hab kaij, "Jewed ka:cim ab t am hu i pi sa:mun," "kwait" g jewed, wesko. "As g su:g u'uhig as so'ig kaij, c as g hejel an a'i niok," b o ep kaidag.

		Ta		sai	waha mu			mu	ki		m	
		Ta		sai	waha mu			mu	ki		m	
	Je	wene we	si	co	cu	ka	ke	n				
Ke		da ke	we		sai	cu	yu	hine kuk	uiwe da	ni	to	
	Je	wene ka		cim		ga	mu pi	sa	mu	ne		m
	Su	hu ga	yu	u	hi		ne	soi newe kai		ce		
	He	je li	ga		mu	we	ne	no	ke.			

Look, and then this [song] says that the sun died. The other [previous song] said that it flooded them [ancient creatures]. At that time the birds didn't know [forgot] their flapping, how to fly, "fly away [as said in English]." Look, and this [song] on the other hand says that the sun died. "Sun dies, sun dies. Just then every kind of bird dropped its cooing," it seems to say, [and] it [next] seems to say, "The laying land nowhere echoes," "quiet [in English]" is the land everywhere. "Merely the mocking bird pitifully speaks, but it merely talks to itself," as it [song] also sounds.

		Su		u	uun	Di		i	ie		s	
		Su		u	uun	Di		i	ie		s	
	La	aand All	O	ver	Da	a	ar	k				
Just	The	en	All		Kind Of	Bi	iird	Coo	iing	Dro	op	Off
	La	aand La		ying		A	way	No	E	cho	in		g
	Mo	oc	king Bi	i	i		ird	Pit	iful	Spe		eaks	
	A	lo	one A			wa	ay	Ta	a	alks.		

Sun dies,
Sun dies.
Earth everywhere dark,
Then every bird stops cooing.
Earth doesn't echo,
A mocking bird speaks pitifully.
Distant and isolated it talks.

From the literary end of the spectrum (Bahr and Hinton are trained primarily in anthropology and linguistics), Larry Evers and Felipe Molina have remarked that "From our perspective, the *sine qua non* . . . is an accurate transcription of a native language text along with an English translation faithful to it" (1987:25). They consider the Yaqui deer songs they have translated, and more recently, Yaqui coyote songs (1989) to be "a native American poetry" (1987:25; 1989:9), one whose ongoing production has been somewhat overlooked by literary critics excited by the so-called Native American Renaissance in writing.[26] Evers and Molina, on the page, look somewhat like Schoolcraft; the difference, an enormous one, is that their collaboration has produced both what seems to be sound "scholarship" and also sound translation. I offer one brief example (Evers and Molina 1987:51):

Maiso Yoleme	Deer Person
Ala inikun maiso yoleme	So now this is the deer person,
hunu kun maiso yoleme	so he is the deer person,
ini kun tua maiso yolemeee	so he is the real deer person.
Ala inikun maiso yoleme	So now this is the deer person,
hunu kun maiso yoleme	so he is the deer person,
ini kun tua maiso yolemeee	so he is the real deer person.
Ala inikun maiso yoleme	So now this is the deer person,
hunu kun maiso yoleme	so he is the deer person,
ini kun tua maiso yolemeee	so he is the real deer person.
Ayaman ne seyewailo	Over there, I, in the center
fayaliata naisukuni	of the flower-covered opening,
weyekai	as I was walking,
im ne yo siali vata paku	here in the open green water,
weyekai	as I was walking,
Hunu kun maiso yoleme	So he is the deer person,
hunu kun tua maiso yolemeee	so he is the real deer person.

Many others, of course, are also currently working to reconcile the principles of accessibility and authenticity, of Identity and Difference in the translation of Native American song and story—so many others, indeed, that to mention all of their work would soon expand my theorized history almost to the dimensions of that would-be comprehensive history I prefer to leave unattempted. I will therefore conclude by repeating my belief that it is not possible to imagine the discovery or invention of any ultimately and absolutely correct or fully adequate way to translate from oral performance to page of text. Spinden's "double standard" will always provide a tension, as I have called it a dialectic, with which translators must work. But this is not to say that each age must, in an outmoded vernacular, simply "do its thing." To the contrary, what I believe this theorized history of translation should demonstrate is that for the foreseeable future, the conditions for any approximation to translational adequacy will be, first, competence, command, or in a phrase Dell Hymes has stated, varied, and repeated, a basic philological *control* of the language of the original; second, competence—in the sense of detailed knowledge—of the culture of the original, an ethnographic control; and, third, some developed sense of the strategies of literary expression both oral and textual in general. Although I am wary of both inadvertent and intentional shifts to the mode of prophecy in criticism, I would nonetheless venture to predict that the current conditions of possibility for the translation of Native American song and story are decidedly hopeful.

Acknowledgments

I would like to acknowledge the part a number of people played in bringing this essay into being, and to offer them my thanks. I first prepared a brief version of this history in response to Rosalind Cutforth's invitation to address the United Nations International School Native American Studies Colloquium in October of 1989, and then, as a result of the efforts of Professor Shamoon Zamir, I had the opportunity to revise it for the University of Chicago conference "Cultural Diversity and Liberal Education: Negotiating Difference in the Academy" in November of the same year. I am grateful to them both. My longtime literary co-worker and friend Brian Swann persuaded me that some further development of those talks could be useful to this volume; I thank him for that encouragement, for his editorial suggestions, and as well for an abundance of more intangible but much-valued support. Encouragement, suggestions, and support of a kind and quality not easily measured or matched also been offered by my anthropologist friends Donald Bahr and Peter Whiteley. I am grateful to them. Finally, I would like to dedicate this essay to Dell Hymes and Roy Harvey Pearce, who have long served to provide for me, each in his own way, models both of careful scholarship and critical ingenuity.

Notes

1. It may be useful to indicate my understanding of the differences between oppositional and dialectical terms. Oppositional relations are the constructions of logic, deriving perhaps foremost from Aristotle's principles of identity, non-identity, and the excluded middle: there is "A" and "not-A," which, for any given discussion in which they appear, are to one another as positive and negative. "A" is fully itself: "not-A" is in no way whatever "A" is. Dialectical relations, however, present terms which inevitably overlap and intersect, each needing—or, better, unavoidably including—the other for its own meaning. Differences between terms, thus, are matters of degree not kind. The principle of logical opposition requires that we must choose *either* "A" *or* "not-A," that choice removing from consideration the term rejected; dialectically, we may *emphasize* "A" or "not-A," that emphasis in no way negating the term de-emphasized. (For an interesting discussion of this matter in feminist terms, see Nancy Jay, "Gender and Dichotomy.") I have taken the time to make this point because I believe it bears importantly on how we think about translation, informing us, for example, that such a question as, "Is it accurate, is it authentic?" cannot be answered with a

simple yes or no. In the same way, it informs us that the observation, "It's lovely, it's powerful," cannot disqualify the question, "Is it accurate, is it authentic?"

2. See my "Post-Structuralism and Oral Literature."

3. The quotation from Spinden appears in Tedlock's 1983 version of this essay in his *The Spoken Word and the Work of Interpretation*. The essay was originally published in 1971.

4. See Bahr's "Oratory," and pages 22–25 of Wiget's *Native American Literature*.

5. Strachey's text, dating from 1612, is probably the earliest European account of an Indian "song" in the present-day United States.

6. There are doubtless other of Schoolcraft's song texts that might be chosen, but just here, uncovering the unfamiliar seems less useful than emphasizing what has oft been expressed but not so well attended to. My own discussion will have achieved its best purpose if it persuades the reader to review Dell Hymes's indispensable essay "Some North Pacific Coast Poems: A Problem in Anthropological Philology," first published in 1965, and reworked for his *"In Vain I Tried to Tell You": Essays in Native American Ethnopoetics* (1983). Here is Hymes's retranslation (1981:41) of the Chippewa original:

> Flitting insect of white fire!
> Flitting insect of white fire!
> Come, give me light before I sleep!
> Come, give me light before I sleep!
> Flitting insect of white fire!
> Flitting insect of white fire!
> Light me with your bright instrument of flame.
> Light me with your bright instrument of flame.

Hymes further comments (1981:42),

> Ethnologists *often* can be relied upon; literary versions *often* may be better than literal counterparts; structure may *often* be accessible in translation—but how is one to tell *when?* The only way to tell is by independent control of the results of translation, through access to the original texts, and, preferably, to the linguistic aids necessary for their analysis.

For further commentary on Schoolcraft's work, see William Clements's essay in this volume and his earlier "Schoolcraft as Textmaker."

7. See, for example, John Bierhorst, ed., *The Fire Plume: Legends of the American Indians Collected by Henry Rowe Schoolcraft*.

8. See, for example, Powell's *Anthropology of the Numa* and Voth's "Powamu Songs" (my thanks to Peter Whiteley for calling these to my attention). Also working in this period as government ethnologist was James Mooney, whose *Myths of the Cherokee* (1897–98:1900) offers prose translations of an enormous body of texts. Although the original Cherokee texts are not given, there is a glossary of Cherokee words retained in some of the translations and elaborate notes on linguistic and ethnographic matters. Mooney's *Cherokee Sacred Formulas and Medicinal Prescriptions* (revised, completed, and edited by Frans M. Olbrecht, and published in 1932) consists chiefly of "The Swimmer Manuscript," "a small daybook of about 240 pages . . . about half filled with writing in the Cherokee characters" (Mooney in Olbrecht 1932:1). Mooney obtained it from a Cherokee known in English as "Swimmer," and began work on it in 1888. Although these are "medical prescriptions," and therefore obviously not "literature" as Westerners usually think of it,

some of them are sung, and, in translation, look rather like a good deal of the material that has been presented as "Native American poetry." I give an example of Mooney's translations procedures below (Olbrecht 1932:170–71; I have not included the Mooney/Olbrecht notes):

¡ʋ̈ꞏɑ-ɴ¡ɔ̃ⁿ	ᴅʋ'niskɔ·li'	ᴅʋ'nitłǫ̈ŋǫ̈'.i'			
this-and	their heads	whenever they are ill			

ɑni'sɢú'ya	ɑni'lɔ¡i'		ʋtsʋ''nɑwa'	ɑnɔ̃''nʋ·ɢa'	ɑ'niᴅɑ·'ᵘwẽ
they men	they just passed by		beyond-it-stretched	they have come and said it	they (are) wizards

ɑni'lɔ¡i'		ʋtsʋ''nɑwa'	ɑnɔ̃''nʋ·ɢa'	ʋtsʋ''nɑwa'	ɢɔ̃'tłtɑ¡aⁿ'	
they just passed by		beyond it stretched	they have come and said it	beyond it stretched	It (has been) rubbed	

ʋtsʋ''nɑwa'	ɑnɔ̃''nʋ·ɢa'		yǎ'
beyond it stretched	they have come and said it		Sharp!

¡ʋ̈ꞏɑ-ɴ¡ɔ̃ⁿ	nɑ.'sɢwɔ̃ⁿ'	ᴅʋ'niskɔ·li'	ᴅʋ'nitłǫ̈ŋǫ̈'.i'		¡ʋ'a'	nʋ·ʋsti'	
this-and	also	their heads	whenever they are ill		this	so far like	

ɔ·'ᴅali-ɢú'ᴅli	ɑnǫ̈·'skɔ̃tł¿'.i	ᴅʋᴅzɔ·'·t'ʋstɔ.ti'
mountain-he climbs	it (sol.) used to be held in the mouth—H	they to be blown with it

And This Is (for) When Their Heads Are Ill

(free translation)

The men have just passed by, they have caused relief,
The wizards have just passed by, they have caused relief,
Relief has been rubbed, they have caused relief. Sharp!

Now that we have William Powers's work on Lakota "Yuwipi" curing songs (e.g., "Text and Context in Lakota Music" [1986] and *Sacred Language* [1986], etc.) along with the work of his teacher David McAllester (e.g., "The first snake song" [1980] and "'The War God's Horse Song,' An exegesis in Native American Humanities" [1980], etc.) among others, it might be interesting to return to Mooney's "prescriptions" not only as ethnography/science but also as poetry/art.

9. Cf. Burlin 1968 [1907]: 535,

> The interlinear translations here given have been made with care in the hope that the book may be of some aid in the comparative study of the linguistic stocks of the North American continent; yet they are offered as approximate only, for philological accuracy requires full and intimate knowledge of the Indian languages—a knowledge which the recorder [Burlin] does not possess. Whenever an authority on the language of a given tribe has been found his criticism has been solicited, as follows, and the recorder wishes here to express her grateful acknowledgment of the services so kindly rendered.

Burlin's list of "authorities" includes Franz Boas, James Mooney, and the Rev. H. R. Voth, among others.

10. Cf. the following example from Fletcher's *Indian Story and Song from North America* (1900), from the Navajo:

A Prayer for Rain

"Music Bars"
Song

(Chapman 1975: 237)

11. See, for example, Drinnon's general attempt to recuperate Austin's reputation, as well as, most recently, the approving words of Michael Castro (in Coltelli 102–3ff).

12. Austin's note to this text, in an appendix (1930:173), reads, "The personal song is an expression of a man's own philosophy, or a note of his consummate spiritual experience. It is often sung going into battle, or on the approach of death, in which case friends of the singer will often gather around his bed and sing it for him.

I am no expert on Lakota culture, but I have my doubts about some of this—or perhaps I should only note that Austin's remarks are at best very vague in their ethnographic content. And she gives nothing whatever as a guide to the Lakota original. In relation to my comments on the Cherokee "prescriptions," in note 8 above, it should be said that Austin has indeed reworked four of them from Mooney's literal translations, "with the help of Leota Harris, a woman of Cherokee descent, who had the formulas almost in the original form from her mother." Typically, Austin notes that she refrained from doing her own versions "until [she] had additional material which [she] thought would bring out their poetic values" (1930:173). As typically, she has no hesitation in stating which one of the four "is most poetic in concept" (ibid). Her standards for determining "poetic values" and "concepts," as expressed in the lengthy introduction to *The American Rhythm,* have not worn very well.

13. See Castro's *Interpreting the Indian: Twentieth-Century Poets and the Native American* (1983).

14. See "Anthropology in the Ironic Mode: the Work of Franz Boas."

15. The "comparative method" in anthropology, if not "literary anthropology" strictly speaking, was attacked by Boas in an influential early paper called "The Limitations of the Comparative Method in Anthropology" (1896).

16. An early harsh critique is the well-known essay by William Bevis, "American Indian Verse Translations" (1974). William Clements's "Faking the Pumpkin . . ." (1981) also takes the cudgel to Rothenberg, perhaps a bit excessively. Rothenberg offers a thoughtful and nondefensive defense of his ongoing commitment to "total translation" in this volume. I have suggested that Rothenberg's work may also be seen in the context of criticism, specifically what I call ethnocriticism, quite as well as in the context of translation. See my " 'Literary' Criticism/Native American 'Literature'" (1991).

17. As Swann notes, John Swanton's original Indian language text, with a literal, and a free/literary translation is given in Dell Hymes's "Some North Pacific Coast Poems. . . ," in which Hymes retranslates it (cf. Hymes 1981:45; Swann 1985:127) as he did Schoolcraft's "Chant to the Fire-Fly."

18. Kroeber's "Turning Comparative Literature Around: the Problem of Translating American Indian Literatures," the essay from which I have quoted, seems quite different from the position he had earlier taken in his Introduction to *Traditional American Indian Literatures* (1981), although that essay, in some measure at least, seemed to conflict with still earlier positions Kroeber had taken in his "Poem, Dream, and the Consuming of Culture," published in 1971.

19. See Bevis's "American Indian Verse Translations."

20. For Hymes's method, and the distinction between "metered verse" and "measured verse," see his "Discovering Oral Performance and Measured Verse in American Indian Narrative," originally published in 1977.

21. If I am not mistaken, Hymes published his first commentary on this narrative (originally recorded by Melville Jacobs and published in 1959) in 1971. He retranslated it in "measured verse" six years later, in the paper cited just above: most recently, he has commented on it again, in a study of change in oral narrative called "Notes Toward (an understanding of) Supreme Fictions" (1991). The version of the story appended to this latter essay differs only in very slight degree from the 1977 verse translation. For an account of the "Literary uses and related versions" of the story, see Hymes, 1981, 300.

22. See, for example, William Bright (1979), Virginia Hymes (1987), M. Dale Kinkade (1983, 1984), Joel Sherzer (1983, 1987) and Barbara Tedlock (1980, 1982), among others.

23. For that, see Mattina's introduction to *The Golden Woman*. Wendy Wickwire's edition of the work in English of another Northwestern storyteller, Harry Robinson, is also interesting in these regards. See *Write it on Your Heart: The Epic World of an Okanagan Storyteller* (1989).

24. See, for example, Hinton and L. Watahomigie, eds., *Spirit Mountain: An Anthology of Yuman Story and Song* (1980).

25. There is also a literary translation by Swann (in Bahr 1987:213–14):

Free Translations (Swann)

1 (1)   Jesus descends to this vile earth.

      Here I descend,
      here I descend,
      Descend to this vile earth.

My poor heart,
I don't know what will happen.

26. The phrase is the title of a book by Kenneth Lincoln (1983).

References

Austin, Mary. *The American Rhythm: Studies and Reexpressions of Amerindian Songs.* Boston: Cooper Square, 1930 [1923].

Bahr, Donald M. "A Format and Method for Translating Songs." *Journal of American Folklore* 96(1983): 170–82.

———. "Oratory." *Dictionary of Native American Literature,* ed. Andrew Wiget et al. Westport, Ct: Greenwood Press, forthcoming.

———. *Oriole Songs.* Unpublished ms.

———. *Pima and Papago Ritual Oratory: a Study of Three Texts.* San Francisco: The Indian Historian Press, 1975.

———. "Pima Heaven Songs." In Swann and Krupat 1987: 198–246.

Berman, Judith. "Oolachan-Woman's Robe: Fish, Blankets, Masks, and Meaning in Boas's Kwakw'ala Texts." In Swann 1992: 125–61.

Bevis, William. "American Indian Verse Translations." In Chapman 1975: 308–23.

Bierhorst, John, ed. *The Fire Plume: Legends of the American Indians Collected by Henry Rowe Schoolcraft.* New York: Dial, 1969.

———, ed. *Four Masterworks of American Indian Literature.* New York: Farrar, Straus & Giroux, 1974.

Boas, Franz. *Kutenai Tales.* Bureau of American Ethnology Bulletin 59. Washington: Government Printing Office, 1918.

———. "The Limitations of the Comparative Method in Anthropology." *Race, Language, and Culture.* New York: Macmillan, 1940, 270–80.

Bright, William. "A Karok Myth in 'measured verse': The translation of a performance." *Journal of California and Great Basin Anthropology* 1(1979): 117–23.

Burlin, Natalie Curtis. *The Indians Book: An Offering by the American Indians of Indian Lore, Musical and Narrative, to form a Record of the Songs and Legends of their Race.* New York: Dover, 1968 [1907].

Castro, Michael. *Interpreting the Indian: Twentieth-Century Poets and the Native American.* Albuquerque: University of New Mexico Press, 1983.

Chapman, Abraham, ed. *Literature of the American Indians: Views and Interpretations.* New York: New American Library, 1975.

Clements, William. "Faking the Pumpkin: On Jerome Rothenberg's Literary Offenses." *Western American Literature* 16(1981): 193–204.

———. "Schoolcraft as Textmaker." *Journal of American Folklore* 103(1990): 177–92.

Clifford, James. "Histories of the Tribal and the Modern." *The Predicament of Culture: Twentieth-Century Ethnography, Literature, and Art.* Cambridge, Mass.: Harvard University Press, 1988, 189–214.

Coltelli, Laura, ed. *Native American Literatures.* Pisa: Servizio Editoriale Universitario, 1989.

Dauenhauer, Nora and Richard. "Haa Shuka, Our Ancestors: Tlingut Oral Narrative." *Journal of American Folklore* 103(1990): 108–11.

Evers, Larry, and Felipe S. Molina. "Coyote Songs." In Coltelli 1989:9–38.

———. *Yaqui Deer Songs: Maaso Bwikam, A Native American Poetry.* Tucson: University of Arizona Press, 1987.

Fletcher, Alice. "The Relation of Indian Story and Song." [1900] In Chapman 1975:235–39.

Foster, Michael. *From the Earth to Beyond the Sky: An Ethnographic Approach to Four Longhouse Iroquois Speech Events.* Canadian Ethnology Service Paper 20. Ottawa: National Museum of Man, 1974.

Hale, Horatio. *The Iroquois Book of Rites,* with an Introduction by William M. Fenton. Toronto: University of Toronto Press, 1963 [1883].

Hinton, Leanne, and L. Watahomigie, eds. *Spirit Mountain: An Anthology of Yuman Story and Song.* Tucson: University of Arizona Press, 1984.

Hymes, Dell. *"In Vain I Tried to Tell You": Essays in Native American Ethnopoetics.* Philadelphia: University of Pennsylvania Press, 1981.

———. "Notes Toward (an understanding of) Supreme Fictions." In press.

Hymes, Virginia. "Warm Springs Sahaptin Narrative Analysis." Joel Sherzer and Anthony Woodbury, eds. *Native American Discourse: Poetics and Rhetoric.* Cambridge: Cambridge University Press, 1974, 62–102.

Jay, Nancy. "Gender and Dichotomy." *Feminist Studies* 7(1981): 38–56.

Kinkade, M. Dale. "Bluejay and his Sister." In Swann and Krupat 1987:255–96.

Kroeber, Karl. "An Introduction to the Art of Traditional American Indian Narrative." *Traditional American Indian Literatures: Texts and Interpretations.* Lincoln: University of Nebraska Press, 1981, 1–24.

———. "Turning Comparative Literature Around: the Problem of Translating American Indian Literatures." In Coltelli 1989:39–52.

Krupat, Arnold. "Anthropology in the Ironic Mode: the Work of Franz Boas." *Social Text* 19/20 (1988): 105–18.

———. "'Literary' Criticism/Native American 'Literature'." *Ethnocriticism: Ethnography, History, Literature.* Berkeley: University of California Press, forthcoming.

———. "Identity and Difference in the Criticism of Native American Literature." *Diacritics* 13(1983): 2–13.

———. "Post-Structuralism and Oral Literature." In Swann and Krupat 1987:113–28.

León-Portilla, Miguel. *Pre-Columbian Literatures of Mexico,* tr. Grace Lobanov and M. León-Portilla. Norman: University of Oklahoma Press, 1969.

Lincoln, Kenneth. *Native American Renaissance.* Berkeley: University of California Press, 1983.

Matthews, Washington. "The Mountain Chant: A Navajo Ceremony." Bureau of Ethnology, Fifth Annual Report. Washington: Government Printing Office, 1887, 385–468.

Mattina, Anthony. "North American Indian Mythography: Editing Texts for the Printed Page." In Swann and Krupat 1987:129–48.

———, and Madeline de Sautel, trs. *The Golden Woman: The Colville Narrative of Peter Seymour.* Tucson: University of Arizona Press, 1985.

McAllester, David. "'The War God's Horse Song,' An Exegesis in Native American Humanities." In *Music of the North American Indians,* ed. Charlotte Heth. Berkeley, University of California Press, 1980, 1–22.

Mooney, James. *The Swimmer Manuscript: Cherokee Sacred Formulas and Medicinal Prescrip-*

tions, rev. and ed. by Frans M. Olbrechts. Bureau of American Ethnology, Bulletin 99. Washington: Government Printing Office, 1932.

————. *Myths of the Cherokee*. New York: Johnson Reprint, 1970 [1900].

Powell, John Wesley. *Anthropology of the Numa: John Wesley Powell's Manuscript on the Numic Peoples of North America*, ed. Don D. Fowler and Catherine S. Fowler. Washington: Smithsonian Institution Press, 1971 [1868–80].

Powers, William. *Sacred Language: the Nature of Supernatural Discourse in Lakota*. Norman: University of Oklahoma Press, 1986.

————. "Text and Context in Lakota Music." *Explorations in Ethnomusicology: Essays in Honor of David McAllester*, ed. Charlotte Frisbie. Detroit Monographs in Musicology, no. 9.

Robinson, Harry. *Write It on Your Heart: the Epic World of an Okanagan Storyteller*, ed. Wendy Wickwire. Vancouver: Talonbooks/Theytus Books, 1989.

Rothenberg, Jerome. "Total Translation: An Experiment in the Presentation of American Indian Poetry." In Chapman 1975:292–307.

————, ed. *Shaking the Pumpkin: Traditional Poetry of the Indian North Americas*. Garden City, N.Y.: Doubleday, 1972.

————. " 'We Explain Nothing, We Believe Nothing': American Indian Poetry and the Problematics of Translation." In Swann, 1992, 64–79.

Schoolcraft, Henry Rowe. *Historical and Statistical Information Respecting the History, Condition and Prospects of the Indian Tribes of the United States. . .* , Part I. Philadelphia: Lippincott, Grambo, 1851.

Sherzer, Joel. *Kuna Ways of Speaking: An Ethnographic Perspective*. Austin: University of Texas Press, 1983.

————. *Verbal Art in San Blas: Kuna Culture Through Its Discourse*. Cambridge, Cambridge UP, 1990.

Swann, Brian, ed. *On the Translation of Native American Literatures*. Washington: Smithsonian Institution Press, 1992.

————. *Song of the Sky: Versions of Native American Songs and Poems*. N.P.: Four Zoas Night House Press, 1985.

————, and Arnold Krupat, eds. *Recovering the Word: Essays on Native American Literature*. Berkeley: University of California Press, 1987.

Tedlock, Barbara. "Songs of the Zuni Kachina Society: Composition, Rehearsal, and Performance." *Southwestern Indian Ritual Drama*, ed. Charlotte Frisbie. Albuquerque: University of New Mexico Press, 1980, 7–35.

————. "Sound Texture and Metaphor in Quiche Maya Ritual Language." *Current Anthropology* 23(1982): 269–72.

Tedlock, Dennis. *Finding the Center: Narrative Poetry of the Zuni Indians*. Lincoln: University of Nebraska Press, 1978 [1972].

————. *The Spoken Word and the Work of Interpretation*. Philadelphia: University of Pennsylvania Press, 1983.

Timberlake, Henry. *Memoirs: 1756–65*. Salem, N.H.: Ayer, 1971.

Voth, H. R. *The Oraibi Powamu Ceremony*. Chicago: Field Columbian Museum Publication 61, Anthropological Series, III, 2, 1901.

Wiget, Andrew. "Oratory." *Native American Literature*. Boston: Twayne, 1985, 23–25.

Suggested Reading

Anyone who reads through some of the work referred to in my historical account will very quickly develop a sense of the range and variety of translations of Native American song and story into English. Here, what might usefully be added is a listing of some of the anthologies of these materials currently available. These are eclectic in their selections—as, indeed, they cannot help but be—and the reader/user of these anthologies will do well to keep in mind the various sorts of translation options and problems I have tried to detail.

The earliest general anthology is that by George Cronyn, called *The Path on the Rainbow,* published in 1918 and reissued by Liveright in 1934. I accept Dell Hymes's view that the "two major anthologies in English are [those of Margot] Astrov (1946) and [A. Grove] Day (1951)" (Hymes 1981:37). The full titles are *The Winged Serpent: An Anthology of American Indian Prose and Poetry* (New York: John Day, 1946; rpt. Capricorn Books, 1962) and *The Sky Clears: Poetry of the American Indians* (New York: Macmillan, 1951). Also worth looking at is the very uneven textbook edited by Thomas E. Sanders and Walter W. Peek called *Literature of the American Indian* (New York: Glencoe, 1973). John Bierhorst's collections previously cited are also important sources to be consulted, along with his *In the Trail of the Wind: American Indian Poems and Ritual Orations* (New York: Farrar, Straus & Giroux, 1971; rpt. Sunburst Books, 1987), and *The Red Swan: Myths and Tales of the American Indians* (New York: Farrar, Straus & Giroux, 1974). William Brandon's *The Magic World: American Indian Songs and Poems* (New York: Morrow, 1970) is "not recommended" by William Bevis (Chapman 1975:323) for the liberties it—like Rothenberg's work—takes. But the canny reader might consult it. More recently, there is *American Indian Myths and Legends,* edited by Richard Erdoes and Alfonso Ortiz (New York: Pantheon, 1984), a valuable collection, yet one that has been incisively criticized by Dell Hymes (Swann and Krupat 1987:41–84).

"Tokens of Literary Faculty": Native American Literature and Euroamerican Translation in the Early Nineteenth Century

William M. Clements

Henry Wadsworth Longfellow had good reason to be concerned with how texts of Native American oral literature were translated and presented to Euroamerican readers. His epic poem *Song of Hiawatha* (1855)—one of his most commercially successful works—drew extensively on the Ojibwa oral narratives which had appeared in *Algic Researches*, a collection of translations published by Henry Rowe Schoolcraft in 1839. Contrary to the opinions of most twentieth-century commentators on Schoolcraft's work (e.g., Thompson xv; McNeil 117) and even some contemporary critics, Longfellow apparently assumed the material in *Algic Researches* to be very reliable. Shortly after its publication, he sent a copy of his poem to Schoolcraft as "an acknowledgment of my obligations to you; for without your books I could not have written mine." His letter accompanying the poem urged Schoolcraft to notice how "very faithfully" he had adhered to "the old myths" (Hilen 3:509). Longfellow's interest in Native American literature had anticipated the publication of *Hiawatha* by over a decade. In 1843 he sent Ferdinand Freiligrath, who was later to translate Longfellow's epic into German, a copy of "a wild ballad, with the war-whoop in it," which had been translated from the original Choctaw by "a gentleman from Mississippi." One stanza of the three comprising the "Song of the Ancient Choctaws" suffices to give its flavor (Hilen 2:516):

> I slew the chief of the Muskokee,
> And burned his squaw at a blasted tree,
> By the hind-legs I tied up his cur,
> He had no time to fondle her.
>> Hoo! hoo! hoo! the Muskokee!
>> Wah! wah! wah! the blasted tree!

From this we get a sense of what Longfellow, the nineteenth century's most ambitious adapter of Native American literature into his own creative efforts, conceived American Indian poetry to be. More importantly, for present concerns, the text provided by the still unidentified "gentleman from Mississippi" represents the typical results of Native American textmaking—the conversion of American Indian oral performances into printed texts (cf. Fine 1984)—throughout the first two-thirds of the nineteenth century.

Translators had begun converting Native American verbal performances into written European languages as early as the seventeenth century, when the Jesuits in New France incorporated occasional orations, stories, and songs into accounts of their mission work among the Hurons and Iroquois. While most New England Puritans—except for rare dissenters such as Roger Williams—evinced little interest in the oral literary culture of beings whom they considered demonic, their contemporaries in the middle and southern colonies were more likely to make an effort to describe performances, especially singing and speechifying. Yet few texts emerged even from the middle and southern colonies, Henry Timberlake's translation of a Cherokee war song (*Memoirs* 56–58) being a notable exception. A relatively systematic program of Native American studies did not begin until the late eighteenth and early nineteenth centuries. Influenced by an interest in American languages among European philologists, the emergence of an indigenous intellectual class of post-Enlightenment figures such as Thomas Jefferson, the continued expansion of the new nation westward into Indian lands, and the need by the federal government for an Indian policy founded on reliable information about Native Americans (see Bieder 1986), students of American Indians found an increasingly receptive audience for their books and essays, in which oral literature—performance descriptions and texts—figured more and more prominently. Even the most casual observers of frontier America in the early nineteenth century were likely to refer at least in passing to Native American verbal art.

Yet translations of that art by Euroamericans in the first half of the 1800s fall far below modern criteria. As records of oral performances, the translations fail in terms of text, texture, and context—the trinity of dimensions which ethnographers of speaking have come to regard as fundamental in documenting artistic communication (Dundes 1964). But ignoring these translations may result not only in a failure to understand nineteenth-century attitudes toward Native American cultures, but also in the loss of the insights into American Indian oral literature that can be salvaged from them. Consequently, this essay aims at reconstructing some of the ideas that shaped how translators in the early nineteenth century went about their work with the ultimate purpose of suggesting how useful those translations may be in documenting Native American oral literature. These shaping ideas—seldom articulated in straightforward statements of method—emerge in opinions about literature and about Native American cultures, especially languages, on the part of translators, critics, and even casual observers of Indian America. They represent components of the intellectual and esthetic milieu that were particularly significant for the textmakers.

The principles which shaped the work of Native American textmakers during the early nineteenth century developed primarily from perceptions of the probable effects of the impact of Euroamerican civilization on Indian cultures. The prevailing opinion held that Native Americans as representatives of "savagism" stood in direct and inescapable opposition to civilization (Pearce 1988). Native cultures appeared to be the obverse of Euroamerican ways of life and were destined to be totally obliterated as civilization progressed westward (Dippie 1982). The songs, stories, and orations of the Indians had so little literary merit that they deserved the same fate as the cultures in general. Since they could be consigned to oblivion with no esthetic loss, translating them served at most the purposes of those who sought to understand Native Americans for the sake of efficiently subjugating them. Representing this point of view was Lewis Cass, who as governor of Michigan Territory had begun a systematic study of that region's Native cultures in order to place their governance on a sounder footing than that provided by the reports of eastern armchair ethnologists (Brown 1953). In an essay in the *North American Review* in 1826, Cass, who became one of his era's most knowledgeable students of Native Americans, found little to recommend itself in their mental culture, especially language, the principal key to a society's collective intellect according to contemporary philologists (cf. Bieder 1986:16–54, 155–60). Of the speech of the Wyandots, for example, he wrote (1826:74):

Of all the languages spoken by man, since the confusion of tongues at the tower of Babel, it least deserves this character [of being harmonious and musical]. It is harsh, guttural, and undistinguishable; filled with intonations, that seem to start from the speaker with great pain and effort.

The debility of Native American languages symptomized for Cass a profounder problem for these "savages," the weakness and narrowness of their intellects. He drew the conclusion (1826:79):

The range of thought of our Indian neighbors is extremely limited. Of abstract ideas they are almost wholly destitute. They have no sciences, and their religious notions are confused and circumscribed. They have but little property, less law, and no public offences. They soon forget the past, improvidently disregard the future, and waste their thoughts, when they do think, upon the present.

While Cass himself had translated a couple of war songs from the Algonquin language of the Miami ("Indian Customs," 1), he apparently agreed in principle with his protégé C. C. Trowbridge, who replied to an item about Native American poetry on a questionnaire that Cass was distributing in the early 1820s that "at most it is nonsense. They have no poetry or rhyme in any shape" (quoted in Weslager 1978:184). For Cass, Trowbridge, and indeed the majority of Euroamericans who shared their views, attempts to translate Native American verbal art into print were futile and useless except for immediate political advantage.

A more positive attitude maintained a precarious coexistence with the idea that the Indians and their way of life amounted to little more than an obstacle to the progress of civilization. Inspired by the historical philosophy of such Enlightenment figures as Adam Ferguson, some Euroamericans believed that Native Americans were not necessarily the direct antithesis of civilization, but possessed—often, to be sure, in small portions—the spiritual and intellectual raw material to become civilized themselves. The idea that the Native American was a "European *manqué*" (Pearce 1988:4) had emerged quite early, an example being the account of Virginia Indians published by Alexander Whitaker in 1613. Whitaker, addressing an appeal for funds to the Virginia Company in London, perceived in the Natives living near his church in Henrico "unnurtured grounds of reason" (27). As evidence of their potential for becoming civilized, he cited the Natives' archery skills, devotion to a (false) religious faith, concept of property, system of morality and law, and "rude kinde of Common-wealth" (25–27). Always a decidedly minority position, Whitaker's view was even more definitely so by the time the new nation took shape in the late eighteenth century, but it continued to provide the philosophical foundation for the efforts of some missionaries and others who glimpsed occasional intimations of civilizable potential among Native Americans.

While the belief that Indians possessed the raw materials of civilization only awaiting the molding influence of the Euroamerican seems a natural parallel to the "virgin land" image, which represented the New World as a fecund wilderness that needed only civilized cultivation to become an Edenic garden, supporters of the theory of Indian potential could cite some particulars of Native American cultures to demonstrate their position's validity. Most prominent among these particulars was that which Cass cited as evidence of Native American savagism: language and literary expression. The "natural eloquence" of the Indians—a trait recognized as early as the seventeenth century by the French Jesuits—became an article of faith for many observers of Native American cultures. For instance, a firsthand account such as that of Moravian missionary John Heckewelder, published in 1819, could heap praises on the unstudied oratorical style of Lenape public speakers:

The eloquence of the Indians is natural and simple; they speak what their feelings dictate without art and without rule; their speeches are forcible and impressive, their arguments few and pointed, and when they mean to persuade as well as convince, they take the shortest way to reach the heart (132).

A generation later, in 1849, Mary Henderson Eastman, an Army wife who had lived among the Dakota in Minnesota, offered similar testimony. About the speaking of orator Shah-co-pee, she exclaimed (1849:115),

We could but admire his native eloquence. Here, with all that is wild in nature surrounding him, did the untaught orator address his people. His lips gave rapid utterance to thoughts which did honor to his feelings.

An anonymous reviewer for the periodical *Ariel* in the 1820s could echo these sentiments from a secondhand perspective. With no apparent effort, the reviewer contended, the Native American " 'speaks as he doth ruminate,' in the simplicity of his heart." The language of Indians, the reviewer continued,

is the more beautiful, from its very simplicity and brevity. . . . Himself the child of Nature, he speaks her eloquent language. He has no far-fetched and pointless expressions—no poor and insufficient similes—but without circumlocution . . . he images forth his eloquence in every sentence ("Indian Eloquence," 142).

Such simplicity, while appealing to ears tuned by romanticism and jaded with the pomposities of Euroamerican rhetoric, represented only the beginnings of truly literary expression. Native American oratory, the special admiration of sympathetic Euroamericans, reflected "the infancy of language," according to a contemporary reviewer of Heckewelder's book (1819:72), and stood ready to be guided to maturity by a sensitive, civilized intelligence.

If Native Americans as persons possessed the fundamentals requisite for becoming civilized, and if their languages evinced the natural eloquence that lay at the base of civilized expression, their oral literature also exhibited potentialities. One of the earliest citations of these potentialities appeared in the first volume of the *North American Review* in 1815. In an essay in which he blamed the lack of a truly American literature on the sad circumstance of America's having no distinctive national language, Walter Channing suggested that "the oral literature of its aborigines" had to suffice as America's literary heritage. He portrayed Indian speech as being "the very language for poetry" and argued that its "objects are the very elements for poetry" (313). Continuing his praise of the literary potentials of Native American oral discourse, Channing rhapsodized,

it is as bold as his [the Native American's] own unshackled conceptions, and as rapid as his own step. It is now as rich as the soil on which he was nurtured, and ornamented with every blossom that blows in his path. It is now elevated and soaring, for his image is the eagle, and now precipitous and hoarse as the cataract among whose mists he is descanting.

American Indian oral literature, Channing asserted, provides "genuine originality." All who encounter it are delighted with "what appears its haughty independence" (314).

According to the perception of advocates of the Indians-as-European-*manqué* view as Channing seems to have been, Native American verbal art constituted as inchoate literature, rich in raw material that only needed the disciplinary guidance of the civilized literary artist to take its rightful place among the world's literatures. In the words of William Gilmore Simms, the Indian "was not without very decided beginnings of a literature. This may have been rude enough . . . but it is sufficient that he had made a beginning" (137).

That beginning—the inchoate features of Native American oral literature—was evident to many observers in the early nineteenth century in a variety of manifestations, the most frequently mentioned being a wealth of imagination, the employment of figurative tropes, rhythm, and parallelism.

Simms, who, like Longfellow, was heavily influenced by Schoolcraft's translations of Ojibwa narratives in his own treatments of Indian themes in fiction, built a case for the richness of the Native American imagination in an extended review, published originally in 1845, of two of his mentor's books. He called attention to the "vast pneumatology" of the Indians "which found spirits, divine and evil,—as numerous as those of the Greeks or Germans—in their groves, their mountains, their great oceans, their eternal forests, and in all the changes and aspects of their visible world" (132). Simms believed that closer investigation of Native American supernatural systems would reveal a complexity of design that only bold and active imaginations could create. Pantheons of spiritual beings in various Native American cultures, particularly among Schoolcraft's Ojibwa, "attest all the preliminary conditions of an intellect" with literary tendencies (144). The tendencies of Native Americans to imagine the existence of beings beyond their sensory perception constituted, according to Simms, "the literary susceptibilities of a people" (132).

Another indication of Native American literary potential, the figures of speech—especially metaphors—employed by Native American orators and other verbal performers, caught the attention of many early observers. Even Lewis Cass has singled out the use of metaphor in a Miami lyric: " 'A clear sky' is a metaphorical expression, and conveys to an Indian the same ideas which are conveyed to us by the words good fortune" ("Indian Customs," 1). But for the Michigan governor, such usage was a symptom of the Indians' "poverty of language," which required the use of concrete images where more civilized speakers had relevant abstractions at their disposal.[1] For others, though, figures of speech in Native American oral performances indicated the performers' literary capabilities. Of Cass's contemporaries, missionary John Heckewelder devoted the most systematic attention to tropes in Native American oral literature. Chapter XII of his study of the Delaware, one of the earliest ethnographies of a Native American group, is devoted to "Metaphorical Expressions." Now finding them tasteful himself, Heckewelder regarded the Lenape fondness for metaphors as "to their discourse what feathers and beads are to their persons, a gaudy but tasteless ornament." However, he admitted that many literary traditions "[e]ven in enlightened Europe" viewed the use of metaphor highly and "the immortal Shakespeare, himself, did not disdain" to use this figure (137). Heckewelder then listed forty-nine examples of metaphors used by Indians—presumably Delaware—beginning with "*The sky is overcast with dark blustering clouds*" (meaning that some sort of trouble lies ahead) (137) and ending with "*To bury deep in the earth*" (meaning to dismiss something totally from one's memory) (140). For most commentators the copious supply of figures of speech, most of them involving comparisons between abstract concepts and natural phenomena, which came readily to Native American lips, testified to the literary potential of Native American minds.

While metaphor was the most frequently cited figurative device among nineteenth-century commentators on Native American oral literature, others were occasionally mentioned. For example, an anonymous essayist, writing on Indian oratory in *The Knick-erbocker* in 1836, cited an example of irony. The Onondaga leader Grangula, in reply to a blustering Frenchman who was trying to persuade him not to trade with the British, responded to his interlocutor's empty threats by facetiously claiming that the Onondaga menfolk had had to restrain their women and children from attacking the very heart of the French garrison in Quebec ("Indian Eloquence," 386–87).

Rhythm and parallelism also received some attention from the Euroamericans who found tokens of literary potential in the stories, songs, and speeches of Native Americans. Heckewelder noticed that when Delaware warriors assembled to recount their battle-field exploits, they narrated in "a kind of half-singing or *recitative*" with a drumbeat regulating the rhythm of their presentations (210). Occasionally, literary critics tried to plug the rhythms used by Indian performers into Euroamerican concepts of patterned repetition, as did the anonymous writer who, in an 1840 *Southern Literary Messenger* article, asserted that "the trochee predominates" in all Native American song texts, because "The polysyllabic character of the language is adverse to short lively metres" ("North American Indians," 192). More often observers were content with vaguer descriptive terms—for example, the "expressive cadences" used by Rufus B. Sage to describe a Brulé oration (57)—when they emphasized the rhythm extant in Native American oral literature. Even more vague, but still indicative of a recognition of literary rhythm, was Heckewelder's characterization of Delaware songs as "not without some kind of measure" (210). For most writers on the subject, the literature—or perhaps from their perspective "*pre*-literature"—of Native Americans demonstrated clear traces of rhythm, which suggested literary tendencies, but ones which only rarely had achieved sufficient sophistication to merit the metrical designations used by civilized poets and their reviewers.

In a similar manner, hints of parallelism suggested Native American literary potential. In a letter to Ferdinand Freiligrath, Longfellow justified his stylistic appropriation of this device for the Finnish *Kalevala* for *The Song of Hiawatha*: "*parallelism* belongs to Indian poetry as well as to Finnish, and not only belongs to it, but in like manner is the 'rule and law of it'" (Hilen 3: 517). Oft-cited comparisons between Native American oral poetry and the Hebrew psalms frequently focused on parallelism as the literary feature shared by the two (e.g., "North American Indians," 192).

Yet these traits of Native American oral literature lacked what was needed to be truly literary in the Euroamerican sense—the only sense recognized by the textmakers of the early nineteenth century. Consequently, in supposed fairness to the Indians and their groping efforts toward literary artistry, translators did what was necessary to convert the products of Native American oral performances into full-fledged literature. That meant adding rhyme to song texts as well as regularizing their meters, extending metaphors and other figures to a more complete realization than the Native performers had been wont to do, fleshing out features of narration—especially scenic description and rounded characterization—that were absent or presented cursorily by Indian storytellers, deleting unsuitable materials such as vocables ("meaningless nonsense syllables") from songs and scatological elements from tales, and emphasizing features of narratives that conveyed straightforward or allegorical moral messages. In short, many translators who were sympathetic to Native American cultures saw their responsibility as one of molding pre-literature into true literature. Their attitude toward Indian oral literature paralleled that of the Reverend Samuel Parker toward Indian singing. In the mid-1830s Parker undertook a journey at the behest of the American Board of Commissioners for Foreign Missions that led him across the Great Plains and Rocky Mountains all the way to the Oregon coast. Parker was impressed with most of the Indians he met along the way. He characterized the intellectual power of the Oglalas, for instance, as "above the ordinary stamp" (63) and of the Pawnees as "very good, but [in] need [of] cultivation" (53). Remarking upon the singing of Plateau groups such as the Flatheads and Nez Perce, he mentioned their "flexible and sweet-toned voices." Parker was delighted to encounter in the western wilderness "the sounds of melody and harmony, even in the most simplified strains." Yet the singers, he added, "are conscious of the inferiority of their tunes to ours, and wished to be instructed in this department of knowledge" (241). Most Native oral performers might not be so reasonable as these Plateau singers who recognized the truncated development of their art, but certainly those Euroamericans who admired their literary potential were. William Gilmore Simms's opinion that Native American verbal art "needed but little help from civilization to grow into a vast and noble literature" (144) and could "be wrought into symmetry and shape with the usual effects of time and civilization" (132) represented a viewpoint shared by many appreciative critics of Native American cultures during the first half of the nineteenth century.

In her preface to Mary Henderson Eastman's *Dahcotah; or, Life and Legends of the Sioux Around Fort Snelling*, a Mrs. C. M. Kirkland articulated this set of ideas fully by calling attention to the literary powers of Native Americans as well as to their need for Euroamerican guidance:

The Indians themselves are full of poetry. Their legends embody poetic fancy of the highest and most adventurous flight; their religious ceremonies refer to things unseen with a directness which shows how bold and vivid are their conceptions of the imaginative. The war-song—the death-song—the song of victory—the cradle-chant—the lament for the slain—these are the overflowings of the essential poetry of their untaught souls. Their eloquence is proverbially soaring and figurative. . . . They, indeed, live poetry; it should be ours to write it out for them (x).

The idea that responsible textmakers, eager to represent Indian narratives, songs, and orations as literature, should do whatever was necessary to enhance their texts' literary features resulted in the publication of material whose Native qualities were usually obscured beneath a heavy veil of Euroamerican accretions. Consider, for example, a Brulé tale made into a text by Rufus Sage (90–91) from the oral narration of an "old man" who told it in response to some heavy betting on a game of hand.[2] After an introduction in which he boasts of the rarity of his martial failures, the storyteller proceeds with his tale:

We were proceeding against the Crows, and, like experienced warriors, had sent our spy in advance to look for the enemy. Hurrying on, in momentary expectation of a conflict, the stout hearts of our braves were appalled by his return without robe or arms, and scalpless—and with a face suffused in blood.
     This was his story: The enemy, aware of our approach, were awaiting us in great numbers.

Encountering their scouts, he had been robbed and scalped, and left for dead. In this situation he lay till darkness shut down upon the mountain and the night-breeze gave him strength to meet us and advise our speedy return.

The party returns to camp in humiliation to face mockery for their lack of success. After "Three moons sped," they go back to the field. Once again, the scalpless warrior acts as spy, but this time comes back triumphantly bearing two scalps. The party follows his lead, successfully engages the enemy, and finds among the dead "one whose scalp was wanting." The spy explains:

"Behind yon hill," said he, "a fountain chants melody fit for warriors' ears,—let's to it, that we may drink."
     Following his direction, he led to a silvery spring overhung by crags and shaded by cottonwoods.

Here had occurred the event that accounted for the earlier humiliation of the spy, the two scalps he now possessed, and the scalpless dead Crow. The spy continued:

"Three times has the night-queen turned her full face to smile upon the prowess of Lacota arms, since at this very spot I met an enemy. We rushed towards each other for the attack. 'Twas then he cried:
     "'Are we not both braves? Why should we fight? When our people meet in the fray, then may we join arms,—till then, a truce.'
     "To this I replied,
     "'Says Crowman peace?—then, be there peace.'
     "Thus said, we shook hands and sat down by the fountain.
     "Willing to amuse the foe, I gathered a pebble and proposed a game of hand. The challenge was accepted, and we played,—first, arrow against arrow, then bow against bow, robe against robe, and scalp against scalp.
     "I was unsuccessful and lost all,—arrow, bow, robe, and scalp. I gave up all, but with the extorted promise that we should here meet again for another trial of skill.
     "True to the word, we did meet again. We played, and this time, the Good Spirit showed me kindness.
     "Winning back arrows, bow and robe, I staked them all against the lost scalp. The game was a close one; but again the Good Spirit favored me, and I won.
     "'Crowman,' said I, 'scalp against scalp.'
     "The banter was accepted, and the play continued. He lost, and I, with my winnings, arose to leave.
     "'Warrior,' exclaimed the luckless player, 'meet me in the fight, that we may try the game of arms.'
     "'Thy words please me,' I answered. 'Will the Crowman name the place?'
     "'A valley lies beyond this hill,—there my people await their enemies, and there let me hope to see you with them.'
     "To that place I led you. We fought and conquered. My opponent at play was among the slain. Need I tell you who took his scalp?"

Several elements of this text probably derive more from Sage than from the oral narrator. For instance, the scenic description (the "silvery spring overhung by crags and shaded by cottonwoods") must reflect the romantic literary esthetic of Sage's time. The careful pacing of the narrative with each phase of its progress fully explained and related to earlier phases suggests the hand of the textmaker, as does the attention to detail in the dialogue, especially the story-within-the-story. Throughout the text, the language strikes twentieth-century ears as too formal for a story of this sort—a personal anecdote devoid of apparent ritual associations. And one must wonder to what extent the English words Sage has employed in his text represent what the narrator actually said. For example, Sage uses the English terms "conflict," then "fray," and then "fight." Are these translations of the same Lakota word? If Sage's three words, in fact, reflect real variations in the narrator's diction, do they catch the different shadings of the original Lakota vocabulary? The mixture of somewhat formal, "literary" English usages (for instance, "a face suffused in blood") with stereotypical "Indianisms" ("Three moons sped") also raises questions about the tonal level of the text. Yet Sage did not see himself as being unfaithful to his originals. Regarding another text he made from a Brulé story, he wrote, "In penning the above I was guided solely by the leading incidents as related in my hearing" (95). In truth, though, he was also guided by his sense of the literary—of what was necessary to make a good tale in a written European language.

Another example of how nineteenth-century Euroamericans handled the Native American oral literature they translated and published comes from the work of Henry Rowe Schoolcraft, certainly the most influential figure in the study of American Indians and their cultures of the early 1800s.[3] Though most well known for his translations of Ojibwa narratives which appeared in *Algic Researches*, Longfellow's principal influence, Schoolcraft actually worked with other major genres of Native American oral literature, including poems (that is, songs without music) and oratory. Usually he reshaped the poems to fit his own conceptions of what constituted literature. Consider the following lines—a war song, presumably Ojibwa—from the 1848 reissue (224) of Schoolcraft's *Oneóta*, which had appeared serially in 1844:

> The eagles scream on high,
>   They whet their forked beaks,
> Raise—raise the battle cry,
>   'Tis fame our leader seeks.

Although Schoolcraft claims that this "expresses no more than the native sentiments," he readily admits that what he calls a "stanza" consists of "expressions brought into connection, from different fragments" (224). In this collation process, he has added alternating end rhymes and has—through unknown Procrustean adjustments—fitted the material into regular lines of iambic trimeter. In regard to these particular embellishments, it is worth noting the questions about "Indian songs" that Schoolcraft circulated to obtain data for a major study of Native American ethnology and history that he was making under the direction of the United States Congress in the late 1840s and early 1850s: "Is there any rhyme in them? Are the words collocated so as to observe the laws of quantity? In other words, are they measured, or are the accents in them found to recur in fixed and regular intervals? (1851:555). These questions suggest what Schoolcraft expected to find in Native American oral poetry: the very features that characterized written verse in the England and America of his day. When he did not find such features in the material he was translating—such as the Ojibwa war song, if we are to use Native-language texts published by Schoolcraft himself (1848:411–12) and by, for example, Frances Densmore (1910:137–46, 176–80; 1913:87–134, 185–95) as touchstones—he added them, primarily for the purpose of making them "literary" in the only sense he recognized.

Though still subject to the "improving" processes which characterized treatments of all Indian oral literature at the time, Native American oratorical texts, which proliferated in the wake of such famous speeches as that of Logan, celebrated by Thomas Jefferson, may have fared slightly better in the hands of early nineteenth-century translators than narratives and poetry did. Virtually every publication on American Indian life from the period had at least one example of "Indian eloquence," and many travelers along the frontier who had no special interest in Native American cultures still found space for a speech or two in the published accounts of their adventures. For example, John Bradbury, who toured the "Interior of America" for a couple of years beginning in 1809, appended the text of an oration which Big Elk, an Omaha, delivered "over the grave of the Black Buffalo," a Teton leader, in the 1819 edition of his travel journal. The first few lines of Big Elk's speech (228) addressed the inevitability of death and of concomitant grief in universal terms:

Do not grieve—misfortunes will happen to the wisest and best men. Death will come, and always comes out of season: it is the command of the Great Spirit, and all nations and people must obey. What is passed, and cannot be prevented, should not be grieved for.

The remainder of Big Elk's short address, apparently intended for the Euroamerican military officers who were present, dealt with his own death, which he predicted would be inglorious, and the disposition of his body—"my flesh to be devoured by the wolves, and my bones rattled on the plain by the wild beasts" (229).

Although the text of this oration in Omaha is just as lacking as the Native-language versions of the Brulé story translated by Sage and Schoolcraft's Ojibwa poem (and although evidence exists of the latitude with which Euroamericans handled oratorical texts by Indians in the nineteenth century [see Kaiser 1987]), fewer reasons for doubting the reliability of the translation immediately suggest themselves. Though reflecting early nineteenth-century English vocabulary, no obvious stylistic accretions from literary romanticism stand out.

One of the ironies of Native American textmaking during the early nineteenth century was that translators who regarded American Indian oral literature as the product of savagism—and perhaps the unknown person who rendered Big Elk's speech into English was among them—probably produced more reliable texts than their more sympathetic contemporaries. Though fragmentary, Lewis Cass's handling of a Miami lyric may be nearer to what was actually performed than the texts from Sage and Schoolcraft reproduced above: "I will go and get my friends—I will go and get my friends—I am anxious to see my enemies. A clear sky is my friend, and it is him I am seeking" ("Indian Customs," 1). Not only does this seem close to the texts in Ojibwa—like Miami, an Algonquin language—that Schoolcraft and later Densmore published, but Cass and others sharing his view had no reason to embellish their texts. They regarded them as merely exhibits in the case against the savages of the American frontier and were consequently quite willing to preserve elements in them that did not meet Euroamerican literary expectations.

Yet except for orations, the texts translated by proponents of the savagism view are few. Textmaking was more likely to be done by someone attuned to the civilizable potential of Native Americans. Our records of Native American oral literature from the early nineteenth century thus are marked by a massive encrustation of Euroamerican embellishment. That embellishment involves the addition of features essential to literature, as it was defined by the vaguely romantic esthetics of the early nineteenth-century textmakers and their contemporaries. Consequently, we can probably assume that such features of Native American song texts as rhyme and rhythms which fit neatly into the Euroamerican metrical system represent translators' outright additions. The same can be said of most attempts at characterization and scenic description that appear in narrative texts, especially when romanticized Euroamerican traits such as an abstract appreciation of natural beauty and a willingness to die for love are attributed to American Indians. Embellishment also included enhancing features that were already present in the Native American originals. For example, figures of speech were extended, and moral messages were enhanced. Consequently, we must admit that stylistically the texts created by most translators in the early nineteenth century probably offer little that is truly Native American.

However, they do have some value. Though early nineteenth-century texts of Native American oral literature are clearly inadequate in most cases for characterizing *how* the material was rendered in performance, they can provide insights into *what* was being performed. I think we can trust, for example, Kirkland's list of song types among Eastman's Dakota as affording insights into what kinds of songs were being sung. We can also trust the general content of the Brulé narratives that Rufus Sage included in his account of his travels. Most of them, in fact, have more recent analogs, recorded in situations where their accuracy can be verified. For example, Nicholas Black Elk related a close parallel to the hand game story treated above to John Neihardt in 1944 (DeMallie 341–45). Twentieth-century versions and related texts for other narratives in Sage's book—even a Lover's Leap story—also exist (Deloria 261–62, 266–68; Around Him 23).[4]

Even Schoolcraft's war song may be able to tell us something about Ojibwa oral literature in the 1820s and 1830s, when Schoolcraft likely heard the original(s). A particularly useful document for examining Schoolcraft's textmaking methods and principles is an essay entitled "Indian Music, Songs, and Poetry," which appeared in the 1848 republication of *Oneóta* (221–29). The "war song" translated (perhaps created) by Schoolcraft appears in a section of that essay entitled "Oral Composition" and in a paragraph dealing expressly with imagery. There Schoolcraft writes, "In war excursions great attention is paid to the flight of birds, particularly those of the carnivorous species," presumably for prognostic purposes. Moreover, he adds, Ojibwa warriors who distinguished themselves on the battlefield received wing and tail feathers from raptors as marks of their accomplishments. Consequently, he concludes, leaders of war parties "are naturally led to appeal to the agency of this class of birds" when they are arousing the martial ardor of their followers (224). This explains the use of bird imagery in the quoted example and in another quatrain which Schoolcraft includes (224):

> The birds of the brave take a flight round the
>   sky,
>   They cross the enemy's line,
> Full happy am I—that my body should fall,
>   Where brave men love to die.

Schoolcraft follows these lines with a comment pertinent to their literary potential: "Very little effort in the collocation and expansion of some of their sentiments, would impart to these bold and unfettered raphsodies [sic], an attractive form, among polished war songs." What we learn from all of this has nothing, of course, to do with Ojibwa poetic style, but we do learn something about the valences of a specific image, which School-craft—almost in anticipation of contemporary symbolic anthropologists—has "un-packed" by associating it with something else within the culture itself.

Yet the most value to be derived from examining the work of early nineteenth-century textmakers may come from outside their texts themselves in the realm of context and performance. Many textmakers and commentators on Native American oral literature presented relatively thorough depictions of the conditions under which they heard stories, songs, and speeches, as well as of the ways the storytellers, singers, and orators rendered their material. These records of natural performance contexts afford insights often un-available from later textmakers, who may have recorded and translated texts more scien-tifically, but who frequently did so in highly artificial situations devoid of natural context and performance variables.

Examples abound in the writings of almost every figure whose opinion has been sampled above, even Lewis Cass. For example, the Michigan governor described in some detail how a Miami warrior would characteristically narrate his martial exploits during a war dance:

He speaks with great emphasis and violent gesticulation—describes the number of the enemy whom he has killed; the mode in which he accomplished it, and the dangers he encountered. He relates the most minute circumstances, and shows the manner in which he crept silently upon his enemy, and took aim at his heart. He exhibits his scars, and relates the occasions upon which he received them ("Indian Cus-toms," 2).

John Heckewelder portrayed a similar context, but focused on the pattern of performance among several participants during a Delaware storytelling session (210):

The oldest warrior recites first, then they go on in rotation and in order of seniority, the drum beating all the time, as it were to give to the relation the greater appearance of reality. After each has made a short recital in his turn, they begin again in the same order, and so continue going the rounds, in a kind of alternate chanting, until every one has concluded.

Rufus Sage (57) conveyed the style of the Brulé orator Marto-cogershne:

He commenced in a low, distinct tone of voice. His robe, d[r]awn loosely around him, was held to its
place by the left hand, exposing his right arm and shoulder. As he proceeded he became more animated,
and seemed to enter into the full spirit of his discourse. The modulations of his voice, its deep intonations and expressive cadences, coupled with a corresponding appropriateness of every look and gesture,
presented one of the most perfect specimens of delivery I ever witnessed.

Even the most casual observer of Indians might provide valuable records of the contexts
for oral literary performance and its style. For example, Edwin James, who accompanied
Stephen H. Long's expedition to the Rocky Mountains in 1819 and 1820, wrote of storytelling among the Omaha (329–30):

The narrator proceeds with a degree of gravity of feature suitable to the nature of the events of his story,
and notes a variety of little circumstances in detail, which contribute much to give the whole an air of
truth to his auditors, who listen with an undivided attention, uttering occasionally an interjection, as the
feelings are excited.

Such descriptions of context and performance style provide insights into the nature of Native American oral literature that even the most accurately translated text cannot.

The idea that translators should transform Native American oral performances
into Euroamerican literature achieved its fullest realization in the work of Schoolcraft,
whose major publications spanned the period from 1839 until 1856. But the attitudes toward American Indian oral literature that shaped this approach to textmaking persisted.
For example, the quotation in this essay's main title comes from the early 1880s, when
John Reade used it in an address "The Literary Faculty of the Native Races of America,"
delivered to the Royal Society of Canada (25). Reade also asserted that the Indians' literary faculty existed as a "*germ* in the legend of the tribe, the story-telling of the wigwam,
and the speech-making of the council" (26; my emphasis). Many of Reade's contemporaries, though, had begun working from a different set of textmaking principles. At about
the same time Reade was addressing the Canadian learned society, Daniel Garrison Brinton, for example—though he seems to have despaired at the feasibility of translating oral
material at all—was preparing a number of influential translations of Mesoamerican texts
from a much more "scientific" perspective than that of Schoolcraft and his predecessors.
The late nineteenth-century ethnologists working for the Bureau of American Ethnology
and those who learned their discipline from Franz Boas also approached Native American
literature as the data of science and filled government bulletins and the professional journals in anthropology and folklore with Native-language texts and literal, interlinear translations. Yet despite the partial eclipse which the textmaking principles from the early
1800s experienced at least among academics, the idea that American Indian oral literature
could assume the textual form of Euroamerican literature has not been totally supplanted.
For example, during the second decade of the twentieth century translators and literary
critics such as Mary Austin saw parallels between the words of Native American songs
and imagist poetry and made texts of those songs accordingly (Castro 5–45). More re-

cently some critics of the ethnopoetics movement, one of whose aims is to produce texts reflecting the Native esthetic, have argued that some contemporary translators are actually imposing their own postmodern poetics on the texts they create (e.g., Bright 83). Even if that view does a disservice to specific textmakers working from the perspective of ethnopoetics, it reminds us of a danger that any translator faces—a danger exacerbated when the material to be translated comes from a culture the translator regards as undeveloped and emerges from a medium the translator considers inappropriate for literary expression.

The early nineteenth-century textmakers could not avoid this danger. The rhyming, regularly metered Choctaw war song that Longfellow sent to his friend Freiligrath illustrates in the extreme what usually happened to Native American literature in the hands of a Euroamerican translator of the time.[5] Consequently, the insights into American Indian oral literature gained from examining translated material from the early 1800s seem slight when compared with what we wished we knew and with what commentators, using material that is often no better, have sometimes claimed they did know. Yet while we should not try to use the work of early nineteenth-century translators in ways for which it is not equipped, we should not completely ignore the worthwhile data which it does afford. An early step in the study of any literary tradition must be an evaluation of its texts. These comments on textmaking in the early 1800s may contribute to our developing appreciation of exactly what is available as we seek to understand the rich traditions of Native American verbal art.[6]

Notes

1. The idea that figurative language resulted from a primitive, childlike inability to articulate in abstract terms was a commonplace in the cultural evolutionism that dominated anthropology and its intellectual forebears until the early twentieth century. The idea's sources lie in the foundations of modern social science. Note, for example, the following from Giambattista Vico's *New Science* (1744): "Now the sources of all poetic locution [i.e., concrete figures] are two: poverty of language and need to explain and be understood" (Bergin and Frisch 1970:6).

2. For a recent description of this guessing game, see Black Bear and Theisz 1976:133. I am grateful to Julian Rice for this reference.

3. For a specific and fairly detailed consideration of Schoolcraft's textmaking principles, see Clements 1990.

4. Julian Rice located these analogues to the narratives in Sage for me. He has also written at some length on Black Elk's hand game story (212–19).

5. Whether this piece was ever oral literature remains questionable. In Longfellow's letter to Freiligrath, he says that it was "written by a Choctaw" and translated by the Mississippian (Hilen 2:516). Whether Longfellow actually meant to be taken literally or was using "written" in the loose sense of "composed" is unclear. I have found nothing like this text in major published collections of Choctaw songs.

6. Most of the research for this paper occurred under the auspices of Arkansas State University's Research Reassignment Program. I especially appreciate the support of Charles Carr and

Lawrence Boucher in ensuring my participation in this program. I am also grateful to Frances Malpezzi for stylistic suggestions and particularly to Brian Swann for important, useful suggestions regarding focus and content.

References

Around Him, John. *Lakota Ceremonial Songs*. Trans. Albert White Hat, Sr. Rosebud, S. Dakota: Sinte Gleska College, 1983.

Bergin, Thomas Goddard, and Max Harold Frisch. *The New Science of Giambattista Vico: Abridged Translation of the Third Edition (1744)*. Ithaca, N.Y.: Cornell University Press, 1970.

Bieder, Robert E. *Science Encounters the Indian, 1820–1880: The Early Years of American Ethnology*. Norman: University of Oklahoma Press, 1986.

Black Bear, Ben, Sr., and R. D. Theisz. *Songs and Dances of the Lakota*. Rosebud, S. Dakota: Sinte Gleska College, 1976.

Bradbury, John. *Travels in the Interior of America, in the Years 1809, 1810, and 1811*. 2nd ed. London: Sherwood, Neely, and John, 1819.

Bright, William. *American Indian Linguistics and Literature*. Berlin: Mouton, 1984.

Brown, Elizabeth Gaspar. "Lewis Cass and the American Indian." *Michigan History* 37 (1953): 286–98.

Cass, Lewis. "Indian Customs." *The Columbian Star* 20 Apr. 1822: 1–2.

———. Review of *Manners and Customs of Several Indian Tribes* by John D. Heckewelder and *Historical Notes Respecting the Indians of North America* by John Halkett. *North American Review* 22 (1826): 53–119.

Castro, Michael. *Interpreting the Indian: Twentieth-Century Poets and the Native American*. Albuquerque: University of New Mexico Press, 1983.

Channing, Walter. "Essay on American Language and Literature." *North American Review* 1 (1815):307–14.

Clements, William M. "Schoolcraft as Textmaker." *Journal of American Folklore* 103 (1990): 177–92.

Deloria, Ella. *Dakota Texts*. Publications of the American Ethnological Society No. 14. New York: Stechert, 1932.

DeMallie, Raymond J., ed. *The Sixth Grandfather: Black Elk's Teachings Given to John Neihardt*. Lincoln: University of Nebraska Press, 1984.

Densmore, Frances. *Chippewa Music*. Bureau of American Ethnology Bulletin No. 45. Washington: Government Printing Office, 1910.

———. *Chippewa Music—II*. Bureau of American Ethnology Bulletin No. 53. Washington: Government Printing Office, 1913.

Dippie, Brian W. *The Vanishing American: White Attitudes and U. S. Indian Policy*. Middletown, Conn.: Wesleyan University Press, 1982.

Dundes, Alan. "Text, Texture, and Context." *Southern Folklore Quarterly* 28 (1964): 251–65.

Eastman, Mrs. Mary. *Dahcotah; or, Life and Legends of the Sioux Around Fort Snelling*. New York: John Wiley, 1849.

Fine, Elizabeth. *The Folklore Text from Performance to Print*. Bloomington: Indiana University Press, 1984.

Heckewelder, Rev. John. *History, Manners, and Customs of the Indian Nations Who Once Inhabited Pennsylvania and the Neighbouring States*. 1819. Philadelphia: Historical Society of Pennsylvania, 1876.

Hilen, Andrew, ed. *The Letters of Henry Wadsworth Longfellow*. 6 vols. Cambridge: Harvard University Press, 1966–82.

"Indian Eloquence." *The Ariel* 27 Dec. 1828: 142.

"Indian Eloquence." *The Knickerbocker* Apr. 1836: 385–90.

James, Edwin. *Account of an Expedition from Pittsburgh to the Rocky Mountains, Performed in the Years 1819 and '20, by Order of the Hon. J. C. Calhoun, Sec'y of War: Under the Command of Major Stephen H. Long. . . .* 2 vols. Philadelphia: H. C. Carey and I. Lea, 1823.

Kaiser, Rudolf. "Chief Seattle's Speech(es): American Origins and European Reception." *Recovering the Word: Essays on Native American Literature*. Ed. Brian Swann and Arnold Krupat. Berkeley: University of California Press, 1987, 497–536.

McNeil, William K. "A History of American Folklore Scholarship Before 1908." Ph.D. diss., Indiana University, 1980.

The Memoirs of Lieut. Henry Timberlake, (Who Accompanied the Three Cherokee Indians to England in the Year 1762) Containing Whatever he observed Remarkable, or worthy of public Notice. . . . London: For the Author, 1765.

"North American Indians." *Southern Literary Messenger* 6 (1840): 190–92.

Parker, Rev. Samuel. *Journal of an Exploring Tour Beyond the Rocky Mountains, under the Direction of the A.B.C.F.M. Performed in the Years 1835, '36, and '37. . . .* Ithaca: By the Author, 1838.

Pearce, Roy Harvey. *Savagism and Civilization: A Study of the Indian and the American Mind*. Berkeley: University of California Press, 1988.

Reade, John. "The Literary Faculty of the Native Races of America." *Publications and Transactions of the Royal Society of Canada* 1st ser. 2.2 (1884): 17–30.

Review of *An Account of the History, Manners and Customs of the Indian Nations. . . .*, by John Heckewelder. *Western Review and Miscellaneous Magazine* Sept. 1819: 65–74.

Rice, Julian. *Lakota Storytelling: Black Elk, Ella Deloria, and Frank Fools Crow*. New York: Peter Lang, 1989.

[Sage, Rufus B.]. *Scenes in the Rocky Mountains, and in Oregon, California, New Mexico, Texas, and the Grand Prairies; or Notes by the Way, during an Excursion of Three Years . . . .* Philadelphia: Carey and Hart, 1846.

Schoolcraft, Henry Rowe. *Historical and Statistical Information, Respecting the History, Condition and Prospects of the Indian Tribes of the United States . . . Part I*. Philadelphia: Lippincott, Grambo, 1851.

———. *The Indian in His Wigwam, or Characteristics of the Red Race of America*. New York: W. H. Graham, 1848.

Simms, William Gilmore. *Views and Reviews in American Literature, History and Fiction. First Series*. Ed. C. Hugh Holman. Cambridge, Mass.: Harvard University Press, 1962.

Thompson, Stith. *Tales of the North American Indians*. Cambridge, Mass.: Harvard University Press, 1929.

Weslager, C. A. *The Delaware Indian Westward Migration with the Texts of Two Manuscripts*

(1821–22) Responding to General Lewis Cass's Inquiries About Lenape Culture and Language. Wallingford, Penn.: Middle Atlantic Press, 1978.

Whitaker, Alexander. *Good Newes from Virginia. Sent to the Counsell and Company of Virginia, Resident in England*. London: William Welby, 1613.

Suggested Readings

The most important study of the attitudes of Euroamericans toward Native Americans during the period treated in this paper remains Roy Harvey Pearce, *The Savages of America: A Study of the Indian and the Idea of Civilization*, (Baltimore: Johns Hopkins University Press, 1953), which appeared in a revised edition in 1965. Issued in a Johns Hopkins Paperbacks edition in 1967 under the title *Savagism and Civilization: A Study of the Indian and the American Mind*, Pearce's volume covers the years 1609 through 1851. Its most recent republication (by the University of California Press as *Savagism and Civilization*) includes a new final chapter by Pearce and an introduction by Arnold Krupat, who has also written on Pearce's work in *The Voice in the Margin: Native American Literature and the Canon* (Berkeley: University of California Press, 1989). Other books that deal with the same topic from slightly different angles include Robert F. Berkhofer, Jr., *The White Man's Indian: Images of the American Indian from Columbus to the Present* (New York: Knopf, 1978), and Brian W. Dippie, *The Vanishing American: White Attitudes and U.S. Indian Policy* (Middletown, Conn.: Wesleyan University Press, 1982). Works that focus particularly on the attitudes of those who studied Native American cultures include Robert E. Bieder, *Science Encounters the Indian, 1820–1880: The Early Years of American Ethnology* (Norman: University of Oklahoma Press, 1986), and William K. McNeil, "A History of American Folklore Scholarship Before 1908" (Ph.D. diss. Indiana University, 1980). The latter provides biographical data on several of the figures treated here. The concept of "textmaking" which informs this paper is worked out in Elizabeth C. Fine, *The Folklore Text from Performance to Print* (Bloomington: Indiana University Press, 1984).

Incorporating the Native Voice: A Look Back from 1990

John Bierhorst

When a translation has gone to the printer, the translator's job is done; but the translation process as a whole, from its cause to its ultimate effect, is not yet complete.

In his work on translation theory, *After Babel*, George Steiner has enlarged on this truism, suggesting that translation be compared to the four-stroke cycle of an internal combustion engine. The translation itself is the power stoke, preceded by a kind of compression, representing the translator's act of faith, or commitment of resources to a project that may or may not turn out well. Two strokes accomplished, the cycle is half over.

During the third, or exhaust, stroke, the translation escapes into the recipient culture, which absorbs the new material and becomes permanently changed. Following this, there is an intake stroke, whereby the donor culture must swallow a result that the ethical translator hopes will be seen as a gain, not a loss. Steiner calls these third and fourth strokes "incorporation" and "restitution."

Translators do not always live to see such a cycle completed, since newly introduced texts may have to rest awhile before they are found worthy of incorporation. Or, as in the case of H. R. Schoolcraft, whose Ojibwa myths were picked up almost immediately by Longfellow and pumped into the English-speaking mainstream, the business may seem happily concluded, leaving it for future generations to discover problems in the area of "restitution."

Direct literary adaptation is not the only means by which a translated text may alter its new environment, but it is a useful indicator, offering inarguable proof of influence. With regard to the literature of the American Indian, one perhaps ought to emphasize that Indianist, or *indigenista*, works do not necessarily incorporate Indian verbal art.

A few years ago, when I was participating in a discussion panel on this subject, a member of the audience expressed irritation that no one had mentioned Gabriela Mistral. Probably the heckler was thinking of Mistral's passionate *America* ("Sun of the Incas, sun of the Mayas, / ripe American sun, / where Mayas and Quichés / reconnoitered and worshipped . . ."). But the truth is that the luscious poems in *America* evoke Indian phantoms without making contact with the song, narrative, and rhetoric that constitute Native American literature. The same could be said of many another New World literary effort, going all the way back to Alonso de Ercilla, author of *La Araucana*.

Historically, the Native literary voice—in translation necessarily—has contributed precious little to the formation of English, Spanish, and Portuguese letters in the New World. This is true even in so-called Indoamerica, the region stretching from Mexico to the Central Andes. Literary oddities of interest mainly to scholars might be rounded up in an effort to dispute this observation. But to come quickly to the point, I would prefer to consider just three waves of influence that have actually touched the mainstream.

The first is Longfellow's experiment, really a single breaker, which gobbled up most of the North American Indian material available in the mid-nineteenth century and survives today principally as a memento of romantic nationalism.

The second is that series of primitivist ripples heard in the 1920s as part of a quest for poetic renewal led by Ezra Pound and T. S. Eliot. Naturally, the expatriates Pound and Eliot avoided Indian material. But the gap was filled by Amy Lowell, Mary Austin, Mário de Andrade, and the temporarily American D. H. Lawrence.[1] An argument for lasting influence in this instance might include the observation that American anthropology would become more attuned to poetics, notably during the 1930s. And, in the literary sphere, writers like D'Arcy McNickle, José María Arguedas, and Rosario Castellanos would begin to slip Native texts into their novels, even if less to embrace Indian literature than to illustrate *costumbre*.

A third wave—which will be the subject of this essay—begins approximately in 1960 and continues, somewhat abated, to the present vantage point of 1990. The movement draws upon powerful currents (Indianist, Latin American nationalist, environmentalist, feminist, non-Christian spiritualist, anti-elitist, anti-ethnocentric) that would stir up a revolution against the literary establishment in the major languages. If in fact it does not divert the mainstream, it may help widen it.

Politics aside, the influence of Native literature has been strengthened in recent years by the sheer increase of new material and by the appearance of new translations of older texts. In his novel of 1986 *Cuzcatlán*, Salvadoran writer Manlio Argueta could insert a two-page adaptation of the Popol Vuh, confident that readers would catch the allusion. They do; but this would not have been possible fifty years ago, before the widely available Recinos translation, which Argueta used.

It is too early to know whether the translated word has at last formed a permanent channel of influence from the Native literatures to the Euroamerican. But a review of significant developments over the past thirty years would seem to indicate a new, higher standard of accomplishment with possibilities for the future.

Narrator into Poet

In his verses entitled "This poem is for bear," published in 1960, Gary Snyder took English translations of the Northwest Coast Bear Mother story—including Tsimshian variants ("Now her companions had disappeared, and she had to gather the spilled berries alone. . . . While busy, she did not notice that someone was beside her, but when she looked up, behold! a very handsome young man stood there")—and shaped them into a personal statement that included the lines:

> The others had all gone down
> From the blackberry brambles, but one girl
> Spilled her basket, and was picking up her
> Berries in the dark.
> A tall man stood in the shadow, took her arm . . .

At about the same time, Octavio Paz was versifying the Aztec salamander myth, using an old Spanish translation ("he hid himself among the magueys . . . but he was seen . . . and was put to flight, and he placed himself in the water and turned into the fish called axolotl [salamander], and from there they took him, and they killed him . . . and then the wind began to blow . . . the sun began to travel . . . "). Englished, after Paz, this becomes:

> . . . he hid himself in the maguey but they found him
> he fell into the water and became the fish axólotl
> the Double-Being
>   "and then they killed him"
> Movement began, the world was set in motion . . .

In verses dated 1962, W. S. Merwin reworked a Cashinawa myth on the adventures of a severed head that eventually becomes the moon:

> . . . So the head started to think what it would turn into.
> If it turned into water they would drink it.
> If it turned into earth they would walk on it.
> If it turned into a house they would live in it . . .

Later, Merwin would again use a verse technique in preparing new English renditions of Crow and Tzotzil Maya narratives.

Indian narrative reshaped as verse was by no means an unknown quantity. But artists like Snyder, Paz, and Merwin were among the first to rescue it from balladry, showing that it could be sent forward as poetry in the modern sense.

Myth into Novel

The late twentieth century, finally, is ready for the novel that deals seriously with the complex intellectual culture of the Native American. Changed attitudes may be traced to controversial works of scholarship and popularization (such as those of Claude Lévi-Strauss and Carlos Castaneda) that for all their excesses succeeded in planting the notion of a New World alternative to Western philosophy.

In his novel *Maíra*, published in 1978, the Brazilian Darcy Ribeiro tips his hat to Lévi-Strauss in a single passage ("We live divided according to rules of yes and of no; of heat and of cold; of luck and of hazard; of life and of death; of joy and of pain; of raw and of cooked . . ."), and it is probable that Lévi-Strauss's *The Raw and the Cooked* helped pave the way for *Maíra*'s wide acceptance in Europe in the early 1980s and its publication in the United States in 1984.

But *Maíra*'s deeper roots go back to translations of Tupian myths brought out mostly during the period 1900–1950. Of these the most important is the so-called Twin Myth, from which Ribeiro's novel takes its main plot.

According to a Tenetehara version that appeared in English in 1949, the god Maira, having impregnated his wife, set out to travel and did not come back. Speaking from the womb, Maira's child, who himself is called Maira, tells his mother to go in search of the father. She takes this suggestion, but, losing her way, comes to the house of Opossum, who impregnates her a second time. Now carrying twins, she travels on, still lost, to the house of the jaguars, where the principal jaguar kills and eats her, delivering her twins in the process.

In Ribeiro's story a Brazilian woman from Rio de Janeiro becomes the mother of the twins; the fictional Mairun tribe is her house of the jaguars; and the story is told in part by the elder god Maira.

The elaborate plot and its subplots revolve around a puzzle: Why are the twin gods stillborn and how was the mother killed? For the non-Indian characters in the novel the mystery is repeatedly and insistently unfathomable. But as Ribeiro spins a widening web of myth—incorporating not only the Twin Myth but the warrior women, the backward-walking *kurupiras*, the anusless food-inhalers, the *jacuí* flutes, and other motifs from Amazonian oral literature—the reader enters the intellectual world of the Mairun and moves toward a solution, or choice of solutions.

In a later work entitled *El hablador* (1987), a more skeptical novelist, Mario Vargas Llosa, has also spun a web of myth, inviting the reader to solve a puzzle. In this case the stories are borrowed from the Machiguenga of Amazonian Peru, and the question is why the teller of these tales—a Christ-like Jew from Lima—apparently has renounced

Western culture in order to merge with a primitive tribe. The novelist himself, in the person of an old chum, attempts to trace the renunciation from afar, finally confessing that it "shatters my heart more than terror or love has ever done." But the joke, if there is one, is that the ex-Limeño, unbeknownst to his worried friend, has become a kind of missionary whose recitals in the jungle are laced with Machiguenga-style retellings of the life of Christ, the history of the Diaspora, and Kafka's *Metamorphosis*.

In late 1989 an English translation of *El hablador* was published in New York as *The Storyteller*. Its virtue, for the subject at hand, is to demonstrate that even an establishmentarian like Vargas Llosa—who almost became President of Peru in 1990—can become enmeshed in Native literature.

The Chantway Novels

A young Pueblo man, who has served in World War II, returns to his home in New Mexico, where he is tormented by a male witch. Oddly, the witch seems to be an accepted member of the community. The young man nevertheless attacks his tormentor, with the result that he himself becomes an outcast and is forced to leave. Away from home, deeply troubled and out of tune with non-Indian society, he is comforted by a young woman, who offers him a more satisfying relationship than the one he had had earlier with an older lover. During his exile, he comes in contact with a Navajo chanter and is exposed to a Navajo healing ceremony. Strengthened, he returns home. By now the elder man in his household has died, and the hero is faced with new responsibilities, which he accepts. At least for the time being, his problems have been resolved, and the story ends with a benediction that echoes the Navajo ceremonial prayers.

Some readers, no doubt, will recognize this as a summary of N. Scott Momaday's novel of 1968, *House Made of Dawn*. Or, with equal validity—and in every detail—it may be taken as a synopsis of Leslie Marmon Silko's *Ceremony*, which appeared nine years later. In folkloristic terms, Silko's work is a variant of Momaday's, while both are distant variants on the basic Navajo chantway myth, in which an eccentric exile witnesses a new ceremony and comes back to his people with the gift of healing.

In Momaday's work, the ceremony that serves as the story's turning point is the Navajo Night Chant, known through a famous English translation of 1902. One of the prayers from that version is used by Momaday without change in a scene that begins the healing process:

> . . . House made of dawn,
> House made of evening light,
> House made of dark cloud,
> House made of male rain,
> House made of dark mist,
> House made of female rain,
> House made of pollen . . .

And in a typical gesture of reiteration, the lines "House made of pollen, House made of Dawn" are given again as the novel's closing prayer.

Echoing the same translation of the Night Chant that Momaday used, but with reference to a different prayer from that work—the one that ends with the formula

> It is finished in beauty,
> It is finished in beauty,
> It is finished in beauty,
> It is finished in beauty

Silko's *Ceremony* closes with a charm against the witchcraft that plays a considerably greater role in *Ceremony* than it does in *House Made of Dawn*:

> It is dead for now.
> It is dead for now.
> It is dead for now.
> It is dead for now.

Allowing herself greater freedom than Momaday, Silko does not acknowledge the Night Chant, or any other canonical Navajo ceremony. Indeed, she invents her own chant, because, as her fictional chanter explains, "only this growth keeps the ceremonies strong."

Incorporating not only Navajo material but massive infusions of Pueblo and other lore, both these superlative novels—which are more attuned to ritual than the myth-oriented *Maíra* of Darcy Ribeiro—draw the reader into a realm whose governing power is the infinitely subtle intellect of the Native American.

The Politics of Revolution

Among the better-known poets of the hemisphere, the most assiduous student of Indian literature has been Ernesto Cardenal. Using translations of Maya, Guaraní, Lakota, and Aztec texts that appeared during the period 1930–1965, Cardenal has crafted elaborate, often witty indictments of the governments of Guatemala, Paraguay, the United States, Mexico, and his own Nicaragua prior to the revolution of 1979.

With reference to Guatemala, the background text for Cardenal is a Spanish version of the Maya prophecy called Cuceb: "Mayapan, Deer-Banner, will be the place where the katun changes . . . he vomits that which he swallowed . . . from the poor, from the wretched he comes to receive his donation . . . the skulls are heaped up. . . ."

Altered, but still recognizable, the old phrases reappear in the poem "Squirrel of the Tuns of a Katun":

> . . . Military juntas on heaps of skulls . . .
> and the United Fruit Co. came to pierce with arrows
> the orphan, the widow, the wretched one . . .

> [But] the first full moon of the katun has already arrived
>> pregnant moon
> The time in which the President vomits what he swallowed . . .
> Mayapan will be the place where the katun will change
> *Cuceb* means Revolution.

Paraguay is the setting for Cardenal's "Children of the Forest of Word-Souls," a long poem built on generous samplings of Paraguayan Indian lore, including passages from the standard Spanish version of the Guaraní creation myth, *Ayvu Rapyta:* "Our father created the foundation of human language and made it a part of his own sacred being . . . created a small portion of love . . . the origin of a sacred song he created in his solitude. . . ." In part, this becomes:

> . . . In solitude he created the foundation of human language.
> In solitude he created a small portion of love.
> It was he who passed down the sacred song of man and of
>> woman . . .
> [But] captured children are sold for the price of a cow . . .
> In Paraguay it is no crime to kill them.
> Captured children generally dying before the age of fifteen.
> And the skull of a little girl in the Museum of
>> Ethnology. . . .

Turning to the United States, the poet-politician makes use of the well-known Lakota Black Elk texts in his "Sacred Pipe Recordings":

> . . . Our tepees were round as nests . . .
> [but} now they have put us in square boxes. . . .

Mexico is the subject of Cardenal's book-length poem of 1985, *Quetzalcoatl,* which utilizes a vast array of translated Aztec sources—including the myth of Quetzalcoatl and the dead-land lord, which reads in part: "Quetzalcoatl went where the death god rules . . . the bones of the man were in one place, those of the woman in another place . . . upon them Quetzalcoatl bled his virile member. . . ."

A few excerpted lines will give the flavor of the finished work (which draws not only on Native texts but on the interpretations of such scholars as Samuel Martí and Pedro Carrasco):

> . . . He went there to get the bones of men . . .
> They were there together, those of the man and those of the
>> woman.
> He watered them with the blood of his penis.
> And they revived.
>> Those of the man and those of the woman.
> . . . Quetzalcoatl Liberator
> . . . the one who awakens the Indian, said Martí . . .
> Carrasco calls him subversive.

As for prerevolutionary Nicaragua, Cardenal has treated the theme with an almost playful sarcasm in large-scale poems derived from Spanish translations of sixteenth-century Aztec songs. Echoes of the old phraseology ("Not forever on earth but briefly here: though it is jade, it is shattered; though it is gold, it is broken. . . .") recur unmistakably, often adapted to fit the situation at hand:

> though you be jade,
>> though you be gold. . . .

Here the allusion serves as a veiled threat to a particular "tyrant," ostensibly the cruel Aztec king, Tezozomoc. But "tyrant" (*tirano*) is also a code word, formerly used by Nicaraguan poets to mean whichever Somoza happened to be in power.

Although the dictatorship of the Somoza family came to an end in 1979, Cardenal continued to write political verse and to mix politics with Indian literature—as did his countryman and fellow poet Pablo Antonio Cuadra, who brought out a poem after the revolution comparing one of its martyrs to the twin heroes (in the Recinos translation) of the Popol Vuh.

"A hero struggled against the lords of the House of Bats . . . and a *doncella* whose name was Ixquic [Blood Woman] knew this history . . . and approached," Cuadra wrote, prophetically; and in February of 1990 the "hero's" widow, Violeta Barrios de Chamorro, was elected president of Nicaragua.

Aftereffects

In Steiner's phrase a translation in the process of being incorporated, even if only marginally, "can potentially dislocate or relocate" the whole of the recipient culture. Such a result may be impossible to measure and even difficult to perceive. But lines of influence are traceable, sometimes stretching far from the translation itself.

Ultimately the effect may extend into the open-ended, if ephemeral, world of popular culture. In the case of mid-century Spanish translations of the Quetzalcoatl texts, one line of development leads to Cardenal's *Quetzalcoatl*, which in turn helped to produce Eduardo del Río's *Quetzalcóatl no era del PRI* [Quetzalcoatl was not of the PRI], available in Mexican news shops and grocery stores in the late 1980s.

The cartoonist del Río, better known by his pen name Rius, has acknowledged Cardenal as a predecessor. Moreover, he appears to have absorbed some of Cardenal's documentary-polemical style in this new picture-book version with its glancing reference to Mexico's governing Institutional Revolutionary Party (PRI).

Or an effect may be felt in the self-contained yet potentially durable world of academe. By 1970 a small, articulate group of linguistic anthropologists had begun to produce translations of Indian narratives that looked very much like the poetic versions made earlier by Snyder, Paz, Merwin, and others. The linguists based their line breaks on reiterative features uncovered by the precise analysis of discourse or on the ad hoc phrasing conveniently preserved in tape recordings.

But since the need for precision had been proclaimed repeatedly over the previous hundred years, and sound recordings had been possible for nearly as long, poetic translation per se looms as an immediate precursor, if not a cause, of the new scholarship on narrative art. In that event specific translations, such as those quoted above, become points of reference in themselves. Among them may be included Jerome Rothenberg's 1967 *Flight of Quetzalcoatl* ("Another stop along the line / This time / THE CITY OF THE SLEEPERS / And runs into a shaman. . . ."), complete with the Poundian majuscules that would be used by the precisionists to represent vocal emphasis.

Rothenberg's poem, and in turn the work it may have helped to create, carry forward another line of descent traceable to the mid-twentieth-century Spanish versions of the Quetzalcoatl narratives.

In some cases the lineage may be less direct than it seems. When Paula Allen writes

> May we walk in beauty,

she preserves the sound of Washington Matthews's hundred-year-old translations of the Navajo chantway prayers. But she is not merely picking up where Matthews left off. It would be more correct to say that she is echoing the larger meaning the phrase acquired during the 1960s, when the Matthewsian "Walk in beauty" or even "Walk in beauty, man" became one of the watchwords in a gentle war of values.

A more apparent form of syncretism occurs in Carlos Fuentes's novel *A Change of Skin*, where the poet-hero conjures up a vision of the four elements of Greek lore, changed into suns: earth-sun, fire-sun, water-sun, and air-sun, each with its power to destroy the world. Readers acquainted with one or more translations of the Aztec myth of the cosmogonic suns, widely available since the 1940s, can recognize four destructive powers far removed (at least geographically) from Greek learning: earthquake, rain of fire, water, and wind.

Sometimes the endpoint of a line may be blurred even further, as when Anne Waldman in a small piece entitled "Silver E" writes

> I'm a mischievous woman,

not quoting but indistinctly echoing her own signature poem "Fast Speaking Woman," which in turn was based on a 1957 translation of medicine chants by the Mazatec wise woman María Sabina.

It is important to keep in mind that a writer may be harking back to a particular *translation* of the chantway prayers or a particular *translation* of María Sabina. In fact the version can make all the difference.

Some of the most characteristic borrowings in Anne Waldman's compelling chant ("I'm an atmosphere woman . . . I'm a speech woman . . . I'm a ready woman") were not confirmed by later translators of the same Mazatec material. If Waldman had seen only the revised version, she would have written a different poem, perhaps no poem at all.

And in that case Jerome Rothenberg, in a piece dated 1982, would not have been able to write

> Maria poet of these hills
> fast speaking woman,

alluding both to María Sabina and to Anne Waldman. Nor, perhaps, would an anthology of Latin American women's poetry, which appeared in 1987, have been given the title *Woman Who Has Sprouted Wings*—by an editor who acknowledges familiarity with Waldman's work.

Another unclear, but arguable, line of descent begins with the primitivist poets of the 1920s, mentioned at the beginning of this essay, who helped set the stage for the anthropologist Dorothy Lee's 1935 translations of Wintu songs, which, in turn, echo in Ursula Le Guin's verse-and-prose novel of 1985, *Always Coming Home*.

In other cases an endpoint, or point of rest, blurs into the surrounding culture, while the vanished line moves on. The borrowed words are no longer present, not even in disguise, having been changed to new words and phrases. An effect of this kind lingers in my own upstate New York village after a reading here by the poet Bob Steuding, whose lines

> Let the strength of my song
> pass into the people

reflect an attitude derived in part from the oral poetry of the Inuit and, I am told, from specific translations of Inuit songs. There are no politics in Steuding's poetry, yet he has acknowledged that poems carrying the directness and clarity for which he strives are created so that "we may live our lives with greater mindfulness." Bob Steuding's recitations draw sizable audiences here in these Hudson Valley neighborhoods. As I look around the room I see people I know to be descendants of Dutch and Huguenot settlers, participating comfortably—three hundred years after the Esopus Wars—in the Native American's incremental progress toward restitution.

Note

1. Lawrence's "Song of Huitzilopochtli" (1925) apparently derives from the *huitzilopochtli icuic* (song of Huitzilopochtli), long available in the translation of D. G. Brinton; this and other Aztec-inspired verses are in Lawrence's *Collected Poems* (Viking, 1959). The most ambitious Indianist poetry of the period, inspired by the translations of Franz Boas, Washington Matthews, and others, is in Amy Lowell's *Legends* and in her *Ballads for Sale* (reprinted in *The Complete Poetical Works of Amy Lowell,* Riverside, 1955). The most graceful efforts, hovering between translation and original poetry, are in Mary Austin's still admirable *The American Rhythm* (1923, rev. 1930, reprinted 1970 by Cooper Square). Andrade's mythopoetic novel *Macunaíma* (1928, English

ed. 1984) is based on translations of Amazonian and Guiana myths prepared by Couto de Magalhães, Capistrano de Abreu, and others.

Notes on Sources

Most of the examples mentioned in the preceding essay were presented in a translation workshop held at the Woodstock Guild, Woodstock, New York, in the summer of 1988. (Acknowledgment is made to the Woodstock Guild and the New York State Council on the Arts, which provided funding.) It was not anticipated that writers attending the sessions would be familiar with Native American languages, but rather that they would participate in the incorporative stage of translation, so to speak, taking cues from the various poets and novelists whose work could be traced to Native texts. Principal sources, both secondary and primary, are as follows.

Snyder

"This poem is for bear" appears in Gary Snyder's *Myths and Texts* (New York: New Directions, 1978 [1960]), 23–25. A source containing material that Snyder used, including Tsimshian versions of the Bear Mother myth, is Marius Barbeau's *Totem Poles* (National Museum of Canada, 1950), vol. 1, 191–206.

Paz

The Spanish text of "Salamander" (dated 1958–61), with an English version by Denise Levertov, is in *The Collected Poems of Octavio Paz, 1957–1987,* ed. Eliot Weinberger (New York: New Directions, 1987), 138–49. Bernardino de Sahagún's sixteenth-century Spanish translation of the Aztec salamander myth, with English and Aztec versions, may be consulted in Sahagún's *Florentine Codex,* ed. Arthur J. O. Anderson and Charles E. Dibble (Salt Lake City: University of Utah Press, 1950–82), Bk. 7, 54–59.

Merwin

"The Creation of the Moon" (dated 1962 and based on an intermediary French version) is in W. S. Merwin's *Selected Translations, 1948–1968* (New York: Atheneum, 1975), 28–30. The ultimate source is João Capistrano de Abreu, *Rã-txa hu-ni-ku-i* (Rio de Janeiro: Leuzinger, 1914), 479–80.

For Merwin's poetic version of a Crow Coyote tale see *Alcheringa* 1 (1970), 31. The source is Robert Lowie's *Crow Texts* (Berkeley: University of California Press, 1960), 195–96.

Two Tzotzil tales, versified by Merwin in *Review* [now called *Review: Latin American Literature and Arts*] 7 (1972), 48–49, may be compared with the subsequently published Tzotzil and English texts in Robert M. Laughlin's *Of Cabbages and Kings* (Washington: Smithsonian Institution Press, 1977), 141–42 and 151.

Ribeiro

The novel is Darcy Ribeiro's *Maíra,* trans. E. H. Goodland and Thomas Colchie (New York: Vintage/Random House, 1984, after the Portuguese edition of 1978). A primary source for the Twin

Myth is Charles Wagley and Eduardo Galvão, *The Tenetehara Indians of Brazil* (New York: Columbia University Press, 1949), 137–40. Other versions of the Twin myth may be traced in John Bierhorst, *The Mythology of South America* (New York: Morrow, 1985).

Momaday and Silko

N. Scott Momaday's *House Made of Dawn* (New York: Harper and Row, 1968) and Leslie Marmon Silko's *Ceremony* (New York: Viking, 1977) may be compared with the copiously summarized chantway myths in Katherine Spencer's *Mythology and Values: An Analysis of the Navaho Chantway Myths* (Philadelphia: American Folklore Society, 1957) and with the reconstruction of Washington Matthews's translation of the Night Chant in John Bierhorst's *Four Masterworks of American Indian Literature* (New York: Farrar, Straus & Giroux, 1974).

Cardenal

The Cuceb poem, called "Squirrel of the Tuns of a Katun," is in Ernesto Cardenal's *Homage to the American Indians*, trans. Monique and Carlos Altschul (Baltimore: Johns Hopkins University Press, 1973), 61–62, after the Spanish in *Homenaje a los indios americanos* (Santiago, Chile: Editorial Universitaria, 1970), 78–79. The Cuceb text used by Cardenal appears in *El libro de los libros de Chilam Balam*, trans. Alfredo Barrera Vásquez and Silvia Rendón (México: Fondo de Cultura Económica, 1948), 101–20: an English version is in Bierhorst, *Four Masterworks*.

For "The Children of the Forest of Word-Souls," in Spanish only, see Cardenal, *Los ovnis de oro* (México: Siglo Veintiuno, 1988), 217–23. The source is *Ayvu rapyta*, ed. León Cadogan (São Paulo: Universidade de São Paulo, Faculdade de Filosofia, Ciências e Letras, boletim 227, 1959), 19–23; and the same material is reprinted as poetry in the more widely available *La literatura de los guaraníes*, ed. Cadogan and A. López Austin (México: Joaquín Mortiz, 1965), 53–57.

"Sacred Pipe Recordings," translated into English by the Altschuls, is in *New World Journal*, vol. 1, nos. 2–3 (1977), 85–93. This may be compared with the original English text of Black Elk's testimony in *The Sixth Grandfather*, ed. Raymond J. DeMallie (Lincoln: University of Nebraska Press, 1984), 290–91; or the reworded version, which Cardenal used, in John G. Neihardt's *Black Elk Speaks* (University of Nebraska Press, 1961 [1932]), 198–200.

Cardenal's *Quetzalcoatl* (Managua: Editorial Nueva Nicaragua, 1985) may also be read in *Los ovnis de oro*, 75–118. A Spanish translation of the myth of Quetzalcoatl and the dead-land bones, available to Cardenal, is in Angel M. Garibay's *La literatura de los aztecas* (México: Joaquín Mortiz, 1964), 18–20; for an English version see Bierhorst, *Four Masterworks*, 17–21.

The excerpt "though you be jade, / though you be gold" is from Cardenal's "Netzahualcoyotl," *Homenaje*, 96 (*Homage*, 79); the Aztec source, available in numerous Spanish versions, may be read in Garibay's *La literatura de los aztecas*, 63, or in English (and in Aztec) in *Cantares Mexicanos: Songs of the Aztecs*, trans. John Bierhorst (Stanford: Stanford University Press, 1985), 184–85.

Cuadra

"The Calabash Tree," celebrating the revolutionary martyr Pedro Joaquín Chamorro, may be read in Spanish and in English in Pablo Antonio Cuadra, *The Birth of the Sun*, ed. Steven F. White (Greensboro, North Carolina: Unicorn Press, 1988), 130–35. The Adrián Recinos work, revised, has been published in English as *Popol Vuh*, trans. Delia Goetz and Sylvanus G. Morley (Norman: University of Oklahoma Press, 1950); recent English versions of the Popol Vuh have been published by Munro Edmonson (New Orleans: Tulane University, 1971) and by Dennis Tedlock (New York: Simon and Schuster, 1985).

Rothenberg

Jerome Rothenberg's *The Flight of Quetzalcoatl*, first published by Unicorn Book Shop, Brighton, England, 1967, was reprinted in his *Technicians of the Sacred* (Garden City, New York: Doubleday, 1968), 92–97.

Allen

For "walk in beauty" see Paula Gunn Allen, *The Sacred Hoop* (Boston: Beacon Press, 1986), v.

Fuentes

The cosmogonic suns are in Carlos Fuentes's *A Change of Skin*, trans. Sam Hileman (Farrar, Straus & Giroux, 1968, originally *Cambio de Piel*, 1967), 191. For the Aztec myth see Primo F. Veláz-quez, *Códice Chimalpopoca* (Mexico, 1945), 5.

Waldman

"Silver E" is in Anne Waldman's *Journals & Dreams* (New York: Stonehill, 1976). Compare Wald-man's *Fast Speaking Woman* (San Francisco: City Lights, 1975; reprinted in Waldman's *Helping the Dreamer,* Minneapolis: Coffee House Press, 1989); and note that a phonograph record of Waldman reading "Fast Speaking Woman" was issued with *Alcheringa*, n.s., vol. 1, no. 2 (1975). The trans-lation of María Sabina that Waldman used is by Eunice V. Pike and Sarah C. Gudschinsky, as pub-lished in the booklet accompanying *Mushroom Ceremony of the Mazatec Indians of Mexico* (Folk-ways Records, album no. 8975, 1957); for the later translation see Alvaro Estrada, Henry Munn, et al., *María Sabina: Her Life and Chants* (Santa Barbara: Ross-Erikson, 1981). Rothenberg's poem on María Sabina is "The Little Saint of Huautla" in his *Altar Pieces* (Barrytown, New York: Station Hill Press, 1982). See also Daniel C. Noel, "Shamanic Ritual as Poetic Model: The Case of María Sabina and Anne Waldman," *Journal of Ritual Studies*, vol. 1, no. 1 (1987), 57–71.

Le Guin

D[orothy] Demetracopoulou [Lee]'s "Wintu Songs," *Anthropos*, 1935, 483–94, may be compared with some (though not all) the verses in Ursula K. Le Guin's *Always Coming Home* (Harper, 1985).

Steuding

The quotations are from Bob Steuding's *Ashokan* (Olive Bridge, New York: Pasture Horse Press, 1976), reprinted, in part, in Steuding's *A Catskill Mountain Journal* (Fleischmanns, New York: Pur-ple Mountain Press, 1990), 66–78.

"We Explain Nothing, We Believe Nothing": American Indian Poetry and the Problematics of Translation

Jerome Rothenberg

> Likeness, as [Walter] Benjamin rightly says, is not at issue here; if one requires that the translated work resemble the work to be translated, no literary translation is possible. What is involved, rather, is an identity that takes off from an alterity: the same work in two languages foreign to each other, and this mutual foreignness thus making visible the movement by which this work always becomes *other*, the very motion from which must be drawn the light which will transparently illuminate the translation.
>
> —Maurice Blanchot (1990:84)

There is a mysticism about translation, and a mystery. It all goes together, finally, and I would be wrong, when dealing with a poetry as grounded in the sacred as the Indian, to treat translation as merely literal, a mechanical act, for which the rules need only be laid down and the intended results will follow. I do not mean that we work without precision or without some rules or limits—without reference beyond that to the source from which translation comes—but that we must also work in ways that do not lend themselves to easy explanations. If we translate poetry, we should be ready, as with poetry, to break the rules that keep us from the poem itself.

My poetry, like my life, has proceeded over the years by various acts of translation, not only that part where translation is evident (from text to text, so to speak), but equally where the work is personal and introspective or personal and looking for a link into a given social nexus. I speak to a stranger and he asks me to repeat myself in different words until he gets the drift of what I'm saying. "Do you mean this? Do you mean that?" we ask each other. It isn't much different with a friend, except that we take our common speech and common terms for granted. As a poet too I find myself engaging in translation every moment that I write: experience, perceptions, thoughts, and feelings brought into a language that we take as common and that isn't. The table in the poem is not a table ("this pipe is not a pipe"—Magritte). The shock of feeling—standing in the empty field one summer morning in Treblinka—is translated into words. The language of the dream's translated into speech, the speaking voice translated into writing, then back to speech again. Myself translated to myself, from there to others, who will read or hear me; so that every act of reading is also, finally, an act of translation—a balancing between what is "there" and what I read/misread of what is there.

This is the continuum into which translation proper enters: the move between one (human) language and another, or within a single language, from dialect to dialect or time (the past) to time (the present). The problematics of translation have been most discussed at this level, and there is for me a sense too that translation itself involves precisely such a discourse on its own problematics. This means that translation, as we have sometimes tried to practice it, is not the reproduction of, or stand-in for, some fixed original, but that it functions as a commentary on the other and itself and on the differences between them. It is much more a kind of question than a summing up.

Such are the problematics in all (serious) translation. But in the approach to American Indian works—their comprehension and translation by whatever means at our disposal—the problems for those of us so engaged are complicated in ways that can throw the whole enterprise into a state of doubt. The points at issue are at least threefold: those that center on orality, those that center on the sacred, and those that center on the question of imperial displacement. It seems quite likely to me that these are not only questions to be asked about translation, but that translation as a process is a principal means by which they can be explored, though probably not answered. I don't mean here to argue against more confidently literal approaches to translation, but to suggest that the kinds of prob-lematics raised by the American Indian works are a crucial part of their attraction to me as both a poet and translator.

As such a poet and translator, I have worked with a range of poetries that might seem different on their face from the traditional Indian poetries in question here, and I have to a degree brought that experience into such works—partly assemblage, partly translation—as *Technicians of the Sacred* and *Shaking the Pumpkin*. Over the last two years in fact my engagement has been with two translation projects of some considerable extent, neither of them connected in any way to Indianismo: a 250-page translation of Federico García Lorca's previously untranslated *Suites* and a 300-page volume (with Pierre Joris) of Kurt Schwitters's selected poetry and other writings.[1] My attraction to these and other, largely contemporary works is as a poet, not a scholar—although the work of scholars has been of great use in considering the nuances of languages and cultures that are foreign to me. I have sought engagement with the work, to lose myself inside it. Lorca and Schwitters are as sacred to me—as near to the sources of poetry and speech—as any more religiously specific poetry; and it is this sense of the numinous or sacred that forms a common thread, for me, between the poets and the shamans.

When I translate poets like these I find myself drawn to certain ideas about their work that the translation itself begins to open up for me. Sometimes these are in conflict with older views about the poet, not only those of others but views I myself may have shared. The underlying problems here are those familiar to anyone who translates seriously: a face-off between the demands of literalism and interpretation, tied as a poet to that kind of ("spiritual") exercise that forms the basis for the kinds of poetry I want and need. Nor is this a question of "free translation," as some would have it. The work of translation in our time—from Pound to the present—is, if anything, less arbitrary, in a certain sense less free, than at any time in western history. One has only to compare the frame-by-frame approach of modernist poets like Pound to the truly open practice of a Pope or Chapman.

There is still a third project to which I've recently returned and which brings me even closer to the translation work from American Indian sources. In 1978 I published a large gathering of texts, covering a four-thousand-year span, under the title of *A Big Jewish Book: Poems & Other Visions of the Jews from Tribal Times to Present*, reprinted in 1989 in a condensed version called *Exiled in the Word*. Both versions involved a great number of translations, for which Harris Lenowitz served as my cotranslator and guide into languages like Hebrew and Aramaic that I barely knew. And in both I followed the same lines of attack as with the Lorca and Schwitters but veered further from the literal in order to bring the work into a new context, not so much to "modernize" as to use the translation itself as a way of pointing to potentialities and hidden forms of poetry in the original that had previously been ignored.

Translation here becomes active, not passive: I am doing something in the process, not just responding to what someone else has done. I am doing it also within a cultural nexus in which I think of myself as a participant or in which I'm trying to come to terms with the nature of my own participation. There is a further tension in the work between the frequently religious nature of the original poems and the secular ambience in which I live as a poet and translator. But I don't experience that as a burden so much as an incitement to transform and to reveal—to connect that revelation to the nature of the poetic process itself in a way that evokes the religious and mystical sense from which I'm otherwise cut off. For doing that I can be harshly reproved from within the culture, but I can also, with a little ingenuity (even ingenuousness), respond on my own as one within that nexus. The crux of the Jewish work for me is that of a disengaged engagement, as in the great statement by Franz Kafka that I quote early in *A Big Jewish Book*: "What have I in common with Jews? I hardly have anything in common with myself."

A statement by Simon Ortiz makes a telling contrast with that by Kafka: "[My grandfather] and the grandmothers and grandfathers before them," he writes, "thought about us as they lived, confirmed in their belief of a continuing life, and they brought our present beings into existence by the beliefs they held. The consciousness of that belief is what informs my present concerns with language, poetry and fiction" (Ortiz 1987). I can certainly accept Ortiz's view, though I have no doubt that there are problematics in the Indian position that have still to be explored. I also know that the Indian differences offer ways for us to question assumptions about reality within the dominant culture: to subvert aspects of that reality that fetter both "them" and "us." The position of dream, the figure of the trickster and the sacred clown, the experience of the other-than-human and of what

Eliade spoke of as "earth as a religious form"—these sacred mythologies and ecologies mark both our separation from a living center and our desire to return.

I translate, as I write, from where I am. Would I want to claim that the translations like the poems themselves create a kind of sacred space for me? Often I would, but more often I settle for viewing them as commentary on our distance from, or closeness to, a world enlightened by our thoughts or words about it. The Yaqui Deer Dancer emerges from his Flower World and the language with its measured repetitions resonates a sense of what that world entails (Rothenberg 1986:143):

> flower
>   with the body of a fawn
>   under a cholla flower
> standing there
>   to rub your antlers
>   bending
> turning where you stand to rub
>   your antlers
>   in the flower world
> the dawn
>   there in its light
>   under a cholla flower
> standing there
>   to rub your antlers
>   bending turning where you stand
> to rub your antlers . . . .

It is what Senghor, fashioning a real but half-created Africa, spoke of as the "traditional surreal" (Rothenberg 1983:119–20), and it corresponds at moments to the imago mundi and the mental sets that poets of my own lineage have struggled, while often failing, to sight and/or create.

> Nothing, only an image, nothing else, utter oblivion. Slanting through the words come
>   vestiges of light.
>   —Franz Kafka (1954:313, 161, in Rothenberg 1989)

> This summer the roses are blue; the wood is made of
> glass. The earth wrapped in its foliage makes as
> little effect on me as a ghost. Living and ceasing
> to live are imaginary solutions. Existence is
> elsewhere.
>   —André Breton, 1924 (in Lippard 1970:27)

> I have brought the great ball of crystal;
>   who can lift it?
> Can you enter the great acorn of light?
>   But the beauty is not the madness
> Tho' my errors and wrecks lie about me.

And I am not a demigod,
I cannot make it cohere.
    —Ezra Pound (1970:795)

The claim then would have to be—take it as you will—that what we are engaged in is not so much a search for the primitive (quote-unquote) as a search for the sacred; and what draws us to Indian and other traditional poetries is the sense of the development over millennia of a relation to that in the human and other-than-human worlds.

If the sacred—or some version thereof—is or should be at the heart of what we do, it remains a still more elusive quality for the translator—and the most difficult to elucidate in terms of method. In Charles Olson's terms it is confounded with that "stance toward reality" that relates to, both informs and emerges from, the act of poesis, of composition and projection. A familiar stance in Indian poetry—as song and myth—identifies the poem (the song) as itself "alive," emerging into language through a "sacred action," as Breton called it also for the poem he sought. "I / the song / I walk there" runs a Modoc poem in the song's voice, and Richard Johnny John's version of a Seneca poem-chant sequence speaks of the song as traveling: "it's off in the distance / it came into the room /it's here in the circle" (Rothenberg 1991:21). It is this idea of the word-come-alive—as beauty and/or terror—that defines the sacred for both them and us.

Where the poem is alive—its existence *elsewhere* and its emergence *here*—we are left to ask how far it can enter into language, in particular the language of translation. This is no different at heart from how we ourselves make poems, or try to—at least since Blake's perception in his own case that "the authors are in eternity," the poem's voices separate from the poet's voice itself. Something like this may put us in a condition to make the poem or the translation, while recognizing that the difference, when translating, is that the terms have changed: that a voice or text is now before us, that it stands between us and its source, becomes our source in turn, or leads us to another source within us. It is at this point that the literal, on which we have depended until now, falls away, or seems to, and that the act of translation becomes a poetic act once more. In short, a sacred action.

With this the problematics that I have spoken of come in as well. For there is no literal here and no copy, rather an ironic relation to a primal "source" that may be duplicable in experience but clearly not in language. Every translation is a divergence, and the interest of translation as such is as a record of its own divergences: a comment on its failure to be source. It is something different from our interest in the source itself, although the two may join together or attempt to do so. Scholars on the whole may pretend to a greater objectivity, to the presentation of the source, the thing, itself, but what they're most likely to deliver is information *about* the source, without the force, the power, that the source has. Their sometime success will lack the interest *as translation* of the poet's sometime failure, for it will be a success based on the denial of divergence and of point of view.

My own relation to American Indian poetry has been a part—but only a part—of a search for a poetics and for the origins of poetry in the time in which I live. Much of this has probably not been clear to others coming at it from other points of view. In *Techni-*

cians of the Sacred (1968) and in the work leading up to it, the native poetry of the Americas was presented alongside traditional, largely oral works from Africa, Asia, Oceania, and, in the revised edition (1985), Europe. The anthology as a structure allowed me to present a range of poetries that challenged dominant assumptions about the form and function of the poetic act. Because of the central role poetry played in my own view of things, I could also extend the challenge and exploration to assumptions about the nature of reality, of social and mental processes, and of the ways in which we might relate to all of these through language. The strategy throughout was one of collage: the juxtaposition of disparate examples ("radical discontinuities"), supported elsewhere by a series of "commentaries" (often collages in their own right) that gave some sense of context—of the works' relations both to their own times and to ours. In *Shaking the Pumpkin* (1972) I limited myself for the first and last time to the poetry of the Indian Americas as such.[2]

In these large assemblages I was as much compiler and arranger as translator. What I was compiling mainly were earlier translations—therefore interpretations—of what was or may have been original: the work at origin; the source. My own selections and placements were also interpretations, even those that faithfully retained the words of the earlier translator. There were times in fact when I thought of the anthology as an assemblage, largely, of outsiders' views, so that even "mistranslations," which I could scarcely distinguish over so wide a range, created new and useful works. Some translations (like Tedlock's "The Boy and the Deer" in *Shaking the Pumpkin*) I presented at greater length than in most anthologies; others I sliced from longer pieces and sometimes freely retitled, to highlight some particularity I wanted to deliver.

For all the collaging I did, I was early—I think—in stressing the value of translating *fully*, to bring across elements of breath and sound, of gesture and repetition, insofar as that was possible or useful. I was also deliberate in calling attention to a range of previously neglected modes and genres: wordless sound-poems and picture-poems (what Frances Densmore had earlier called "song pictures"), performance works and rituals presented as performance, trickster narratives (unbowdlerized) and sacred clown dramas, spoken narratives approached as oral poetry, and song-poems with contemporary subjects (trains, pickup trucks, urban scenes, moon shots, and so on). And, because I was bothered by assumptions about tribal anonymity, I tried persistently to identify singers and poets by name, not only literary contemporaries like Leslie Silko or Simon Ortiz, but traditional contemporaries like Andrew Peynetsa or María Sabina.

The work of translation, as carried on by poets within the ethnopoetic enterprise, has centered on the translation itself and has been carried on largely through intermediaries—either collaborators or earlier translated texts or both. (There is no question in my mind but that this puts any such translations into question, except—I would like to think—as guidelines for a new poetics, a newly considered way of making poetry, that the poet-as-translator is seeking to explore.) In working with earlier translations, then, the editor-collagist may leave them as he finds them or, like Marcel Duchamp with his ready-mades, introduce a range of alterations. The titling of oral poems is the most widespread form of innovation practiced both by editors and by some of the most "literal" of scholarly translators. Excision (the presentation of a cut or segment from a longer work) is still another. Both are so common as not in general to be felt as alterations. In addition many, particularly earlier translators and editors, omitted elements of the original, and many, particularly more recent translators, have (re)introduced them.

My own practice, both as translator and assembler, has tended to be pragmatic and open, motivated both by an interest in the original and by a search for new poems and forms in English. I have generally tried, in the accompanying commentaries, to indicate the degree of divergence from the found text—by the identification of such works as "versions" or as "workings," the latter a kind of buzzword for those with a more singular approach to the idea of translation.[3] Textual modifications in my own practice or that of related poet-translators have ranged from the invention of a style or voice for the translation to the reintroduction of omitted elements or, more rarely, to deliberate divergences or elaborations, utilizing additional materials (from notes or other prose descriptions) or exaggerating certain qualities in the source poem that seemed to relate to the presence or absence of such in contemporary non-Indian works.

Nor is it a question only of distance from the source, of letting one's unknowing or cultural separation create a sense of strangeness that may or may not correspond to the original's own mystery or aura. Even when positioned closer to the source—as in those field-translations that I've sometimes wandered into—I have tried as much to cultivate the mystery as to dispel it. It is my own urge toward a *Verfremdung* that I feel operating here, most strongly in those acts of composition that I chose (working close to Dennis Tedlock but with my own approach to them) to present as instances of "total translation." In that project of the early 1970s, Tedlock worked (quite independently) with spoken narratives and I worked with oral chant-poems. In retrospect, I can speak only of my own experience here, which may have been different from his, not only as a question of temperament but as a reflection of the kinds of poems with which we each were working. His project ended with a claim, I thought, to an essential closeness—a literalness that I have questioned elsewhere but here was ready to believe—while my own seemed to involve both the sense of a new form—and hence of a new content—and of an ironic distancing that I only slowly came to understand.

My two principal works in this area, both from the late 1960s to early 1970s, were "Poems from the Society of the Mystic Animals" and "The 17 Horse-Songs of Frank Mitchell."[4] The objective here was threefold: (1) to develop special means for recreating oral works within a literate culture; (2) to comment on their relation to and/or divergence from new areas of writing; and (3) to push them, where possible, to a new completion in performance. The means employed, in the first two instances at least, were more formal and conceptual than experiential, and the success of the final work was to be measured, I thought, by the interest both of the original (however oblique it might now seem to be) and of the resultant English, along with the relation between them. I was aware throughout of a movement from a sacred text as such to the reflection of a sacred text as poem—a difference (in the light of Breton's "sacred action") that I hoped would someday disappear.

In the summer of 1968 I began to work simultaneously with two sources of Indian poetry. Settling down a mile from the Cold Spring settlement of the Allegany (Seneca) Reservation at Steamburg, New York, I was near enough to friends who were traditional songmen to work with them on the translation of sacred and secular song-poems. At the same time David McAllester was sending me recordings, transcriptions, literal translations, and his own freer reworkings of a series of seventeen "horse songs" that had been the property of Frank Mitchell, a Navajo *hatali* (sacred singer) from Chinle, Arizona (born 1881, died 1967). My first concern in both instances was with the translation process itself. While I'll limit myself to that right now, I should at least say (things never seem to be clear unless you say them) that if I hadn't also come up with matter that I could "internalize," I would have floundered long before this.

The big question, which I was immediately aware of with both poetries, was if and how to handle those elements in the original works that weren't translatable literally. As with much Indian poetry, the voice carried many sounds that weren't, strictly speaking, "words." These tended to disappear or be attenuated in translation, as if they weren't really there. But they *were* there and were at least as important as the words themselves. In both Navajo and Seneca many songs consisted of nothing but those "meaningless" vocables (not free "scat" either but fixed sounds recurring from performance to performance). Most other songs had both lexical and non-lexical elements, and such songs (McAllester once told me for the Navajo) were often spoken of, qua title, by their "meaningless" burdens.

So there were these and other indications that the exploration of "pure sound" wasn't beside the point of these poetries but at or near their heart: all of this coincidental too with concern for the sound-poem among a number of modern poets. Accepting its meaningfulness here, I more easily accepted it there. I also realized (with the Navajo especially) that there were more than simple refrains involved: that we, as translators and poets, had been taking a rich *oral* poetry and translating it to be read exclusively for meaning, thus denuding it, to say the least.

Here's an immediate example of what I mean. In the first of Frank Mitchell's seventeen horse songs, the opening "line" comes out as follows in McAllester's transcription:

> dzo-wowode sileye shi, dza-na desileye shiyi, dzanadi sileye
> shiya'e

but the same segment given "as spoken" reads:

> dząądi silá shi dząądi silá shi dząądi silá shi

which translates as "over-here it-is-there (and) mine" repeated three times. So does the line as sung if all you're accounting for is the meaning. In other words, translate only for meaning and you get the threefold repetition of an unchanging single statement; but in the Navajo each time it's delivered there's a sharp departure from the spoken form: thus three distinct sound-events, not one-in-triplicate!

The most important group of songs I worked on from the Seneca was a sacred cycle called *Idos* (ee-dos) in Seneca—in English either "shaking the pumpkin" or, more ornately, "the society of the mystic animals." Like most Seneca songs *with* words (most Seneca songs are in fact *without* words), the typical Pumpkin song contains a single statement, or a single statement alternating with a string of vocables, which is repeated anywhere from three to six or seven times. Some songs are nearly identical with some others (same melody and vocables, slight change in words) but aren't necessarily sung in sequence. In a major portion of the ceremony, in fact, a fixed order for the songs is completely abandoned, and each person present takes a turn at singing a ceremonial (medicine) song of his or her own choice. There's room here too for messing around.[5]

Richard Johnny John, a Seneca singer and songmaker, was my collaborator on the Pumpkin songs, and the basic wording is therefore his. My intention was to account for all vocal sounds in the original but—as a more "interesting" way of handling the minimal structures and allowing a very clear, very pointed emergence of perceptions—to translate the poems *onto the page*, as with "concrete" or other types of minimal poetry. (In other words: to use the analogy to concrete poetry as a signal of the developed, not "primitive," nature of the original, and conversely to put modernist forms as such into a clearly sacred context.) Where several songs showed a concurrence of structure, I allowed myself the option of treating them individually or combining them into one. I deferred singing any of these until a later occasion.

Take the opening songs of the ceremony. These are fixed pieces sung by the ceremonial leader (*hajaswas*) before he throws the meeting open to the individual singers. The melody and structure of the first nine are identical: very slow, a single line of words ending with a string of sounds, etc., the pattern identical until the last go-round, when the song ends with a grunting expulsion of the breath into a weary "ugh" sound. I had to get all of that across: the bareness, the regularity, the deliberateness of the song, along with the basic meaning, repeated vocables, emphatic terminal sound, and (in following Johnny John's reminder to play around with it "if everything's all right") a little something of my own. The song whose repeated verse is:

The animals are coming *heh eh heh* (or *heh eh-eh-eh heh*)

can then become:

```
  T
  h            H E H E H H E H
  e
The animals are coming  H E H E H H E H
  n
  i            H E H U H H E H
  m
  a            H E H E H H E H
  l
  s            H E H E H H E H
```

and the next one:

```
T                    H E H E H H E H
h
e                    H E H E H H E H
The doings were beginning
    o                H E H UH H E H
    i
    n                H E H E H H E H
    g
    s                H E H E H H E H
```

and so forth: each poem set, if possible, on its own page, as further analogue to the slowness, the deliberate pacing of the original.

In other songs I used similar, largely visual methods to allow a play between
vocables and words: calligrammatic, as in a series of owl-songs, in which I pick up the
vocables suggesting the animal's call and shape them into an outline of a giant owl, within
which frame the poems are printed; decorative, with vocables serving as a border or frame
for words or titles, as in the following:

```
hiiiiiiiiiiiiiiiiiiiiiiiiiiiiiiiiiiiiiiiiiiiiiiiiiiiiiiiiiih
e                                              e
e    THREE WAYS TO SCREW UP    e
e ON YOUR WAY TO THE DOINGS e
e            THREE WAYS            e
e                                              e
hiiiiiiiiiiiiiiiiiiiiiiiiiiiiiiiiiiiiiiiiiiiiiiiiiiiiiiiiiih
```

(1)
I fell down

(2)
I got lost

(3)
I lost my bucket

or punning (in the manner of Louis Zukofsky), where *yehgagaweeyo* (lit. "that pretty
crow") becomes "yond cawcrow's way-out," while trying at the same time to let something of the meaning come through.

With the Navajo horse songs my decision—in a very different way from
Zukofsky (1969)—was to work with the sound as sound: a reflection in itself of the difference between Navajo and Seneca song structure. For Navajo (as already indicated) is
much fuller, much denser, twists words into new shapes or fills up the spaces between
words by insertion of a wide range of "meaningless" vocables, making it misleading to
translate exclusively for meaning or, finally, to think of *total* translation in any terms but
those of sound. Look, for example, at the number of free vocables in the following excerpt from McAllester's assertively literal translation of the 16th Horse Song:

(Nana na) Sun-(yeye ye) Standing-within (neye ye) Boy

(Heye ye) truly his horses
('Eye ye) abalone horses
('Eye ye) made of sunrays
(Neye ye) their bridles

(Gowo wo) coming on my right side
(Jeye yeye) coming into my hand (yeye neyowo 'ei).

Now this, which even so doesn't show the additional word distortions that turn up in the singing, might be brought closer to English word order and translated for meaning alone as something like:

Boy who stands inside the Sun
with your horses that are
abalone horses
bridles
made of sunrays
rising on my right side
coming to my hand
etc.

But what a difference from the fantastic way the sounds cut through the words and between them from the first line of the original on.

It was the possibility of working with all that sound, finding my own way into it in English, that attracted me now—that and a quality in Mitchell's voice I found irresistible. It was, I think, that the music was so clearly within range of the language: it was song and it was poetry, and it was possible at least that the song issued from the poetry, was an extension of it or rose inevitably from the juncture of words and other vocal sounds. So many of us had already become interested in this kind of thing as poets, that it seemed natural to me to be in a situation where the poetry would be leading me toward a (new) music *it* was generating.

I began with the 10th Horse Song, which had been the first one Mitchell sang when McAllester was recording him. At that point I didn't know if I'd do much more than quote or allude to the vocables: possibly pull them or something like them into the English. I was *writing* at first, working on the words by sketching in phrases that seemed natural to my own sense of the language. In the 10th Song there's a division of speakers; the main voice is that of Enemy Slayer or Dawn Boy, who first brought horses to The People, but the chorus is sung by his father, the Sun, telling him to take spirit horses and other precious animals and goods to the house of his mother, Changing Woman. The literal translation of the refrain—(*to*) *the woman, my son*—seemed a step away from how we'd say it, though normal enough in Navajo. It was with the sense that, whatever distortions in sound the Navajo showed, the syntax was natural, that I changed McAllester's suggested reading to *go to her my son*, and his opening line

Boy-brought-up-within-the-Dawn It is I, I who am that one

(lit. *being that one*, with a suggestion of causation) to

> Because I was the boy raised in the dawn.

At the same time I was, I thought, getting it down to more or less the economy of phrasing of the original.[6]

I went through the first seven or eight lines like that but still hadn't gotten to the vocables. McAllester's more "factual" approach—reproducing the vocables exactly—seemed wrong to me on one major count. In the Navajo the vocables give a very clear sense of continuity from the verbal material; that is, the vowels in particular show a rhyming or assonantal relationship between the "meaningless" and meaningful segments:

'Esdza shiye'	e hye-la	'esdza shiye'	e hye-la	ŋaŋa yeye 'e
The woman,	*(voc.)*	*The woman,*	*(voc.)*	*(voc.)*
my son		*my son*		

whereas the English words for this and many other situations in the poem are more rounded and further back in the mouth. Putting the English words ("son" here but "dawn," "home," "upon," "blown," etc. further on) against the Navajo vocables (*e hye-la ŋaŋa yeye 'e*, etc.) denies the musical coherence of the original and destroys the actual flow.

I decided to *translate* the vocables, and from that point on was already playing with the possibility of *translating* other elements in the songs (e.g., the word distortions and the music) not usually handled by translation. It also seemed important to get away as far as I could from *writing*. So I began to speak, then (with enough text in front of me) to sing my own words over Mitchell's tape, replacing his vocables with sounds relevant to me, then putting my version on a fresh tape, having now to work it in its own terms. I created my own vocables, then, by carrying simple English words like *one, none,* and *gone* into something like the area of pure vocal sound (the difference, if it's clear from the spelling, between *one, none & gone* and *wnn, nnnn & gahn*): soundings that would carry into the other songs at an even greater remove from the discarded meanings:

Because I was thnboyngnng raised ing the dawn NwnnN go to her my son N wnn N wnn N nnnn N
  gahn
etcetera.

What I was doing in one sense was contributing and then obliterating my own level of meaning, while in another sense it was as if I was recapitulating the history of the vocables themselves, at least according to one of the standard explanations that views them as remnants of archaic words that have been emptied of (lexical) meaning: a process that I could still sense elsewhere in the Horse Songs—for example, where the sound *howo* turns up as both a "meaningless" vocable and a distorted form of the word *hoghan* = house. But even if I was doing something like that in an accelerated way, that wasn't the real point of it for me. Rather what I was getting at was the establishment of a series of sounds that were assonant with the range of my own vocabulary in the translation, and to which I could refer whenever the Navajo sounds for which they were substitutes turned up in Mitchell's songs.

With the word distortions too, it seemed to me that the most I should do was approximate the degree of distortion in the original. McAllester had provided two Navajo texts—the words as sung and as they would be if spoken—and I aimed at roughly the amount of variation I could discern between the two. I followed therefore where McAllester and Mitchell led me, responding to any of Mitchell's moves of which I was aware and letting them program or initiate the moves I made in translation. All of this within obvious limits: those imposed by the field of sound I was developing in English. Throughout the six songs I worked out before desisting, I proceeded in pretty much that way: the relative densities determined by the original, the final form by the necessities of the poem as it took shape for me. To say any more about that—though the approach changed in the later songs I worked on, toward a more systematic handling—would be to put greater emphasis on method than any poem can bear. More important for me was actually being in a stimulus-and-response situation, certainly the most *physical* translation I've ever been involved in. I hope that that much comes through for anyone who hears these sung.

In the performance versions—which came later and were no more Navajo music than the words were Navajo words or the vocables Navajo vocables—I was always careful to explain the degree to which they did or didn't relate to the originals. That much was also a reflection of my sense that the more *total* the translation—the more elements I could attend to—the more the songs departed from the Navajo.[7] I was aware, too, that the written versions of the Horse Songs risked, even courted, unreadability, that they became the markers of an attempt to translate the untranslatable, as if the act of translation was less a carryover than a rupture. For all of that, it was precisely the sung versions that achieved the impact—nearly immediate—of the kind of poetry at issue here, and an entry into spaces that my work had scarcely touched before this. Nor did I continue to translate in this vein—however promising I took this vein to be, however much it revealed (to me at least) about the possibilities and limits of translation. Unlike Tedlock's or Dell Hymes's approach to spoken narrative as a readily duplicable kind of verse, what I was proposing was a mode of translation, an experimental poetics that could only be carried on by other poets—by those engaged with poetry as a precise yet strangely open sound art.

Behind it too, as I noted first in 1969, there was another, hidden motive: not simply to make clear the world of the original, but to do so at some remove from the song itself: to reflect the song without the "danger" of presenting any part of it (the melody, say) exactly as given: thus to have it while not having it, in deference to the sense of secrecy and localization that's so important to those for whom the songs are sacred and alive. So the changes resulting from translation are, in this instance, not only inevitable but desired, or, as another Seneca said to me: "We wouldn't want the songs to get so far away from us; no, the songs would be too lonely."

It's something like this of course that gets us into the problematics of translation in an imperialist or postcolonialist context. If I've managed to explain my reasons for pursuing an ethnopoetics—translation and all—there's no denying that once having entered this field, the questions that face the poet-translator are very much those that have faced others as well. Is it possible or proper to translate here with the same assumptions as with translations and adaptations from western or contemporary work? Do such translations conceal a claim to power and authority on the translator's part—a forced displacement of the "other" from control of his or her own life and work? Is there a general problem in translating via others from languages not known to the translator, and is it still more problematic under the conditions named? Are translations by scholars less (or more) of an imperial intrusion than those by poets? Is what we do translation in the ordinary sense, or is it—should it be—a commentary on the problematics of translation and a calling into question of dominant attitudes in the colonizing culture? And finally, is such a questioning compatible with the idea of the poem as "sacred action"? Can it help to foster the conditions for a new, even a newly *sacred* sense of poetry and life?

I have no desire to offer self-justifying answers or to present my own work as more appropriate or correct than the work of others, but I long ago decided (not without some apprehension and some turning from the work at hand) that the doubt I felt was more an incitement to continue than an injunction to desist. Clearly I have no sense that I've provided answers to the questions raised. (Nor would I expect anyone to trust such answers if I claimed to have them.) Besides which, I've long found questions to be of greater interest to me than answers, while recognizing that as a further symptom of my own necessary unbelief. For that reason I have, more than once, cited Edmund Carpenter's version of the account Knud Rasmussen gave of his conversation with the Inuit shaman, Aua:

Asked by Rasmussen to explain why life was as it was, [Aua] took him outside and, pointing to hunters returning emptyhanded after long hours on the ice, himself asked, "Why?" He then took him into a cold igloo where hungry children shivered and into another igloo where a woman, who had always worked hard and helped others, now lay miserably ill. Each time he asked, "Why?" but received no reply.

"You see," said Aua, "you are equally unable to give any reason when we ask why life is as it is. And so it must be. All our customs come from life and turn toward life; we explain nothing, we believe nothing, but in what I have just shown you lies our answer to all you ask" (Rothenberg & Rothenberg 1983:481).

As an answer it remains enigmatic enough to have, for me, the ring of truth.

Notes

1. The first of these will be published by Farrar, Straus & Giroux as part of collected translations of Lorca by various hands, and the second will be published by Temple University Press in 1992.

2. I am here not counting later essays and interviews that followed in large part from the discourse initiated by *Shaking the Pumpkin*. Other anthologies and the magazine *Alcheringa*, which I edited with Dennis Tedlock, included but were never wholly devoted to American Indian texts. In

my own poetry, *A Seneca Journal* (1978) comes off two years at the Allegany Seneca Reservation but remains primarily a spinoff from work begun a decade earlier in *Poland/1931*.

3. In the revised edition of *Shaking the Pumpkin*, I dropped the "workings" designation in favor of the more general "English version," a decision with which I still don't feel entirely at home.

4. See the author's *Shaking the Pumpkin* (revised edition, University of New Mexico Press) for both of these. Additional "horse songs" were published in a limited edition by Tetrad Press in London and in a sound recording, *6 Horse Songs for 4 Voices*, by New Wilderness Audiographics in New York. A more detailed account of what follows is in my essay, "Total Translation" (1969), the most complete version of which appears in *Pre-Faces & Other Writings* (New Directions, 1981) and *Symposium of the Whole*.

5. Looking back at this, it strikes me again just how suggestive and contrastive it all is when set against our conventional ideas of the structure, tone, and venue of serious and extended works of poetry. I assume that this much is evident here and in the other examples given, so that nothing further need be said about it.

6. McAllester's approach in his own version of the Horse Songs was the exact opposite of this: to go with Navajo syntax, no matter how twisted the English became in the process. Syntactically his versions are—in that sense—more radical than mine. (See his essay, "The Tenth Horse Song of Frank Mitchell," in Rothenberg and Rothenberg 1983:393–98.)

7. By the time I came to do group versions of the songs (but really of my own voice multiplied four times on tape and in live performance), I felt much more at home with the translations, much freer to work those up as the English texts seemed to demand. Some hints from McAllester contributed to this, but the divergences likely went beyond the limits of translation as such.

References

Blanchot, Maurice. 1990. "Translating," *Sulfur 26*, 82–86.

Kafka, Franz. 1954. *Dearest Father*. New York: Schocken Books.

Lippard, Lucy. 1970. *Surrealists on Art*. Englewood Cliffs, New Jersey: Prentice-Hall, Inc.

Ortiz, Simon J. 1987. "The Language We Know," In *I Tell You Now*, ed. Brian Swann and Arnold Krupat. Lincoln: University of Nebraska Press.

Pound, Ezra. 1970. *The Cantos of Ezra Pound*. New York: New Directions Publishing Corp.

Rothenberg, Jerome. 1968. *Technicians of the Sacred: A Range of Poetries from Africa, America, Asia, & Oceania*. New York: Doubleday & Company.

———. 1972. *Shaking the Pumpkin: Traditional Poetry of the Indian North Americas*. New York: Doubleday & Company.

———. 1978. *A Big Jewish Book: Poems & Others Visions of the Jews from Tribal Times to Present*. New York: Doubleday & Company.

———. 1981. *Pre-Faces & Other Writings*. New York: New Directions Publishing Corp.

———. 1985. *Technicians of the Sacred: A Range of Poetries from Africa, America, Asia, Europe, & Oceania* (revised edition). Berkeley: University of California Press.

———. 1986. *New Selected Poems 1970–1985*. New York: New Directions Publishing Corp.

———. 1989. *Exiled in the Word* (revised edition of *A Big Jewish Book*), with Harris Lenowitz. Port Townsend, Washington: Copper Canyon Press.

———. 1991. *Shaking the Pumpkin* (revised edition). Albuquerque: University of New Mexico Press.

Rothenberg, Jerome, and Diane Rothenberg. 1983. *Symposium of the Whole: A Range of Discourse Toward an Ethnopoetics*. Berkeley: University of California Press.

Zukofsky, Louis, and Celia Zukofsky. 1969. *Catullus*. London: Cape Goliard.

Part Two:
North America

Use
All
There
Is to
Use

Dell Hymes

My title is from Kenneth Burke.[1] I cannot now recall when I first learned it from him—perhaps as long ago as the summer I met him, a student in his class at the School of Letters at Indiana University in 1952. If there is a motto that sums up and informs my work, it is this. To use Burke's pregnant vocabulary, it serves as a strategic, stylized answer to situations in which I have found myself.[2] It names an attitude toward what counts as anthropology (as against "that's not anthropology"); toward what counts as linguistics (as against "that's not linguistics"); toward the scope of competence in the use of language (as against "that's just performance"); toward administering a School of Education; toward ethnopoetics.[3]

Let me use this saying now as the title for an apologia. When even those whose work one admires publish portraits one doesn't recognize, an attempt at clarification may be justified. What follows, then, is part response to what others have said, part a general view of work ahead.

Someone who studies narratives ought not to object when others construct one that gives him a prominent role. Still, as an historian, I would like to resign from the role of "Hymes" in the drama "Hymes vs. Tedlock." To be sure, there are differences in what we do and prefer to do. It might be a fair summary to say that Dennis is concerned most of all with the moment of performance, and I am much concerned with the competence that informs it. Dennis trusts most of all the speaking voice, I evidence of recurrent pattern. That means I run the risk of finding pattern that isn't there (but I have Virginia Hymes [e.g., 1987] to keep pointing that out). Dennis runs the risk of missing pattern that is.

What is not so is that there is a fundamental difference between us with regard to the importance of the oral life of narrative. Dennis regarded his Tulane dissertation (1968) on Zuni narrative as the first dissertation in the ethnography of speaking, an enterprise I had launched, and correctly so. Both of us contributed to an issue of *New Literary History* with titles that stress oral performance (Hymes 1977, Tedlock 1977).

What is particularly not so is the equation, Tedlock : Hymes = pause : particle. Dennis has sometimes attended to particles as relevant, and I have never attended to particles alone.[4] The point of method is not to look for any single feature, but to look for what counts in the text and tradition. In the article just mentioned, I put it this way (1981 [1977]:318).

Verses are recognized, not by counting parts, but by recognizing repetition within a frame, the relation of putative units to each other within a whole. Covariation between form and meaning, between units and a recurrent Chinookan pattern of narrative organization, is the key.

With regard to features that count, the principle is that which Roman Jakobson (1960) called *equivalence*. With regard to patterns of narrative organization, the principle is that which Kenneth Burke called "arousal and satisfying of expectation" (1925, 1941 [fifth paragraph of the forword]). Lines, equivalence, arcs of expectation: these are the three keys (see Hymes 1987a:49–51).

What counts as equivalence is always to be determined. When Ralph Maud thrust a set of Bella Coola texts into my hand at the Vancouver airport some years ago, a little before I was to talk to his class at Simon Fraser, what counts turned out to be a non-final quotative suffix (Hymes 1983b). In the Koasati texts analyzed by Geoffrey Kimball, a small set of initial particles, turns at talk, and a word-final quotative string figure prominently (see Kimball 1989). When I turned from the Wishram Chinook texts of Louis Simpson to the Clackamas Chinook texts of Victoria Howard, Mr. Simpson's explicit pairs of initial particles were seldom to be found. The two varieties of Kiksht (the native name for the language) are closely related; the two narrative styles seemed not to be. I was forced to discover something beyond overt signals. In Chinookan that something is a small set of alternative relations.

Not that there are no overt markers at all in Mrs. Howard's stories. As put in 1977 (1981:319):

Mrs. Howard often makes use of "Now," "Soon now," and other such elements, but often does not. To determine the organization of her narratives, one has to recognize and abstract features that co-occur with the use of initial particle pairs in the narratives of Louis Simpson. Especially salient and important are statements of change in what Kenneth Burke calls the "scene-agent ratio"—indications of change of scene in either location or lapse of time, and indication of change among participant in the action.[5]

The long myth that is the subject of the final chapter of *"In Vain I Tried to Tell You:* "Grizzly Woman Deceives and Kills Women" (Hymes 1980) shows the preponderant importance of these considerations. Reading it, one would see at once the recurrent marking of units by time expressions ("In spring," "In the morning," "It became evening," "At daybreak," "Now it was day"), and the dramatic organization of scenes in terms of turns at talk.

If one organizes Mrs. Howard's stories in the order of their dictation (Jacobs's notes identify the sequence of notebooks), her way of using initial particles turns out to have evolved in the course of her two seasons of work with Jacobs. What proves basic in her narratives is not any one kind of marker of units, but a set of rhetorical relations. It is a set shared with the other Chinookan narrators known to us, a way of accomplishing what Burke has called the fundamental principle of style, the arousal and satisfying of expectation. I have discussed the Chinookan pattern at length in other places. Suffice it to say that it offers narrators certain options for grouping sequences of incident, event, and image. The normal options are sequences of three or five. (Often enough a sequence of five is an interlocking double sequence of three, the third unit being a pivot, completing a first series and initiating a second.) My work with Mrs. Howard's narratives has depended upon (a) recognizing a variety of kinds of equivalent features in the identification of verses, and (b) recognizing the recurrence of rhetorical relations. These rhetorical relations, indeed, pervade the narratives; they relate verses, stanzas, scenes, acts.

Particles, then, are not the alpha and omega of my work. Historically, they were the alpha, but no more than that, not even the beta.

II

There remains the general question: how should texts be put on the page? We have pretty well escaped a phase in which oral narratives were put on the page in paragraphs, because narratives were assumed to be prose. It is pretty well recognized that putting a narrative on the page implies an assumption as to its form, and that form involves lines. But in what way? And with what else?

A fundamental issue is the extent to which a presentation can combine different kinds of information. The issue arises in several ways. Let me consider first the relation between the kind of information focused upon by Tedlock and some others (e.g., Facey 1988), on the one hand, and the kind focused upon by myself and some others, on the other hand.

(1) A narrative involves pace shaped by pause and intonation, and pace shaped by rhetorical proportion and point. There is the speed or slowness, the length or brevity of

lines, their clustering or separation. There is speed or slowness of progression through a formal part, the length or brevity of verses, stanzas, scenes, their interconnection.

Can both be presented on the same page? Where the two dimensions coincide, as Bright has found them to do in Karok (1984:93–94),[6] and as Virginia Hymes has found consistently in English, or complement each other, as Kroskrity (1985) has found them to do in Arizona Tewa,[7] or intersect, as Sherzer (1982) has found in San Blas Cuna, there is of course little problem. Where the two do not coincide, as appears to be the case in the Zuni text we have from Tedlock (and also in Hopi and Nguna),[8] the two kinds of account may appear quite different on the page. If one experiments with presenting both kinds of information, however, the degree of difference seems to depend on the starting point: lines shown in terms of pauses, or lines shown in terms of rhetorical patterns.

I have examined the one Zuni text published by Tedlock, "Coyote and Junco," and the Nguna (New Hebrides) story of "The Heron" (Facey 1988:250–53).[9] One comparison has been to put the texts on the page so as to show verses and rhetorical patterns, while introducing brackets to indicate the scope of the lines with which they were first published. The brackets permit recovery of the information as to what is part of such a line, but not an easy inspection of those relations (and possible insight from seeing them).

If one starts from the other side, and introduces information as to verses into a presentation in terms of pause, my own impression is that this second experiment works better than the first with the Nguna "The Heron." The Nguna lines are usually short, and one can usually display relations of verse, scene, and stanza at the right. In two instances a verse begins in the middle of a line so defined (8, 15).

When the two experiments are tried with the Zuni "Coyote and Junco," again the first result does not seem very effective. The lines as defined by Tedlock are too variable to be easily perceived as performance within the showing of underlying relations. Information as to rhetorical relationships is more intelligible, again, as with the Nguna text, with occasional exceptions in which a verse or stanza begins in the middle of a pause-defined line (20, 75, 81). Still, the lines defined by rhetorical relations are not easily perceived, or taken into the mind for comparison.

Two texts, two narrators, two languages, accidentally chosen, are of course not adequate for a general conclusion. And others may form different impressions from the same presentation. On this showing, however, it seems to me that in those cases, perhaps exceptional, when the two kinds of information differ notably, then the foregrounding of one does allow one to document the other, but for interpretation it is best to provide each separately. If one mode of presentation must be chosen, it may be easier to show rhetorical relations within a presentation in terms of vocal lines, than conversely.

These questions of mode of presentation arise because ethnopoetics involves not only translation but also transformation, transformation of modality, the presentation of something heard as something seen. The eye is an instrument of understanding. Still, questions of translation itself do enter as well. When the purpose of presenting a text is to convey its rhetorical relationships, one translates in the service of that aim. Insofar as possible, signals that are the same in the original are kept the same in the translation. In "Coyote and Junco," for example (as indicated in n. 8) *Taachi* is always "meanwhile,"

Taas always "again" in my verse translation. When Sapir published Louis Simpson's Wishram Chinook myths, *Aga kwapt* was variously translated, according to context and taste, from "Now" and "Then" to "And" and nothing. In the verse translation it is always "Now then." That is a little awkward in English, but one asks the reader to come to take it for granted.

This indeed is a hallmark of the understanding of narrative structure that has emerged in the last two decades. When taken as ingredients of prose, such elements did not seem to matter. One would translate them ad hoc, certainly not always the same, and might often leave them out. If all that is of concern is what the story is about, and if one believes that what it is about is not affected by an original structure, of course, that is all right. Even if one knows that the point of the story depends in part on its shape, and on the marking of that shape, one may want to convey it in English that is idiomatically effective. Still, the translation may be a reader's only access to the original lines and relationships. If so, adaptation to the target language may conceal the otherness of the text, and some of its interest. There is no single answer to the question, how much to adapt, how much to preserve, but some degree of teaching is often necessary. One must often ask the reader to learn.

(2) The question of "what else" arises just because we must teach as well as show. Local hearers of a narrative usually share with the teller the idiom employed, along with knowledge of conventions of form and expression, of references and allusions, of a taken-for-granted world.[10] Readers generally do not, and generally lack access to other sources of information. What they see, together with whatever else may be found in the publication, is what they get.

The kinds of information that may be helpful are diverse. Because much of ethnopoetics involves other languages and other cultures, information about those languages and cultures obviously has a part. It may be relevant as well for narratives from parts of the vast network of English use not one's own.

Many linguists incorporate linguistic information within a translation. At least one pioneer of ethnopoetics has incorporated contextual information. Let me consider each in turn.

(a) A way of presenting texts quite popular with linguists working on American Indian languages is interlinear translation. (Part of the popularity may have to do with the availability of a useful computer program.) Each phrase or sentence of a text is represented three times, as a triplet of lines—one the original language, one a morpheme-by-morpheme analysis with grammatical information, one a full translation. Here is an example from a Klamath text collected by Theodore Stern, as edited by Noel Rude.[11]

1   coy hok lmelamlis   cii-ya
     and the thunderbird   SG.live-IND
     And the thunderbird lived.

2   coy hok lmen-damn-a
     and the thunder-HAB-IND
     And he thundered all the time.

3   coy hok w'a-k'a   ho-n-k   domn-a   lmelamlis-as
    and the coyote-DIM the-OBJ- hearken-IND   thunderbird-OBJ
    And Little Coyote hearkened to the thunderbird.

4   coy w'a-k'a   g-en-a   hadakt-dal
    and coyote-DIM   go-TRL-IND   there-ALL
    And Little Coyote went there,

5   coy ho-n-k   sle-pga-pg-a   lmelamlis-as
    and the-OBJ-   see-DUR-DUR-IND   thunderbird-OBJ
    and watched the thunderbird.

6   coy hok lmelamlis   b-awal-lG-a
    and the thunderbird   throw.PL-upon-down-IND
        mna lolp blay-dal
        his   eye up high-ALL
    And the thunderbird threw his eyes up toward the sky,

7   na?as   t'ikt'ik t t t hrrrrrr
    thus
    [saying] thus, "T'ikt'ik t t t hrrrrrr

8   coy hok lolp he-tGi-bli
    and the eye PL.fall-down-back
    And the eyes fell back down,

9   he-wy'aq-bli   lolb-at   lmelamlis
    PL.fall-into a container-back   eye-LOC   thunderbird
    fell into the eye sockets, thunderbird.

Such a presentation is helpful in making sure of the linguistic underpinnings of translation and interpretation. It is less helpful in detecting narrative form. It dictates pauses on the part of the reader, but for information, or to pick out the line that continues the story. Picking out, it is hard to sustain a sense of rhetorical form, of the arousal and satisfying of expectation. And insofar as an inquiring eye must take the place of a cultural ear, there is not enough on a page. The passage just given runs over one manuscript page onto another, yet is just three pairs of verses. Here they are, the pairs identified by a closing brace at the end of each:

> And the Thunderbird lives.
> And he thunders all the time.}
> And Little Coyote hearkens to the Thunderbird.
> And Little Coyote goes there,
>   and watches the Thunderbird.}
> And the Thunderbird throws his eyes up toward the sky,
>   (speaking) this way: "T'ikt'ik t t t hrrrrrr."
> And the eyes fall back down,
>   fall into Thunderbird's eye sockets.}

However useful the interlinear program and presentation for linguistic analysis, concordances, and documented lexicons, a separate presentation is needed to show rhetorical form.

(b) We tend to forget that the usual way of writing languages on the page is one that implies, or, one might say, conceals, linguistic information. It is phonological, or phonemic, in the sense that it abstracts from spoken qualities and represents words as part of a grammar. One who knows the grammar, one who knows the language, may be able to infer the spoken qualities from the abstract representation. Many may not be able to do so, and any reader not a user of the language may forget the spoken qualities.

We are concerned to convey the voice of performance in various ways, by indicating loudness, quietness, raspiness, and the like. It is in keeping with such concern to convey the words in a phonetic, rather than phonological, way as well. To do so is to reverse (for the purpose at hand) the accomplishment central to the rise of linguistics, phonemic analysis. But it is easier to infer phonemic status from phonetic symbols than the reverse, and insofar as the quality of performance and its effects involve actual sounds, not structural abstractions, desirable.

Here is an example (translation first) from Louis Simpson's "Coyote and Deer" (cf. Hymes 1984). As the myth ends, Coyote's wife reproaches him.

Then the woman told him:
   "You are bad, Coyote.
   "I for my part am not Deer.
   "Look at the Deer;
   "Everyone will swallow *his* meat   60
   "I do not have good meat.
   "Likewise you, Coyote, are different;
   "You are a poor thing, Coyote.
   "No one would swallow your meat.
   "This is what people will say: 65
      " 'Dead things are Coyote's food.' "

A phonemic representation would be:

Kwapt gagiulxam aǧagilak:
   "Imik'amla Isk'ulya.
   "Našqi náit'a Ič'ánk.
   "Yaxtau sik'lutk Ič'ánk;
   "Kánawi šan luq ałgiuxwa iáǧiwaq.
   "Našqi naika it'ukti ičgiwaq.
   "Daukwa maika Isk'ulya mxlúidat,
   "Mguałilx Isk'ulya.
   "Naqi pu šan luq ałgiuxwa imigiwaq.
   "Qidau alugwagima idlxam,
      "Iłmimlušt iałxlm Isk'ulya."

Stress is marked only where it is an exception to the prevailing rule that stress occurs on the next to last syllable. Length of vowel is not phonemic and is not shown. The final [a] or [i] of a word is often elided before a word beginning with a vowel, especially [a] before initial [i], but all words are shown in full. The back stops, palatal [k] and velar [q] are pronounced with an audible fricative release [x, x̣, respectively]. When [l] and

[m] follow a consonant, a vocalic transition usually precedes them, written by Sapir (who recorded the text) with schwa [ə], but that is not phonemic and shown. Phonemic /a/ is sometimes heard as schwa. The language has two high vowels, phonologically /i u/. When these vowels occur next to a velar consonant (q, x̣), their quality is that of a mid-vowel (e, o). Next to a velar consonant, the quality of [a] is commonly somewhat further back and higher [ɔ]. All this is regular and not shown. Here is the text, then, with phonetic detail:

> Kx̣wópt gagiúlxam agagílak:
> "Imik'ámǝl(a) isk'úlǝyǝ.
> "Ná·šqx̣i náit'(a) ič'ánk.
> "Yáx̣tau sík'ǝlutk ič'ánk;
> "Ká·nauwe· šan lúqx̣ ałgiux̣wa iágewɔq.
> "Ná·šqx̣i náik(a) it'ukt(i) ičgéwɔq.
> "Dáukwa máik(a) isk'úlǝyǝ mx̣lúidǝt,
> "Mgoáłix isk'úlya.
> "Ná·qx̣i pu šan lúqx̣ ałgiúx̣w(a) imigéwɔq.
> "Qé·dau alugwagím(a) idólxam,
>   "'Iłmé·mǝlušt iáłxlǝm isk'úlǝyǝ."

Much of this one could predict. Some of it is not regular and so not recoverable from a phonological presentation: the schwa in "Coyote" (5, 7, 11) and the last syllable of line 7, the [o] in the first word of line 8. The elision of vowels is expectable in a fluent style of speech, but could have been otherwise.

Vowel length on the first syllables to lines 3, 5, 6, 9, 10 is expressive. Notice the words it emphasizes: "Not, all (every), not, not, thus." The stress on the third syllable from the end of the last word in line 5 ("his-meat"), rather than the second from the end, is contrastive. Expressive length and stress can be shown in a phonological representation, to be sure, and the last example ("*his* meat") has been. Still, a phonetic presentation seems desirable, in that expressive features are inherently shown, along with other details that could not be inferred. One has the phonetic texture as a whole.

(c) Melville Jacobs preserved much of what can be known about several narrative traditions of Oregon and Washington (Northern Sahaptin, Miluk Coos, Santiam Kalapuya, Clackamas Chinook), and pioneered in conceiving of such narrative as dramatic performance. In presenting the Clackamas Chinook narratives of Victoria Howard, he sought to make clear the meanings by incorporating contextual detail. Footnotes served for information about the recording of the text, linguistic comments, comments on and from Mrs. Howard, interpretive remarks, etc. Some explanation of what was being said and done or referred to also appears in the footnotes, but a very great amount is in parentheses within the translation. For the myth of "Tongue" (Jacobs 1959:369–75), one footnote comments on the recording of the story, the other recounts the opening (nn. 314, 315 on p. 635). All other information is supplied in parentheses. Here are the opening scenes (Jacobs 1959:369–70). (The numbers are those provided by Jacobs to key portions of translation and text to each other.)

1. Those persons who lived at their village right here (a little above Willamette Falls at Oregon City) were always playing. Now their wealthy headwoman died, and they put her away, they hung her up (on branches of a tree, inside a canoe with small holes punched in it). Then when it became nighttime now they saw something just like fire. It came out (from an island in the river) high up in that direction on one side from the river. At that place then they placed two of them (two Fish persons), they remained there, from both sides they watched that (fire-like) thing as it came there. 2. Their name was ____ Fish (a fish with some kind of sharp cutting edge) from the river.

Explanatory information is at hand as one goes along, but the rhythm of going along is not that of the story, even taking the story as prose. With a presentation in lines, one can key needed information to the pertinent point in the story in a separate set of notes. Victoria Howard's narratives, the fullest body of Chinookan narrative we have, have long been out of print. I hope eventually to be able to republish them, presenting them in lines, but without losing useful information provided by Jacobs. There seems to be two kinds of information indeed. Some seems to reflect a sense on Jacobs's part of a need to help the reader make connections, as in "they watched that (fire-like) thing." Some, such as "(a fish with some kind of sharp cutting edge)" is from the notebooks, obtained from Mrs. Howard. The first such item "(a little above Willamette Falls at Oregon City)" is indeed telling for interpretation. The opening words and the supplementary remark identify the people of the story as predecessors of the Clackamas in their own place, as perhaps then representatives of the fate of the historic Clackamas. The opening words indeed have special force and an alliterative ring in Clackamas: dáyčka dába nuxílayt idálxam, "Those-people here they-lived, their-community." Not the common "They lived there" or "They lived at X," but "here." (See the use of the opening scene as illustration of rhythm in the next section.)

In sum, both three-line interlinear translation and Jacobs's parentheses provide information that is useful. Neither could readily accomodate the information of the other. Just so a translation shaped on the page by rhetorical form, by composition, may not be able to offer the eye and mind the sense of a translation shaped by pause and intonation, by overt performance, and conversely.

There is a way to show the composition of a narrative compactly, separate from the presentation of the narrative itself. One can show the relations, the verses, stanzas, scenes and acts, their sequence and hierarchy in relation to each other and their lines. I have often myself wanted to present a story with little or no apparatus, so that the reader can experience it for its own sake, and can perhaps detect relations independently of what I had found, relations perhaps that I had missed. To some extent, then, a profile might be an adequate complement to a story presented with no marking of relations other than those of lines. (For an example, see the profile of "Coyote and Eagle's Daughter" at the end of this essay.)

When one is interpreting a story, such a profile works well as a test of completeness and consistency. Missing lines, skewed relations, become evident. One can see pattern, or lack of it.[12] Providing the information is of course not the same as experiencing the unfolding of the story in terms of it. It may be hard to merge the two mentally. One may still want to see the story itself with relations explicitly marked.

There is one more important question as to how to put a story on the page. Passages that are alike in general pattern may yet differ in internal rhythm, and one can find visual equivalents for such differences. This question can be addressed best toward the end of the next section. Let me end this section with a short peroration.

One often reaches a point at which more than one presentation of a story may be desirable, if not essential. Of course it is difficult to publish such narratives at all, let alone in more than one form. The justification of our work is to make the narratives accessible, interpretible by others, and to make clear what we ourselves have done. That is not usually possible. One can accept that, given the human needs of the world, but it is hard to accept, when great sums go not to human needs, but to armaments, ostentation, and greed. Still, we must be as responsible as we can. Ours is the laying of foundations and we should make them as secure as we can. Ultimately, others will be free to experiment, to recreate, to respond as the spirit may move them to what they can grasp of the often astonishing and moving oral literatures of other peoples. But much of the time an oral literature is not able to defend itself. The world's literatures are not on equal footing. If someone takes liberties with a poem by Verlaine, others need not depend on that willful version. Someone who cares can likely find the original, find even a bilingual edition. Someone who does not know French can likely learn it, or pick up a dictionary and grammar to help make out what goes on. That is possible for several modern languages, and for the languages our civilization has accepted as classical. A novice can find resources with which to compare and interpret translations of the Hebrew Bible and the New Testament. There are handbooks and dictionaries with information as to places and persons and customs. There are diverse translations, interlinear translations, even guides to the assessment of the original manuscripts. It is not so for most languages with which ethnopoetics is concerned. Here the dialectic between original and adaptation is acute. The original text is normative, yet one wants it to speak to places and people not its own. One wants to establish a connection between different languages and settings, without reducing either to the other. In ethnopoetics we have almost everything to do ourselves, and with little support. Still, whatever compromises in presentation are required, the goal of full accessibility to original texts can be kept as a standard.

III

The years have seen a step-by-step recognition of the architecture oral narratives can have. There has been a progression from overt markers to implicit patterns, and from cultural uniformity to individual diversity.

(a) Writing in the fall of 1957, I recognized that initial particles had a structural role in Wishram Chinook (Hymes 1958). Commenting on the presentation of my paper in a symposium at the American Anthropological Association meetings that fall, Melville Jacobs declared that it would be impossible to pursue such an approach. In 1971, however, I analyzed one of the myths that Louis Simpson had told in Wishram to Edward Sapir in such terms, "The News about Coyote" (Hymes 1975). Analysis consisted simply of recognizing initial particle pairs as identifying segments of the text.

(b) In the course of a year's leave in Oregon in 1972–73, thanks to the National

Endowment for the Humanities, I convinced myself that there was more than the marking of segments. There was systematic relationship among segments, relationships of a kind involving the Chinookan pattern number (five). At the time Virginia Hymes thought I must be making it up, if not mad, but close analysis of another of Louis Simpson's dictations to Sapir ("The Deserted Boy") showed consistent and telling patterning, not at just level (groups of verses), but at levels beyond that (Hymes 1976). I would now revise the last portion of that analysis, but the difference would not change the general finding, that of pervasive patterning. "The Deserted Boy" remains the first full-scale demonstration.

(c) At this point narrative patterning appeared to have a strict correlation with cultural patterning. It has long been known that cultures are to have preferred "sacred," "ceremonial," pattern numbers. It has long been known that in a story with a series of siblings, say, or repeated actions, the number of siblings and actions will accord with such a number. The ethnopoetic discovery showed such accord to exist within the formal organization of narrative itself. Where the pattern number of the culture was five, narrative units would occur in series of five. Where the pattern number was four, narative units would occur in series of four. But narrative proved subtler than a single pattern. In narrative the pattern number was found to have a correlate. Five would have three, and four would have two.

This double correlation has indeed been sustained. Five- and three-part relations go together in all the Chinookan varieties (Wishram-Wasco, Clackamas, Kathlamet, Shoalwater-Clatsop); in several of their neighbors along the Columbia River (Nez Perce, Sahaptin, Chehalis and Cowlitz Salish), and in the Willamette Valley (Kalapuya); in some other Native American traditions (e.g., Coos, Klamath, Tlingit); in Xhosa of southern Africa; and now in Nguna of the Pacific and in much English-language narrative. Two- and four-part relations go together in Coos of the Oregon coast, Takelma of the Rogue River Valley in Oregon, Karok and Hupa of the Klamath River Valley, Zuni, Tonkawa of Texas, and elsewhere.

(d) The double correlation points to more than a reflection of cultural pattern generally. It appears to point to something in the nature of human narrative ability. In Chinookan, as said, the cultural pattern number is five, and known by members of the culture to be so. They are not particularly aware, however, of three-part patterning, although certain forms of it are so salient as to have led Henry Morrison to call one of them "the Chinookan triplet." (As in "Coyote went, he kept on going, he arrived.") In English, of course, three is a recognized pattern number, but not five. It was a surprise to Charlotte Ross, an Appalachian storyteller, to find that her Märchen and legends had five-part relations as well as three.

It seems, then, that if one starts, as it were, from either five or three, one will get the other too. It seems that such patterning in narrative always involves alternatives. One can imagine the mind of the narrator at work in performance, coordinating two kinds of sequence, one of incident, the other of rhetorical form (cf. Hymes 1981:327). Alternatives allow for flexibility, and increase expressive possibilities as well.

The world has seemed partitioned almost between three and five, on the one hand, two and four, on the other. Empirically, of course, it is rash to say so. Only a small portion of the world's traditions have been analyzed. Theoretically, however, one can imagine grounds for it being so. Suppose that part of the point of narrative is not to provide news, but satisfying form. Surely this must be so for myths and tales told many times, as it is for music listened to again. The interest is not so much in what will happen as in how it will happen. As C. S. Lewis put it (1947; cf. also 1961).

The re-reader is looking not for actual surprises (which can come only once) but for a certain surprisingness. . . . In the only sense that matters the surprise works as well the twentieth time as the first. It is the *quality* of unexpectedness, not the *fact* that delights us.

And as Kenneth Burke put it in a seminal essay (1925):

The methods of maintaining interest which are most natural to the psychology of information . . . are [the fact of] surprise and suspense. The method most natural to the psychology of form is eloquence. . . . The contemporary audience . . . is content to have facts placed before it in some more or less adequate sequence. Eloquence is the minimization of this interest in fact, *per se,* so that the "more or less adequate sequence" of their presentation must be relied on to a much greater extent. Thus, those elements of surprise and suspense are subtilized, carried down into the writing of a line or sentence, until in all its smallest details the work bristles with disclosures, contrasts, restatements with a difference, ellipses, images, aphorism, volume, sound-values, in short all that complex wealth of minutiae which in their line-for-line aspect we call style and in their broader outlines we call form.

At any point, then, the teller and re-teller, the hearer and re-hearer of a myth may assume that in its smallest details it will again and again complete an arc of culturally satisfying form, and at the same time may choose, or find, that there is more than one way to realize such form. If there are to be relations of form at all, indeed, there must be something to relate—two elements at least, or three. These are the minimal relations for narrative art. Four can be two taken twice. Five, indeed, can be three taken twice, when, as often in Chinookan, and independently, it appears, in other traditions, the third element of five counts as a pivot, facing two ways, completing an initial three-part arc, and initiating a second. And if it is to be possible to subtilize surprise and suspense, and point and emphasis as well, work them into the line by line achievement of style, one wants the recurring relations to be, as these are, the smallest possible.

I am suggesting that such relations arise in response to a use to which narrative is put, that they are the result of selective adaptation of an aspect of language. It is only fair to acknowledge that they might be innate. After all, such relations begin to appear universal; they take just a few possible forms; that they occur and take the forms they do is not explained by common historical origin. That is the sort of thing Noam Chomsky, Jerry Fodor, and others would expect of an aspect of language with an innate basis. A child could be imagined as born with the kind of ability, or relation, in question, settling upon a specific form in response to the linguistic input it encounters. Verse relations may be innate in that sense. Still, the argument for innateness is most convincing when the property in question does not seem something that can be acquired through experience, and when there is no consistent, current functional reason for it to be what is, when it appears independent of use. Since it seems possible that children could extract verse relations from experience of stories, that they could be explained in terms of current use, innateness is less likely.

(e) It was clear early on that narrators need not confine themselves to expected patterns and markers. If one analyzes a text entirely in such terms, it may fight back. Just counting particles, say, of threes and fives, or twos and fours, can make hash of a text. The principle of method, after all, is not simply one of counting, but one of discovering form/meaning covariation.

In Victoria Howard's "Tongue" (Jacobs 1959:369–75), the scene in which the chief's son recreates the people ends with what would have to be two verses, one ungainly, if only initial particles were considered. Freed from the cramped confines of a prose paragraph, the lines clearly express the repetition three times of a ritual outcome: "they became people." It would be foolish of an analysis not to show that:

> Then now, he transformed them:
>   they became people.
> Those feathers there,
>   bones,
>   they became people—
>   those other feathers were for canoes.
> Now they became people.

John Rush Buffalo's Tonkawa telling of "Coyote and Eagle's Daughter" was an early instance (first published 1980, revised 1987b). I analyzed Tonkawa to honor a late teacher, Harry Hoijer, in a series dedicated to him at UCLA, the institution at which he had taught for so long, and where I had studied with him. Mr. Buffalo made use of a kind of double initial particle, the base 'e- followed by another element, to mark verses. The myth opens with clear four-part relations. The first two stanzas have a common pattern of four lines: Coyote goes, goes up (down), arrives at a point, perceives something (sees a camp, hears weeping). Each of the next stanzas has a two-part exchange between Coyote and a woman in the camp. He says he will fight the monster that has destroyed the people, and sets off to prepare ritually. The next stanza is patterned in, not four, but six lines:

> When it was evening,
>   he went down to the river, and
> cutting off a piece of hard wood,
>   he burned it black, and
> putting it away,
>   he went to sleep, they say.

The succeeding stanzas of this part have four or two lines. I know no reason for the intervening six, but there they are.

In Victoria Howard's "Gitskux and his older brother" (Hymes 1983a) the story proceeds in sets of three and five, as one would expect. At one point there are ten lines which stand by themselves. Any attempt to subdivide them would destroy their unity. They occur in the second part of the myth. The older brother (Panther) is the only free survivor of the destruction of his village. He comes to a house, then sees someone enter at the other end, bringing a deer and going out. Later he sees a woman enter, who washes and twists her hair into braids. She allows him to stay, and at night, causes fleas to bite him and bring him from the corner to her bed and beside her, joining five nights together. She becomes his wife. He does not know that the one bringing deer was her.

> Now the two stayed.
>> She told him,
>>> "Now you will be doing the hunting.
>>> "You will have thought,
>>>> Perhaps there is some man."
>>> "Here I have lived alone,
>>> "I would be the one hunting."
>> "Indeed,"
>>> he told her.
> Now that is what the two did.

The shape is that of a chiasmus:

> the two stayed
>> she told him
>>> you hunting
>>>> you
>>>>> some man
>>>> I alone
>>> I hunting
>> he told her
> the two did.

The shape seems a beautiful expression of interchange within duality. The man will be the hunter, not by right, but by gift.

(f) Some years ago it became apparent that the two kinds of basic pattern were not mutually exclusive. Both could occur in the same text. One would be the normal, "unmarked," kind of relation. The other would enter as a "marked" pattern, intensifying the action.

In John B. Hudson's Kalapuya account of "Coyote releases water dammed up by the frogs" (Hymes 1987a), there are three scenes. In the first (five verses) Coyote prepares to deal with the Frogs, who charge people to drink; in the second (three verses) he trades them a money bead. In the third he drinks. The third scene has eight verses, organized as three sets of two, followed by two others. The three pairs correlate the three steps of a pair of actions, the denouement in which Coyote, on the one hand, drinks as expected, and on the other surreptitiously destroys the dam:

> Now then indeed he drank, Coyote.
>> Now then he put one hand down in.
> Now then he drank.

> Now then he put his hand down in the water where it
> > was dammed up.
> Now then he stopped drinking water.
> > Now then he got up,
> > > he scooped the dirt aside,
> > > > he scooped it out.
> Now then the water went through.
> Now then Coyote said,
> > "All the time water will be everywhere."

In Charles Cultee's two tellings to Boas of the Kathlamet Salmon myth (Hymes 1985a) intensification by pairing is at the heart of the difference between them. Both tellings have two parts, in the first of which Salmon and his party come up river in the spring, are hailed five times from the shore in an insulting way, recognize an elder relative, and go ashore to give gifts and place the plant where it will be. All this is a striking acknowledgment of the importance in winter of a woman's domain of food by a figure symbolic of male pride and men's role as suppliers of the food that made the people well off relative to others lacking direct access to the Columbia. In the second part Salmon and his party continue, encounter an odd trio coming down river, whose claims he rejects, twisting their necks, and, in the second telling, telling them where they will be. In the second telling Salmon regains the upper hand, for the myth ends with his telling Flounder to be in the river. It will no longer be entirely true what the insulting relatives had said, "Without me your people would have died," that the people had to rely on plants until salmon returned up river in the spring. There will be food from Salmon's domain, fish, in the winter as well.

The second telling proceeds unhurriedly with three- and five-part patterning throughout. It is only the second telling that has the placing of the trio, Flounder last. The first telling has only the twisting, and the insistence that the trio are wrong in saying it took them only a day to come from The Dalles. And in the first telling Cultee was evidently in a hurry to get to the second part, but not in the second. In the last scene of the first part, he omitted one line, one step of the action, and went right on. In contrast, when he omitted a line of quoted speech in that scene in the second telling, he paused to add it (so the field notebook shows).

The unhurried, rhetorically unmarked second telling goes, I think, with Cultee having remembered the second phase of dealings with the trio in the second act, and knowing that so far as the emblematic dignity of Salmon is concerned, male vs. female domains, he has a flounder up his sleeve. In the first telling the part about the flounder in the river had not been remembered, was not in store. Salmon's dignity is restored by dramatic assertion of control, intensification by pairing, as soon as the first act is over.

(g) The use of patterns may differ in another way as well, by gender. Elizabeth Jacobs (1959, 1990:116, n. 21) noted that "four is the pattern number of feminine contexts, five of masculine contexts, in Tillamook folklore." [13] As it turns out, the contrast is not only a matter of four women in a set or series, but five men. It obtains in the formal organization of a story (Hymes 1990a). In Clara Pearson's fine telling of "Split-His-

Own-Head" there are nine scenes. The first five have to do with the younger brother of the title taking literally what his sister had told him, and making a fool of himself as a result. That there must be five times is shown in the fact that in this telling to Mrs. Jacobs five is achieved by having the fifth duplicate the third, whereas in an earlier telling to May Mandelbaum Edel, five is again achieved by duplication, although not the same duplication. The last four have a different theme, getting a wife, and each is distinct. (The two patterns are further interwoven, in that they alternate as between levels of organization. In either part of the story, whether scenes are five in number or four, the number of stanzas within scenes is four or two, while the number of verses within stanzas is five, three, or one.)

Such an association of a most general level of patterning with gender may occur in Tonkawa also, but reversed. Four goes with male, five with female, at least in John Rush Buffalo's "Coyote and Eagle's Daughter" (Hymes 1987b). The first major part, in which Coyote restores the people destroyed by a monster, has four main sections, themselves paired: Coyote promises to defeat the monster, Coyote prepares; Wolves (actually) defeat the monster, Coyote restores the people. The one woman is a source of information, but the action is focused on male actors. The second major part has five main sections. Having been given a wife, Coyote leaves her to go gambling; she follows, a young man is intermediary, one commands the other, she leaves. The five-part pattern is repeated, with the difference that the second time it is the woman who commands Coyote, and when she leaves, she leaves for good. Here the focus is on the woman, and indeed a contrast is carefully drawn between the two acts as to her behavior toward Coyote.[14]

(h) The preferred relations may differ among individuals within a community, and indeed, from one telling to another by the same individual. I discovered this a few summers ago when working through Bright's fine Karok texts as a way of keeping sane in the Mt. Hood National Forest while learning to use a computer. One and the same myth, "Coyote's journey," is told with three- and five-part patterning by one of the women with whom Bright worked, Julia Starrit, but with two- and four-part patterning by another. Conversely, the narrator, Nettie Reuben, who used pairing pervasively in telling "Coyote's journey," uses three- and five-part grouping in telling "Coyote's homecoming" and "Coyote trades songs" (see Hymes 1985b:47–53).

In sum, one or the other of these two widely occurring matrices of relationship may dominate a cultural tradition, but that can not be taken for granted of the next story one hears or sees. One may contrast with another within the same tradition—to foreground and intensify a point in the story, as appropriate with one gender rather than another, as a difference among persons or occasions for which we may not have an explanation. Some cases of unexpected use of a pattern may be due to acculturation, as when Timothy Montler (p. c.) reports that his principal source for Saanich Salish patterns stories in terms of two and four, but her son, influenced by English, shows three. Probably there are many cases of Indian people having learned stories, and a patterning with it, from one of their elders from a different tradition. I suspect that the prevalence of pairing in Victoria Howard's early dictations to Melville Jacobs have such a source, as does what seems a reversion in the midst of her telling of a Clackamas counterpart to Cultee's Salmon myth to four verses within a stanza, seemingly just by not making the effort to add the pro forma fifth turn at talk that she occasionally supplies.[15] Acculturation or some other factor may explain the presence of three- and five-part patterning in several Tlingit texts, despite the pervasiveness of even-numbered patterning otherwise in the culture.[16]

IV

There are further differences, differences that can affect the way one puts a text on the page. Two passages may have the same formal patterning, the same number of elements, at a given level, and yet display a difference in balance, a difference in rhythm. One may find oneself wanting to reflect a sense of this in the way one places the lines. I have done so often enough in publishing texts in articles and books, and want here to be somewhat more explicit and systematic.

Here we are very much in the midst of the transformation of something heard into something seen. The differences may or may not have audible characteristics. Often the differences have to do with composition, with balance of content. A verse with four lines, for example, might be balanced 3 + 1, 1 + 3, 2 + 2, or as a straight run of 4.

There is an example of the first possibility in the Tonkawa "Coyote and Eagle's daughter." The sequence in which Coyote revives the people proceeds steadily in terms of stanzas each having a pair of verses. The verses, however, differ. The first has three lines, quite like a Chinookan triad. The second, describing the outcome (futile in each case until the fourth and last) has one. Possibilities of three-part patterning seem exploited here for a comic anti-climax. Here are the last two stanzas:

> Then again he went off, and, (D)
>   coming at a run,
>   "Hurry! This camp is on fire!" they say he said.
> Then, they say, nothing happened.
> Then the last time he went off, and, (E)
>   coming at a run,
>   "Hurry! This camp is on fire!" they say he said.
> Then, they say, many people ran out.

As said, as one grows in sensitiveness to a text, to local movement and rhythm, one senses that something of the "voice" of the narrator is lost if lines are aligned all the same way. This sense does not come from hearing the voice itself, but from becoming intimate with the disposition of words, phrases, and markers in relation to each other. A desire to have a visual analog to one's sense of relations increases when one does want to display as little as possible of the machinery of analysis, explicit labeling of verses and stanzas, with the text. I would like to show several types of cases that have arisen in connection with Victoria Howard's dictations in Clackamas Chinook, types that may be suggestive and useful to others, and then to display the true complexity of the Tonkawa text just quoted, a complexity I failed to grasp in previous analyses of it.

Victoria Howard

Victoria Howard's Clackamas texts indeed exhibit a variety of local rhythms. Units may be formally equivalent (e.g., the stanza) and the principles of grouping the same (three- or five-part relations), yet the rhythm within such formal equivalence not be the same.

Recognizing such differences among them, I find myself almost instinctively representing them differently on the page.[17] Here is an overview, citing instances. The examples are almost entirely from "Tongue" (Jacobs 1959:369–75), whose analysis is otherwise unpublished.

Step by step run. Sometimes in a stanza the sequence of verses seems to proceed in a 'linear' fashion, rapidly, from first to third, or first to fifth. Each verse is a short step in a continuous sequence of action. It seems right to set such a stanza on the page with each unit successively indented. Lines 73–77 of "Tongue" are such a case.

> Now to be sure,
>> now she went into labor,
>>> now she brought out a baby boy.
>> Now it dawned five times,
>>> now she bathed.

And (181–85):

> Now he goes,
>> morning,
>>> now he goes,
>>>> now there . . . he is in the mountains,
>>> now he trains to the end.

Partial internal pairs. Sometimes in a stanza of an odd number of verses, the actions seem not to be a straight line sequence as a whole, but to have parts grouped in pairs. It seems appropriate to indent the second member of a pair. There are two kinds of case.

The usual case in Chinookan is one in which the final verse has no partner. The procession is pair, pair, singleton. Lines 105–13 (III ii A) of "Tongue" are such a case. Each of the first four lines is marked as the start of a verse by initial particle. The paired alternation (Now again : now, Now again : now) suggests the stepwise placement of these four verses.

> Now again he goes about,   105
>> now he hunts.
> Now again he comes back,
>> now he says to her,
>>> "Mother! If only my bow were a little bigger,
>>>> "I could kill something big,   110
>>> spotted all over."

"O. . . ,"
        she told him.[18]

Sets of pairs: reported action. Sometimes in a stanza, all the verses enter into pairs. Sets of three (or five) pairs are indeed not uncommon in Chinookan narrative. When the pairs of a stanza are reported action, it is appropriate to indent the second member of each. Lines 124–29 (III iii), in which each line is also a verse, marked as such, are an especially clear and appropriate case.

> Now again he goes,
>   now the boy hunts all the time.
> Now he would bring back deer,
>   sometimes he would kill two deer.
> Now she would take a little of it,
>   now she would give all (the rest) to it.

Sequences of quoted speech. Sequences of quoted speech do not lend themselves to the indentation just shown. That is due in part to a convention of indenting what is said. It is also often because speech of more than a line or two obscures the visual relation signaled by indentation. With such a convention, it seems best to put each turn at talk flush left. The opening three stanzas of the first scene of Act IV of "Tongue" (131–53) illustrate the difference. The three verses of the first stanza seem a run served by indentation. The three verses of the last stanza of talk between the boy and his mother "Tongue" might be shown this way (and I will do it as an example), but the three verses of the middle stanza would be ill-served.

> Now they lived on there.   (A)
>   Now that is the way the two did to him.
>   Now her son became a man.
> Now he asked his mother.   (B)
>   "How does it happen we are the only ones?"
> She told him,
>   "Ahhh. I had not thought it would be so soon,
>   "(but) a little later before I would tell you about it."
> Now she told him all about it,
>   she told him,
>   "That thing you look at there is not a person.
>   "He devoured our village,
>   he ate all the people,
>   when you were not yet a person."
> Now he told her,   (C)
> "How could you not have told me about it already?"
>   Now . . . she told him.
>   He told her,
>   "Now I will go from here.
>   "I will not get back for a day or two.
>   "I will camp overnight before I get back."

If quoted speech itself is not indented, and is brief, then it might be possible to indent verse in the same way as for reported action. Extended sequences of paired verses, however, involving quoted speech, seem not to lend themselves to this.

Extended sequences of pairs: reported action and quoted speech combined. The final lines of "Tongue" (286–308) are a moving example. Due to their folly, the people of the village had all been eaten by Tongue. One woman, the chief's other wife, survived, having been out digging roots. She copes with Tongue, and bears her son; he grows rapidly and together they kill Tongue. Then in the mountains he gathers feathers and bones from which he recreates the people. On return to the village, where his father teaches them to fish, they mock him. This scene follows. Its pairing is in terms of the relation of action to actors. The person in focus changes with each pair of marked verses: son, mother, son, people, son. Change is clear in the first verse of the fourth pair (the people speak), not clearly in the second. Still, the "No" of the second verse continues a point of view that the son, although grammatical subject, is not initiating, but responding.

> Now——— his heart became bad.
> Now he went,
>   he waded.}
> Now his mother saw him,
>   going.
> Now she ran,
>   she scolded the people,
>   "It is he himself who has made you,
>   "He brought you back here."}
> Now in vain he was followed,   295
>   he was told,
>   "Come back!"
> No.
>   He went further.}
> Now he wept,   300
> Now there he stood in the water.}
> Now his mother wept.
> Now she told the people,
>   "Now then.
>   "Had you not done like that to him,   305
>   "You would have lived on here.
>   "Now then.
>   "Now we shall make our separation."}

Another example is at the beginning of Victoria Howard's "Grizzly Woman began to kill people" (Hymes 1981:356). There are five pairs of verses, the last three turns at talk. Again the relationships of the scene seem shown best by beginning each verse flush left. Of course one could put space between each pair, but the presence of the pairs can also be shown by putting a closed brace at the end of each.

```
Soon now,
   a woman reached him.
They said,
   "Some woman has reached our headman"}
Now they lived on there.
In spring,
   she went I don't know where,
      she came back at evening:
         Oh dear! she brought back camas;
            now she began to share it about.}
They told her,
   "Where did you gather them?"
She told them,
   "Well, I reached a burned-over place,
      it's just camas there,
         the camas stand thick."}
They told her,
   "Goodness, whenever you go again,
      we'll follow you."
"Very well,"
   she told them,
      "Perhaps tomorrow."}
"Indeed. We will follow you too."
"All right,"
   she told them.}
```

Coordinate series. Sometimes in a stanza of marked verses, there is continuity without either a run of action, or internal pairing. For such a set of verses it seems appropriate to put each verse flush left. Lines 67–71 of "Tongue" are such a case. Three groups of lines are marked each with initial "now." The first is a general condition, the second has two quoted lines of thought and decision, the third has a pair of actions.

```
Now the two stayed there, (she and) that thing.
Now she thought,
   "Now it's nearly time for my labor,
   "now I'll carry in moss."
Now she carried in wood also,
   she filled up her house.
```

Partial parallelism within pairs. As we have seen, what is possible and desirable depends in part on how much there is to accommodate line by line on the page. Victoria Howard sometimes pairs verses one way, content another. She presents tristichs, as it were, two of which are related as marked verses, and two of which are related as semantic parallels or elaborations. The opening of "Tongue" has several such. One could choose to make the verses parallel on the page, or the semantic parallelism, or neither. Here are the three alternatives for the second pair: (a-1, a-2) no relation shown on the page, (b) pairs of verses aligned, (c) semantic content aligned.

Now their head-woman died,
now she was put away,
she was hung up.

Now their head-woman died,
  now she was put away,
    she was hung up.

Now their head-woman died,
now she was put away,
  she was hung up.

Now their head-woman died,
  now she was put away,
    she was hung up.

In the case of "Tongue," and Victoria Howard's style of narration generally, a choice is hard to make, but I have adopted the second possibility. It seems important to make clear the presence of marked pairs within larger sequences by putting them to the left, especially if space can not be used to separate them. To align such pairs also is consistent with aligning the pairs that sometimes occur within five-element sequences within the same longer sequences. The amplified third verse of the second scene of "Tongue" is a case in point.

Here, then, are the three scenes of the first act of "Tongue." End braces, rather than space, are used to indicate the pairs of verses, and the two extended five-member sequences that alternate with them in scene [ii]. To present them consistently in one of these ways has the virtue of showing the consequence of a practice, even if one's response is to want another.

It was here those persons lived,   [i]
  had their village.
Always they were playing.}
Now their head woman died.
Now she was put away,
  she was hung up.}
Now it became night.
Now a thing just like fire was seen,
  it came out high on one side of the river.}

Then now, two were gotten   [ii]
  they stayed,
    they watched from both sides
      (as) the thing comes—
        (their name was 'Cut-fish' from the river).}
Soo · · · n while they are there
now something comes like fire.}
Now they are there,
  there they watch:
      straigh · · · t where · · · that dead person hangs it goes,
      straigh · · · t there that thing gets,

                now its tongue,
                now it carries all of it.
                    It is lying on its tongue.}
        Now the two clip the tongue,
        now that thing draws all the way back.}
        Now the people go,
            they go to take the dead one;
        now the dead one is put away again.}
        Now they lived on (there).   [iii]
        Now that thing,
            indeed its name is "Tongue,"
                now da · · · y,
                    night,
                        "Give me back my tongue."}
        Now he made them tired.
        Now they said,
            "Let's give it back to him."}
        Now then they gave it back to him.
        Now he put an end to the village.
            he ate all · · · the people.}

In terms of rhythm we have here a case in which paired relations are not an intensification, against a background of three- and five-part relations, as in Cultee's "Salmon myth" (Kathlamet Chinook), John B. Hudson's account of Coyote and the Frogs (Santiam Kalapuya), and elsewhere. Quite the reverse. The pairs are the norm in this passage. It is the five-part relations that enter as intensification, a mode of elaboration that allows for additional marking. Notice that the second and third pairs of the first scene display the "this, then that," initiation and outcome, effect often associated with narrative pairing: died, put away; night, something seen. The same is true of the three pairs in the second scene: they are there, something comes; they clip, it draws back; people go, the dead one is put away, and of the pairs in the third scene: they live on, the thing pleads (elaborated in form, but with only one action in its five lines); he makes them tired, they say; they give it back, he eats them up.[19]

    At the same time this prevalence of two-part rhetorical form and meaning is interwoven with the three- and five-part logic one expects in Chinookan. The three pairs of the first scene are an arc of ongoing, onset, outcome, the outcome being an object of perception, as is often the case in Chinookan narratives. The second scene, which begins with a marked reversal of the usual particle order, "Then now" rather than "Now then," has also a three part sequence ending in perception in its five lines: the two are gotten, they stay, they watch the thing coming. The extended third group uses pairs in an elaborated three-part sequence: there, watch; goes, gets there; carries it, has it lying on its tongue. Pairs of lines that correspond to a step in the progression are marked in parallel fashion (straight, straight; now, now). The five parts of the scene are related by the rhetorical logic by which the third part completes one arc and begins another. The two who are gotten watch the thing coming, see it coming like fire, watch as it gets the corpse (onset, ongoing, outcome). The thing gets the corpse, they clip its tongue and it goes back, the people put the corpse away again (onset, ongoing, outcome). And of course the three pairs in the third scene have such a logic: "give it back," "let's give it back," eaten up.

Here we have something more than a question of segmentation into appropriate parts. We have an interweaving of rhythms. One might say that Victoria Howard was like Brahms in liking to play off 3 against 2.

John Rush Buffalo

Such complexity is not unique. In John Rush Buffalo's telling of "Coyote and Eagle's daughter" an interplay between pairing and tripling is commonly marked within individual stanzas. A decade ago I discovered that the initial particles that so often marked verses in pairs gave way at one point in the story to marking them in sets of three (1980b; cf. 1987b). There could be no doubt; the form of the narrative was clear in a classical way. Coyote's wife, coming after him, stops at each of a series of camps and exactly the same details are repeated. To insist on grouping verses in pairs would violate the obvious coherence of the story. But elsewhere I accepted the evident pairing as matrix, and published the result. Of course I noticed that a pair of verses often had three word-final quotative suffixes. That was striking, but it did not lead me to suspect three- and five-part relations as having any organizing role beyond their use to intensify one scene.

While preparing this essay and turning to my earlier analysis for that example, I noticed what might be a loose end in the fit between form and meaning: the way in which even-numbered relations had been posited might be forced in, for example, the first act when Coyote prepares to fight. Why did there have to be four groups? Why not five, one for the preparation by the river, and one each for each of the directions in which he howled? And while Coyote comes running to revive the people four times, perhaps the scene really begins in the preceding verse, and has five elements also. I had already revised analysis of the encounters between Coyote and his wife in the second and third acts, with success in recognizing a recurrent relation in regard to Coyote peering in. But the passage in which a young man acts as intermediary had not fitted easily. Perhaps there did not have to be four parts of an act. Perhaps there could be five. And having a single element in a unit at a large level makes some sense, it seems to occur naturally enough, in three- and five-part (odd-numbered) patterning, but seemed unmotivated in the instance or two in which it had seemed necessary in this story.

All this led to a reconsideration, and a recognition that three- and five-part relations are pervasive in the organization of the narrative. An incidental benefit was a neatening or tightening of the disposition of a line or two. Most importantly, whatever may have led Victoria Howard to interweave even- and odd-numbered patterning, such a phenomenon could be not explained (away) simply as mingling of traditions. Here it was in Tonkawa, intricately accomplished, explicitly marked, and, as mentioned above, having an apparent appropriateness, offering a contrast to Tillamook: there broad four-part relations for women, five for men; in Tonkawa, the reverse.

Such a case makes one want particularly to display the relations, and their marking, in an abstract form. I have done so in an appendix. Here is the story itself, doing fuller justice, I hope, to John Rush Buffalo, its teller, and to Harry Hoijer, who sought him out and recorded it.

[Part One. Coyote Restores the People]

[i] [He discovers an empty camp]

They say Coyote was going along;   (A)
In doing so, he went up a mountain.
They say he stood there;
When he did, they say, there was a large camp at the mountain's foot.

Coyote went down,   (B)   5
he went to that large camp; and
when he went to the tipi on the edge,
there was weeping inside, they say.

Then Coyote went in.   (C)
   "What is it?" they say he said.   10
Then that woman,
   "Here all the people in this camp are gone," they say she said.
   "A fearsome being destroyed them," they say she said.

Then Coyote,   (D)
   "Now, do not weep," they say he said.   15
   "Tomorrow I shall fight it," they say he said.
Then that woman went outside, and
   "Coyote says he will fight it tomorrow," they say she said.

"Tomorrow when I fight it,   (E)
   "Do not run away," they say he said, Coyote.   20
   "Watch me closely," they say he said.
Then,
   "Yes," they say she said.

[ii] [He prepares to fight]

When it was evening,   (A)
   he went down to the river, and   25
cutting off a piece of hard wood,
   he burned it black, and
putting it away,
   he went to sleep, they say.

And at daybreak, arising,   (B)   30
he went outdoors, and
sitting to the east,
he howled loudly, they say.

And then again, to the south,   (C)
again he howled, they say.   35

And then again, to the west,   (D)
again he howled, they say.

And then, last, sitting to the north,   (E)
he howled, they say.

                                                      [iii] [He meets the monster]
This done, they say, Coyote joined some women going after wood.   40
As he did,
    "That one is coming!" they say was said.

As it did, that fearsome being from the waist up, they say, was red;
And there, from the waist down, they say, it was black.

Then, they say, those women were afraid.   45
Then, they say, Coyote hid.

As he did, it came in that direction at a run;
Coyote fought it, they say, that fearsome being.

As he did, a great many Wolves,
catching that fearsome being,   50
were fighting it, they say.
Doing so, they killed it, they say, that fearsome being.

                                                      [iv] [He restores the people]
And then, they say, those Wolves left.
Then Coyote went toward that camp that had no people.
    "Close all those tipis tight!" they say he said.   55
All those tipis were closed, they say.

And then Coyote went off from the place, and,
galloping,
    "Quick! This camp is on fire!" they say he said.
When he did, they say, nothing happened.   60

Then again he went off, and,
coming at a gallop,
    "Hurry! This camp is on fire!" they say he said.
When he did, they say, nothing happened.

Then again he went off, and,   65
coming at a run,
    "Hurry! This camp is on fire!" they say he said.
Then, they say, nothing happened.

Then, the last time he went off, and,
coming at a run,   70
    "Hurry! This camp is on fire!" they say he said.
Then, they say, many people ran out.

[Part Two] [Coyote Goes Gambling]

                                          [II] [i] [He leaves his wife for another camp]
Then, they say, they made Coyote marry a beautiful girl.
Then, after staying a while, to that woman,
    "I'll go to the other camp over yonder," they say he said, Coyote.   75
Then that woman,

"Oh!" they say she said.

"Don't go!" they say she said.

Then Coyote,

"I won't stay long," they say he said.   80

"In two days I'll come back," they say he said.

Then that woman,

"All right," they say she said.

        [ii] [She follows him]

Then, they say, Coyote went off.

And, getting to a large camp,   85

they say he stayed for a long while.

It was then that woman went after them, they say;

getting to that large camp,

"And Coyote?" they say she said.

Then,   90

"He's joined a bunch of gamblers over there," they say they said.

Then she got to a place nearby, and

entering the tipi,

"Water," they say she said.

Then,   95

"There is none," they say they said.

        [iii] [Young man as intermediary]

Then she picked up the bucket, and,

they say, she went to get water.

As she did so, one young man at the gambling place:—

"Oh!" they say he said.   100

"Coyote's wife!" they say he said.

"She comes this way!" they say he said.

Then Coyote saw her, and,

they say, he was laughing.

Then the young man,   105

"We heard that you left her," they say they said.

Then Coyote,

"No," they say he said.

"Watch me!" they say he said.

"She'll give me water to drink," they say he said.   110

        [iv] [She refuses him water]

And then, getting to where that woman was,

they say, he touched her.

Then that woman, seeing Coyote,

"Leave me!" they say she said.

Then Coyote,   115

"Give me water to drink!" they say he said.

Then, that woman, not giving him water to drink,

went off, they say.

        [v] [She decides to go]

When night came he came to that woman,

and as he talked with her, the young men,   120

"Let's not let Coyote sleep tonight," they say they were saying.
"Let's steal that woman," they say they were saying.
And then that night, they say, they danced with him.
And, they say, they didn't let him sleep until daylight, Coyote.
Then, they say, that woman was angry;   125
And,
    "I'll go," they say she said.

[II] [i] [He goes north to gamble]

Then Coyote,
    "I'll go to gamble in the north," they say he said.
And, they say, he went away, Coyote.   130

And he got to a large camp, and
    "I go to gamble in the north," they say he said.
And then, going away,
    they say, he got to a large camp.

And the next day,   135
    "I go to gamble in the north," they say he said, Coyote.
The next day, they say, he went off;
    getting to a large camp,
    they say, he joined a bunch of gamblers.

[ii] [She follows him]

While he did, that woman,
    "I'll go after Coyote," they say she said.
And, they say, she went after him;
    getting to a large camp,
    "And Coyote?" they say she said.
Then,   145
    "He's gone to gamble in the north," they say they said.

Then, they say, that woman went after him.
And again, getting to a large camp,
    "And Coyote?" they say she said.
Then,   150
    "He's gone to gamble in the north," they say they said.

Then, they say, that woman went after him.
And getting to a large camp,
    "And Coyote?" they say she said.
Then,   155
    "He's gone to gamble in the north," they say they said.

Then, they say, that woman went after him.
And getting to a large camp,
    "And Coyote?" they say she said.
Then,   160
    "He's gambling here," they say they said.

Then,
    "Go to him, and

"Tell him,
    "Come!" they say she said.   165

[iii] [Young man as intermediary]
Then, going to him,
    "Your wife is summoning you," they say he said.
Then Coyote,
    "You're lying," they say he said.
Then,   170
    "I speak the truth," they say he said;
    "Now come!" they say he said.

[iv] [He refuses her command to come in]
Then Coyote went with him, they say;
the two got to the tipi, they say;
    "She is staying here," they say he said.   175
Then, they say, Coyote peered inside.

Then that woman,
    "Come in!" they say she said.
Then Coyote, they say, not going in,
    was laughing.   180

Then again,
    "Come in!" they say she said.
Then Coyote, they say, not going in,
    was laughing.

Then again, that woman,   185
    "Come in!" they say she said.
Then Coyote, they say, not going in,
    was laughing.

Again as he peered in,
    "Come in!" they say she said.   190
Then when Coyote laughed, that woman,
    "I shall go away," they say she said.
    "Back," they say she said;
    Going outside, she flew away, they say.

[v] [She goes for good]
Then Coyote peering in,   195
    "And my wife?" they say he said.
Then,
    "She has gone away," they say they said.

Then, they say, Coyote came running,
    back.   200
As he did, that woman was getting home;
    "I left him," they say she said.

Then her father and mother,
    "You are doing the right thing," they say they said;
    "Let us go," they say they said.   205

And, they say, she flew away with them up into the air.
　　She was an Eagle, they say.

　　So it is.

Composing this narrative, John Rush Buffalo used all there was to use, I think. His words were not fitted to a simple, single template, his verses and stanzas not a sequence of verbal cookies all the same. Nor were they words simply off the cuff, darted out in the excitement that congenial performance can have. These words were dictated slowly to a linguist, writing them down to preserve what has proved all we know of the verbal heritage John Rush Buffalo had survived to share. A heritage, we can now see, that could vary texture and shape to a purpose; integrate several levels of organization of incident and relationship; that could differentiate large-scale relationships as between male or female the focus (four scenes for male, five scenes for female); alternate at another level to highlight forthcoming change (the two pairs of verses in scene [iv] of Act II, amidst groups of three and five, the triplets of verses in scene [ii] of Act III where pairs had prevailed); double a plot, as between Acts II and III of Part Two, and play the second off against the first, so as to let details of interaction show a wife, given by a community as reward to its reviver, loyally seeking her husband, but respecting herself, in the end, taking charge. Perhaps anyone in the Southwest could have said that a Coyote can't keep an Eagle for a wife; this narrative treats that truth, not as a categorical *a priori,* but as something learned and earned.

　　Would we not want to know these things because there is no tape recording? Not use this narrative? Some schools of linguists have rejected information about language because it was not obtained in an approved way: "that's not linguistics." Are we to say of all we can ever know about the imagination of people like John Rush Buffalo, "that's not ethnopoetics"? Philology, I submit, can do something to make known a voice worth knowing.

V

The worth of the texts makes worthwhile our worry about how to present them.[20] More fundamental than how it is done is whether it is done. Means are scant in relation to need. Texts published years ago should be edited in the light of the field notebooks and republished in ethnopoetic terms. There are texts collected years ago that have never been published at all (Frachtenberg's Molale from Oregon, Swadesh's Chitimacha from Louisiana, to name two). There are texts collected in recent years that are not published for lack of funds and series in which to place them (the native-language originals of Tedlock's Zuni, Ellen Basso's Kalapalo, for example, and who knows whether the unique Apache myth cycle recorded fifty years ago by Hoijer and now prepared in close collaboration with Apache speakers by Keith Basso can find a publisher?). Computers make it possible to do many things that would once have been impossible or lifelong. Perhaps ethnopoetics will be a field in which the basic materials are privately published and distributed—a field for the elderly and established then, since younger people could not expect to gain recognition and employment that way. Texts, of course, are not important to the hungry and homeless, although there are those of us who love them, and descendants who would value having them in appropriate form. If the funds of the country all were going to meet the needs of children, women, schooling, health care, one could have no complaint.

Let me close with a plea as well for readers. Of course field work with ongoing traditions is vital. Documentation of living performance is absorbing. But reading matters too. It is the way we can recreate something of the imaginative world, the intertextuality, in which a given telling arose, and so recognize and appreciate a teller's aesthetic and moral imagination. If all one has is the one occasion, one may miss important aspects of what is there. Narrators create in performances, but also between performances. Stories are good to hear, but also good to think. John Rush Buffalo's "Coyote and Eagle's daughter" did not come to him as an inspiration as Harry Hoijer opened his notebook. Surely "all that complex wealth of minutiae which in their line-for-line aspect we call style and in their broader outlines we call form" (Burke 1925) had a history, marked by moments of reflection as to how such a relationship between a woman and a man, an Eagle's daughter given as wife to Coyote, might be true to inherent natures and lived experience.

The resources in such moments are not one's voice and audience, but experience reflected upon, stories reflected upon, experience and stories acting upon each other. We need to recover as much as possible of that experience, of that horizon of stories. Other stories may inform us of meanings, possibilities, inventions, and transformations, even though new performances are not to be heard. It is here that Lévi-Strauss stands as a permanent example, however one may criticize particular interpretations. He has read widely with close attention to detail, and so approaches particular stories with a sense of alternative possibilities and sources of creative change.[21]

Such reading is essential because the standard sources of comparison and context are fundamentally inadequate. One does learn from them. The contributions to naming of recurrent plots by Kroeber (1908) and Lowie (1908a, 1909) early in the century are still something to read, as are comparative studies by them and Boas (notably, *Tsimshian Mythology* (1916), and the next generation (e.g., Lowie 1908b, Reichard 1921, Demetracopoulou 1933, Gayton 1935). The notes to Thompson's 1929 *Tales of the North American Indians* are still indispensable. There are insights and comparisons in a great many publications (e.g., Demetracopoulou and Du Bois 1932, Adamson 1934, Reichard 1947). One needs to be acquainted with the classificatory schemes of motif and tale type (see Thompson 1951, 1961, Wycoco [Moore] 1951), and with what Lévi-Strauss has proposed (1964–71, 1979 and other works) as transformational relationships. But the critical point is that for a given starting point, what proves relevant, but comes into view, may not have been brought together by anyone else. What one can discover as to informing context and intertextuality will depend on one's own reading and recollection, and, to be frank, chance.

This situation could be improved by new guides. Motifs and tale-types are helpful, but knowing that a story is about Coyote, say, is about as helpful as knowing that a statue is one of Jesus. Is it Jesus lying in a mother's lap as baby, Jesus erect upon mother's knees as Pantocrator, Jesus as emaciated corpse? More specifically, the fine details, the explicit frames, the implicit themes that are relevant are often not mentioned in the comparative guides available. Part of the problem is that their scope is not sufficiently local, not sufficiently fine. Part of the problem is that their sources may exclude nonprofessional material that yet provides crucial information.

Let me briefly offer four cases in point: two have to do with framing sequences of action, one characterizes tricksters in relation to one kind of act, one validates two kinds of transformational relationship in the recasting of a myth.

Sequence of action (1). In 1975 Donald Bahr published an analysis of ritual oratory among the Pima and Papago. I first saw it at the Cultural Center at Warm Springs Reservation, Oregon, when visiting its then director, Nathan Jim. Bahr found a pattern he summarized as DTAX: departure, travel, arrival, outcome. In the orations the pattern governs whole texts. In John Rush Buffalo's telling of "Coyote and Eagle's daughter," it governs two opening stanzas (and confers pattern on the second stanza, which itself is without markers). In the midst of a myth of Eagle and Grizzly Woman that France Johnson told Edward Sapir in Takelma (Rogue River, Oregon), the device governs that stanza in which Eagle first discovers the Grizzly girl.

Three separated cases lead one to inquire. It becomes evident that frames for the moments of a sequence of travel may be characteristic of every tradition. The ingredients may differ. Moments may be recognized in common, but kept as distinct steps in one tradition, combined in a single step in another. (Not unlike the relation between distinctions that enter into aspect categories across languages.) In Saanich Salish (Vancouver Island) preparation can be a major element. (See the discussion of these matters in Hymes 1990c.)

Sequence of action (2). By accident of reading, again, I know a recurrent device for getting people together in bed. In the Clackamas Chinook myth "Gitskux and his older brother" (Willamette Valley, Oregon) Victoria Howard tells how the woman to whom Panther comes allows him to sleep inside her lodge far in the corner. At night he is bitten by fleas until, step by step (five steps in all, of course) he comes to her bed, and then beside her. Jarold Ramsey called my attention to Clara Pearson's account of brother-sister incest in a Tillamook myth (Oregon coast). The sister takes the initiative in a step-by-step progress involving leaks in the roof (E. Jacobs 1959:48–49, Ramsey 1983:96–126). Working through Tonkawa to honor a late teacher, I discovered that this device is not peculiar to Oregon. John Rush Buffalo knew it as well. In the partner to the myth given above, "Coyote, Jack Rabbit, and Eagle's Daughter," when Eagle's daughter and Rabbit are in bed, Coyote makes his way there step by step by pretending he is being bitten. The result is that the couple leave (Hoijer 1972:16–17). Such step-by-step biting must have been a narrative device over a wide stretch of North America.

Characterizing tricksters. Working on a notebook of texts that Philip Kahclamat dictated in Wishram Chinook to Sapir's student, Walter Dyk, in 1933, I came upon one new to me. The trickster Coyote has killed his partner, Deer, intending to eat him, but has propped him up as if sick but still alive, and calls on Owl to lead singing to cure him. Owl's song says that the curing is a waste of time, but it is in Chinookan. Then Coyote laments for Deer in Sahaptin. Evidently the truth in Chinookan is not to be understood by those to be taken in by the falsehood in Sahaptin. The narrative assumes a Sahaptin-speaking audience for Coyote, a bilingual audience for itself.

At first I thought the story unique. Working through texts in Quileute (from the northwestern corner of the State of Washington), I found a story, evidently popular, since told to three different collectors over the years by different narrators, in which the trickster Q'wati kills the chief of the Wolves, and when confronted by other wolves, sings first in Makah, then in Quileute, about what he has done. Like Coyote, his choice of language can't conceal the death (Andrade 1931:46–50, 94–98; Clark 1953:121–22). As it happened, finding a copy of Barbeau and Beynon (1987:20) in the bookstore in the Hoodland Shopping Center near Rhododendron, I discovered a Tsimshian story in which the trickster Raven has his slave speak for him when he comes as a great chief to visit another chief. Officially, Raven does not understand the local language. As a result, he loses out on the food his hosts provide. And rereading Clark (1953:100), I rediscovered a story that Melville Jacobs's Kalapuya collaborator, John B. Hudson, had told to Clark in English. It explains why the falls that make a rich harvest of salmon possible on the Willamette are in the territory of the Clackamas, not further upriver in the territory of the Kalapuya. When Meadowlark called across to Coyote to make the dam, she spoke in Clackamas and Coyote did not understand, since he knew only Kalapuya. Later she used sign language too. Clark was an amateur who did not always publish full versions of what she was told (David French, p.c.) and who focused on the kinds of things local whites thought romantic about Indian legends: the origins of mountains, rivers, waterfalls, and the like. But perhaps asking in terms of that interest is why we owe to her a story Hudson did not tell Jacobs in all the years he worked with him.

The hypothesis that emerges is association of a trickster-figure with bilingualism, but with bilingualism that does not benefit. In Kalapuya (Willamette Valley, Oregon) and Timshian (Alaska) the trickster loses out on food because of someone else's bilingualism. In Wishram (Columbia River, Washington) and Quileute (northwest corner of Washington) the trickster cannot conceal death and loses out on food, despite his own bilingualism, presumably because of that of other people. The nature of things, it would seem, is not monolingual. Not to be or to pretend to be is to lose out; to presume that others are is to lose out. And one can see a connection between the trickster's inability to control this skill of language with the widespread premise that a trickster cannot control a song (songs being serious also, a source of power and sign of status).

Validation. The figure of Salmon is of central importance to the narrative imaginations of those who lived along the Columbia and its tributaries, just as the food salmon was of central importance to the sustenance of life. Salmon indeed proves a contested figure, as between the Kathlamet Chinook narratives of Charles Cultee and the Clackamas Chinook narratives of Victoria Howard. In the latter Salmon is displaced, once in the very course of dictating a story (Hymes 1984), whether by Victoria Howard alone, or by the tradition she acquired from her mother-in-law and mother's mother. Most remarkably, there is the story of "Tongue." The association of the father with teaching others to fish and the pride of the son suggest a chiefly actor such as Salmon. As it happens, Ramsey (1977:94–95; cf. Lyman 1900) has reprinted an early account, taken down by a local historian and antiquarian from a half-breed, Louis Labonte. Not authentic performance, but authentic information. The man who goes into the river is indeed Salmon, and where he goes explains which streams have salmon today and which do not. But he is shamed, not by the people, but by his father. Victoria Howard has changed a story focused on a father and son into one in which the active parent is the mother—the only one to survive the destruction of the people by Tongue, and that through her diligent provision of food (digging roots). She fends off Tongue for the first and bears and raises the heroic son.

In the story first mentioned, the Clackamas counterpart to Cultee's Salmon Myth (Hymes 1985a), the contested role is that of pronouncer of the foods that will be provided for the people. It is in that role that Salmon is explicitly supplanted by Coyote in the Howard telling. In the story of Tongue something else is going on. It appears that the virtuous son of a virtuous mother can be Salmon and source of salmon. The role is not contested, although the name is suppressed: neither Salmon the actor nor salmon the food is named as such.

There is a second transformation, one of the Lévi-Strauss type. The opening of "Tongue" is a transformation, partly the same in details, partly inverted, of a major part of William Hartless's telling of Coyote's attempt to copulate across a river with a long and borrowed penis (Hymes 1987a). Why? For some time I could think of no reason. The formal relation was there, but not a motivation. I now think that the transformation and inversion has to do with chiefly status. Coyote's attempt to copulate across the river (the same river, the Willamette, indeed—the Kalapuya were up river from the Clackamas, as the story of where the falls were put indicates) is with the daughter of a chief. When he subsequently pretends to be a shaman who can cure her (the tip of the penis has been cut off and is still inside her), much is made of the way in which he deceives the chiefly father, pretending to be old, experienced, famous, and reluctant. When he crawls inside the place in which the girl lies, of course he is deceiving, and humiliating, the chiefly father, having a cohort of raucous birds sing to help him with his song, while he in fact copulates, gets the penis parts to rejoin, and runs away.

"Tongue" has quite another view of chiefs and chiefly families. It begins with Tongue wanting the corpse of one chiefly wife. The other (chiefs in this area often had two wives) is the only virtuous survivor, and due to that, the only survivor at all. Her son is a chief's son, and the restorer of his people. When at the end he enters the river, and all must change into what they will be in the next age, it is the people who have injured his pride. The story suggests that the Clackamas themselves, who lived at the same spot, the spot highlighted in the story's first words, might still be there if they had heeded their chiefly family.

One myth that mocks chiefly honor, as ordinary people might, and one that sustains it against the foolishness of ordinary people.[22] The formal connections are detailed, and a meaning can be given to the transformation. The Coyote story being so widespread in the region, the story of Tongue unique so far as we know, the former is presumably the starting point. And in this case the interest of an antiquarian provides a validation.

H. Lyman reports (1903:126–27) the Clackamas version of a widespread story in which Coyote creates a fish trap. Coyote offends the trap, and it will work no more:

So the people were left to simply spear the fish. The story, which is also a continued one, proceeds then to tell of the great tribe that flourished on the shore, one great man being chief. The village was on the right bank. In his days there came a monster, or Skookum [Chinook Jargon for "strong"] from the mountains, and devoured all the people but the wife and unborn son of the chief.

Now the Hartless Kalapuya story ends with a brief scene in which Coyote marries, has children, and makes a fish trap. It ends, that is, with an allusion to just the story that in Clackamas, according to Labonte, precedes the story of Tongue. The two stories are related not only by transformation. According to Labonte, they are related by succession.

Others can no doubt supply similar examples, and no doubt there are many more to be discovered. One has to read all there is to read, whatever its source. Each fresh venture will require fresh reading, because what is relevant now may not have been relevant then. Much will have been forgotten, and is not to be recovered from secondary guides. Only so can we reconstruct the imaginative narrative resources and surrounds of the stories we give attention. Doing so, we can bring analysis to the focal point it must have, the named narrator, not the named tribe. Perhaps doing so, we will create guides for others that begin with the frames and characteristics that emerge from such close reading, the workings of style that emerge from the analysis of rhetorical form we can now undertake.

Each time we seek to understand a particular myth, we find ourselves tracing a new path among what we can remember and can find. We can be guided by expectations as to rhetorical form, but the workings of the particular text may always surprise us. And each text attracts to itself its own constellation of analogues. In this regard, the slogan, *use all there is to use,* is vital. Scholars are likely to be prejudiced for and against certain sources, may value certain kinds of relations and not others. But in the name of all that is oral, when there is so little, who can refuse any part?

The true work of ethnopoetics, certainly as it addresses the many and manifold oral traditions of Native Americans, is barely begun.

Appendix: Profile of "Coyote and Eagle's Daughter"

At the right side of the page are the indications of the two parts, of the acts [I, II, III] and of the scenes [i, ii, iii, iv, v]

At the left side of the page the columns show stanzas (ABCDE), verses (abcde), lines, and markers other than initial particles. Line numbers for different verses are separated by a comma. Markers that belong to different verses are separated by a semicolon; here, a comma indicates separate lines. The indications of markers usually are P for initial particle, - for no marker, " for quoted speech, Q for quotative. Occasionally "-and" indicates a connective ending to a line, and 'Time' indicates an initial time word.

[i] [He discovers an empty camp]

A	ab	1–2, 3–4	Q, P;	Q, PQ
B	ab?	5–6, 7–8	-and;	- Q [same framework as A]
C	ab	9–10, 11–13	P, "Q;	P, "Q, "Q
D	ab	14–16, 17–18	P, "Q, "Q;	P -and, "Q
E	ab	19–21, 22–23	-, "Q, "Q;	P, "Q

[ii] [He prepares to fight]

A	abc?	24–25, 26–27, 28–29	-and, -and,	-Q
B	ab	30–31, 32–33	P, -and;	-and, Q
C		34–35	P, -and;	Q
D	ab	36, 37	P;	PQ
E		38–39	P, -and;	Q

[iii] [He meets the monster]

A	ab	40, 41–42	PQ;	P, "Q
B	ab	43, 44	PQ;	PQ
C	ab	45, 46	PQ;	PQ
D	ab	47, 48	P;	-Q- [fearsome being final]
E	ab	49–51, 52	P, -, Q;	P -Q- [fearsome being final]

[iv] [He restores the people]

A	ab	53, 54–56	PQ;	PQ, "Q, Q
B	ab	57–59, 60	P -and, -, "Q;	Q
C	ab	61–63, 64	P -and, -, "Q;	Q
D	ab	65–67, 68	P -and, -, "Q;	Q
E	ab	69–71, 72	P -and, -, "Q;	Q

[Part Two] [Coyote Goes Gambling]

[II] [i] [He leaves his wife for another camp]

abcde	73	Q
	74–75	P, "Q
	76–78	P, "Q, "Q
	79–81	P, "Q, "Q
	82–83	P, "Q

[ii] [She follows him]

ab	84, 85–86	PQ;	P -and, Q
cd	87–89, 90–91	PQ, -, "Q';	P, "Q
ef	92–94, 95–96	P -and, -, "Q;	P, "Q

[iii] [Young man as intermediary]

abcde	97–98	P -and, Q
	99–102	P, "Q, "Q, "Q
	103–104	P -and, Q
	105–106	P, "Q
	107–110	P, "Q, "Q, "Q

[iv] [She refuses him water]

| ab | 111–12, 113–14 | P -and, Q; | P, "Q |
| cd | 115–16, 117–18 | P, "Q; | P, Q |

[v] [She decides to go]

abcde	119–22	Time, -, "Q, "Q
	123	PQ
	124	PQ

		125	PQ
		126–27	P, "Q

[III] [i] [He goes north to gamble]

	ab	128–29, 130	P, "Q;	Q
	cd	131–32, 133–34	P, "Q:	Q
	ef	135–36, 137–39	P, "Q;	P, Q

[ii] [She follows him]

A	abc	140–41, 142–44, 145–46	P, "Q; P, -, "Q; P, "Q
B	abc	147, 148–49, 150–51	PQ; P, "Q; P, "Q
C	abc	152, 153–54, 155–56	PQ; P, "Q; P, "Q
D	abc	157, 158–59, 160–61	PQ; P, "Q; P, "Q
E		162–65	P, ", ", "Q

[iii] [Young man as intermediary]

	abc	166–67, 168–69, 170–72	P, "Q; P, "Q;	P, "Q, "Q

[iv] [He refuses her command to come in]

	ab	173–75, 176	PQ, -Q-, "Q;	PQ
	cd	177–78, 179–80	P, "Q;	P, Q
	ef	181–82, 183–84	P, "Q;	P, Q
	gh	185–86, 187–88	P, "Q;	P, Q
	ij	189–90, 191–94	P, "Q;	P, "Q, "Q, Q

[v] [She goes for good]

	ab	195–96, 197–98	P, "Q;	P, "Q
	cd	199–200, 201–202	PQ, -;	P, "Q
	ef	203–205, 206–207	P, "Q, "Q;	PQ, Q

Close

Notes

1. I want to thank Brian Swann for encouraging me to contribute these reflections.

2. See the opening pages of the title essay in Burke 1941.

3. On the first four, cf. Hymes 1972, 1962 and 1964, 1974, and the chapters "What is Ethnography" and "Educational Ethnology" in Hymes 1980a.

4. I will discuss the details of this point in another place.

5. These relationships have been important to Bright in his work with Karok (1984).

6. "Carefully re-listening to Mrs. Starritt's taped narration, along with analysis of the type proposed by Hymes, permits identification of the following features of structure: (a) *Verses* . . . are marked syntactically by the presence of 'sentence-initial particles' at the beginning, and phonologically by a falling pitch and audible pause at the end'. . . . Lines . . . are marked syntactically by the occurrence of predications. . . . Most lines are marked by a final falling pitch without audible pause. However, lines containing verbs of saying may end in a final mid or high pitch, with or without pause before a following quotation. . . . Tedlock's and Hymes' approaches . . coincide 90 percent of the time in their identification of basic units—the verse (Tedlock's strophe) and the line. Because of this, occasional ambiguities in the application of one approach can be resolved by reference to the other."

7. "Lines of narrative speech are marked by both particle and pause, whereas lines of quoted speech are distinguished solely on the basis of pause critiera" (186).

8. See Tedlock (1972:76–83), where the Zuni telling of "Coyote and Junco" by Andrew Peynetsa is presented, and Wiget (1987), where a Hopi telling of an analogue of "Coyote and Junco" by Helen Sekaquaptewa is given.

9. I hope to display the two comparisons in full in another place.

10. Presumbly North American Indian myths do not describe the world at least in important part because their hearers know what it looks like. It may be relevant how large a house is and how many fires it has, but not that it is made of wood. When Coyote goes upriver, he goes up a river most hearers have traveled many times. Even in imagined worlds, like that of the dead, what is said and done declares the nature of the place. There is no scene-painting for atmosphere. The images are of action. Often indeed, one senses that a narrator is picturing a scene, and hearers may indicate that they picture it as well. This then would authorize a freedom in interpretation in the very process of transmission. This is the story as I heard it, yet the picture in my mind may be my own, and affect the retelling.

11. We are fortunate to have Stern's texts, and fortunate that Rude has been able to do some work with them. The famous nineteenth-century Swiss linguist Albert Gatschet collected almost no narratives. When M. A. R. Barker worked with the language a generation ago, he did not obtain very many. Stern worked earlier than Barker and much of what can be known about Klamath tradition will depend on the eventual publication of his materials. I am grateful to Rude for sending me copies of his work.

12. For example, one would see and wonder about the lack of apparent consistency in the number of sections within major parts and of relations within major sections of Muluku's "Saganafa" as analyzed in Basso 1985:41–54 (cf. n. 4).

13. The page reference in the preceding part of the note is to page 52, not 48, as the original edition and the reprinting both have it.

14. This account revises my published analysis, in which the coordinate status of the scene involving the young man as intermediary was not recognized.

15. The myth is "Štank'íya," the name of a certain mythical Coyote.

16. I am grateful to Richard Dauenhauer for pointing out this pervasiveness in commenting on my finding five-part patterning in one of the texts published by himself and Nora Dauenhauer (cf. Hymes 1990b).

17. I have done this for a long time, and Virginia Hymes long ago pointed out to me the variety of relations that appear within sets of four in various languages. There are some remarks in my paper "Some subtleties of measured verse." Yet it is the work of Henri Meschonnic that has encouraged me to address the practice explicitly here in terms of the notion of rhythm. See his *Critique du rhythme* (1982). I am grateful to Professor Meschonnic and to the Commonwealth Center for Literary and Cultural Change for the opportunity to consult with him during the course of his seminar at the University of Virginia in the fall of 1989.

18. In "Tongue" lines 186–91 are another example, as are lines 204–14. In the former, the five markers all are "now"; in the latter, the markers are "now, now; all day, now; now."

19. This is one of the reasons I suspect that there was a two- and four-part tradition in Victoria Howard's background. She did, after all, have Molale relatives and know some Molale, and if the Molale texts recorded early in the century by Leo Frachtenberg are ever published and analyzed, they may shed light on her heritage of resources.

20. For a book-length discussion of such issues, addressing much that is not touched on here, see Fine 1984.

21. For Lévi-Strauss's response to criticism of mine, see his "De la fidélité au texte," *L'Homme* 27(1):117–40 (1987).

22. On the mocking of chiefs in Kalapuya Coyote myths, see the last section of Hymes (1987a).

References

Adamson, Thelma. 1934. *Folk-tales of the Coast Salish*. New York: American Folklore Society.

Bahr, Donald M. 1975. *Pima and Papago Ritual Oratory: A Study of Three Texts*. San Francisco: The Indian Historian Press.

Basso, Ellen B. 1985. *A Musical View of the Universe: Kalapalo Myth and Ritual Performances*. Philadelphia: University of Pennsylvania Press.

Boas, Franz. 1916. Tsimshian mythology. Bureau of American Ethnology, Annual Report 31. Washington, D.C.

Briggs, Charles L. and Julián Josué Vigil. 1990. *The Lost Gold Mine of Juan Mondragón: A Legend from New Mexico Performed by Melaquías Romero*. Tucson: University of Arizona Press.

Bright, William. 1982. Poetic Structure in Oral Narrative. In Deborah Tannen (ed.), *Spoken and Written Language: Exploring Orality and Literacy*. Norwood, N.J.: Ablex.

———. 1984. *American Indian Linguistics and Literature*. Berlin: Mouton.

Burke, Kenneth. 1925. Psychology and Form. *The Dial* 79(1)(July):34–46. Reprinted in his *Counter-statement* (New York: Harcourt, Brace, 1931). 3rd edition, Berkeley & Los Angeles: University of California Press, 1968.

———. 1941. *The Philosophy of Literary Form*. Baton Rouge: Louisiana State University Press. 3rd edition, Berkeley & Los Angeles: University of California Press, 1968.

Clark, Ella E. 1953. *Indian Legends of the Pacific Northwest*. Berkeley: University of California Press.

Cove, John J. & George F. MacDonald (eds.). 1987. *Tricksters, Shamans and Heroes: Tsimshian Narratives I*. Collected by Marius Barbeau and William Beynon. (Canadian Museum of Civilization, Mercury Series, Directorate Paper No. 3). Ottawa.

Demetracopoulou, D. 1933. The loon-woman myth: A study in synthesis. *Journal of American Folklore* 46:101–28.

Dundes, Alan. 1964. *The Morphology of North American Indian Folktales*. Helsinki: Academia Scientiarum Fennica.

Edel, May M. 1944. Stability in Tillamook folklore. *Journal of American Folklore* 57:118–27.

Facey, Ellen E. 1988. *Nguna Voices: Text and Culture from Central Vanuatu*. Calgary: The University of Calgary Press.

Fine, Elizabeth C. 1984. *The Folklore Text: From performance to print*. Bloomington: Indiana University Press.

Gayton, A. H. 1935. The Orpheus myth in North America. *Journal of American Folklore* 48:263–93.

Hoijer, Harry. 1972. *Tonkawa Texts*. Berkeley & Los Angeles: University of California Publications in Linguistics, 73.

Hymes, Dell. 1962. The Ethnography of Speaking. In Thomas Gladwin & William C. Sturtevant (eds.), *Anthropology and Human Behavior*. Washington, D.C.: Anthropological Society of Washington.

———— (ed.). 1964. *Language in Culture and Society.* New York: Harper & Row.

———— (ed.). 1972. *Reinventing Anthropology.* New York: Pantheon.

————. 1974. *Foundations in Sociolinguistics.* Philadelphia: University of Pennsylvania Press.

————. 1977. Discovering Oral Performance and Measured Verse in American Indian Narrative. *New Literary History* 8:431–57.

————. 1980a. *Language in Education.* Washington, D.C.: Center for Applied Linguistics.

————. 1980b. Particle, Pause and Pattern in American Indian Narrative Verse. *American Indian Culture and Research Journal* 4:7–51.

————. 1981. *'In Vain I Tried to Tell You'.* Philadelphia: University of Pennsylvania Press.

————. 1982. Narrative Form as 'Grammar' of Experience: Native American and a Glimpse of English. *Journal of Education* 164(2) (Spring), 121–42. Boston: Boston University.

————. 1983a. Victoria Howard's "Gitskux and his older brother": A Clackamas Chinook myth. In Brian Swann (ed.), *Smoothing the Ground: Essays on Native American oral literature.* 129–70. Berkeley & Los Angeles: University of California Press.

————. 1983b. Agnes Edgar's "Sun's Child," Verse Analysis of a Bella Coola Text. In William Seaburg (compiler), *Working Papers for the 18th International Congress of Salish and Neighboring Languages,* 239–312. Seattle: Department of Anthropology, University of Washington.

————. 1984. Bungling host, benevolent host: Louis Simpson's "Deer and Coyote." *American Indian Quarterly* 8(3):171–98.

————. 1985a. Language, memory, and selective performance: Cultee's "Salmon's myth" as twice told to Boas. *Journal of American Folklore* 98:391–434.

————. 1985b. Some subtleties of measured verse. In June Iris Hesch (ed.), *Proceedings 1985* (15th Spring Conference, Niagara Linguistics Society), 13–57. Buffalo: The Niagara Linguistics Society.

————. 1986. A discourse contradiction in Clackamas Chinook. Victoria Howard's "Coyote made the land good." *21st International Conference of Salish and Neighboring Languages,* compiled by Eugene Hunn, 147–213. Seattle: University of Washington, Dept. of Anthropology.

————. 1987a. Anthologies and Narrators. In Brian Swann and Arnold Krupat (eds.), *Recovering the Word.* Berkeley & Los Angeles: University of California Press.

————. 1987b. Tonkawa Poetics: John Rush Buffalo's "Coyote and Eagle's Daughter." In Joel Sherzer and Anthony C. Woodbury, *Native American Discourse: Poetics and Rhetoric.* Cambridge & New York: Cambridge University Press.

————. 1989. Three Wishram texts, told by Philip Kachlamat to Walter Dyk. *24th International Conference of Salish and Neighboring Languages,* compiled by Nile Thompson, 120–62. Steilacoom, Washington.

————. 1990a. Verse retranslation of "Split-His-Own-Head." In E. Jacobs, *Nehalem Tillamook Tales,* 220–28.

————. 1990b. Tlingit poetics: A review essay. *Journal of Folklore Research.*

————. 1990c. Thomas Paul's "Sameti": Verse analysis of a (Saanich) Chinook Jargon text. *Journal of Pidgin and Creole Languages.*

Hymes, Virginia. 1987. Warm Springs Sahaptin Narrative Analysis. In Joel Sherzer & Anthony C. Woodbury (eds.), *Native American Discourse: Poetics and Rhetoric.* Cambridge & New York: Cambridge University Press.

Jacobs, Elizabeth Derr. 1959. *Nehalem Tillamook Tales*. Eugene: University of Oregon Books. Reprinted, Corvallis: Oregon State University Press, 1990.

Jacobs, Melville. 1959. *Clackamas Chinook Texts, Part II*. Research Center for Anthropology, Folklore and Linguistics, Publication 11; International Journal of American Linguistics 25(2), Part 2. Bloomington: Indiana University.

Kimball, Geoffrey. 1989. Peregrine Falcon and Great Horned Owl: Ego and Shadow in a Koasati Tale. *Southwest Journal of Linguistics* 9:45–74.

Kroeber, A. L. 1908. Catch-words in American mythology. *Journal of American Folklore* 21: 222–27.

Kroskrity, Paul V. 1985. Growing with stories: line, verse, and genre in an Arizona Tewa text. *Journal of Anthropological Research* 41(2):183–200.

Lévi-Strauss, Claude. 1964–71. *Mythologies, vols I–IV*. Paris: Plon. Translated 1969–81, New York: Harper & Row.

———. 1979. *La voie des masques*. Paris: Plon. Translated as *The Way of the Masks*. Seattle: University of Washington Press, 1982.

Lewis, C. S. 1947. On Stories. In C. S. Lewis (ed.), *Essays Presented to Charles Williams*. Oxford: Oxford University Press. Reprinted, Grand Rapids, Michigan: William B. Eerdmans, 1966. Also in Walter B. Hooper (ed.), *On Stories and Other Essays on Literature*. New York: Harcourt Brace Jovanovich, 1982.

———. 1961. *An Experiment in Criticism*. Cambridge: Cambridge University Press.

Lowie, R. H. 1908a. Catch-words for mythological motifs. *Journal of American Folklore* 21: 24–27.

———. 1908b. The test theme in North American mythology. *Journal of American Folklore* 21:97–128.

———. 1909. Additional catch-words. *Journal of American Folklore* 22:332–33.

Lyman, Horace S. 1900. Reminiscences of Louis Labonte. *Oregon Historical Quarterly* 1: 167–88.

———. 1903. *History of Oregon. The Growth of an American State*. Vol. One. New York: The North Pacific Publishing Society.

Ramsey, Jarold. 1977. *Coyote Was Going There: Indian literature of the Oregon country*. Seattle: University of Washington Press.

———. 1983. *Reading the Fire: Essays in the Traditional Indian Literatures of the Far West*. Lincoln: University of Nebraska Press.

Reichard, Gladys A. 1921. Literary types and dissemination of myths. *Journal of American Folklore* 34.

———. 1947. *An Analysis of Coeur D'Alene Indian Myths*. Philadelphia: American Folklore Society.

Sherzer, Joel. 1982. Poetic structuring of Kuna discourse: The line. *Language in Society* 11:371–90.

Tedlock, Dennis. 1968. *The Ethnography of Tale-Telling at Zuni*. Ann Arbor: University Microfilms.

———. 1972. *Finding the Center: Narrative Poetry of the Zuni Indians*. New York: The Dial Press. Reprinted, Lincoln: University of Nebraska Press, 1978.

———. 1977. Toward an Oral Poetics. *New Literary History* 8:507–19.

———. 1983. *The Spoken Word and the Work of Interpretation*. (Conduct and Communication Series). Philadelphia: University of Pennsylvania Press.

———. 1985. *Popol Vuh: The Definitive Edition of the Mayan Book of The Dawn of Life and the Glories of Gods and Kings.* New York: Simon & Schuster.

Thompson, Stith. 1929. *Tales of the North American Indians.* Cambridge: Harvard University Press. Reprinted, Bloomington: Indiana University Press, 1966.

———. 1946. *The Folktale.* New York: Dryden.

———. 1955. *Motif-index of Folk-literature.* 6 vols. 2nd ed. Bloomington: Indiana University Press. (1st ed. 1932–36, Helsinki).

———. 1961. *The Types of the Folktale.* 2nd revision. (Folklore Fellows Communications No. 184). Helsinki: Academia Scientarium Fennica.

Wiget, Andrew. 1987. Telling the Tale: A Performance Analysis of a Hopi Coyote Story. In Brian Swann and Arnold Krupat (eds.), *Recovering the Word.* Berkeley & Los Angeles: University of California Press.

Wycoco (Moore), Remedios. 1951. The Types of North-American Indian tales. Ph.D. dissertation, Indiana University.

Oolachan-Woman's Robe: Fish, Blankets, Masks, and Meaning in Boas's Kwakw'ala Texts

Judith Berman

The mythical value of the myth is preserved through the worst translation. Whatever our ignorance of the language and the culture of the people where it originated, a myth is still felt as a myth by any reader anywhere in the world (Lévi-Strauss 1963:210).

On October 4, 1894, Franz Boas was told a lewd story and didn't know it.[1]

The story was a *nuyəm,* or "myth," which described how a being named Oolachan-Woman created a magical abundance of herring. Boas dutifully transcribed and translated the story, but he didn't understand it. Though there are few actual mistakes, his misinterpretations are so extreme that in the English version the story seems incoherent.

The story is in fact perfectly coherent, if somewhat ribald. While Boas's translation may not be the worst conceivable, it is still a very bad one, and we are left wondering how much of the "mythical value" of a myth really does emerge in a bad translation. Boas was oblivious not only to the disingenuous sexual humor of this story, but also to the more serious notions about cosmogony and etiology on which that humor is a commentary. The nature of the mythical conflicts, and the plot through which these conflicts are expressed and developed, are nearly invisible in Boas's English.

This is strange, since Boas should have been the ideal translator for this story—at least as far as technical accuracy is concerned. He knew the language, folklore, and traditional culture of the "Kwakiutl," or Kwagul, perhaps better than any other white man before or since. The worst his Kwagul contemporaries could say about his command of their language was that he spoke too slowly (Codere 1966:xxv).

Boas's problem with this story was that he understood the words but not what was being said. The truth about the origin of herring is bound up in word play and metaphor, as well as in cultural concepts which Boas never, to the end of his life, seemed to compass. In his many years of translating Kwakw'ala texts, Boas probably never strayed as far afield as with this story about herring. Nevertheless, the *kind* of mistake he made here is quite common throughout his work. In both translation and ethnography, Boas suffered from a kind of conceptual tone-deafness, an insensitivity to the categories and interconnections of Kwagul culture. This handicap kept him from integrating his vast knowledge of language and custom, and from arriving at deeper insights into the myths he collected. The story about herring underscores the point that merely translating words and sentences may communicate nothing at all. Without a sense of the delicate *relationships* between linguistic form and cultural meaning, the translator may mistake the meanings of the myth on all levels, from the semantics of the individual morphemes to the nature of the cosmogonical transformations which those morphemes describe. In the worst case, the myth might scarcely be "felt as a myth" by anybody.

Franz Boas: Myth, Translation, and Ethnography

Franz Boas's name is well known to every student of American anthropology and folklore, but may be unfamiliar to readers outside of those fields. He is considered both the institutional and intellectual founder of modern American anthropology. His immensely productive career, spanning over fifty years, ended only with his death in 1942. His research interests covered a wide theoretical and geographical range, but his ethnographic fieldwork focused on the North Pacific Coast, specifically on the group of Indian tribes known as the Kwakiutl or Kwagul.

Boas's output on the Kwagul was enormous: the first articles came out in 1888, and thereafter publications appeared regularly and in quantity until the posthumous *Kwakiutl Grammar* (1947) and *Kwakiutl Ethnography* (1966). His lengthy bibliography, however, obscures the fact that relatively little print was devoted to description and analysis. The bulk of his Kwagul publications consisted of texts, eleven volumes in all, in the Kwakw'ala language (Boas and Hunt 1905, 1906; Boas 1909, 1910, 1921, 1925, 1930, 1935–43).

In his seemingly endless accumulation of texts, Boas had a serious aim in mind:

I have spared no trouble to collect . . . [texts] in the language of the Indians, because in these the points that seem important to him are emphasized, and the unavoidable distortion contained in the descriptions given by the casual visitor and student is eliminated (Boas 1909:309).

What we today think of as ethnography—description by a "participant-observer"—was for Boas already too far removed from the experiential world of the Indian. While Boas clearly felt there was a place for scholarly description, analysis, and comparison, in the end only the expressions of the Indian's *own* mind—myths and masks, prayers and songs—could accurately convey the nature of his world.[2]

Given such an outlook and aim, it is ironic that Boas's translations of the texts are far better read than the texts themselves. In fact, the many re-analyses of the Kwagul use Boas's translations as raw data (e.g., Locher 1932; Müller 1955; Reid 1974, 1979; Goldman 1975; Dundes 1979; Walens 1981). Such work is an act of faith. However, Boas was neither omniscient nor infallible, and his translations are far from perfect.[3]

By and large the deficiencies in Boas's translations do not stem from a faulty knowledge of Kwakw'ala. As noted above, the Kwagul commented that he spoke slowly, not that he spoke badly. Boas was a great and innovative linguist for his day, and his Kwakw'ala grammars (1911, 1947) are still highly usable.

Boas's biggest difficulty is with the cultural categories, concepts, and analogies which are expressed in the texts. Since he did not always understand these well, there is sometimes a highly problematic relationship between the Kwakw'ala of the texts and his English gloss. Scholars search for clues to Kwagul culture in Boas's English, but many vital clues did not survive translation.

For example, Boas is not consistent in his glosses of terms for Kwagul cultural categories. He translates the Kwakw'ala word *nuyəm* variously as "myth," "story," "legend," and "tradition." Curiously, Boas's emphasis on the need to record the native's thinking in his own words did not seem to apply to the native's *English* words. All of Boas's glosses for *nuyəm* differ from the native speaker's gloss—"Historie" (George Hunt, letter to Franz Boas, February 7, 1894).

Or, conversely, Boas's translations contain Kwakw'ala terms which appear to correspond to Kwagul cultural categories but do not. Consider the following passage:

The people speaking the *Kwaguł* dialect inhabit many villages, each of which is considered as a separate unit, a tribe. . . . Setting aside the tribes speaking the Bella Bella dialect, whose social organization differs from the *Kwaguł,* we may distinguish two closely related dialects among the *Kwaguł* tribes (Boas 1966:37).

In this passage, $\overset{w}{K}$aguł is at one and the same time a language (the old sense of "dialect"); a group of "tribes" defined according to language; and a group of "tribes" defined according to type of social organization. All three are *ethnological* definitions, imposed by the analyst, and not native cultural understandings of what $\overset{w}{K}$aguł means. Originally, $\overset{w}{K}$aguł applied only to a single high-ranking descent group dwelling at a village site called Half-Circle Beach. The name was transferred first to all the villagers at Half-Circle Beach, then to the four tribes at the new settlement at Fort Rupert, and finally came into vogue as an ethnic self-designation.[4] The meaning of the term lies in a complex history of social schisms and amalgamations, and Boas never explains that history—though it can be traced out in his texts.

Sometimes Boas will translate metaphors literally without explanation. Since his Kwagul narrators tended to use a highly metaphorical style, especially when speaking on such topics as rank, wealth, and religion, this practice can produce a bewildering effect. Giving away furs is "swallowing the tribes" (1966:193), the elder of twin brothers is the "head fish" (n.d.: 102), the assistant to a dance society novice is a "mouth healer" (n.d.: 103). Even when Boas explains such metaphors in footnotes, his explanations rarely include the *concepts* behind the metaphor, the underlying analogies which his speakers are drawing. *Why* is the older twin the "head fish"?

More frequently, Boas will replace a rich Kwakw'ala metaphor with a non-metaphorical term. For instance, one text describes a conflict over control of the weather, fought between the thunderbirds of heaven and the birds of earth. The chief of the latter is named G̓ə́ldəm (Boas and Hunt 1905: 295–317). The literal meaning of G̓ə́ldəm is "Fiery," but in Boas's translation, he calls the character "Woodpecker." Clearly it is significant that the chief fighting for summer and sunny weather is named "Fiery," but Boas characteristically did not perceive this.

Boas has particular difficulties with the topological specificity of Kwakw'ala. Boas's grammars and glossaries (1911, 1921, 1947) and his dictionary (n.d.) show that he understood how such information was expressed from the standpoint of morphology, grammar, and lexicon. However, his translations do not reveal a similar understanding of its importance in narrative imagery. In one of Hunt's texts, the hero reaches what Boas calls the "edge of the world" (Boas and Hunt 1905: 72). This "edge of the world" is not, as Western readers would expect, the edge of a horizontal plane which overhangs nothingness. In Kwakw'ala, the word used is kʼuk̓-, meaning "edge of a vertical plane." The Kwagul "edge of the world" is a wall which *encloses* the world.

Another example is Boas's treatment of the spirit name Bax̌bak̓alanux̌siui?. Boas's gloss, "Cannibal at the rivermouth," is based on a folk etymology interpreting bax̌bak̓ala- as "eating humans," and the suffix -xsiu as "rivermouth." The spirit name actually comes from the neighboring and related language Oowekyala, in which bax̌bak̓ala means "becoming increasingly human" and -xsiu means "passing through an aperture" (Hilton and Rath 1982), probably in reference to the process of initiation.[5] Now, the Kwagul folk etymology clearly expresses concepts important to the *Kwagul*. However, Boas's gloss of this etymology does not communicate these concepts. A non-human spirit eating humans is not cannibalistic, merely predatory. Further, Boas's gloss of "rivermouth" for -xsiu, while not, strictly speaking, incorrect or inadequately specific, has led to a misapprehension by English-speaking anthropologists, fueling commentary on "orality" in Kwagul culture (Dundes 1979; Goldman 1975; Walens 1981; cf. Sanday 1986). A "rivermouth" in Kwakw'ala is *not* a mouth. A mouth is the opening to a bag, bottle, house, or room, or the entrance to a bay—the opening into a hollow object. A river is a long object like a branch or a pole, and the headwaters of a river are ?ug̓ɛxtoi?, "place on top of a long vertical object." A better, if unwieldy gloss of the Kwagul folk etymology of Bax̌bak̓alanux̌siui? might be "[the spirit who] eats humans at the river's end."

Another characteristic is Boas's tendency to focus on detail rather than pattern. This exacerbates the problems already discussed. For example, the names of Kwagul supernaturals are often descriptive of their attributes, i.e. Mig̓atəm, "Seal face" for a supernatural seal; Ṅəmĉaqiu, "One horn on forehead" for a supernatural mountain goat; Mɛisila, "Fish-maker" for a salmon-woman who can create fish; Hayəlbalisəla, "Going from one end of the earth to the other in a single day" for a Loon who can do exactly that.

If Boas had perceived the pattern in this practice, he might have realized that the Woodpecker chief's name, "Fiery," is probably intended as description of an actual attribute of this character; this chief really does burn like the sun. He might then have been less likely to drop the name from the translation and substitute "Woodpecker."

These characteristics do not affect all of Boas's translations the same way. In some of Boas's translations, the distortions of the Kwakw'ala originals are relatively minor, affecting only details of interpretation. In others, the general outlines of the story are present, but important elements are missing and invisible, and other, alien features placed to seem as if they belonged. In the text we will examine in this essay, the story about herring, plot and imagery have been altered almost out of recognition.

Provenience of the Text

On that day in October 1894, Boas was confined in bad weather on a steamship bound for Kincolith, British Columbia, to continue his survey of British Columbia Indians for the British Association for the Advancement of Science (Rohner 1969:81–83). Boas was suffering badly from boredom, inactivity, and the expectation of seasickness. He was a workaholic deprived of his work, and the *Barbara Boskowitz* was so crowded with stacks of wood and oil barrels that he couldn't even pace the deck (Boas, letters to Marie Boas, October 3, 1894, 1 and 2; letters to parents, October 3, 1894, 1 and 2; see also Rohner 1969:148–51).[6]

His only solace were some Indians on the boat. Initially, Boas doubted that these particular Indians could produce anything of interest to him. "I know their legends and songs better than they do," he complained (letter to parents, October 3, 1894, 2). However, one man promised to tell him some "legends" (*Sagen*) which he hadn't heard yet (letter to Marie Boas, October 3, 1894, 1). Boas quickly pressed this Indian, a Kwakw'ala-speaking Ṅaqemgilisəla villager named Q̓umgiləs (Boas 1910:186–87), into the service of Science. He pumped Q̓umgiləs for three days, rain or shine, ceasing only when the Indian left the boat at Alert Bay, with, we can imagine, some relief (letter to parents, ibid.).[7]

In those three days of miserable autumn weather, Boas had obtained, among other things, a series of traditional stories in Kwakw'ala, most of which were eventually published sixteen years later in a volume called *Kwakiutl Tales* (1910:187–244). These stories recount certain of the cosmogonical efforts of Q̓ániqiła̋k (Q̓ániqiła̋x̌), the Kwagul Transformer. They are rare among Boas's texts in that they were collected in the field by Boas himself, rather than written down and mailed to Boas by native speaker George Hunt. They are also unusual in that they were dictated to Boas in the Tl'astl'asiqwala dialect of Kwakw'ala, which has not been well described.

Boas's surviving field notes from 1894 show that his acquaintance with Kwakw'ala was as yet brief and superficial, and his transcription skills undeveloped. The fact that he did not transmit these texts for publication in 1900 with others obtained by George Hunt (Boas and Hunt 1905, 1906) seems to indicate that he was waiting for the oppor-

15   "Ḡē'la," ⁸nē'x·⁸laē Ts!ā'ts!ō, "qaE'nts a'młē," ⁸nē'x·⁸laē
Ts!ā'ts!ō lāx Dzā'dzaxwītElāga.   Lā'⁸laē ts!â'ᴇ Ts!ā'ts!ō
yîsēs k!u'taałdē lāx Dzā'dzaxwītElāga.   Lā'⁸laē k!utā'ał-
⁸îdᴇsēs ėg·â'nᴇm.   Lā'⁸laē Q!ā'nēqî⁸laxᵘ ⁸nē'x·⁸laē: "Gwa'-
dzēs ⁸yā'lag·ilîs," ⁸nē'x·⁸laē Q!ā'nēqî⁸laxᵘ.   Lā'⁸laē yā'q!eg·a⁸łē
20 Dzā'dzaxwītElāga: "Gwa'la hē'k·!āla g·ā'xᴇn, ā'g·anē,"
⁸nē'x·⁸laē Dzā'dzaxwītElāga.   " 'Tsē'x̣⁸ōstēs q!ᴇ'mxᴇxstix,'
⁸nē'x·la g·ā'xᴇn, ā'g·anē."   Lā'⁸laē

"Tsē'xwistē', tsē'xwistē'; q!ᴇ'mxᴇxstē', q!ᴇ'mxᴇxstē';" ⁸nē'x·⁸la g·ā'xᴇn, ā'g·anē'

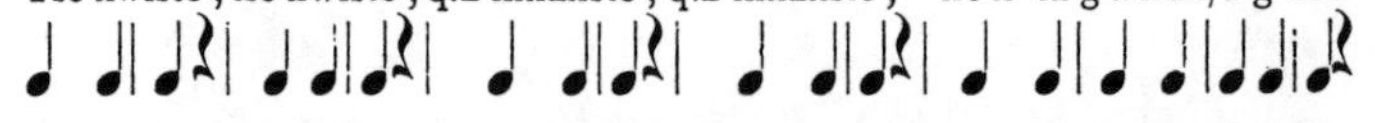

Lā'⁸laē ʟ!ā'psta lā'xē dᴇ'msx·.   Q!ᴇ'mxᴇxstē; s+⧾xa⁸laē
25 q!ā'ma; tsē'x̣⁸ōstēs lā'xē awî'nagwis.   Ax⁸ē'tsᴇ⁸wēs g·ō'kulōt.
Lā'⁸laē łā'x̣⁸wīlālaē gᴇnē'mas Ō'⁸māł, yîx ᴇ'lx̣sâayūgwa qa⁸s
k·inā'la lā'xē q!ā'ma.   Lā'⁸laē ax⁸ē'd lā'xēs habā'gaē⁸ qa⁸s
yîx⁸ē'dēx qa⁸s ax⁸ē'dēs lā'xē q!ā'max·.

Q!ā'nēqî⁸laxᵘ and Ts!ā'ts!ō.

"Come," said Ts!ā'ts!ō, "that we may play!" Thus said
Ts!ā'ts!ō to Olachen-Woman.   Then Ts!ā'ts!ō gave his
blanket to Olachen-Woman.   Then she put on the blanket
that she had gained in gambling.   Q!ā'nēqî⁸laxᵘ said,
"Don't go on the beach." Thus said Q!ā'nēqî⁸laxᵘ. Then
Olachen-Woman spoke.   "Don't say that to me, lord!"
Thus said Olachen-Woman.   "Say to me, 'Dried herrings
are jumping on the beach,' lord." (Then he said,) " 'Jump
on the beach, jump on the beach! Dried herring, dried
herring,' say to me, lord." Then she put the corner of
the blanket into the sea.   Behold! dried herrings made
a noise, "Ssss!" Shoals of herrings were jumping ashore
on the land.   They were taken by the tribe.   Then the
wife of Ō'⁸māł, Fog-Woman, found it difficult to scoop
up the herrings.   Then she took her pubic hair and
netted a net to take the herrings.

Figure 1. "Q́ániqiłax̱ʷ and Ćáću," from Boas 1910: 190–91.

tunity to revise his transcription. He subsequently undertook such revisions, perhaps with
the assistance of Hunt, or perhaps with William Brotchie, a half-Nəmgis resident of Alert
Bay whom he had consulted extensively for the 1905 volume of texts (Boas and Hunt
1905:3).

    If indeed Boas consulted Hunt or Brotchie on Q́umgiləs' texts, he does not seem
to have been very thorough. He seems to have paid the most attention to transcription, but
there are still several uncorrected errors. The translation shows very little change. He does

not appear to have checked the original glosses from his field notes, and the eventual 1910 publication preserves a number of mistakes and misinterpretations. One error persisted in glossary and dictionary throughout his whole life (Boas 1921: 1436–37; Boas n.d.: 441).

Figure 1 shows the text of one of these Q̓ā́niqilax̌ stories, "Q̓ā́niqilax̌ and Ćáću," as it originally appeared in the 1910 volume (1910: 190–91). I have altered it only to the extent of placing the Kwakw'ala above the English; the two were situated on facing pages in the original.

A casual glance leaves the reader with many questions. Why does Q̓ā́niqilax̌ command Oolachan-Woman to stay off the beach? What is their relationship that Q̓ā́niqilax̌ cares one way or another about her actions? What's the significance, whether in ordinary narrative logic or in nonlogical mythical symbolism, of the dried herring? What do the herring have to do with gambling?

There are two methods for getting at the truth about the herring, neither of which is sufficient by itself. One is retranslation, the other is "rhetorical" analysis (cf. Hymes 1981). Translation in the strictest sense looks at what words and sentences mean. Rhetorical analysis looks at the way the narrator uses words and sentences to tell a story: the way in which topic and setting are established and then change, the way in which imagery and the actions and responses of story actors are patterned. Though rhetorical analysis deals with a "higher" level of linguistic organization than translation, let us begin first with it.

"Q̓ā́niqilax̌ and Ćáću": Rhetorical Structure

The body of Boas's text is printed as a prose paragraph. As the first step in rhetorical analysis, let us rewrite text and translation (using an orthography more modern than Boas's),[8] so that each numbered English line corresponds with a single, numbered Kwakw'ala clause:

Q̓ā́niqilax̌ and Ćáću

[*Version 2*]

"Gíla,"	1
ńíxlai Ćáću.	2
"qaə́nc ʔámłi,"	3
ńíxlai Ćáću lax Zázax̌itəlaga.	4
Láłai ćóə Ćáću yəsis x̌ə́taʔałdi lax Zázax̌itəlaga.	5
Láłai x̌ə́taʔałʔidəsis ʔigónəm.	6
Láłai Q̓ā́niqilax̌ ńíxlai	7
"Ǧázis ýálagiləs,"	8
ńíxlai Q̓ā́niqilax̌.	9
Láłai yáq̓əgaʔłi Zázax̌itəlaga,	10
"Ǧála híx̌kala gáxən, ʔágani,"	11
ńíxlai Zázax̌itəlaga.	12
"'cíx̌ʔustis q̓ə́mxəxstix,' ńíxla gáxən, ʔágani."	13

Laĺai   14
　　"‘Cíx̌istí, cíx̌istí,   15
　　　q̓ə́mx̌əx̌stí, q̓ə́mx̌əx̌stí,’   16
　　　　níxíla gáx̌ən ʔáganí."   17
Láĺai X̌ápsta láx̌i də́msx.   18
Q̓ə́mx̌əx̌sti;   19
Sss . . . xaĺai q̓áma.   20
Cíx̌ʔustis láx̌i ʔawínag̓is.   21
ʔax̌ʔícoʔis gúk̓əlut.   22
Láĺai łáx̌ʷilalai gənə́mas ʔúṁał, yəx̌ ʔə́lx̌soayug̓a,   23
　　qaś kinála láx̌i q̓áma.   24
Láĺai ʔax̌ʔíd láx̌is habágaiʔ   25
　　qaś yəx̌ʔídix̌   26
　　qaś ʔax̌ʔídis láx̌i q̓ámax   27

"Come,   1
　　said Ćáću,   2
　"that we may play,"   3
　　thus said Ćáću to Oolachan-Woman.   4
Then Ćáću gave his blanket to Oolachan-Woman.   5
Then she put on the blanket she had gained in gambling.   6
Q̓ániqiĺax̌ said,   7
　"Don't go on the beach,"   8
　　thus said Q̓ániqiĺax̌.   9
Then Oolachan-Woman spoke: 10
　"Don't say that to me, lord,"   11
　　thus said Oolachan-Woman.   12
　"Say to me 'Dried herrings are jumping on the beach,' lord."   13
(Then he said,)   14
　"‘Jump on the beach, jump on the beach,   15
　　dried herring, dried herring,’   16
　　　say to me, lord,"   17
Then she put the corner of the blanket into the sea.   18
Behold! dried herrings;   19
Herrings made a noise, "Ssss!"   20
Shoals of herring were jumping ashore on the land.   21
They were taken by the tribe.   22
Then the wife of ʔúṁał, Fog-Woman,   23
　found it difficult to scoop up the herrings.   24
Then she took her pubic hair   26
　and netted a net   26
　to take the herrings.   27

Let us begin by looking at changes in topic, setting, and character.

　　The first few clauses of the text (clauses 1–6) appear to describe a scene in which two actors, Ćáću and Oolachan-Woman, are gambling. We are not told *where* they are gambling.

　　Then a new character is introduced—Q̓ániqiĺax̌ (clause 7). Seemingly out of the blue, he commands "Don't go on the beach!" We guess that he is addressing Oolachan-

Woman, because she responds "Don't say that to me, lord!" The next few clauses (7–17) are taken up with the interaction of Oolachan-Woman and Q̓ániqiḷax̌; Ćáćᶸ is no longer on stage.

In the first part of the text, the narrator is not explicit about setting, but on the basis of changes in topic, and in the characters who appear onstage, we can divide the first part of the text into "scene A" and "scene B":

A: Ćáćᶸ and Oolachan-Woman are gambling
B: Q̓ániqiḷax̌ and Oolachan-Woman are talking

The topic of scene B is obscure. Q̓ániqiḷax̌ and Oolachan-Woman are discussing something, but we can't tell exactly what it is or why they are discussing it. Yet there are several hints. Given the overall circumstances of the story, and knowledge of Q̓ániqiḷax̌'s nature from other stories (e.g. Boas and Hunt 1906: 192–95, 225–27), we suspect that Q̓ániqiḷax̌'s speech has magical power. If he forbids Oolachan-Woman from going onto the beach, she will not be able to do it. But when Q̓ániqiḷax̌ says the magic words—literally—she is able to go down to the water's edge.

Their argument and the events which follow it only make sense if we posit a metaphoric/magical identity between herring and oolachan. This is not farfetched (see figure 2). Both are small, silvery, oily ocean fish with forked tails. Oolachan (pronounced *OO*-la-kn, also called eulachon, olachen, oulakan, hooligan, etc.) are more slender and somewhat smaller than herring, commonly measuring no more than six or seven inches, while herring usually reach about ten inches when mature. Both come inshore in vast numbers to spawn, oolachan to freshwater rivers in early spring, herring to shallow salt water in spring or summer (*Encyclopedia Americana* 1986).

For some reason, Q̓ániqiḷax̌ appears to be ignorant of this magical relationship. This is how Oolachan-Woman is able to trick him: how she is able to go on the beach after he has sung his song, and how she is able to create herring once she is on the beach.

Scene A could be understood as an *Invitation* (clauses 1–4) plus a *Consequence* (clauses 5–6). Scene B could also be understood as two *Speech-Response* pairs, a *Prohibition* and a *Protest,* a *Permission* and a *Consequence.*

Figure 2. Herring and oolachan.

A. 1. Ćáću invites Oolachan-Woman to gamble with him.
   2. Oolachan-Woman wins their game.
B. 1. Q̓ániqiɬax̌ forbids Oolachan-Woman to go on the beach.
   2. Oolachan-Woman protests.
   3. Q̓ániqiɬax̌ inadvertently permits Oolachan-Woman to go on the beach.
   4. Oolachan-Woman does it.

Dell Hymes has used words like *line, verse,* and *stanza* to label various units of rhetorical structure. Here, let us refer to each numbered unit as a *verse.* The relationships could be represented in the following way (for brevity's sake the Kwakw'ala is omitted here):

A. 1. (Invitation)
      "Come,"   1
         said Ćáću,   2
      "that we may play,"   3
         thus said Ćáću to Oolachan-Woman.   4

   2. (Consequence)
      Then Ćáću gave his blanket to Oolachan-Woman.   5
      Then she put on the blanket she had gained in gambling.   6

B. 1. (Prohibition)
      Q̓ániqiɬax̌ said,   7
      "Don't go on the beach,"   8
         thus said Q̓ániqiɬax̌.   9

   2. (Protest)
      Then Oolachan-Woman spoke: 10
      "Don't say that to me, lord,"   11
         thus said Oolachan-Woman;   12
      "say to me 'Dried herrings are jumping on the beach,' lord."   13

   3. (Permission)
      (Then he said,)   14
      "Jump on the beach, jump on the beach,   15
         dried herring, dried herring,'   16
            say to me, lord,"   17

   4. (Consequence)
      Then she put the corner of her blanket into the sea.   18

In many oral-narrative traditions, such rhetorical structures are linguistically marked. It will be noted that up to this point, each main clause in "Q̓ániqiɬax̌ and Ćáću" except the very first has begun with the auxiliary form *laɬai.*

Boas translates *laɬai* consistently as "then," except for clause 7, where he omits it. "Then" is as good a gloss as any; *laɬai* has no concrete meaning. The main function in narrative of *laɬai* and other auxiliary forms is to mark the movement of the narrator's focus from one character, locale, or activity to another, and to relate the events causally and temporally (Berman 1982). However, such auxiliaries do also function, in a limited way, as a marker of rhetorical units (Berman 1983). Elaboration of these points need not concern us here; let it suffice to say that auxiliaries usually mark what could be called *lines*—the most basic rhetorical element which forms *verses* and *stanzas* of what are often intricate patterns of four-fold and four-stage action (Berman 1991). As a rule, auxiliaries are present in every main clause of a narrative. They are only absent from the very first line of a narrative and from the quoted speech of story actors, and, sometimes, during the climactic action of a story.

The next few clauses of the text, 19–22, lack auxiliaries. This is because they describe the climactic moments of the story—the moments in which Oolachan-Woman is creating herring for her tribe. But what is the place of these clauses in the story's overall rhetorical structure? Do they form a separate scene C or do they topically and organizationally belong to scene B?

Certainly clause 22 is the end of a scene, whether a scene B or a scene C. The following clause 23 introduces a new actor, Fog-Woman, and a new topic, Fog-Woman's inability to catch herring.

But there seems to be more than one possible analysis of the clauses describing the appearance and resuscitation of the dried herring. Consider a scene B which includes these clauses:

B.	1.	Q̓ániqiłax̌ said,	7
		"Don't go on the beach,"	8
		thus said Q̓ániqiłax̌.	9
	2.	Then Oolachan-Woman spoke:	10
		"Don't say that to me, lord,"	11
		thus said Oolachan-Woman;	12
		"say to me 'Dried herrings are jumping on the beach,' lord."	13
	3.	(Then he said,)	14
		" 'Jump on the beach, jump on the beach,	15
		dried herring, dried herring,'	16
		say to me, lord,"	17
	4.	Then she put the corner of her blanket into the sea.	18
	5.	Behold! dried herrings;	19
		Herrings made a noise, "Ssss!"	20
		Shoals of herring were jumping ashore on the land.	21
		They were taken by the tribe.	22

The foregoing analysis is unsatisfactory for several reasons. First, the preference of Kwagul narrators for the number four in all levels of narrative organization is quite striking. This is not to say that four-fold patterning is rigidly adhered to in absolutely every instance, and that no narrator would ever add a fifth verse. But clauses 19–22 do not seem to belong with the rest of scene B for other reasons. They have a different topic and different actors. In the preceding clauses of scene B, Q̓ániqiłax̌ and Oolachan-Woman are arguing about whether she should go on the beach or not; in these clauses Q̓ániqiłax̌ is absent and irrelevant and the main action is with the herring.

At the same time, there are arguments against these clauses standing by themselves as verse C. First, it would be unusual, I believe, for a Kwagul narrator to begin a major rhetorical unit, to make a scene shift, without some rhetorical marker. There is no such marker whatsoever in clause 19. Second, all other scenes in this text share an action–response pattern. In scene A it is *Invitation-Consequence*. In scene B, it is *Prohibition-Response*. In the final scene, clauses 23–27, it is *Problem-Solution*. Here, the action which causes the magical manifestation of herring occurs in clause 18, which the previous analysis has put with scene B. An analysis which would seem to better reflect the organizational realities of the text is:

C.	1.	Then she put the corner of her blanket into the sea.	18
	2.	Behold! dried herrings;	19
		Herrings made a noise, "Ssss!"	20
		Shoals of herring were jumping ashore on the land.	21
		They were taken by the tribe.	22

In this scheme, scene C begins when Oolachan-Woman leaves Q̓ániqiⅼax̌ʷ and goes down to the waterside to dip her blanket in the ocean; a change of setting, character, and topic. Such an analysis, however, destroys the (previously argued) four-part action–response symmetry of scene B.

I believe the solution to these difficulties lies in reconsidering Oolachan-Woman's role in the story. Though the title of the text leaves her out, Oolachan-Woman is surely the main character, the main mover of the action in this story.[9] If we look at the action from *her* point of view, the story becomes a series of her victories and accomplishments. First, she wins Ćáću's blanket. Second, she tricks Q̓ániqiⅼax̌ʷ so that it becomes possible for her to go on the beach. Third, she manifests herring for her tribe. In the final sentences of the text, another woman, Fog-Woman, achieves a minor victory of her own.

From this point of view, the action is clearly and unambiguously organized into four scenes, and each scene has a two-part structure of *Problem–Problem Solved*. In the first verse of each scene (labeled 1 below), a problem or difficult task is presented. In the second verse (labeled 2), the problem is solved or the task accomplished:

A.	1.	"Come,"	1
		said Ćáću,	2
		"that we may play,"	3
		thus said Ćáću to Oolachan-Woman.	4
	2.	Then Ćáću gave his blanket to Oolachan-Woman.	5
		Then she put on the blanket she had gained in gambling.	6
B.	1.	Q̓ániqiⅼax̌ʷ said,	7
		"Don't go on the beach,"	8
		thus said Q̓ániqiⅼax̌ʷ.	9
	2.	Then Oolachan-Woman spoke:	10
		"Don't say that to me, lord,"	11
		thus said Oolachan-Woman.	12
		"Say to me 'Dried herrings are jumping on the beach,' lord."	13

	(Then he said,)	14
	"'Jump on the beach, jump on the beach,	15
	dried herring, dried herring,'	16
	say to me, lord,"	17
C. 1.	Then she put the corner of the blanket into the sea.	18
2.	Behold! dried herrings;	19
	Herrings made a noise, "Ssss!"	20
	Shoals of herring were jumping ashore on the land.	21
	They were taken by the tribe.	22
D. 1.	Then the wife of ʔúṁaɫ, Fog-Woman,	23
	found it difficult to scoop up the herrings.	24
2.	Then she took her pubic hair	25
	and netted a net	26
	to take the herrings.	27

In scene A, the task at hand is to win in the game with Ćáću. In scene B, the problem is how to get round Q̓ániqiɫax̌'s prohibition. In scene C, the task is to bring the herring into being. And in scene D, the problem is how to catch the herring.

"Q̓ániqiɫax̌ and Ćáću": Retranslation

Close attention to organizational logic—to rhetorical structure—has brought the apparent incoherencies of the text into focus but has not converted them into sensible narrative. We still do not understand the significance of the first gambling scene. Does this supply the reason why Q̓ániqiɫax̌ orders Oolachan-Woman to stay off the beach? Logically, it must. Oolachan-Woman's trick with the herring must also be related to her gambling, but how? What is the substance of the conflict between Q̓ániqiɫax̌ and Oolachan-Woman?

We can only discover this if we understand that the narrator of this text was deliberately punning with sound and image, in most cases giving a sexual meaning or association to words for which the primary meaning is not sexual. Careful retranslation will make some of this punning obvious, and allow us to guess at the rest.

Scene A begins with an invitation from Ćáću to "play." Boas interpreted this "play" as gambling play. Actually, no explicit mention of gambling is found in the Kwakw'ala original, despite Boas's English of clause 6.

In Kwakw'ala, Ćáću's initial speech consists of three words: *Ǥila qaənc ʔamɫi.* The critical word is *ʔamɫi,* which derives from the stem *ʔamɫ-,* "to play." Now, in English, "to play" has multiple connotations, as is evidenced by such words and phrases as "children playing," "to play cards," and "foreplay." As it happens, a comparable or even wider semantic range exists in Kwakw'ala. There appear to be four main uses of *ʔamɫ-,* "to play" in the Kwakw'ala textual corpus: "child's play," "gambling play," "sexual play," and "shamanic play." [10]

The first verse of "Q̓ániqiɫax̌ and Ćáću" does not reveal to us which of these four senses of "play" is intended. However, clause 6 in verse 2 contains the answer. This clause contains three Kwakw'ala words, Láƚai ƙ‘ətáʔaƚʔidəsis ʔigónəm. The first word, laƚai, is an auxiliary and contains no concrete meaning. The second word, ƙ‘ətáʔaƚʔidəsis, is the verb, and the third word, ʔigónəm, is a noun in the oblique case.

The clause as a whole is difficult to translate. The only clue as to who is the subject of the sentence, Ćáću or Oolachan-Woman, is the possessive marker -is at the end of the verb ƙətáʔaƚʔidəsis.[11] This marker signifies that the possessor of the oblique noun and the subject of the sentence are the same person.

The thing possessed, the oblique noun, is ʔigónəm. This word is derived from a stem ʔiko-, "to be victorious," and a nominal suffix -anəm, "obtained by an action."[12] Together stem and suffix mean "the thing obtained through victory"—that is, "the prize, the thing won." Boas interprets this "thing won" as the blanket Ćáću gave to Oolachan-Woman in the preceding clause. Indeed, a blanket is apparently mentioned in clause 6, in the verb ƙətáʔaƚʔidəsis. Since this blanket is no longer ƙətáʔaƚdi "[Ćáću's] former blanket," as in the previous clause, but simply ƙətáʔaƚ-, "blanket," it would seem that Oolachan-Woman is the possessor of the blanket, and Boas is right to make her the subject of the sentence.

However, the meaning of the verb ƙətáʔaƚʔidəsis is somewhat tricky. Boas interprets this verb as deriving from the stem ƙətáʔaƚ-, "robe, blanket," and an inchoative aspect marker -[x]ʔid, "to start doing an action, to become something"; he translates the whole form as "she put on a blanket." At first glance this is a likely interpretation. Since the stem ƙətáʔaƚ- occurs in two adjacent clauses, it would make sense that the stem means the same thing in both places. The boundary in Kwakw'ala between noun and verb is not a very distinct one, and there is no grammatical or syntactic reason why "blanket" cannot function as a verb.

However, given this interpretation, ƙətáʔaƚʔidəsis cannot mean "she put on a blanket." It would have to mean "she became a blanket," a bizarre scenario! We begin to wonder if Boas's interpretation is incorrect all around.

Let us look more closely at the stem of this verb form. Ƙətáʔaƚ, also ƙəƚáƚ, is a Tl'astl'asqwala dialect form deriving from the Kwakwʔala root ƙət(a)- meaning "to stick to, to stick on, robe, blanket worn as clothing," and a nominal suffix -(!)aƚ. In other words, one's robe is a "thing which sticks on."

While "robe" is the common and expected meaning of ƙətaʔaƚ, there are other possible interpretations. The root ƙət(a)- can mean "sticking together, joined by sexual intercourse." It is used in this sense in the word ƙatoxsd, "sticking together behind," a term for informal and irregular marriage unions. "Like dogs sticking together," George Hunt explains (Boas 1921:1075). Further, the nominal suffix -(!)aƚ in ƙətaʔaƚ, "robe," is formally identical to an adverbial suffix -(!)aƚ which means "quickly, easily."

In other words, if the *expected* interpretation ƙəta ʔaƚ is "robe," a *possible* interpretation of ƙəta ʔaƚ is "sticking together easily, joining together quickly or easily in sexual intercourse."[13] In ordinary circumstances, context would allow us to separate which meaning was intended; but here the narrator deliberately confuses the two. We think we are hearing about someone's clothing, and all of a sudden we discover we are hearing about a sexual act.

The whole word, ǩ̇ataʔałʔidəsis, can be analyzed as follows:

ǩ̇ət(a)-   "to stick on, to join in sexual intercourse"
-(!)ał   "quickly, easily"
-[x]ʔid   "inchoative aspect marker" ("to start doing an action, to become something")
-əs   "oblique case marker"
-is   "possessive case marker; possessor same as subject"

No, it does not make sense for Oolachan-Woman to "become a blanket," but it does make sense for her to "begin sticking onto something in sexual intercourse." The pair of clauses can now be translated as:

A. 2.   Laİai ćóə Ćáću yəsis ǩ̇átáʔałdi laẋ Zázaẋitəlaga   5
         Laİai ǩ̇átáʔałʔidəsis ʔigónəm   6

A. 2.   Ćáću gave his robe to Oolachan-Woman.   5
         She quickly stuck [herself] onto that thing she had won. 6

The reader will now begin to guess that the "thing she had won" is not a blanket.

Nor are Ćáću and Oolachan-Woman gambling in the normal sense of the word. Instead, in scene A, the narrator is slyly using the *idiom* of gambling to describe a sexual encounter. The stem *ʔamł-,* "to play," in the form *ʔamłi,* the appearance of the form *ʔiko-,* "to be victorious," and an apparent transaction involving Ćáću's clothing, actually refer to sexual play.

In this light, Q̇ániqiİaẋ's anger in scene B begins to make sense, but there are still several confusing details. Clearly, some relationship exists between Q̇ániqiİaẋ and Oolachan-Woman that gives Q̇ániqiİaẋ the right and the need to control her sexual activities. In a closely related story from the Ṅaqəmgilisəla village, a character named Oolachan-Woman is Q̇ániqiİaẋ's mother (Boas 1895:319). In yet another story from the nearby Yuẋinuẋ village, Oolachan-Woman is Q̇ániqiİaẋ's paternal grandmother (1906: 188). The best we can say about the relationship of the two in "Q̇ániqiİaẋ and Ćáću" is that Oolachan-Woman is probably some kind of older kinswoman. Of course, as the myths tell us, she would be an adoptive kinswoman only, since Q̇ániqiİaẋ is human and Oolachan-Woman belongs to the magical animal-people.

But Q̇ániqiİaẋ's command—"Don't go on the beach!"—seems somewhat nonsensical. What does going on the beach have to do with improper sexual activities? Let us examine what he says more closely.

The phrase consists of two words, Ǧ̇ázis ýálagiləs. The first term, ǧ̇azis, is relatively straightforward, an imperative meaning "don't you do it!" The second term is problematic, containing what may be either a transcription error or dialectal variant. The stem could be ya-, meaning "to do, to be, to move." This is clearly what Boas had in mind. If the stem is ya- the word can be analyzed as following:

ya-   "to do, to be, to move"
-la   "continuative suffix"
-gəɫ   "continued or repeated motion"
-is   "outside, the beach, the world"

Ya-la-gəl-is could be translated as "to move continuously/exist with continuous motion throughout the world," or as "to do something continuously outside/on the beach."

The first gloss has a somewhat cosmic ring to it, and in fact, Yálagəlis happens to be a name of a Kwagul warrior deity (Boas 1897:713). The suffix combination -gəlis, "continual motion throughout the world" is very often used as an epithet descriptive of divine nature. Given that Oolachan-Woman has magical powers, given that (in the context of the myth-age world in which these stories take place) she is a fish-supernatural, g̈ázis yálagiləs might mean "Don't act according to your divine nature!"

The more concrete and restricted meaning would be "Stop doing things on the beach!" (cf. Boas n.d.: 44). Traditionally, the beach—not, obviously, the shore right in front of the village, but a more private location—was the usual site for hanky-panky (Jay Powell, personal communication). A woman's legitimate trips to gather food might be used as a cover for her illicit affairs, as they were in another Kwagul story, in which a woman has intercourse with her husband's brothers while collecting cockles (Boas and Hunt 1905:282–87). In this concrete sense, Ḱániqiḷax̌ is saying to Oolachan-Woman, "Don't go off to 'work' on some secluded beach, I know what you're really up to!"

The tricks that the narrator plays elsewhere in the text suggest that yet another interpretation is possible here. The clue is a small mark (ʼ) over the /y/ (Boas's ᵋ). This mark is not found in Boas's field notes, but does appear in the published version. It represents glottalization, which is a distinctive feature in Kwakw'ala. There are dialectical differences between the two dozen Kwakw'ala-speaking "tribes," and this was even more true in the nineteenth century. It may be that the form from the Kwagul dialect, yálagəlis, was legitimately ýálagəlis in the Tl'astl'asiqwala dialect of the narrator of this text. However, it is also possible that the narrator was playing with the sound of a stem similar to ya-, "to do, to be, to move."

This stem is ýəɫ- "to spread legs for intercourse." The form ýəɫagəlis would be analyzed as follows:

ýəɫ-   "to spread legs for intercourse"
-gəɫ   "continued or repeated motion"
-is   "beach, world"

Ýəɫagəlis would mean "Don't fornicate all the time on the beach!" [14] In Tsaxis Kwakw'ala, at least, the form which occurs in the text, ýálagəlis, is halfway between this ýəɫagəlis, and the standard yálagəlis, "Don't be doing that on the beach all the time!"

Again, at first glance, Oolachan-Woman's reply to this command is rather odd. "Cíx̌ʷʔustis ḱə́mxəxstix̌," Oolachan-Woman says, and Ḱániqiḷax̌ repeats "Cíx̌istí ḱə́mxəxstí"—the difference is subtle.

The first word in Oolachan-Woman's speech is *cíx̌ʷʔustis,* which Boas translates as "jump on the beach." It can be analyzed as:

cix̌ʷ- "to flap (like a fish when caught); to be stranded" [15]
-w, -ẃ "(moving) out of"
-sta "in the water"
-is "outside, beach, world"

One would expect this form to read *cíx̌ʷʔusdis;* the irregularity may be due to transcription error.

The second word, *q̓ə́mx̌əxstix̌,* can be analyzed as:

q̓əmx̌- "herring"
-əxsta "mouth, to do with mouth, to talk, entrance to an inlet or enclosure"
-ix̌ "2nd-person demonstrative (this visible thing near you)"

The first word of this speech is relatively straightforward; it can be translated as "to flap on the beach (moving) out of the water." On the face of it, this refers to herring becoming stranded when they come inshore to spawn.

The second word requires caution from the translator. The suffix -*əxsta* has several meanings, and we might be tempted, from previous reference to geographical features such as water and beach, to choose the meaning "entrance to an inlet." However, there are two objections to such an interpretation. First, -*əxsta* only takes this "inlet" meaning in the form -*əxstalis.* Second, if -*əxsta* means "entrance to an inlet," the coordinates expressed by the locative and demonstrative elements of each word, *cíx̌ʷʔustis* and *q̓ə́mx̌əxstix̌,* would conflict. The herring cannot simultaneously be offshore, at the entrance to an inlet, and at the beach (-*is*), stranded near the person Oolachan-Woman is talking to (-*ix̌*), that is, near Q̓ániqiɫax̌ʷ.

The word *q̓ə́mx̌əxstix̌* is a complex pun, and we need to look in the next scene for the key to its meanings. Exactly what the herring are, and why it makes sense for Oolachan-Woman to bring them up at this juncture, is revealed at the beginning of scene C (clauses 18–20).

Boas's translation of clause 18, "Then she put the corner of her blanket in the water," is completely wrong. The clause consists of four words, *laɫai x̌apsta lax̌i dəmsx.* The critical word here is the verb, *x̌apsta.* It can be analyzed as a root *x̌ap-* and a suffix -*sta,* "into the water." Boas glosses *x̌apsta* in his 1921 Kwakw'ala-English glossary, and again in his unpublished dictionary (Boas n.d.: 441) as "to dip into water"; but the only reference he gives in each case, C190.24, is this very page and line.

Boas probably arrived at "to dip into water" via the related story from the Na̓qəmgilisəla, in which Oolachan-Woman is Q̓ániqiɫax̌ʷ's mother. Oolachan-Woman keeps all the fish in her blanket, and Q̓ániqiɫax̌ʷ, concerned that there should be abundance in the world, borrows it and dips it into the water. The fish are thus released into the ocean (Boas 1895:319, see also 332–33; Maud n.d.: 4). Boas evidently collected this version of the story in English. At any rate, Boas seems to have assumed that he already knew Q̓umgilə́s's story well enough to guess how Oolachan-Woman would create herring. The mention of a blanket at the beginning of the story probably reinforced his belief.

A glance at other occurrences of X̌ap-, in Kwakw'ala and its closest relatives, shows that the meaning of the root X̌ap- has nothing to do with blankets, or dipping, or water (Lincoln and Rath 1980:192). It means "to pull limbs close to the body." Derivatives of X̌ap- in Kwakw'ala mean variously "to clutch something to one's body," and "to climb a smooth pole, tree, or steep bank." A Heiltsuk word derived from the same root is X̌xX̌ṕs, "to squat on the ground outside" (Lincoln and Rath ibid.; Boas 1921:1437; n.d.: 436). Boas does give examples with a correct gloss in his glossary and unpublished dictionary, but with the stem spelled X̌əp-. With his original misunderstanding in place, he never connected this X̌əp- with Oolachan-Woman's X̌apsta.

To repeat, X̌apsta has nothing to do with blanket corners, or dipping. The most literal translation of clause 18 would be "she pulled her limbs close to her body in the saltwater." The most probable interpretation of this is that Oolachan-Woman is squatting down. The next line makes the matter completely clear: "'Sss . . .' said the herrings." The herring are Oolachan-Woman's labia, and she is urinating into the water.

"Don't keep fooling around on the beach," Q̓ániqiláx̌ orders his kinswoman. "Oh, no, lord," says Oolachan-Woman, "tell me 'herring *are* flapping on the beach."

And Q̓ániqiláx̌ dutifully repeats, "Lord, tell me, 'herring are flapping on the beach.'" This bit of buffoonery is not typical of Q̓ániqiláx̌, who is usually a fairly dignified character, but the motif is found elsewhere in North Pacific Coast oral literature (e.g. Davis and Saunders 1980:165–66; cf. Maud n.d.: 6).

Q̓ániqiláx̌ does not repeat the phrase exactly as Oolachan-Woman tells it to him. He alters it, perhaps in part to make his song more euphonious (see Boas 1966:352). What Q̓ániqiláx̌ says is cíx̌istí q̓ə́mx̌əxstí. The difference lies in the suffixes. Cíx̌istí is missing the locative suffixes -w̓ and -is found in the word as Oolachan-Woman says it, and q̓ə́mx̌əxstí has a different terminal demonstrative suffix. Q̓ániqiláx̌'s speech can be analyzed as:

cix̌-	"to flap (like a fish when caught), to be stranded"
-sta	"in the water"
-i	"prenominal 3rd-person subject marker"
q̓əmx-	"herring"
-əxsta	"mouth, to talk, entrance"
-i	"3rd-person demonstrative (that visible or invisible thing over there)"

What Q̓ániqiláx̌ sings is "in the water over there, those herring—which are at the entrance to an enclosure—are stranded/flapping."

Again, Oolachan-Woman says "these herring which you can see, near you," while Q̓ániqiláx̌ is saying, "those herring over there." [16] Q̓ániqiláx̌ does not realize that the herring are on the body of Oolachan-Woman, that the entrance they are stranded at is her vagina. The consequence of his change seems to be that Oolachan-Woman is compelled to go down to the water to flap her herring, instead of doing it on the spot. It may be that if Q̓ániqiłax̌ had not so erred, the multitude of herring would not have been created. Oolachan-Woman must immerse a body part in saltwater to manifest fish, as we will discuss later.

In Kwakw'ala, the moment in which the herring come to life reads:

Q̓ə́mx̌əx̌sti;   19
Sss . . . xałai q̓áma.   20
Cíx̌ʔustis láx̌i ʔawínag̈is.   21

Clause 19 in its entirety is the same word as we saw in Q̓ániqiła̍x̌'s magical song, q̓əmx̌əx̌sti, which we translated roughly as "herring at the entrance." In clause 19 it is used as a verb.[17] Here it is well to remember, from the narrator's fun with the blanket, that such noun–verb shifts may not be as innocent as they initially appear.

Let us examine this herring word a little more carefully. The stem, q̓əmx̌- "herring," is not polysemic, and presents no problem. It is the primary suffix, -əx̌sta, "mouth, to do with mouth, to talk, entrance" which is difficult. Certainly one intended meaning of q̓əmx̌əx̌sti is "herring at the entrance," that is, "herring at the entrance to the vagina." However, q̓əmx̌əx̌sti can also mean "herring talking," and in clause 20 the herring really do talk, sss . . . xałai, "saying 'sss.'" In other words, clauses 19–20 can be read as: "The herring talked. 'Ssss,' said the herring."

In addition to all this, the narrator also is making at least one sound-play with q̓əmx̌əx̌sti. The sound-play rests on the similarity of q̓əmx̌əx̌sti to q̓əmx̌asdi, "dried herring"; we will return to this topic shortly.

Another possible sound-play is with the Kwakw'ala form meaning "herring on someone's behind," which would probably be written q̓əmx̌ʔəx̌sdiʔ. In fact, the suffixes -əx̌sta, "mouth, entrance" and -!x̌sd, "tail, behind, hind end" are at least formally related; the latter suffix occurs with the meaning of the former in a number of instances (Boas 1947:373, e.g. bə̃k'ə̃x̌sd, "man's voice"). Otherwise, there is little direct evidence for this pun, but the interpretation of q̓əmx̌əx̌sti as "herrings on one's behind" actually makes more sense, initially, than "herrings at the entrance to an inlet"; it draws the connection between the herring and Oolachan-Woman's "tail" in a more obvious and literal way.

The three clauses, 19–21, describe the moment of transformation. We have discussed clause 19; clause 20 is straightforward, a verb followed by a subject. The verb stem is sss . . . xa, "to say 'sss . . .'"; the subject is q̓áma, "herring" (or, correctly transcribed, q̓amax̌; see footnote 18 below).

In clause 21, the third-person pronominal subject, referring to the herring, is unmarked; and the verb, cíx̌ʔustis, is the same as we saw in Oolachan-Woman's speech in clause 13: "to flap like a stranded fish, while moving out of the water onto the beach." The last two words form what could without too much distortion be thought of as a prepositional phrase: láx̌i, "into, onto," and ʔawínag̈is, "country, beachside."

The three clauses can be translated as:

The herring at the entrance talked.   19
"Ssss," said those herring.   20
[Now] they were flapping all along the shoreline.   21

The narrator does not describe the transformation directly. Rather, he obliquely indicates the magical event through a contrast in locative coordinates. As the herring move between -əxsta, "at the entrance," clause 19, and -ʔustis, "moving out of the water onto the beach," clause 21, they are detaching themselves from Oolachan-Woman, multiplying magically.

It is possible to add on an additional layer of interpretation in this scene. This layer of interpretation rests on Boas's original gloss of the word q̓ə́mxəxsti. In his field notes, and again in publication, Boas translates this word as "dried herring." Q̓əmxəxsti means "herring at the entrance"; it does not and cannot mean "dried herring." However, since the gloss appears in Boas's field notes, we assume that his narrator is the source. What does all this mean?

The most likely Kwakw'ala rendering of "dried herring" would be q̓ə́mxasdi, q̓əmx- "herring" plus a suffix -asdi, "dried meat of something." Q̓əmxəxsti, "herring at the entrance," and q̓ə́mxasdi, "dried herring," sound somewhat similar. I believe Boas transcribed the first, and was then given the gloss for the second. Perhaps the narrator even slurred the sounds together, as punsters often do.

Boas could not figure it out. Later in life, he decided his transcription was in error, that he must really have heard q̓əmxasdi. When entering data for this particular text into his dictionary, he put down q̓ə́mxasdi for q̓əmxəxsti (Boas n.d.: 349).[18]

We, however, now know that our narrator is fond of word-play, and that it is perfectly probable that *both* interpretations were intended. With the latter interpretation— the "dried herring" option—the passage would be translated as:

The dried herring talked.   19
"Ssss," said those herring.   20
[Now] they were flapping all along the shoreline.   21

It is in this version that Oolachan-Woman's urination becomes meaningful. Urine in Kwagul stories has magical properties; it is the "water of life" (Furst 1989). Generally, the water of life is used to resuscitate the dead and to cure the mortally wounded; in many, but not all cases, it is the property of a woman. In one Kwagul story, a chief uses his water of life to resuscitate a salmon-twin-woman, in order that his tribe should have abundance of food (Boas and Hunt 1905:211–330). Sometimes seawater can be substituted for urine: in the same story, the dried salmon obtained by the chief are insulted, and jump down into the ocean, where they become live fish again and swim away. In another story, a woman rescues her husband and his tribe, who have been caught and eaten in the form of salmon, by placing their remains in the ocean; they become live fish and swim away (Boas and Hunt 1905:390–92). In everyday life outside of myth, this was the customary means of disposing of fish remains, guaranteeing as it does that the fish-people will be able to reincarnate in fish form and return to the rivers and streams year after year.

In "Q̓ániqiíax̌ʷ and Ćáću," the "dried herring" are immersed in both urine and seawater to bring them to life. On one level of meaning, it is this immersion which transforms dead herring into live jumping herring. The implication that herring are Oolachan-Woman's labia suggests yet another level of interpretation: it is not so much dried, dead herring as *dry* herring, and what transforms dry herring into wet, slippery, and flapping herring is the moisture of sexual arousal; another kind of water of life.

Along these lines, it is possible, too, that the narrator intended an aural as well as a visual and tactile analogy between herring and female genitalia. I am told that the *sound* of herring flapping on the beach closely resembles the sound of intercourse (D. Berman, personal communication).

Bearing all this in mind we can see why Fog-Woman needed a net of pubic hair to recontain the herring (clauses 22–26). This coda to the story, along with the other myths to which this story is related, points to a moral about woman's sexuality and productivity; but more of this later. There is one last point about the translation of this text to be raised, and that is the translation of names.

The three men named, Ćáću, Q̓ániqiíax̌ʷ, and ʔúm̓ał, have names which are difficult to translate. Q̓ániqiíax̌ʷ and ʔúm̓ał are characters found in a number of other myths. Boas translates Q̓ániqiíax̌ʷ's name as "Born to soar," from q̓ani-, "to soar" (Boas n.d.: 358). Lincoln and Rath derive the name from an untranslatable stem q̓ax- (1980:371).

Ćáću is a character who appears in only one other myth, in which he is identified as a bird skilled at spearing (Boas 1895:332–33). Ćáću may be the onomatopoeic name of the bird species, or it may be the character's own name. In the latter case it is probably identical with ćáću, "gut harpoon line" (Boas n.d.: 206, 218).

Boas translates ʔúm̓ał as "Chief-of-the-ancients" (1905:322 passim), probably deriving it from a stem ʔúm̓-, "great, chiefly, high" and an undetermined suffix.

Boas's gloss of ʔə́lxsoʔayuǧa as "Fog-Woman" is incorrect. ʔə́lxsoʔayuǧa can be analyzed as:

ʔəl-	"secure, fast, tight, firm; to bury"
-xso	"[pass] through; through a hole or enclosed space"
-yuǧa	"woman"

In a later volume Boas glosses ʔə́lxsoʔayuǧa as "Revenging-Woman" (Boas and Hunt 1906:170), presumably deriving it from the sense in which ʔəl- means "to bury." I would suggest, however, a better reading might be "Something stuck inside a hole" and that the name refers to an unorthodox ploy ʔə́lxsoʔayuǧa uses to hide her lover when they are surprised by her husband *in flagrante*. Note that in "Q̓ániqiíax̌ʷ and Ćáću," it is *herring* which would be stuck in—or at least near—the hole in question.

The most interesting of the names is Zázax̌itəlaga, which Boas translates as "Oolachan-Woman." The full meaning of this name is actually more subtle and complex:

zazax̌ʷ-   "oolachan (distributive plural)"
-[g]it   "all over surface of body of person"
-əla   "multiplicity of parts"
-g̣a   "woman"

Oolachan-Woman is the "Woman whose body has oolachan all over its surface."

Analysis of this name suggests that our earlier assumption of a metaphoric identity of herring and oolachan is correct. Not only are Oolachan-Woman's genitalia made of herring/oolachan, her whole body-surface is. Somehow Q̣ániqiłax̌ʷ doesn't realize this, doesn't fully guess her powers.

"Q̣ániqiłax̌ʷ and Ćáću": Reprise

[Version 3]

A.	1.	"Hey,"	1
		said Harpoon-Line,	2
		"let's have some fun,"	3
		that's what Harpoon-Line said to Oolachan-Woman.	4
	2.	Harpoon-Line gave his robe to Oolachan-Woman.	5
		She quickly stuck herself onto her prize.	6
B.	1.	Q̣ániqiłax̌ʷ said,	7
		"Stop your fooling around on the beach,"	8
		that's what Q̣ániqiłax̌ʷ said.	9
	2.	Oolachan-Woman began to speak;	10
		"Don't say such a thing to me, sir,"	11
		that's what Oolachan-Woman said.	12
		"Say 'These herring at the entrance are flapping on the beach,' sir."	13
		He sang,	14
		" 'Flapping in the water, flapping in the water,	15
		herring at the entrance, herring at the entrance,'	16
		say to me, sir,"	17
C.	1.	She squatted down in the seawater.	18
	2.	The dry herring at the entrance talked;	19
		"Sss . . ." said those herring.	20
		Now they were flapping all along the shoreline.	21
		They were taken by the villagers.	22
D.	1.	The wife of ʔúṁał, Stuck-inside-Woman,	23
		had a hard time scooping up those herring.	24
D.	2.	She took her pubic hair	25
		and knotted a net.	26
		to take the herring.	27

Despite Boas's poor translation of it, "Q̓ániqiⱡaẇ and Ćáću" is a coherent, well-formed story. The story opens on Oolachan-Woman and her lover "playing." The lover disrobes, and offers a "prize" to Oolachan-Woman. Then Q̓ániqiⱡaẇ discovers what his adoptive kinswoman has been up to. "Stay at home!" he orders. "Stay off the beach, away from the waters' edge! Don't fornicate! Don't act like what you are, a divine being who is constantly on the move!" He wants this fish-being to keep away from the water, perhaps to act like a human.

But Oolachan-Woman is of no mind to obey. She wants sex and she wants the ocean—she is an oolachan woman, after all. She knows that Q̓ániqiⱡaẇ's commands have considerable force in the world, and that even she is bound by what he says. She also knows, however, that being human, Q̓ániqiⱡaẇ might not really know the myth-people, might not know their nature or powers. Perhaps he can't see that her skin is covered with numerous small, silvery fish. "Oh, no, lord," she says, deceptively humble. "I think you could come up with a better Transformation than that. Try this one instead, lord: 'Herring are flapping on the beach, these herring here are flapping at the entrance.' Say that to me, lord."

This sounds good to Q̓ániqiⱡaẇ. Perhaps he sees an image of fish helplessly stranded on land—precisely the fate he is trying to impose on Oolachan-Woman. However, he gets the words somewhat muddled, repeating more of Oolachan-Woman's speech than is necessary. "Flapping in the water, flapping in the water," he sings. "Over there, over there. Herring at the entrance, herring at the entrance. Say that to me, lord."

Though it is not precisely what she had in mind, Oolachan-Woman accepts this song. She walks down to the water's edge (surely to Q̓ániqiⱡaẇ's dismay?), and squats down until her vulva is in the water. She urinates—"sss. . . ." Water of life renews the herring. The ocean restores her divine nature, perhaps arouses her sexually. The fish on her skin slip off into the water, multiplying fantastically. All around her in the shallows, little silvery fish are jumping, smacking, wriggling, flapping.

Does the village come running to look? What an incredible abundance of food! But difficult to catch; these fish show little affinity for ordinary nets. Then Stuck-inside-Woman, thinking, perhaps, about where the herring came from, has an idea: in order to recapture them, one needs the substance which kept them confined in the first place. So she makes a special net and with it manages to catch the herring.

And there the narrator ends his story.

"Q̓ániqiⱡaẇ and Ćáću": Background

Though Boas's Kwakw'ala texts were offered as an insight into the Kwagul experience of the world, no single one, by itself, tells us a great deal. Nor is Boas much help: he rarely offered interpretation or commentary beyond the bare translation. It is often a frustrating task trying to relate the texts to anything else he said about the nineteenth-century

Kwagul. Fortunately, he did publish enough material, and enough in Kwakw'ala, that it is possible to say more about the texts than he did.

"Q̓ániqiḷax̌ and Ćáću" belongs to the Kwagul ethnoliterary category called *nuyəm* "myth, tradition, history." The main criterion for membership in this category is that the events of the story take place before the end of the so-called myth age (cf. Boas and Hunt 1905:111). The category is extremely diverse, and includes several subdivisions which had different functions in social life.

One of these subdivisions was sometimes called *nuyəmił*, literally "tradition in the house" (Boas 1947:250). House-stories describe how a descent-group ancestor acquired certain names, crests, and other important privileges in the myth age. House-stories are owned by the descent group (or by the chiefly lines within the descent group) in the same way that chiefly names and crests are. One type of house-story features an adolescent hero who journeys across the sea or into the mountains to encounter a supernatural being. This being for one reason or another eventually yields the hero the treasure he seeks. Another common type has a supernatural hero who descends to earth, takes off his spirit mask and sends it back to the sky-world, and then settles down to live as a human being.

A second major subdivision of *nuyəm* are the animal stories (I do not know if this subgenre is named). In these the actors are the *nŭx̌nimis*, or "story-people," animal-beings who possess odd powers and abilities, such as the buffoonish Mink X̌isəlagiḷa, son of the Sun, and the much sought-after Merganser-Woman. The story-people linger on the threshold between human and animal form, and live in beachside villages more or less like humans. The narratives about them do not name crests or descent groups or often even tribal names, though many refer to particular village sites. If they have an etiological theme it generally refers to something which affects a wide range of people: wind, weather, currents, tides, fish, and so on.

These two subdivisions stand in opposition to each other. House-stories explain the public symbols of rank, wealth, and privilege, while the audience of animal stories is usually informal and domestic. Both have an etiological component, but these components refer to opposing processes in cosmogony. Speaking very generally, the etiologies in the animal stories describe *change*. The outcomes of these stories—the barrenness of mountain summits, the cyclicity of the tides—are states of existence which did *not* exist at the beginning of time, but were brought about by the narrated events. In contrast, the etiologies in the house-stories describe *continuity*. The importance of the chiefly crests and privileges acquired in the stories is that they *did* exist at the beginning of time, and have been handed down to the present unchanged. At most they were merely transferred from spirit to human ancestor. That is probably the reason house-stories are sometimes also called *nuyəmbalis*, "stories from the (beginning-)end of the world" (Boas 1921:1351–52).

A third subdivision are the stories about Q̓ániqiḷax̌. Q̓ániqiḷax̌ is the Transformer (not a Kwakw'ala term) whose actions in sum bring an end to the myth age. Q̓ániqiḷax̌ journeys from village to village, encountering all kinds of characters on his way, including the animal-people and descent-group ancestors.

"Q̓ā́niqiꞏlax̌ʷ and Ćáću" is a Q̓ā́niqiꞏlax̌ʷ story in which the central dramatic conflict lies between Q̓ā́niqiꞏlax̌ʷ and one of the animal-people, viz., Oolachan-Woman. In the text, the conflict between them is expressed in sexual terms, as a conflict between her desire for sexual freedom and his outraged morals. However, there is a larger context in which this action takes place. Q̓ā́niqiꞏlax̌ʷ and Oolachan-Woman have opposite natures, belong to opposite camps. The animal-people belong to an age when the most bizarre permutations of form are possible, when the sun is kept in a box, when a mink's musk-bag can talk, when a fart can cause a gale. Q̓ā́niqiꞏlax̌ʷ was adopted and raised by animal-people, but he is explicitly human and secular (bax̌əs). His purpose in life is to bring an end to these permutations, to "set everything right in the world" (hixhəlisəla), to create a world of order and plenty where humans can safely dwell. It is no coincidence that the words for "human," "secular," and "male," derive from closely related roots (bək̓-, bax̌-). Q̓ā́niqiꞏlax̌ʷ exemplifies these qualities.

Q̓ā́niqiꞏlax̌ʷ makes war on the animal-people, and tangles with the powerful nonsecular ancestors, but he never succeeds in completely ending the myth age. What he seems to accomplish is a zone of order at the center of the world. Outside this zone, the myth age still persists in the scattered, hidden villages of the animal-people in the forest or under the sea. Generally, though, Q̓ā́niqiꞏlax̌ʷ gets the best of the animal-people he encounters. Oolachan-Woman is a rare case, an animal-person who bests Q̓ā́niqiꞏlax̌ʷ. It is important to note, however, that the outcome of their conflict is in accord with one of Q̓ā́niqiꞏlax̌ʷ's overall goals, which is to create an abundance of food for humans.

The *nuyəm* genre as a whole is most variable where the names, form, and other attributes of characters are concerned. For example, there is no "sea god" whose attributes are consistent over a wide range of stories, but instead a whole range of different supernaturals in some way associated with the sea, whose attributes overlap from story to story. Q̓ā́niqiꞏlax̌ʷ is only a partial exception to this. He is acknowledged to be the same personage in the various versions of his life. Certain attributes, for instance his humanness, are consistent from story to story. Others vary widely. For instance, Oolachan-Woman is Q̓ā́niqiꞏlax̌ʷ's (adoptive) mother in one Ṅaqəmgilisəla story but, in a story from the nearby Yux̌inux̌, his paternal grandmother (Boas 1895:319; Boas and Hunt 1906:188).

Plots and thematic material, on the other hand, tend to repeat from *nuyəm* to *nuyəm*. There are two stories in the Boas corpus which are thematically very similar to "Q̓ā́niqiꞏlax̌ʷ and Ćáću." We have already mentioned the other Ṅaqəmgilisəla story featuring Q̓ā́niqiꞏlax̌ʷ and Oolachan-Woman. To repeat, in this story, Oolachan-Woman is Q̓ā́niqiꞏlax̌ʷ's mother, and keeps all the world's fish in her robe. Q̓ā́niqiꞏlax̌ʷ wants to see the waters alive with fish, so he borrows his mother's robe, and dips the corner of it in the water. Fish appear in the water and soon populate the rivers and ocean.

The second story is from the Nak̓axda²x̌ʷ village. This story is longer and more-complex. The hero is ²úmiɬ, a chief who is troubled because there is neither river nor fish where his tribe lives (Boas and Hunt 1905:322–30). He creates the river, and then plans to marry a twin, that is, a changeling (x̌ax̌ayaćaýa), a salmon-person who has incarnated in human form. He searches until he finds one among the dead. He sprinkles her with his water of life and she comes alive. Her name is Mέisila ("fish-maker," from mε-, "fish, especially salmon"). She is beautiful, and ʔúm̓iɬ's brothers warn each other not to think about committing adultery with her. She nevertheless favors the brothers over her husband. She refuses to make salmon for ʔúm̓iɬ, but will produce them to feed his brothers when he is away. She creates salmon by putting her little finger in her mouth and then into a kettle of water. In the end, ʔúm̓iɬ discovers her deception and he compels Fish-maker to fill the river with salmon. She creates salmon in the river by walking into the water; if she were to immerse herself entirely, she warns ʔúm̓iɬ, the river would dry up with such a huge mass of salmon. So ʔúm̓iɬ gets what he wanted. But his marital difficulties are not over. He grows proud from his new wealth, insults a salmon-bone, and then speaks angrily to his wife. She calls "her tribe, the dried salmon"; they all return into the sea (though salmon eventually come back again to ʔúm̓iɬ's river).

There are several elements which "Q̓ániqiɬax̌ and Ćáću" shares with these two stories. In all three stories we find a woman with supernatural powers who possesses fishy abundance. She is either wife or kinswoman of the male hero. In two of the stories, there is either a suggestion or fact of extracurricular sexual activity by this woman, which leads to friction with the hero. In all of them, the fish are released by dipping part of her body or clothing into the water.

Let us examine this last element more closely. In "Q̓ániqiɬax̌ and Ćáću" Oolachan-Woman dips (dried) herring, that is, her labia, into saltwater. The herring are resuscitated by ocean water and the water of life, multiply magically, and populate the ocean. In the related version from Ṅaqəmgilisəla, Q̓ániqiɬax̌ dips Oolachan-Woman's *robe* into the water to achieve a similar result. Now, Oolachan-Woman's full name, Záxax̌itəlaga, means "many oolachan all over the surface of her body." The name allows some ambiguity as to whether the fish on her body are attached to her skin, as they appear to be in "Q̓ániqiɬax̌ and Ćáću," or merely covering her skin, as they would be if she wore her robe full of fish in the related story.

That these two conditions are essentially the same is, I believe, is an important insight into the notion of human and animal physiology which underlies all transformations in the *nuyəm*. This notion comes into focus when we turn our gaze from Boas's English translations to the Kwakw'ala of the original.

Kwakw'ala has a poorly described shape-gender system which classifies all objects and beings into several shape-categories. The most important of these categories are long, round/bulky, flat, and hollow/dishlike. In some circumstances, such as counting, a shape-suffix is grammatically obligatory, but generally the system is used more in derivation than in grammar. For example:

1. *uǧextoiʔ*, "headwaters of river," from *u-*, "empty root," *-[g]ɛq*, "side of hollow object, riverbank," *-xto*, "end of vertical long object."
2. *ƛ̓anxstənd*, "to poke branch or pole in water," from *ƛ̓ax-*, "long object is somewhere," *-sta*, "in the water," *-nd*, "inchoative."
3. *hənizas*, "where canoe is on beach," from *hən-*, "hollow object/vessel is somewhere," *-is*, "on beach," *-as*, "place of something."
4. *həm̓azu*, "food mat" from *ham̓-*, "to eat," and *-zu*, "flat object."

Not only are there suffixes and stems which express the basic meaning of the shape category (long, flat, hollow, etc.), but there are also many suffixes and stems which express more specific ideas about shape. For instance, "to carry" is a different stem depending on whether one is carrying a long object (e.g. a pole) or a round, bulky object (e.g. a bundle). "End" can be either "end of horizontal object," or "end of standing object."

This topological specificity is quite idiomatic and is ubiquitous in Kwakw'ala. The suffix -[g]it used in Oolachan-Woman's name, which means "covering surface of person's body," is yet another example. By paying close attention to how these suffixes are used in Boas's texts it is possible to glean some hints as to how the narrators of the text conceived of human and animal physiology, and of the nature of transformation between the two.

Generally, humans are classified grammatically as long objects, animals as round, bulky objects. The basic classifying suffix for animals is -sgəm, "round object," as in, for instance, musgəmi miǧat, "four seals" (mu-, "four," -sgəm, "round object," -i, demonstrative suffix, miǧat, "seal").

Now, in the texts, animal-people generally appear in human form, and are described as such, standing on two feet (ƛax̌-) as opposed to four feet (gal-), and so on. Their animal nature—their animal flesh—is a costume which they can put on or take off as they please. This animal flesh-costume is usually called -[g]əmł, glossed by Boas as "mask" (e.g. miǧatəmł, "seal mask," from miǧat, "seal").

We might think of a *mask* as portraying only the *head* of the animal, and indeed, there is a strong relationship between these two concepts in Kwakw'ala; the suffix -[g]əmł, "mask," is almost certainly derived from the suffix -[g]əm, "face, head." However, in Kwakw'ala, an animal flesh-costume is apparently conceptualized as including both head and body. The body of the flesh-costume is a removable robe or covering, in one text pasʔəni, "fur blanket" (Boas and Hunt 1905:33).[19] Interestingly, terms for many of the different sorts of robes or blankets are derived using the suffix -sgəm, "round object"; as for example ʔəlagəmsgəm, "robe of dressed deerskin" (from ʔəlagəm, "dressed deerskin"). In other words, the head (-gəm) plus the robe (-sgəm) together make the mask (-gəmł) of the animal (-sgəm). These suffixes are linguistically as well as conceptually related.

There is a closely related fourth suffix, -gəmiʔ, "in front of, first of its kind."[20] This form would seem to derive from a close conceptual relationship between the head (-gəm), being first or in front of, and the animals (-sgəm), who are first in time, as well as first in a synchronic moral hierarchy. Note the probably similar relationship between the stems gəl-, "first, to come first, to lead, the ancestors," and gal-, "to crawl on all fours, animal."

The flesh-costume of an animal, its mask/robe, is like clothing. Animals dress— q̓ux̌ćud, literally "[go] inside clothing"—in their masks and then undress—q̓ux̌əlćud, literally "[go] out from inside clothing" (e.g., Boas and Hunt 1905:165–66; these terms use the suffix -ćo, "inside hollow object").

This is why Oolachan-Woman's robe, which is full of fish, and her skin, which is covered with fish, are essentially the same. She is a supernatural being who can remove her animal shape, which then becomes a robe.

The mask is a covering, but to human eyes, the mask appears as the flesh and bone of the animal. *The mask is both the thing which transforms and the end result of the transformation.* Only the core, the bones, intestines, blood, fins, etc., of an animal are substance separate from the mask (cf. Boas and Hunt 1905:304–5.) Since the mask is the food that humans depend on for their sustenance, from the human perspective, the mask is the valued element of the transformation. It is the mask which, in traditional Kwagul culture, signifies wealth. But the important thing about the mask is that it is in a sense disposable. The animal is not destroyed by human consumption. After its mask has been eaten and it has been reduced to bones and offal, after it becomes a "ghost," it can be reincarnated.[21]

Consider the fate of Méisila, the Fish-maker. She begins as a salmon, incarnates among humans as a twin, and then dies. As a human, she is buried. ʔúm̓iɫ revives her by sprinkling his water of life on her bones. She calls her tribe, the salmon, and they are taken and dried by ʔúm̓iɫ's people. Later, ʔúm̓iɫ mistreats a salmon bone. Insulted, the dried salmon-tribe returns into the water, resuscitating, and swims away.

This particular text depicts the problems both of the *origin* and the *maintenance* of abundance. Like Q̓ániqiła in the second Ṅaqəmgilisəla story, ʔúm̓iɫ wishes to introduce fish in the waters. He must first seek out one of the animal-people—specifically a fish-woman—who has the power to make the fish, since he himself does not. Fish-maker's power in and of itself is of no benefit to him. It is his marriage with her, which establishes a relationship between his tribe and the salmon-people, that creates plenty.

During the myth age the animal-people are generally inaccessible to humans, unavailable as game. Even Q̓ániqiła, raised among the animal-people, is denied food by his adoptive parents (Boas and Hunt 1906:185–92; Boas 1910:187–90). In the new dispensation brought by Q̓ániqiła—in the secular age—the animal-people have become something that humans, as long as they remain within the narrow zone of order, can hunt, kill, and eat. But the animals still have the power to refuse to visit that zone of order. This is the problem of *maintenance*. Humans must treat the essential remains—bones and offal—correctly. Otherwise the animals will not be able to resuscitate, and come back to feed humans again.

The proper way to dispose of fish bones is in seawater. Once the bones are immersed, the fish-people come to life again. Compare the following passage with Oolachan-Woman's actions in "Q̓ániqiła and Ćáću":

Then she gathered the backbones, fins and the blood of all the salmon and put them into an old mat. She carried the mat out of the house. She walked to the beach. Thunderer went out and called to her. He said, "Oh, mistress! Don't take it to the beach; just throw it down the embankment," thus he said. But Thrush-Woman just walked to the beach. She said [to Thunderer], "This is the way of our tribe." . . . Then she waded into the sea. When her knees were covered with water, the pretty woman poured the contents of the old mat into the water. As soon as the bones, intestines, and blood went into the water, the little silver-salmon came to life again; and all the salmon came to life. All the salmon jumped in the [shallow] water on the beach. And then Thrush-Woman disappeared, because she was taken away by [the salmon] (Boas and Hunt 1905:307; cf. 390–92).

Animal-flesh masks are not so much disposable as they are transitory representations of a durable transformative idea. Each animal-shape that is consumed by humans is but one iteration, one exemplification of this idea, which remains in the possession of the animal. Such a mask-idea is not a Platonic ideal, because the idea has a physical, perceptible existence—it is the ur-mask, if you will. It exists as part of the "supernatural" power of the animal, though of course it is not outside of nature; it is the essence of nature.

That is how fish-women such as Oolachan-Woman and Fish-Maker create great plenty by simply immersing their body parts. Oolachan-Woman's robe, her skin, *is* fish: it is the notion of fish, the form of fish. When placed in water, this ur-form generates thousands of representations, fish-masks which at the same time are part of the robe itself, but different, transitory, expendable.

One curious point about Oolachan-Woman is that her robe does not take the form of a single fish, but rather a multiplicity of fish. Texts dealing with other kinds of animals suggest that *their* masks are in the form of a single creature. For instance, a grizzly-person takes off his mask and robe, the shape of a single grizzly bear (Boas and Hunt 1905:33). Fish, on the other hand, except for halibut, seem to come most typically in numbers. This may supply the reasoning behind why twins are thought to be salmon-people: when humans arrive in the world in multiples, they are like fish.

Among the animal-people, predators and game animals are usually depicted as male, while many birds, especially ducks and geese, are depicted as female. Occasionally, fish-people appear as male characters (e.g. Boas and Hunt 1905:302–3), but in general, fish are linked to female sexuality, and the ur-mask which creates fishy abundance is a feminine prerogative. There is apparently a feeling of sensory similarity between fish and female genitalia. The analogy is suggested in a variety of texts. One of Mink's misadventures involves a village of women who keep their genitalia in a box (Boas and Hunt 1906:124–27). Mink gets into the box, soils Merganser-Woman's vulva, then hastily washes it to prevent discovery. Unfortunately, while it is laid out to dry, an eagle mistakes it for a fish and carries it off.

Another thread in the symbolic linkage may derive from the role of women as food-preparers and providers. If women are food-providers, and food *par excellence* is fish, then, perhaps, women are like fish. Then, too, it may derive from the role of women as disposers of fish offal. In the story about Thrush-Woman, she places the fish offal in the ocean, making it possible for the salmon to come back to life. In everyday life this was commonly a female task.

The woman watches to make sure all the guests throw on the mat all the bones [and refuse] left after eating. . . . After they have finished eating . . . and gone home . . . the woman scrapes off . . . the rest of her guests' food, and puts it on the mat. . . . and she carries it down to the beach and shakes it out in the saltwater (Boas 1921:246).

It is likely that the image of a woman wading into the water to provide for the resuscitation of the fish was a strong one.

Yet another thread no doubt derives from the reproductive role of women—from the fact that it is women who give birth. The life-cycle of anadromous fish such as salmon and oolachan suggests more clearly than that of any other animal the notion of reincarnation and cyclicity: they run, die, and then return. Similarly, each generation of humans is (re)-born through the wombs of women.[22] But, again, the theory of reproductive physiology expressed in these texts is very different from that of Western culture. A womb is a container, literally *boči,* "box or bag for fetus." It is not the woman's womb which creates wealth and plenty; wealth may be *stored in* and *brought forth from* containers, but it is *generated by* and *constituted in* coverings.

There are a number of texts in which male humans with supernatural power, such as Q̓ániqiḷax̌, create an abundance of fish. These men, though, create fish by placing rotten wood or wooden carvings in the water (e.g. Boas and Hunt 1905:94–99, 390–92). Humans, even those with supernatural power, must "imitate," manifest some of the original ur-fishiness by making the closest possible exemplification of it.

Kwakw'ala terms which express this effort are *nanax̌co* and *hayigiʔ,* both usually glossed by Boas as "imitate." *Nanax̌co* derives from the stem *nanaq-,* "to coincide or be correct in all parts," and the suffix *-čo,* "inside, inside hollow object"; it could be glossed "to do in the right way in all parts, to be entirely correct in all parts inside." *Hayigiʔ* derives from the root *hi-, ya-,* "to be the case, to exist, to live, to go," and a suffix *-igiʔ, -iga, -ika,* "back, in back of, afterwards, to follow behind"; it could be glossed "to follow, to use someone else's existence as a model."

It is interesting that "to obey" and "to reply" are formed from the same elements as these two words for "imitate." *Nanax̌mi,* "to reply," is *nanaq-,* "to coincide or be correct in all parts" and the discourse suffix *-m̓,* which signifies that the action of the stem to which it is attached is not separate or discrete from a previous action. A reply coincides with or is correct after the question, it is an inseparable part of the question. *Nanagiga,* "to obey," is *nanaq-,* "to coincide or be correct in all parts," and the suffix *-igiʔ, -iga, -ika,* "back, in back of, following," which occurs in *hayigiʔ,* "to imitate."

It is instructive to compare forms which use this suffix:

nanaq-	"to be correct in all parts, to coincide or meet in all parts, to do straightaway"
	nanagiga "to obey"
hay-	"to be, to exist, to go"
	hayigiʔ "to imitate"
duǧ-	"to look"
	duǧigiʔ "to look back and imitate deeds of one's ancestors: to watch what others are doing"
x̌iǧ-	"to err, to miss, do wrong, disagree"
	x̌ilǧika "to miss one's way, to not take after parents"
	x̌aliǧigiʔ "to disobey, to refuse"

The suffix *-igiʔ,* "in back of, following," has more than a purely locative meaning. The notion of "following" contains, or gives rise to, a political and moral meaning. "To obey" is "to follow correctly"; "to disobey" is "to fail to follow." In all these forms with *-igiʔ,* the action taken is not original or authoritative, it depends upon a prior state of being or doing in another—in one's ancestors, parents, rulers. First (*gǝla*) came the animal-people (*gal-*) and the ancestors (*gəlzəs*), who lead (*gəlaba*). The chief (*gigami?*) is the one in front (*-gəmi?*) with the mask (*-gəmɫ*), imitating them (*nanax̌co, hayigi?*). Commoners watch *duᵂgigi?*) and obey (*nanagiga*).

In house-stories, the more public, prestige-oriented myths, the primary thematic concern is with acquiring "imitations" of the transformative power of the spirits. The "imitations" acquired by the ancestors—masks, dances, crests designs, names, and so on—are known as *k̓ík̓əs?u* (sing. *k̓is?u*), which Boas glossed as "crests" or "privileges." In the secular age, privileges are associated with a body of ranked positions, somewhat like an aristocracy, called the "seats" (*k̓ᵂa-*) of a descent group. Each incumbent of a seat uses the set of privileges belonging to that seat. Privileges link the present with the myth age, and are both the index and the producer of wealth among humans.

The body of seats is the essential part of the descent group (cf. Boas 1966:50). The welfare of the descent group depends upon these positions being perpetuated—or, perhaps better, reinvigorated—in each generation. In the words of a Kwagul noble:

I . . . told you people that we are going to be scattered . . . [but] here now is the grandson of our chief. He is young, while our chief was going on to old age; he is new, and he will grow up to be the same as his grandfather. I have taken back what I said; we will not scatter, for we have our new chief here who will take his grandfather's place (Ford 1941:165).

It is not that the chief himself is reincarnated in his heir. Rather, when an aging chief installs his vigorous younger heir into his seat, the heir *becomes* "the same as" the chief. Each succeeding heir is incarnated into the same *form,* in a line of such chiefly incarnations stretching back to the myth age.

This cycle of social transformation is analogous to the transformative cycle of the animals. Just as the individual chief is the latest transitory and cyclic version of the durable ancestral form, the salmon running in the rivers is a transitory and cyclic version of the immortal's mask. Similarly, the so-called "potlatches" held during a chief's installation—which included large-scale prestations of fur or textile blankets (coverings)—are analogous to the gift of masks salmon-people make when they die and are reborn.[23]

There is a term which encompasses both social and spirit transformation: *ƛayu* (also *ƛaya*). *ƛaya* means "to change to, to exchange":

?awaw̓a . . . aɫmai lai *ƛayuᵂx̌ƛɛ Gigəlgəm* . . . "the [descent group called] ?awaw̓a . . . just recently exchanged this name (*ƛayu-xƛɛ*) for [the name] Gigələm" (Boas 1935–43:189).

ƛayu also means "to transform," as in the word which Boas glosses as "Salmon twin," *ƛaƛayćí*. Literally, *ƛaƛayaćí* is *ƛaƛaya-,* "to change, transform (distributive plural?)," and *-aćí,* "hollow object, receptacle for some object or activity." The twin is a "receptacle for transformation," the physical receptacle in which the transformation was accomplished—the salmon-person now in human flesh.

From a Western point of view, social continuity is accomplished in part through sexual reproduction. However, in Boas's texts, these two themes seem to be disjunct, even opposed. Sexual imagery is present in many of the animal stories but is rare in Kwagul house-stories. In part this may be because animal stories deal with change, house-stories with continuity. Copulation creates a new, different being, but the rituals of chiefly succession work to clothe this new being in the original ancestral shape.

When present, though, copulatory imagery, like the imagery of social continuity, often "follows after" the model of animal transformation. Recall from "Q̓ániqiłax̌ and Ćáću" that the term for "robe," ǩata?ał, is a homomorph of ǩata?ał, "to stick on quickly in sexual intercourse." They share the root ǩat-, "to stick to, to stick on." Another word for "to copulate," ńax̌ala, is derived either from ńax̌-, "near to, next to," or from ńax̌-, ńax̌-, "to cover" (or both: the stems may be related).

Wɛ, laamławis ńix qaś ńax̌alax?idi . . . wax?amłaxaawusu q̓amsi ?álxsoyuǧa . . . "Well, then he said he would cover/get close to [copulate with] her. . . . ?álxsoyuǧa tried to demur once more . . ." (Boas and Hunt 1906:172).

These tropes suggest a pattern of thought in which copulation is conceived as a "covering" rather than, as Western observers might expect, a "penetrating" action: the "covering" of a woman by a man, or, as we saw in "Q̓ániqiłax̌ and Ćáću," of a man by a woman.

Conclusion

In this essay I have re-examined a short Kwakw'ala-language myth text, "Q̓ániqiłax̌ and Ćáću," collected by Franz Boas in 1894 from a Kwagul man named Q̓umgiłas. The language of the text is not straightforward, and Boas's translation of it is seriously flawed. However, through careful analysis of the language, from the meaning of individual morphemes to the way in which words and sentences are used to construct the narrative action, it is possible to recover much of the story's meaning. Further, the language of other texts provides many clues to understanding the conceptual background of the story.

Lévi-Strauss once claimed that it was unnecessary to read mythology in the original language, or even to have good translation, because the underlying structure emerged no matter what. Not to beat a dead horse to death, as a professor once phrased it, but it just ain't so. "Q̓ániqiłax̌ and Ćáću" is to some extent is an extreme example, because the narrative hinges on word play, which in turn depends on culturally based concepts and analogies which will not exist for the translator's audience. But all literature depends largely upon language; even oral literature, which can be theater as much as pure narrative. Language, especially in literature but in daily life as well, is full of association and imagery: a robe is also a quick and eager coupling; "dried herring," to some minds, sounds like "herring at the entrance to an enclosure"; seals are round; the chief is the one in front; oolachan cover the surface of her body.

Lévi-Strauss to the contrary, the meaning of a myth lies within the narrator's use of language, not outside it. Boas knew this, which was why he left us eleven volumes of

Kwakw'ala texts. If Boas's translations to those texts are unreliable, I believe it is at least in part because he did not intend for them to be relied on. For Boas, the texts were in and of themselves the end products of ethnography, and the translations a necessary evil, an aid to those without fluency in Kwakw'ala. The translations were never intended to be the primary source they have become.

Though Boas did not write about it, he must have felt that translations were like the ethnographer's descriptions of which he was so wary, full of bias and distortion. Translators run certain inevitable risks, because translation inevitably alters the narrator's words, and so changes the story's meaning. Today we may feel that translation can be something more than a necessary evil. But we should not forget that the *real* story was told in the narrator's own words, in his or her own language. No matter how satisfying, the translation should never come to substitute in our minds for the original.

This essay has been critical of Boas, but it is also, more fundamentally, in praise of him. Boas's methods may have been faulty, and his results sometimes unreliable, but I believe his goals were sound. Too often ethnographers tell us what they think people are like, without telling us what people say themselves. Literature is one of the ways people talk about their experience. We may no longer agree that texts without significant commentary or annotation, like Boas's, are terribly useful. Still, long after Boas and George Hunt and the Kwagul they talked to are gone, we have some words that were said by someone, instead of a record only of what Boas thought those words might have meant.

Guide to Pronunciation

The characters used to write Kwakw'ala words denote sounds both familiar and unfamiliar to English-speakers. For the vowels, /i/ sounds as in American *beet,* /ɛ/ as in *bet,* /a/ as in *pot,* /ə/ as in *but,* /o/ as in *bought,* and /u/ as in *boot.*

The consonants are somewhat more complex. The diacritic /'/ and the character /ʔ/ represent glottalization (the catch in the throat at the beginning of vowels in *I ate eight eggs*); thus the difference between /m/ and /m̓/. The barred /ɬ/ is pronounced like Welsh *ll;* the lambda (/λ/) is affricated, somewhat like pronouncing a *d* and an *l* simultaneously (the barred lambda /ƛ/ is *tl*). /X/ represents a fricative sound similar to Russian *x* or German *ch* in *ich.* /K/, /k'/, /g/, and /x/ are always pronounced as if an /i/ or /y/ were following: /K̫aguɬ/ = *Kwagyuł.* The corresponding series, /q/, /q̓/, /g/, and /x̣/ are not so palatalized, but otherwise are pronounced similarly, from a position further back in the throat. /C/ is like English *ts* and /z/ like English *dz.*

Notes

1. My attention was first called to this text and to the existence of field notes and correspondence from the time of the collection of the text, by Ralph Maud, who has written his own paper on it (n.d.). Goldman's *The Mouth of Heaven* (1975) first suggested to me the importance of

the mask in traditional Kwagul thought. An earlier version of this paper, under the title "The origin of herring: reexamination of an 1894 Kwakw'ala text," was given at the XXIVth International Conference on Salish and Neighboring Languages, Steilacoom, Washington, August 16–19, 1989, and I am grateful for Jay Powell and Nile Thompson, especially, for comments and suggestions. All interpretations, however, are unless otherwise indicated my own.

2. There are difficulties with Boas's methodology, chief among them, perhaps, that the "Indian" who produced most of his texts, George Hunt, was not, strictly speaking, Kwagul (see Berman 1991 for further discussion of these issues).

3. Only two short articles have subjected Boas's translations to serious scrutiny, in this case his etymologies (Hilton and Rath 1982; Compton and Rath 1988).

4. See Berman (1991) for a more detailed discussion of this point.

5. The Oowekyala suffix -xsiu, "through," relates to Kwakw'ala -xso, "through," but not to Kwakw'ala -xsiu, "river's end."

6. The date could be October 5th.

7. The port of departure may have been Fort Rupert.

8. I am following the orthography used in Lincoln and Rath 1980. This substitutes ' for !, ʔ for ᶜ, c for ts, z for dz, ƛ for L, and so on. The only significant point of departure is in the usage of ə (Boas E), which is nonphonemic in Kwakw'ala. Whether because of transcription errors, expressive factors, or dialectal variation, the relationship of ə and a is often difficult to determine in Boas's texts. Also, as Boas leaves out word-initial and intervocalic occurrences of glottal stop (ʔ), the placement of these may be somewhat irregular.

9. The title does not occur in Boas's field notes. It is probably a later addition by Boas, or, perhaps, Hunt or Brotchie, with whom Boas would seem to have consulted in the revisions he made of this text before publication.

10. E.g., Wɛ, lákasⱡaxai dúx̌ax̌əlakasxi bəkəmála ƛuk̓ási ćədáxi ʔiáx̌əm̓alakasxis ʔiaʔáwəmi . . . lákasⱡaxai ʔámⱡəliskas m̓áqap̓aiskaci yáǧaʔi. "Well, [Q̓ániqiⱡax̌] discovered a man and woman wearing head-rings of red-cedar bark . . . they were playing (ʔámⱡəliskas), throwing toredo worms at each other [i.e. throwing supernatural power at each other]" (Boas and Hunt 1906: 210–11, cf. 195).

11. Gender is not marked in Kwakw'ala pronouns, and in any case the third-person subject pronoun is always unmarked.

12. There are some difficulties in morphology and grammar in the text which may be connected to the fact that the narrator spoke the Tl'astl'asiqwala dialect of Kwakw'ala, which is less well described in the literature than the Tsaxis (Fort Rupert) dialect. The forms do not always correspond to what one would expect in Tsaxis Kwakw'ala.

13. Boas in fact gives the gloss "old blanket, it sticks on easily" to the related form k̓ʷəduⱡ (Boas n.d.:304; 1947:334).

14. Another stem, ýaⱡ-, "to dig clams," would render a similar form, ýáⱡagəlis, "Don't go digging clams on the beach all the time!" (Lincoln and Rath 1980:268). This, too, would apply to the situation.

15. In Tsaxis Kwakw'ala this would be cəx̌ʷ-.

16. The two phrases may also differ syntactically. The case marker in Oolachen-Woman's speech is missing; we don't know whether the noun's case is subjective, objective, or oblique. The simplest analysis seems to be to treat the noun as a subject as it is in Q̓ániqiⱡax̌'s speech.

17. The final suffix on q̓əmxəxsti in this clause is the demonstrative -i, third person

visible/invisible, because the frame of reference is the world of the third-person narrative, rather than a story actor's (first person) frame of reference.

18. Boas realized later that he had not corrected all transcription errors in this text. For instance, the published version of the text follows his field notes in showing an apparent contrast between a stem $\acute{q}\partial mx$-, "dried herring," and a stem $\acute{q}am$-, "shoals of [live] herring." The latter occurs in the forms $\acute{q}\acute{a}ma$ and $\acute{q}\acute{a}max$ (with the front x) in clauses 20, 24, and 27. However, there is no occurrence of a stem $\acute{q}am$-, "shoals of [live] herring," anywhere outside this text, and $\acute{q}\partial mx$- always means "[live] herring" elsewhere. All the $\acute{q}\acute{a}ma$ and $\acute{q}\acute{a}max$ forms should actually be $\acute{q}\acute{a}max$ (with the back x with subposed diacritic), that is, deriving from $\acute{q}\partial mx$-. In his transcription, Boas lost or misheard the final x. Boas realized all this when entering the data from this text into his dictionary file, where all the references to this text are under $\acute{q}\partial mx$-.

19. Note the relationship between $p\partial s\acute{?}\partial ni$, "fur blanket," literally, "softened skin blanket" (derived from $p\partial s$- "to soften by soaking" and -$[k]!\partial n$ "skin, surface of body"), and $\acute{n}\acute{a}\overset{w}{x}\acute{?}\partial ni$, "blanket worn on body" (derived from $\acute{n}\acute{a}\overset{w}{x}$- "to cover" and -$[k]!\partial n$ "skin, surface of body)". In the first, the "surface of body" is the animal's the robe is *taken from;* in the second, it is the human's the robe is *worn against.*

20. E.g., $\acute{n}\acute{u}las\!f\partial g\partial mi\acute{?}$, "eldest one," $xamag\partial mi\acute{?}$, "head chief." There is also a fifth suffix, -$g\partial manu$, which is used only for "head·of animal."

21. This suggests a line of inquiry as to why the Kwakw'ala swearing recorded by George Hunt refers to death and bones, etc., instead of sex and body effluvia, as in English (Boas 1921: 793–94).

22. Kwagul children were often suspected of being the reincarnations of particular deceased relatives (Ford 1941:167).

23. They are alike, but not the same. The transactions of inanimate goods only "imitate" spirit transformations: feasting your neighbor on salmon is only an approximation of the salmon's own sacrifice to you.

References

Berman, Judith (1982). "Deictic Auxiliaries and Discourse Marking in Kwakw'ala Narrative." In *Working Papers for the XVIIth International Conference on Salish and Neighboring Languages,* Portland State University, Portland, Oregon, August 9–11.

—— (1983). "Three Discourse Elements in Boas' Kwakw'ala Texts," in *Working Papers for the XVIIIth International Conference on Salish and Neighboring Languages,* University of Washington, Seattle, Washington, August 10–12.

—— (1991). *The Seals' Sleeping Cave: The Interpretation of Boas' Kwakw'ala texts.* Ph.D. dissertation, Department of Anthropology, University of Pennsylvania, Philadelphia.

Boas, Franz (1895 [1975]). *Indian Legends of the North Pacific Coast of America.* Unpublished translation by Deitrich Bertz of *Indianische Sagen von der Nord-Pazifischen Küste Amerikas.* Victoria, B.C.: British Columbia Language Project.

—— (1897). *The Secret Societies and Social Organization of the Kwakiutl.* Report of the U.S. National Museum (Smithsonian Institution). Washington: Government Printing Office.

—— (1909). *The Kwakiutl of Vancouver Island.* The Jesup North Pacific Expedition, Memoir of the American Museum of Natural History, vol. V. New York: Stechert.

———— (1910). *Kwakiutl Tales*. Columbia University Contributions to Anthropology, vol. 2. New York: Columbia University Press.

———— (1921). *Ethnology of the Kwakiutl*. Bureau of American Ethnology Annual Report 35, parts I and II. Washington: Government Printing Office.

———— (1925). *Contributions to the Ethnology of the Kwakiutl*. Columbia University Contributions to Anthropology, vol. 3. New York: Columbia University Press.

———— (1930). *Religion of the Kwakiutl Indians*. Columbia University Contributions to Anthropology, vol. 10 (Part 1, Texts; Part 2, Translations). New York: Columbia University Press.

———— (1935–43). *Kwakiutl Tales, New Series*. Columbia University Contributions to Anthropology, vol. 26 (Part 1, Texts [1935]; Part 2, Translations [1943]). New York: Columbia University Press.

———— (1947). *Kwakiutl Grammar, with a Glossary of the Suffixes*. New York: AMS Press.

———— (1966). *Kwakiutl Ethnography*. Edited by Helene Codere. Chicago: University of Chicago Press.

———— (n.d.). *Kwakiutl Dictionary*. Edited by Helene Boas Yampolsky. Unpublished typescript in the Franz Boas Collection of American Indian Linguistics at the American Philosophical Society, Philadelphia.

Boas, Franz, and George Hunt (1905). *Kwakiutl Texts*. The Jesup North Pacific Expedition, Memoir of the American Museum of Natural History, vol. III. New York: Stechert.

———— (1906). *Kwakiutl Texts, Second Series*. The Jesup North Pacific Expedition, Memoir of the American Museum of Natural History, vol. X. New York: Stechert.

Codere, Helene (1966). "Introduction" to Franz Boas, *Kwakiutl Ethnography*, edited by Helene Codere. Chicago: University of Chicago Press.

Compton, Brian, and John Rath (1988). "The translation of the name 'Kwakiutl,'" in *Working Papers for the XXIIIth International Conference on Salish and Neighboring Languages*, University of Oregon, Eugene, Oregon, August 11–13.

Davis, Philip W., and Ross Saunders (1980). *Bella Coola Texts*. British Columbia Provincial Museum Heritage Record #10. Victoria: British Columbia Provincial Museum.

Dundes, Alan (1979). "Heads or Tails? A Psychoanalytic Look at Potlatch," *Journal of Psychological Anthropology* 2:395–424.

Encyclopedia Americana (1986). "Candlefish" and "Herring." International Edition. Danbury, Conn.: Grolier.

Ford, Clellan (1941). *Smoke From Their Fires: The Life of a Kwakiutl Chief*. New Haven: Yale University Press.

Furst, Peter (1989). "The Water of Life: Symbolism and Natural History on the Northwest Coast," *Dialectical Anthropology* 14:95–116.

Goldman, Irving (1975). *The Mouth of Heaven: An Introduction to Kwakiutl Religious Thought*. New York: John Wiley.

Hilton, Suzanne, and John Rath (1982). "Objections to Franz Boas's Referring to Eating People in the Translation of the Kwakw'ala Terms *baxubakwelanuxusiwe* and *hamats!a*," in *Working Papers for the XVIIth International Conference on Salish and Neighboring Languages*, August 9–11, Portland State University, Portland, Oregon.

Hymes, Dell (1981). *"In Vain I Tried to Tell You": Essays in Native American Ethnopoetics*. Philadelphia: University of Pennsylvania Press.

Lévi-Strauss, Claude (1963). "The Structural Study of Myth," in Lévi-Strauss, *Structural Anthropology*, 206–231. New York: Basic Books.

Lincoln, Neville, and John Rath (1980). *North Wakashan Comparative Root List*. National Museum of Man, Mercury Series, Canadian Ethnology Service, Paper #68. Ottawa: National Museums of Man.

Locher, G. W. (1932). *The Serpent in Kwakiutl Religion*. Leyden: Brill.

Maud, Ralph (n.d.). "Herrings Jump on the Beach: The Humorous Side of a Northwest Coast Creation Myth." Simon Fraser University, Vancouver, British Columbia.

Müller, Werner (1955). *Weltbild und Kult der Kwakiutl Indianer*. Wiesbaden: F. Steiner.

Reid, Susan (1974). "Myth as Metastructure of the Fairytale." In Pierre Maranda, ed., *Soviet Structural Folkloristics*, 151–72. The Hague: Mouton.

——— (1979). "The Kwakiutl Maneater," *Anthropologica* 21:247–75.

Rohner, Ronald, ed. (1969). *The Ethnography of Franz Boas*. Chicago: University of Chicago Press.

Sanday, Peggy Reeves (1986). *Divine Hunger: Cannibalism as a Cultural System*. New York: Cambridge University Press.

Walens, Stanley (1981). *Feasting with Cannibals: An Essay on Kwakiutl Cosmology*. Princeton: Princeton University Press.

Archival Sources:

American Philosophical Society, Franz Boas Collection of American Indian Linguistics (Fieldnotes and Dictionary), Philadelphia.

American Philosophical Society, Franz Boas Papers in the Boas Collection (Boas's Family Letters, translated by Helen Boas Yampolsky, and Letters of George Hunt to Franz Boas), Philadelphia.

Suggested Reading

The literature on the Kwagul is vast. The following list is not intended to do justice to it, only to touch on some of the work most relevant to this essay (I have included short references for those books not cited above).

A good short anthropological overview of the 19th-century Kwagul is Clellan Ford's introduction to *Smoke From Their Fires*. The most important published sources from this period are Boas's many volumes of Kwakw'ala text and translation, which include not only Kwagul myths and tales, but genealogies, prayers, oral histories, dreams, swearwords, and even dinner menus. Edward S. Curtis produced an ethnographic volume on the Kwakiutl in 1915, illustrated with his photographs (volume 10 of his series *The North American Indian*). While George Hunt served as the chief informant for both Boas and Curtis, the flavors of their work are quite distinct. Finally, Clellan Ford recorded and edited the autobiography of Charley Nowell, a Kwagul chief and near-contemporary of George Hunt, which gives quite a different perspective on the period.

Of the many interpretive works on the Kwagul, Irving Goldman's *The Mouth of Heaven* is the most insightful. However, there are many problems with his treatment of Kwakw'ala-language terms, and this aspect of the book cannot be relied upon.

Boas recorded not only Kwagul oral literature but also that of many other native groups of the North Pacific Coast, and he encouraged others such as J. R. Swanton (e.g. *Haida Texts and Myths*, 1905), Edward Sapir (*Nootka Texts*, 1939), and James Teit (e.g., *Mythology of the Thompson In-*

dians, 1912) to do the same. Boas's major comparative analyses of this literature are *Indianische Sagen* (1895), *Tsimshian Mythology* (1916), and *Kwakiutl Culture as Reflected in Mythology* (1935). Ralph Maud's *A Guide to B.C. Indian Myth and Legend* (1982) describes the published collections of North Pacific Coast oral literature, as well as the often fascinating history behind these collections.

No one should read about Kwagul *concepts* of the mask without having looked at the masks the Kwagul carved (and continue to carve today). There are numerous publications on native North Pacific Coast art: Audrey Hawthorn's *Art of the Kwakiutl Indians* (1967) and Bill Holm's *Smoky-Top: The Art and Times of Willie Seaweed* (1983) are two which deal specifically with the Kwagul. Edward S. Curtis filmed an early motion picture, *In the Land of the Head-Hunters* (1914), based on a Kwagul myth and using Kwagul actors and Kwagul-made costumes, sets, and props. This film has been restored, dubbed with Kwagul voices, and renamed *In the Land of the War Canoes*, and it is available from ethnographic film libraries. There is also a film *about* the filming of this movie; see also Bill Holm and George Irving Quimby's book *Edward S. Curtis in the Land of the War Canoes* (1980). Curtis's folio volume of Kwagul photographs is rare, but some photographs appear in a biography co-authored by his granddaughter (Florence Curtis Graybill and Victor Boesen, *Edward Sherriff Curtis: Visions of a Vanishing Race*, 1976).

Translating Pentlatch

M. Dale Kinkade

Pentlatch is a Salishan language that was spoken on the east coast of Vancouver Island between Nanaimo and Courtenay, British Columbia.[1] It is the most poorly documented Salishan language, known only through vocabulary and a few texts collected by Franz Boas in 1886. Even then there was only a handful of speakers of the language left. The Pentlatch had long been vulnerable to raids by neighboring tribes, particularly the Kwakiutl and Nootka, and the survivors at the end of the nineteenth century had intermarried with the Comox to their north or the Sechelt across Georgia Strait (both Salishan groups speaking similar languages). One speaker survived into the early 1940s, but he had been unwilling to work with ethnographers or linguists; hence the Boas data were the last ever collected.

Virtually nothing on Pentlatch was ever published. Boas did not prepare his materials for publication, and what little ethnographic data Homer Barnett collected in 1935 and 1936 was in actuality obtained from the Comox wife of the last Pentlatch. Boas did, however, publish three Pentlatch texts in German in 1892. Even in his manuscripts, though, there are only six texts, and these are quite short: one is only some eleven clauses long, four are between two and three dozen clauses long.[2] What is curious about the Pent-latch texts published in German is that they do not match the manuscript texts.

Two of the Pentlatch manuscript texts are reflected by texts in German. The other four are not, although very similar versions of their contents can be found in the Comox texts in German that immediately precede the Pentlatch texts in the same publication. The third text in German is not represented in the Pentlatch manuscripts, nor do the two that are there fully match the German versions—one is much less similar than the other. Given this lack of match between these two very small corpora, the question arises as to the origin of the German versions.

First of all, there is no doubt about the identification of the texts as Pentlatch. Those in the original language are unmistakably Pentlatch; each German version contains just a few words in the original language, and these suffice to identify them as non-Comox (the only other likely source of the texts). Two of the German versions also contain refer-ences to specific sites that were located in original Pentlatch territory. Thus there is no need to be concerned that Boas might have gotten some of his papers mixed up.

One of the problems with Boas's Pentlatch data is that there are several versions of both word lists and texts. It was Boas's practice to copy his notes as quickly as possible, usually on the same day they were collected. His Pentlatch notes are curious, however. There are several versions of the word list: one is Pentlatch-German (as is one set of the texts), one is Pentlatch-English, and one is English-Pentlatch. The latter two are in alpha-betical order, the first is not. Since the order of the first is more or less random, it is proba-bly the original. This means that Boas was writing material down in Pentlatch and provid-ing on-the-spot German glosses. Only when he recopied materials did he convert to English and alphabetize his data. Certainly Boas's informants were not providing him with German glosses, and if they provided English ones, there is no obvious reason for him to have then translated them into German. It is therefore most likely that yet another language was involved: Chinook Jargon, the native-language based lingua franca used throughout the Northwest. During the nineteenth century a great many native Indians in the northwest would have known Chinook Jargon quite well. Boas states explicitly in the foreword to his *Indianische Sagen* (1895) that a large number of these texts were told to him through the medium of Chinook Jargon (although he does not tell which ones, nor does he give there other details of their collection); it is left unclear whether he even heard some of the texts in the original language. A careful reading of his letters and diaries from the field during his early years of field work (as published in Rohner 1969) makes it fairly clear that he was in fact working with many native informants through this medium. For example, on Sep-tember 29, 1886 (from Victoria) he writes:

Conversation among the Bella Coola is of course in their own language. I generally understand just about enough to know what they are talking about. As soon as friends from other tribes are present, conversation is in Chinook [Jargon]. I am gradually learning to understand this language quite well. Unfortunately the language is incomplete, even more so than the jargon among the Eskimos, although the latter contains fewer words. The people speak very rapidly, a rapidity which I can by no means approach. I understand everything that is in any way to be understood, however. It is characteristic of Chinook that one must guess the meaning of a sentence; one never knows what is subject and what is object. Even verbs and nouns can often not be distinguished, and one has to be very alert in listening to their mythical tales. When I get to Alert Bay I shall try as quickly as possible to pick up something of the language so that I can make myself understood. A mixture of Chinook and the native language is quite useful for purposes of communication (Rohner 1969:28).

Even after working in the area for a few years, he still relied on Chinook Jargon. From Seaside, Oregon, where he collected some Tillamook data, he writes on July 6, 1890:

Only one old woman understands the language, but she does not speak English, so that I have to rely on my Chinook. I really get along all right with it, but unfortunately it is hard to get people to speak slowly" (Rohner 1969:119).

Four years later, while studying Nishga, he writes from Kinkolith, British Columbia, on October 17, 1894:

I then went to an old man and let him dictate texts to me all day long, and I shall continue with this tomorrow. I want to translate the texts later with my informant. I know so few words that I don't understand anything, and the old man doesn't know any English and very little Chinook (Rohner 1969:160).

These passages suggest that Boas collected some Pentlatch texts through Chinook Jargon alone, without hearing the Pentlatch originals (and the same is almost certainly true for other languages). Unfortunately, the original manuscripts that provided the basis for his *Indianische Sagen* do not seem to have been preserved (they are not among his papers at the American Philosophical Society Library, which is the main repository for Boas materials), so there is no way to check the language of original collection. Given that the vocabularies are Pentlatch-German, it is not unlikely that Boas heard the texts in Chinook Jargon and translated them directly into German, without ever preserving the Chinook Jargon version.

In any case it seems likely that Boas did embellish his German versions of Northwest texts, presumably to make them more acceptable to his German audience. His concern at this point was not the form and style of the texts, but the content. It is quite clear from other publications during this early part of Boas's career that he was interested in comparing myths and tales to help him deduce the origins of motifs and tales and hence even of peoples. A comparison of a Pentlatch text for which there is both a Pentlatch and a German version can therefore be instructive about Boas's methods and presuppositions when translating. This may also show what can happen to a story when it goes through two or three languages if translations are not made directly from an original.

One of the Pentlatch texts in German has a fairly close correspondent among the Pentlatch language texts. This is the one he calls "Der Donnervogel" ("The Thunderbird"). This is the title of the Pentlatch version as well as the German one; Boas does not give titles in Pentlatch for this and three other stories. In spite of major and general similarities between these two versions of the story, there are interesting and significant differences. These are obvious just by reading the German version, then the line-by-line translation (actually mere glossing) that Boas gave in both German and English for the Pentlatch version. The former is a much more polished and flowing account, whereas the latter—never intended as a good translation in any case—is quite rough and ready.

In terms of genre, this story appears to belong to a special variety found commonly among neighboring Wakashan groups. This is a type of story told to explain and validate the history of a particular family, and to tell how its special crests, songs, and names were acquired. They are thus not truly mythical. Boas refers to this class of legends as one of two major types told by the Kwakiutl (who lived a few miles north of the Pentlatch, and were expanding southward during the nineteenth century):

There are two classes of these legends . . . the second telling how he [an ancestor] encountered certain spirits and by their help became powerful. The latter class . . . [is] based entirely on the custom of the Indians of acquiring a guardian spirit after long-continued fasting and bathing. The guardian spirit thus acquired by the ancestor became hereditary, and is to a certain extent the crest of the division,—and there is no doubt that these traditions, which rank now with the fundamental myths of the tribe, are based on the actual fastings and acquisitions of guardian spirits of ancestors of the present division (Boas 1896:432).

Stylistic features and motifs of this and other types of legends do not appear to differ, and only content keeps them apart. The Pentlatch version of the story by itself does not make it clear that this is a family-validation story, although the German version seems to do so. Both begin with a trip to the mountains with the bathing and self-purification typical of quests for a guardian spirit. Boas adds to the German version explicit information on family names, and specifies that members of this family can calm storms with their spirit power. This extra information may have been added by one of Boas's translators as commentary on the story, allowing him to turn it into a more explicit validation legend.

These validation legends were of considerable importance in this region where social rank was all-important. A recent clear account of how a family might be validated at a potlatch tells us:

Usually a speaker was hired to speak on behalf of the host. He thanked the guests for coming, explained the purpose of the potlatch and then delivered a long eulogy on the renowned ancestors of the host—one of the few occasions when the modest bearing of a high-status person was put aside! Several other men stood and responded to the speaker, reaffirming the status of the host and his illustrious family. Even more speeches were made complimenting the host for upholding the honour of his family and setting an example for all the people. Then the host sang his family's song and his children and other relatives, fully costumed in masks and dancing regalia, danced, some carrying implements suggesting the occupations that had brought wealth to the family" (Kennedy and Bouchard 1983:63).

Throughout the Northwest rank had to be confirmed continually (as by giving potlatches), and there was a constant effort to increase one's status. The upper classes were the rulers, and had considerable power. Evidence of this power among the northern Coast Salish can be seen in the fact that some of the last known Pentlatch were chiefs in a Comox village (their northern neighbors) after their own communities had been wiped out by raiding parties. At the bottom of the social ladder were the slaves. There was frequent raiding all along the coast, particularly by northern people such as the Haida, Tlingit, and Kwakiutl, in part to acquire more slaves and hence increase the social status of the raiders in their home communities. These raids, along with introduced European diseases, were the cause of the rapid decline of the Pentlatch. Their remnants were incorporated into neighboring Comox and Sechelt (and probably Nanaimo) communities, where their separate identity disappeared.

In what follows, I give an English version of "The Thunderbird" based on the Pentlatch original, then compare this with the German version. The English version I give here is my own rendition of the text based on Boas's manuscript glosses and what I can make of the Pentlatch material itself.[3] It is a fairly close translation. The text is presented in a verse format, following principles best formulated in Hymes 1981. For this presentation, the equivalent of each Pentlatch clause is given in a single line; these are then grouped into verses, scenes, and acts (these seem to be enough levels to represent this very short text). Justification for some of these groupings follows the texts, although full explication is omitted to concentrate on the translation.

Act I. Scene 1.

He goes to bathe in the lake.
  He bathes for many days.
    The young man becomes handsome.

Act I. Scene 2.

Then he goes to the mountain.
  It isn't long
    and he sees the house.

He stands at the door.
  He is called in by the woman.
    He goes inside.

"It will be good for you
    to hide yourself in the corner."

Act I. Scene 3.

He is not hidden long
  when there is a noise.

He comes inside.
  He asks his wife,
    "Human odor!"

"It is true!
  A person is inside."

Act I. Scene 4.

He takes off his clothes.
  He takes off his belt.
    He hangs his robe over the drying-pole.

Act II. Scene 1.

The man stays inside for one summer.
   All his people (summer-)dance,

   And he carries him away.
     He is on the other side.

Act II. Scene 2.

Then all the people know.
   Then the people launch the boat.
     They go to the other side.

All his people go over.
   They go ashore
     and they see nothing.
       They only hear his call.
       "Hoo, hoo, hoo!"

Act II. Scene 3.

The people go ashore.
   The men go ashore.
     Then they surround him.

And they do not see
   how he goes into the boat.
     They only hear
       how he calls in the bow [of the boat].

Act II. Scene 4.

The people row.
   They come home.
     They sweep the house.
       All the men are inside.

They do not see
   where he sits.
     They only hear
       how he calls
         "Hoo, hoo, hoo."

Although the text is short, it shows considerable structural integrity. Its brevity does not detract from the story, but may even be seen to lend it power. The division into two acts can be justified as representing the two phases of the life of the man who goes away: his self-purification and entry into the house of the powerful Thunderbird in the first half and his return to his people in the second. The first act is probably an allusion to the acquisition of a Thunderbird spirit power by a semi-mythical Pentlatch, and the second to his benevolent use of that power as the founder of one family of the Pentlatch people. The four parts (scenes) of Act I are (1) the man's purification, (2) his arrival at Thunderbird's house and entry therein, (3) Thunderbird's return and discovery of the alien, and (4) the removal of Thunderbird's garments. The first scene of Act II then sets a new time and place. Scene 2 moves the people to "the other side," where they hear, but cannot see, the man. In scene 3 they locate him and perceive that he has gotten into their boat, although they still cannot see him. The last scene has them return home, ritually cleanse a house for him, and perceive him in their midst. The last three scenes are strongly marked by parallel endings, where the people do not see, but only hear, their returned hero.

Although one might choose other divisions and structuring of this text, the general outlines seem reasonable enough. The major break between the two parts is supported further by the German version, which is presented by Boas in two paragraphs corresponding to these two acts. The division into four scenes for each act can be justified both on the grounds of their contrasting content and the fact that the pattern number in Pentlatch is four. Hymes has shown that the pattern numbers which are found in cultures all over the world are commonly reflected directly in the organizational structure of narratives, not just in terms of the number of persons or objects involved. If the pattern number is four, then narratives are structured in units of two and four; if the pattern number is five, the units are in threes and fives. In "The Thunderbird" there are two acts of four scenes each.

A roughly similar structure can be assigned to the German version of this story. I give this version in my own translation from the German, again staying as close as possible to the German while maintaining smooth English. I have omitted several parenthesized passages which appear to have been added as explanations to the German reader.[4]

Act I. Scene 1.

Two brothers went into the woods
and stayed hidden there for a month.
Every day they bathed in a lake
and then washed themselves with spruce[5] boughs,
until they had become completely cleansed
and had no more human smell about them.

Act I. Scene 2.

Then they climbed up onto the mountain Kwlénas
and there found the house of the thunder-god Wálxwm.

They stepped inside the door
and saw a woman sitting in the house.
She invited them to come in,
and told them
that her husband and his brother had flown out.

Before they returned
she hid the visitors in a corner of the house.

Act I. Scene 3.

It wasn't long,
  before they came flying in
    and set down in front of the house.
      It sounded as if a tree was being blown down by a storm.

When they came into the house,
  they at once smelled the visitors
    and asked the woman
      where she had hidden them.

She called them forth.

Act I. Scene 4.

Then the Thunderbirds took off their belts,
  which gleamed like fire
    and were made of Aihos[6] skin,
      they hung up their feather cloaks
      and took on human form.

Act II. Scene 1.

Toward the end of the summer the Pentlatch tribe celebrated a feast.
  Then the Thunderbirds came flying
    and brought back the young men,
      whom they had given the names Xwúmt'iq and Qápnats.

The dancers heard
  how they called,
    "hoo, hoo, hoo, hoo."

Act II. Scene 2.

Then they tied two boats together,
  laid boards across them
    and went out
      to look for them.

But they couldn't see anyone,
  although they reached the place
    where the voice came from.
      Suddenly they heard
        how something settled on the high prow of the boat,
          but still couldn't see anything.

Act II. Scene 3.

Then they returned to the village,
  cleansed the house,
    and now Xwúmt'iq came in,

danced with the Thunderbird mask
and sang.

Act II. Scene 4.

He was the founder of the Xwúmt'iq family.

His daughter was called Sixsíxawit.

His descendants can see the thunderbird,
and, when there is a bad thunderstorm,
they are able to persuade him
to return to his house.

In the German version, a new last scene is added, giving information that might well be understood by a Pentlatch listener without having it explicitly stated. The whole structure of the second act is changed; instead of three parallel scenes ending in the hearing without seeing, there are only two such references, and both come in one scene. (These might alternatively have been placed in separate scenes. This would then either require a very long scene 4 or a fifth scene; this would have disrupted the overall structure in yet a different, less desirable, way.) The difference in dramatis personae is also very peculiar. Nothing in the Pentlatch version suggests that there are two men or two Thunderbirds. In fact, the German version loses one of the men by the end, since only one is referred to as an ancestor of a family.

Other differences are not as obvious, but require familiarity with traditional style features found in Northwest myths and legends. Jacobs 1972 identifies twenty-one classes of such features, not all of which need be found in any one story. A comparison of ten of Jacobs's class features which do occur in the Pentlatch version of this story with their equivalents (or lack of them) in the German version show other important ways in which Boas's translation is both similar to and departs from the original.

Both versions can be seen to have a "play structure" (Jacobs feature 1), although this seems to break down toward the end of the German version. The pattern number (Jacobs feature 5) in Pentlatch is four, and this is nicely reflected in the Pentlatch version; the German version can be expressed in units of four, although the effort is clearly much more forced. The German version twice refers to two of something (two brothers, two boats), and two is an expected corollary of four in myth structure (according to Hymes); yet neither of these specifications of duality occurs in the Pentlatch version.

Little variety is found in the expression of distances or locations (Jacobs feature 6). There are about a dozen such expressions in the Pentlatch version, and they are all minimal—the sort of thing expected in Northwest myths. The German version keeps the location references in the first act, but elaborates several of them, and adds others ("into the woods" in Scene 1, the name of the mountain, the owners of the house, and where the woman is sitting in Scene 2, and where the Thunderbirds set down in Scene 3). The second act of the German version retains few of the locations specified in the Pentlatch version, most notably all the repeated references to going ashore that are important to the rhythm of this part of the story. Such repetition is desirable in Pentlatch, but not in German.

Few expressions of time occur (Jacobs feature 7). There are only four in the Pentlatch version ("many days," "it isn't long," "he is not hidden long," "one summer"). The German version adds "for a month" in the second line, changes "many days" to "every day," omits reference to the time the hero hides, and changes "one summer" to "toward the end of the summer." In Pentlatch, the specification of one summer at the beginning of Act II is only a stylized indication of the passage of time. The specification of one summer need not be taken literally, although the man's return does occur during the summer, as indicated by the fact that the dance is specifically a summer dance, rather than one of the better documented winter dances. Thus the total number of time references remains unchanged, although the overall impression given is of much more explicit time periods than is found in Pentlatch, or than would be expected in Northwest myths in general.

Feature 8 pertains to motifs used in a story. These are essentially the same in both the Pentlatch and the German version, and it is primarily this that makes them the same story. Feature 12 concerns the absence of references to features of nature (such as flowers, weather, mountains), and feature 13 the absence of references to moods and feelings. Indeed the Pentlatch version lacks any such references; the German version is faithful in this regard except for the quite unnatural (in Pentlatch terms) addition of the line "It sounded as if a tree was being blown down by a storm." This line seems strikingly out of place for any Northwest story. Feature 14 notes that description of movement and travel is minimal, and expressed with only a word or two; here the two versions do not differ significantly.

Feature 15 has to do with the absence of personality characteristics in Northwest stories. They are indeed absent from the Pentlatch version, except for the mentioning of the young man becoming handsome (implying spiritual purity) after his bathing ritual. This specific point is elaborated in German. One of the most striking differences in the two versions, however, is the elaborated description of the belts and cloaks of the Thunderbirds (and thus an indirect description of them)—a glaring departure from Northwest norms.

Perhaps the most striking difference between the two versions stems from a lack of laconicism in the German version. Jacobs's feature 19 notes that "all the evidence points to an extreme of laconicism in depiction of action, movement, travel, feelings, relationships, and personalities . . ." (1972:16). The German version is very wordy and longer by nine lines (fifty-eight as opposed to forty-nine in Pentlatch). In fact, the German version as a whole uses a rather awkward style, and often seems stilted and unnatural. Some of this awkwardness is the result of language change in the past hundred years, although much is because it is a translation from yet another language and presumably tries to retain some of the characteristics and style of the original. Clauses are longer in the German version, and it is much more formal than the Pentlatch, using far more dependent clauses and indirect discourse. The Pentlatch has short, terse sentences, few dependent clauses, and direct discourse, and fits Jacobs's expectation of laconicism perfectly.

The two presentations are clearly the same story, although the style of the two is strikingly different. The Pentlatch is terse, the German is wordy. This, however, does not make Boas's translation bad. Boas was writing for a German audience, one that would be quite unfamiliar with the sorts of stories being presented. It would have had certain expectations about what folktales are like, since the Grimm Brothers's stories were well known. These Northwest myths would have presented quite different types of characters, different customs, and different geography. All these had to be made reasonably clear while still telling the story correctly. Boas was not trying to replicate the form and style of the Pentlatch original, but told a Pentlatch story in German. That he came as close as he did to the verse structure of a Pentlatch original is probably accidental and hence is remarkable. Indeed, we can be grateful for this version, since it gives some extra details not included in the Pentlatch version; these tell us more about the Pentlatch people and their beliefs.

Boas's translation is thus a useful addition to our knowledge of the Pentlatch people, although not to what we would want to know about myth form and style. This can be learned only by looking at stories in the original language. Presenting them, as has been done here, in yet other translations may well introduce further distortions, but can at least be justified on the grounds that they show something about Pentlatch narrative structure. To a native audience that was probably as important for a well-told tale as its content. The fresh translation offered here shows that form, as well as content, can be preserved in a translation.

Notes

1. I wish to thank William R. Seaburg for helpful suggestions about various points in this paper and Ingrida Brenzinger for advice on my translation of the German text.

2. The reason for indicating the size of these texts in clauses will become clearer later when a specific text is discussed. Pentlatch clauses tend to be quite short, and provide a useful basis of comparing the length of individual texts either in Pentlatch or German.

3. No Pentlatch grammar exists. However, since Pentlatch shares much of its structure (and vocabulary) with neighboring Comox and Sechelt, comparisons with these two languages make it possible to reach fairly reliable conclusions about how best to analyze and phonemicize most of Pentlatch.

4. The German original is as follows, including archaic spellings:

"Zwei Brüder gingen in den Wald und blieben dort einen Monat lang verborgen. Jeden Tag badeten sie in einem See und wuschen sich dann mit Fichtenzweigen, bis sie ganz rein geworden waren und nichts mehr vom Geruche eines Menschen an sich hatten. Dann stiegen sie auf den Berg Kulē'nas (im Pɛ'ntlatc-Thale) und fanden dort das Haus des Donnergottes Wā'lek·um. Sie traten in die Thür und sahen eine Frau im Hause sitzen. Diese lud sie ein, hereinzukommen, und erzählte ihnen, dass ihr Mann und dessen Bruder ausgeflogen seien. Ehe jene zurückkamen, versteckte sie die Ankömmlinge in einer Ecke des Hauses. Es währte nicht lange, da kamen jene angeflogen und liessen sich vor dem Hause nieder. Das tönte, wie wenn ein Baum vom Sturme niedergeworfen wird. Als sie in's Haus traten, rochen sie sogleich die Besucher und fragten die

Frau, wo sie jene versteckt habe. Diese rief sie herbei. Dann legten die Donnervögel ihre Gürtel ab, die wie Feuer glänzten und aus Aihōshaut gemacht waren, hingen ihre Federkleider auf und nahmen menschliche Gestalt an.

"Gegen Ende des Sommers feierte der Stamm der Pɛ'ntlatc ein Fest (an der Stelle, wo jetzt das Werft von Comox ist). Da kamen die Donnervögel geflogen und brachten die jungen Männer, denen sie die Namen Qū'mt'ik· und K·ā'penats gegeben hatten, zurück. Die Tänzer hörten, wie jene riefen: "hū, hū, hū, hū" (jedes Mal eine Quinte herunter gezogen). Da banden sie zwei Boote zusammen, legten Bretter darüber und fuhren hinaus, sie zu suchen. Sie konnten aber niemand erblicken, obwohl sie die Stelle erreichten, von der die Stimme herkam. Plötzlich hörten sie, wie etwas sich auf dem hohen Bootschnabel niederliess, konnten aber noch nichts sehen. Da kehrten sie zum Dorfe zurück, reinigten das Haus, und nun kam Qū'mt'ik· herein, tanzte mit der Maske des Donnervögels und sang. Er war der Stammvater des Geschlechtes Qū'mt'ik·. Seine Tochter hiess Siqsē'qawit. Seine Nachkommen können den Donnervögel sehen, und, wenn es stark gewittert, vermögen sie ihn zu bewegen, nach seinem Hause zurückzukehren."

5. The German here says "Fichtenzweigen," which would probably usually be translated as "spruce boughs." The ethnographic literature, however, suggests that other trees were used for this cleansing purpose, but which one specifically (if a single variety was indeed used) is unclear. Barnett (1955:95) mentions cedar and hemlock; Kennedy and Bouchard (1983:47) mention cedar. Fir is also sometimes cited.

6. The Aihos was a mythical double-headed monster (i.e., with a head on each end), usually translated as a snake or serpent. It was considered very powerful, and could turn people to stone. It is better known by its Kwak'wala name "Sisiutl."

References

Barnett, Homer G. *The Coast Salish of British Columbia*. University of Oregon Monographs: Studies in Anthropology No. 4. Eugene: University of Oregon, 1955.

Boas, Franz. [Pentlatch materials.] American Philosophical Society Library, Philadelphia, Pennsylvania, 1886.

———. Sagen aus Britisch-Columbien IX. Sagen der Pɛ'ntlatc. *Verhandlungen der Berliner Gesellschaft für Anthropologie, Ethnologie und Urgeschichte, Jahrgang 1892*, 65–66. Berlin: Verlag von A. Asher & Co., 1892. Republished in *Indianische Sagen von der Nord-Pacifischen Küste Amerikas*. Berlin: Verlag von A. Asher & Co., 1895.

———. The Growth of Indian Mythologies. In Franz Boas, *Race, Language and Culture*, 425–36. New York: The Free Press, 1940. [Slightly altered reprinting from *Journal of American Folk-Lore* 9:1–11, 1896.]

Hymes, Dell. *"In Vain I Tried to Tell You": Essays in Native American Ethnopoetics*. Studies in Native American Literature I. Philadelphia: University of Pennsylvania Press, 1981.

Jacobs, Melville. Areal Spread of Indian Oral Genre Features in the Northwest States. *Journal of the Folklore Institute* 9(1):10–17, 1972.

Kennedy, Dorothy and Randy Bouchard. *Sliammon Life, Sliammon Lands*. Vancouver: Talonbooks, 1983.

Rohner, Ronald P., ed. *The Ethnography of Franz Boas: Letters and Diaries of Franz Boas Written on the Northwest Coast From 1886 to 1931*. Chicago: The University of Chicago Press, 1969.

Suggested Reading

Little is known about the culture of the Pentlatch because of their disappearance at the end of the nineteenth century before much ethnographic data could be collected. What little there is can be found in Barnett 1955, although even this is secondhand. Barnett's source was the Comox wife of the last Pentlatch, who refused to work with any anthropologist. It is probable that Pentlatch culture was very much like that of their northern neighbors, the Comox-Sliammon, whose villages were on both sides of the Strait of Georgia. Descriptions of Comox-Sliammon life and culture can be found in Barnett 1955 and Kennedy and Bouchard 1983.

Legends and myths of the Pentlatch and surrounding groups can be found in Boas 1895. For style and structure of native American mythology, see Hymes 1981 and Jacobs 1972.

The Discovery of Nursery Tales in Twana

Nile Robert Thompson

It began as a simple project. I wanted to take a text in Twana, the Native American language I was researching, and translate it into English.[1] Since this was my first attempt at translation, I naturally selected the shortest story I had heard. What could be easier than translating a seven-word text into English? I knew of only one story from the language that had been published with its original text and the translation. My goal was to translate a new story and give it the same meaning and the same flavor in English.

Unfortunately, shorter is not always easier. The translation process did not go smoothly. For each piece of new data I gathered in trying to resolve a seemingly minor problem, I received a greater number of new problems. This essay will follow my trail in trying to solve the dilemmas associated with translating the Skokomish Twana story of Louse. An examination of my scholarly trek may assist others who find their simple translation task turning into an exponentially expanding project.

The Twana (*tuwaduq*) were the aboriginal residents of the Hood Canal region of western Washington State. Their language (*tuwaduqucid*), also known as Twana, is a member of the Salish language family. In precontact times, it was probably spoken by no more than two thousand individuals. Decline began with the introduction of European-brought diseases in the eighteenth century. Following the signing of the Point No Point Treaty in 1855, most Twana relocated on the Skokomish Reservation near the mouth of the Skokomish River, home of the largest aboriginal dialect group, the Skokomish (*sqo-qobəš*, "big-river people"). By 1881 there were only about 150 speakers of Twana on Hood Canal. Educational, economic, and religious factors of cultural subjugation reduced the number of new speakers in each successive generation. The last fluent speaker of Twana died in 1980.[2]

Little published information is available on narration in the Twana language. Although there have been a number of Twana stories printed in English, only one brief story has been published with the original Twana text and an English translation.[3] The genres of Twana stories have therefore received little attention.

In the particular Skokomish Twana story I selected the main character is *bəščəd*, "head louse" (*pediculosis capitis*). Mrs. Louisa Pulsifer (ca. 1886–1979), a Skokomish Twana, first told me the story in early 1977. My phonetic transcription and the translation I subsequently set out for it appear as Version I.

Louse Version I   LJP/NT/01/08/77

1. buščə'd   ʔəd   biʔiəq'o'lw'altxʷ.
    It's Louse   and   she is sweeping her house.

2. ʔəda'q'ʷ   wəʔæ'txʷəlwəsəb.
    She got just halfway.

3. ʔəd   ca'yay.
    And   she got mixed up.

The most puzzling part of translating this short story is the part that is not there. A portion of the storyline seems to be missing from the final sentence. In an effort to clarify what was meant in stating that Louse was getting "mixed up," Mrs. Pulsifer indicated without prompting that Louse got mixed up "with the dirt" (*ʔač ti sqələbalbuš*).[4]

The gender of Louse presents another problem. While there are numerous ways of showing gender in Twana, none are used in the story.[5] Louse's age is also not set out. From the character's housecleaning activity I figured Louse to be an adult female and therefore translated each instance of the third-person ending (-∅) as "she" rather than "he" or "it."[6]

Several months later I had Mrs. Pulsifer retell the Louse story in Twana. The result was a second version that contains the same elements as the first version.

Louse Version II   LJP/NT/06/01/77

1. ʔiəq'ʷolwəltxʷduxʷ buščə'd.
    Louse was sweeping her house now.

2. ʔəda'q'ʷ wəʔæ'txʷəlwəsəb.
She got just halfway.

3. ʔəd hoy ca'yayduxʷ.
And then she got mixed up now.

For Version II, however, she offered no addendum regarding how Louse got mixed up.

A month later I decided that the third time might be a charm. I had her retell the same simple story. Her response, Version III, turned out to be a cross between Versions I and II; Line 1 combines elements of I and II, Line 2 as in both I and II, and Line 3 as in I:

Louse Version III　　　　　　　　LJP/NT/07/28/77

1. biəq'ʷo'lwəltxʷduxʷ bɪščəd.
Louse is sweeping her house now.

2. ʔəda'q'ʷ wəʔæ'txʷəlwəsəb.
She got just halfway.

3. ʔəd ca'yay.
And she got mixed up.

In the process of going over Version III with me Mrs. Pulsifer added "in the mud" (ʔač tə šč'aꞏqolbɪš), only to switch it to "in the dirt" (ʔač ti sqələba'lbɪš). The solution for how to handle Sentence 3 was still not clear.

I also discovered a new problem. Rather than a paucity of information I now had a surplus in terms of syntax and morphology. This situation had come about by requesting the narrator to repeat the story. What I wasn't hoping for, but got, was multiple versions of the same story.

Fearing that I might get more differing versions if I asked her to repeat the story more times, I turned to examining whether other researchers who had worked with her had recorded the same story. I found that Ghulam Hasnain, a research associate on the Twana Language Project, recorded a version from her. The phonetic transcription of the Louse story from his unpublished field notes appears here as Version IV, although it was recorded after the time I recorded Version I (to which it is nearly identical) but before her telling of Version II.

Louse Version IV　　　　　　　　LJP/GH/05/19/77

1. bɪščə'd ʔəd biəiq'ʷulwəltuxʷ.

2. ʔədaʔqʷ wəʔatuxʷwəsəb.

3. ʔəd hoy cayayduxʷ.

Hasnain too notes that she had explained in English that Louse had been mixed up "in the dirt."

To account for the missing and changing information in the story's final sentence, I was tempted to use parentheses, as in (3a) or (3b).

3a. ʔəd hoy   cayay(duxʷ)   (ʔač ti sqələbalbɪš)
      And then   she got mixed up (now) (in the dirt).

3b. ʔəd hoy   cayay(duxʷ)
      And then   she got mixed up (now)   (in the dirt).
                                      (ʔač ti sqələbalbɪš).

By adding information, however, I concluded that I would be, intentionally or not, making one of two claims: that the original version is incomplete and has to be supplemented (contrast 3a with 3 in Version I) or that cultural differences require that an explanation be included (contrast 3b with 3 in Version I). Being uneasy about adding anything to the story, I chose to add nothing.

I then moved on to try to resolve a syntactic discrepancy in the versions. As is readily apparent, there is a difference in the retellings of the Louse story in word order (and thus translation) between Versions I and IV, on one hand, and Versions II and III, on the other. Chronologically, the order Mrs. Pulsifer gave the versions was I, IV, II, and then III. She thus initially provided the first sentence with a raised subject in focus position and then in later version began it with the verb, the unmarked word order. The difference in translation is analogous to English "It's beans I like" versus "I like beans."

As I struggled with how to account for the differences between these four versions, I knew that I had to consider the storyteller's age as a possible factor contributing to variation. Although she was in her nineties, she had demonstrated a fantastic memory for details in recounting her personal history. Additionally, both of the word orders used for the initial sentence are grammatical. Thus, the use of one rather than the other might have something to do with storytelling rather than memory. Still, I chose to disregard the difference as associated with narrative style.

Instead, I made the assumption that Mrs. Pulsifer had changed the word order in Versions I and IV because of the influence of the normal subject-initial structure of English. Perhaps the absence of regular interaction with the other few remaining speakers of Twana might have had a greater impact on her storytelling than her age. I hypothesized that since there were few Twana speakers with whom to interact and since she had not worked with a linguist for approximately a decade, her Twana was highly susceptible to language interference. The absence of conversational data was hampering my own research and, I reasoned, must also have a negative impact on her maintenance of narrative skills. My reasoning was borne out by a shift in word order over time in her single sentence utterances similar to her shift in the initial sentence word order.

Some time later I was given access to the field notes and tapes of the linguist who had worked with Mrs. Pulsifer over a decade earlier. When I found they contained information on the Louse story I figured it would provide the template on which to critique my assumptions. The following is my transcription and translation of the story as recorded by Gaberell Drachman in 1963:

1. ʔiəq'o'lwəltxʷ ʔo bʊščə'd.
   Louse was sweeping her house.

2. ʔən he·' dabduxʷ.
   And she moved on now.

3. ʔədaq'ʷ wæʔtwəlsəb.
   She got just halfway.

4. bica'yay tə q'ʷiłu'cad.
   She is mixing up in the dust.

5. ʔəd špəqs.
   And that's the end.

Sentence 1 of this earlier version appears to support my assumptions regarding word order. Like Versions II and III, the first sentence of Version V is verb initial. Unlike Versions I–IV, however, it contains an additional particle. The particle ʔo marks the agent within a clause. For example, *biəqo' ʔostəbčud ʔo meri* means "I am being given water by Mary," even though it contains the subject ending *-čəd* "I" rather than the object ending *-bəš* "me."

Version IV contains three pieces of information not found in the 1977 versions. Sentences 2 and 5 are not essential to the storyline and appear to have been forgotten in the intervening years. Sentence 4 specifies that Louse got lost in the dust. The version does not shed light on Louse's gender.

The brevity of the story and the fluctuations in the story between the years suggested to me that there might originally have been even more to the Louse story. It was especially puzzling that the main character was not developed as were many of the subjects of other Twana stories. I began my search for a longer version by researching the story's central character.

Comparative research revealed that the head louse was not a common character in Salish legends. A Nooksack story, told by Mrs. Louise George and recorded in English by Norman Lerman (1952), contains Louse as a main character who is the partner of Flea. The story shows that there is nothing inherently short about Louse stories and verifies that Louse can be a male. Among the Tillamook of the central Oregon Coast head lice are discussed in three Nehalem Tillamook stories presented in English in Jacobs (1959) but do not appear as characters. Farther to the south, the unrelated Karok also have a story in which lice appear without human attributes, although they are changed into human babies (see Kroeber & Gifford 1980:38, 141). To the east, a Sahaptin story that explains the creation of landmarks in the Hanford area of eastern Washington has Louse as an elderly woman who lived in a house with her husband Tick (Consortium 1974:10–24).

The greater Puget Sound Basin (i.e., the watersheds leading into Puget Sound and Hood Canal) was home to a large number of Native Americans in precontact times. In fact, it is felt to be one of the most heavily populated areas north of Mexico City before the coming of the white man (Deloria 1977:12–13). Although there were a number of dialects, the region was divided into but two languages, the Twana language around Hood Canal and Puget Sound Salish surrounding neighboring Puget Sound proper. The speakers of these two languages had very similar cultures and societies, and much of their oral tradition was related, particularly in terms of the creation epic of Dukwibahl, the Transformer.

I was therefore not surprised to find a story containing Louse in the Puget Sound Salish language. In a Puyallup story, Louse (*bə'ščad*) was a pretty woman who was married to Loon's son (Ballard 1929:101–3). Nor was I surprised to find that a version nearly identical to the Skokomish Twana story of Louse was recorded in the same language.

Only a few months before Drachman made his Twana recording, Thom Hess recorded the Louse story from Mrs. Elizabeth Krise (Hess 1972). Mrs. Krise was a Snohomish Indian from *sba'daʔɬ,* the town of Snohomish (Hess 1976:xiv). This version, too, is but a few sentences in length. The partial English translation is from Hess's glossary.

Louse Version VI Lady Louse Cleans House EK/TH/11/18/62

1. [əs]ɬaɬlil   kʷsi bsč'ad ʔal tə hikʷ ʔalʔal.
   dwell, live   louse   in the big   house

2. dayayʔ.
   be alone

3. xʷi   kʷi gʷəsyayʔs.
   no, not   relative(s)

4. huy   gʷəl   kʷədadəxʷ.
   then, next and, not she took it

5. gʷəl,   ʔuʔik'ʷidəxʷ tiʔə hikʷ ʔalʔal.
   and, next she swept it this   big   house

6. [qa   sč'iq'ʷil]
   much, many, a lot filth

7. xʷuʔələʔ   gʷəʔudgʷičiləxʷ ʔal ti ʔalʔal.
   maybe, I guess   in   a   house

8. huy,   x̌ʷil'əxʷ.
   then, next lost

9. šəbšub   bsč'ad.
   disappear forever   louse

10. [diɬ shuys.]
    That is the end.

Although the Snohomish version is approximately twice as long as the Skokomish story, it too appears to have been told with a minimum of information. I interpreted Hess's use of square brackets as indicating that the material they contain was material he, not the teller, had inserted. If so, he too would have struggled with the same problems I had with Twana. He, then, seemingly chose to add information. My interpretation seems to have been borne out in a work by his frequent collaborator, Vi Hilbert, who explains the use of bracketing as follows (Hilbert 1980: ii):

[ ] indicates the translator's explanation
( ) indicates the storyteller's explanation

In Line 1, an aspect marker has been added to the verb. The insertion of Line 6 was probably done to explain in advance how Louse got lost, equivalent to the situation in Skokomish where Louse got mixed up. Here "filth" was added rather than "dirt," "mud," or "dust." The insertion of Line 10 was probably to give the story a traditional ending, such as he described in Hess (1985: xxiii). This is the same ending Mrs. Pulsifer used in Twana for her Version V.

Sentence 4, which I translated as "And then she grabbed it," fails to convey what it was that Louse grabbed, a conifer branch used as we would use a broom. In the glossary, Hess adds the information in parenthesis for the reader:

kʷədadəxʷ . . . "she took it" (a broom,
                    səxʷʔix̌ʷicut)

Taken in its totality, the sentence would read:

4a. huy   gʷəl   kʷədadəxʷ
     then, next   and, then   she took it   (a broom)
                                    səxʷʔix̌ʷicut

Clearly he did not intend this as comprising a grammatical sentence, in that the object lacks an article. Instead, he was supplying the information he felt to be missing.

As with the Twana, the Puget Sound Salish text does not clarify whether Louse is male or female, young or old. Hess's attribution in the title of Louse as an adult female matched my own estimation.

Hilbert (1980: 143) presents a slightly different version of the story Hess recorded from Mrs. Krise. Of no little interest to me was also the inclusion of a free translation in English (although it was not interlinear, as presented here):

Louse Version VII Lady Louse Cleans House EK/TH/1962

1. ʔəsɫaɫlil kʷsi bsč'ad ʔal tə hikʷ ʔalʔal.
    Louse lived there in that huge big house!

2. dayayʔ.
    All alone, by herself.

3. xʷi kʷi gʷəsyayaʔs.
    She had no friends or relatives

4. huy gʷəl, kʷədadəxʷ.
   Then she took it.

5. gʷəl, ʔuʔik'ʷidəxʷ tiʔə hikʷ ʔalʔal.
   And she swept it. This huge house.

6. qa sč'iq'ʷil.
   There was lots of dirt!

7. x̣ʷuləxʷ uʔudəgʷiǰiləxʷ ʔal ti ʔalʔal, huy, x̣ʷil'əxʷ.
   When she got to the very middle of the house, she got lost.

8. šəbšub bsč'ad.
   And that was the end of Louse!

9. diɬ shuys.
   That is the end.

Hilbert, a native speaker of Puget Sound Salish (see Hess 1985), kept all of Hess's bracketed information. The brackets, however, were deleted. Additionally, the initial clause of Line 7 has been altered from the original but is almost identical to an updated version provided by Hess (1976:680):

> x̣ʷul'əxʷ ʔuʔu'dəgʷiǰiləxʷ ʔal tiʔiɬ ʔalʔal.
> She only got to the middle of the house.

The presence of the seemingly inserted information indicated to me that the truncation was not just problematic to non-Indian linguists such as Hess and myself but also to a Puget Sound Salish speaker such as Hilbert. I was still very puzzled by why such a short story would appear to be truncated and why it would happen in both languages. It would take me several more years until I would discover that the missing information was not really a problem after all.

The evidence that changed my mind came in the form of a rediscovered fuller version of the Louse story, recorded in Twana only by Leon Metcalf about 1951.[7] The storyteller was Mrs. Liza Purdy, a Hoodsport Twana born about 1874.[8]

The following is my phonetic transcription and translation of the Louse story as told by Mrs. Purdy. Blanks in the transcription represent problem areas on which I am still working. The title appears as Mr. Metcalf introduced the story on tape.

Louse Version VIII   Louse Sweeping the House   LLP/LM/ca. 1951

1. daqtəduxʷ ʔo bɨščəd.   Louse was alone now.

2. bɨščəd daqtə, ɬe·.   Louse was alone now, you folks.

3. daqas waw'iʔɨct.   He first heard about it.

4. ʔiəq'olwəltxʷ tə bɨščəd.   Louse swept the house.

5. ʔəd ʔiəq'olwəltxʷ.   And he swept the house.

6. ʔəd ʔiəq'olwəltxʷ.   And he swept the house.

7.	ʔi'q'olwəltxʷ.	He swept the house.
8.	daqtəduxʷ.	He was alone now.
9.	lalʔabacəduxʷ tə siʔə.	He took care of his house now.
10.	ʔiəq'olwəltxʷ.	He swept the house.
11.	lalʔabacəduxʷ.	He took care of it now.
12.	hoy, łaqalduxʷ ti siʔə.	Then he spun around the house.
13.	q'ʷəsæ q'ʷasiʔɩs	
14.	łaqalduxʷ ʔəd ʔa·'čłduxʷ əʔd la'lʔabətəbduxʷ bɩščəd.	Louse sat, waited and watched.
15.	tə siʔə ʔiəq'olwəltxʷ.	The house he swept.
16.	he·'dabduxʷ.	He went on now.
17.	ʔeq'o'lwəltxʷəb ʔačduxʷ tə šuw'ał.	He swept the house to the door.
18.	bəq'ʷa'bduxʷs tə sqələba'lbɩš.	He piled the dirt.
19.	bəq'ʷa·'bduxʷ ʔač tə šuwał.	He piled the dirt at the door.
20.	ʔačduxʷ bɩščəd ʔə ti siʔə.	Louse went into the house.
21.		
22.	qʷəla·'bduxʷ.	He sank down now.
23.	x̌ʷe'lduxʷ	He was lost now.
24.	x̌ʷe·'lduxʷ.	He was lost now.
25.	x̌ʷe·'lduxʷ.	He was lost now.
26.	ʔəd ƛ'ə'ʔətəb.	And they looked.
27.	ʔəxʷɔ·'ča·duxʷ tə bəščəd?	"Where did it go, the louse?"
28.	ta·'tałbətəbduxʷ	They hollered:
29.	dɩča'duxʷč ʔu bəščəd?	"Where are you, Louse?"
30.	dɩča·'duxʷč?	"Where are you?"
31.	dɩča·'duxʷč?	"Where are you?"
32.	xʷa·'qəqs qʷa'w'aqs.	There was no answer.
33.	ʔaxʷɔ'ča·duxʷč qaʔwi ʔə bəščəd?	"Where did you go, anyway, Louse?"
34.	ʔaxʷɔ'čaduxʷč?	"Where did you go?"
35.	xʷa·'qəqs qʷa'w'aqs.	There was no answer.
36.	ʔəd hoy . . .	And then . . .
37.	. . . ʔiəq'olwəltxʷ	
38.		

39.	ca·'yay ʔæč tə sqələbalb ɨš ʔæč ti stabixʷ.	He was mixed up in the dust on the ground.
40.		
41.	xʷa'ʔqa·duqʷs toqʷo'təbs.	He never was found.
42.	x̌ʷe'lduxʷ.	Now he was lost.
43.	x̌ʷe'lduxʷ.	Now he was lost.
44.	———	That's the last.

New transcription problems arose with this new version. The poor quality of the recording coupled with my never having heard Mrs. Purdy in person caused difficulties. Additionally, her dialect had virtually disappeared in the intervening quarter century. I therefore had difficulty with forms in the story that were distinct from Skokomish Twana. At least one other researcher also had problems with the collection in terms of the "lack of clarity and the dialect difference" (Hilbert 1974:50).

If I heard correctly, Lines 4 and 27 contain some startling information. In both cases a non-female article *tə* is used, rather than the female counterpart *cə*. I looked through Drachman's notebooks. There I found a transcription of Mrs. Purdy's story with word by word translation that did not completely correspond with mine (for example, his Line 1 reads *co'təduxʷo bəsčʌ'd* "Louse said" and appears to be in error; compare with Version VII, Line 2). However, Drachman did transcribe *tə* in both Lines 4 and 27. Therefore it appears that the Twana character, contrary to my assumption based on chores associated with sex roles, is probably a male.

Even more startling was Line 3, which is a familiar one in Twana stories. It cues the listener that what follows is one of a number of accounts related to the coming of Dukwibahl, the transformer figure whose journey through the area is chronicled in a multi-episode legend:

They have a tradition that a long time ago a great supernatural being called Dok[w]ibatl came here and told them to give up all bad habits (Eells 1985:206).

A long time after the creation, say the Indians, the world became bad and the people became bad and foolish, whereupon Dok[w]ibatl determined to come here and rectify affairs—to punish the world and to change the foolish into something else.

According to them, the animals had been first made as men, but they were foolish. If a person stubbed his toe and fell down, he died. The hummingbird tried to fight the rain (Ibid:363).

At least one modern version states that Dukwibahl sent Bluejay to get "word to all beings, that I am going to change things" (Miller ms.). A number of the episodes in the Dukwibahl saga open with a statement that indicates that the individual heard about his coming. This is true for deer, beaver, band-tailed pigeon, loon, and cormorant. Eells (1985:363–64) recounts in English two of these episode introductions as follows:

". . . one man, knowing he was coming . . ."
"A boy knew that Dok[w]ibatl was coming . . ."

Drachman (1965) provides both the Twana and English translation for the episode where Loon and Cormorant are preparing themselves for a visit by Dukwibahl:

to'lastəbduxʷ   ʔo qʷoʔo'la wuɬ ba'čad.
They heard about it, Loon   and Shag [Cormorant]

The news Louse heard was this same news, that Dukwibahl was moving through the region changing the way of life for the inhabitants of that period. Thus Louse, like many of the others, was busy cleaning her house in preparation for the arrival of Dukwibahl. That the story of Louse was a portion of the Dukwibahl saga explains why there was no development of Louse as a character. Dukwibahl was actually the central character and Louse was only a new character introduced briefly in this particular episode.

The traditional opening found in Version VIII (as in Version VI/VII) identifies the main character of the myth and that character's situation. In direct contrast to Mrs. Pulsifer's versions (I–V), the notion of sweeping is delayed until Line 4. Much more information that is found in Version VIII is absent from Versions I–V.

It is doubtful that the absence of details in the Skokomish Twana versions should be attributed to poor recollection on the part of the storyteller. But should it be viewed as being omitted by the storyteller as part of the situation of the storytelling?

According to Snyder (1964:21–22), a story must be considered to be complete to the teller's knowledge if the teller does not say it is incomplete:

But that they considered their own renditions complete, unless otherwise specified, is certain. . . . Skagits were compulsive about telling stories "right." If a story was imperfectly recalled it was wrong for them to "guess," meaning to pad, improvise, paraphrase or omit. It was better not to tell it at all for it was dangerous to omit scenes and to shorten myths. Nubile women in the audience might then give birth to deformed children, incomplete or malformed like the abbreviated or truncated story. And shortening of myths would shorten the lives of all listeners.

Mrs. Pulsifer did not state that the Louse story she told was a fragment. On the contrary, she stated that it was complete. There were other stories that she would not relate because she said she could not remember them in totality. Her adherence to the traditional practice described by Snyder indicates that she believed her version to be complete. The Snohomish version of the Louse story, which is equally brief, offers additional evidence that the Skokomish version is complete.

The riddle I had before me was: When is a whole story only part of a story? This led me to examine the genres of stories among the Twana and Puget Sound Salish. It was there I decided upon my final solution.

Elmendorf (1961:7–9) divides Twana folk literature into three categories: myths, or tales from the myth period; semi-mythic tales; and semi-historic tales. The Hoodsport version of Louse falls under the myth category because it contains Dukwibahl

(Ibid: 7). Hess (n.d.) also identifies the Snohomish version as belonging to this category. Therefore all of the versions of the Louse-sweeping story appear to be set in the same time period. But they are very much different.

The complete Dukwibahl epic provides Native people with explanations regarding their relationship to nature and geography. It was used as part of the general training provided to the youth. While the Skokomish and Snohomish versions do appear to have an unstated moral, they do not contain the same teaching materials as the Hoodsport story. Therefore it could be that they differ from the Hoodsport version because they were intended for different audiences.

I went back to my field notes. There I saw that after Mrs. Pulsifer told the story she classified it as "a little kids' story" or "a story for little kids" (Thompson, n.d.). Suddenly I began to see the Skokomish version of Louse as a nursery tale, intended for very young children, that had long ago been condensed from a fuller version like the one found among the Hoodsport Twana.

While my positing a new subtype provided a solution for why Mrs. Pulsifer's versions seemed to lack information, such a claim needed to be supported. There should be other brief stories that are similar in nature. But I could find no examples in other Salish languages nor could I find such a category of story listed for them. I turned my search to a review of my Twana field notes.

I was successful in finding what I believe to be a further example of the subgenre: the story of Boil (*spus*), Mrs. Pulsifer's favorite story as a young child. The following is her Skokomish Twana version of that story and her free English translation.

Boil Story: Spus   LJP/NT/11/14/75

1. biʔičʼud ci spuʼs.

2. ʔən bicututut tə kʷtaʼbac.

3. "ʔəsuɬ ʔæʼɬ. ʔəsuɬ ʔæʼɬ."

4. hoy, ʔæʼɬduxʷ spus.

5. ʔəndoy yəx̌ʷax̌ʷəduxʷ.

Boil was getting big and getting big and getting big.
And her husband told her to bathe, bathe, bathe.
So she got in the water and she bathed.
The Boil just disappeared.

The Boil story is comparable to the Louse story she told in length and lack of character development. It has no traditional introduction. It is quite interesting that Boil is specified as a female through the use of the feminine article *cə*.

The Skokomish stories of Louse and Boil are readily seen as having the same structure. These nursery tales are all set in the myth period and appear to be part of a subset of the stories from that period. They are both of limited length (eleven to sixteen words within three to five sentences), have an absence of main character development, and deal with an aspect of cleanliness. Additionally, they each appear to present a single lesson in cultural training:

> Louse: keep house clean to avoid lice
> Boil: wash frequently to avoid boils

Ascertaining that the Skokomish Louse story was complete even when it seemed to lack certain portions of the storyline provided me with the final piece of the puzzle. I did not have to add information to make it complete beyond what was inadvertently left out by the storyteller. I did not have to account for details presented in the Snohomish or Hoodsport versions.

Thus, I now consider Version V to be the Louse story as told by Mrs. Pulsifer when she was about eighty-two years of age and the following composite to be the story she told when she was about ninety-six. The differences between these versions are then, I feel, attributable to the age of the storyteller. It is probably the case that in 1977 she could not recall the word for "dust" while she was telling the story and felt uncomfortable about substituting another word. Likewise she probably felt uncomfortable about not including mention of what it was Louse got mixed up in; therefore her parenthetic inclusions of "dirt" or "mud." I now feel comfortable about adding that information to the composite version. Likewise, the Hoodsport Twana version convinced me that Louse should be treated in Twana as a male.

Louse Story/Composite Version LJP/NT/1977

1. ʔiəqʼʷoʼlwəltxʷduxʷ bɪščəʼd.
    Louse was sweeping his house now.

2. ʔədaʼqʼʷ wəʔæʼtxʷəlwəsəb.
    He got just halfway.

3. ʔəd hoy caʼyayduxʷ   ʔal tə qʼʷiɫuʼcad.
    And then he got mixed up now in the dust.

Notes

1. My work with the Skokomish Indian Tribe regarding the Twana language was from 1975 to 1980. Support came through various grant and contract sources, including the Melville and Elizabeth Jacobs Research Fund and the U.S. Department of Social and Human Services. Symbols used for vowels in Native American words have the following values:

> a   as in "m*a*"
> æ   as in "gl*a*d"
> ə (ʌ) as in "c*u*t"
> e   as in "cl*ay*"
> i   as in "b*ee*"

ι	as in "gr*i*t"
o	as in "g*o*"
ɔ	as in "*ou*ght"
u	as in "d*o*"
ʊ	as in "p*u*t"

The letters *b, d, h, l, m, n, p, r, s, t, w,* and *y* represent the same sounds that they do in the English alphabet. Other symbols are used as follows:

c	as in "ca*ts*"
č	as in "*ch*ew"
gʷ	as in "*Gw*endolyn"
ǰ	as in "*j*am"
ł	a breathy *l* like the Welsh *ll*
kʷ	as in "*qu*it"
q	as in "*c*old"
qʷ	as in "*qu*ote"
š	as in "*sh*oe"
ƛ	a sound that combines *t* and *l*
xʷ	as in Spanish "*Ju*an"
x̌ʷ	an xʷ pronounced farther back in the mouth, where the northern Germans pronounce "i*ch*"
ʔ	the catch in the vocal chords found in the middle of "huh uh"
ˀ	a catch in the vocal chords that occurs within the pronunciation of the preceding consonant

2. For a more detailed description of the death of the Twana language, see Thompson 1985.

3. Elmendorf (1961) presents a number of Skokomish tales in English only. Drachman (1969) provides an episode of the Twana transformation cycle.

4. The attachment of commentary of this sort onto the end of a myth is noted elsewhere in the Pacific Northwest (e.g., Hymes 1981:128).

5. See Thompson (1984) for a discussion of a female speech register used by the Twana.

6. A third person singular subject (i.e., "he/she/it") is detected by the absence of any other person marker such as the first person singular subject (-čəd) or the second person singular subject (-č).

7. I would like to express my appreciation to Burke Museum for access to the Metcalf Collection.

8. The Hoodsport people (*čtslalʔałʔałtəbixʷ*) were one of nine Twana village communities (Elmendorf 1960:263–64). Each of the communities spoke a different dialect (e.g., in Skokomish, the largest and best recorded dialect, the word for "big" was *sisid* while in the Hoodsport dialect it was *hikʷ*) and those with winter housing near Hood Canal also had temporary houses akin to today's summer cabins where they spent their summers. The Hoodsport people had their permanent homes along Finch Creek, just north of the modern day reservation. Their temporary fishing, hunting, and berry picking grounds with accompanying camping site was at Steelhead Creek (*duxʷkʷawələp;* Robert Lewis statement, May 12, 1942). Mrs. Purdy's parents moved from Hoodsport to the Skokomish Reservation in 1859 (Tenth Census of the United States, Skokomish Reservation).

References

Ballard, Arthur C. 1929. Mythology of Southern Puget Sound. *University of Washington Publications in Anthropology* 3:31–150.

Consortium of Johnson O'Malley Committees, Region IV, State of Washington. 1974. *The Way It Was: Anaku Iwacha* (Yakima Legends).

Deloria, Vine, Jr. 1977. *Indians of the Pacific Northwest: From the Coming of the White Man to the Present Day.* Garden City, N.Y.

Drachman, Gaberell. 1969. Twana Phonology. *Ohio State University Working Papers in Linguistics* 5.

————. n.d. Twana Field Notes. Unpublished manuscript.

Eells, Myron. 1985. *The Indians of Puget Sound.* Seattle.

Elmendorf, W. W. 1960. The Structure of Twana Culture. *Research Studies,* Monographic Supplement 2.

————. 1961. Skokomish and Other Coast Salish Tales. *Research Studies* 29:1–37, 84–117, 119–50.

Hasnain, Ghulam. 1977. Twana Field Notes. Unpublished manuscript.

Hess, Thom. 1972. Puget Salish Texts. Unpublished manuscript.

————. 1976. *Dictionary of Puget Salish.* Seattle.

————. 1985. Introduction to Hilbert, *Haboo: Native American Stories from Puget Sound.*

Hilbert, Vi. 1974. On Translating the Metcalf Tapes. *Papers of the IXth International Conference on Salishan Languages,* 49–52. Vancouver, B.C.

————. 1980. *Huboo.* Seattle.

————. 1985. *Haboo: Native American Stories from Puget Sound.* Seattle.

Hymes, Dell. 1981. *"In Vain I Tried to Tell You": Essays in Native American Ethnopoetics.* Philadelphia.

Jacobs, Elizabeth Derr. 1959. *Nehalem Tillamook Tales.* Eugene.

Kroeber, A. L. and E. W. Gifford. 1980. *Karok Myths.* Berkeley.

Lerman, Norman Hart. 1952. Folk Tales of Lower Fraser Indians. Unpublished manuscript.

Miller, Gerald B. 1975. Changer: A Puget Sound Myth of the Coming of Man. Unpublished manuscript.

Snyder, Sally. 1964. Skagit Society and its Existential Basis: An Ethnofolkloristic Reconstruction. Ph.D. dissertation, University of Washington.

Thompson, Nile. 1984. Female Indicators in the Twana Language. University of Victoria, *Working Papers of the Linguistics Circle* 4:331–36.

————. 1985. Twana Baby Talk and its Theoretical Implications. Ph.D. dissertation, University of Washington.

————. n.d. Twana Field Notes, 1975–1980. Unpublished manuscript.

Translating Form in Classical American Indian Literature

Toby C. S. Langen

Several years ago, I had the experience of watching a volume of stories translated from several Indian languages go through the process of evaluation and publication. The manuscript was examined by three scholars of American Indian literatures who were also expert in American Indian languages (though not in the source languages of the translations, since there are not three such experts available). Reports pronouncing the translations good came in from the readers, and the book was published to favorable reviews. During the entire period of pre- and post-publication evaluation, however, not one person had ever asked to see glossed versions of the Indian-language originals from which the translations had been made. In the case of this book, then, the name of a reputable publisher on the title page and the presence of favorable reviews in reputable journals were no guarantee that the translations had been held to any kind of account.

While I express dismay at the fact that publisher's readers and reviewers will evaluate a translation without attempting to consult the original work, I do not mean to imply that literal fidelity to that original is the measure to which a translation must be held. But surely the relation of the translation to the original, whatever that relation may be, ought to be of interest to an evaluator. The relation of the translation to the target language and literature ought to be of interest, too. In the particular case under discussion here, the English into which the stories had been translated was not entirely competent. No reviewers ever mentioned this, and I suspect that silence was the product of an (un-evaluated) assumption that the translator, following the model of many scholarly transla-tions, had decided to devalue literary quality in the target-language version and to privi-lege fidelity to source-language syntax and lexicon. The assumption was, however, invalid: many of the problems sprang from the fact that the translator had attempted to break free of the kind of interlanguage that results from literal fidelity to the original by following models of folktale and fairy tale that the target culture no longer values in the way that one would like to see classical American Indian works valued.

For those who are interested in seeing classical American Indian narrative be-come more available for an audience that includes Indian people whose first language is English, general readers, and students in classrooms, the absence of widely accepted stan-dards in the evaluation of translations for publication is disabling. I find myself wary of any translation that does not offer some sort of access to the translation process as well as to the original (which, because I need to do close readings, means something on the order of a morpheme-by-morpheme gloss, not just a facing-page source-language text). My atti-tude is not solely due to an awareness of critical nonfeasance, but also to an appreciation of the problems faced by translators working with transcriptions of American Indian nar-ratives. Unlike classical Greek texts, for example, which have had the benefit of hundreds of years of scholarly attention, the texts of classical American Indian literature are still comparatively unexamined and unestablished. Very few have had the attention of more than one editor, and there are not crowds of scholars fluent in any Indian language waiting to evaluate the quality of anyone's translation. In addition, source-related problems are often immense. In my case, I work with tape recordings that are thirty years old. There are very few stories in this collection that are intelligible all the way through, whether because of bad recording conditions at the outset, tape deterioration over the years, or the fact that fluent elders in the 1950s used a kind of Lushootseed no one any longer speaks. As trans-lator of these stories, I am forced from time to time to intervene in such a way as to re-create the source (for example, to guess at which might have filled what is now a lacuna). As a reader familiar with such problems, then, I want to know as much as possible about what the source performance was like: in the final presentation of a translation, access to the original-language text will reveal the existent problems and annotation will detail the process of intervention.

In his article "Poetic Retranslation and the 'Pretty Languages' of Yellowman" (Toelken and Scott 1981), Barre Toelken has described a process of change in his own practice of translation, a process that began as a response to issues raised by Dell Hymes in "Discovering Oral Performance and Measured Verse in American Indian Narrative" (1977). In the course of reworking his translation of a Navajo story, Toelken tried out a lineated format, similar to the one Hymes uses, in order to make available to the reader such features of the original as "parallelism, redundancy and grouping"—that is, inter-linear relations that carry meaning (65). As a result of his retranslating, Toelken says, "I have discovered patterns, words and meanings that I did not see before; I have been forced to deal directly with matters I had easily buried in prose explanation; worst of all, I realized I had failed even to hear some words because I didn't think they were there" (70). A look at the beginnings of the two versions of his translation will illustrate the kinds of problems he is talking about:

1968 Prose Translation

(style: slow, as with factual conversational prose; regular intonation and pronunciation; long pauses between sentences, as if tired) Ma'i was walking along once in a one-forested area named after a stick floating on the water. He began walking in the desert in this area, where there were many prairie dogs, and as he passed them by they called him mean names, but he ignored them (75).

1979 Poetic Retranslation

(1) Ma'i was trotting along [having always done so].
(2) At a place I'm not familiar with called "Where the Wood Floats Out" he was walking along, it is said.
(3) Then, also in an open area, it is said, he was walking along in the midst of many prairie dogs.
(4) The prairie dogs were cursing him, it is said, all crowded together, yelling.
(5) He went along further into their midst.
(6) Then he walked further.
(7) He got angry and soon began to feel hostile.

(97–98)

In quoting from the 1968 version, I have omitted a footnote that explains how "walking along once" can quite reasonably become "trotting along [having always done so]" in the 1979 version. From the 1979 version I have omitted the scene labels, pause-length markers and diacritics, since I am discussing only the rhetoric, not the performance values, of the two versions.

In the 1968 version we can see that Toelken actually attempted less to translate than to retell the story. The sentence structure obscures the *inclusio* we see in lines 1–2 of the 1979 version, prevents us from considering the information in line 3 as a sort of pendant to the *inclusio* and falsifies the pace (and perhaps humor) of Yellowman's depiction of Coyote's growing anger. If the sentence structure of the 1968 version is an effort to connect the parts of the original that are separated by pauses and might seem choppy in translation, then an inadvertent result of this silent intervention is the reinforcement of the stereotype of oral style as helplessly paratactic. While I disagree with Toelken's (and Hymes's) assumption that the presence of parallelism, chiasmus, *inclusio,* and other "line-based" figures in a story means that the story is a "poetic" rather than a prose work (see Mattina 1983 and Langen 1989), I think they are right, at this moment in the process of Indian/white cultural exchange, to call attention to the kinds of iterative structures that they find in their sources and to privilege these structures in their translations.

The goals and emphases of translation practice change as the relations between source culture and target culture change. What it is most important for a translator of classical American Indian literatures to do at any particular moment ought to be a response to unsatisfactory aspects of past practice as well as to current needs, needs that have been created in part by the failings of past practice. A list of the qualities that any translator, past or present, might wish to be able to transfer from the source document (let's say, a tape recording) to the target document (let's say, a printed text) might look like this:

Style
    The "voice" of the storyteller:
        Diction (register, rime and rhythm as the results of capitalizing on aleatory phenomena, idiolect, language competence, etc.)
        Delivery (pause, gesture and expression, vocal mimicry, mime, interaction with audience, sound effects, pitch, intensity, mannerisms of movement, etc.)
        [These qualities are all means to ends; if the mode of translation cannot reproduce the qualities, perhaps the ends can still be retrieved.]
    The "voice" of the narrator:
        Validation (right to tell the story, etc.)
        Point of view
        Plotting and characterization as they yield a motivated train of events
        [These items, of course, may be traditional and not reflect individual decisions of the particular narrator.]
    The "voice" of the occasion (the circumstances under which the performance takes place, as these circumstances affect the performance)
    The "voice" of the language:
        Etymology
        Morphology
        Syntax
        Characteristic cadences
        Phonemic catalogue
        [Attempts to transfer language-specific qualities usually result in interlanguage: we translate *la plume de ma tante* as "the pen of my aunt" only for laughs; why do we have a different rule for American Indian literature?]
Content
    Story (catalogue of events, as opposed to motivated train)
    Characters
    Setting (insofar as different from validation)
    Information included in story (as distinguished from validation)
    Lexicon
Form
    Order (flashbacks, variation in episode-patterns, etc.)
    Pace (iterative patterning of content)
    Meter (prescribed iterative patterning of sound)
Literary history
    (Proportion of individually contributed elements to traditional elements)
Reception
    The esteem granted to
      the particular storyteller
      the subject matter of the story
      the activity of storytelling

traditional practices of storytellers
the activity of listening to stories
Significance
Storyteller's purpose in telling the story
Storyteller's accommodation of the cultural expertise of the audience (punning, use of proverbs, allusions, allegory, ambiguity, foiling of expectations, etc.)

No translation can transfer all of these qualities of the source, not least because some of the qualities become mutually exclusive when considered as goals of translation. Literal fidelity to the source lexicon, for example, is the surest enemy of stylistic equivalence in the target-language version. What a glance at the list shows is that certain items in the content inventory—plot, for example—have been privileged in past translation practice to the extent of eclipsing entire other categories—form, for example. What we need to ask at this point is whether past translators' emphasis on content is reflective of the ways in which the source cultures valued their stories.

There is plenty of evidence that Lushootseed classical storytelling did not privilege plot over form. Most members of any audience already knew the plot, and we have lengthy versions of stories in which parts of the plot are not narrated, but only alluded to. Instead, the audience for a classically told narrative was interested in what the narrator made of the story. A storyteller still famous around Puget Sound, though he has been dead for many years, is Casimir Sam. People who tell me about Mr. Sam have gone to the length of acting out how he told portions of this or that story: even when they cannot remember the plot, they may still retain a vivid recollection of the delivery. In speaking about storytelling as it used to be, people invariably stress the quality of attention paid to the narrative, the training of children to enable them to achieve a high degree of attentiveness, and the fact that storytellers left audiences with the task of figuring things out. Elders today, in fact, may remember the significance they found in a certain telling of a story even when they no longer entirely recall how the story went.

From elders' testimony we get a picture of the storytelling event as an occasion for the exercise of a disciplined, practiced attention directed to connoisseurship of performance and decipherment of codes. And we get an idea, too, of a story as a means of training for hermeneutic activity. In a textbook called *The Sacred: Ways of Knowledge, Sources of Life* prepared at Navajo Community College, there is a section on listening to stories, and part of that section is entitled "Not Asking Why" (Beck and Walters 1977: 50–63). The title is explained in part by a quotation from information given by a Keres man, Larry Bird, to Dennis Tedlock: "You don't ask questions when you grow up. You watch and listen and wait, and the answer will come to you" (51). Though he is speaking about pueblo culture, Mr. Bird's remarks describe the kind of attentiveness that was fostered by storytelling in Lushootseed culture as well. We can tell this because the formal properties of classically told stories repay precisely that kind of patience.

At present in Lushootseed storytelling practice I do not know of anyone who attempts to replicate the formal qualities of traditional narration. I know of no one who speaks of the act of listening as training. Plot is routinely laid out in linear fashion, repetition is avoided, and various kinds of meaning that used to be conveyed in code are now made explicit. Present practice, along with remarks I have heard made about the old tape-recorded narrations, convey to me the impression that Lushootseed people are somehow ashamed of the amount of repetition in classical performance and no longer understand how it works. This shame, it seems to me, is a by-product of the devaluation of form and the privileging of plot in past translation practice, for it is largely through the products of past practice that people have arrived at a notion of what a "presentable" literature ought to be. Nor has it been without effect that much of the attention directed to Lushootseed literature has been in a context of curriculum development, not of presentation of stories to audiences of adults. At the present time, therefore, as a translator of classical Lushootseed narrations, I choose the rehabilitation of form as the goal I most desire to achieve, and in doing so I am aware that the privileging of form will have the attendant effect of drawing regard to certain other qualities of the source literature: literary history, reception, and significance.

II

Ranking one's goals is a way of determining priorities among the criteria that govern decisionmaking. But in setting to work, the translator soon discovers a need to decide something about means as well as goals, for it soon becomes evident that the narrative voice in the translation cannot be that of the translator, nor even the voice that expresses itself as narrative point of view in the story (something perhaps analogous to the omniscient author of written literature). The narrative voice in the translation turns out to be the representation of the person who tells the story.

Anthony Mattina has discussed the reasons for his decision to use "Red English" to represent the Colville-speaking voice of Peter Seymour, narrator of *The Golden Woman* (Mattina 1985:9–13). For this story, which uses a European fairy tale to poke fun at European culture, the irreverent and at times *faux-naïf* tone of Red English is very successful. But it is a marginal English and carries with it a certain freight. In fact, in the example of the use of marginal English in the work of Leslie Silko quoted by Mattina in support of his decision, it is evident that Silko is characterizing her speaker as of a certain social class and not highly educated.

For me, as I undertook the translation of the narrative I am about to discuss, Susan Sampson Peter's story about the Sockeye Salmon wife, the use of Red English was not an option. In terms of her culture, Mrs. Peter had received the best of educations: she was an Indian doctor, a trained historian, and a storyteller noted for the vividness of her delivery. The Lushootseed she spoke is sophisticated beyond the capabilities of current speakers, and it may also be a little archaic in its lexicon. (Whether because she herself was old when the recordings were made or because there was an archaic storytelling diction is something we do not know.) There is a problem with trying to represent her utterance in formal, perhaps a little archaic, English, however: Mrs. Peter is speaking to us, not writing for us. In English-language tradition, the speaking voice is rarely the vehicle of highly competent, formalized utterance outside the court or the academy, neither of which is customarily considered a forum for art narrative. My goals for the English I would use to represent Mrs. Peter's voice were that it be not only competent, but also supple; that it reflect her ability to characterize the voices of different people; and that it embody the gusto of her narration. I felt it was necessary to find an English that would command respect for Mrs. Peter, as her Lushootseed commands respect.

Since my goals for the translation as a whole were to reveal the traditional poetics and to make it possible for a reader of the English version to appreciate the quality of the narrative as an example of that poetics, a literary analysis of the story had to be the first step. (A synopsis of the story in the form of excerpts linked by passages of summary is appended to this article. Limitations of space preclude the inclusion of the Lushootseed original with morpheme-by-morpheme analysis.)

Earlier in this discussion I used terms such as *inclusio* and chiasmus to name the kinds of iterative structures characteristic of Lushootseed literature. This is because the most interesting studies of the modes and functions of repetition have been made in the fields of European classical and Biblical literatures (cf. Berlin 1985, Thalmann 1984). But when it comes to discussing specific stories, I have hesitated to use the established terms, because I want to leave myself free to define structures of repetition as they function in American Indian classical literature, and my impression is that circular figures (a-x-a) and concentric figures (a-b- . . . x . . . -b-a) as they overlap (a-b-x-b-a-z-a) and interlace (a-b-x-c-b-a-z-c) are more fluid in their variety than are their analogues in European classical and Biblical figuration (cf. Langen 1991).

In Mrs. Peter's story of how it is that sockeye salmon are to be found in the Baker River, the main characters—Qidaqi?, the young man, and CʔIilh, the sockeye woman— are both introduced by means of passages of intricately figured narration. Here is the introduction of Qidaqi?, which I give only in Lushootseed for the time being so that the figuration may be as evident to the eye of a non-Lushootseed reader as it is to the ear of a listener:

1. gʷel ʔeslhalhlil kʷesi? ti?ilh ?i qidaqi?
2.   ?al ti?ilh ?alhXaducid ?e dxʷqelb,
3.   ?al ti?e? ilh?alhXad dxʷqelb.
4.   ʔeslhalhlil ti?e? qidaqi? ?i ti?ilh yelyelabs.
5.   ?absuqʷsuqʷa? ?e ti?e? bebuus.
6.   ?absuqʷsuqʷa? ?e ti?e? ?i ?ad?ad
              bebuus, bedbeda? ?e tsi?e?
              skʷuys.
7.   ?al ti?e? ?al?als helgʷe?,
8.   ?al ti?ilh lheqʷucid ?e ti?ilh ?e
              qaLelgʷilh qiqixʷ.
9.   ?a kʷi ?eslhalhlil ?e ti?e? qidaqi? ?i ti?ilh
              yelyelabs.
10.   Luxʷi?xʷi? ti?e? suqʷsuqʷa?s. . . .¹

This passage is in the form of two overlapping circular figures, each with its own cap or pendant. By "circular figure" I mean an organization of information in which the narrator circles back to what came first before going on to what comes next. Lines 1–4 constitute a circular figure: 1) People are living there—among them, Qidaqiʔ; 2–3) below the mouth of the Baker river, downstream from the Baker (on the Skagit); 4) they are living there, Qidaqiʔ and his relatives. The core of the circular figure (the information in lines 2–3) is restated in lines 7–8 after the figure is closed, and this device I call a "cap": the cap to the first circular figure (lines 7–8) gives additional information about the location of Qidaqiʔ's home. Lines 4–9 constitute the second circular figure, which overlaps the first in that it shares line 4 with it: 4) Qidaqiʔ and his relatives are living there; 5–6) he has four brothers; [7–8) location of the home, cap of the first circular figure]; 9) that is where he and his relatives are living. The second figure has what I call a "pendant" rather than a cap: lines 10 ff, which take up the subject of the brothers introduced at the core (lines 5–6) of the figure and does not just restate it, but continues with it.[2]

The passage in which CʔiIh, the sockeye woman, is introduced, is also highly figured. It comes just after Qidaqiʔ has announced to his mother that he is planning to go to CʔiIh's village and take her away from her husband:

1.   lecuyayus tsiʔeʔ:
2.   lecuCelh jecgʷicʔeʔ;
3.   huyud tiʔeʔ jecgwicʔeʔ;
4.   huyud tiʔeʔ sLalabac;
5.   huyud tiʔeʔ sqaSed,
6.   tiʔeʔ bitaʔs, tiʔeʔ Ludaʔteb
            degʷdegʷalep [. . .][3]
9. dilh suyayuss—
10.   ʔi tiʔeʔ puʔted, gʷeputedes [. . .]
13. dilh shuyayadis.

1. She was always working, this woman:
2.   she finished blanket after blanket;
3.   she made blanket after blanket;
4.   she made all kinds of clothing;[4]
5.   she made moccasins,
6.   women's leggings—what they used
        to call "degʷdegʷalep" [. . .]
9. This was what she kept working on—
10.   shirts, also, a kind of shirt [. . .]
13. This was what she kept doing.

Again, there are two overlapping circular figures (lines 1–9 and lines 9–13). This time the pendant of the first (lines 10–12) is the core of the second, and the second has no pendant of its own; the cores are parallel-constructed. Compared to the circumference-lines of the Qidaqiʔ circular figures, the circumference-lines here depend less on the repetition of words than on the repetition of concepts.

The circular figures concerning CʔiiIh themselves form the core of a larger, concentric, figure, which introduces her husband, Seltups. The concentric figure consists of a circular figure (B) with its core (C) inside another circular figure (A). But something else is going on here: in the interstices of the concentric figure, Mrs. Peter is interlacing the beginning of the next part of the story, which tells how Qidaqiʔ gets to CʔiiIh.

A-1.   qʷulＬel—qʷulＬel tiʔeʔ diʔeʔ seltups.
A-1.   Point Roberts—This Seltups was a Point Roberts man.

B-1.   lecuʔuXʷ tiʔeʔ seltups dxʷdiʔi.
B-1.   Seltups used to travel all over.

       lecuCelhXeCeb ckʷaqid bekʷ sleXil, bekʷ
       sleXil, sʔuʔuXʷs.
       He used to make new plans every day, every
       single day, about these travels of his.

    [Inter-   cugʷukʷexʷ tsiʔeʔ Cegʷass tsiʔeʔ
    lace]   Luʔalʔalʔal, ʔi tiʔeʔ yelyelabs.
           And his wife is home alone with
              his parents.

C [core].   [CʔiiIh's circular figures
           quoted above.]

    [Inter-   ʔa huy ʔuXʷexʷ, ʔibeSexʷ. . .
    lace]   Now (Qidaqiʔ) goes on his way . . .

B-2.   lecuCelhXeCeb tiʔeʔ seltups.
B-2.   Seltups was making plans as usual.

    [Inter-   huy ʔeＬaxʷ tiʔeʔ qidaqiʔ.
    lace]   Qidaqi' is coming closer now.

A-2.   sbaliʔxʷ—sbaliʔxʷ tiʔeʔ qidaqiʔ.
A-2.   Sbaliʔxʷ village—Qidaqi' is a sbaliʔxʷ village man.

Lushootseed verbs are not marked for tense; I have felt comfortable using the historical present—a technique frequent in oral narrative the world over—to render the lines involved in the interlace above, because they tell us what is happening in the story now, while the concentric figure gives us the background situation. (Line 1, I think, is about Cʔiilh as Qidaqiʔ's quarry, not about her as a good wife.)

It is evident from the fact that Mrs. Peter took pains to introduce Cʔiilh and Qidaqiʔ by means of the same narrative technique—overlapping circular figures—that she meant to bring them into some sort of parity. At the beginning of the story, it is clear that although they are equally important, they are on opposite sides of a moral fence, Qidaqiʔ engaged in a course of action of which people do not approve, and Cʔiilh leading an exemplary life. However, this relation changes, and Mrs. Peter charts the change by means of a series of parallel speeches. When Qidaqiʔ announces to his mother that he plans to steal Cʔiilh from Seltups, his mother says, "tiʔilh gʷel saʔ gwadshuy (That's a terrible thing you are going to do)." When Qidaqiʔ is trying to force Cʔiilh to come with him, she says, "saʔexʷ tiʔilh adshuyuc (This is a terrible thing you are doing to me)." So far, the women are in agreement. However, when Cʔiilh confronts her parents-in-law with her decision to leave, she takes as her excuse "hiqebexʷ saʔ tiʔilh seshuy ʔe tiʔilh seltups (It has really been a terrible thing, what Seltups has been doing)"; and her mother-in-law replies, "saʔexʷ kʷi gʷadsyayus, dbedaʔ (It's a terrible piece of work that you're planning to do now, my child)." Now Cʔiilh is on the same side of the question as Qidaqiʔ, the very word "work (syayus)" that is usually used to praise her now is being thrown in her face. Although it requires some departure from the strict letter of the Lushootseed, maintaining a noticeable parallelism among these speeches in English is crucial to the revelation of Mrs. Peter's formal intent.

The end of the story is noticeably less figured than the rest. No longer can translators take comfort in being able to check the accuracy of their work by comparing each line against its counterpart in a pattern. The frame of reference is now the whole story: we must check the end against the beginning and middle.

We notice a number of puzzling things about this last part of Mrs. Peter's story. Qidaqiʔ, who once replied to his mother's advice with an abrupt "*paLaL*" (akin to "phooey"), now at the end of the story couches his utterance in the dignified speech of a pillar of society. Has he grown up, as people who go into the forest and come back bearing a prize often have done in Lushootseed literature? Or does the orotundity of his speech have a hollow sound that reflects badly on him? Qidaqiʔ's mother, once so opposed to his course of action, is now spoken of as happy; but there is a sarcastic tone to Mrs. Peter's voice as she tells us about this. Is Qidaqiʔ's mother now being portrayed as a foolish old lady, too impressed by her new daughter-in-law's blonde hair? We notice also Mrs. Peter's use of the word "squeezed" when as narrator she talks about Cʔiilh's new home ("ʔuXʷ tsiʔeʔ gʷel leʔuXʷ, gwel leLuLuqwagʷ": she journeyed and journeyed far, and now she is squeezed in along the river), whereas her quarters are described as spacious and warm when Qidaqiʔ and his brothers speak of them. At the very end of the story, when Qidaqiʔ's mother asks, "lhuʔeXidexʷ kʷesi cedilh lhudxʷCadexʷ kʷi lhudexʷaʔs? (What are things going to be like for that woman where she is supposed to stay?)," the only reply she gets is about the permanence of Cʔiilh's residence.

During her lifetime, Mrs. Peter had seen the Baker River dammed and the sockeye disappear. The fishing rights of her people had been curtailed, and the first salmon ceremony was no longer performed. At the time when she told this version of the story, Mrs. Peter may have been in the process of repointing it to accommodate her attitudes to the changes in Sockeye's environment and in her people's relationship to the salmon. The characterizations of Qidaqiʔ as having a good opinion of himself upon his return, and of his mother as so overjoyed to see him that she forgets her scruples, were probably present in the story as it was told before any dam on the Baker River was built. But I suspect that the fact that these characterizations now contrast with the way the characters are presented at the beginning of the story may be something that Mrs. Peter has emphasized.

Her story ends, as it probably always had done, with the brothers' speech to their mother, telling her that Sockeye will be in the river for all time, and that the people will always come there looking for food. As things stood in 1952, storytellers had the choice of leaving out the speech, of including the speech because they believed that the salmon would come again, or of leaving it in and dealing with the irony that now accompanied it. For those storytellers who left the speech in, the behavior of Cʔiilh and Qidaqiʔ had to come under a new kind of scrutiny, because the effect of their actions had changed. Like most narrators who made heavy use of formal figures, Mrs. Peter did not usually explain what her stories meant. But midway through the homecoming scene, after she has said that the sockeye salmon will always spawn in the Baker River, she adds: "dex^w tuX^{w}s ti sex^{w}k^{w}edibelh ʔe qidaqiʔ tsiʔeʔ Cʔiilh teɬudex^w lhCils dx^{w}ʔal tiʔeʔ diʔeʔ swatix^{w}ted (The only reason for this is Qidaqiʔ's having become the abductor of the Sockeye woman—the reason for their repeated return to this particular country)." This is obviously something she wants us to think about.

What we notice about Mrs. Peter's version, then, is an access of ambiguity in its last part. It is not enough to translate the meaning of Mrs. Peter's words: the tone here is more important than the literal meaning, and if in achieving a good English translation there should arise some conflict between the goal of reproducing tone and the goal of reproducing lexicon, then tone should prevail. The register of Qidaqiʔ's later speeches, for example, must be replicated in English so that the contrast with his earlier rude brevity is available to the reader. Close attention to the tape recording is indispensable here, for the expressiveness of Mrs. Peter's voice must guide the English version no less than it does the Lushootseed. Certainly, the English version of the end of Mrs. Peter's salmon story should be as open to various interpretations as her Lushootseed version is.

Appendix: Summary of Mrs. Peter's Story

Note: A complete text of the salmon story runs over thirty pages and is too long to include here. I have instead provided a summary with excerpts from the translation. Summary narration appears within square brackets, along with information that might appear as annotation to a full translation. Cruces have been silently dealt with, though if this were a full translation, they would be identified and discussed.

[It is traditional to open a story with a circular figure introducing the main character; in using reduplicated and overlapping circular figures, Mrs. Peter has elaborated on the traditional opening in a manner that is characteristic of her. At the close of the introductory patterning, Mrs. Peter tells us that somehow Qidaqiʔ heard something about the wife of a man called Seltups. Qidaqiʔ decides then and there to go and get the woman. He announces his decision:]

He talked to his mother about it, and his mother talked right back:
    "That's a terrible thing for you to do, to pick a woman who has a husband. Instead, why not pick a single woman?"
    "I don't care, I'm going after her. I'm going to take her from that Seltups." Point Roberts— Seltups was a Point Roberts man.

[The rush of Qidaqiʔ's mother's speech shows her agitation. The implication of her words is that she is even willing to cede a parent's privilege of choosing her child's future spouse, if only Qidaqiʔ will come to his senses. An elder recently commented about this passage: "In the old days, when a young person misbehaved, people didn't say, 'Oh, So-and-so is misbehaving'; they said, 'Your child is misbehaving': they laid it on the parents." The fact that Seltups lives where the salmon first come into Puget Sound, while Qidaqiʔ lives far up on the Skagit River, may be a factor in Qidaqiʔ's decision.

    [The story goes on to tell how Qidaqiʔ sets off and how the salmon woman is a hard

worker, always being left alone by her wandering husband. The evening after Qidaqiʔ's departure,
the magpie boys, his brothers, arrive home from a hunting trip. They are boisterous, always kidding
around, a little hard on their mother:]

"Now, where's that son of yours, since he's not here?"

"Oh, it's a terrible thing your older brother is doing, absolutely terrible! That's why I am
totally distraught—I haven't slept, I haven't eaten—he's going after this married woman, and he's going
to get her and bring her here! Is she the only woman in the world?"

[The magpie boys set off after their brother.

[Now the story comes to the point at which the salmon woman gathers up the ingredients
for her shampoo and goes out to take a bath:]

She went upstream to a certain place and bathed. She was not ashamed, because there was nobody
around. She took off her clothes and went wading out and was washing her hair—

Qidaqiʔ jumped out of the woods. He landed on the woman's clothes.

There he is now, planted on them—

There she was now, and she was washing her hair, and her eyes were stinging, and she is
there just washing her hair.

She bathed: she was diving, she dived, shook her head, washed her hair—

(That must be Qidaqiʔ there, planted on her things, her *Sadets*.)
—and she saw something just downstream there where she was looking. She wrung out her hair and
was going to tie it and was turning her head—some person is sitting there!

"Oh! This is a terrible thing you are doing to me. What gives you the right to plant
yourself on top of my clothes?"

"It's not terrible at all, what I'm doing. You're the reason I came here: I want to
take you home to Dxʷqelb."

"Well, I'm not single, I'm married. I have a husband."

"I know that, but I came after you anyway. I'm going to take you away. Just say
yes, and I'll give you back your clothes. But if I don't get any cooperation from you, you
won't get any clothes back from me, even if it starts to get dark. There you'll be, still sitting
out in the water."

This woman thought it over for a long time.

"Am I the only woman in the world, that I have to be put on the spot by this man's
bad behavior? Here I am spied on by him when I don't even suspect a thing and am standing
up without any clothes on, walking around, washing."

She thought it over for a long time:

"All right, then. It's just that it will take me a long time to do everything I have to
do before I leave. I want to hang up that blanket I made. I'll put it out, and when Seltups—
and it will be out there in plain sight. I'll take only my own things, nothing else."

"Fine. Over there is where I'll wait, right over there. I'll be waiting for you."

So that's how it was: she went on her way, got home, and began getting herself ready;

she let down all her hair, which had been tied up, and began to dry it;

she got dressed.

She got things ready: despite her wet hair, she got ready.

She put out that certain item for Seltups.

She set it out so that it would be the first thing he saw that was different.

So that's how it was;

now she combed her hair

and put on red face paint.

She put on her clothes.
She put on her leggings.
She put on her moccasins.
She packed her tallow, her ochre.
She took her comb and put it in.
She took her moccasins and those *deg^wdeg^walep* I mentioned—
everything went in to be tied up; she was going to carry it that way.

Now she talked to the old people:

"The day has come when I shall leave you.
You will not see me again, ever.

It has really been a terrible thing, what Seltups
      has been doing;
He doesn't stop to think that I might be hungry;
he is always leaving me, every day;
he doesn't get any wood—I might as well be
      single, the way we fight over firewood.
And it's not that I don't work hard.

Well, he can go as often as he wants to whatever
place it is that he goes, wherever it is, now that
I'm leaving you."

"Oh, that would be a terrible thing for you to do, my daughter, a terrible piece of work. It would be better if you gave up this idea you're talking about: there's no one else to look after us."

"Well, I'm just going anyway. No one can stop me.
  I'm going anyway.
  I'm going to leave you
I hope you get along all right after I've left.

Seltups can go as often as he wants to, wherever
he wants, wherever it is he goes every day.

He is always staying away overnight,
      staying away overnight,
         on these trips of his."

She packed her things and picked them up and went outside.

The old woman was told by her husband: "Go on out and keep an eye on your daughter-in-law; see where she goes."

Sockeye salmon: these people are Sockeye.
The young woman is Sockeye.
Seltups is Sockeye.

The old woman was peering out, and her daughter-in-law got to the place at the edge of their land where the trees begin and was standing there. Suddenly the young man stands up and is taking hold of the things the young woman has brought.

Off they go, over there, walking together.

[The next part of the story tells how Qidaqiʔ and the young woman make their way back to Dx^wqelb, with the magpie boys a day behind, tracking them. Mrs. Peter tells this part of the story as four narrations of a single pattern-episode. Each day the woman tears off a piece of her *Sadets* and throws it away beside the trail. The magpies coming along find the pieces and pick them up. They sing a song that ends with their characteristic laughter.

[The *Sadets* is some kind of garment, but the exact meaning of the word has not been recovered, as far as I know. It is on a *Sadets* (perhaps the one she has with her now) that Qidaqiʔ landed when he jumped out of the woods as the woman was bathing. Perhaps the sight of him there suggested to the woman her future course of action. The audience's freedom to speculate about this and about the intention of the woman as she marks her trail is carefully preserved by Mrs. Peter. She provides a detailed portrait of the woman through interior monologue and dialogue and then leaves the audience to search the portrait for evidence of the woman's intent. Some storytellers simply state that the woman is leaving a trail for her husband; but they present a story less compelling than the one Mrs. Peter is asking us to attend to.

[The narration of the last pattern-episode is interlaced with an account of the arrival of Qidaqiʔ and the salmon woman at Dxʷqelb. Next, the magpie boys arrive and find that they now have a beautiful blonde sister-in-law. Their mother frets about the fact that her daughter-in-law has to be kept squeezed below the falls, forever hiding from Seltups:]

"Will that woman be all right where she is going to stay?"

"It is forever that she will be there, Mother, for all time.
That will become the gathering place of the people in the future
whenever they come looking for food
to the place where she is, there inside."

Acknowledgment

Some of the research for this essay was done at the 1987 NEH Summer Seminar on American Indian Verbal Art and Literature. The author wishes to thank the National Endowment for the Humanities and Larry Evers, who directed the seminar, for their support.

Notes

1. The orthography used for the Lushootseed text in this paper contains some symbols modified from the International Phonetic Alphabet:

italicized consonants are underlined
ʔ   glottal stop
C   voiceless palatal affricate (/ch/ as in church)
e   schwa
lh   voiceless lateral alveolar fricative (sound resembles a lateral lisp)
L   voiceless glottalized lateral alveolar affricate (/t/ and /lh/ pronounced together)
S   voiceless alveolar fricative (/sh/)

X   voiceless uvular fricative (/ch/ in German *ach*)

x^w   voiceless labialized velar fricative (/wh/ in when)

In the course of making the transcription I consulted a transcription done by Vi Hilbert of Lushootseed Research, Inc., and I thank her for making this available to me. Discussion of linguistic problems in my transcription and of principles of lineation must, because of space limitations, be taken up elsewhere.

2. Some critics call circularity "framing." I would distinguish between circularity, which is a reflective way of organizing the flow of material, and framing, which is essentially a technique for setting something off from its context and belongs more properly to linear narrative. Lushootseed narrative does use framing, too—at the beginnings and ends of speeches, for example.

3. Ellipses indicate that there is something on the tape recording that I cannot translate. In each case in this passage Mrs. Peter has added some information about the garment she is talking about, and her statements are parallel in form, each beginning with the word "just" and having something to do with lacing.

4. Mrs. Peter says only "blanket" and "clothing," but she draws out the vowels to indicate many items of each.

References

Beck, Peggy V. and Anna L. Walters. 1977. *The Sacred: Ways of Knowledge, Sources of Life.* Tsaile, AZ: Navajo Community College.

Berlin, Adele. 1985. *The Dynamics of Biblical Parallelism.* Bloomington: Indiana University Press.

Hilbert, Vi. n.d. Manuscript transcription of Susan Sampson Peter's story about Sockeye Salmon from a tape recording made by Leon Metcalf on November 2, 1952, and now Reel #24 in the Metcalf Collection, Thomas Burke Washington State Memorial Museum.

Hymes, Dell. 1977. "Discovery of Oral Performance and Measured Verse in American Indian Narrative." *NLH* 8:431–57.

———. 1981. *"In Vain I Tried to Tell You": Essays in Native American Ethnopoetics.* Studies in Native American Literature, I. Philadelphia: University of Pennsylvania Press.

Langen, Toby C. S. 1989. "Lineation and Translation." Paper presented at the annual meeting of the International Conference on Salishan and Neighboring Languages. Steilacoom, Washington, 16–18 August.

———. 1991. "The Organization of Thought in Lushootseed Narrative." *MELUS,* vol. 16, no. 1 (1991).

Mattina, Anthony. 1983. "North American Indian mythography." In *Working Papers* for the XXVIII International Conference on Salishan and Neighboring Languages, University of Washington, Seattle, August 10–12.

———. 1985. Introduction. *The Golden Woman: A Colville Narrative by Peter J. Seymour.* Tucson: University of Arizona Press.

Thalmann, William G. 1984. *Conventions of Form and Thought in Early Greek Epic Poetry.* Baltimore and London: Johns Hopkins University Press.

Toelken, Barre and Tacheeni Scott. 1981. "Poetic Retranslation and the 'Pretty Languages' of Yellowman." In *Traditional Literatures of the American Indian: Texts and Interpretations*. Edited by Karl Kroeber. Lincoln: University of Nebraska Press.

Suggested Reading

Collections

Because of their methods of collection and/or the amount of editorial emendation they contain, the few extant volumes of stories from the Lushootseed-speaking region are not very useful for students of narrative art. On the other hand, some such collections do present the variety of points of view about stories within and among tribal communities. Three of the most interesting collections available are Vi Hilbert, *Haboo: Native American Stories from Puget Sound* (Seattle: University of Washington Press, 1985), which contains thirty-three stories, including the Sockeye story discussed in this article, along with a valuable introduction and bibliography; Arthur C. Ballard, *Some Tales of the Southern Puget Sound Salish* (University of Washington Publications in Anthropology 2 [3]: 59–81) Seattle: University of Washington Press, 1927; and the same author's *Mythology of Southern Puget Sound* (University of Washington Publications in Anthropology 3 [2]: 3–150) Seattle: University of Washington Press, 1929.

Reception

Two volumes, neither concerned with Lushootseed literature, are nonetheless of interest in establishing the context in which the appreciation and interpretation of Puget Salish literature has gone on in the academic community: Melville Jacobs, *The Content and Style of an Oral Literature: Clackamas Chinook Myths and Tales* (Chicago: University of Chicago Press, 1959) and *Haa Shuká: Our Ancestors,* edited by Nora Marks Dauenhauer and Richard Dauenhauer (Seattle: University of Washington Press and Juneau: Sealaska Heritage Foundation, 1987). Jacobs was an early advocate of the artistic quality and psychological depth of Indian literatures, and his views influenced several generations of students of Puget Sound cultures; his Freudian bias seems out of date today, but his enthusiasm for the literature is still worth encountering. *Haa Shuká* is an offering to the general reader from within the Tlingit community; it presents texts in such a way as to recreate for the reader several aspects of an unmediated encounter with Tlingit narratives; editorial comment is kept for introductions and annotations, and the general reader is aware that he is sharing the texts with Tlingit-language learners, as well as the Tlingit people themselves. The Dauenhauers' work has been seen as a model by some scholars seeking to present Lushootseed stories to a general audience.

For Lushootseed literature specifically, three forthcoming publications are of interest: Crisca Bierwert's "Apparent Differences: A Study of Surface Texture in 'The Marriage of Crow' as Narrated by Lushootseed Storyteller Martha Lamont," in *Studies in American Indian Literatures* vol. 3, no. 1 (Spring 1991), presents an original-language text, poetic translation, and commentary on a story that invites multiple interpretations; in "The Organization of Thought in Lushootseed Narrative: Martha Lamont's 'Mink and Changer,' in *MELUS* vol. 16, no. 1 (1989–1990), I have tried to provide an introduction to Lushootseed poetics; a complete text and translation of "Mink and Changer," along with seven other stories, will be available in *Lushootseed Texts,* vol. I, edited by Vi Hilbert, Thomas M. Hess and Crisca Bierwert, tentatively scheduled for publication in 1992.

Translation

A good introduction to translation studies for the general reader is Susan Bassnett-McGuire's *Translation Studies* (London: Methuen, 1980), but the bibliography it provides is minimal. More helpful in this regard is a 1981 issue of *Poetics Today* (2 [4]) devoted to translation theory. Many of the scholars who cooperated on that volume are now publishing in a new journal, *Target: International Journal of Translation Studies.*

Cultural Background

For Mrs. Peter's own tribal group, the Upper Skagit, June Collins's *Valley of the Spirits: The Upper Skagit Indians of Western Washington* (Seattle: University of Washington Press, 1974) is the only book-length ethnography. Though published in the 1970s, it is based on fieldwork done thirty years earlier. A more recent study of northern Lushootseed religious beliefs, Pamela Amoss's *Coast Salish Spirit Dancing: The Survival of an Ancestral Religion* (Seattle: University of Washington Press, 1978), provides information essential to an appreciation of the spiritual context of the literature. In *Indians of Skagit County* (Mount Vernon, Washington: Skagit County Historical Society, 1972), Martin Sampson, Mrs. Peter's son, has provided a memoir of his mother and information not available elsewhere about the Skagit people during the century from 1870 to 1970.

Archives

At the present time, much Lushootseed material, including stories, remains unpublished. A good starting place for investigation is William Seaburg's *Guide to Pacific Northwest Native American Materials in the Melville Jacobs Collection and in the Archival Collections in the University of Washington Libraries* (Communications in Librarianship, 2), Seattle: University of Washington Libraries, 1982.

Hopitutungwni: "Hopi Names" as Literature

Peter Whiteley

. . . [N]o proper name of place or person names any place or person as such; it names *in the first instance* only *for* those who are members of some particular linguistic and cultural community, by identifying places and persons in terms of the scheme of identifications shared by, and perhaps partially constitutive of, that community. The relation of a proper name to its bearer cannot be elucidated without reference to such identifying functions.

—Alasdair MacIntyre (1985:7).

The old pond;
A frog jumps in, —
The sound of the water.[1]

—Bashō

If the naming of cats is a difficult matter, the naming of persons is assuredly more so.[2] Naming practices vary widely across cultures. From an anthropological perspective, names may individuate "persons"; they may designate positions in a social order; they may class individuals into social groups; or, in use, they may serve performative negotiations of personal identities and relationships.[3]

The idea that personal names might comprise a literary genre in some cultural contexts does not seem immediately obvious. In the "West," personal names have generally been regarded as signs without semantic content. John Stuart Mill's view that "proper names are meaningless marks set upon things and persons to distinguish them from one another" retains currency in philosophical and linguistic inquiry (Willis 1982:227; Basso 1988:103). Within anthropology, Lévi-Strauss's interpretation (1966:172–216) of names in "primitive" societies as instruments of social classification has been very influential. Consequently, in those societies where personal names have individual meanings, their full interpretive potential remains largely unplumbed.[4]

In many instances Native American personal names[5] carry semantic content that narratively denotes cultural or natural occurrences, or historical or mythological events. Moreover, name-composition may reflect a formal poetics; some Hopi names, I shall argue, are "tiny imagist poems." As narrative figures poetically composed, such names are oral texts, and "require exegesis in addition to translation" (Kendall 1980:261).

Hopi personal names do a number of things simultaneously. First, since they derive from totemically named clans (albeit indirectly—see below), they reflect a pattern of social relations that articulates with the kinship and ritual systems. Second, names serve to individuate persons—each name is unique and confers a unique identity on the bearer.[6] Third, and my central concern here, Hopi names are individually authored poetic compositions that comprise a literary genre. In concert, these three aspects bespeak a Hopi conception of their society as comprised of conscious individual agents, who use the figures that are names to construct personal identity, cultural meaning, and interpersonal relations—within, of course, received structures of social (and natural) organization.[7] Let me begin with the social background.

The Social Context of Hopi Naming

In August 1989, in order to supplement other accounts I had gathered over the years, I asked Herschel Talashoma from Bacavi to provide a formal account in Hopi on naming practices. We then produced a translation, mostly in his own English idioms. Part of this discourse (which I will explicate subsequently) went as follows:

Nu' hapi Niiti'yvaya. Ina hapi tapwungwa. Pu' inay oovi angqwat put sinomat puma ikyam. Pu' puma hapi hakiy tungwayangwu hakiy inayat angqwat. Niiqe oovi pu' puma nuy pan tungwaya nuy tiitiwaqw, nuy sunattaqw, Niiti'yvaya. Pumuy nu' oovi kyamuy'ta tapngyamuy. . . .

My name is Niiti'yvaya[8]—it means "brought a lot." My father is a Rabbit clan. So from my father's side, his relatives, they are my aunties. They are the ones that name you, from your father's side. And so, they are the ones who named me when I was born, when I made the twenty days— Niiti'yvaya. Those are the ones who are my (naming) aunts, the Rabbit clan. . . .

Noq put yu'at itanay hapi pam oovi yu'at pu' itaakya yu'at pam nuy yaw pan tungwa, Niiti'yvaya. Pu' pam pi tapwungwa niiqe pu' pam oovi put aqw taykyangw naatoylay aw taykyangw: yaw maqwise' a'ani qöqöye' ahoy ökye' pu' taataptuy, sowituy niiti'yvayangwu. Put nu' aw Niiti'yvaya.

It was my father's mother who named me, and my auntie's mother who named me that, "brought a lot." Because she was a Rabbit clan, so she was looking up to that, her clan [-totem]: when they go out hunting, and if they kill a lot, and come back with a lot of cottontails and jackrabbits. That is the reason why she named me "brought a lot". . . .

Pantikyangw pu' paasat hak
piw naat wimkyatingwu, wimkyate',
paasat pu' piw aqw naat pas
sukwat piw aqw naat nay'tangwu,
nay'vangwu. Pu' nu' pantiqe'
paasat pu' nu' tsu'ngyamuy,
tsu'wungwat nu' nay'taqe aw
paasat pu' tsu'ngyam ikyam
piw. Pu' puma piw nuy oovi
tungwaya. Pu' pam pay naap
hiisa'niiqam hakiy asnayangwu:
pay pi naamahin sen piw
suukyaningwu, piw qa suukya,
lööyöm, paayom, pam pay qa
tuwaniy'tangwu. Puma piw
paasat pu' hakiy tuwat
naatoylay panwat tungwayangwu.
Noq pu' pay pi itam soosoyam
Hopisinom naatoylay'ngwu—
hiihiita. Pu' peetu pay himu
naatoyla pay piw pay sukw
amumningwu puma pay naama
yantaningwu. Kur nu' uumi
pangqawni nu' honanwungwa;
itam poovolwungwat enangwye'. . . .

Pu' niikyangw itam Hopiit pay
aqw sutsep yuy amumningwu hakiy
yu'at himuwungwa niqw pay hak
put amumningwu. Pay qahisat
hopiitsay haqam nay amum. . . .

Paasat pu' nu' oovi wimkyatiq
paasat pu' puma tsu'ngyam
puma paasat pu' pi nuy tuwat
asnaya, nuy wimkyate'.
Paasat pu' puma pi tsu'ngyam
niiqe pu' puma naatoylay
oovi pu' pi aw nuy tuwat
tungwaya. Pu' put nu' hakiy
nu' Joseph nay'ta,
katsinnay'ta, put niqw put oovi
pas yu'at ephaqam naat qatu,
hak Nasiwunqa pam nuy Tahooya
yan tungwa, ispi naat nu'
ephaqam pay naat tsayniqw oovi
hoyat pam aw nuy tungwa Tahooya.
Noq pu' paasat i'i pas naap ina
niiqe pu' pamwa pu' nuy
Tsu'leetsiwma yan tungwa. . . .

After that, then you have to be
initiated. When you are
initiated then you have to have
another father, you will be given
another father. After that I
received a father from the Snake
clan, a Snake clan man. So, from
there on, my aunties were the
Snake clan. So they named me
also. There is no set number of
them who will wash your hair: it
could be one, not just one, it
could be two, three, there is no
limit to that. Then they name
you according to their
clan-totem. And then, all of us
Hopis, we have clans—*all* kinds.
And also some of these clans can
join together, they go along with
each other. For example, let me
tell you, I'm a Badger; we go
along, we also have Butterfly
with it. . . .

But us Hopis all the time,
whatever your mother's clan is,
you go along with that clan, you
go with your mother's clan.
Never a Hopi child goes along
with his father's clan. . . .

So that's why when I was
initiated, it was them, the Snake
clan, who washed my hair then,
when I was initiated. And since
they were the Snake clan, they
named me according to their clan.
And so, from there on my god-
father was someone by the name of
Joseph, he was my katsina god-
father. At that time, his
real mother, Nasiwunqa, was
still living; it was her who
named me "little blue racer
snake," because at that time I
was still a young one, and
small, so she named me "*little
blue racer snake.*" And then my
god-father himself named me

Pu' paasat i' qööqa'at inay	"Snake-dancers in line." And
qööqa'at pam pu' nuy paasat	then my god-father's older
Tsuu'a yan tungwa.	sister [later amended to younger
	sister] named me "rattlesnake."

Hopis are given names in a sequence of ritual initiations through life. Hopi is a matrilineal society, that is, clan membership is inherited from the mother.[9] But a baby's namegivers are female members of its father's clan (Niiti'yvaya's "aunties"), not of its own clan; in fact you never receive a name from your own clan. Gathering in the house of the newborn (traditionally twenty, but nowadays often only ten days after birth), several paternal clanswomen each bestow a name associated with their clan. Typically, a child receives half a dozen different names, only one of which will *huurta,* "stick."

At about ages six to ten, every Hopi child is initiated into either the *Katsina* or the *Powamuy* ritual society (for summary accounts of the Hopi ritual order, see Frigout 1979, or Whiteley 1987)—a practice still strongly maintained at all three Hopi Mesas. If male, new names are conferred by an initiating "godfather" and his close female relatives; if female, by a "godmother" and her close female relatives. Naming and initiation by a "godparent" create formal relationships with another clan (and group of clans or "phratry"); the named now applies the appropriate (patrilateral) kin terms and role-behavior to members of this clan (and phratry), who reciprocate in kind. Moreover, the godparent–godchild relationship is more than notional; the godparent holds a tutelary role in the child's learning of ritual knowledge, especially.

The new namegivers must be of another clan than *either* of the child's parents.[10] Still at Second Mesa and formerly at First and Third Mesas, a male receives an "adult" name on initiation by a godfather (who may be the same as the first one, but sometimes another, perhaps from a different clan again, is chosen) into one of the four *Wuwtsim* ("Manhood Initiation") societies. Yet other names will be conferred if he is inducted into one of several "Second Order" religious societies (notably, Blue Flute, Drab Flute, Antelope, Rattlesnake). Likewise, if a girl is initiated into one of the three women's societies (*Mamrawt, Lalkont, O'waqölt*)—and most were in the past initiated into at least one (the same Mesa breakdown applies here too)—she receives a new name.

There are other occasions for name-giving as well—such as being accidentally doused with someone's wash-water or urine. In the past, a boy also received a name at his first participation in a hunt, and a girl at her puberty initiation; Oraibi men returning from a (post-*Wuwtsim* initiation) salt expedition to the Grand Canyon received new names; and at death, clan "aunts" conferred new names, preparatory to the "soul's" (*hikwsi,* literally "breath") journey to Maski, the home of the dead.[11]

Names are conferred ritually while the subject's hair is washed in yucca suds. An ear of corn is wafted over him or her, and the namegiver enunciates the name in a short ritual formula (Voth 1905b provides a detailed account). The name a male receives during *Wuwtsim* initiation supersedes all others, marking the assumption of adult status. With the end of *Wuwtsim,* of the Second Order societies, and of the women's societies (the *O'waqölt* persists in modified form) at Third Mesa (Whiteley 1988a), child-names or names conferred at *Katsina/Powamuy* initiation remain operative in those contexts where Hopi names are used. These contexts are principally in ritual, and as terms of third-person reference in everyday discourse. Kin terms, English names, nicknames, or abbreviated versions of formal names are the usual forms for address, and English names serve bureaucratic requirements such as school and tribal enrollments.

The Poetics of Naming

All formal Hopi names refer to clan associations of the name-giver. Naming images are myriad. A proliferation of associations—by no means limited to finite repertoires—with one's *naatoyla,* clan emblem or "totem," are drawn upon from the namegiver's clan or phratry. Some names are straightforward clan eponyms: for example, Hoonaw (bear), Taawa (sun), Koyongo (turkey, associated with the Eagle clan), Honani (badger), Kuukutsi (lizard), or Tsuu'a (rattlesnake). A few others metaphorically combine a totemic species with an observed personal characteristic, as in Herschel Talashoma's explanation of Tahooya (*taaho,* a whipsnake or "blue racer"—a totemic association of the *tsu'ngyam,* [Rattle]snake clan—plus -*hoya,* a diminutive suffix, apt because of his age and size). But more often, the namegiver has a specific event or instance in mind which is not semantically presented in full in the lexical components of the name. Meaning is thus typically oblique, and not inferable from literal translation. A name's sense may not be widely known beyond the particular donor and receiver. Asked the meaning of certain names, my consultants often indicated this was impossible to discern from the morphemes themselves, though these were easy enough to identify; the *express intentions* of the namegiver would have to be known (cf. Voth 1905c:68).

Let me provide some examples (see Voth 1905c for many more). Lomayayva literally means "beautiful climbed (pl.)" or "beautifully ascended" from *lolma,* "beautiful" or "beautifully" and *yayva,* "climbed," "ascended" (pl.). This name belonged to an Oraibi Lizard clan man. There is absolutely no way to infer phenomenal sense (it could refer to any number of entities ascending something) from the literal translation, nor the clan-identity of the namegiver. In the concrete case, it is a Badger clan name—though, I hasten to add, it does not refer to "climbing badgers." As part of its ritual prerogatives, the Badger clan "owns" the *Powamuy* ceremony—a grand February pageant featuring numerous different *katsinam* (masked representations of spirits, in this case). A connected ceremony, *Patsavu,*[12] is performed at the end of *Powamuy* when there have been initiations into the *Wuwtsim* societies the previous November. During *Patsavu,* an elaborate procession of many different kinds of *katsinam* ascended into the village of Oraibi, in the afternoon, along a path from below the southwest side of the mesa on which Oraibi sits. "Beautifully ascended" refers to the aesthetic splendor—in terms of color, costume, and movement—of the procession of *katsinam* at *Patsavu* coming up into Oraibi as seen from the perspective of someone standing on the mesa.[13]

The condensed evocation this name conjures—a typical feature—displays the same quality that Keith Basso (1988:126, n. 17), borrowing from Edward Sapir, attributes to Western Apache placenames, as "tiny imagist poems." The almost photo-graphic quality of the captured image and the emphasis on process and movement are also reminiscent of some Japanese haiku.[14] But the poetic form of Hopi names is even more compact than haiku. Maria Chona's remark about Papago songs that "the song is very short because we understand so much" (Underhill 1979:51, cited in Krupat 1989:47) illustrates a widespread tendency toward condensation in some Native American narrative genres. This is very markedly the case with Hopi names.

Syntactically, and this too is a common feature, the name is elliptical: a com-pacted phrase in which the subject (the *katsinam*) is suppressed, leaving a predicate com-posed of a contraction of verb and adverb ("ascended" and "beautifully") to accomplish the poetic task.[15] Meaningful translation thus hinges, in the first place, on the identifica-tion of a lexically absent subject.

Another example: a widely known name, Sikyakwaptiwa,[16] is similarly oblique in denotation. Morphemically, it is composed of *sikyangpu,* "yellow," "yellowness," *kwapta,* "he/she put some things (pl.) above on high," and *-tiwa,* a male name suffix.[17] "He/she put yellows above on high" may be a reasonable translation. The namegiver's clan was Coyote, and the reference is to *sikyaatayo,* "yellow fox" (or, as C. and F. Voe-gelin [1957:18] record it, "brown, colorful fox with white-tip on tail"; I mention this for the acuteness of Hopi perceptual distinctions it reveals, a quality echoed in the strong vi-sual emphasis of many name-images; see below). *Sikyaatayo*'s color and habits are associ-ated in Hopi thought and tradition with the appearance of *sikyangnuptu,* a perceptually discrete stage of yellowish dawn light that follows *qöyangnuptu,* first gray light of dawn, and precedes *taalawva,* full daylight. The name, then, images the distant eastern appear-ance of a yellow fox in the completed act of putting the yellowness of postcrepuscular auroral light up onto the sky.[18]

If William Carlos Williams is "correct" that, "so much depends upon a red wheel barrow glazed with rain water beside the white chickens," then a "yellow fox put-ting up the yellow dawn light" similarly speaks of as it celebrates a powerful aesthetics that centrally animates Hopi cognition and cultural values. A "pure" translation of the morphemes would miss not only the intended meaning but also the aesthetic force of the poetic image.

Associations between this name and some traditional concepts occur in myths referring to sunrise. The personified (male) sun, Taawa, rises by climbing out of a kiva in the east. At the top of the kiva ladder, he puts on a gray foxskin tied to one of the ladder-poles, at which point the gray dawn light appears. He then puts on, from its position on the ladder pole, a yellow foxskin, creating the yellow dawn light, before beginning his journey across the sky to a western kiva, into which he descends at dusk (Voth 1903:351; 1905a:1). Voth (1903:351, n. 1) records a further association in this context with the two Flute societies (which have a ritual concern with the sun's movements); according to myth, the Drab Flute (*Masilelent*) society was brought to the Hopi mesas from its original loca-tion in the eastern kiva where the sun rises, and the Blue Flute (*Sakwalelent*) from the western kiva where it sets. The gray foxskin is the *naa'tsi* (ritual standard) of the Blue Flutes, and the yellow foxskin that of the Drab Flutes; these standards are tied to the ladder-poles of the societies' respective kivas when they are in session. The mythological prototypes of the Flute societies continue to perform in the sunrise and sunset kivas, but instead of putting up foxskins on the kiva ladder-poles, they magically raise up the live animals. I have not been able to discover any specific connection between these myths and the namegiver's intention, but clearly a nexus of mythological ideas associating yellow foxskins and yellow dawn light informs the name.

In this way, then, names may excerpt an image from an ideational complex more fully embodied in mythological narratives. Moreover, Hopi myth and ritual are mutually integral (as above with the Flute societies). Name images evoking ritual activities simultaneously invoke correlated myths. Lomayayva may be further unpacked by reference to the *Patsavu* ritual's accompanying mythology. The ascent of the *katsinam* into Oraibi in part reenacts the original arrival of the Badger clan. Each Oraibi clan, having completed its migrations undertaken after emergence from the "third" world below, had to seek entry to the village from the first arrivals, the Bear clan, and in particular their leader, the *Kikmongwi,* "village chief." Each clan had to demonstrate special ritual or other abilities before the *Kikmongwi* would accept them. At first the Badger clan, whose skills pertained to medicine and seed-fertility, were refused admission and went off to live at Tuuwanasavi ("earth-center place"), a few miles south in the Oraibi Valley. Finally, the *Kikmongwi* decided he needed their skills, and went four times (the archetypal number in Hopi sacred narrative, but in this case also because the Badgers were miffed by their earlier rejection) to persuade them to move into the village. To mark the significance of the event, the Badger clan entered Oraibi dressed as *katsinam,* along the same route from below that is retraced in the *Patsavu* ritual. To translate the name Lomayayva, then, is to image a moment of the *Patsavu* ritual, and simultaneously to evoke and recapitulate the Badger clan's mythological narrative of arrival.

Lévi-Strauss's structuralist approach to Amerindian myth, widely influential as it has been, has obscured vital connections with ritual. In many instances, of course, ritual enactments of myths are no longer observable in North American social life. Likewise, myths, recorded in written texts, or recalled in oral traditions, often no longer speak directly to ritual practice. All I am suggesting is that in those cultures, and Hopi is one, where many ritual practices are still very much alive, a major dimension of mythological meaning will be located in ritual performance. Translating names which evoke ritual and myth together requires an explicit attention to particular forms of this interplay.

A similar neglect of ethnographic context characterizes some recent literary treatments of North American mythological narratives (e.g., Ramsey 1983). It seems to me that any separation of myth from its empirical grounding in social, cultural, and historical contexts seriously vitiates culturally significant interpretation.[19] What holds for myth is true of the densely laconic narratives in Hopi names, as Alasdair MacIntyre's epigraph is intended to highlight. Accordingly, my claim for interpreting Hopi names as literature is diametrically opposed also to various poststructural theoretical emphases on the free play of signifiers, that give no import to authorial intention, no possibility of language as referential, and no relevance to the sociocultural and historical sites of the literary production. For "Lomayayva," without a basic knowledge of the namegiver's intention, or of the *Patsavu* ritual and the Badger clan migration myth (and of the Hopi linguistic practices, naming conventions, clan and ritual system, and natural environment, in which name, ritual, and myth are constructed)—but *with* only an oblique, silent subject—"beautifully ascended" is utterly fathomless, even to the most linguistically competent translator.

Although many Hopi names are composed, like Sikya-kwap-tiwa, of three morphemes, complex events may be rendered by a simple lexeme. For example, Voth records a name U'na[20] that literally just means "recall it," "remember it." In the specific case, it was given by a Coyote clan member, and the intended image is a coyote's habit of burying tidbits of food in different locations. The name denotes a coyote in the mental and physical act of remembering the locations of buried food.

We can take this example, U'na, to highlight the multiplicity of possible connotations if the namegiver's intention were not known. Let me turn to a conversation with Herschel Talashoma of the Badger clan:

PW: You also said that, for example, that name U'na could be a Badger clan name and it could refer to a badger going and remembering medicine plants.
HT: Where he got his medicine the previous, the last time.
PW: That's because a badger is a *tuuhikya* ("medicine man")?
HT: Yes, yes.
PW: And is in charge of *ngahu* ("medicine").
HT: Right. [Pause] *Or,* where he ate the last corn!—at which field! Because, well, according to a porcupine it would work, because a porcupine really does that.
PW: So a porcupine could be "U'na?"
HT: "U'na," right: "Oh! I remember that—that's where I got the last good corn!" *

Speculative play with the conceivable meanings of names, or with how a name might be applied from a particular clan's perspective (i.e., possibly entailing a free play of signifiers), nonetheless takes its place within an entrenched, observed convention that the name as given means something specific. As such, the convention dictates that the grounds of its meaning shall not be trespassed upon, during the life of the individual to whom the name has stuck, by any additional application of the same lexical combination to another individual. I will return to this below.

Female names are as imagistic and unique as the male names in the foregoing examples, equivalently *poems,* so to speak, in themselves. For instance, Qöyangöynöm is composed of *qöya,* "light gray," *ngöyta,* "he/she/it keeps chasing [it]" and *-nöm,* a fe-

---

*Porcupines lie within the Badger clan's totemic compass. The porcupine is notorious among Hopi farmers for descending upon cornfields toward the end of the labor-intensive four or five months it has taken to produce a crop. It may be the most wasteful—as well as perhaps the most heartbreaking for the farmer—of crop pests, since it goes from clump to clump of corn breaking off the ears and stripping away the husks in search of a few ripe ones. In this way, a single porcupine can devastate a large field in one night's work. Many a Hopi farmer at this time of the year (August and September) spreads his traps well and spends night after night in a fieldhouse with his shotgun. The porcupine's memory, then, is a matter of vital concern!

male name suffix. This was conferred by a member of the *Piikyas-Patki* ("Young Corn" and "Divided Water") phratry, whose totemic sphere includes clouds. The image is of two small gray clouds, one chasing the other across the sky.

Talashongsi, a female name conferred by a Badger clan-member, displays another dimension of the breadth of potential imagery available to this clan. The components are: *talasi,* "pollen," *hoongi,* "standing" (pl.), and *-si,* a female name suffix. The sense is of a pollen-laden flower standing up straight. The association with the Badger clan is via its consociate Butterfly clan; the perspective is that of a butterfly's interest in a pollen-laden flower. In this example, as is perhaps most clearly the case with Lomayayva, the visual (or perhaps "apperceptive" is better for a butterfly) perspective is intrinsic to the image. But simultaneously, the name evokes a double identification: with the butterfly and its "eye-view" of the pollen, and with a viewer's witnessing of this scene. This is also the case with the mind's (and stomach's) eye of the coyote in U'na. Again, a "pure" translation is inadequate for this perspectival dimension of the image too.

The aesthetics of sensory, especially visual, imagery are key features in name composition; upon learning the sense of a name, Hopis often comment on its relative "beauty." So Puhuhoynöm, a Rabbit clan name, refers to the perception of the beauty of a newly made rabbit-fur blanket. Nowhere in the morphemes themselves is there a direct reference to either rabbit-fur or a blanket. *Puhu-* (*puuhu* in non-combinatory form) means "new" or "newly," *hoy-* comes from *hooyi* meaning "separated," "taken off," and *-nöm* is the same female name suffix as above. The reference is to the cottontail and jackrabbit skins that have been newly taken off the animals' bodies in the process of making a blanket. The visual beauty Hopis associate with fresh rabbit fur is foregrounded in the image. Or, in Herschel Talashoma's words, "After when they are finished with a blanket, new blanket from all the rabbit fur, I guess it's pretty, that's why she is called Puhuhoynöm, 'newly-made rabbit-fur blanket.'"

Hopis no longer make rabbit-fur blankets, and as I indicated above, at Third Mesa no longer practice the central *Wuwtsim,* or indeed Snake-Antelope, Flute, *Maraw,* or *Lakon* rituals. In some instances, oral narratives commemorating practices formerly central to Hopi life provide a storehouse of namegiving imagery, that no longer directly reflects experience. But in many cases, the passing of traditional quotidian or ritual practices has seriously curtailed the variety of possible images, and so, of names. When discussing with younger Hopis a name, the meaning of which I had learned from an older person or from a written source, several times the response I received was a nostalgic delight at the "beauty" of the name and a wistful observation that nowadays people had lost the ability to invent such beautiful names. But while the variety of available images has receded somewhat, names—at least in my (outsider's) impression of some recently conferred ones—continue to be richly imagistic, indeed poetic in the "West's" sense of the term.

The literary qualities of some Hopi names should by now be apparent in several respects. First, names constitute a marked use of language that involves an intentional construction of imagery that exceeds ordinary discourse. This "surplus of signification" calls conscious attention to the image depicted, as, for example, in "My love is like a red,

red, rose." This is true with Hopi names, despite the fact that signification is formally opaque without a knowledge of the namegiver's intentions. Of course, *any* perception of "surplus signification" will depend on the cultural context of language usages. In the context of Hopi discourse, the surplus of signification in a name is ineluctably bound to a determinate "meaning"—in E. D. Hirsch's (e.g. 1976, 1984) terms—dependent on authorial intention, and independent of its farther fields of extratextual (or extracultural) "significance." Second, names are individually authored creative "texts" that have in mind a "readership"—at least of the name-receiver. Third, there is a central element of delight, enchantment, or aesthetic pleasure in many names—a key criterion of "literature," as Arnold Krupat (1989:39) points out: "Poetry, by its rhyme and meter, or—this is the case in literary prose—by its figures and structure—*delights* us; it is pleasurable beyond what can be accounted for rationally." And fourth, another axis of the "literary," Hopi names *instruct*—about clan tradition, ritual, myth, natural event, even about a particular kind of perceptual perspective. Moreover, they instruct reflexively—for the namer in fixing an image—as well as for the "reader" (i.e., the name-receiver or another who learns the name's sense). Again, following Krupat (1989:40), "the surplus of signification, the excess that pleased, ha[s] cognitive value."

The conjunction of aesthetic and cognitive value is especially clear with Talashongsi, U'na, and Lomayayva. To the butterfly, the discovery of a pollen-laden flower is very pleasurable. To the Hopi viewer (especially namer and named), the captured image is both beautiful to behold, and simultaneously communicates an observation of natural history and, as with all names, an axiom of social amity (i.e., between named and namer, and namer's clan). Likewise, the coyote delights in remembering the food burials, and the intended Hopi imaginer of this scene is supposed to find it intriguing and delightful (and perhaps on reflection, though here I am speculating, also amusing and morally instructive, in that Coyote as Trickster—an idea complex that is not at all exclusive to the Coyote clan, but that significantly informs its totemic associations—serves as a hilarious exemplar against, among other things, self-serving canniness and gluttony). And again, the viewer on the mesa top will be enchanted by the picture of *katsinam* coming up from down below, and instructed by the associated myth the name invokes—resocialized, as it were.

Many names begin with adjectival or adverbial forms that overtly signal aesthetic, especially visual, beauty. *Loma-* (from *lolma*, above) is one of these (e.g., Lomaventiwa [beautifully painting], Lomaheptiwa [looking for something beautiful], Lomawayma [beautifully walking]). *Kuwan-*, "brightly and beautifully colored"—of, say, butterfly wings, parrot feathers, coyote-pup fur—begins many names. Likewise, *puhu-*, "new, fresh" often denotes beauty of something that gives the appearance of fresh color, for example, again, of young animal fur, butterfly wings (which can be thought of as "newly decorated" as in Puhuvey'ma, "going along with freshly decorated wings"), or newly painted *katsina* masks. Specific color prefixes—*sikya-* (above), *sakw[a]-*, "blue-green," *pala-*, "red," *qöya-*, "light gray," *qöma-*, "black," *qöts[a]-*, "white,"—appear in many names.

Aesthetics of motion are also commonly emphasized, presenting for the viewer a processual, rather than a static, image (a movie, if you will, rather than a still photograph).[21] In addition to the examples mentioned, other images include a sparrowhawk in flight, a spider making a web, an eagle's wings alighting, a bear walking around, a person beginning to complete a rabbit-fur blanket, the colorful movement of masked *katsinam* successively turning around in a line at a particular point in a line-dance, a rainshower "walking" across the landscape, corn-tassles waving in the breeze, abruptly rising miniature columns of water produced by the force of heavy raindrops on a puddle (this last from Voth 1905c:94), and snow settling down. In each, a story is told that centrally involves action and the perception of it. Moreover, every case involves significant condensation and overdetermination in both the creative practice of the story's author and the interpretive practice of its auditor/"reader."

The range of possible subjects (although to list these as such risks a misconceived emphasis on entities rather than the actions they are engaged in—see note 21) includes individuals, pairs, or groups of animals, insects, birds, plants, humans, clouds, rain, other meteorological phenomena, spirits, mythological figures, geographic forms, etc. More abstract notions, like a clan's reputation (e.g., Maataq'ya, "they are famous for it [i.e., a specific behavioral trait or traditional practice]") also appear.

Finally, humans are not the only creatures who are regularly and poetically named. Eagles are gathered in late spring, and kept on house-tops until the *Niman*, "home-going," ceremony in July, when the *katsinam* depart for their spiritual homes around Hopi country. The captured eagles are "baptized" and named after the clan of the namegiver, just like human children. Eagle names reflect the same conventions as human names, and unless given by a member of the Eagle clan, may refer to numerous other species and practices. For example, one recorded eagle name given by a member of the Spider clan is Hayyiwma, "coming down," the sense denoting a spider descending on a single filament (Page and Page 1982:194).[22]

Poesis and Consciousness, Selfhood and the Social Order

Hopi names derive from the clan-system and are thus integral to the social structure. Name senses represent aspects of Hopi "totemic" classes and processes. For the name-receiver the totemic figure of the name is a mental image evoking a natural and social association of the (paternal or godparental) clan the name ties him or her to. The social relationship is thus culturally enframed in a narrative "picture" that lives and resonates in the mind of the named.[23] In this nonliterate society, the name is a poetic sign instantiating attributes of Hopi traditional knowledge—about the environment, ritual practices, clan histories, and so forth—that are inseparable from the organization of society. Reflection on a name's form and meaning thus serves to re-delight and re-teach an aspect of Hopi knowledge. Effective translation must address this range of social, cultural, and cognitive contexts in which names have their meanings constituted.

The classifying function of personal names which Lévi-Strauss (1966) postulates (one of his principal examples is Hopi) seems borne out by the totemic references. But the great degree of authorial latitude and creativity within totemic spheres, on the one hand,

and the intentional uniqueness of each name, on the other, add strongly individuating elements simultaneously for namer and named. The namegiver is a genuine author, who, in inventing a new name, inscribes, as it were, his or her personal "signature" onto it. Moreover, the esoteric nature of meaning produced simply by the frequent (though not prescribed) absence of public explications of exact sense, keeps the names "special"; the mystery produced merely from denotative opacity, vouchsafes the individuality of the name and its author. Authorial individuality, as it must do elsewhere, takes its place within an "intertextual" context of other images and other authors. Appropriate imagery derives from a collective consciousness of the general parameters of totemic associations. If one were to take all the names conferred by members, or individual "authors," of a particular clan, these would constitute a canonical genre of the narrative depictions of clan tradition.

For the receiver, a name confers a unique individual identity, in addition to the roles ascribed by kin, clan, and sodality membership. Within a Mesa group of villages, no two individuals will share the same name. There is a clear desire to avoid duplicates—even of homonyms which, conferred by members of different clans, would have entirely different meanings (cf. Voth 1905c:69). For example, Lomavuyawma, "beautifully going along flapping," could be conferred by members of any clan with totemic interests in birds, in each case referring to a different image. But if one person had been given this name, specifically, say, referring to an eagle flying high in the sky easterly in the morning sunlight, another would not choose the same lexeme, even if the reference intended would be, for example, to a duck flying low over a specific lake away from the viewer in the afternoon, or to a roadrunner in flight. The resultant individuation of identity names serve to mark, and partially constitute, is pronounced.

The effect of names that individuate both authors and subjects, selves and others, is well drawn by David Parkin (1982:xxxix, implicitly critiquing Lévi-Strauss 1966:181) discussing Fipa and Omaha personal naming systems:

. . . [T]he choices made by a namer reflect on himself as well as on the bearer and those who may or may not use the name. Naming then defines selfhood as well as others' personhood. Putting this another way, the subject objectifies himself through the act of defining or objectifying another.

In the first three decades of this century, government officials, missionaries and schoolteachers insisted that Hopi children adopt English forenames and their fathers' names (in a few cases, mothers' names), in many instances butchered by Anglo pronunciations, as hereditary patronymics. So in "Herschel Talashoma," "Talashoma" is a corruption of his father's father's Hopi name, Talashoyiwma. (In "Talashoma" principal stress falls on the third syllable, and 'sh' is a single phoneme as in English "*ship*"; in "Talashoyiwma" principal stress falls on the second syllable—the usual case with Hopi polysyllabic names—and the "sh" is two phonemes as in English "mi*sh*ap"). The clan association of the original namegiver and her or his relationship to the original name bearer are entirely confounded by this process. Moreover, the name's intended meaning is often simply lost. Many seemingly Hopi names have thus become English names, as Hopis describe this, and are now the untranslatable, "meaningless marks" of Mill's depiction. Some Hopis have taken on English surnames, or used their fathers' English forenames (Sidney, George, Charlie, etc.) as surnames, because of the difficulty non-Hopis experience with Hopi phonology and morphology. Nonetheless, each child also still receives several ("true") Hopi names which are generally not used for the dominant society's bureaucratic purposes that require a "forename" and "surname." Some people, conscious of the hegemony present in accepting the national society's naming conventions, have rejected inherited patronymics and substituted their own Hopi names as surnames. Thomas Banyacya (or Paangaq'ya according to the orthography I follow), for example, the widely known spokesman for the Traditionalist movement, replaced the surname "Jenkins" his father had adopted by his own *katsina* initiation name.

The avoidance of duplicating Hopi names is pursued also with English forenames, resulting in an extraordinary range and variety: Aquila, Lemuel, Starley, Ebin, Orin, Lovina, Kylene, Marietta, Charmetria, Aldena are just a few. Here again, the sense aspect of a Hopi name is absent, but in order to maintain the individuative function, Hopis have purposefully found access to a store of English, and some Spanish, names that greatly outstretches the average name-list in the Anglo Southwest. Sometimes English forenames are passed on to the next generation, or after a gap of one or two generations, and the intention is to foreground the relationship of the nameholders. But often the name spelling is deliberately changed, or the name is applied to a member of the opposite sex, in order to differentiate as well as associate; never is the name regarded as reincarnating a social person.

In addition to both individuated Hopi and English names, most people have at least one nickname which is commonly used for address and reference in ordinary conversation. Nicknames are often mildly insulting. They may poke fun at personal habits or appearances; for example, Kutuksona, "parched-corn craver," Kwaa'töqti, "eagle's call," the name of the Hopi newspaper (for a gossip), Tseemoni, "Germany," (for a person who worked for the German Mennonite missionaries), Wunavutsqasi "planklike thighs." Also, child-names are sometimes long remembered and used as quasi-nicknames, especially by the namegiver and his or her close relatives, after the acquisition of initiation names.

Concluding Remarks

"Literature," as Arnold Krupat (1989:43) puts it, "is that mode of discourse which foremost seeks to enact and perform its insights, insisting that we understand with affect, feel with comprehension." Partially constituted in a naming genre that seems genuinely literary in its imagistic qualities, Hopi selves are consciously marked in the intersubjective naming process that links an individual namegiver and a name-receiver. Hopi names provide vivid images and tell stories that commemorate their storytellers, and individuate and identify the sites of their telling, that is, the named subjects. Elsewhere (1988b:2), I have drawn attention to a Hopi conception of marked narrative form as an active mnemonic device for important events and traditions, or "Making a story out of it, to remember it by." This, it seems to me, is what Hopi names do for Hopi persons: "tiny imagist poems" or narrative mental-pictures through which the subject as author delightfully and instructively marks the individual identity of another subject. And in turn, Hopi persons thus marked are walking poetic metaphors of cultural, social, and natural experience:

Pay yan itam it ayangqaqw	This is how we've been doing it
yuupahaqaqw tumalay'ngwu.	all the way along from the past.
Niiqe oovi hak naatoylay aw	And so you name a person
hakiy tungwangwu; meh, nu'	according to your clan-totem;
honanwungwa, pu' kur nu'	see, I'm a Badger clan, so if I
hakiy tungwanik pu' nu'	want to name someone, I would
inaatoylay aw taykyangw pu'	have to look at my own clan in
nu' hakiy tungwani. Pu' son	order to name someone in a
nu' hakiy naatoylayat aw hakiy	certain way. I will not name
tungwantani, nawusni himuy'sa	anyone looking at someone
aw put taykyangw hakiy	else's clan-totem; I will
tungwamantani.	only look at my own clan's
	prerogatives in order to name
	that person, give that person a
	name.

Notes

1. Translations of this famous haiku proliferate (Sato 1983); mine is taken from R. H. Blyth (ibid.: 154).

2. My special thanks go to Herschel Talashoma for the text he provided for this inquiry, and for graciously putting up with me over the years. Other Hopi consultants prefer to remain anonymous. For the same reason of privacy, most of the names discussed herein are not those of living people. Earlier versions of this paper were presented at "Persons and Selves in Pueblo and Northwest Coast Societies," a session of the 1988 American Anthropological Association annual meetings in Phoenix, and at Sarah Lawrence College in February 1990. A number of people have helped greatly to clarify some issues; in particular, remarks by discussants Alfonso Ortiz and Ray Fogelson in Phoenix, and by Lina Brock, Roland Dollinger, and Danny Kaiser at Sarah Lawrence are much appreciated. My deep thanks for extensive written comments go to Arnold Krupat (most especially), Armin Geertz, and Bob Zimmerman. None but I, however, bear the blame for what remains.

3. Recent considerations of naming practices that discuss one or more of these features and/or others include Ramos 1974; Kendall 1980; Barnes 1980, 1982; Dalforo 1982; Willis 1982; Moore 1984; the articles by Maybury-Lewis, Maxwell, Rosaldo, and Mithun in Tooker 1984; Harrison 1985; Lindstrom 1985; Glasse 1987; Revard 1987; Kuschel 1988, and several articles, among which that by Godfrey Lienhardt is particularly noteworthy, in a Special Issue on Names of the *Journal of the Anthropological Society of Oxford,* 1988.

4. Some recent exceptions to this are to be found in the references cited in note 3. To be sure, many English names originally had denotative meaning; Peter, for example, derives from the Greek *petra,* "a rock" (and see Dunkling and Gosling 1983). And there are other exceptions. Lienhardt (1988:107) indicates women's names denoting flowers or spring and summer months and also some Puritan names with semantic content; clearly such names as Faith, Hope, and Charity

betoken moral precepts. Some people name their children for sporting events or social luminaries. Likewise, writers from Shakespeare (Sir Toby Belch) to Sheridan (Mrs. Malaprop), from Joyce (Stephen Dedalus) to Pynchon (Isaiah Two Four) have used names, often semantically significant, to evoke character, mood, or social conditions. And then there is rock star Frank Zappa's daughter, Moon Unit Two. But for the most part, it remains true that in ordinary life, proper names point out, refer or address, they do not denote images constituted apart from the subject's identity.

5. Two articles by Ralph Barnes (1980, 1982) are particularly useful recent treatments of Native American naming systems.

6. The resurrection of Marcel Mauss's 1938 essay on "the person" (Carrithers, Lukes, and Collins 1985) has renewed a misconception of naming practices in Pueblo societies. Mauss characterizes Pueblo names as drawn from a limited fund conferred by clans on their own members. Names then designate social characters in a fixed *dramatis personae* reproduced from one generation to the next—reflecting an underdevelopment of individuated persons and of selves as conscious agents (by contrast to the developed Western versions). Mauss's principal Pueblo examples are Zuni and Hopi, and, while he may be more accurate on Zuni names (whether this entitles him to infer inchoate persons and selves is a different matter), he is quite wrong with regard to Hopi—in a way, I believe (this was my theme in earlier versions of this paper), that substantially undermines his overall argument.

7. I owe the inspiration for this emphasis on the "narrative" construction of Hopi social persons to Armin Geertz (personal communication and 1990), who, in a rather different way, has persuasively argued for "narrated ethics" in the construction of persons in ritual contexts.

8. Hopi is traditionally an unwritten language, so the kind of proper-name marking of initial-capitalization is not present as such in Hopi discourse (cf. Mithun's [1984:40] remarks on Mohawk naming). Nonetheless, Hopi marks proper names both nominally by the term *tungwni* (pl. *tuutungwni*) "name," and verbally by *tungwa*, "to name it." *Maatsiwa*, "be named," is commonly used to identify the name of a person, e.g., *ya um/pam hin maatsiwa?*, "how are you/he-she named?" to which I would respond, *nu' Peter yan maatsiwa*, "I Peter this way am named." Likewise *maatsiwa* is used in the ritual conferring of a name, which ends with *X yan um maatsiwni*, "you will be called X" (Voth 1905b:54).

9. I have criticized conventional usages of the terms "clan" and "phratry" in Hopi ethnography (Whiteley 1985, 1986, 1988a). They are still useful shorthand terms for Hopi social groups, so long as the usage is not taken to imply formally and functionally discrete social-structural units.

10. Some accounts indicate a tendency to choose a member of the father's clan to serve as godfather/godmother (cf. Nagata n.d.:8, n. 3). This does not correspond with my experience or with most published accounts.

11. In addition to what I have learned from Hopi consultants, I am drawing here, particularly for the salt expedition and for death-names, from a very useful, as yet unpublished, paper by Shuichi Nagata (n.d.) that combines his own research with that of several prior accounts. Maitland Bradfield (1973:passim) also provides informative summary remarks of published accounts of Hopi naming. I have not personally inquired into whether namegiving at death still occurs (a sensitive ritual matter I prefer to stay away from).

12. Voth (1901:122–25) and Titiev (1944:222–26) provide the best available accounts of *Patsavu* at Oraibi.

13. This very image—a rare one indeed—is captured in a photograph by Kate Cory at Oraibi (Wright et al. 1986: photograph 4).

14. The association between imagist poetry and haiku is not accidental. Ezra Pound, for example, was explicitly influenced by Japanese styles and imagery, and was responsible for bringing some Japanese poetry to a Western audience (see, e.g., Ueda 1965).

15. Barnes (1982:221) points out a similar pattern with some Siouan names.

16. This male name (spelled Sekaquaptewa) was taken as a marital surname by the bearer's wife, Helen, the subject of a well-known autobiography (1969); it is now the inherited patronymic of their sons, who include Abbott, a former chairman of the Hopi Tribal Council, and Emory, an anthropologist and linguist at the University of Arizona.

17. Despite some claims that -*tiwa* is an unusual verbal form (e.g., Voth 1905c:71), I follow Malotki's position here (1979:371). I thank Armin Geertz (personal communication) for pointing out this, and some other linguistic discrepancies.

18. This account of the name—the fullest I have heard—derives from the son of the namegiver, who assured me his mother explained it to him. Slight modifications on this account exist within the extended family of those who bear the name as an inherited patronymic.

19. By leaving out here the specific performative context of myth in the telling (for which, e.g., Sherzer 1987 has so persuasively argued), I do not mean to underplay its significance. It just seems less important for the interpretation of names, which are spoken in numerous genres of discourse and depend more on the ideas of myth rather than their specific narrative utterances.

20. Voth spells it variously Úuna (1905b:59) and Úna (1905c:81).

21. Ekkehart Malotki (1983) has trenchantly critiqued Whorf's characterization of the Hopi language as "timeless." Whorf (1956:147) contends also that the Hopi language formally configures an emphasis on "events" (or "eventings") which "are expressed mainly as outlines, colors, movements, and other perceptive reports"—as opposed to the static "things" emphasized by SAE (Standard Average European languages). While Whorf's assignment of intrinsic perceptual qualities to the Hopi language itself is in some disrepute, the phenomenological emphasis he has identified in Hopi worldview is nonetheless clearly foregrounded in the cognitive style of name-images.

22. Voth (1905c:73) also records the formal naming of a pipe in the context of the Blue Flute ceremony. The naming of kivas shares some features of personal naming too, but names of ritual objects and places are beyond my scope here.

23. Keith Basso's emphasis on the mental-pictorial features of Western Apache place-names (1988) is resonant here also. As one of his consultants explains (ibid. 107–8), characterizing a conversation centrally involving placename usage:

> We gave that woman . . . pictures to work on in her mind. . . . We gave her clear pictures with placenames. So her mind went to those places, standing in front of them as our ancestors did long ago. That way she could see what happened there long ago. She could hear stories in her mind, perhaps hear our ancestors speaking. She could reknow the wisdom of our ancestors.

References

Barnes, R. H. 1980. Hidatsa Personal Names: An Interpretation. *Plains Anthropologist* 25: 90:311–31.

———. 1982. Personal Names and Social Classification. In *Semantic Anthropology*, D. Parkin ed., 211–26. London: Academic Press.

Basso, Keith. 1988. "Speaking with Names": Language and Landscape among the Western Apache. *Cultural Anthropology* 3:2:99–130.

Bradfield, R. Maitland. 1973. *A Natural History of Associations: A Study in the Meaning of Community,* vol. 2. London: Duckworth.

Carrithers, M., S. Collins, and S. Lukes, eds. 1985. *The Category of the Person.* Cambridge: Cambridge University Press.

Dalforo, A. T. 1982. Logbara Personal Names and their Relation to Religion. *Anthropos* 77:1/2:113–33.

Dunkling, Leslie, and William Gosling. 1983. *Everyman's Dictionary of First Names.* London: Dent.

Frigout, Arlette. 1979. Hopi Ceremonial Organization. In *Handbook of North American Indians,* vol. 9, *The Southwest,* Alfonso Ortiz, ed., 564–76. Washington: U.S. Government Printing Office.

Geertz, Armin. 1990. Hopi Hermeneutics: Ritual Person Among the Hopi Indians of Arizona. In *Concepts of Person in Religion and Thought,* H. K. Kippenberg, Y. B. Kuiper, and A. F. Sanders, eds., 309–36. Berlin: De Gruyter.

Glasse, R. M. 1987. Huli Names and Naming. *Ethnology* 23:3:201–8.

Harrison, Simon. 1985. Names, Ghosts, and Alliance in Two Sepik River Societies. *Oceania* 56:2:138–46.

Hirsch, E. D. Jr. 1976. *The Aims of Interpretation.* Chicago: University of Chicago Press.

———. 1984. Meaning and Significance Reinterpreted. *Critical Inquiry* 11:2:202–25.

Kendall, Martha B. 1980. Exegesis and Translation: Northern Yuman Names as Texts. *Journal of Anthropological Research* 36:3:261–73.

Krupat, Arnold. 1989. *The Voice in the Margin: Native American Literature and the Canon.* Berkeley: University of California Press.

Kuschel, Rolf. 1988. Cultural Reflections in Bellonese Personal Names. *Journal of the Polynesian Society* 97:1:49–71.

Lévi-Strauss, Claude. 1966. *The Savage Mind.* Chicago: University of Chicago Press.

Lienhardt, Godfrey. 1988. Social and Cultural Implications of Some African Personal Names. *Journal of the Anthropological Society of Oxford* (Special Issue on Names and their Uses) 19:2:105–16.

Lindstrom, Lamont. 1985. Personal Names and Social Reproduction on Tanna, Vanuatu. *Journal of the Polynesian Society* 94:1:27–45.

MacIntyre, Alasdair. 1985. Relativism, Power, and Philosophy, *American Philosophical Society, Proceedings,* 5–22.

Malotki, Ekkehart. 1979. *Eine sprachwissenschaftliche Analyse der Raumvorstellungen in der Hopi Sprache.* Tübingen: Gunter Narr.

———. 1983. *Hopi Time: A Linguistic Analysis of the Temporal Concepts in the Hopi Language.* Berlin: Mouton.

Maxwell, Allen R. 1984. Kadayan Personal Names and Naming. In Tooker 1984 (q.v.), 25–39.

Maybury-Lewis, David. 1984. Name, Person and Ideology in Central Brazil. In Tooker 1984 (q.v.), 1–10.

Mithun, Marianne. 1984. Principles of Naming in Mohawk. In Tooker 1984 (q.v.), 40–54.

Moore, John H. 1984. Cheyenne Names and Cosmology. *American Ethnologist* 11:2:291–312.

Nagata, Shuichi. n.d. Being Hopi in the Twentieth Century. Manuscript.

Page, Jake, and Susanne Page. 1982. *Hopi*. New York: Harry N. Abrams.

Parkin, David. 1982. Introduction. In *Semantic Anthropology,* D. Parkin, ed., xi–li. (Association of Social Anthropologists Monograph 22.) London: Academic Press.

Ramos, Alcida. 1974. How the Sanuma Acquire Their Names. *Ethnology* 13:171–85.

Ramsey, Jarold. 1983. *Reading the Fire: Five Essays in the Traditional Indian Literatures of the Far West.* Lincoln: University of Nebraska Press.

Revard, Carter. 1987. Traditional Osage Naming Ceremonies: Entering the Circle of Being. In *Recovering the Word: Essays on Native American Literature,* B. Swann and A. Krupat, eds., 446–66. Berkeley: University of California Press.

Rosaldo, Renato. 1984. Ilongot Naming: The Play of Associations. In Tooker 1984 (q.v.), 11–24.

Sato, Hiroaki. 1983. *One Hundred Frogs: From Renga to Haiku to English.* New York: Weatherhill.

Sekaquaptewa, Helen. 1969. *Me and Mine,* Louise Udall, ed. Tucson: University of Arizona Press.

Sherzer, Joel. 1987. Strategies in Text and Context: The Hot Pepper Story. In *Recovering the Word: Essays on Native American Literature,* B. Swann and A. Krupat, eds., 151–97. Berkeley: University of California Press.

Titiev, Mischa. 1944. *Old Oraibi: A Study of the Hopi Indians of Third Mesa.* Peabody Museum of American Archaeology and Ethnology, Papers, 22 (1).

Tooker, Elizabeth, ed. 1984. "Naming Systems." *Proceedings of the American Ethnological Society,* 1980.

Ueda, Makoto. 1965. *Zeami, Basho, Yeats, Pound: A Study in Japanese and English Poetics.* The Hague: Mouton.

Underhill, Ruth M. 1979 [1936]. *Papago Woman.* New York: Holt, Rinehart, Winston.

Voegelin, Charles F., and Florence M. Voegelin. 1957. Hopi Domains: A Lexical Approach to the Problem of Selection. Supplement to *International Journal of American Linguistics* 23:2.

Voth, H. R. 1901. The Oraibi Powamu Ceremony. *Field Columbian Museum Publication* No. 61, *Anthropological Series,* vol. III, no. 2.

———. 1903. The Oraibi Summer Snake Ceremony. *Field Columbian Museum Publication* No. 83, *Anthropological Series* vol. III, no. 4.

———. 1905a. The Traditions of the Hopi. *Field Columbian Museum Publication* No. 96, *Anthropological Series,* vol. VIII.

———. 1905b. Oraibi Natal Customs and Ceremonies. *Field Columbian Museum Publication* No. 97, *Anthropological Series,* vol. VI, no. 2.

———. 1905c. Hopi Proper Names. *Field Columbian Museum Publication* No. 100, *Anthropological Series,* vol. VI, no. 3.

Whiteley, Peter. 1985. Unpacking Hopi "Clans": Another Vintage Model Out of Africa? *Journal of Anthropological Research* 41:4:359–74.

———. 1986. Unpacking Hopi "Clans", II: Further Questions about Hopi Descent Groups. *Journal of Anthropological Research* 42:1:69–79.

———. 1987. Southwest Indian Religions. In *The Encyclopedia of Religion,* Mircea Eliade, ed., vol. 10, 513–25. New York: MacMillan and Free Press.

———. 1988a. *Deliberate Acts: Changing Hopi Culture through the Oraibi Split.* Tucson: University of Arizona Press.

———. 1988b. *Bacavi: Journey to Reed Springs.* Flagstaff: Northland Press.

Whorf, Benjamin Lee. 1956 [1939]. The Relation of Habitual Thought and Behavior to Language.

In *Language, Thought and Reality: Selected Writings of Benjamin Lee Whorf*, John B. Carroll, ed., 134–59. Cambridge, Massachusetts: MIT Press.

Willis, Roy. 1982. On a Mental Sausage Machine and Other Nominal Problems. In *Semantic Anthropology*, D. Parkin ed., 227–40. London: Academic Press.

Wright, Barton, Marnie Gaede, and Marc Gaede. 1986. *The Hopi Photographs: Kate Cory, 1905–1912*. La Cañada, California: Chaco Press.

Suggested Reading

Studies of proper names converge from philosophy, anthropology, and linguistics; I cannot pretend to offer more than sample suggestions. John Stuart Mill's classic discussion occurs in chapter two of his *A System of Logic* (1843). Some other influential treatments within philosophy include A. H. Gardiner's *The Theory of Proper Names: A Controversial Essay* (1940, London: Oxford University Press), Bertrand Russell in his *Human Knowledge* (1948, New York: Simon and Schuster), P. Strawson's "On Referring" (1950, in *Mind*, 49:320–44), John Searle in his *Speech Acts: An Essay in the Philosophy of Language* (1969, Cambridge: Cambridge University Press), and more recently in his *Intentionality, an Essay in the Philosophy of Mind* (1983, Cambridge: Cambridge University Press). S. P. Schwartz's (ed.) *Naming, Necessity and Natural Kinds* (1977, Ithaca: Cornell University Press), and M. Devitt's *Designation* (1981, Chicago: University of Chicago Press) are also significant. R. H. Barnes's "Personal Names and Social Classification" (1982, and see also his 1980 article on interpreting Hidatsa names), as well as providing a fine synthetic consideration of Native American naming systems, centrally opposes Mill's argument by drawing on philosopher Gottlob Frege's notions of sense and reference.

From the perspective of linguistics, John Lyons's discussion in his *Semantics* (1977, Cambridge: Cambridge University Press), Nancy Parrott Hickerson's "On the Sign Functions and Sociocultural Context of 'Personal Names'" (1977, *Proceedings of the Semiotic Society of America*, 1:44–150), and J. M. Carroll's "Toward a Functional Theory of Names and Naming" (1983, *Linguistics*, 21(2): 341–71) are recommended.

Within anthropology, sources cited in Note 3—especially the collection edited by E. Tooker and the "Special Issue on Names" of the *Journal of the Anthropological Society of Oxford*—are particularly recommended, as well as the passages cited from Lévi-Strauss's *The Savage Mind*. In addition, some other influential considerations include: E. E. Evans-Pritchard's "Nuer Modes of Address" ([1948] reprinted in Dell Hymes's (ed.) *Language in Culture and Society*, 1964, New York: Harper and Row), Ward Goodenough's "Personal Names and Modes of Address in Two Oceanic Societies" (1965, in Melford Spiro [ed.], *Context and Meaning in Cultural Anthropology* (New York: Free Press), Rodney Needham's "Penan Friendship Names" (1971, in T. O. Beidelman's (ed.) *The Translation of Culture* (New York: Barnes and Noble), and T. O. Beidelman's "Kaguru Names and Naming" (1974, *Journal of Anthropological Research*, 30:281–93).

Accounts of particular Native American naming systems (see also Note 3) are myriad: again Barnes's 1982 article provides an excellent starting point that considers a number of these, and contains a good bibliographic resource. Lévi-Strauss's aforementioned discussion focuses on several Native American cases. Keith Basso's work on Apache placenames (particularly 1988 and his "'Stalking with Stories': Names, Places, and Moral Narratives among the Western Apache" in E. Bruner [ed.], *Text, Play and Story: The Construction and Reconstruction of Self and Society*

[1984, Washington, D.C.: American Ethnological Society]) provides superb insights into Native American naming practices (albeit specifically of place rather than person). Kiowa author N. Scott Momaday's personal memoir *The Names* (1976, New York: Harper and Row) includes some powerfully evocative considerations of Native American names. And, to repeat, the classic source on Hopi names is H. R. Voth's *Hopi Proper Names* (1905).

A Hopi Song-Poem in "Context"

David Leedom Shaul

Interpretation has always been at the heart of the study of any literature, or literature in general. Such *knowledge about literature*, whether a culture-specific or crosscultural poetics, is distinct from *information about literature*, which makes interpretation available as discourse (Todorov 1981). Literature that is primarily intended as an unselfconscious reflection *of* (rather than *on*) social or natural life should, reasonably, have an interpretation sufficiently transparent to the native audience as to preclude any need for an extensive discourse about interpretation. One reason for this is that recurrent patterns highlight important structures and arrays of (emotional) information in a given piece (Hymes 1981; Tedlock 1983; Sherzer and Woodbury, eds., 1987). This essay analyzes a single Hopi song-poem, linking external situating information about the text to internally generated knowledge about the song-poem which allows for variable interpretation. In doing this, I will be using structuralism not as a heuristic for interpretation, but to organize the interpretable.

My central idea is that a higher level structure is needed in order to help interpret a structure on a lower level. Here, the notion of *level* in linguistic parlance is important: the essential idea is that a structure on a lower level is incorporated as part of an array in a larger structure. The smaller unit is thought of being on a *lower level*, with the larger, integrative structure being seen as the *higher level*. This higher level provides a context for any of its constituent parts; the ultimate context is the actual situation in which a discourse takes place. The most usual unit in discourse analysis is a *line* (a prosodically defined unit, most often a clause or elaborate phrase; cf. Sherzer 1987 and Hinton 1984: chapter 4). Clearly such units are amenable to interpretation in some larger, more inclusive context. This is the central theme of this essay, but I will first illustrate the notion of levels of structure.

One of the most clear cases that comes to mind of levels of structure is the classic phoneme: the test of phonemic status is made by referring to the next higher level. The phonemes of a language are its essential sounds. Compare the English words *bit* and *pit*. They are identical, except for the initial consonant; hence /b/ and /p/ are distinctive sounds in English (i.e., they are phonemes of English). We know this not by looking at the level of speech sounds, but by looking at a higher level (the word). It is only in words that one can discern phonemes. Another example of what I mean is the Hopi modal *so'onqa*, "surely/inevitably/undoubtedly." This word has, from Whorf's time on, been presented as a compound word (*so'on*, the negative marker that occurs with the tense marker -*ni*, which marks predicates as future or hypothetical, and *qa*, the negative for the other tenses). Yet the true significance of *so'onqa* escapes one, if one only considers the word level. When one looks at the distribution of *so'onqa* in sentences, it is clear that it is a framing device that highlights other parts of the sentence.

Son pi	nu'	ung	put	ahoy	*qa*	nawkini.
not indeed	I	thee	it	back	not	will:take

This sentence is from a story (Malotki and Lomatuwa'yma 1984:182). The word-by-word glossing gives almost no clue as to the functional meaning of *so'onqa*, which appears in the editors' English translation: "*Believe me*, I'll have to take it away from you." Seen this way, *so'on . . . qa*, "indeed" signals a sentence that must be interpreted on a higher discourse level; the translation "believe me" (in lieu of "indeed") is possible only by referring to context, which supplies the reason why one actor wants to take away something from another character.

Structuralism is characterized by contrasts and possible combinations on different levels that exist in a hierarchy (for example: speech sounds, words, sentences). Here again, the notion of level as a hierarchy must be taken as integrative: simpler units are subsumed into larger units. Rather than implying dominance or subordination, the use of the word hierarchy here means larger, encompassing structure. As such, structuralism is an inductive device that helps to define what words (signs, symbols, configurations) are salient (that is, potentially interpretable). Dennis Tedlock (1983) has argued that the interpretation of Native American literature is essentially a hermeneutic enterprise; interpretation depends on knowing about the culture in which the particular piece is situated, noting that each text carries structural clues to its own meaning. Seen this way, a structural analysis of a given piece is potentially hierarchical, an expanding series of contexts. The significance of (particular) words is seen from the sentence and higher levels, the significance of sentences from the vantage of paragraphs, sections or episodes, and so on. Discourse marking cues (marked prosodic and syntactic partials) allow for production and processing of structures to which meaning can be assigned (for narratives, see Lord 1960; Hymes 1981; Tedlock 1983; Kroskrity 1985; Shaul 1987a and 1987b; Woodbury 1987). Such cues are also the partial basis for successful performances (Bauman 1986). A performance implies interaction of participants in a kind of context. Some types of context require more predetermined behavior than others. In conversation, there must exist conventions for turn taking. In storytelling, there is a narrator and audience; the former has the floor, but listeners may (and often do) still interact. In live and spontaneous narration, then, it is logical to expect some sort of culture-specific narrative schema known to both storyteller and audience. At section boundaries and other major features, the passive participants in a narrative context often affirm the authenticity or worth of the story they are hearing. When the structuring behavior of a given kind of context is fairly predictable, we may distinguish *genres*. The more a performance adheres to a genre schema, the more comfortable the context will be to participants. Thus, predictable expectations for behavior (such as genre schemata) help interactants perceive a common ground, creating a linguistic habitus (Hanks 1987).

The hierarchy (or amalgam) of structures in a text helps to provide points for interaction, or point out major motifs or symbols, some of which are nested in others, the entirety creating a holistic array of meaning. A narrative or poem schema, then, is

durably installed generative principle of regulated improvisations, [which] produces practices [discourses] which tend to reproduce the regularity immanent (Bourdieu 1977:18).

That is, there must be some preexisting shared (cultural) knowledge for how to expect participants in a given context to interact; this dynamic reading of structuralism allows for the mutual negotiation of contextual reality, and the dynamic expectations account for observed regularity. For Bourdieu, the focus on dynamism is the central issue in structuralism. He does not take to standard focus that structuralists have taken on structure as a product of interaction, but investigates the interaction itself. With this vision of structuralism, one will expect variation at each level. This is because some aspects (the overall structure) of a text/performance are predictable, following a genre schema. Content may be static (as with a conventional or set piece, or traditions motif[s] or theme[s]), but content is more likely to have variation, simply because there are more cultural concepts and vocabulary items than there are structural conventions. For example, the formal structural elements of a story (beginning formula, section boundary markers, quotation markers, etc.) will be fewer than the actual words of the same story. When variations occurs in what is usually predictable and regular (in our example, narrative structure as opposed to narrative content), the structural variation is pointing to something of high semantic salience, but one must interpret this meaning from the vantage point of a higher level.

The texts of song-poems in Hopi culture, like much poetry, seemingly create their own context by virtue of minimalist language. These texts lack the modals ubiquitous in other Hopi discourse, such as modals are lacking in Piman song texts (Bahr and Haefer 1970; Shaul 1991). Modals relate the linguistic content to some context external to the text. Modals are, roughly, adverbs that contextualize the sentence or utterance in which they occur. For example, the presence of "perhaps" in a simple sentence (for example, *Perhaps they all went bankrupt*) is radically different in meaning from the same sentence without "perhaps"; the sentence without the modal must be taken on truth value alone. Lyrics that (almost) entirely lack modals create a text world that is inherently true or universally pervasive, especially if the lyric is a fairly short text. Lacking modals like "certainly" or "could have" makes a song-poem inward looking; it becomes an autonomous text world.[1]

Like much Native American poetry, Hopi song-poems use some words exclusively as *genre signatures*; this is like the use of quotative particles ("they say/it is said") as genre signatures in narratives in most Native American traditional narratives. These two qualities (short, seemingly self-contained texts; genre signatures) have made Native American song-poems (which natively are not divorced from music) popular as poetry in English translation in various guises: standing naked in anthologies; in supported analysis of a single piece like Wiget's analysis of Sayatasha's night chant (1980); in supported gatherings of a single tradition such as Spinden's admired *Song of the Tewa* (1933, though Underhill's *Singing for Power* [1983] is superior); or through experiments such as Simon Ortiz's transferring of traditional Native American poetry technique to English language texts (mirroring Momaday's and Silko's narrative work). The song-poem is an ideal target for translation, indeed an invitation for translation, because of the unique structural properties outlined above.

The problem of translation into English or another language, however, remains a fundamental one. A major recent collection of Yaqui deer songs, was translated from at least one native point of view.

Acquiring "the native standpoint" is, we agree, a more difficult matter. Felipe Molina's collaboration ensures that *a* native standpoint is represented here. Moreover, we have asked all the deer singers with whom we worked to comment on their songs (Evers and Molina 1987:27).

Note that Evers and Molina do not indicate their scansion convention (what is a line? when is a line indented?); neither do they relate the linguistic artifact to its musical fabric. This issue is addressed by another major study of a Southwestern native music (Hinton 1984), which holds that semantic highlights correlate with phonological stress or musical high pitch. Such cognitive (and measurable) cues to lines or correlation with musical structure are suggested in observations that native and outsiders both have made about the overall structure of Pueblo song-poems. In general, one may discern a five-part AABBA structure as the basic musical and textual form. Herein, the B is higher in range, syncopated, and often choreographed by an increasing density of movement which visually suggests increasing tempo (Frisbie 1980:309).

This five-part song-poem schema is common to Tewa (Kurath and Garcia 1970), Keresan (Kurath 1959), Zuni (B. Tedlock 1980), and Hopi musical cultures. The music is an envelope, a larger structure and context into which the linguistic text fits. It will be shown that the most variable part of translations provided by native experts of the same Hopi song-poem text are not musically highlighted.

I will present the text of a well-known butterfly dance song-poem (Curtis 1907:480–84) with a translation attributed to the composer (Chief Tawakwaptiwa) which is compared with readings by two other Hopi experts (Emory Sekaquaptewa, Leigh Jenkins). I have chosen this piece because it is popular, and because it is accessible in published form with its musical context.

Here is the English version attributed to Tawakwaptiwa, with the original text preceding; there is some phonological restoration.

> Humisita singöylawu.
> Morisita singöylawu.
>
> Itam tootim niikyangw
> uysonaq ngöytiwmani,   4
> tuvevolmanatu amumi.
>
> Peyo, peyo!
> Umumutani, tayayatani.
> Uyimantu oomi naawungwinani.   8
>
> Now for corn-blossoms we wrestle.
> Now for bean-blossoms we wrestle.
>
> We are youths, 'mid the corn,
> chasing each other in sport,   4
> playing with butterfly maidens.
>
> Hither, hither!
> Thunder will hither move, we shall summon thunder here,
> that the maiden-plants upward may help each other to grow. 8

This is the translation of Emory Sekaquaptewa (in Black 1984).

> Wrestling for the corn blossoms,
> wrestling for the bean blossoms.
>
> Since we are boys
> we go along the field playing,   4
> and teasing the colorful butterfly maidens.
>
> To here, here
> the storms will come thundering, the ground will tremble.
> Upward the corn maiden plants will help each other to grow. 8

Leigh Jenkins (p.c.) remarked that the first two lines' wrestling theme could alternatively refer to the blossoms on the plants swaying in the breeze or tumbling along on the ground, that *tuvevolmanatu* (line 5) could variously be rendered in English as the butterflies or the cheeks of the female dancers, and that *naawungwinani* (line 8) could mean two different things in English ("help each other up," "help themselves up").

The least variable semantics of all three translations are on lines 3 and 4, and on lines 6 and 7. By least variable semantics I do not mean different wording that is essentially synonymous (compare Tawakwaptiwa's "thunder will hither move" to Sekaquaptewa's "the storms will come thundering" in line 7). I am concerned with different ways of viewing the scene of the text world. In Tawakwaptiwa's and Sekaqupatewa's renderings, it is the boys who are wrestling for blossoms in the first two lines, but in Jenkins's conception it is the blossoms swaying in the summer breeze. The butterfly maidens of line 5 are ambiguously either the female dancers or the actual butterflies invoked by the text. The playing versus chasing action in line 5 is also a case in point; both imply different participant roles. Jenkins's conception differs with the other two in the last line (line 8) in that he can consider both an individual as well as collective focus for the activity of growing.

The lines with the least variation of viewpoint or actor roles are lines 3–4 and lines 6–7. All three readings agree in lines 3–4 that the boys are among the plants, either chasing or playing. In lines 6–7, the thunder is progressing to the location of the song-poem, with the earth trembling (*tayayata* at the end of line 7 in the Tawakwaptiwa version must be a mistake; the verb means "be trembling" and has no connotation of "summon"). In both instances, all three versions agree on actor (the boys in lines 3–4; the thunder in lines 6–7) and focus (the location of the boys amid the plants; the direction of the thunder).

It is on these two pairs of lines that the B phrases of the musical fabric begins. At the beginning of the B phrase, significant musical variation takes place. The octave leap to c″ extends the range of the tune up a fifth (from a-f′ to a-c″)—the technical term for it is *oomi* "upwards/above." Furthermore, just before the B phrase begins, there is hemiola (shift of beat). Lastly, the B phrase has more syncopation (staggered beats) that distinguishes it from the rest of the musical package. The most variation (in terms of actor and focus) in the three translations are outside of this highlighted area; the musical climax is fairly stable in its meaning, as represented in the English translations by knowledgeable Hopis. Please refer to the appended score; note that the music that goes with lines 3–4 and 6–7 of the lyric is the tonal apex of the piece, that within seven beats the melody cascades downwards an octave (a feature unusual in Native American music), that there is considerable (more?) ornamentation here, and that the rhythm involves a shift of beat (hemiola).

The recognition of a core part of the Hopi song-poem means that adaptations of lyrics from Native American sources can indeed reflect some of the native expectations about form expected by Bourdieu and pursued by ethnopoetics; see, for example the treatment of the lyric examined here in Swann (1985:31). Recognizing this patterning also has importance for pioneering a study of Hopi song-poems. In this regard, it is noteworthy that the parts of the musical envelope for the lyric have names in the Hopi language. The

A phrase is called *atkyamiq*, "down," and the B phrase is called *oomiq*, "towards up"; most Hopi music conforms to this general schema (AABBA), though with melodic variation. Recognition of a semantic core in Hopi song-poems also contributes a hypothesis for the comparative study of song-poems in Western Pueblo cultures (Hopi, Zuni, Laguna, Acoma); this is a wider context into which the present example would fit. Finally, the present analysis shows the fundamental importance of ethnomusicology for the study of Native American song-poems.

The musically highlighted, semantically stable material of the opening of the B phrase of the song-poem schema related to cultural meaning external to the text. The text alludes to the practice of *ngöytiwa*, where boys enticed girls with bundles of flowers as part of the "vacation" that followed the serious endeavor of the Snake or Flute rituals that celebrate high summer and attract late summer rains. It is also significant that the butterfly dances also typically follow the Snake or Flute rituals (which themselves alternate by year), and that the butterfly dance uses some of the same imagery as the *ngöytiwa*.

When the corn and melons are ripe, the youths in the field hold high the fairest fruit and summon the maidens with a call. Then the butterfly-girls come running, and try to wrest the prize. . . . So the thunder [and] rain will come, that the corn maidens may grow high (Tawakwaptiwa, in Curtis 1907:481).

The part of the text that relates the most to this cultural knowledge that is external to the song-poem itself are lines 3–4 and lines 6–7. It is clear from the translations of the linguistic text that these two pairs of lines are the most semantically stable. It is not clear why this should be until one considers the musical level above the linguistic text. Then one realizes that these two pairs of lines (couplets?) are highly salient; they are marked structures. Structuralism tells us that the lines are significant in a special way, but we must refer outside the song-poem itself for interpretation.

Only reference to the culture or to other song-poems would make interpretation of the genre possible. From the present analysis, it can only be suggested that central thematic material is stated at the beginning of the B sections of the AABBA form, and that these sections are marked on the musical level (preceding hemiola, syncopation, jump in pitch, higher range of pitch). It is worth noting that vocables (emotive syllables that are not actual words), which appear to have conventional emotive meanings in a given culture (Hinton 1980), surround the linguistic text of the song-poem, comprising most of the AA . . . A portions of the schema, creating yet a larger context for interpretation than I have considered here.

The envelope and simultaneity of text and sound make the song-poem a three-dimensional experience. This expands its emotional impact and interpretation. Some parts of the schema allow for semantic variation; these parts will mean slightly different things to individuals. Other parts of the schema are used for major cultural themes which vary less in interpretation within a given culture. This putative inherent stability and variability is a strength of genres. It is a basis for the predictable knowledge that allows for variable behavior, to calque Bourdieu's calque on structuralism cited above. In the future, it should be obvious that studies of Native American poetics cannot afford to exclude the musical dimension, and that structuralism still has a contribution to make in the milieu of post-structuralism and related agendas.

Appendix
A New Transcription of the Curtis Text

Please note that only the first part of the song-poem (the AAB of the AABB′A) has been transcribed. The last portion of the piece is three repetitions of the B part with vocables and then the descent into the A part, which is also repeated. This variation of the AABBA form is characteristic of Butterfly dance form. I have given the relative range of the two final parts (B repetitions, A and repeat of A). Since the rhythm follows the text in Hopi song-poems, no barlines are used. Instead, musical-textual phrases are presented as cohesive units. A separate staff has been used to show the fundamental rhythm, recorded by Curtis as a gourd rattle. Also note that vocables are underscored, while actual text in Hopi is not underscored. Rhythmic and pitch notation are, of course, approximate. The parts of the retranscription are labeled (A, A′, etc.).

Retranscription of Curtis Text
(First Part)

Poli Tiwa Tawi
Butterfly-Dance Song
Composed and Sung by Tawakwaptiwa

* This triplet is a downward sweep of the voice.

Note

1. The idea of a modal is distinct from the idea of a *vocable* or nonsense syllable. Vocables are common in both western folk music (a prosaic example is the *tra-la-la* of song refrains in the English tradition) and are quite common in Native American music; see the review of the literature on this topic in the paper by Powers in this volume, and also Hinton (1980). Vocables may have conventional cultural meanings, but these meanings are emotive, while modal meaning is at least partly linguistic (probability, intention, obligation) relative to some context (a sentence or larger context).

References

Bahr, Donald M., and J. Richard Haefer. "Song in Piman Curing." *Ethnomusicology* 22 (1978): 89–122.

Bauman, Richard. *Story, Performance and Event*. London: Cambridge University Press, 1986.

Black, Mary E. "Maidens and Mothers: an Analysis of Hopi Corn Metaphors." *Ethnology* 23 (1984): 279–88.

Black, Robert. *A Content Analysis of 81 Hopi Indian Chants*. Dissertation, Indiana University, 1965.

———. "Hopi Grievance Chants: a Mechanism of Social Control." *Studies in Southwestern Ethnolinguistics*. Edited by Dell Hymes and William E. Bittle. The Hague: Mouton, 1967.

———. "Hopi Rabbit-Hunt Chants: a Ritualized Language." *Essays in the Verbal and Visual Arts*. Edited by June Helm McNeish. Seattle: University of Washington Press, 1967.

Bourdieu, Pierre. *Outline of a Theory of Practice*. Trans. by R. Rice. Cambridge: Cambridge University Press, 1977.

Chesky, Jane. "Indian Music of the Southwest." *The Kiva* 7 (1941): 9–12.

Curtis, Natalie, ed. *The Indians' Book*. New York: Harper and Brothers, 1907.

Evers, Larry, and Felipe Molina. *Yaqui Deer Songs: Maso Bwikam*. Tucson: University of Arizona Press, 1987.

Frisbie, Charlotte J. "Epilogue." *Southwestern Indian Ritual Drama*. Edited by Charlotte J. Frisbie. Albuquerque: School of American Research and University of New Mexico Press, 1980. 307–43.

Gilman, Benjamin Ives. "Hopi Songs." *A Journal of American Ethnology and Archaeology*, 5. Edited by Jesse Walter Fewkes. Boston: Houghton and Mifflin, 1908. 1–26.

Hanks, William F. "Discourse Genres in a Theory of Practice." *American Ethnologist* 14 (1987): 668–92.

Harvey, Byron. "Song of the Dog Kachina." *Masterkey* 40 (1966): 106–8.

Herzog, George. "A Comparison of Pueblo and Pima Musical Styles." *Journal of American Folklore* 49 (1936): 283–417.

Hinton, Leanne. "Vocables in Havasupai Song." *Southwestern Indian Ritual Drama*. Edited by Charlotte J. Frisbie. Albuquerque: School of American Research and University of New Mexico Press, 1980. 275–305.

———. *Havasupai Songs: a Linguistic Perspective*. Tübingen: Gunther Narr, 1984.

Hymes, Dell. *"In Vain I Tried to Tell You": Essays in Native American Ethnopoetics*. Philadelphia: University of Pennsylvania Press, 1981.

Jeancon, Jean A. "Indians of the Southwest: Music and Drama." *Pro-Music Quarterly* 5 (1927): 16–24.

Kroskrity, Paul V. "Growing on Stories: Line, Verse, and Genre in an Arizona Tewa Text." *Journal of Anthropological Research* 41 (1985): 183–99.

Kurath, Gertrude P. "Cochiti Choreographies and Songs." *Cochiti: A New Mexican Pueblo Past and Present*, by Charles H. Lange. Carbondale: Southern Illinois University Press, 1959.

———. and Antonio Garcia. *Music and Dance of the Tewa Pueblos*. Museum of New Mexico Research Records 8. Santa Fe: Museum of New Mexico, 1970.

List, George. "The Hopi as Composer and Poet." *Centennial Workshop on Ethnomusicology, Proceedings*. Vancouver, British Columbia: University of British Columbia, 1967.

Lord, Albert B. *The Singer of Tales*. Cambridge, Massachusetts: Harvard University Press, 1960.

MacLeish, K. "A Few Hopi Songs from Moenkopi." *Masterkey* 15 (1941): 178–84.

Malotki, Ekkehart, and Michael Lomatuwa'yma, eds. *Hopi Coyote Stories: Una'ihu*. American Tribal Religions 9. Lincoln, Nebraska: University of Nebraska Press, 1984.

Rhodes, Robert William. *Selected Hopi Secular Music: Transcription and Analysis*. Dissertation, Arizona State University, 1973.

———. *Hopi Music and Dance*. Tsaile, AZ: Navajo Community College Press, 1977. 34 pages.

Rhodes, Willard. "Acculturation in North American Indian Music." *Acculturation in the Americas*. Edited by Sol Tax. Chicago: University of Chicago Press, 1952.

Shaul, David Leedom. "Piman Song Syntax." *Berkeley Linguistic Society, Proceedings* 7 (1981): 275–83.

———. "Cohesion in Hopi Narrative." *Proceedings of the First International Conference on Pragmatics*. Edited by J. Verschueren. Amsterdam: John Benjamins, 1987. 96–105.

———. "Pragmatic Constraints on Hopi Narrative Discourse." *Berkeley Linguistic Society, Proceedings* 13 (1987): 263–69.

Sherzer, Joel. "Poetic Structuring in Kuna Discourse: the Line." *Native American Discourse: Poetics and Rhetoric*. Edited by J. Sherzer and A. C. Woodbury. Austin: University of Texas Press, 1987. 103–39.

Spinden, Herbert J. *Songs of the Tewa*. New York: Indian Tribal Arts, Inc., 1933.

Swann, Brian. *Song of the Sky: Versions of Native American Songs and Poems*. Ashuelot, New Hampshire: Four Zoas Night House Ltd., 1985.

Tedlock, Barbara. "Songs of the Zuni Kachina Society." *Southwestern Indian Ritual Drama*. Edited by Charlotte J. Frisbie. Albuquerque: School of American Research and University of New Mexico Press, 1980. 7–35.

Tedlock, Dennis. *The Spoken Word and the Work of Interpretation*. Philadelphia: University of Pennsylvania Press, 1983.

Todorov, Tzvetan. *Introduction to Poetics*. Theory and History of Literature 1. Trans. by R. Howard. Minneapolis: University of Minnesota Press, 1981.

Underhill, Ruth M. *Singing for Power: the Song Magic of the Papago Indians of Southern Arizona*. Berkeley: University of California Press, 1938.

Voegelin, Carl F., and Robert C. Euler. "Introduction to Hopi Chants." *Journal of American Folklore* 70 (1957): 115–36.

Wiget, Andrew O. "Sayatasha's Night Chant: a Literary Textual Analysis of a Zuni Ritual Poem." *American Indian Culture and Research Journal* 4 (1980): 99–140.

Williams, James. *Tribal Education of the Hopi Indian Child*. Master's thesis, Arizona State College, 1948.

Woodbury, Anthony C. "Rhetorical structure in a Central Alaskan Yupik Eskimo Traditional Narrative." *Native American Discourse: Poetics and Rhetoric*. Edited by J. Sherzer and A. C. Woodbury, Cambridge: Cambridge University Press, 1987. 176–239.

Suggested Reading

The major works on Southwestern Native American musics include a comparison of Pueblo and Piman musical styles (Herzog 1936), works cited above in the text by Evers and Molina, Hinton, Kurath, Kurath and Garcia, and work on Navajo music by McAllester. Hopi music and song-poems have received only cursory treatment in scholarly journals; the most important items are by Chesky (1941), Jeancon (1927), MacLeish (1941), and W. Rhodes (1952). Although there is no published book-length treatment of Hopi music, there is a small literature on the related genre of chanting (Voegelin and Euler 1957; Black 1965, and two articles published in 1967). The most important published studies on Hopi musical structure and the composition process are by List (1967), Gillman (1908), who considers only the musical structure; and by R. Rhodes (1967), which is primarily about the social matrix of Hopi song-poems and their appropriate use. There are also two important unpublished studies of Hopi song-poems: R. Rhodes (1973) and Williams (1948).

Navajo
Poetry
in
Print
and in the
Field:
An
Exercise
in
Text
Retrieval

Paul G. Zolbrod

When I undertook to examine Native American literature twenty-five years ago, I had to confront the effects of my print-oriented bias—typical, I think, of those of us conditioned to assume that great poetry resides only on the written page, and typical too of those whose literary orientation comes from Anglo-European traditions. As something of a newcomer to Native American cultures with no training whatsoever in ethnography, I had presumed that by working in the field I could explore the depth and range of tribal poetic narrative by building a standard written version of the Navajo creation story. I presumed further that the resulting text would be definitive in its length and in its details, like *Beowulf* or the established written versions of the *Odyssey* and the *Iliad*.

I had already located Washington Matthews's English rendering of the Navajo creation story in *Navajo Legends*, and thus found something to build on.[1] And although I sensed that his translation of one tribe's account of its origins reflected little of the poetic quality that resides in oral performances of Native American stories and knew that it was by no means complete, I naively believed that all I had to do after becoming familiar with the Navajo language was listen to informants to supplement whatever was missing either artistically or substantively. Thus I could produce a comprehensive, authentic text that might reflect the poetic quality which, I imagined even more presumptuously, resided in the way that particular cycle could be performed. Significantly, I acquired that impression from reading books, having been trained as a literary scholar. I had found other translated versions of what Navajos often call the emergence myth, which for the most part indicated that Matthews had not recorded the whole story. But the combined additional published accounts still created the impression that I was dealing with a single, unified work and was studying literature in a fairly conventional way.[2]

The more I talked with people across the reservation, however, and the more I learned about the Navajo language beyond basic patterns of sound and syntax, the more apparent it became that I was not doing conventional literary research. Nor was this enterprise merely a matter of translating, as difficult as that itself can be. Orally transmitted material requires a perplexing mediation between performance and print.

For one thing, the relationship between poet and listener is always direct and often intimate in a non-print community. Audiences are frequently small, and the performer is likely to know its members personally. Something as simple as a gaze becomes a subtle rhetorical device; a storyteller can point with special impact to a listener who bears a resemblance to some character; whether he sits cross-legged or rests on his haunches contributes a tonality that print can scarcely replicate. When the audience is larger the presentation grows more formal. The storyteller then may fall under the careful scrutiny of elders who might see fit to interrupt with a correction, in which case speech may be more deliberate. Pitch then rises slightly, speech actually slows, and there may be less body movement. But whether the audience is large or small, a dynamic immediacy links poet and listener which does not exist between the mutually remote reader and writer in the transmission of printed literature. Hence, body language, eye contact, voice modulation, and even posture can supplement or even supplant stylistic features and poetic devices conventional to print, ranging from purely mechanical matters like punctuation to the most subtle applications of meter and rhyme.

Also, oral poetry cannot as easily be isolated from the other arts as it is in our own literate culture. It coexists with song and dance and the plastic arts. The great chantway ceremonies, which are dramatic reenactments of mythic events, require sand paintings, songs, masks, and other carefully crafted paraphernalia, for example. Nor are audiences as stratified in an oral setting as they tend to be where literature circulates by way of print. No social or intellectual distinction separates the literate from the nonliterate. There is no division whatsoever between so-called high and low art or culture or between intellectuals and non-intellectuals. People come to listen or to watch or to participate, partaking equally of a tradition without the slightest self-consciousness about doing so. That reality may not at first seem germane to a translator. However, it does ultimately influence wording and syntax; it calls for an idiom which is not only accurate but which balances accessibility against the subtleties of voice and gesture resonating in a performance the way the subtleties of, say, diction or imagery can reside in a written text but emerge only after careful reading and re-reading.

If transplanting poetry from a tribal setting intensifies the challenges a translator faces, gathering it adds new ones. Navajo country is nothing like a library and in many ways nullifies the convenience of lexicons or a printed grammar. Relative to the distance I was accustomed to travel to visit academic and public libraries, the reservation is small and sparsely populated. Originally I assumed that I could get around easily and locate informants who would all more or less agree with each other the way standard dictionaries do. But the seemingly small size of the reservation turned out to be deceptive. I found few paved roads and relatively few radios, television sets, and telephones. I was unprepared for other conditions of reservation life where presumed assumptions do not always apply. Cash needed to get back and forth is in short supply. Post offices are widely scattered. Books, newspapers, and other printed items do not circulate freely. A standard Navajo script had only recently been established, and traditional Navajos fail to see the value of writing things down. In other words, conditions relative to preliteracy still prevailed.

Assembling material is not easy, I thus discovered, for a print-oriented literary scholar suddenly working with no long-established alphabet, no catalogs, no bibliographies, no official dictionary, no standard libraries.[3] Many Navajos were baffled by my interest in their storytelling, and some opposed the idea of writing material down. To those who could not read or write, print seemed too remote from stories they knew, and all too lofty. What connection could there possibly be between their own seemingly commonplace traditions and the kind of written text I wished to generate? Once a semiliterate Navajo man I got to know began repeating to me a narrative he had heard an elder recite in a sweatlodge the previous night. A certain power intrinsic to the story had obviously been transmitted by its telling, for he repeated it eloquently in language not characteristic of his own speech. I made the mistake, though, of interrupting to comment that I would like to see that episode in print, whereupon he replied defensively, "But that's just one of our stories; it's not like the literature you find in your books." And with that he stopped reciting.

Among the widely scattered Navajos, where assumptions vary sharply from one part of the reservation to another, customs and taboos could hamper my efforts to get material and interpret it. One December night during a discussion with an elder in his family's ceremonial hogan in the Tuba City area, a bird suddenly flew in the smokehole overhead, circled round the room several times, and flew out again. When we began that particular session, my informant had promised to talk all night if needed; we were working on an important passage, and he was eager to have me understand it. But now he announced without explanation that he had to stop; would I take him home?

Several months later, I recalled that incident to two Navajos from different parts of the reservation. One said that the bird would not have bothered him since the incident occurred during storytelling season. The other speculated that my informant may have wanted to quit because he was giving sacred information to an outsider precisely then. The literary scholar accustomed to the indelible permanence of print does not have to deal with problems like that. Once written down, poetry ceases to register shyness, distrust, cultural ambivalence, or regional idiosyncrasies. The printed page does not overlook appointments and is not indifferent to the necessities of scholarship. In the possession of a wary traditionalist or an old shaman who cannot read or write, poetry can be as remote and as unyielding as a hieroglyphic. Or so it would seem to a naive outsider whose ingrained assumptions about the employment of print in the production of poetry seem somehow out of place.

As I went from locale to locale, I met with differing opinions on what belonged to the Navajo creation story and what did not. Some accounts varied so much that I could scarcely believe every informant was talking about the same cycle. In some settlements portions of the narrative had acquired Christian overtones. In others I found accretions resulting from Spanish contact. Some medicine men favored older versions that predated the coming of Europeans; others accepted more recent versions such as those that accounted for the origin of horses and sheep. Different clans placed different emphases on different portions of the story. One informant might declare that something I had heard from another was wrong. To still another I would summarize two varying accounts of a particular episode and ask which was correct. The reply? Neither. Get in contact with so and so up at Kayenta for the right one.

I must admit, too, that locating material in the field can befuddle someone accustomed only to grappling with a mute, inanimate book that simply awaits the patient reader's mastery. I look back now at certain disorienting experiences which I had, and part of me disbelieves that they ever occurred, so inimical are they to the reasoned skepticism that critical reading and empirical method condition us to accept.

My very first venture into the field, for instance, took me up the Rio Grande valley, where I dumbly went from village to village asking Pueblos to share their traditions with me. Unaware of my intrusive tactlessness in doing so, I was turned away again and again, sometimes with doors literally being slammed in my face. After receiving that kind of treatment at Santo Domingo, I was so deadeningly discouraged that I was ready to give up entirely the idea of investigating Native American poetry. Had I done so, of course, I would never have gotten my project underway. Absolutely dejected after being rebuffed for the sixth or seventh time, I headed back to my car, ready to drive away from the Southwest and never return, consigning myself to the study of conventional printed poetry. There, however, I spied a little Pueblo girl of perhaps six; she stood smiling shyly before me, her arm outstretched and her fist upturned at eye level. Once she got my attention, she slowly opened her fingers without a word, disclosing in her hand a small, smooth pebble. Obviously she wanted me to take it, which I did, whereupon she scampered out of sight. For some reason, that simple gesture prompted me to try one more stop at Tesuque before I abandoned the idea of undertaking to seek a corpus of Native American poetry. And that is where Martin Vigil, then governor of that village, issued the first real encouragement I received by directing me to the less secretive Navajos.

It is as easy to make too much of that incident as it is to wonder nearly twenty-five years later if it really happened at all. My whimsical side craves to fancy that the little girl who saved me with a pebble from my own discouragement was some kind of spirit-being common in the narratives of tribal peoples. My reader's skepticism, however, prompts me to wonder if the event ever occurred; after all, I cannot pick up such an experience the way I can handle a book, reexamining its contents to verify them. Meanwhile, the realist in me begs me to rejoin that I had simply encountered a little girl who wanted to give a stranger a pebble: no big deal one way or the other when taken at face value. So here I am, wavering uncertainly between conflicting possibilities.

I would not make so much of that incident if I hadn't experienced other improbable ones which likewise baffled me. Late one January night, for example, after a particularly intense session in the high country toward Navajo Mountain with a storyteller who had agreed to let me hear him tell several stories about the trickster Coyote, I began the long trip back to Flagstaff to rejoin my family after a week out in the field. I was tired and my head was full of images. I had just heard how Coyote refused to plant corn in neat rows when everyone else did; how he had insisted that mortals should not be allowed to live forever; how he scampered from spot to spot urinating with delight after successfully seducing a woman who swore she wanted nothing to do with him; how he then initiated her into the ways of witchery. And now as I drove through the darkness, I could not stop wondering about the way he defied tribal values, about how Navajos alternately scorned and admired him, and about the capacity of well-told trickster tales to fascinate listeners.

Highway 160 south through Tuba City where it joins U.S. 89 to Flagstaff is a long, lonely route, especially at night. You descend nearly two thousand feet and cross the Little Colorado between Cameron and Gray Mountain, listed on the map respectively as a junction and a trading post, but at night indistinct from the surrounding desert: there are no lights, no markers, no landmarks visible between dusk and dawn. South of Gray Mountain begins the long climb up again to Summit Pass, overlooking Flagstaff and its wide grid of lights which contrast starkly with the vast, empty desert to the north.

Following that route as I fought sleep and vainly tried to pick up an all-night radio station, I felt the storyteller's lingering effect. He had recited quietly, depending on sibilants and nasals to underscore Coyote's cloying whine. The rhythm of his language obtruded where Coyote persisted most doggedly in winning the diffident maiden. For me, this had been an exercise in oral narrative at its poetic best. I listened and watched in the hushed darkness, virtually hypnotized by what I simultaneously heard and saw, especially once I recognized how the storyteller orchestrated the movement of his hands. Seated cross-legged on the floor, the rest of his body virtually immobile, he extended his forearms belt high and alternately turned his palms up and then down with the rhythm of his speech—depending, it seemed, upon whether or not Coyote was speaking; or he alternately held them fast to one spot on his thighs, then moved them slowly up and down, depending on whether Coyote was going somewhere or stayed put. Speech was muted, the voice soft, so that the audience had to strain to listen, which seemed to heighten concentration, drawing listeners all the more fully into the story's action and thus summoning all the more readily clear illusions. Language and physical presence merged perfectly to bring Coyote veritably to life. The whole session had made a startlingly powerful imprint on me, so graphically had this man described Coyote stalking and preening and taunting. Now his voice and my memory of having envisioned Coyote's obtrusive features remained lodged between my ears the way a country-and-western tune lingers long after it is heard.

Meanwhile, I headed uphill into flurrying snow and heavy winds which drove large tufts of tumbleweed across the road ahead. Resisting fatigue and the sound of that voice, I suddenly imagined seeing a coyote dash across the road in front of my car, and then another, and yet one more. They were not real coyotes, though, but more like over-sized, animated caricatures of Coyotes darting ethereally through the blowing snow ahead, their semihuman faces grinning and leering. Overwhelmed for an instant by such visual disarray, I had to stop the car, get out, and rub my eyes in the cold wind until I could regain control of my sight. I had hallucinated those creatures, to be sure, as I tried to see through the blowing mélange of snow and tumbleweed with the voice of someone now not present still in my ears. I managed to make my way across the remaining thirty miles to Flagstaff alertly enough, but not free of the vivid yet disorienting illusion of Coyote streaking across my path.

"Too many Coyote stories," I found myself saying when trying to explain the experience to others. Now, more than a dozen years later, I vacillate between doubting that I had ever imagined seeing those coyotes and flinching because I bear so sharp a recollection of them. Such, I think, is the impact of hearing well-recited tales in a vastly different cultural setting during storytelling season among people who take them literally. Even in retrospect incidents like that drive home the difference between hearing narratives in a tribal context and reading them in a book. Stories retold aloud in the darkness and in their native setting can place a trained reader like myself in a state of disarray. Orally transmitted works have their own kind of permanent immediacy; how, I continue to wonder, does one convey that peculiar permanence by way of the silent, inanimate page? Is the indelibility of print alone sufficient? Or else is the barrier too great between orally transmitted narratives on the one hand where listeners actually believe what is described, and printed stories on the other where disbelief is only temporarily suspended?

But then I also had to contend more straightforwardly with linguistic barriers. As a holophrastic language with a verb system offering no easily visible pattern of inflections, Navajo comes slowly—paradigm by grudging paradigm.[4] Tense, mood, and aspect seem to call for an entirely new conception of motion and change. By the addition of certain particles to a given verb, actions can occur in a mythic pre-past over a period of time whose duration is seemingly without end. Depending on how verb stems are matched with inflections, movement takes place circularly or in straight lines, in wide arcs or narrow ones. A morphemic infix can determine whether someone or something moves in one direction, its opposite, or there and back. Special tense markers for ceremonial use crop up in performances but go unnoticed in the few available written grammars. Person and number impose a different way of classifying groups and social units. Added to our simple categories of singular and plural are separate distinctions for pairs, small groups, and larger groups, along with pronominal markers to designate who in a group does or does not participate in an action that affects everyone. As for pronunciation, I quickly found that Navajo contains consonants especially difficult to hear or to pronounce, along with levels of pitch and tone not easily gleaned by a non-native speaker. Thus, progress came with unrecognized slowness; I kept imagining that I was learning faster than I indeed was at first because I couldn't distinguish high tone from low, rising from falling, or long vowel from short.

I finally faced that fact when I picked up a Navajo hitchhiker in Leupp, Arizona, which lies in a remote western corner of the reservation. He had had too much to drink and was in no frame of mind to do what many of my Navajo acquaintances had taken to doing as I attempted to learn to speak. When my pronunciation was so far off that I could not easily be understood, they would, by replying in English, prompt me to speak English in return, thereby gaining access to what I wished to say. Or, if they knew no English they would finesse by drawing out the discussion until my meaning became clear. But they were generally too polite to indicate that I was speaking badly. But not this man. Alcohol had overwhelmed his Navajo propensity for reticent politeness, and as I struggled to introduce myself in the customary Navajo way by giving my name, telling him where I was from, and stating my business on the reservation, we had traveled the full sixty miles to Flagstaff, his destination. For he kept repeating to me in Navajo, "I can't understand." When he finally did make out what I was saying, he would ask a follow-up question and the struggle to communicate resumed. I knew then that I had to refine the way I listened to pick up distinctions of tone and length and to increase my inventory of options available to chanters and storytellers seeking to make their speech esthetically effective.

But the inherent poetic features of Navajo do not easily disclose themselves to a linguistic outsider who naively believes that because he can recognize an Old English caesura or scan a Petrarchian sonnet he can quickly spot the artistry in a given Navajo passage. Navajo storytelling can be a subtle, intricate art inscrutable to anyone with no firm command of the language, especially among individualistic, locale-oriented performers.[5] For a long time I could not even be sure that there was even a standard dialect. I recall hearing words and phrases in the Tuba City area or around Leupp or Bird Spring on the western edge of the reservation that I did not remember hearing around Fort Defiance, Shiprock, or Pueblo Pintado further East. Sometimes I even fancied that pronunciation could vary significantly within a distance of thirty miles. Was I witnessing a dialect shift or a shift in style? Was I hearing deliberately preserved archaic pronunciations? Or was my own linguistic inadequacy playing tricks on me?

In my struggle to absorb all too much all too quickly I could never be sure of such things, and I am left with an impression of noticing more than I could actually absorb. Just when I thought I was becoming fluent enough to hear well, I would recognize another feature, such as the exaggerated use of nasality or the careful positioning of parallel phrases among passages of more loosely constructed syntax. But when I fixed my attention on some new pattern of speech or gesture, I too easily lost track of what was being said. Sometimes the struggle to appreciate while straight out trying to understand seemed impossible. And there was always the question of how I could put all of that into my own written English. I kept recalling old Martin Vigil's warning at Tesuque back in 1969. "If you want to learn our poetry, you need fifty years," he had said. "The traditions of each village are more complex than you could ever imagine, not to mention the language."

Ironically, it was printed material that ultimately provided me with a grasp of the Navajo creation story sufficient to assemble a text suitable for Anglo readers conditioned by the circumstances of history and cultural hegemony to assume that there was no such thing as Navajo poetic tradition or anything like a Native American literature. Somewhat by accident, I located a set of some four dozen manuscripts at the Museum of Northern

Arizona in Flagstaff.[6] Adding up to a total of more than twenty-five hundred pages, they ranged in length from thirteen to seven hundred sheets each of material originally recorded on cylinders or tape and then transcribed both in a crudely devised Navajo script and a compacted literal English.

For the most part, these were important "fragments" of the emergence cycle which Matthews had either overlooked, ignored, or compressed for the sake of brevity. After all, he was interested in content, not poetic texture, and his assumptions about what constituted a complete version were apparently as crude as my own had been. The remaining texts were miscellaneous narratives that may not have supplemented the creation story very fully but did complement it. Many of the stories were never printed elsewhere. Others were published in fairly obscure places and treated as anthropological source material.[7] None had been acknowledged as poetry by the two researchers who had gathered them or by those who later edited some of them for publication.

The manuscripts had been compiled earlier in this century by Father Berard Haile and Gladys Reichard. Haile's share includes twenty different stories typewritten in makeshift orthography and repeated in accurate but unliterary English. He, too, was retrieving what he saw only as data. Added to all of that are four similarly arranged bilingual transcriptions prepared by Reichard, likewise an ethnographer rather than a literary critic. In addition there is a story which Father Haile recorded but was translated by her. Most of the manuscripts also contain informative introductions, detailed linguistic glosses, end various textual notes which ethnographers sometimes consult but which have gone unnoticed for any poetic information they might yield, much as have the transcriptions assembled by other ethnographers who consider narratives data instead of poetry.

Obviously, Haile and Reichard had devoted their entire professional lives to research spanning many more years than I had as yet put in. Both had mastered the Navajo language, and both approached Navajo culture with unparalleled receptivity. Their work, in fact, underscores the kind of partnership needed between ethnography and literary study if viable Native American poetic texts are to be recovered. Occasionally I would come across some oldtimer on the reservation who had known one or the other and who validated that impression. "She was the only White person I was willing to tell exactly what my grandmother told me," one woman said of Reichard. Another of my informants turned out to be the grandson of one of Father Berard's chief sources. When I asked him to help me gloss several passages he was amazed to find that such sacred lines had been put into print. Then I told him that they were recorded by Haile in 1937, and he seemed less surprised. Medicine men like his grandfather regarded the Franciscan as one of them, he revealed, and the "skinny little priest" was able to record material nobody else could have acquired, including background information.[8]

So I could rely on the manuscripts to help me overcome some of the frustration I had experienced in the field. Barriers I initially faced now seemed less formidable. I could read and reread relevant material in the kind of solitude that permitted a more bookish kind of concentration. I could cross-reference separate passages and make careful comparisons. I could confirm things I thought I had heard myself. What the manuscripts contained had been recited by people like Slim Curly, River Junction Curly, Frank Mitchell, or Red Moustache, names I recognized because old timers I met sometimes mentioned them as those who last recited stories in the traditional way.

Together the documents indicated something that I had not fully appreciated yet, even after struggling to get material in the field—something that anyone wishing to recover important poetic material from a tribal setting needs to understand. A major narrative does not necessarily have a fixed shape or length in a preliterate culture. It may begin where a particular storyteller wants it to for a particular storytelling occasion, end where it may seem appropriate to end at the time of recitation, and include details that might suit one immediate purpose but not another. Very often it is part of a larger issue, such as curing an illness or exercising some negative force to restore harmony in the world. In that case it assumes, so to speak, a new identity as a distinct, purposeful ceremony, incorporating song and dance and drama and graphic or plastic art and adding sacred depth to its broad secular dimensions.

Such a story—if it can really be called a single story—is actually an entire tradition residing collectively in the minds of all who hear it over a span of many generations. Furthermore, that tradition is not accurately identified by older translations, and certainly not adequately recognized by mainstream literary scholars and critics whose print-based conception of American literary culture is obviously incomplete. In fact, when I studied them, the Navajo manuscripts cast a new light on standard Old World literary texts common to my earlier training. *Beowulf*, too, comes ultimately from an oral tradition and might conceivably emerge from a ceremonial context like the *Shootingway* or any one of the many other Navajo chantway myths. *Chanson de Roland* could owe its origins as much to music and song as any chant from *Blessingway*. The assumptions I inherited as someone trained only to read could very well be too narrow.

Now I recognized my editorial mission. I could coordinate the Haile-Reichard manuscripts with what I discovered in the field and produce a text suitable to compare with the great texts that constitute our own literary tradition. It was my good fortune to have observed enough on the reservation to appreciate the rich poetic source Washington Matthews had drawn from and to understand better the encounter between oral tradition and print. But I was also lucky to have located products like the Haile-Reichard manuscripts, which allowed me to affirm my observations and match firsthand the benefits of print with the effects of preliterate performance.

By analyzing the manuscripts I could reexamine poetic qualities which I thought I had witnessed in the field. Each storyteller on record in the archives had a unique style which he might apply freely at times, just as I believed each of my informants had. Not always able to distinguish features sharply when I listened, I could verify them when studying the manuscripts. Because he employed archaic terms, for example, and because his sentences were stately in their measured length and heavily parallel structure, River Junction Curly spoke in what Haile identified as classical Navajo, which I could now recognize. By contrast, Red Moustache relied on dialogue to tell his stories, which thus sound more colloquial. Indicating in a textual note that Curly relied heavily on nasal vowels when representing Coyote, Haile confirmed what I had noticed when I had listened to those Coyote stories north of Tuba City. That was the kind of confirmation I needed.

Seeing variations in print, too, reassured me that what I first considered discrepancies were part of the cycle's larger scheme after all. Differences similar to those I noticed were now on printed record and I could deliberate over them. In one account of Coyote's exploits, for instance, he incites swallows to attack him. But in another it is the otters who kill him. Likewise, in one version describing a quarrel between the sexes, First Woman's mother-in-law goads her to argue with her husband First Man; in another, though, the mother-in-law is not even mentioned. But the manuscripts suggested that certain other details must remain constant from telling to telling, just as the style in which they are described varies less, and they are key ones. Coyote is inevitably killed. The quarreling First Man and First Woman are reconciled after four years of separation, but not until after the birth of voracious monsters resulting from the quarrel. The monsters are subsequently killed by warrior twins. It would seem that the authenticity of the overall cycle is reflected best in such passages, which can be considered sacred because of what they imply. Those are the passages which I was especially happy to read closely in the museum library. Written down, they somehow seemed much more reliable than oral testimony, at least to someone with my literary orientation and my lingering difficulty in speaking and understanding Navajo, with its six variations in tone, its repetitive holophrastic syntax, its seemingly unpatterned morphophonemic scheme, and its confounding array of inflections.

Not that I wish to diminish what I managed to acquire in the field. To the contrary, I became convinced that my work there and the archival work enriched each other. By listening I became familiar with the sound of the language, with the cadence of a storyteller's voice, with the way speech and gesture are orchestrated, with the part that music and dance play in a ceremonial narrative—all of which contributed to my growing sense of what the manuscripts fully implied and of how I could shape a credible idiom as I assembled a written English version. By getting to know Navajo people I found out why storytelling remains an important activity on the reservation; I saw firsthand how values defined by the stories managed to endure considerable cultural change; I gained new insight into the dynamics of oral performance and its esthetics; and I fostered a heightened respect for that kind of discourse. All of that fortified me with a secure understanding of what I could and could not do on the printed page. At its best, my text would stand as just one more performance—albeit written—of a narrative cycle whose poetic strength resides in its elasticity. It lives as art not because one version overshadows or supplants all others, but because it resonates in the daily lives of those who wish to hear it told and retold. My version might reflect the character of an orally transmitted prototype, but by no means could it serve as a definitive text.

On several occasions I got help from native speakers able to read and write Navajo in working my way through passages whose literary quality I hoped to spot. As a result, I am all the more persuaded that a viable Navajo poetic tradition exists. But I also realize how little I still know about it, and how unlikely it is that any one book could fully encapsulate a living oral tradition. There is more "literature" out there on the reservation than anyone could uncover in three professional lifetimes, and more still among other Native American communities whose poetry prevails more resiliently than we allow ourselves to believe. But if we are to appreciate it and to learn from it, we need to revise our assumption that poetry exists only where there is literacy, to say nothing of how we define the term literature.

A more complicated merger than we might at first suppose, the union of oral tradition and print can be achieved in an effort to recover the lost tradition of Native American poetic narrative. Or so the Navajo example suggests. First, however, we have to recognize that individual tribes have produced poetry without print. We must also learn to respect the esthetic dimensions of oral transmission. Then we have to balance listening against reading with a growing awareness of how those two kinds of discourse may vary but without presuming that one is necessarily superior to the other. Meanwhile, we would do well to review earlier written scholarship produced by ethnographers, whether or not they were seeking literature so-called. All of that makes for an interesting exercise in translation, to say nothing of the discovery—yet to be fully explored for its ramifications—that classical poetry indigenous to the New World does indeed exist.

Notes

1. Matthews's proper place in American intellectual history has not yet been recognized. The story of harvesting and translating Native American poetry will remain incomplete until his work is accounted for and appreciated (see Zolbrod 1983). Virtually everything he wrote is out of print, although his collected papers are on microfilm. See Halpern and McGreevy. For an annotated bibliographical guide to earlier published versions of the Navajo creation story, see Spencer, 12–30. Subsequently published accounts include King, Oakes and Campbell; Link; O'Brien; and Zolbrod (1984).

2. After first undertaking this project, I encountered various responses to the difference between written poetry and orally transmitted poetry, especially from Native American sources. See, for example, Greenway; Hymes (1965, 1975); Kroeber; Rothenberg; Tedlock. Attention to the topic has increased during the last decade or so. See, for example, the excellent anthologies compiled by Swann (1983) and Krupat and Swann (1987), where some of the above mentioned material has been reprinted. Also see Friedrich; Sherzer; and Sherzer and Woodbury. As yet I know of no one who has treated the differences systematically and in a broader context which includes studies of Old World and tribal material alike, although that fascinating topic too is receiving wider attention than it had drawn when I first began my own study. The work of Walter Ong had provided some early direction. Helpful, too, were Havelock and Lord.

3. Compiled by Young and Morgan in 1980 and revised in 1989, an official dictionary does now exist.

4. Textbook grammars include Blair, Simmons, and Witherspoon; Haile; Hoijer; Goosen; Sapir and Hoijer; Wilson; Witherspoon; and Young and Morgan.

5. For a notable example of how the poetics of Navajo discourse can be ferreted out by

patient, open-minded field work, see Toelken and Scott. See Sherzer's discussion of the process with the Kuna Indians of Panama, too. Apparently without being aware of the relevance to poetics of what she had observed, Reichard (1944) also attained an astute appreciation of the poetic dimensions of Navajo prayer.

6. The manuscripts are housed in the library of the Museum of Northern Arizona, Flagstaff. Duplicates exist in the Special Collections Division of the University of Arizona Library and in the archives of the Wheelwright Museum of the American Indian, Santa Fe, New Mexico. Listed as Accession #63, they are indexed and contain thirty-one folders numbered consecutively. See, for example, Haile (1938, 1943, 1978, 1979); Wyman (1962, 1965, 1970, 1973, 1975, 1979) and Wyman, Oakes and Campbell.

8. It is still possible, however, to retrieve Navajo material presumed no longer to exist. See, for example, Luckert (1978, 1979). Interestingly enough, however, Luckert, too, had to rely on the Haile manuscripts to supplement what he located in the field, although he was not seeking to recover poetic material. It was he who first called the manuscripts to my attention, and I acknowledge his help in locating them. I am indebted to him more generally for the direction I acquired from some challenging and stimulating discussions we had during the course of my field work. I also acknowledge the expert assistance of Ms. Katherine Bartlett, Archivist at the Museum of Northern Arizona, and Ms. Dorothy House, Museum Librarian, in helping me work through that material.

References

Austin, Mary. 1930. *The American Rhythm: Studies and Reexpressions of Amerindian Songs.* Boston: Houghton Mifflin Company.

———. 1931. Aboriginal American Literature. *American Writers on American Literature*, ed. John Macy. New York: Horace Livewright.

Barnes, Nellie. 1922. *American Indian Verse, Characteristics of Style.* Lawrence: Bulletin of the University of Kansas, vol. 22, no. 18.

Bierhorst, John. 1974. *Four Masterworks of American Indian Literature.* New York: Farrar, Strauss, & Giroux.

Blair, Robert W., Leon Simmons, and Gary Witherspoon. 1969. *Navajo Basic Discourse.* Provo, Utah: Brigham Young University.

Boas, Franz. 1925. Stylistic Aspects of Primitive Poetry. *Journal of American Folklore* 67:333–49.

Brinton, Daniel. 1881–1933. *Library of American Aboriginal Literature.* 5 vols. Washington, D.C.: Bureau of American Ethnology.

Eisenstein, Elisabeth L. 1979. *The Printing Press as An Agent of Change.* Cambridge: Cambridge University Press.

Fishler, Stanley A. 1953. *In the Beginning: A Navajo Creation Myth.* Salt Lake City: University of Utah Anthropological Paper No. 13.

Friedrich, Paul. 1986. *The Language Parallax: Linguistic Relativism and Poetic Indeterminacy.* Austin: University of Texas Press.

Goosen, Irvy. 1977. *Navajo Made Easier.* Flagstaff: Northland Press.

Greenway, John. 1964. *Literature Among The Primitives.* Hatboro: Folklore Associates.

Haile, Berard. 1926. *A Manual of Navajo Grammar*. St. Michaels, Arizona.

———. 1938. *Origin Legend of the Navajo Enemy Way*. New Haven: Yale University Publications in Anthropology No. 17.

———. 1943. *Origin Legend of the Navajo Flintway*. Chicago: University of Chicago Press.

———. 1978. *Love Magic and Butterfly People*. Flagstaff: Museum of Northern Arizona Press.

———. 1979. *Waterway*. Flagstaff: Museum of Northern Arizona Press.

Halpern, Katherine Spencer, and Susan Brown McGreevy. 1985. *Guide to the Microfilm Edition of the Washington Matthews Papers*. Albuquerque: University of New Mexico Press.

Havelock, Eric A. 1963. *Preface to Plato*. Cambridge, Mass.: Harvard University Press.

Hymes, Dell. 1965. Some North Pacific Coast Poems: A Problem in Anthropological Philology. *American Anthropologist* 67:316–41.

———. 1975. Breakthrough Into Performance. In *Folklore, Performance and Communication*, ed. Dan Ben-Amos and Kenneth S. Goldstein. The Hague: Mouton.

King, Jeff, Maud Oakess, and Joseph Campbell. 1943. *Where the Two Came to Their Father*. New York: Pantheon Books.

Kluckhohn, Clyde, and Dorthea Leighton. 1962. *The Navajo*. Garden City, New York: Doubleday & Co.

Kroeber, Karl. 1978. Poem, Dream, and the Consuming of Culture. *Georgia Review* 32:266–79. Reprinted in Swann: 98–111.

Krupat, Arnold. 1989. *The Voice in Margin: Native American Literature and Canon*. Berkeley: University of California Press.

———. and Brian Swann, eds. 1987. *Recovering the Word: Essays on Native American Literature*. Berkeley: University of California Press.

Link, Margaret Schevill. 1956. *The Pollen Path*. Palo Alto: Stanford University Press.

Loomis, Roger Sherman, 1959. *Arthurian Literature in the Middle Ages*. Oxford: Oxford University Press.

Lord, Albert B. 1960. *The Singer of Tales*. Cambridge, Mass.: Harvard University Press.

Luckert, Karl. 1975. *The Navajo Hunter Tradition*. Tucson: University of Arizona Press.

———. 1978. *A Navajo Bringing-Home Ceremony*. Flagstaff: Museum of Northern Arizona Press.

———. 1979. *Coyoteway: A Navajo Holyway Healing Ceremonial*. Tucson/Flagstaff: University of Arizona Press and the Museum of Northern Arizona Press.

Malotki, Ekkehart. 1978. *Hopitutuwutsi/Hopi Tales*. Flagstaff: Museum of Northern Arizona Press.

Matthews, Washington. 1897. *Navajo Legends*. Boston: American Folklore Society.

McNeley, James Kale. 1981. *Holy Wind in Navajo Philosophy*. Tucson: University of Arizona Press.

Newcomb, Franc Johnson. 1967. *Navajo Folk Tales*. Santa Fe: Museum of Navajo Ceremonial Art. Reprinted by the University of New Mexico Press, 1990.

O'Bryan, Aileen. 1956. *The Diné: Origin Myth of the Navajo Indians*. Washington, D.C.: Bureau of American Ethnology Bulletin No. 163.

Ong, Walter J. 1977. *Interfaces of the Word*. Ithaca: Cornell University Press.

Opland, Jeff. 1980. *Anglo-Saxon Poetry: A Study of the Traditions*. New Haven: Yale University Press.

Ramsey, Jarold. 1983. *Reading the Fire: Essays in the Traditional Indian Literatures of the Far West*. Lincoln: University of Nebraska Press.

Reichard, Gladys A. 1944. *Prayer: The Compulsive Word*. New York: J. J. Augustin.

———. 1950. *Navajo Religion: A Study of Symbolism*. Bollingen Series XVIII. Princeton: Princeton University Press.

Rothenberg, Jerome. 1972. *Shaking the Pumpkin: Traditional Poetry of the Indian North Americas*. Garden City, New York: Doubleday & Co.

Sapir, Edward, and Harry Hoijer. 1967. *The Phonology and Morphology of the Navajo Language*. Berkeley: University of California Publications in Linguistics, vol. 50.

Sherzer, Joel. 1987. A Discourse-Centered Approach to Language and Culture. *American Anthropologist* 84:295–309.

Sherzer, Joel, and Anthony Woodbury, eds. 1987. *Native American Discourse: Poetics and Rhetoric*. Cambridge: Cambridge University Press.

Spencer, Katherine. 1947. *Reflections of Social Life in the Navajo Origin Myth*. Albuquerque: University of New Mexico Press.

———. 1957. *Mythology and Values: An Analysis of Navajo Chantway Myths*. Philadelphia: American Folklore Society.

Swann, Brian, ed. 1983. *Smoothing the Ground: Essays on Native American Oral Literature*. Berkeley: University of California Press.

———. 1986. *Song of the Sky: Versions of Native American Songs & Poems*. Ashlot Village, New Hampshire: Four Zoas Night House.

Tedlock, Dennis. 1971. On the Translation of Style in Oral Narrative. *Journal of American Folklore* 84:114–33. Reprinted in Swann: 57–77.

———. 1972. *Finding the Center: Narrative Poetry of the Zuni Indians*. New York: Dial. Reprint, Lincoln: University of Nebraska Press, 1978.

———. 1983. *The Spoken Word and the Work of Interpretation*. Philadelphia: University of Pennsylvania Press.

———. 1985. *Popol Vuh*. New York: Simon and Schuster.

Toelken, Barre, and Tacheeni Scott. 1981. Poetic Retranslation and the "Pretty Languages" of Yellowman. In *Traditional American Indian Literatures: Texts and Interpretations*, ed. Karl Kroeber. Lincoln: University of Nebraska Press.

Underhill, Ruth, et al. 1979. *Rainhouse and Ocean: Speeches for the Papago Year*. Flagstaff: Museum of Northern Arizona Press.

Welsh, Andrew. 1978. *Roots of Lyric: Primitive Poetry and Modern Poetics*. Princeton: Princeton University Press.

Wilson, Alan. 1971. *Breakthrough Navajo*. Gallup, New Mexico. University of New Mexico, Gallup Branch.

Witherspoon, Gary. 1977. *Language and Art in the Navajo Universe*. Ann Arbor: University of Michigan Press.

Wyman, Leland. 1962. *The Windways of the Navajo*. Colorado Springs: The Taylor Museum.

———. 1965. *The Red Antway of the Navajo*. Santa Fe: Museum of Navajo Ceremonial Art.

———. 1970. *Blessingway*. Tucson: University of Arizona Press.

———. 1975. *The Mountainway*. Tucson: University of Arizona Press.

———. 1983. *Southwest Indian Drypainting*. Santa Fe: School of American Research.

———, Maud Oakes, and Joseph Campbell. 1957. *Beautyway: A Navajo Ceremonial*. New York: Pantheon Books.

Yazzie, Ethelou. 1971. *Navajo History*. Many Farms, Arizona: Navajo Community College Press.

Young, Robert W., and William Morgan. 1969. *The Navajo Language*. Salt Lake City: The Deseret Book Company.

———. 1980, 1989. *The Navajo Language: A Grammar and Colloquial Dictionary*. Albuquerque: University of New Mexico Press.

Zolbrod, Paul G. 1983. Poetry and Culture: The Navajo Example. In *Smoothing the Ground: Essays on Native American Oral Literature*. ed. Brian Swann. Berkeley: University of California Press.

———. 1984. *Dine bahane': The Navajo Creation Story*. Albuquerque: University of New Mexico Press.

Suggested Reading

In addition to consulting works cited in the endnotes, readers wishing to gain a general overview of how poetry fits into the broader context of Navajo culture can consult Kluckhohn and Leighton, 121–38; McNeley; Reichard, 1944, 1950; Spencer, 1957; Witherspoon; and Wyman, 1983. Bear in mind that none of these works deals specifically with poetry and poetics, leaving the reader to draw inferences as I have done. Each in its significant way, however, can add understanding. Recommended also are works dealing concertedly with tribal poetics, especially those of Hymes; Ramsey; Sherzer; and Tedlock, 1972a, 1981, 1983. Recently published noteworthy translations from other tribes include Bierhorst; Malotki; Tedlock, 1972, 1985; and Underhill et al. In addition to the anthologies of Swann and Swann and Krupat, a good contemporary work to use as an entree into Native American poetics is Krupat. Well worth noticing is the effort by Swann (1986) to use print graphics literally to reshape earlier translations. To his great credit, he draws his selections from earlier efforts to translate Native American discourse. Such material is too easily overlooked because of its age. Much of it remains invaluable, however, even if the contemporary reader may wish to winnow out assumptions that now seem outdated. See the works of Austin; Barnes; Boas; and Brinton (whose century-old material remains fresh in some surprising ways despite his "noble savage" pronouncements). A useful work that links Native American material with mainstream poetry ancient and modern is Welsh. Relevant, too, is Opland, although he connects Old English poetry not with Native American traditions but South African tribal analogs. And, for those who wish to stretch even further the horizons of their appreciation for the encounter between print and preliterate poetry, I recommend a careful exploration of Arthurian tradition. See Loomis, especially the first twelve chapters, a work that has gone unappreciated for far too long, and one which should be drawn into use if we are to expand our understanding of the relationship with print. In that regard, too, Eisenstein is vital.

Translating Papago Legalese

Donald Bahr

This essay explores two issues in translation, first, what I will call "texted-" versus "textlessness," and second, the more familiar issue of accuracy versus inaccuracy. I discuss examples of textlessness and inaccuracy from the field of law, specifically from the promulgation of law in, and the translation of law from, Native American languages. The examples come from the tribal council of the Papago, or, as it is now called, Tohono O'odham ("Desert Indian"), Nation of southern Arizona.

The issues are not on a par. The first has logical priority over the second in that one cannot judge the accuracy of a translation unless one has a text to go on. The possibility of a textless translation precludes any judgement of accuracy. What, then, is this oddity, a textless translation? Textlessness occurs when a new work in language B is created under the influence of generically but not literally similar works in language A. Textless translations are therefore fresh creations, and this freshness distinguishes them from what we normally expect of translations. We normally expect that the artistic or literary qualities, and the content, of a translation are not fresh, but are carried over from an original text in a source language. Thus, we praise a translation for its felicity, meaning its felicitous conformity with an original, but not for its raw creativity.

Textlessness

There are no original texts in the instances we are interested in. There is only a *genre* in language A which artists in language B have understood to the extent of producing a similar work in their preferred language. It follows that a textless translation is as greatly or little creative as a new work of the same genre in the source language—only the translators have the additional challenge of outfitting themselves with an appropriate vocabulary, semantics, diction, and cadence from resources available to them in B.

Textless translation is a fairly common manner or mode of literary production. It occurs by definition whenever genres (not single works, but productive genres) spread across linguistic boundaries. In Native America, much of what Lévi-Strauss called "transformations," in reference to historically linked chains of prose myths (classically displayed in his article on the myth of Asdiwal, 1967), belongs to this mode; and so does the poignant burst of multitribal Ghost Dance song creation that was studied by Herzog in 1935. On the other hand, the "diffusion" of prose myths, so interesting to early twentieth-century Americanists such as Boas, Lowie, and Kroeber, is not a case of textless translation (the creation of new works in a given genre), but of regular "texted" translation (the presentation of a given work to a new, foreign language audience). Finally, my concept of textless translation overlaps the structuralist or poststructuralist notion of "intertextuality" insofar as the latter pertains to literary works that are formed in reaction to other works (this sense of intertextuality is covered by the notion of "transformation"). Another aspect of intertextuality bears on the present project, namely the idea that literary works are heterogeneous by nature, being variously patchworks of hitherto distinct discourses, or homogenized blends, or (perhaps the most appropriate for understanding Papago legalisms) grafts of foreign "twigs" onto native "root stock" (Culler 1982:134–56, on Derrida's notion of "grafting").[1]

The Example

The present example of Native American legalese is a grafting of English-born intentions onto Desert Indian linguistic custom. It is not an isolated example. Similar cases abound in the New World. This abundance was an accomplishment of the 1980s, a decade in which human-rights movements, native-language literacy, and New World technical linguistics (the writing of grammars and dictionaries) moved apace to encourage and enable Native polities, often for the first time, to enact laws in their languages. (The Fall 1989 number of *Cultural Survival Quarterly* gives a good survey of this activity in Central

America, the Caribbean, and points in South America where the immediately surrounding European language is generally Spanish but where technical and inspirational works written in English play an interesting and controversial role.)

The example that we will study comes from a single electronically published (photocopied) document which, so far as I know, has no overall title in the Desert Indian language. The document was issued concomitantly with a larger English-language photocopied publication called "Tohono O'odham Education Standards October 1987" (Lopez-Manuel 1987). The native language version corresponds to Section II of the English document, which is entitled "Language Policy of the Tohono O'odham Nation." [2] The Desert Indian version has ten subsections (called "Sections" in the English version) and totals seven pages. The English version uses smaller type and totals four pages.

This essay deals with three of the ten subsections: the first, fourth, and ninth, called "Philosophy," "Official Use of the Tohono O'odham Language," and "Legal Application" respectively in English. Those are free ("inaccurate," see below) translations of the Desert Indian titles, respectively *T-Eldadaq, Mat Has Masma, O Hekid O i E-Hekajid G T-Tohonno O'odham Niok* (I retain the document's capitalization throughout this essay, but delete certain diacritics, including some apostrophes that represent glottal stops), and *O'ohona Cihanig Apedag,* which I literally ("accurately") translate respectively as 'Out Thought,' 'How and When Will Be Used Our Desert Indian Language,' and 'Writing Commandment Propriety.' (In this essay, single quotes mark literal translations. Double quotes mark all other quotations.)

I believe that the overall project of Section II, that is, the determination to produce an untitled native-language document that would be called "Language Policy of the Tohono O'odham Nation" in English, was a case of textless translation. The genre in question was the Written Act of Government, the Governmental Resolution, the Edict. The Tohono O'odham Nation (under the name "Papago Tribe") had produced many such documents in English since the 1930s, but this was probably their most ambitious act written in the native language to date, and it may have been their very first. [3]

In judging the native-language version of Section II to be a textless translation, I exclude the possibility that Section II was first written in English and then translated into Desert Indian. Thus, turning to this essay's second theme, accuracy in translation, I will treat the English version as a more or less accurate, texted translation of a Desert Indian original, not vice versa. In fact, although the details are not known, it is certain that the producers of the combined document, who belong to what is called the Papago (not Tohono O'odham, not Desert Indian) Education Committee, were all members of the Desert Indian Nation, were mostly fluent in both Desert Indian and English, mostly believed that their deepest, truest thoughts came to them first and by preference in Desert Indian, and took pains to discuss the wording of the Desert Indian version with elderly persons who by skill and preference spoke almost no English at all. In short, it is certain that the Desert Indian version was intended to be the original and the English version to be a (texted) translation.

Accuracy, or Literalness, in Texted Translation

Literal translation tries to assimilate the language being translated into, English in this case, to the language being translated from (Desert Indian). It does not wish to translate Desert Indian into good English, but to make English imitate Desert Indian. Free translation does the opposite. It frees itself from something in the "from" language (Desert Indian) in order to say more or less the same thing in the "to" language (English). It is fairly clear what the translation frees itself from: the *words,* the very word-for-word sequence, of the original. I am aware of nothing else that a translation can be free of.

The accuracy of literalness is in the matching of words. I will presently discuss some problems associated with this, but will first note that free translation might better attain some kinds, or fruits, of accuracy, for example, accuracies of spirit, dignity, or overall feel. But although these are conventionally opposed to literalness, it is not clear that they are necessarily so. Perhaps literal and free translations are alternative roads to them, and if so the present essay will aproach them in its way while it remains for others to approach them through freeness.

Now, the chief practical problem in literal translation is that the resulting text borders on illegibility; the problem is not in preparing such a translation, but in enabling people to read it. The cause of this problem, I think, is differences in the grammatical structure, or grammatical type, between languages. The classic and still illuminating statement on this issue was by Edward Sapir in his book *Language* (1921). To Sapir, the structure of a language comes down to the architecture of its sentences, and this architecture comes down to the disposition of four types of "grammatical concepts." All languages include two types of grammatical concepts which he termed "concrete" and "pure relational." Some languages use only those types (he called them "simple pure relational languages") and some use those plus either or both of two additional types of grammatical concept. He called the resulting additional architectural types "complex pure relational," "simple mixed relational," and "complex mixed relational." Sapir classed English as a complex mixed relational language. He did not classify Desert Indian, but it seems to be a complex pure relational type.

We do not need to enter the details of Sapir's types. The relevance is this: grammatical concepts tend to be lodged in individual words, but there are some concepts, called relationals, whose force extends beyond the word in which they are lodged. These relationals are particularly vexing for literal translation. Granted that they are lodged in words, the relational solutions of one language are never perfectly translated into the words of another language, at least not of a language of different structural type.

Let me give an example that involves what are in effect relational concepts, but that uses a somewhat different Sapirean vocabulary (also from the book *Language*). Both Desert Indian and English use the grammatical "function" (Sapir) of word order to express important grammatical concepts, but they do so differently. A key rule of Desert Indian sentence architecture is that a word called the "auxiliary," which gives information on the grammatical concepts of person, number, and verbal aspect, normally comes in second position in a sentence (Zepeda 1983:8–9). This auxiliary is neither a noun nor a verb. It is a densely inflected, one-syllable, wordlike particle. English on the other hand has a word order rule that governs the sequence of nouns (or pronouns) and verbs, as follows: subject, verb, object, indirect object—the so-called "analytical word order rule" (Nist 1966:13–15, on Jesperson 1964). Desert Indian does not observe the English rule, and vice versa. Thus, a free translation of Desert Indian will miss the important native auxiliary (English has "auxiliaries," but no precise equivalent to this one with its fixed position and particular information); and a free translation will attend to subject, verb, and object order, which are immaterial in Desert Indian. A literal translation will auxiliarate the English and will fail to observe English subject, verb, and like requirements.

The reader may now fairly ask, What difference does it make if a free translation adds or deletes such features? My answer is that it makes roughly the same difference as when a literal translation "looks funny" because it dresses the "from" language's relational features in the verbal clothing of the "to" language. True, the free translation reads smoothly because the foreign relational features are concealed, and the literal translation reads roughly because those features are retained. This is the cost or price of literal translation.[4]

Presentation and Discussion

The Education Committee rendered its Desert Indian language version in paragraph form, each paragraph consisting of a few, generally quite long sentences. I retain the committee's sentence divisions, capitalization, and punctuation in presenting the Desert Indian texts, but I divide their sentences into shorter segments, typically but not always clauses (segments with a verb). I number the segments and write each as a line.

Below each word of each line of Desert Indian I give, when possible, a one-word English equivalent. I prefer real English words to analytical abstractions, for example, to use the real word "will" instead of analytical abstraction "future" in translating the Desert Indian wordlike particle *o* (the "future marker"). Thus, the reader is given "The boy will run" rather than "The boy future run" (where "future" is not meant to be read as a word, but as an analysis of the meaning of a word). In general this practice succeeds. But there are at least two particles, "*i*" and "*a*", for which I know no plausible one-word English equivalents (indeed I am not sure what the particles mean); and there is the recurrent auxiliary, already mentioned. I label this latter as "s.s.," for "sentence straightener," after the practice of Albert Alvarez on the texts in Bahr et al. 1974; and I enclose in brackets the information encoded in these "straighteners" on person (1, 2, 3, for first, second, and third), number (sing. and plu.), and aspect (perf. and imperf., for perfective and imperfective). This is the principal exception to my preferred practice of giving word for word equivalents.

From the interlineal literal translation, a somewhat freer English translation is next made, again with lines that are numbered to correspond to the segments of the Desert Indian original. This "modified literal" translation is written in capital letters but with the same punctuation as used by the committee for the Desert Indian original. Next to it, to the right, also in capital letters, is placed the committee's "free" translation of the Desert Indian original. I segment this translation to show alignment and nonalignment (or non-correspondence) both with the Desert Indian original and with my more literal translation. The sequence of segments in the committee's translation is never changed, nor are the words changed, with one exception: when the committee uses a Desert Indian word or phrase, for example, *Tohono O'odham,* I use a literal English translation, in this case "Desert Indian"; thus the reader learns that those words are translatable.

Subsection I. T-Eldadag, 'Our Thought,' "Philosophy"

Sentence 1.

(1) Gadhu   as   i amjed
(1) Remote   just   coming

(2) mat   hekid   in i   t-na:to
(2) ss [3, imperf] when   here   us-make

(3) g   t-na:toikam
(3) the   our-maker

(4) at   idam go:k ha'icu t-ma:,
(4) ss [3, perf] these two   things us-give,

(5) mo   wud t-O'odham himdag
(5) ss [3, imperf] are   our-Indian   way

(6) c   t-niok.
(6) and   our-language.

(1) LONG AGO
(2) WHEN DID HERE MAKE US

(A) GIVEN US AS A GIFT

(3) OUR MAKER   (B) FROM OUR CREATOR,
(4) DID THESE TWO THINGS GIVE US,
(5) WHICH ARE OUR INDIAN WAY   (C) OUR DESERT INDIAN WAY
(6) AND OUR LANGUAGE.

(D) HAS ENDURED
(E) THROUGH GENERATIONS.

Sentence 2.

(1) A:cim O'odham wud a'i   hejel   t-nioki
(1) We   Indians are solely ourselves our-language

(2) c   t-himdag,
(2) and   our-way,

(3) c   wud idam go:k ha'icu
(3) and   are these two   things

(4) mo   am   t-gawulkaj
(4) ss [3, imperf] there us-separate

(5) ab   ha-amjed   in i   na:ko   ma:s   hemajkam.
(5) facing   them-coming   here   diverse seeming   peoples.

(1) WE INDIANS ARE ALONE IN   (A) NO OTHER INDIAN TRIBE
    LANGUAGE
(2) AND WAY,
                                      (B) OR NATION
                                      (C) CAN CLAIM IT.

(3) AND THESE ARE TWO THINGS
(4) THAT SEPARATE US
(5) FROM NEARBY DIFFERENT
    PEOPLES.
                                      (D) IT MAKES US DESERT INDIANS.

Sentence 3.

(1) Am   t-O'odham himdag   ed
(1) There   our-Indian way   in

(2) o   s-gewk g   si   ha   eldadag,
(2) ss [3, imperf]   strong   the very some kind intention,

(3) c   ab   t-O'odhamdalig   amjed
(3) and   facing   our-Indianness   coming

(4) mo   ab   e-tasogidc   g   i:mig;
(4) ss [3, imperf] facing gets-made clear the kinship;

(5) cem attp   hasc   wud o'i   we:mkamk,
(5) just ss [1 plu, perf] whatever is   will be helper,

(6) Ban   o   g   Nuwi.
(6) Coyote or   the Buzzard.

(1) IN OUR INDIAN WAY   (A) WITHIN OUR WAY
(2) IS A STRONG THOUGHT,   (B) RESPECT IS STRONG.
(3) AND ABOUT OUR INDIANNESS
(4) IT CLARIFIES KINSHIP;
                                    (C) THIS IS EVIDENT
                                    (D) BY THE RESPECTFUL TERMS
                                    (E) USED IN CLANS
(5) WHATEVER WILL BE THE
    HELPER,
                                    (F) RELATING US TO THE EARTH
                                         AND ANIMALS.

(6) COYOTE OR BUZZARD.

Sentence 4.

(1) Am   a   hia   ep   woho
(1) There of course also true

(2) mac   pi   we:s   t-wepo   kaidam   nenok

(2)   ss [1 plu, imperf]   not   all   us-alike   sounding   talk

(3)   c as hab a   we:s   wud a   hemako   am   t-we:m
(3)   but   al   are   on   there   us-with

(4)   id   eda   t-O'odhamdalig,
(4)   this   in   our-Indianness,

(5)   mac   ab   si   has   elid.
(5)   ss [1 plu, imperf]   facing   very   somehow   wish.

(1)   OF COURSE TRULY
(2)   WE DON'T IDENTICALLY TALK   (A)   OUR DIALECTS SEPARATE
(3)   BUT ALL IS ONE WITH US   (B)   AND YET DIVIDE US AGAIN
(4)   IN OUR INDIANNESS
(5)   AS WE GREATLY WISH.

                                         (C)   THROUGH THE CIRCLE OF LIFE.

Sentence 5.

(1)   Ab   o   we:sijc   t-ab   e-gewssap   i:da
(1)   Facing   ss [3, imperf]   all   us-facing   get-befallen   this

(2)   matt   ab   a'i   o'i   t-we:mt
(2)   ss [1 plu, perf]   facing   each other   will   us-help

(3)   k   ab   o   i-cipk
(3)   and   facing   will very   work

(4)   k   o   nu:kud   g   t-niok   c   t-himdag
(4)   and   will   take care of   the   our-language   and   our-way

(5)   heg   hekaj   matp   heg   a:gkc
(5)   that one   by means of   ss [3, perf]   that one   means and

(6)   ab   t-ma: g   t-na:toikam.
(6)   facing   us-gives   the   our-maker.

(1)   ON ALL OF US FALLS THIS
                                         (A)   IN ORDER FOR OUR WAY TO BE
                                               CARRIED ON,

(2)   THAT WE HELP ONE ANOTHER
(3)   AND REALLY WORK
(4)   AND CARE FOR OUR LANGUAGE   (B)   WE MUST CARE ABOUT OUR
      AND OUR WAY   HERITAGE
(5)   BECAUSE THAT MEANT AND
(6)   GAVE IT TO US, OUR MAKER.

                                         (C)   AND PRESERVE THE GIFT
                                         (D)   THAT WAS GIVEN TO US SINCE
                                               TIME IMMEMORIAL.

Sentence 6.

(1)   Na:,
(1)   Look,

(2) kc   ab   ep   t-ab   w:sij a:cim
(2) and   facing also   us-confronts   all   us

(3) matt   cem hekid   am   o   si   s-gewkam oidad,
(3) ss [1 plu, perf]   just whenever   there will very strongly be following,

(4) c   am   o   himcudad   i:da
(4) and   there will   be driving this

(5) t-O'odhamdalig.
(5) our-Indianness.

(1) LOOK,   (A) THEREFORE
                                        (B) OUR DESERT INDIAN WAY

(2) AND SO IT IS FOR ALL OF US
(3) THAT WE ALWAYS WILL
     STRONGLY FOLLOW,
                                        (C) DEMANDS RESPECT
(4) AND KEEP GOING THIS   (D) AND MAINTENANCE
(5) OUR INDIANNESS.
                                        (E) BY ALL WHO CLAIM IT.

Discussion

In this and subsequent discussions, my literal translations are to be taken as bona fide if eccentric bits of English language. They will be compared as equals with the Education Committee's smoother free translations. No doubt the literal translations could be tightened to make them more literal and closer to the grammar and semantics of the Desert Indian originals. But all that matters is that they be more literal than the committee's translations so as to serve, even uncorrected, as bases to interrogate the latter: "How and why does the committee's translation differ from what the Desert Indian original actually says?" I will call the two versions respectively L (literal) and F (free). We start with the first sentences of the two six sentence versions, and then we briefly consider both versions as wholes.

Each first sentence can be read as a poem:

L	F
LONG AGO	GIVEN US AS A GIFT
WHEN DID HERE MAKE US	FROM OUR CREATOR
OUR MAKER	OUR DESERT INDIAN WAY
DID THESE TWO THINGS GIVE US	HAS ENDURED
WHICH ARE OUR INDIAN WAY	THROUGH GENERATIONS.
AND OUR LANGUAGE.	

Each poem centers on one line, 'our maker' (L) and "our Desert Indian way" (F). Each of those lines has a correspondence in the other poem ('maker' with "Creator," 'Indian way' with "Desert Indian way"), but the centers as centers do not correspond, the L being a 'maker' centered poem and the F being a "way" centered one.

The L poem has a bit of rhyme or near rhyme that is lacking in the F: it flanks its central line with the near rhyming pair, 'when did here make us' and 'did two things give us.' There is no such parallelism or rhyme in the F. The F poem has its own art, however, which I term "line final patriotism." Its entire central line is patriotic, "our Desert Indian way" (equivalent to a U.S. poem centered on "our American way"). Each remaining line of the poem (two above and two below the center) ends with a more or less patriotic word: "gift," "Creator," "endured," "generations." Thus we receive the following patriotic telegram: "Gift/Creator/Desert Indian way/endured/generations." The L poem is far blander when scanned in this manner: "Ago/us/maker/us/Indian way/language."

Thus, the one poem rhymes around 'maker' and is a bit hymnlike, and the other is a patriotic telegram around the national "way." Turning now to the texts as wholes, these first two sentences can be seen as the variant opening parts on *past creation* of two six part texts (I will call them "versions") whose remaining parts deal with the *present distinctiveness* of the Desert Indians (sentence 2), *present kinship* (sentence 3), *present diversity* internal to the Desert Indians (sentence 4), and (sentences 5 and 6) the need for *future care* for the Desert Indian language and way. The two versions share this same outline.

In my opinion, the unexpected, and presumably generically Indian, feature in the outline is the sentence on kinship. One would not expect such a sentence in an American proclamation on language policy; such a sentence is not of the corpus of Americanisms that stand as the hypothetical, textless "source" of the committee's document. The sentence in question comes midway through both versions. It presents us with a task similar to that with the opening sentence: we must contrast the L and the F versions for how they treat this unexpected feature.

Briefly, the L version finds a dualism in Desert Indian kinship, but one needs some ethnological background to understand how this is so. Traditionally the tribal members were divided into two patrilineal moieties ("halves") whose totems are Coyote and Buzzard. These creatures are referred to in the text as 'helpers,' *we:mkam,* but that word that could equally be translated as 'totem.' The text explicitly makes this Coyote/Buzzard dualism stand for 'Indianness' (*O'odhamdalig*): kinship is dualist and dualism is Indian according to the L version and, I believe, the Desert Indian original. The F version, in contrast, gives a greatly weakened, practically imperceptible statement on dualism in its sentence on kinship: ". . . the respectful terms used in clans relating us to the earth and animals" ("earth and animals" might be considered a dualism); and it altogether lacks the word "Indianness," as if the word *O'odhamdalig* had not been said in the original.

O'odhamdalig is put to good use in L version. Introduced in that version's kinship sentence, *O'odhamdalig* is an abstraction on top of, or in addition to, a pair of abstractions common to both versions: 'language' and 'way.' Now, both versions assert in sentence 2 that language distinguishes the Desert Indians from all other peoples—and so language unites them against foreigners. But both versions also admit in sentence 4 that the Desert Indian language is internally diverse—there are dialects. The versions differ in that L has prepared for this admission in its sentence on kinship and its concept of Indianness, so as to say in effect, "We have dialects as we have dualistic kinship; we persist in and through having differences; this is the essence of Indianness." The F version in contrast follows its weakened kinship dualism with the assertion, in sentence 4, "Our dialects separate and yet unite us again through the circle of life." There is no circle of life in the Desert Indian original, nor have I heard this phrase used in the Desert Indian language.

In sum, the L version uses the unexpected sentence on kinship to solve a problem on linguistic diversity. The F version uses a different notion—cycles instead of dualism—to solve that problem, and it recasts its sentence on kinship into a statement of respect toward earth and animals. It is fair to ask why the F version did this, and I respond by resorting to the concept of textlessness. The F version's changes are toward established English-language usages about Indians: cyclicity and respect for nature. Perhaps the changes are toward making the F version read as the Committee believes that Indian proclamations should read. Now, were the F version a literal translation, the Desert Indian original would be a textless (derived from English usages) translation. The F version is not literal, however, and the Desert Indian original is not perfectly textless in the sense of drawing entirely from English-language precedents. It is stubbornly Indian (i.e., drawing from Desert Indian usages) in its kinship dualism.

Subsection IV. Mat Has Masma, O Hekid O i E-Hekajid G T-Tohonno[5] O'odham Nioki, 'How and When Will Be Used Our Desert Indian Language,' "Official Use of the Desert Indian Language"

Sentence 1.

(1) Heg   hekaj
(1) That one by means of

(2) mac   si   has   elid   g   t-niok
(2) ss [3, imperf]   very   somehow   wish the our-language

(3) k   ab   wud   t-elida
(3) and facing is   our-wish

(4) mat   o   e-hekajid g   Tohonno   O'odham   niok
(4) ss [3, perf] will get-used   the Desert   Indian   language

(5) am   eda   g   ge'e   je:ngiga,
(5) there   inside   the big   council,

(6) ceksan   je:ngida,   ki: t-am   je:ngida
(6) boundary   council,   house at-there   council

(7) kc   as   cem   hascu   je:ngida ed
(7) and   just   simply   whatever   council   in

(8) an   we:s   Tohonno jewed   da:m.
(8) there   all   Desert   land   upon.

(1) BECAUSE
(2) WE LOVE OUR LANGUAGE   (A) WITH RESPECT TO OUR FIRST
                                              LANGUAGE

(3)	IT'S OUR WISH	(B)	THE DESERT INDIAN NATION DECLARES
		(C)	THE DESERT INDIAN LANGUAGE
		(D)	AS THE OFFICIAL LANGUAGE OF OUR PEOPLE.
(4)	TO HAVE USE OF THE DESERT INDIAN LANGUAGE	(E)	THE DESERT INDIAN LANGUAGE IS TO BE USED
		(F)	AS THE OFFICIAL MEANS OF ORAL COMMUNICATION
(5)	AT GREAT COUNCIL,	(G)	AT ANY AND ALL TRIBAL COUNCIL
(6)	DISTRICT COUNCIL, HOUSE COUNCIL	(H)	DISTRICT, VILLAGE, COMMITTEE, AND BOARD MEETINGS
(7)	AND JUST ANY COUNCIL	(I)	AS WELL AS IN ANY AND ALL TRIBAL COMMUNITY FUNCTIONS AND ACTIVITIES
(8)	ALL THE DESERT OVER.	(J)	THROUGHOUT THE DESERT INDIAN NATION.

Sentence 2.

(1) Gawul   ma:s   niok
(1) Different   kind of   language

(2) at   as   s-ap   ep   o   e-hekaj
(2) ss [3, perf]   just   well   also   will   get-used

(3) mat   hekid   o   e-taccud.
(3) ss [3, perf]   when   will   get-wanted.

(1)	OTHER KINDS OF LANGUAGE	(A)	OTHER LANGUAGES
(2)	CAN ALSO BE USED	(B)	MAY BE USED
(3)	WHEN THEY ARE WANTED.	(C)	AS DEEMED NECESSARY.

Sentence 3.

(1) Mat   hedai   hab   o'i   elidad
(1) ss [3, perf]   anyone   so   will   be wishing

(2) c   g   cipkan   o   ga:gad
(2) and   the   work   will   seek

(3) t   hemho   am a   he'e   o   s-ma:cid
(3) ss [3, perf]   always   there   somewhat   will   know

(4) g   Tohonno   O'odham   himdag
(4) the   Desert   Indian   way

(5) mat   ab   ab   o   bei   g   cipkan
(5) ss [3, perf]   facing   facing   will   get   the   work

(6) id   eda   Tohonno   O'odham   jewed.
(6) this   inside   Desert   Indian   land.

(1)   IF ANYONE HAS WISHES
(2)   AND A JOB WILL SEEK
(3)   THEN MUST ALWAYS SOMEWHAT   (A)   SOME KNOWLEDGE
      KNOW
(4)   THE DESERT INDIAN WAY   (B)   OF THE DESERT INDIAN WAY
(5)   IF EXPECTING TO GET A JOB   (C)   SHALL BE REQUIRED FOR
                                           EMPLOYMENT
(6)   HERE WITHIN DESERT INDIAN   (D)   WITHIN THE BOUNDARIES OF
      LAND BOUNDARY.   THE DESERT INDIAN NATION.

Sentence 4.

(1)   Idam   Ge'e   Je:nokam
(1)   These   Big   Councilors

(2)   at   am   o   ha-ma   g   apedag   c   gewkdag
(2)   ss [3, perf] there will them-give the   rightness and   strength

(3)   g   Tohonno   O'odham   Mascama   E-Je:nokam
(3)   the   Desert   Indian   Teaching   Get-Councilors

(4)   mat   am   o   o'oho   hegai
(4)   ss [3, perf] there will write   that

(5)   mat   ab   amjed   o   e-tasogi
(5)   ss [3, perf] facing coming will get-clarified

(6)   mat   he'es   o i   s-ma:ck
(6)   ss [3, perf] somewhat   will   know

(7)   ha'icu   ab   t-O'odham   himdag   ab
(7)   something facing   our-Indian way   facing

(8)   mat   hedai   o'   taccud   g   cipkan.
(8)   ss [3, perf] anyone will want   the work.

(1)   THESE GREAT COUNCILORS
(2)   WILL GIVE THE RIGHT AND
      POWER

                                     (A)   PROFICIENCY STANDARDS
                                     (B)   SHALL BE ESTABLISHED
(3)   TO THE DESERT INDIAN   (C)   BY THE PAPAGO EDUCATION
      SCHOOLING COUNCILEES   COMMITTEE/BOARD OF
                                           DIRECTORS
(4)   TO WRITE THAT
(5)   WHICH WILL CLARIFY ABOUT
(6)   HOW MUCH WILL BE KNOWN
(7)   OF THINGS OF OUR INDIAN WAY
(8)   BY WHOEVER WANTS A JOB.

                                     (D)   BY AUTHORITY FROM THE
                                           PAPAGO TRIBAL COUNCIL.

Discussion

This subsection has two potentially far-reaching and controversial provisions: the privileging of the Native language above all others in the conduct of the Desert Indian national business; and the requirement of some knowledge of the Desert Indian 'way' as prerequisite for obtaining employment within the Desert Indian Nation. ('Way' is defined in free English in another subsection as "way of life, inclusive of such terms as culture, heritage, history, values, tradition, customs, beliefs, and language.") At about the same time as the Nation enacted this regulation, the state of Arizona debated the privileging of English in the conduct of state business. Most Desert Indians have rights and duties as Arizonans as well rights and duties as Desert Indians.[6] In a statewide referendum in 1988, Arizona adopted English as its sole official language, that is, the sole language of Arizona's sovereign acts of government. Unknown to most Arizonans, the Desert Indians had preceded them by thirteen months in a similar act.

How similar? Desert Indian language policy occupies two of the four sentences of this subsection and all of subsection IX (discussed below). The present two sentences concern the use of the language in 'councils.' The literal version uses the word 'council' (*je:ngida*) open endedly, and the free version opens the matter still further by calling for Desert Indian language use at "any and all tribal community functions and activities." (The free version uses the word "meeting" in addition to "council." This is a common alternate translation for *je:ngida*).[7] Although the span is vague, this does not create an enforcement problem because both versions state that languages other than Desert Indian may also be used at all the events. Thus, the present Indian law differs from the Arizona statute in that it does not restrictively privilege a language in the conduct of the national business. Nor does this subsection of the Indian law mention those most sensitive of all governmental linguistic acts, the promulgation of law itself and the letting or issuing of contracts. It would seem that any and all languages can be used for any and all governmental actions.

The final sentences of the subsection do impose a restrictive requirement and do name a sensitive issue, but the requirement concerns knowledge of the Desert Indian 'way' (which would seem to include language) and the issue is employment. The Education Committee is empowered to establish employment standards based on knowledge of the 'way.' I don't know if those standards have been established, enforced, complied with, or challenged, but the intention to have them makes the Indian law more radical than its Arizona counterpart.

Subsection IX. O'ohona Cihanig Apedag, 'Writing Commandment Propriety', "Legal Application"

Sentence 1.

(1)	Mat	hekid	am	o	e-hekaj
(1)	ss [3, perf]	when	there	will	get-used

(2)	i:da	Tohonno	O'odham	niok	Cihanig		Apedag
(2)	this	Desert	Indian	talk	Commandment		Propriety

(3)	at		heg	o	hekaj
(3)	ss [3, perf]		that	will	use

(4)	mo		am	o'odhamkaj	o'ohonas.
(4)	ss [3, imperf]		there	indianish	written.

(1) WHENEVER THERE IS USE OF

        (A)   IN ALL CASES,

(2) THIS DESERT INDIAN LANGUAGE
COMMANDMENT PROPRIETY

        (B)   THE DESERT INDIAN TEXT OF
                THIS LANGUAGE POLICY

(3) THE ONE TO USE
        (C)   SHALL BE USED
        (D)   TO ESTABLISH ITS MEANING.

(4) IS THE INDIAN WRITING.

Sentence 2.

(1)	Am	o		hiwigidas
(1)	There	ss [3, imperf]		permit

(2)	mat		na:nko	ma:s	hemajkam	ha-niok		ed
(2)	ss [3, perf]		various	appearing	people	their-language		in

(3)	am	ep	o	e-o'oho
(3)	there	also	will	get-written

(4)	i:da	Tohonno	O'odham	Niok		Cihanig,
(4)	this	Desert	Indian	Language		Commandment,

(5)	k as	ba	hegai
(5)	and	but	that

(6)	mo		o'odhamkaj	o'ohonas
(6)	ss [3, imperf]		indianish	written

(7)	wud	o		si	cihanig.
(7)	is	ss [3, imperf]		very	commandment.

(1) IT IS PERMITTED

(2) THAT IN DIFFERENT KINDS OF   (A)   TRANSLATIONS OF
PEOPLES' LANGUAGES

(3) ALSO WILL BE WRITTEN

(4) THIS DESERT INDIAN LANGUAGE   (B)   THIS POLICY
COMMANDMENT,

        (C)   IN OTHER LANGUAGES
        (D)   MAY BE PROVIDED
        (E)   BY THE INDIAN EDUCATION
                DEPARTMENT,

(5) BUT THE ONE

(6) IN WHICH INDIAN IS WRITTEN

(7) IS VERY LAWFUL.

                (F)   BUT SUCH TRANSLATIONS SHALL
                           HAVE NO LEGAL EFFECT.

Discussion

This subsection justifies the entire present essay by establishing that, in questions of law, it is what is said in Desert Indian, not what is said in English, that really matters. Moreover, unlike the previous subsection, this one plainly privileges the Desert Indian language in acts of government. But it does so only in questions of law pertaining to *these ten subsections,* that is, to the ten subsections that correspond to Section II of the English document, "Tohono O'odham Education Standards October 1987." The present statement, then, is only a toehold into restrictive language policy.

Even so, the literal version is less of a toehold than the free version. The former says that Desert Indian language versions of law are 'very lawful,' but it does not deny the lawfulness, or legal effect, of translations (whether literal or free). The free version unambiguously denies the legal effect of any translation, but it does so without foundation in the lawful text that it claims to speak for. It seems to me that the free version could be challenged on the basis of what the Desert Indian text actually says.

Conclusion

How do the above laws fit in Desert Indian legal history? Since the 1930s this people has been a miniature republic with a constitution modeled on that of the United States. The people's land boundaries had previously been established by negotiations with the United States and Mexico (there have been slight additions to this land during postconstitutional times), but in the 1930s the lands under U.S. protection were divided into several Districts (*ce:cksan,* 'boundaries; border lines') for which elected Councils and a superordinate Tribal Council were established. The Tribe was to be sovereign over the new Districts, the Districts were to be the internal divisions of the Tribe. The United States supplied a written constitution for the tribe-to-be which, after some negotiation, elected to become that districted, centralized Tribe. Desert Indians in Mexico would have no Districts under this constitution, hence no place at the Tribal Council.

The district boundaries were not only written in the constitution, but were a kind of law themselves written on the land like the artist Cristo's fences. Few people read the constitution but everyone saw the new district boundary fences of barbed wire. They were benign. Horses and cattle (Spanish introductions) could not cross them, but all other animals could, and all roads through them either had gates or permanent openings equipped with cattle guards (bars at road level to deter the passage of cattle and horses). I would say that the palpable constitution of the 1930s was this text of fences and gates.

To my knowledge the district governments have done little since their inception.

I wonder if they keep copies of their formal acts which are, I believe, mostly discussions of papers, orders, and proposals sent down from the Tribe. There are no district courts or police, only tribal courts and tribal police outposts. Schools and clinics, as these have developed since the 1930s, are under tribal control.

Independent of the constitutional government, the Desert Indians have governed themselves and settled disputes by 'councils/meetings/smokings' where people assemble after prior notice to plan new or respond to recent past actions. Churches, villages, neighborhoods, cattle owners' associations, orchestras, and multihousehold families hold such meetings more or less in the same form and with the same etiquette. These are what subsection IV called 'just any council' (literal), and "any and all community functions and activities" (free). They enact a kind of local law the proceedings of which, I must say, in this case, have been little studied by anthropology.

As the tribe's activities grew (signaled by a change in name, from "Papago Tribe" to "Tohono O'odham Nation"), the local law has lost its autonomy. The tribe's growth was precisely in the functions that had been controlled by local law: education, health, nutrition, family counseling, substance abuse, elderly programs, recreation, environmental planning, occupational safety, and so forth. The tribe's main activity is those functions. The local, unwritten lawmaking on those issues has devolved into discussing the tribe's involvements in them. Meanwhile the latter's activities are not autonomous, but are the enactment of funded packages sent (with tribal council approval) from the U.S. government. This is what the original constitutional program of the 1930s has grown into. In its mature form, the Indian Desks at various U.S. government departments (Interior, Health, Education, and Welfare, Labor) are the sovereigns (subject to the whims of Congress and a powerful Indian lobby), and the various U.S. Indian Nations (Tohono O'odham, Navajo, Northern Cheyenne) are the districts—and these districts control functions that were formerly controlled by Indian local law.

One more system remains to be described. It governs Desert Indian relations with the 'ways' of 'dangerous objects.' Parallel to the 'Writing Commandment Propriety' of subsection IX, this system can be called 'Dangerous Object Commandment Propriety.' The danger is sickness. When Desert Indians transgress on these 'ways,' they get sicknesses. The commandments establishing the system do not issue from humans, but from gods or God or the Creator (of the free text), as interpreted by medicine men. Humans enter the system not only by suffering its punishments, but also by determining which 'way,' of which 'dangerous object,' is making an individual sick. Medicine men perform that quasijuridical function by divination. (See Bahr et al. 1974 for a full discussion of this system.)

The emphasis is on maintaining the boundaries between Desert Indian humans and nature. Thus, most of the dangerous 'ways' belong to animals (deer, rabbit, butterfly, rattlesnake, etc.). It is not a civil legal system, but it has great prestige and seems to be the source of much of the language, in the sense of discourse, of the language policy statement.[8] I would like to say that the medicine men's habitual reticence is responsible for the modest phrasing of the Desert Indian as compared with the freely translated version of that document.

Notes

1. And in another Derridan intertextual sense, my literal translations will be grafts upon free translations provided by the Papago Education Committee. Thus, if there is to be any adventure in reading these texts, I hope it will be in the tension between the side-by-side translations, the left side being my literal, and the right side being the Committee's free conveyance of Desert Indian law into English.

2. Section I of the English document, three pages long, is called "Introduction and Purpose." Section II is four pages long in English. Section III, "Educational Standards of the Tohono O'odham," has thirty-two pages and Section IV, "Appendices," has eight, making a total of fifty-five pages.

3. Perhaps they had translated their tribal or national constitution previously, but this would have been the translation of a document first written in English, that is, a "texted" translation. The language-policy act was textless in the sense used in this essay.

4. One might think that literal translations are primitive, mindless, and artless. Thus, they are called "ponies" and "trots," terms which suggest temporary, juvenile conveyances. (Pony is less than steed, trot is less than canter, etc.). This judgment is true, I think, only when languages are written, when their words are inventoried, segmented, and stored in dictionaries, and when there are schools that actually teach translation in mass. On the other hand, it is certain that there was translation all over the world long before those conditions were met, and I am confident that this was what we call free or interpretive translation—essentially what our artists and experts (not schoolboys) aspire to. The Papago Education Committee produced such an interpretive translation which is, in my opinion, un- or insufficiently schooled. Thus, I accept that literal translation is artless, but not that it is primitive or mindless.

Toby Langen calls such literalness "interlanguage," and I would like to comment on this term in the context of her article in this volume. The term suggests to me a trot through unschooled territory, which I submit defines the advance guard in Native American translation. Langen values such translations, and calls them "the voice of the language"—one of several "voices" that comprise the subject of Style. This is not the voice that she chose to convey in her article. She opted for the "voice of the storyteller," the competence and suppleness (her judgements, her terms) of which she conveys in a non-literal manner. Characteristically for our profession, she made a morpheme-for-morpheme gloss as the basis for a possible literal translation, but she does not, at least in this article, present the translation. It is a privilege for me to present one, and I owe that privilege to the Education Committee who made a competent and supple free version—into which my literal version could bite.

5. In this subsection the committee spelled the word for 'desert' with two "n's," while in the previous section they spelled it with one.

6. Most Desert Indians are citizens of the United States. The rest are citizens of Mexico. Most of the U.S. Desert Indians are legal residents of Arizona. The rest are residents of other U.S. states. There is no U.S. Desert Indian who is not a legal resident of some U.S. state, and subject to the voting rights and tax duties of other residents of that state.

7. In the most literal, etymological sense the word means '[the act of] smoking,' since tobacco was ceremonially smoked at traditional councils and meetings.

8. The revealed texts of the 'ways' are song-poems that are said to be learned in dreams, but the medicine men's prose expositions of the system resemble the language policy statement.

References

Bahr, D., J. Gregorio, D. Lopez, and A. Alvarez. 1974. *Piman Shamanism and Staying Sickness.* Tucson: University of Arizona Press.

Culler, J. 1982. *On Deconstruction.* Ithaca: Cornell University Press.

Cultural Survival Quarterly. 1989. Vol. 13, No. 3. Central America and the Caribbean.

Herzog, G. 1935. "Plains Ghost Dance and Great Basin Music." American Anthropologist, n.s., 37:403–19.

Jesperson, O. 1964. *Essentials of English Grammar.* University: University of Alabama Press.

Lévi-Strauss, C. 1967. "The Story of Asdiwal." *In* E. Leach, ed., The Structural Study of Myth and Totemism. London: Tavistock Publications.

Lopez-Manuel, R. 1987. Tohono O'odham Education Standards October 1987. Sells, Arizona: Tohono O'odham Education Department.

Nist, J. 1966. *A Structural History of English.* New York: St. Martin's Press.

Sapir, E. 1921. *Language.* New York: Harcourt Brace and World.

Zepeda, O. 1983. *A Papago Grammar.* Tucson: University of Arizona Press.

Suggested Reading

Bahr, D. 1992. Oratory. In A. Wiget, ed., *Dictionary of Native American Literature.* Westport, Connecticut: Greenwood.

Cohen, F. 1971. *Felix S. Cohen's Handbook of Federal Indian Law.* Albuquerque: University of New Mexico Press.

Dauenhauer, N., and R. Dauenhauer. 1989. *Haa Tuwunaagu Yis, For Healing Our Spirit: Tlingit Oratory.* Seattle: University of Washington Press.

Deloria, V. 1983. *American Indians, American Justice.* Austin: University of Texas Press.

Irvine, J. 1979. Formality and Informality in Communicative Events. *American Anthropologist* 81:773–90.

Nader, L., ed. 1969. *Law in Culture and Society.* Chicago: Aldine.

Pospisil, L., ed. 1978. *Ethnology of Law.* Menlo Park, California: Cummings.

Starr, J., and J. Collier. 1989. *History and Power in the Study of Law.* Ithaca: Cornell University Press.

Stoll, D. 1982. *Fishers of Men or Founders of Empire? The Wycliffe Bible Translators in Latin America.* London: Zed.

Strickland, C. 1975. *Fire and the Spirits: Cherokee Law from Clan to Court.* Norman: University of Oklahoma Press.

Tso, T. The Process of Decision Making in Tribal Courts. *Arizona Law Review* 31(2): 225–35.

Wiget, A. 1985. *Native American Literature.* Boston: Twayne.

Narrative Styles in *Dakota Texts*

Julian Rice

Lakota is the living language of thousands of Lakota (Teton Sioux) people now living on the Pine Ridge, Rosebud, Cheyenne River, and Standing Rock reservations in North and South Dakota. At community colleges on these reservations, and at several colleges and universities in the region, Lakota oral narratives are studied in the original language. The best collection continues to be *Dakota Texts* (1932), transcribed and translated by Ella Deloria, a native Lakota speaker and student of Franz Boas at Columbia. While her English translations are scrupulously accurate and clear, they are equally Boasian in their lack of affect and nuance. Her transcriptions, on the other hand, preserve distinct Lakota styles. Although the narrators wished to remain anonymous, their use of storytelling conventions makes it possible to appreciate variations of structure, tone, style, and theme.

Some of the most compelling elements of the stories, experienced as literature, read as well as heard, exist only in Lakota. The criticism that follows is presented in the expectation that Lakota literature will one day be accorded the respect given European texts, bilingually quoted in such journals as *PMLA* and *Comparative Literature*. For teaching purposes, however, it is impractical to suspend the study of *Dakota Texts* until students can read them in the original. Deloria's translations are situated in their cultural context by extensive annotations and can be supplemented by her other works on language and culture (see Suggested Reading).

The present analysis of "White Plume," the nineteenth story of *Dakota Texts*, is meant to suggest an interpretive method for teachers of literature. Deloria's translation of "White Plume" is printed in the paperback edition (Vermillion, South Dakota: Dakota Press, 1978, 37–42), as well as in the AMS reprint (New York 1974, 106–13). The latter also contains the Lakota version, quoted here in the analysis that follows the English text:

White-Plume Boy

A certain man, when his son was born, took him in his arms and planted a white plume in the crown of his head, naming him "White-Plume." Then wishing to hasten his growth, he threw him outdoors several times, and each time he reentered the tipi, somewhat bigger than before, until finally, all on the same day, he attained the stature of a man. Then the father said, "Oh, would that my son had such and such things!" and it all happened, so that the youth possessed handsome apparel and fine things. Then the father talked thus to his son, "These people are in great distress, my son. Four men are abusing them severely. So if there is something you can do, do it." Just as he had said, four men stood outside their tipi the next morning, and called, "White-Plume, we have come to challenge you to a race. Come on out;" to which he answered, "All right." Four men waited for him, and one was painted red, and one was blue and one was white and one was black. And the one who had used red for his paint contended with him first; they ran towards a distant tree, and climbed it; and on getting down, the instant they were landing to run back, the red painted man tossed something out, and it was cattail fuzz. Suddenly the entire meadow became a mass of cattail fuzz which tangled itself into White-Plume's feather. This delayed him long, while he tried to untangle his feather, so that the red-paint man had a good head start. Even so, when White-Plume boy was through, he ran so swiftly that he got home first. And four wooden clubs belonging to the four men, and painted in their respective colors, lay at the base; so White-Plume took up the red club and with it he struck and killed his opponent. So only three men went home. Next morning, the three came again and challenged him to a race. So he went out and raced with the man painted blue. The race included climbing a distant tree, and then coming down, and returning to the home base. But as they were coming down the tree, the man who was painted blue threw something out. It was cockleburs and at once the whole place was filled with bur-bearing weeds. They clung to the head-ornament and made it necessary for White-Plume to stop and rid himself of them. Even so, he was so fleet of foot that he got home first, and taking up the man's blue club he struck and killed him with it. So only two men went home. The third morning the two remaining opponents came and this time it was the man painted white who raced with the boy. And he tossed something about which proved to be choke-cherry stalks. These caught in the white plume, and it took the boy a long time to remove them, while the other man started back, and was almost reaching the goal. But now White-Plume had freed himself, and because his speed was equal to being carried by the wind, he soon caught up with and passed the man. The whitened club lay at the goal; so he took it and killed the owner with it. Now only one man remained. The man who blackened himself came, carrying his black club with him. He placed it at the goal, and started to compete with White-Plume Boy. As they were descending from the tree, he tossed something out; it was crab-apple stalks full of thorns which caught in the boy's headdress, for they suddenly filled the place. He was obliged to take time out to rid his plume of the thorns, so that the blackened man was almost home. But now the boy was through, and starting home. Soon he was nearly touching the blackened man, as he ran. Now he passed him and arrived first at the goal, where he stood with the black club, ready to kill the owner when he got in. From that time, the tribe was free from the oppression of the four tyrants.

Then one day the boy said, "I have decided to go on a journey."—"Alas, my son," his father protested, "though I am aware that you are a man and should travel, still, I am troubled; for on your way you are going to encounter a tricky woman." But the boy didn't hesitate to start, on account of this warning. He was travelling westward when he saw a woman, walking along, carrying something in her arms. "Ah! Undoubtedly this is what my father was speaking of," he thought, and tried to go around, so as to avoid meeting the woman. But she got in his path, and offered to rid him of lice. The boy was insulted. "Say, what do you think I am that I should have lice?" he said to her, "I'm no orphan!" And he tried to go on, but she persisted. By some unexplained method she induced him to yield, so that he lay down to have her look in his hair. She pulled his hair apart here and there hurriedly and jerked out the white plume, leaving behind a poor whimpering puppy, affected with itch. The helpless animal sought out a sunny spot and lay there all day. Of course it was Ikto again, masquerading as a woman. He now set the white plume in his hair, and entered the tribal circle in the role of a boy-beloved. So he was promptly presented with a wife and established in a tipi, in the role of son-in-law. It happened that the woman was a favorite child, in her own right, so the two had their tent inside the camp-circle. And his wife said, "Each morning a red fox runs by, and everyone tries to shoot him, but nobody succeeds in hitting him." It was morning and the camp was in an uproar. "There he is again, the red fox," the wife said. And Ikto replied with a command. "Prop up the door flaps so they will stay," he said, and his wife, thinking how he would doubtless shoot from where he sat, hastened to do his bidding. Instead, just as the fox passed within his range, he pretended to fumble, and said, "Hard luck! the limbs of my robe struck my bow!" and he didn't shoot. Again his wife said, "Now and then, a very scarlet bird goes flying past here, and they all try to shoot it but nobody ever hits it." After a while, the camp was in an uproar again and the wife said, "There now, they are shooting because it is flying by." And Ikto said, "Adjust the poles of the smoke vent so that the opening is clear." Thinking how her husband was about to succeed where others had failed, she hastily adjusted the poles and then came in and sat down to wait. But instead of shooting the scarlet bird when it flew overhead, he evidently had cut nicks in his bow-string, because it snapped just as he placed an arrow. By way of apology he said, "Hard luck! I've broken my bow-string!" and he did not shoot. Then he said, "Have your father send a crier around. I am about to smoke." So a crier made the announcement and soon the tipi was filled with a waiting crowd. He now said, "Each time I puff out smoke from this tobacco, be ready to kill something." So they sat in tense readiness, but nothing magical happened. At last the men took their departure, heavy-hearted from disappointment. During all this, a poor girl who lived alone with her mother, in a tipi outside the camp-circle, went into the woods to gather fuel for their fire. There she found the little helpless dog and was moved by pity. "You poor little dog, how you must suffer!" she said, pulling up quantities of sagebrush to make him a softer bed. But the dog spoke to her, "You are kind; but even better than to make me a bed here would be to take me home." So she took him up in her blanket and carried him home. She laid him down and went outside; but when she reentered the tipi, she found instead a very handsome young man sitting in the place of honor. He said to her, "Go now to Ikto who resides in the tipi within the camp-circle and ask him to return to me the head-ornament which he took from me." So the girl stood outside Ikto's tipi and said, "Ikto, I have come for that head-ornament, on behalf of its owner." Immediately he began, "Hand it out; hand it out; for it is his." She took the plume and carried it home. At once the people derided Ikto with shouts and jeers, and chased him out towards the wild places and left him still going. "Oh, but what's the use?" they said, "It is Ikto. He'll be turning up again, by and by." Once more the red fox ran by; and it was White-Plume's arrow which pierced and killed him. And the next morning, when the scarlet bird soared overhead, it was White-Plume's arrow which brought it down, piercing its heart. They took the scarlet bird and set it up at the very topmost point of White-Plume's tipi. "Now I shall smoke. Ask them to come in," he said, so the men crowded into the tipi. "I shall send out four puffs of smoke, so try to kill them all," he instructed. They sat in readiness and the instant the tobacco smoke came out of his mouth, birds of every sort filled the room; so the men worked hard to kill them all. Finally even blankets, red ones and blue ones and brown ones and black ones, also fell, and then guns and fine possessions came down.

And that was the beginning of such things in the tribe, they say. White-Plume took for his wife the girl who was so humble but so kindhearted, and the tribe caused them to live in a tipi inside the camp-circle and held them in highest esteem and affection, they say. That is all.

Like most of the stories in *Dakota Texts,* "White Plume" is divided into four distinct episodes: 1) White Plume's naming, upbringing, and proving of valor in a warrior contest; 2) his deception and defeat by the trickster; 3) his rescue by the girl preceding his recovery of strength; and 4) the demonstration of his mature power to provide for the people and the fulfillment of his growth in taking a wife. Four is the "pattern number" of Lakota culture in all formal expression. The number has been discussed and explained at length (for a summary see Hassrick 256), but the four-part concepts most applicable here are the stages of a man's growth: *hoksicala*—baby, *hoksila*—boy, *koskalaka*—young man, and *wicasa*—mature man, as well as the four cardinal virtues: *woohitika*—courage, *wawacintanka*—fortitude, *wacantognaka*—generosity, and *woksape*—wisdom. By the end of the story White Plume has achieved wisdom, the power to "make grow," as Black Elk says, qualifying him to generate spiritual confidence in the children he will shape.

Thematic and stylistic balance is a distinguishing feature of Lakota stories. The first of the story's four episodes is itself composed of four events, separately important though of variable length. White Plume is 1) named, 2) strengthened and equipped, 3) made aware of the need to protect the people, and 4) proven as a warrior. In the last and longest part of the first episode, White Plume is established as a warrior by ritually outrunning each of four opponents, after which he appropriates their power for himself, thus completing the first stage of the development his father anticipates when he honors his infant son with an extraordinary name (see Hassrick 312–13). A white eagle plume is attached to the end of the eagle bone whistle carried by a sun dancer (see Densmore 125 and Mails, *Sun Dancing* 69), who is loved and honored for his sacrifice on behalf of the people. Valued as much or more than emblems of courage in battle, the sun-dance plume was placed in the center of a war bonnet where it waved above the ring of upright eagle feathers (see illustrations in Mails, *Mystic Warriors* 344, 379, and 574). The father begins the realization of his son's identity with the name. But the boy must complete the process himself just as Crazy Horse had to earn the name his father already bore (see Ambrose 81).

Naming the hero is central to the story's meaning. When the young man defeats the four enemies, the narrator uses the name repeatedly. But when the hero is tricked in the second episode, the name "White Plume" is not used at all; he is reduced in the language to a verbalized pronoun, and correspondingly in the plot to a mangy puppy. The name returns with the emergence of his compassion through the influence of the girl and is used emphatically at the end to show how a man becomes himself. Unfortunately, Deloria's translation does not match the name to the event but uses the name and the pronoun alternatively in line with standard English usage.

Other aspects of her translation lose some of the techniques employed by the original narrator to convey thematic emphasis. In the story's first sentence, the narrator makes the naming of the child the dominant element, setting it off with pauses, marked by dashes: "Wicasa wan cinca wan kicitunpi yunkan ikikcu na peslete kin el wacinhin wan paslatin na—Wacinhin Ska—eya-caśkitun śke?," "A certain man, when his son was born, took him in his arms and planted a white plume in the crown of his head, naming him "White Plume" (*Dakota Texts,* AMS ed. 106). Deloria emphasizes the placing of the actual plume and makes the naming a grammatical afterthought, subordinating it at the end of the sentence, "naming him White Plume." A literal translation would read: "he put in a head ornament and—White Plume—he said, to name him, it is said" (my translation). This has the right emphasis but sounds awkward, like someone speaking a foreign language, losing the characteristic euphony of the narrative artist. In any case the careful naming of the hero is not conveyed in Deloria's translation.

From the first naming until the child grows enough to face an enemy, the Lakota narrator uses nurturing kinship terms, *cinca,* "child," and both *micinkśi,* "my son," and *cinkś,* "son," in direct address. "White Plume" is next spoken by one of the four enemies, as if to suggest that identity comes into being through challenge. And while Deloria uses the words "white plume" to refer to the plume itself during the racing, the narrator saves those words exclusively for the hero's name, using *wapegnake* or *wacinhin* (both words for head ornament) to refer to the actual plume. For the contest itself, the narrator speaks the name seven times, while White Plume races to validate it. Four of these uses occur in the ritual phrase, *Wacinhin Ska el etunwan,* "White Plume noticed it," which Deloria's translation does not reproduce. Although her omission reflects the premium placed on variety in English prose, White Plume's coming to disciplined manhood represents an ordeal of repetition that the Lakota words reflexively evoke (for a similar use of exact repetition in the development of a hero, see Rice 197–206).

Varying uses of repetition further ritualize the racing. Just after White Plume descends from the tree at the race's midpoint, each opponent throws a different prickly substance in his way to distract him with panic, impatience, or rage. Each obstacle is progressively more painful and difficult to disentangle from his plume. But in each of the four races, he must stop and carefully remove them before he can continue. The implication is that White Plume has no power to run if his plume is contaminated. In each case he must take the time to carefully purify himself before he can compete or even survive, since each race is both physically and spiritually a matter of life and death. And the virtues gained help White Plume to endure the humiliation Ikto has in store. In the course of his development even a hero can be fooled, but the ideal to be remembered as long as possible is voiced by a redbreasted woodpecker in a vision described by Black Elk: "Be attentive as you walk!" (*The Sacred Pipe* 64).

For each of the four obstacles the narrator includes a formulaic reference to the hero's virtue of attentiveness: *taku kala iyeya canke Wacinhin Ska el etunwan* (AMS edition 107–8). The phrase means that the opponent threw something out, *taku kala iyeya,* and that White Plume noticed it, *Wacinhin Ska el etunwan.* It shows that the hero was alert to consider every possible event in a battle situation. He took nothing for granted and could not be surprised. But Deloria omits *el etunwan,* "he looked at it," from the translation in each occurrence, as if it were already implied in the action.

In addition, she varies the Lakota words for *taku kala iyeya:* 1) "he tossed something out," 2) "he threw something out," 3) "he tossed something about." Even these slight variations detract from the ritualized prolongation of ordeal and the corresponding expectation of success. The withstanding of panic or rage is further praised through the words, *Yunkan henakeȟcin* "and so great a number," to qualify the cockleburrs, choke-cherry stalks, and crabapple branches thrown out by the men. The narrator does not use the phrase in the first instance, perhaps because the cattail fuzz is explicitly a first and relatively easy task to remove, but for everything else, he emphasizes the degree of irrita-tion. Again Deloria drops the refrain, reflecting differences of culture as well as style.

The elevation of patience in Lakota culture permeates the style of the first epi-sode: *canke toel hena nazin na kpahihin na gluśtan kin el* (108). In English, Deloria writes that the burr-bearing weeds "made it necessary for White Plume to stop and rid himself of them" (108). But the narrator says that he had to stand *and* ("na") brush them off *and* ("na") finish before he could start running again. This excruciating interruption is preceded by the word *toel*, "time taken for delay with impatience expressed by the speaker" (Buechel, *Lakota-English Dictionary*), though the hero must withstand it. With *toel* the narrator expresses the tension between a potential loss of nerve and the unbroken concentration maintained by the hero.

For the fourth and final delay, the Lakota narrator employs a long single sentence integrating the sense of increasing urgency. Perhaps because it is the culminating test, the narrator calls upon the hero's name to strengthen his effort: *Wacinhin kʔun he ataya ikoyaka canke ena toel gluśpuhin na wanna wicaśa sapa kʔun he glihunnikta hanl nakeś Wacinhin Ska glicu keʔ*, "He was obliged to take time out to rid his plume of the thorns, so that the blackened man was almost home. But now the boy was through, and starting home" (109). In the Lakota sentence the sequence of controlled cleansing followed by violent movement forms one flow of energy, first contained then released. But Deloria's translation makes the actions separate, dividing the delay and resumption. The original narrator situates the whole experience in the consciousness of White Plume, rather than in separate, objective events.

Reversing this contrast, Deloria runs together the culminating acts of victory, while the narrator divides them into an abrupt rhythm. At the end of each race White Plume kills the loser with his own club which has been ritually "set down," *kignakapi*, the Lakota word being repeated four times, while Deloria refers to the clubs unpur-posefully lying 1) "at the base" or 2) omits any reference to their placement, and 3) has them lying "at the goal" and 4) again omits the last reference to the club as *ekignakin*, "set down" according to the ritual of the contest.

The actual killing is also expressed four times in Lakota by the phrase *na un katʔa keʔ*, literally "and he used it to kill by striking, they say" (my translation). In each case the pause marker *keʔ*, to be discussed at greater length later, intensifies the energy and finality of each of the four cleansing acts. In addition to omitting the formal references to the clubs being ceremonially placed before the race, Deloria varies the description of the final victory to significantly lose the spiritual dimension: 1) "with it he struck and killed his opponent"; 2) "he struck and killed him with it"; 3) "so he took it and killed the owner with it"; and 4) "he stood with the black club ready to kill the owner when he got in." Deloria takes the greatest liberty in the last instance which literally says: "Therefore he went over to that blackened club which had been set down and took up his own and used it to kill by striking, they say" (my translation). To have White Plume simply "stand ready" is to omit a ritual completion, which must be overtly enacted in words as well as in the fictional action. The word *icu*, "to take," used in previous races is varied slightly to *ikikcu*, "he takes his own" in order to show that the club now belongs to White Plume, that he has appropriated the power of his enemy in the same way that a warrior would keep an enemy *wotawe*, an object containing sacred power for war (see Walker, *Lakota Belief and Ritual* 264).

The narrator accentuates White Plume's readiness for these feats by using his name four times as the subject of perception, as in White Plume *etunwan*, "saw" (the cattails, cockleburrs, choke-cherry stalks, and crabapple stalks). In the whole of the first episode, the name is used only when his father names him, when the opponents challenge him, when he sets out for home after removing the chokecherry branches in the third race, and when he resumes running after the delay in the fourth race. The last two uses are parallel and make the character's movement stronger after being tested. The principle of strengthening by repetition is initiated by White Plume's father, who throws the infant "outdoors" many times to help him grow into a man "all on the same day" (see analogues in "Stone Boy," *Dakota Texts* 87, 93 and "Falling Star," Riggs 84, 91).

The episode's conclusion comments first on the hero's effect on the people's state of mind and then on their actions when they are free from fear: *Canke hetanhan oyate kin tuweni nagi yewicayeśni ca okablaya unpi ke ?*, "From that time, the tribe was free from the oppression of the four tyrants" (109). A literal reading is helpful here: "Therefore from then on none of the people's souls could be touched with fear, and they spread out to live" (my translation). This connotes both population increase and a release from needing to crowd together for defense. In the immediate experience of storytelling and Lakota religion, these are also the subjective results of ritual repetition. But the story does not end here, as a ceremony does not control events. Both prepare the participants to survive losses in the next episode, wherever it may occur.

From the ceremonial rigor of the race course, White Plume enters the territory of the trickster where he is initially less impressive. He prevails in the end because he and the girl he will marry have been prepared through repetition. Readers of James Welch's novel *Winter in the Blood* (1974), whether they know it or not, are familiar with the traditional quest of the hero in Plains Indian stories to earn a name and win a wife. Welch's narrator is inundated by the buzzing of a protean trickster—contemporary American society. For a long time he lacks the ceremonial discipline to clear his "plume" and realize an identity, but although he is defeated in much of the novel, the little bits and pieces of ritual discipline he has learned from his grandmother, his father, and his brother help to guide him home.

In Welch's novel the trickster episode is magnified in comparison to the hero stories on which it is based. The modern protagonist lives in a world in which the trickster reigns. In the story of White Plume, Iktomi's power, though less encompassing, is far greater than that of one who is alert only to physical threat. The first section of the second episode begins with the young man eager to pursue his "journey," despite his father's anxiety about an inevitable encounter with a "tricky woman." In the form of a woman, the trickster can maneuver a young man into self-indulgent anonymity. In the whole of the second episode of "White Plume," neither the narrator nor Deloria uses the hero's name at all. When Ikto steals White Plume's clothing, he appropriates the appearance of the hero's purposed self, and for an interval takes the power contained in his name.

This loss occurs almost immediately after the boy sets out in his *koškalaka* or adolescent phase (see Powers on the relation between the word *koškalaka* and venereal disease, *Oglala Religion* 196). The delousing has probable sexual connotations. When she (Ikto) "by some unknown method induces him to lie down," the narrator employs a convention of psychologically dangerous sexuality, used elsewhere in North American myth (for a Pueblo version, see Carr and Gingerich, "Vagina Dentata" in Swann, *Smoothing* 195). Losing his white plume and his name, the defining manifestations of his manhood, the hero is reduced to the whimpering, itching puppy, seeking only "a sunny spot" on which to lie "all day." A Lakota warrior might well have demonstrated courage as early as age fourteen, but in the next stage of life he could lose his fighting edge (usually the result of a vision), by excessive preoccupation with sex (see "The Deer Woman," *Dakota Texts* 163–66).

Ikto's disguise is the hero's alternative fate, that of a spoiled "child beloved" who carries a name and lives with a woman of high standing, though he has earned neither name, wife, nor prestige. In the rest of the episode he wears the white plume without absorbing its power. While he tries to excuse his failures to bring the people supernatural protection through killing the red fox and the scarlet bird (see analogues in Beckwith 385 and Deloria, *Teton Myths* 6, 23), he does not even bother to explain his botched pipe ceremony. Meanwhile the people's ability to secure supernatural help has been trapped in the helpless puppy.

The first part of the third episode begins when the compassion imparted by the "poor girl," who lives outside the circle, restores White Plume to his name and purpose. He in turn will restore the people, still "heavy-hearted" from Ikto's repeated failures. After Ikto is "disentangled" from the camp, the name "White Plume" returns as the subject of his first unselfish effort since his victories in episode one. Near the end of the third episode White Plume kills the sacred animals, appropriating their powers for the people just as he had taken those of the four enemies. This time, however, he can give much more, commensurate with his greater maturity and the integration of "feminine" care he has received from the girl.

The description of the pipe ceremonies includes several important stylistic details missed in Deloria's translation. The language of Ikto's ceremony and that of White Plume's involve meaningful parallels and variations. Ikto's language is careless: *Ho, canli blablukta ce takunl kat?ewacin po* (111), literally, "Now! tobacco I will puff so be ready to kill something" (my translation). White Plume's language is respectfully formal, *Le canli kin topa blablukta can iyuha wicakat?ewacin po* (113), literally, "*This* tobacco (*the*) *four times* I will puff so be ready to kill *all* of them" (my translation). Deloria points out in a footnote to another story that Ikto is habitually lazy in speech, omitting phrases of respect, disregarding any attempt to make his hearers understand, using only "the barest skeleton of language" (*Dakota Texts* 13n). Ceremonial language, like that of narrative, is not just an efficient means to a personal end. In White Plume's ceremony, comprising the second part of the third episode, the tobacco as the medium of power is elevated both by the demonstrative *le* and the definite article *kin*. In addition, the tobacco is puffed a ceremonial four times rather than indefinitely.

The resultant gifts, possessed again through the metaphor of killing (as a hunter obtains food) must not be disrespectfully wasted. Killing *iyuha*, "all of them," shows appreciation rather than just *takunl*, "something," as Ikto puts it. After giving the people warmth and confidence, blankets and guns, the hero is ready for the reward anticipated by the narrator of *Winter in the Blood*: "Next time I'd do it right, buy her a couple of cremes de menthe, maybe offer to marry her on the spot" (Welch 175). For getting it right at last White Plume gets the girl, in what may be considered the story's last episode, too brief to be divided into parts.

In episodes two and three the rhythmic repetition used in episode one is largely dropped, except for the parallels between Ikto's failure and White Plume's success. In the fourth episode, the story's last sentences have both alliteration and verbal symmetry to convey the sense of purposeful completion: *ecel śina oowa-śa nais to nais gi, sapa koko kahpapi na hankeya mazawakan na woyuha koko kahpapi śke?. Hetan nakeś oyate kin woyuha waśteśte yuhapi śke?*, "even blankets . . . guns, and fine possessions came down. And that was the beginning of such things in the tribe, they say" (113). For the raining down of blankets and guns, Deloria uses "also fell" and "came down" respectively. But the text twice uses the alliterative and slightly guttural *koko kahpapi*, "also fell," to indicate the impressiveness of those events. Alliteration is also used in the next sentence to refer to the further results of the demonstration (on this type of *wakan kaga*, or non-curative sacred performance, see Powers, *Sacred Language* 183).

Finally the last long sentence incorporates the marriage of the hero and heroine into the harmony of the tribe, building to *tiwicakiyapi na lila tewicahilapi*, meaning literally "they were caused to live in the center" and "were greatly loved," words distinct in denotative meaning but united by a balanced, rhyming sound appropriate to the theme of restoring harmony within the tribe. A similar use of alliteration and balance is also used in the first sentence: *yunkan ikikcu na peslete kin el wacinhin wan paslatin*, "he planted a white plume in the crown of his head" (106). *Peslete* means "crown of the head" and *paslatin* means literally "inserted." Only the Lakota words express the strength of the father committing his son to a certain kind of life (on the predictive intent of Plains Indian naming see Buechel, *Lakota Tales and Texts* 342, Frey 55, and McClintock 395–96). Deloria's "planted a white plume" does not alliterate the same concepts and reduces the seriousness of the act.

The use of narrative conventions to augment meaning occurs frequently in *Dakota Texts*. Among the most effective conventional terms are the quotatives *śke?, keyapi?*, and *ke?*, "it is said" or "they say," phrases used to conclude sentences and to indicate continuity from teller to teller through the generations. The quotative has been recognized as serving these purposes in many Native American languages (see Wiget 329). But it has not often been seen as a structuring principle in the sense that Dell Hymes has explained initial particles in Clackamas Chinook stories (see Suggested Reading). Of the 64 stories in *Dakota Texts,* an intentionally esthetic use of the quotative may be observed in 28 (see Appendix). In these the strong sound *śke?* concludes approximately the first and last two to six sentences. Most of the intervening sentences end in the less emphatic *ke?,* the shortened form of *keyapi?,* though at the end of an episode or after a decisive action, *śke?* may be selected.

The meaningful use of *śke?* is a storytelling style, rather than the practice of a single narrator, since the technique is found in stories Deloria collected from both Rosebud and Standing Rock (for the differentiation, see *Dakota Texts* x). The other major method of using *śke?,* at the end of every sentence throughout a narrative, occurs in 24 of Deloria's texts (see Appendix). At the end of a sentence, *śke?* and *ke?* both take the terminal glottal stop, accentuating the narrative pause with a physical cessation of breath. When *keyapi* refers to characters speaking within a story, it has no glottal stop (see Deloria, *Dakota Grammar* 106–7). While the glottal stop strengthens sentence endings, the fricative *ś* makes *śke?* a stronger sound than *ke?,* and a sentence ending in the former will be more emphatic. A story told with *śke?* at the end of each sentence may be both more intense and more ritualized. Although Deloria notes that *śke?* is used particularly in myths, and *keyapi?* or *ke?* is used in "tribal tales, war, and other stories" (*Dakota Texts* 1), this distinction does not match the texts. In many *ohunkakan* (myths) *śke?* is used variably with *ke?,* though in others *śke?* is used consistently.

Intensely dramatic stories like "Doubleface Steals the Virgin" (51–64) and "The Deer Woman" (163–64) are well served by the use of *śke?* at the end of every sentence, but other short, suspenseful stories like "Meadowlark and the Rattlesnake" use *śke?* only after the first and last sentences. Narrators expected irregular choral responses from the audience such as *hau* and *ohan* (see Jahner, "Stone Boy" 178), particularly after statements affirming fundamental values. Quotatives may be more frequent at the beginning to warm up the listeners, to keep their attention. If not used frequently until near the end, *śke?* will be a signal of the end approaching, like the hard penultimate beat of the drum preceding the soft, trailing beats that end a song. And when the tension of a story has been resolved, the audience is again invited to vocally appreciate its transmission.

The narrator of "White Plume" uses *śke?* only once in the beginning, at the end of the first sentence, already strengthened by the cultural importance of naming and the alliteration of **peslete** *kin el wacinhin wan* **paslatin**, "he placed a white plume in the crown of his head" (106), mentioned earlier. Thereafter *ke?* is used at the end of every sentence until the two separate sentences concerning Ikto's failure in ritual and its effect on the people. The whole sequence reads: *ituhcin winyeya yankapi keyaś takuni hinhpayeśni śke?. Canke wicaśa kin iyuha canl-ececapiśni śke?,* "So they sat in tense readiness, but nothing magical happened. At last the men took their departure, heavyhearted from disappointment" (111). Here *śke?* effectively ends Ikto's masquerade as well as the episode he dominates. *Ke?* is used for the sentence describing White Plume's resumption of power but *śke?* is used once more as much to bid Ikto farewell as to warn of his inevitable return: *Tokśa, ake ukte lo; He Ikto eśnika caś,—eyapi śke?*" (112), liter-ally "soon he will return. That's Ikto, what can you do?—they said, it is said" (my translation).

To express the demonstration of White Plume's mature power, the fulfillment of a young man's story, the narrator saves the repeated use of *śke?* for the concluding events. To indicate the care with which he uses the term, it should be noted that when White Plume kills the red fox, *ke?* is used: *Wacinhin Ska ipahna o ke?*, "White Plume pierced and killed him" (112), but when he completes the task with a remarkable shot, given the size of the target, the narrator verbally applauds with *śke?*: *zitkala wan luta ca wankal okinyan un tkaś cante kin glakinyan o śke?*, "when the scarlet bird soared overhead, it was White Plume's arrow which brought it down, piercing its heart" (112). In a more com-pressed sequence, *śke?* is used again almost immediately after the next six words to ver-bally supplement the triumph: *Canke tice kin el śayela otkeyapi śke?*, literally, "they hung the little red one from the tipi poles, it is said" (my translation).

In the next sentence where White Plume manifests the power Ikto lacked, the narrator confidently anticipates his success with *śke?*: *Hehanl,—Ho, canunmunpinkta ce til uwicaśi po,—eya canke ti otinś ahiyotaka śke?*, " 'Now, I shall smoke. Ask them to come in,' he said, so the men crowded into the tipi" (113). And with the last sentence, long enough to give the flow of power mentioned previously, *śke?* accentuates the wonder expressed in the closely repeated phrase *ko kahpapi*, "also fell" (113). In effect the value of the story's telling is implied as the people's power to live is manifested, both fictionally and immediately through the oral tradition. Appreciation for tribal longevity is voiced in the next seven words followed by another *śke?*: *Hetan nakeś oyate kin woyuha waśteśte yuhapi śke?*, "And that was the beginning of such things in the tribe, they say" (113). The final one sentence episode, containing the hero-gets-the-girl convention, also gets the *śke?*, because it celebrates the continuity of Lakota consciousness. In the final *śke?*, the people's strength to continue is assured: *Wacinhin Ska wicincalala wan unśike ceyaś sanp-waun-śila k?un he yuzin na kici hocokap tiwicakiyapi na lila tewicahilapi śke?*, "White Plume took for his wife the girl who was so humble but so kind-hearted, and the tribe caused them to live in a tipi inside the camp circle and held them in highest esteem and affection, they say" (113).

In "White Plume," *śke?* affirms the making of a hero. It is used after the first sentence as if to accentuate his naming. Much later in the story it is used twice, imme-diately after the failures of Iktomi, as if to lend clarity to his exposure, and then again after Ikto's banishment to express preparedness for his inevitable return. From that point on *śke?* is used to conclude each sentence remaining in the story, six times in succession. The nar-rator uses *śke?* conventionally to mark the beginning and end, and selectively to intensify dramatic events.

The next story in *Dakota Texts* may be by the same narrator. "Blood Clot Boy" (113–20) is the only other story in the collection where the hero's name is carefully used. In the first episode, where he kills a family of bears who have abused a rabbit (his adoptive grandfather), the name We Hokśila is used to accompany its winning four times. In the second episode where Blood Clot Boy, like White Plume, is immobilized by Ikto, the name is used once as he embarks on his journey, and again when he is mocked by Iktomi, who has caused him to stick to a tree. The name does not return until he is freed by his future wife who, like White Plume's, had been an outcast. Thereafter the name is used three times until it gives way to the kinship term, *takoza,* "grandson," upon his return to the rabbit.

In "Blood Clot Boy" *śkeˀ* is used more frequently at the beginning than in "White Plume." It occurs after the first three sentences of the first episode, as well as once more within the first section of the first episode to mark a significant supernatural event—the immediate answer to the rabbit's wish for fine possessions for his son. Then in the challenge comprising the second section of part one, *śkeˀ* is used four times to 1) underscore the audacity of the hero's provoking the bear; 2) to punctuate the one-blow clubbing to death of another bear; 3) to lend force to the collective killing of the other bears; and 4) to conclude the hero's labors at the end of the episode.

In the second episode, *śkeˀ* is resumed after Ikto leaves Blood Clot Boy stuck to the tree, effectively interrupting the hero's progress. From this point on the narrator uses *śkeˀ* after every sentence to the story's close, a significantly different use than in "White Plume." Perhaps the narrator wishes to emphasize the outrageousness of Ikto's lies in the camp, where he marries into a prominent family. *Śkeˀ* follows five sentences concerning Ikto's impersonation and is then used five more times to describe the hero's return. But after being used to complete ten successive sentences, *śkeˀ* significantly gives way to four sentences ending in *keˀ* immediately before the ending.

Following his victorious expulsion of Ikto and his marriage to the kind girl, Blood Clot Boy returns to his own people rather than remaining with his wife's relatives as White Plume does (for the implications of this residential choice, see Hassrick 130). During the journey the tenor changes with the quieter *keˀ* concluding four sentences (seven in Deloria's English version). The girl's spoiled elder sister, abandoned by her husband (Ikto), follows the couple:

*Iś ehakela kiśicapi keyaś nunge wanil yahin na ecel wana We-Hokśila ti kin ikiyela glapi **keˀ**. Otaninyan wana glapi yunkan mato cincalala kˀun he iśnala pahata oksanksan etunwan yankahe ḣcehantu canke wanwicayanka hunśe nazin hiyayin na akoketkiya aiyoḣpeya mahel kigla **keˀ**. Niyaśniśni kihunni na,—Wana mitakoza ku tka winyan wan aku welo,—eya **keˀ**. Hecena Maśtinskala lila wiyuskin na psipsil itkop wicayin na takozakpaku kin kici na glogla **keˀ**.*

They in turn ordered her back but she did not have any ears. And so they came on until they neared Blood Clot Boy's home. The little bear who was sitting on a hilltop saw them. He had been sitting there alone, viewing the country round about. He started up, evidently having seen them, and disappeared downhill in the other direction. Breathlessly he arrived home and said, "Grandson is now returning; but he brings a woman home." Immediately the rabbit, very happy, ran hopping out to meet them; and taking his grandson on his back he carried him the remainder of the way (120).

Finally *śkeˀ* is resumed in the last two sentences to lend the usual conclusive force, as well as to emphasize two diametrically opposed ways of regarding kinship. The smallest bear, whom Blood Clot Boy spared because he had no part in persecuting the rabbit, demonstrates ideal behavior by strenuously honoring his new sister, no small sacrifice considering his size:

*Canke matola kʔun iś-eya takosku kin kici na ihakap gle ceyaś yuhaśni canke wikośkalaka kin si kin makicagogoyela aglapi **śkeʔ**. Cuweku wan waȟʔanicʔila tka kʔun he tuweni el etunweśni canke iyecinka wicihakap i ca caȟol-iȟpeya yuhapi **śkeʔ**.*

The little bear also came to meet them, and he took the daughter-in-law on his back, but she was so heavy (for him) that he could not lift her entirely off the ground; so her feet dragged on behind. As for the proud elder sister, nobody took any notice of her, so she came along behind them, and lived with them there. They kept her to take out the ashes for them (120).

As *śkeʔ* makes this an epitome of the story's values, so it is used in the last sentence to indicate the inverse values of those who consider relatives to be worthless. The elder sister is left to throw out trash instead of the sister she had humiliated, and for this deserves the narrator's final irony.

"Blood Clot Boy" has something of the symmetry Hymes has shown in Clackamas texts. *Śkeʔ* is used four times in the expository first episode, and again to end four more sentences about the scourging of the bears. Then in episode two it is used five times in succession to refer to the antics of Ikto. In episode three *śkeʔ* is again used five times to offset Ikto and to manifest the hero's recovery. Of these uses *śkeʔ* refers once to Ikto's banishment and once to the discomfiture of his wife. The fourth episode, the return of Blood Clot Boy and his wife to his own community, occurs after the tension has been resolved. *Keʔ* carries the sense of quiet confidence through four sentences until *śkeʔ* returns in the last two as a narrative convention, and a pointed reminder to "never treat your relatives like trash."

In this story the selection of *śkeʔ* and *keʔ* is virtually schematic:

Episode 1.
   Section 1. The oppression of the rabbit and the childhood of the hero. *Śkeʔ* is used four times.
   Section 2. Scourging the bears. *Śkeʔ* is used four times.
Episode 2.   Ikto's ascendancy. *Śkeʔ* is used five times.
Episode 3.   Blood Clot Boy's return. *Śkeʔ* is used five times to end sentences and once, atypically, to precede a quote, a possible printing error (p. 119, sentence 21), since all other quotes are preceded or followed by "eya *keʔ*."
Episode 4.   The hero's return. *Keʔ* is used four times. *Śkeʔ* is used twice, at the end of the last two sentences.

Hymes has suggested that such structures in a few stories, even a single story, may be predictive (*"In Vain . . ."* 276). Few stories are as symmetrical as "Blood Clot Boy" or even "White Plume," although another story "Doubleface Tricks the Girl" (*Dakota Texts* 46–50) has four successive *śkeʔ* endings at the beginning and four at the end with only two in succession in the middle, when the heroine suddenly discovers that her lover is a monster (47). Other stories also have this balance. The frequently told story of the woman who lived with the wolves, entitled "She who Dwells in the Rocks" (*Dakota Texts* 238–45), employs *ške*? seven times at the beginning, while the woman prepares to desert her abusive husband, and five times at the end after she has returned to her own camp to demonstrate the supernatural power of the wolves to whom she became related during her long walk home. *Ke*? is used as in most of the other stories through all of the intervening sentences. An additional aspect of the *ške*? convention occurs in its omission from the last three transcribed sentences. The last *ške*? concludes the final reference to her healing power and concludes the story proper. Of the remaining three sentences, the first has *ke*? and the last two have no ending term at all:

*Nakun wapiya can oyas?in okihi s?a keyaś wapiye c?un he hakeya ayuśtan **ške**?. Iglus?aka hanl he glicu canke wicincala wan yuha **ke**?. He le wicaśa wan śicaya kuwa k?un he cinca ca. He wicincala kin wana winuȟcala hanl untipi el hi na tisanp ȟpaya yunkan unkiyunkapi kin ohakap le oyaka ca miye iyatayela nawaȟ? un.*

And whenever she doctored the sick, she was always successful, but, they say, in time she abandoned this practice (*ške*?). She was pregnant when she left, so now she gave birth to a baby, a girl (*ke*?). She was the child of the man who had maltreated her so (no ending). When that girl was now a very old woman, she once came to our home, and spent the night there. She occupied the space on the left of the fireplace, and when we were all in bed for the night, she told this story, so I myself heard it from her lips (no ending) (245).

This modulation from *ške*? to *ke*? to no ending resembles the use of the sweat lodge after a vision quest. It verbally negotiates the transitions from the woman's kinship with spirits, to her human relationships, to the reflexive completion of the immediate telling.

Since *ške*? is used after every single sentence in some of the longest, most highly developed stories in *Dakota Texts* (see Appendix), it cannot be concluded that only the best narrators used the word as a modulatory device with *ke*?. It may be that neither the varied nor constant uses of the quotative are effectively verbalized in English. Elaine Jahner's fine translation of George Sword's "Stone Boy" (Jahner "Stone Boy" 19–85, also Walker, *Lakota Myth* 89–100) shows a predominance of *ške*?, which she translates, "so they tell." *Keyapi*? (they say) also occurs but with far less frequency. Jahner theorizes that *ške*? marks major pauses and *keyapi*? minor ones. She distinguishes between the two quotatives in her translation by putting *ške*? (so they tell) in separate lines each time it occurs, while *keyapi*? (they say) is set off by a comma at the end of a line. Although this is an improvement on Deloria's complete omission, the one syllable *ške*? with its fricative *ś* signals a more distinct pause, enhanced by the glottal stop, while "so they tell," even when set off in a line by itself, is comparatively neutral. The subtle relaxation from *ške*? to *ke*? is also lost in the unrelated sounds of "so they tell" and "they say." Because it includes the glottal stop but lacks the fricative *ś*, the pause after *ke*? is a half beat shorter.

These difficulties are not absolute impediments to understanding traditional stories in English. But if the academic community is to effectively implement its recent curricular inclusions, Native American languages must be more widely taught. Knowledge of any literature cannot advance without knowledge of its tone and texture. A reading knowledge of a Native American language is not impossible to attain. Reading in translation has initiated sincere interest and useful literary criticism. Reading in the original will add the differentiation inevitably obscured in English, and often overlooked by the systematics of folklore and anthropology.

Arnold Krupat has called for a more open approach to Native American texts than social scientists have heretofore been willing to afford: "we must read the texts we have, from Henry Schoolcraft to the present moment, as in need of unfixing, a process by which we acknowledge that any meanings which appear to be present are never fully present" (Krupat 124). This continual supplementation of meaning reflects narrative practice itself. Although singers had to repeat sacred songs exactly as the spirits had given them (see Densmore 59–60), storytellers freely improvised from content motifs and verbal formulas. Their resourceful *bricolage* can be more thoroughly conceived in a criticism that turns artifacts back into art.

Appendix

The infrequent use of *śke* ⁷ does not correspond to narrative skill. *Śke* ⁷ is used to end every sentence in several highly developed stories in *Dakota Texts:* numbers 10, 16, 24, 26, 36, and 39.

Śke ⁷ also concludes every sentence in stories 1, 4, 22, 29, 30, 32, 38, 40, 41, 46, 48, 49, 52, 53, 54, 55, 57, and 63.

The use of *śke* ⁷ at the beginning and end, and at dramatic points within a story occurs in stories 2, 3, 5, 6, 7, 8, 9, 11, 13, 14, 15, 17, 18, 19, 20, 21, 23, 25, 27, 28, 33, 34, 35, 42, 43, 44, 47, and 50. Several exceptions occur. In story 23 *śke* ⁷ is used at emphatic points and concentrated at the end in the last three sentences but not used in the beginning. In story 61 *śke* ⁷ is used only in the last three sentences. In story 12 *śke* ⁷ is absent from the beginning but used four times in the story including the last sentence. In stories 37 and 56 *śke* ⁷ is used only after the last sentence.

In several stories the alternation of *śke* ⁷ and *ke* ⁷ or *keyapi* ⁷ appears to be random, concentrated neither at the beginning and end, nor used to intensify specific situations: 45, 58, 59, 60, 64.

"The Deer Woman," stories 30 and 31, is presented both in the Teton and Yankton dialects. In both versions, the quotative is used after every sentence but where the Teton narrator uses *śke* ⁷, the Yankton customarily uses *keyapi* ⁷, because, Deloria notes, they consider *śke* ⁷ "too indefinite" (*Dakota Texts* 165n).

Suggested Reading

Ambrose, Stephen E. *Crazy Horse and Custer.* New York: Doubleday, 1975.
Beckwith, Martha Warren. "Mythology of the Oglala Dakota." *Journal of American Folklore* 43 (1930): 339–439.

Black Bear, Ben, Sr., and R. D. Theisz. *Songs and Dances of the Lakota*. Aberdeen, South Dakota: North Plains Press, 1976.

Black Elk. *The Sacred Pipe*. Ed. Joseph Epes Brown. New York: Penguin, 1971.

———. *The Sixth Grandfather*. Ed. Raymond J. DeMallie. Lincoln: University of Nebraska Press, 1984.

Brennan, Terry, S. J. *Lakota Woonśpe Wowapi*. Rosebud, South Dakota: Sinte Gleśka College Center, 1973.

Buechel, Eugene, S. J. *A Grammar of Lakota*. Rosebud, South Dakota: Rosebud Educational Society, 1939.

———. *A Dictionary of the Teton Dakota Sioux Language*. Pine Ridge, South Dakota: Red Cloud Lakota Language and Cultural Center, 1970.

———. Ed. *Lakota Tales and Texts*. Pine Ridge, South Dakota: Red Cloud Lakota Language and Cultural Center, 1978.

Deloria, Ella. *Teton Myths* [The George Bushotter collection]. ca. 1937; Philadelphia: MS30 (x8c.3), Boas Collection, American Philosophical Society.

———. *Dakota Texts*. 1932; rpt. New York: AMS Press, 1974.

———. *Dakota Texts*. 1932; rpt. (English only) Vermillion, South Dakota: Dakota Press, 1978.

———. *Dakota Grammar*. 1941; rpt. Vermillion: Dakota Press, 1982.

———. *Speaking of Indians*. Vermillion, South Dakota: State Publishing, 1983.

———. *Waterlily*. Lincoln: University of Nebraska Press, 1988.

Densmore, Frances. *Teton Sioux Music*. 1918; rpt. New York: Da Capo, 1972.

Dorsey, James O. *A Study of Siouan Cults*. 1894; rpt. Seattle: Shorey, 1972.

Fools Crow, Frank. "Fools Crow." LP Recording TLP 100. Denver: Tatanka Records, 1977.

Frey, Rodney. *The World of the Crow Indians: As Driftwood Lodges*. Norman: University of Oklahoma Press, 1987.

Hassrick, Royal B. *The Sioux: Life and Customs of a Warrior Society*. Norman: University of Oklahoma Press, 1964.

Hymes, Dell. "Bungling Host, Benevolent Host: Louis Simpson's 'Deer and Coyote.'" *American Indian Quarterly* 8 (1984): 171–98.

———. *"In Vain I Tried to Tell You."* Philadelphia: University of Pennsylvania Press, 1981.

Jahner, Elaine A. "Cognitive Style in Oral Literature." *Language and Style* (Fall 1982): 32–51.

———. "Finding the Way Home." In *Handbook of American Folklore*. Ed. Richard M. Dorson. Bloomington: Indiana University Press, 1983.

———, ed. Introductory essays. James R. Walker. *Lakota Myth*. Lincoln: University of Nebraska Press, 1983.

———. "Stone Boy: Persistent Hero." In *Smoothing the Ground: Essays on Native American Oral Literature*. Ed. Brian Swann. Berkeley: University of California Press, 1983. 171–86.

Krupat, Arnold. "Post-Structuralism and Oral Literature." In *Recovering the Word: Essays on Native American Literature*. Eds. Brian Swann and Arnold Krupat. Berkeley: University of California Press, 1987. 113–28.

Mails, Thomas. *Mystic Warriors of the Plains*. New York: Doubleday, 1972.

———. *Sundancing at Rosebud and Pine Ridge*. Sioux Falls: Augustana College, 1978.

McClintock, Walter. *The Old North Trail: Life, Legends and Religion of the Blackfeet Indians*. 1910; rpt. Lincoln: University of Nebraska Press, 1968.

Powers, William K. *Oglala Religion*. Lincoln: University of Nebraska Press, 1975.

————. *Sacred Language: The Nature of Supernatural Discourse in Lakota*. Norman: University of Oklahoma Press, 1986.

Rice, Julian. "How the Bird that Speaks Lakota Earned a Name." In *Recovering the Word: Essays on Native American Literature*. Eds. Brian Swann and Arnold Krupat. Berkeley: University of California Press, 1987. 422–45.

————. *Lakota Storytelling*. New York: Peter Lang, 1989.

Swann, Brian, ed. *Smoothing the Ground: Essays on Native American Oral Literature*. Berkeley: University of California Press, 1983.

Taylor, Alan. *Beginning Lakhota*. 2 vols. Boulder: University of Colorado Lakhota Project, 1976.

Walker, James R. *The Sun Dance and Other Ceremonies of the Oglala Division of the Teton Dakota*. 1917; rpt. New York: AMS Press, 1979.

————. *Lakota Belief and Ritual*. Eds. Raymond J. DeMallie and Elaine A. Jahner. Lincoln: University of Nebraska Press, 1980.

————. *Lakota Society*. Ed. Raymond J. DeMallie. Lincoln: University of Nebraska Press, 1982.

————. *Lakota Myth*. Ed. Elaine A. Jahner. Lincoln: University of Nebraska Press, 1983.

Welch, James. *Winter in the Blood*. New York: Harper & Row, 1974.

Wiget, Andrew. "Telling the Tale: A Performance Analysis of a Hopi Coyote Story." In *Recovering the Word: Essays on Native American Literature*. Eds. Brian Swann and Arnold Krupat. Berkeley: University of California Press, 1987. 297–338.

Wissler, Clark. "Some Dakota Myths." *Journal of American Folklore* 20 (1907): 121–31, 195–206.

Translating the Untranslatable: The Place of the Vocable in Lakota Song

William K. Powers

During the twentieth century scholars writing mainly in the English language have taken the liberty of extracting native texts from their original contexts, in this case song, and treating them as if they were the equivalent of Western notions of poetry. This essay takes as its starting point the singular problem of what to do with the nonsemantic residue of song texts once they have been removed from their musical setting. By residue I mean the linguomusical utterances known by various terms—vocable, meaningless syllable, burden syllable, nonsense syllable—that appear either exclusively as the sole utterances of a given song in order to carry the melody or that appear in a number of phonemic environments within the song texts to elongate or otherwise modify textual materials in order to allow them to conform to or coincide with the melody and rhythm of the song proper.

The major problem, then, is not whether song texts may be justifiably considered poetry in the Western sense or whether once lifted from their melodic matrix they gain or lose any of their intrinsic meaning. The question is simply that when songs are composed with vocables, themselves lacking a semantic range, and texts, to what extent should the vocable be at least graphically retained in the translation of the song from the native language into another language in which vocables rarely or never appear?

Obviously, I think that the vocable should be retained, but if this is to be the case, then precisely how do we treat the vocable from a purely pragmatic point of view? How, when, and where does it appear on the translated piece and what rules if any may be applied to systematically retaining a form of text that under normal circumstances is not translatable?

In an earlier article based on empirical research on Plains Indian music, I demonstrated that contrary to much of what has been written in the past about the vocable, vocabalic phrases indeed do have structure and their phonemic characteristics are somewhat constrained by the language of the people who sing them.[1] Therefore, there is a structural relationship between language and vocable. Also, historically some languages may actually employ archaic or foreign words in their songs but treat them as if they were lacking innately in semantic range. Although I think that understanding the relationship between vocable and text is subject to universal testing, the precise relationship between semantic and nonsemantic utterances appearing in song obviously changes from one group of people to another. In the following essay what I hope to do is provide some clear examples of how the vocable is used, and how it may be graphically represented, to illuminate the song texts themselves in a number of ways.

I shall first address the structure of the vocable both paradigmatically and sytagmatically, then move on to what I consider its major poetic function, which serves to enance the natural rhythm of the language expressed in meaningful texts. Further along I will discuss pertinent relationships between vocables and the Lakota language by providing some relevant song translations.

Certainly the presentation of vocables along with the song texts is nothing new. It has been employed by some of the earliest ethnographers of music, such as L. W. Colby, Natalie Curtis, Frances Densmore, Alice C. Fletcher, and James Mooney. Later I will provide some examples of their work mainly to show that although they were frequently inconsistent in their employment of vocables, when they did use them correctly it rendered the song texts more interesting. This is not intended as a criticism of the early fieldworkers without whose careful recording of Lakota song, and others, we would know very little about continuity and change in one important aspect of American Indian culture. Using some of the principles I have referred to at the beginning of this essay, I will reconstruct some earlier songs by incorporating vocables in with the song texts in a consistent manner, rerendering the orthography in a manner consistent with current Lakota usage, and finally provide some translations of more recent Lakota songs. But first I want to discuss what I consider to be the rules of vocabalic structure.

Vocabalic Paradigms

If vocables are to be retained in the translation of song texts then there must be some agreement as to how they are to appear on the printed page. I personally have opted for presenting them phonemically, using an orthography adapted from one used to write Lakota by Eugene Buechel.[2] Since even today there is no strict agreement between linguists as to just what constitutes the proper orthography there is wide agreement among native Lakota speakers that so-called "missionary orthography," one partly based on an earlier orthography used by Protestant missionaries, should be used to represent the Lakota and Dakota dialects. Setting aside for a moment what I elsewhere described as a linguistic battle waged over the "politics of orthography," I find it useful to take in the following considerations when writing vocables in Lakota songs.[3]

First, every vocable should be considered a monosyllable, and every monosyllable should be considered to be the relative equivalent of an eighth-note in music, the minimal metrical unit in which the vocable appears when sung.

Second, when vocables are sustained for more than an eighth-note in the original song, the sustention may be indicated by duplicating the sustained phoneme, which is always a vowel. Thus:

> *a* indicates a vocable held for an eighth note,
> *aa* indicates a vocable held for a quarter note.

In theory the vocable can be extended for even a longer value, but this rarely happens in the actual production of the song except in those introductory phrases found in Plains Indian singing in which the first or second note may be sustained *portamento* for as long as seven or eight beats, or even longer.

Third, among the Lakota, all possible combinations of consonants and vowels that form the basis for constructing all vocables may be reduced to the following paradigm:

> *a e i o u*
> *h*
> *w*
> *y*
> *l*

All consonants in the vertical column may combine with all vowels in the horizontal column to form vocables. All vowels also may form vocables without consonants. These combinations generate the following vocables:

> *a, e, i, o,*
> *ha, he, hi, ho*
> *wa, we, wi, wo*
> *ya, ye, yi, yo*
> *la, le, li, lo*

The last line is specific to Lakota. The L-sound in Lakota distinguishes it from the D-sound in Dakota and in the latter we would find the corresponding line written:

> *da de di do*[4]

Fourth, in Lakota under some circumstances vocables are nasalized. This occurs usually when vocables are used to space words so as to allow the textual material to conform to the melodic material. This partly confirms Nettl's statement that the melody is primary in any song and once composed the melodic line and its inherent meter do not change after the texts have been added, or composed simultaneously along with the melodic line.[5] Thus the following nasalized vocables appear in Lakota songs:

> *an in un*
>
> *y*

Here only one consonant (*y*) may combine with the vowels in the horizontal column but note that only three vowels appear. This is because in Lakota *e* and *o* are never nasalized.

The use of the singular consonant *y* is retained perhaps for stylistic reasons, and is found affixed to Lakota words ending in *un* thus giving the combination of word and vocable a rhyming effect, for example, *oyate k'un* **yun,** "the people."

Syntagmatic Considerations

Once we have established that vocables should be written as monosyllables, we must examine the relationships between those vocabalic monosyllables to each other as they appear in any given song. Of course the original order in which they appear is determined by the composer. However, there are some rules, conscious or unconscious, that the composer must follow in order to create a steady flow of vocables over a melodic line.

The major syntagmatic consideration is that the vocable is always sung in such a way that it is sustained through each strophe of the song. Rarely do we find glottalized vocables except between combinations of vowels without consonants (*a'a'a'*, etc.) or in individual ornamentation in which a singer has developed a personal vocabalic signature that makes him stand out among other singers.[6] Therefore, the major objective in linking vocables together is to make them elide smoothly into each other until the end of the strophe is reached, where we find a tendency toward glottalization on the final note of a set of songs accompanied by a heavy final beat of the drum.

The most typical combinations are those in which we find a consonant (*c*) plus a vocable (*v*) as the second monosyllable in a chain of vocables, such as:

> *h(v)y(v)* as in *he ya* or *ha ya*
> *w(v)y(v)* as in *we ya* or *wi ya*
> *y(v)y(v)* as in *ya ye* or *ye ya*

We do not find duplicated consonants interspersed with vocables (which form glottal stops and thus reduce the flow of the song); therefore *w(v)w(v)* and *h(v)h(v)* do not appear, but *y(v)y(v)* is common.

To recapitulate briefly, paradigmatic and syntagmatic considerations lead to a number of rules that govern the use of the vocable as it appears interspersed before and after textual materials, or in exclusively vocabalic renditions with respect to sound and structure. These are:

1. The distinctive features of the vocable (the phoneme) are homologous to the distinctive features of the native language. Therefore rules governing the sounds of the language also govern the sounds of the vocables.
2. Songs containing vocables only are likely to contain fewer varieties of vocables than those songs composed with meaningful texts (for example, nasalized vowels are functions of word songs).
3. All vocables end with a vowel, either vocal, nasal, or glottal.
4. Pure and nasal *a, e,* and *i* are always followed by *y* plus a vowel unless they are the final vocable in the song.
5. *O* is always followed by *w* unless it is the final vocable in a song.
6. Pure and nasal *u* may be followed by *w* or *y.*
7. Vowels ending in glottal stops may be reduplicated.
8. Only the consonant *y* may be substituted for another consonant.
9. Vocables found in a tribal repertory that are phonemically inconsistent with these rules may be regarded as exotic or idiosyncratic.[7]

Now I would like to turn from the structural features of the vocable to some of its important functions.

Vocabalic Functions

Elsewhere I have demonstrated that the vocable serves a number of signal and symbolic functions in all American Indian song.[8] Vocables actually direct a good part of the song, particularly its beginning and ending; they also serve to set the pitch of the song. But they also have a more important function from the point of view of translation.

Although elsewhere I have divided vocabalic functions into four types, the only one that I consider here is what I have called the poetic function, which refers mainly to the relationship between the vocable and the text.[9] Vocables can be employed in numerous grammatical ways to enhance the text through various poetic features such as rhyme, meter, and alliteration. When combined with texts vocables may appear as prefixes, infixes, or suffixes to words. For example, in a phrase that frequently introduces songs of a similar genre (so-called Omaha dance songs) which appears in Lakota, *Oyate k'un kawita au na iyokipimayaye lo* **he ye he ye,** we may find a vocabalic prefix:

He oyate k'un . . . etc.

or an infix:

Oyate *ye* k'un . . . etc.

or as a suffix:

Oyate k'un *yun* . . . etc.

or in theory, all possible combinations:

He oyate *ye* k'un *yun . . .* etc.

The above examples should not be seen as a singer's option for singing the same song. Once a song has been composed, the relationship between the vocables and texts remain fixed for the life of the song.

Intratextually, then, the vocable may serve a number of stylistic functions such as rhyming, metrical continuity, semantic and syntactic emphasis, spacing of textual materials, pausing, and other prosodic devices.

In particular, with respect to line endings in translation, vocabalic cadential formulas always provide the clue as to when textual materials begin and end. By including vocables along with texts one is insured that the line endings of the translator unequivocally coincide with the intended line endings of the composer. The separation of words and vocables as well as the proper indication of line endings has been a major problem in the translation of American Indian songs in general. It would seem that as long as the translator is aware of the structure and function of the vocable, then the task of making these finer textual distinctions is enhanced. Vocables provide the essential brackets within which textual materials appear.

Vocable Versus Syllable

One must be cautious in the graphic representation of vocables to distinguish them from syllables that have a semantic range. Lakota is replete with a number of enclitics that indicate, among other things, the declarative, imperative, and interrogative forms of a sentence as well as some gender distinctions. A number of syllables in Lakota then are actually identical to the vocables shown in the tables above. For example, in addition to being a vocable:

> *he* is an interogative enclitic (as a noun it means "horn").
> *we* is the female imperative enclitic and male entreaty form (as a noun it means "blood").
> *ye* is a female imperative enclitic and entreaty form (as a verb it means "to go").
> *ho* is a paragraph starter for males and females (as a noun it means "voice").
> *wo* is a male imperative enclitic.
> *yo* is a male imperative enclitic.
> *lo* is used to mark certain kinds of declarative sentences.
> *ya* suffixed to some radical elements renders them adverbs.

All the above not only appear in everyday Lakota discourse, but when used in songs they may also appear adjacent to identical vocables. The following example of a Yankton Peyote song will give some idea of the complexity of the juxtapositions. Again, to help clarify the distinctions between vocables and syllables of meaningful words, only the vocables are underscored:

Wacekiya yo *yo yo yo*
Wacekiya yo *yo yo yo*
Wacekiya yo *yo yo yo*
Wacekiya yo *yo yo yo*
Wacekiya yo
Ho yani kte
He ya na hee yee yoo wee
Maȟpiya kin heciya *ya ya* wiconi *ye ye*
He ya wa na yo
Wacekiya yo
Ho yani kte
He ya na hee yee yoo wee

Pray! *yo yo yo*
Pray! *yo yo yo*
Pray! *yo yo yo*
Pray! *yo yo yo*
Pray!
Ho you will live
He ya na hee yee yoo wee
There in heaven *ya ya* there is life *ye ye*
Ha ya wa na yo
Pray!
Ho you will live
He ya na hee yee yoo wee[10]

Some points of clarification: The first "yo" appearing after "wacekiya" in the first four lines of the song is not a vocable but an imperative enclitic. The subsequent repeats of *yo*, of course, are vocables and serve to set the delineation of each line neatly. The "ho" preceding the text "yani kte" is strictly speaking a paragraph or sentence starter in spoken Lakota. It also serves to reaffirm the statements that have preceded it. Thus the general idea is "pray" (repeated three times); "once you've done that you will live." The single line of vocables following the text are standard formulas in Peyote songs. The appearance of the vocable *na*—from the Lakota standpoint—indicates that this is a foreign song because *na* does not appear as a vocable in Lakota songs. Peyote music is of course intrusive to Lakota culture historically. In theory, it is possible to determine outside influences on tribal music by carefully examining the standard tribal vocables. When *na* appears here it tells the translator immediately that the song has been adopted from an outside source, in this case from the Southern Plains. Finally, the vocables *ya ya* make the listener wait for the punch line: "there is life."

In the past, other translators of Lakota songs have advertently or inadvertently included vocables in their original text renderings. But without hearing the songs it is unlikely that many of these texts can be reconstructed along with their attendant vocables.

Frances Densmore, certainly one of the most prolific of all Lakota translators, provided some clues as to the use of vocables in the translations of her songs mainly from the Standing Rock reservation.[11] Clearly however she did not pay much attention to the vocables as she did to the texts. Where vocables do appear they are italicized in the running text of the song written beneath their respective notes. But once extracted from the melody, she excluded the vocables and arranged only the words in columns. The following examples provide a comparison between her text-with-melody; her text separated from the melody; and my revised text and translation in which the orthography has been slightly modified to conform to the acceptable form of writing by native speakers. The song is titled (by Densmore; Lakota songs have no titles) "The Horseman in the Cloud," and was sung by Lone Man.[12]

1. Text with melody:
   Ma-ka-ta e-ton-wan yo e-ton-wan yo le-na
   ni-ta-wa kte-lo ma-ka-ta e-ton-wan yo le-na
   ni-ta-wa ye-lo *he* ma-ka-ta e-ton
   wan yo le-na ni-ta-wa ye-lo *he yo*

2. Separated text:

maka'ta	the earth
e'tonwan yo	behold
lena	all these
nita'wa	yours
ktelo	will be
maka'ta	the earth
e'tonwan yo	behold
lena	all these
nita'wa yelo	(are) yours

3. My revision:
   Makata etunwan yo
   Makata etunwan yo
   Lena nitawa kte lo
   Makata etunwan yo
   Hee lena nitawa yelo
   Makata etunwan yo
   Lena nitawa yelo *hee yo*

   My translation:
   "Look toward the earth!
   Look toward the earth!
   All these things will be yours.
   Look toward the earth!
   Hee all these things are yours.
   Look toward the earth!
   All these things are yours *hee yo*."

In comparing examples 1 and 2 above, we see that Densmore in the first example writes linearly in such a way that the syllables of the Lakota line up underneath the musical notes. She uses a convention of hyphenating syllables in the same word; and she italicizes the vocables. In the second example however, she simply arranges the lexical items in two columns, Lakota on the left and English on the right, a convention that she uses for all examples in *Teton Sioux Music*. Interestingly enough, Densmore must not have thought of the text as poetry, even though Kenneth Rexroth hailed her as one of the finest translators of American Indian songs. As one can see from comparing the two examples above that Densmore never ventures a free translation of the songs she so assiduously recorded and notated. Her only translations are in the form of glosses.

It should also be noted that in the second example, the repeat of "Maka etunwan yo" in the first line of example 1 is eliminated, probably because Densmore wanted to provide only a translation of the lexical items without giving much attention to their meaning either in the translations per se or in the exegeses provided by her or her respondents. The songs are only loosely placed in a cultural context, but we frequently are confronted with the simple fact that we do not have the slightest idea of what the song means in any context. This probably was acceptable in the past because Densmore's columnar correspondences between Lakota and English renders the disconnected words somewhat mysteriously to the non-Lakota, precisely a position that English-speaking scholars have felt comfortable with when writing about what they perceived to be the "primitive" nature of American Indian verse.

But of course the songs do have meaning, although perhaps it is impossible to reconstruct all of them in Densmore's work, or in those of others who did similar translating in the past. In my revision 3 I attempt to place the fluidity of Densmore's first example of texts as they appear in the musically notated version into a freer context, one which requires some knowledge of Lakota culture as well as song structure so that the texts, once separated from the melody, may be aligned on the page with some sort of defensible structure and translation.

In my revision, I have arranged the line endings to correspond with Lakota enclitics and vocables (even though Densmore provides only three vocables, I am positive that there had to be more in all of the songs). I also retain the repetitious materials in the first stanza of the song (my first two lines).

In lines 1, 2, and 4, the final syllable is a male imperative enclitic. I do not use an exclamation mark in the Lakota because the "yo" serves the same function. However, in the translation of the same lines, I convert the Lakota "yo" into an English exclamation mark.

In lines 3, 5, and 7, "lo" is a male declarative enclitic. In line 3 the line ends with "kta" (which becomes "kte" when penultimate or final in the sentence) which is the future enclitic. The "lo" is an abbreviated form of "yelo" which appears in lines 5 and 7 and which is a male declarative enclitic.

Since enclitics always end the sentence in Lakota (unless there is a direct quote followed by an attributive in which case the attributive is last), then it is clear that the Native composer conceptualizes the lines as they appear in my revision. Also, this justifies placing the vocable *hee* in line 5 as an introduction to the line rather than as an ending to line 4. Alternately, the final vocables probably represent cadential formulas in all of Densmore's translations.

Finally, the entire song is in quotes because of cultural considerations. In Lakota, songs learned in a vision usually comprise words of advice, prediction, or even warnings from the spirits appearing in the visions and who sing the song to the supplicant. Sometimes there is an interchange indicated in the text in which attributives are used. In these interchanges dialogs attributed to the spirits are interspersed with statements of fact. In the case of this song, however, the entire song is a statement by the spirit to the supplicant, therefore I have placed the entire song in quotes. It should be noted that the context of the song, not the texts themselves, indicate the need for quotation marks.

Natalie Curtis's translation of Lakota songs, while frequently offering questionable meaning, are usually very good from the perspective of vocable. Like Densmore, she frequently notated the melody of the song with interlinear translations.[13] The following example will help me make my first point about meaning. This song does not appear notated at all; only these texts and translations appear:

> Hocoka wan cicuqon
> Yutokanl nunwe

which she translates:

> In this circle,
> O ye warriors,
> Lo, I tell you
> Each his future.
> All shall be
> As I now reveal it
> In this circle;
>   Hear ye![14]

Since there is no other information provided by the author, it is difficult to determine whether vocables appeared in the original song, although from cultural knowledge one must assume that they did and that she simply eliminated them from the text because she, unlike Densmore, was more interested in ascribing some kind of poetic virtue to the texts, even though she was apparently driven more by her own sense of what poetry should be, rather than guided by the texts themselves and particularly the context in which they appear. I suspect that vocables may very well have appeared in the Lakota where we find exclamatory words like "O" and "Lo" which Curtis frequently uses in other translations, as if English exclamations were in fact glosses for Lakota vocables.

As to the actual translation of the song above, my revision reads:

> Hocoka wan
> Cic'u k'un
> Yutokanl
> Nunwe

which, translated, reads:

> The center of the universe
> That I once gave you

Is somewhere else
So be it.

Curtis has of course missed the point completely. In this vision song, the spirit is making the comment about white encroachment on Lakota land and culture. But the point here is that if Curtis were to have notated the song, from what we can observe from the next song, then at least the spacing of the texts would have more or less conformed to the original song because the vocables justify line endings and spacing.

As a much better example of Curtis's work I choose a Fox Society song, which Curtis presents along with the melody as well as extracted from the melody. In the first case, interestingly, Curtis faithfully records not only the melody and texts of the song, but she indicates the entire introductory part of the song which is sung in vocables only.[15]

E ha e. . . . yo e. . . yo he yee
E ha e. . . e. . . . yo he ye ye ye
E ha e. . . . e. . . . yo he-ye yo yo
E ha e. . . . yo e. . . . he ye yo
He ye e ye yo!
To-ka-la-ka mi-ye ca- . . ya ya,
Na-ke-nu-la wa-on we - . . lo . . ,
We ha e . . . yo e . . . yo . . . he ye yo!

She translates the text:

Lo, the Fox, the Fox am I. . . . . . . yea, yea,
Still a Fox, a moment yet, . . . then,
Then the Fox shall be . . . no . . . more. . . . . . .

When Curtis writes the text without the melodic transcription, however, it appears:

Tokalaka miye ca,
Nakenunla waon we

which she translates:

Lo, the Fox, the Fox am I!
Still the Fox a moment yet,
Then the Fox shall be no more.

A better rendering of the original and translation would be:

Tokala k'un miye ca
Nakenunla waun we

I am a Fox
I am here out of choice[16]

With respect to the placement of vocables in the texts accompanying the melodic transcription, it is possible to superimpose the texts upon the vocables appearing in the notated form, and assuming that Curtis's rendering of the vocables are acceptable (which I believe they are) then we can reconstruct the entire song (with new orthography and translation) in the following way:

> *E ha ee yo ee yoo he ye ye*
> *E ha ee yo ee yoo he ye ye ye*
> *E ha ee yo ee yoo he ye yoo yo*
> *E haa e yo ee yoo he ye yo*
> *He ye e ye yo*
>
> *E ha ee yo ee yoo he ye ye*
> Tokala k'un miye ca *ye ye*
> Nakenunla waun welo
> *E haa e yo ee yoo he ye yo*
> *He ye e ye yo*

The only liberty I have taken is to make lines 4 and 5 of each rendition coincide. This is based not on my knowledge of the song per se but of my understanding of the structure of these types of songs.

L. W. Colby,[17] who collected Ghost Dance songs at Pine Ridge, provides a good example of how the inclusion of vocables as well as other semantic features, might have contributed to a better understanding of how the lines to this one song should end.

Colby's rendering:

Howo micinkxi, howo micinkxi.
Le cico qon wanna, yahi ye, yahi ye;
Maka kin le icu wo, maka kin le icu wo
Akal inicagin kte, akal inicagin kte;
Haye eyayo, haye eyayo.

Colby's translation:

My son return now thou art come,
My son return now thou art come;
Take this land, take this land;
Thou shalt live on, thou shalt live on.
Tell this, tell this.[18]

My revision:

Howo micinkši
Howo micinkši
Le cico k'un wana yahi *ye*
Yahi *ye*
Maka kin le icu wo
Maka kin le icu wo

Akanl inicagin kte
Akanl inicagin kte
Ha ye e ya yo
Ha ye e ya yo

My translation:

All right my son
All right my son
I called you and now you've come *ye*
You've come *ye*
Take this earth
Take this earth
Grow upon it
Grow upon it
Ha ye e ya yo
Ha ye e ya yo

It is not clear from Colby whether the last two lines of the song are composed of vocables or a mistranslation of *Ate heye lo, Ate heye lo,* "The Father said that, The Father said that," which is a typical Ghost Dance song ending, as are the vocables that I have underscored in my revision. If they are texts, then Colby's translations are far off the mark.

Now I would like to turn to my own work and give some examples of the use of the vocable and other grammatical considerations in the translations of some more modern Lakota songs.[19]

World War II Song

Kawita au welo
He ye he ye ye
Ohitika weksuye lo *yo*
He ye he ye ye
Kola toki iyaye lo
He ye he ye yo

Translation:

When the people gather
He ye he ye ye
I remember Brave *yo*
He ye he ye ye
My friend who passed away
He ye he ye yo

Here lines 2, 4, and 6 are cadential formulas quite typical of songs of this genre. In line 3 note the contrast between "lo," a declarative enclitic, and *yo,* a vocable. This song dates back to prereservation days but is still sung for soldiers who died in World War II. The expression *toki iyaye,* "gone away," is a metaphor for passing away.

Giveaway Song

Wamniomni k'un blihic'iya yo
Lakol wicoȟ'an kin waštewalake c'un
   Oteȟike lo *yo*
    He ye he ye ye
Maka kin hecena tehan yunke lo
He ye he ye ye
Wanbli Wašte k'un heyin na iyaye lo
He ye he ye yo

Translation:

"Whirlwind, take courage.
I love the Lakota way
But it's hard to do *yo*
He ye he ye ye
My son, only the earth lasts forever."
Good Eagle said this and started off
He ye he ye yo

In this song, line 1 ends with a male imperative enclitic, but the *yo* seen in lines 3 and 8 are vocables. Lines 3 and 5 are standardized cadential formulas found in Giveaway and other types of social dance songs. This is a peculiar song in that two proper names appear. Although not indicated in the text per se, cultural knowledge informs me that the two are related. Good Eagle is the father of Whirlwind, hence the addition of "my son" in line 5.

Omaha Dance Song

Wanbli Wašte k'un *yun*
Cangleška kin yuha yahi cana
Iyokipimayaye lo
He ye he ye o-oi
Tehan yaun eyaš
Ohinniyan ciksuya waun kte lo
He ye he ye yo

Translation:

Good Eagle *yun*
When you come with your hoop
You make me happy
He ye he ye o-oi
Even though you are far away
I will always be remembering you
He ye he ye yo

In line 1 we have an example of the vocable *yun,* which rhymes with the previous word. "K'un" conventionally follows a proper name but as such has no translation value. In ordinary discourse, "k'un" is a form of the definite article "kin" and indicates that the subject that it modifies has been mentioned before in the conversation. It also mildly suggests past tense. When used in songs however, "k'un" simply sets a proper name apart from the remainder of text in which it appears.

Also noteworthy is the vocable written *o-oi.* I have hyphenated it to indicate that the entire vocable falls on two eighth-note beats, but that the second part of the vocable is actually a diphthong, the only one found in Lakota vocables.

Rabbit Dance Song:

Deary ye miye ca *ya* miye ca *ya*
Waci waun *we yo he ye he ye ye*
Heȟag winyan *miye ca ya*
Ohinniyan acitun waun *wee yee*
We ya ha ya we ya ha ya yo

Deary *ye* it is me *ya* it is me *ya*
I am here at the dance *we yo he ye we yo he*
Elk woman it is me *ya*
I am always staring at you *wee yee*
We ya ha ya we ya ha ya yo

This song provides a good example of vocables interspersed rather evenly through every strophe in the song. In line 1 the first word is the English expression *deary.* When sung it sounds more like *a te a re.* Note that some vocables rhyme with the preceding word. Elk woman in this case is not a proper name but a slang expression in Lakota for a flirtatious woman. It is the female counterpart of *heȟaka,* "elk," which is in colloquial Lakota equivalent to "stud."

Conclusion

What I have attempted to do in this essay is simply to call attention to the structure and the function of the vocable and demonstrate how they affect the translation of the songs in which they originally appeared. I suggest that the retention of the vocables in the graphic translations of the songs similarly enhances the subject matter and meaning of the attendant texts through various prosodic devices that I have labeled poetic functions of the vocable.

Since Lakota traditionalists find unacceptable the whole idea of separating texts from the melodies in which they are an integral part, I cannot in all fairness suggest that the addition of vocables to the translation of songs will be totally acceptable to them. I do know, however, that younger Native Americans have been experimenting with a number of different literary and musical forms, not the least of which is the wide inclusion of vocables in folk songs largely composed with English or Native texts and sung to the accompaniment of guitar or other recently introduced instruments.

Whether acceptable or not in an ethnographic sense, I still want to emphasize that vocables are subject to a great deal of rigorous structure, and form an integral part of the song structure of all American Indian songs today. Vocables are not related to particular musical notes as they are say in the Indian ragas of the Asian subcontinent. However, once composed, American Indian songs are at least partly recognizable on the basis of the particular configuration of vocables that the Native songmaker chose to compose the song, and the relationship between vocables, and between vocables and texts, is governed by rules.

There is a strong inclination in modern performance studies to suggest that Native American song texts can be recited in public and that the inclusion of vocables in the performance will make the poetry have a more dramatic effect. I do know that when reading to college students, vocables certainly do have a dramatic effect perhaps because the vocables sound so distinctly "Indian" to an audience that usually knows little about American Indian culture and even less about American Indian music and dance.

American Indian poets, like their folk-singer counterparts, do of course employ vocables in their own poetry, but it is unlikely that even they will have the power to change the minds of their traditionalist forebears. It is unknown just what kind of lasting effect any contributions made in the name of the vocable will have on those people who have invented them and used them so poetically. Nevertheless, I believe that a better understanding of the structure and function of the vocable will be useful in understanding fundamental principles of composition and performance, since vocables do seem to be a universal feature of song.

Acknowledgments

Research on the methodological considerations of the vocable has been made possible by a generous grant from the Translations Division, National Endowment for the Humanities (AY 1989–91), for which I am sincerely grateful.

Notes

1. For a more detailed study of the vocable see Powers 1987: Chapter 1. Other important works include Frisbie 1980, which focuses on Navajo vocables but which also contains the most comprehensive bibliography on the subject. See also Halpern 1976; Nettl 1953; and Powers 1961a and 1961b.

2. The essential works are Buechel 1939 and 1970.

3. My argument is condensed in Powers 1990.

4. For other examples of dialectal influences on the vocable see Powers 1987.

5. For his most recent work on the Blackfeet see Nettl 1989: 70.

6. For example, the vocable *c'e,* which is used by William Horncloud, a prominent Lakota singer from Pine Ridge.

7. This contains a slight revision of my earlier work on the vocable in Powers 1987.

8. Signal functions are those that are related to the melodic line: they serve to carry the tune, emphasize rhythmic patterns, identify genres of songs, and cue singers and dancers.

9. The other three are mimetic, ornamentative, and mnemonic functions discussed in Powers 1987.

10. This is a revision of a review of Yankton Peyote songs in Powers 1981.

11. Densmore 1918.

12. Densmore 1918:160–61.

13. Curtis 1907.

14. Curtis 1907:49.

15. Curtis 1907:73–74. I have underscored the vocables for consistency. Curtis writes them in her own hand beneath the music notation. She uses dots and hyphens to separate vocables so that they appear directly beneath their respective notes.

16. "Nakenunla waun we" has many connotations. The expression was used by warriors belonging to the Fox society, who had the option of staying at home but instead chose to go to war. It is not so far removed from the English sentiment, "You've made your bed, now lie in it."

17. Colby 1895.

18. Colby 1895:145.

19. The remainder of songs were collected by me at Pine Ridge beginning in 1950. All of them are still sung at contemporary celebrations.

References

Buechel, Reverend Eugene, S. J. 1939. *Grammar of Lakota.* St. Louis: John S. Swift Company.
———. 1970. *Lakota-English Dictionary.* Edited by Reverend Paul Manhardt. Pine Ridge, South Dakota: Red Cloud Indian School.
Colby, L. W. 1895. Wanagi Olowan Kin. *Proceedings and Collections of the Nebraska State Historical Society* 1(3): 131–50.
Curtis, Natalie. 1907. *The Indians' Book.* New York: Dover.
Densmore, Frances. 1918. *Teton Sioux Music.* Bureau of American Ethnology Bulletin 61. Washington, D.C. Government Printing Office.
Frisbie, Charlotte J. 1980. Vocables in Navajo Ceremonial Music. *Ethnomusiciology* 24(3): 347–92.
Halpern, Ida. 1976. On the Interpretation of "Meaningless-Nonsensical Syllables" in the Music of the Pacific Northwest Indians. *Ethnomusicology* 20(2): 253–71.
Nettl, Bruno. 1953. Observations on Meaningless Peyote Song Texts. *Journal of American Folklore* 66:161–64.
———. 1989. *Blackfoot Musical Thought.* Kent, Ohio: Kent State University Press.
Powers, William K. 1961a. The Sioux Omaha Dance. *American Indian Tradition* 8(1): 24–33.
———. 1961b. American Indian Music: Contemporary Music and Dance of the Western Sioux. *American Indian Tradition* 7(5): 158–65.
———. 1981. Toward a Sound Ethnography of Native American Music. Discographic Review Essay. *Ethnomusicology* 25(1): 159–62.

———. 1987. *Beyond the Vision: Essays on American Indian Culture*. Norman: University of Oklahoma Press.

———. 1990. Comment on the Politics of Orthography. *American Anthropologist* 92(2): 496–98.

Suggested Reading

Given the predominance of the vocable in American Indian (and other) music, there is a relative paucity of literature on the subject. However, those interested in theories of the evolution of the vocable and music in general should consult my "The Vocable: An Evolutionary Perspective" in *Beyond the Vision: Essays on American Indian Culture* (Oklahoma, 1987) and "Incomprehensible Terms" in my *Sacred Language: The Nature of Supernatural Discourse in Lakota* (Oklahoma, 1986).

The earliest mention of the vocable is in Alice C. Fletcher's *Indian Story and Song from North America* (Boston: Small and Maynard, 1900) and in Frances Densmore's classic *Teton Sioux Music* (Bulletin 61, Bureau of American Ethnology, Washington, D.C., 1918). The most definitive article on the place of the vocable in song of a singular tribe is that of Charlotte J. Frisbie's "Vocables in Navajo Ceremonial Music" (*Ethnomusicology* 24(3): 347–92, 1980).

Part Three:
Central
and
South
America

Have
We
Really
Translated
the
Mesoamerican
"Ancient
Word"?

Miguel León-Portilla

Archaeological vestiges, including glyphic inscriptions, mural paintings, and a few colored pictoglyphic books, are the only per se unobjectionable extant testimonies left by Mesoamerican civilization. Certainly, among the archaeological evidence, ruins of magnificent temples and palaces and the many other objects described today as "the art of Mesomerica" stand out. But for testimonies truly pre-Hispanic telling something more explicit, one has to restrict oneself to the inscriptions in stone or on ceramics and to the pictoglyphic books. The rest, that is, the other testimonies, shall be described as compilations and productions, either pictorial, or written in Spanish or in an indigenous language in the years following European domination. Although obviously more explicit, they are elaborations in one way or another, produced in the colonial epoch.

The achievements of Mesoamerican archaeological research are already great. They have unveiled an impressive cultural skeleton whose scattered bones appear to be waiting for a breath of life that would restore their spirit, flesh, and meaning. But, where may such breath of life come from? Will it arrive only from the per se unobjectionable, though still not fully deciphered, messages of the inscriptions, and from the no more than fifteen extant pre-Hispanic pictoglyphic books?

Many researchers have believed that to rescue the spirit and meaning of ancient Mesoamerica, the other testimonies, those produced in the colonial years, must also be taken into account. And every day more and more such testimonies have been consulted, interpreted, and translated. Working in this manner, one thought the ancient word had been approached, that some of the skeleton's scattered bones had been reassembled and the obscurities of the inscriptions and the pictoglyphic books illumined.

But now, influenced by perhaps more penetrating critical considerations originally expressed by scholars concerned with other cultures, challenging questions are being addressed to those scholars who believed they had approached and translated at least something of the Mesoamerican ancient word, to those scholars working with testimonies claimed to be reliable, even though produced in colonial times. The challenge implies a gamut of possible consequences. The most serious would be that one had been working on the false premises of testimonies deeply contaminated by the Euro-Christian presence. We have believed the ancient word had been approached, its meaning disclosed, rescued, and translated. But now some researchers say that such has not been the case.

Challenging Questions

Several scholars concerned with classical Greek studies and also with contemporary ethnological research have focused their attention during the last few decades on what is described as "orality" vis-à-vis the written word. One scholar in particular has subjected to rigorous critical analysis the consequences of the process through which what is orally transmitted becomes committed to permanently fixed linear alphabetic writing. Erik Havelock has studied such a process in the case of Greek culture during that time (around the seventh century B.C.) during which the originally sung poems of the *Iliad* and the *Odyssey* were committed to an unalterable linear alphabetic script. It was the time when, as Havelock puts it, "the muse learned to write." In such a process, many of the original attributes of the classical poems were lost. Spontaneity, which allowed for enrichment and the introduction of various other changes in the poems, including the music that accompanied their recitation, the living nature of that which is communicated orally, disappeared. In contrast, a text forever fixed, committed to alphabetic writing, resulted from the process (Havelock, 1986).

Parallel considerations have been discussed by researchers such as John A. Goody, whose field is ethnology or cultural anthropology. All processes of obtaining "texts" from native informants belonging to a different culture, they say, involve a long series of risks. The informant, who may be in possession of traditions belonging to his people, once exposed to interrogations from a researcher who is foreign to him, will react in a nonspontaneous manner. He may say what he feels is going to please the researcher or fit what he is looking for. The informant, confronted with questions derived from a different world view, may not only misunderstand them but may also try to conceal what he considers sacred to him and therefore not to be communicated to foreigners (Goody 1977).

In both cases, in the processes of conversion from orality to fixed script within the same culture, as in the Greek case, or in situations of intercultural contact, as in the anthropologist-informant relation, many of the original and perhaps essential attributes of the oral tradition become lost or deeply contaminated. The underlined consequence is that the written texts thus obtained do not correspond to the cultural tradition which for hundreds of years was communicated through orality.

Drawing from these arguments, several contemporary Mesoamericanists have come to question the reliability of the testimonies in Nahuatl, Yucatec-Maya, Quiché, and other languages committed after the Conquest to linear alphabetic writing. It is said that by the mere act of converting indigenous orality into fixed texts, that which was recited or sung becomes radically altered. Orality, open always to enrichment and adaptations within changing circumstances, cannot be incarcerated, reduced to linear alphabetic writing, transformed into something totally alien to the native culture. Such a transformation did not fit into the mental procedures associated with the indigenous world view (Grusinskey 1988, 51–70). Besides, in the process of trying to convert oral tradition into written "texts," many cultural contaminations take place. The process was provoked by a person belonging to another culture, who asked questions according to his own preconceptions and with aims also alien to his informant. The latter most probably felt disturbed and, forced or insistently induced, came to tell what he considered adequate to satisfy his inquirer, concealing what could be risky to reveal. Even in cases in which the relation of inquirer-informant occurred in more friendly circumstances, as with Indians already converted to Christianity, the process would not escape alienation or cultural contamination and many other kinds of possible distortions, including those resulting from the not insignificant circumstance of having an already "converted" informant (Klor de Alva 1988, 45–47).

The conclusions reached by those contemporary Mesoamericanists—conscious or unconscious followers of the critical approaches of Havelock, Goody, and others—are negative for the most part. In a few words, they can be stated as follows: the extant "texts" in Nahuatl, Yucatec-Maya, and other native languages, resulting from post-conquest ethnohistorical inquiry, cannot be taken as testimonies of the pre-Hispanic culture. At best they can reflect something of the situation of cultural confrontation and trauma in which they were written, obtained from the induced interrogations to which not a few natives were submitted (Burkhart 1989, 5). Therefore, to believe that "texts" or compositions like those in the *Florentine Codex*, the *Cantares Mexicanos*, or the *Annals of Cuauhtitlan*, among others, can be trusted as true pre-Hispanic testimonies is not only naive but extremely dangerous, leading to fictitious representations of a culture that did not exist in the manner depicted in those texts.

Such a conclusion is equally dramatic for those of us who, patiently applying available linguistic and philological resources, have translated some of those texts into European languages. In dealing with them, translating them, or quoting from them for historical purposes, we have not understood what in fact they are. Instead of being testimonies of the ancient Native word, they reflect the forced answers of the vanquished vis-à-vis the imposed attitudes of the invaders and foreign lords, civil and ecclesiastical, anxious to know about Indian beliefs, practices, riches, tributes, and so on, anxious to seize what may be of profit and to expurgate whatever was designated as evil from the native's soul.

So what can we say, those of us who believe we were translators of the ancient word? Will it be worthwhile to try to retranslate "the texts" in view of such a new understanding of how they were obtained and what they conveyed?

The Book as Seen by the Mesoamericans

As a point of departure to consider the conclusions at which some Americanists have arrived concerning early colonial indigenous written texts, I deem it pertinent to pay attention to the existence not only of orality, including that derived from the formal memorizing in the priestly schools or *calmecac*, but also of books or codices in Mesoamerica. And in order to do so more effectively, I will compare the Mesoamerican experience with that of the Quechuas in the Incan days of splendor. The Peruvian Quechuas kept various kinds of records by means of their quipus, arrangements of cords variously colored and knotted. But while the utility of the quipus has been duly appreciated, it is also recognized that the Quechuas had neither writing nor books.

When the first encounter between the Inca Atahualpa and Francisco Pizarro took place in Cajamarca on November 16, 1532, something occurred which reveals the Inca's reaction at the moment a Spanish book was put in his hands. The episode is recounted by the chronicler Francisco de Jerez and by the Quechua Guamán Poma. According to the latter, once Pizarro had spoken to Atahualpa, assisted by the Guancabilcan Indian interpreter Felipe, the chaplain, Father Vicente Velarde, began to preach. He told Atahualpa he had been sent to Christianize him and his people. The Inca responded that he knew very well whom he should worship: the Sun and his other gods.

And the said Inca asked Father Vicente what he preached. Friar Vicente answered that it was the Gospel, the Book. And Atahualpa said: Give it to me, the book, in order for it to tell me. And it was given to him. And he looked at it and turned its pages. And the Inca said: It does not tell me anything. Then, with great majesty, seated on his throne, Atahualpa threw the book from him (Guamán Poma de Ayala, fol. 385 1987, II, 392).

Atahualpa's reaction to the silent book brought on tragic consequences. Father Velarde, who was not only conscious of what a book was, but knew this book was the Bible, exclaimed: "Quick, *caballeros*, let us fight these gentile Indians, enemies of our faith!" Thus, ignorance of the nature of a book resulted in a battle and the imprisonment of poor Atahualpa who, even with all the gold he gave to Pizarro, could not move him to spare his life.

The reaction of a Mesoamerican native when he first contemplated a Spanish book was different. We owe the story to the chronicler Peter Martyr of Anghiera who, in the service of the Catholic Kings, collected all sorts of information from the lips of those coming from the New World whom he could interview. He tells of a certain Corrales who, around 1514, served in the civil administration of Darién in Panama. He informed Peter Martyr about the following experience:

> One day he met a native who had escaped from the vast lands of the interior [probably from an area where Mesoamerican culture extended]. Corrales was reading. The native jumped, full of joy, and by means of an interpreter, exclaimed: How is this? You also have books and use painted signs to communicate with the absent? And saying this, he asked to see the book in the belief that he was about to see the writing he was familiar with, but he discovered it was different (Pedro Martyr de Anghiera 1964, I, 381–82).

The Mesoamericans had an idea of what a book was; it was something close to a book in Western culture. The Nahuatl word *amoxtli* conveys such an idea. Derived from *ama(tl)* and *oxitl*, it literally means "glued sheets of paper." On those glued pieces of paper made of the mashed bark of the *amate* tree (a ficus), paintings and glyphs were drawn.

It is significant to find that the *tlamatini*, "the one who knows," that is, the Nahuatl sage, is described as "he who possesses the *amoxtli* and the black and red inks" (*Florentine Codex* 1979, III, X, fol. 19 v.). A more vivid picture of the relation between sage and book is offered by the words some ordinary people addressed to the twelve Franciscans who arrived in Mexico in 1524. When the friars began their preaching, telling the Nahuas that they did not know the true God, the people responded by confessing their ignorance but adding that there were others, their guides, who were the possessors of wisdom. They were described as both masters of the word and of what was recorded in their books (*Libro de los Colloquios* 1986, 140–41):

> There are those who guide us . . .
> The priests, those who make the offerings . . . ,
> The *tlahtomatinimeh*, sages of the word . . .
> who contemplate,
> follow the contents of the books,
> noisely turn their pages, who possess
> the red, the black inks,
> who keep with them the paintings. . . .
> They carry us, guide us,
> those who keep the order of the years
> and know how the days and destinies
> follow their own way.

Among these sages and priests, who, according to the same account, came to confer with the friars in defense of their beliefs, there were some who, according to the *Florentine Codex*, "taught the young people all their songs, their divine songs, *teocuicatl*, following the contents of their books (*amoxotoca*)" (1979, III, lib. III, fol. 39 r.). *Amoxotoca* is a compound of *amox*(tli), "book" and *o-toca*, "follow the way," (from *oh-tli*, "way," and *toca*, "to follow"). By this word a process is delineated in which the sages' eyes followed the paintings and "characters," that is, the pictoglyphic sequences of the codex. One must note that the quotation states precisely that "following the contents of the books," the sages "taught the young people all their songs, the divine songs." In other words, a relation of book and song is indicated, that is, between what is orally transmitted and what is pictoglyphically registered.

To investigate the nature of such a relationship seems of prime importance as it can shed light on the theme under discussion. It is true that in Mesoamerica most of the extant indigenous "texts" committed to alphabetic linear writing were orally transmitted. But here we have a reference—and there are many others from the central highlands, from Oaxaca and the Maya area—which state that what was orally transmitted derived from "following" the sequences of the pictoglyphic contents of the books. Let us therefore consider the relationship prevailing in Mesoamerica between books and songs, or more amply, books and the "ancient word."

The Relationship of Book to "Ancient Word"

The testimonies, both Spanish and indigenous, concerning the existence of books and libraries (*amoxcalli*) in ancient Mexico are rather abundant. Above all it has to be recalled that, notwithstanding burnings and other forms of disappearance, there are today some fifteen codices of unquestionable pre-Hispanic origin. They come from the central highlands, the Mixtec area and the Maya zone. From their contents they can be described as *tonalamatl*, or books of the counts of the day-destinies, *Xiuhamatl* and *tlacamecayoamatl*, books of the years and lineages, thus of a historical nature, and *teoamatl*, books about divine things.

The fifteen extant pre-Hispanic codices provide examples of these genres. We know in addition, either by references to them or because of the existence of other pictoglyphic productions from the early colonial years, that several other book-genres existed. Among these were the *tequi-amatl* or tribute records, the *tlal-amatl*, landbooks or a kind of cadastrial record, as well as maps and charts of towns, provinces, and larger regions with precise indications of their most salient geographical features. And there are references (provided, among others, by Bernardino de Sahagún's informants) to *cuica-amatl*, "books of songs," and *temic-amatl*, "books of dreams"—the latter probably related to the *tonal-amatl*, or books of the day-destinies employed to formulate astrological diagnosis and predictions. And, as we will see later, according to Friar Andrés de Olmos, there were even books which conveyed more complex compositions such as the *Huehuehtlahtolli*, or testimonies of the "Ancient Word." Later I will discuss whether in this case the "reading" was only a mnemonic device to stimulate the recalling of what was learned by heart in the schools as a sort of formal oral tradition.

The Spanish Conquest did not mean the end of book-production in Native Mesoamerica. Several scores of very important codices have been preserved which are either copies of pre-Hispanic books or derive from them (some convey to various degrees the influence of European culture). These postconquest codices include at times glosses in Nahuatl, Mixtec, Otomi, Spanish, and even Latin. Thus they appear as a sort of bridge that links the indigenous culture with intrusive elements of a new dominant society. While those culturally Mestizo codices were sometimes employed as a sort of Rosetta Stone to approach the contents of the truly native books, they also may have provided culturally contaminated and, therefore, misleading information.

Today, more than ever before, researchers are working to decipher the glyphic contents of extant pre-Hispanic books. Undoubtedly, substantial knowledge has been gained, relating in particular to the more complex and precise Maya system of writing. But while this has been taking place, the question which interests us here remains open: What was the relationship of book to "ancient word," the relationship between orality and the pictoglyphic sequences included in the books and the inscriptions? Any inquiry about such a relationship has much to do with the subject of indigenous orality and its commitment to linear alphabetic writing in colonial Mesoamerica.

As we will see, the natives, the friars and other Spaniards, living in different places within Mesoamerica (mainly the central highlands, Oaxaca, and the Maya area), coincide in their assertions about the character of the books as repositories of knowledge. They all insistently repeat that the sages and priests taught in their schools the songs, discourses, prayers, and so on by means of these books. In the case of the Nahuas they even use words like "read" the book, or in Nahuatl *tlapoa*, "recite" that which is inscribed therein.

Obviously it will be necessary to introduce distinctions between the "reading" of the pictoglyphic books of the Nahuas and Mixtecs vis-à-vis the contents of the Maya books and inscriptions. In the case of the Maya, it is today universally recognized they had developed an authentic logosyllabic system of writing. By logosyllabic writing I mean a system structured by two kinds of glyphic elements: logograms representing whole words or a variety of morphemes, mainly affixes, and phonograms denoting syllabic sounds. Maya writing is therefore a mixed system in which complex graphemes can be structured in the shape of a "cartouche." By means of such logosyllabic graphemes, Maya writing can represent a variety of specific denotations: substantival, verbal, adjectival, and so on. In other words, it is an authentic writing system.

For their part, the Mixtecs and Nahuas were in possession of a system, if not as developed as that of the Mayas, effective enough to convey what they wanted to communicate. It has often been repeated by most researchers that the effectiveness of such a system depended on its being linked to oral tradition, in particular to that which was formally memorized in the pre-Hispanic schools. To discern the potentials of the script which, with minor differences, was shared by the Mixtecs, Nahuas, and others, poses a real problem. Contrary to the idea of the large majority of researchers, the group headed by Professor Joaquín Galarza claims that such script was so developed that, by itself, it could convey all kinds of messages (Galarza 1972).

Perhaps the main difficulty in appreciating the full potential of such script derives from the fact of the limited number of extant pre-Hispanic books and inscriptions from the Mixtecs and Nahuas. In the case of the Maya, to compensate for the paucity of extant codices, there are thousands of inscriptions on monuments and various objects.

Nevertheless, the study of the writing in the Mixtec historical codices, conducted mainly by Alfonso Caso (1960, 1964, 1966, and 1973) and Mary Elizabeth Smith (1963, 1966, and 1972) is particularly revealing. Caso identifies a rich ensemble of graphemes, some of them ideograms and others of a logosyllabic character, although not as frequent nor as semantically expressive as those developed by the Maya. The ensemble includes precise chronological ideograms, names of persons and places, and geographical symbols. Other ideograms denote celestial bodies; metereological and geological phenomena, such as earthquakes; religious concepts and practices; a range of objects such as flowers, plants, trees, animals, dresses, ornaments, instruments, and metals; a variety of stones; diverse genres of cultivated fields, houses, palaces, temples, and marketplaces; as well as attributes of the gods and dignitaries, performances of several ceremonies, including those related to a person's birth, marriage, and death.

The study of the extant Nahua pre-Hispanic codices permits us to extend to them what Caso, Smith, and others tell us about Mixtec writing. Besides, one has to note that in both Mixtec and Nahua scripts there are graphemes which represent abstract ideas such as movement, direction, authority, nobility, war, penance, and many others. An incipient logosyllabic character in the script can be observed through the employment of graphemes with phonetic connotations to which other elements are attached as kinds of affixes, above all in the case of place names and in those accompanied by reverential or minimizing denotations.

The existence of graphemes with verbal connotations has been also documented in both the Mixtec and Nahua manuscripts. Among others, one can cite those for "to obey," "to push," "to conquer," "to walk," "to die," "to be born," "to smell," "to smoke," "to escape," "to speak," "to sing," "to cry," and so on. Taking into account not only the truly pre-Hispanic Mixtec and Nahua books but also the more abundant books from the early colonial period, many more elements pertaining to indigenous writing can be noted.

Some of these elements have been the subject of contrasting critical approaches. Some scholars see in them an outgrowth of the pre-Hispanic system, but already influenced by the Euro-Christian presence, as in the case of the so called "Testerian Catechisms," in which a rebus is amply employed. But we may doubt that many of those elements are found in the pre-Hispanic system, precisely because of the scarcity of the extant codices. If this were the case, and it seems to be in some instances in which the extant colonial codices appear to be early copies of pre-Hispanic books, one can accept as genuinely native those other graphemes appearing therein. One example of those graphemes, rich in actually exploited derivational or compositional potentials, is that which denotes the syllable *ix*. The grapheme has the aspect of an eye, thus revealing it was conceived after the word *ixtli*, which means "eye" in Nahuatl. Alone, or as part of a composition, such a grapheme—as Orozco y Berra has demonstrated (1880)—could denote a gamut of ideas and objects, among them the verbs "to see or observe" and "to cry," as well as substantives like *coaix*, "serpent's eye" (a penetrant eye), *ixayotl*, "tear," *ixpopoyotl*, "a blind person," as well as the idea of "surface," mainly in place names like *xal-ix-co*, "on the sandy surface," *atl-ix-co*, "on the surface of the water," and so on.

To all these glyphic elements one has to add, of course, the complex semantic value of the pictorial representations included in the indigenous books. Most of them convey ensembles of other symbolic elements, of which colors are not the least important.

Images of the universe, like those appearing on page 1 of the *Codex Fejérváry-Mayer* or *Tonalamatl of the Pochtecas* (merchants), and on pages 75–76 of the Maya *Codex Tro-Cortesiano*, portrary a universe of symbolic references at least as rich as those of the Medieval charts, such as the so-called maps of the *Beatus*, conceived to represent the terrestrial universe from the metaphysical perspective of the New Testament *Apocalypse* or *Book of Revelations*.

Other examples of colorful paintings concerning the world of the gods, and the ultimate origins of the ancestors from which a whole indigenous nation descended, are found, respectively, in several pages of the *Codex Borgia* and of the *Codex Vindobonensis*. The allusion to European medieval manuscripts in which many colored pictures accompany a written text, seems pertinent as a distant and totally independent cultural parallel. If those medieval manuscripts can be labeled picto-written books, those of Mesoamerica, because of their character as conveyors of "pictures and signs" intrinsically interrelated, certainly deserve to be named pictoglyphic books.

This brief summary of the most obvious attributes of the script employed by Mixtecs and Nahuas does not pretend to answer the question concerning the plenitude of its potential. Nevertheless it will suffice, I believe, to show that describing such writing as a mere "mnemonic device" to assist the recalling of oral tradition seems far from adequate.

It is true that, parallel to the transmission of knowledge by means of books, oral tradition played an important role in Mesoamerica. But can we say that the compositions which later, in the early colonial years, became committed to linear alphabetic writing, derive only from an orality linked to the memorizing of songs, prayers, discourses, and the like, in pre-Hispanic schools? Or was such orality, at least in some instances, the result of "reading a codex"? When there are indications or vestiges that can lead to the assertion that one or the other was the case, which procedures should be taken to detect possible Euro-Christian contaminations?

The enunciation of these questions demonstrates the complexity of what can be meant by orality and writing in the case of Mesoamerica. To take as merely colonial fabrications the extant texts in the Native languages committed to linear alphabetic writing, without applying distinctions or critical analysis, will indeed be so naive as to attribute to them all a pre-Hispanic origin.

Trying to answer these questions, I will adopt a triple procedure. First, the principal testimonies of those who contemplated how the books were consulted or "read" will be discussed. A second procedure will be to present cases of actual "readings," in particular by natives, early in colonial times. The third path to be followed has to do with some external evidence which eventually may be indicative of pre-Hispanic authenticity in the case of "texts" committed to the alphabet.

Testimonies of People Who Saw Mesoamericans "Reading" Their Books

For the first time, the existence of Mesoamerican books was noted and reported with admiration in a volume printed as early as 1516, three years before the landing of Cortés in

Veracruz. It was the Italian humanist Peter Martyr of Anghiera, in the service of the Catholic Kings, who, in his *De Orbe Novo* (Alcalá, 1516) included the already quoted passage concerning the Indian who affirmed that his people also had books similar to the books of the Spaniard Corrales. Only three years later, the cosmographer Martín Fernández de Enciso, in his *Summa de Geografía*, published in Seville in 1519, describing his explorations around the Gulf of Uraba (and referring probably to the Pipil-Nicaraos), wrote that "there is a land about which the Indians say that people have books and write and read as we do" (Fernández de Enciso 1987, 230).

Direct evidence of the native books was demonstrated by several people, including Hernán Cortés himself, who sent some books to Charles V (Cortés 1963, 407), Gonzalo Fernández de Oviedo saw some produced by the Pipil-Nicaraos (1945, XI, 65), and Peter Martyr of Anghiera contemplated the books Cortés sent to Charles V in 1519 (1964, I, 425–26). In that same year the nuncio of the Pope in Spain, Archbishop Juan Ruffo de Forli, also inspected these books (Bataillon 1959, 140). The list of those who refer to them includes the soldier-chronicler Bernal Díaz del Castillo (1955, I, 143), as well as many of the missionary friars, some of whom praise them, while others condemn them as conveyors of the Devil's falsehoods and idolatries.

Among these testimonies, there are some of particular relevance, since, besides reporting the existence of books, they describe how the natives "read" them and communicate to others what is contained in them. Such is the case with the testimony of friar Toribio de Benavente Motolinía, one of the twelve Franciscans who arrived to Mexico in 1524. In a letter of introduction, signed in 1541, preceding the text of his *Historia de los Indios de Nueva España*, he declares:

And they had five genres of books, as I said, of figures and characters. The first dealt with the years and different times. The second was concerned with the days and feasts during the whole year. The third was about the dreams, enchantments and vanities and auguries in which they believed. The fourth dealt with the *baptism* [the pouring of the Rain God's water] and the names given to babies. The fifth was about the rites, ceremonies and auguries concerning marriages (Motolinía 1985, 52–53).

To be more precise, Motolinía adds that the first kind of books, "are worthy of credit as in them there is the truth . . . because with much order they counted the different times, days, weeks, months, years and feasts." In them they included

the deeds and stories, victories and wars and successes of the principal lords and any remarkable happening in the skies, and the pestilences which occurred during their reigns . . . All this they had inscribed with their characters and figures, from which it is understood (Motolinía 1985, 53).

Antedating this information signed by Motolinía in 1541, there are three other testimonies, perhaps the earliest we have about how knowledge was drawn from the indigenous books. Two of these testimonies are due, most probably, to the same Motolinía who addressed them to Charles V at the request of the conqueror Juan Cano and his wife Isabel Tecuichpo, daughter of Motecuhzoma. A reference to the yet to be consecrated bishop Juan de Zumárraga, who, it is stated, "will carry with him this communication" (*Origen de los Mexicanos* 1983, 745), permits us to establish the date at which it was written. 1533 was the only time at which Zumárraga traveled to Spain to receive his episcopal consecration. He returned to Mexico the next year.

In the two testimonies attributable to Motolinía, many references are made to the "books of characters and figures," as the primary sources consulted to provide the required historical antecedents in support of the request made by Motecuhzoma's daughter and her husband. Also, in both texts the friar expresses his concern for the loss of many of the books, as "we have burned many of them" (1983, 718, 731–32). Nonetheless, he adds that some survived to which he had access: "And we have confronted the contents of several of them and found conformity in them" (1983, 718). As to how this consultation and confrontation took place, he declares:

Writers or learned men, (as we should call them), who understand this well [the contents of the books] are many, and they do not dare to appear, as we have burnt the books. . . . They answer that they have no more books because they are burnt, and ask why we need them (1983, 732).

The friar, as Motolinía himself had done in his 1541 epistle, describes the various genres of books and affirms that those in which the time records, years, months, and days, the annals, are inscribed, should not be censured. On this assumption, he consults them, assisted by the "learned" natives, and, making a number of explicit references, indicates that "the books say it" or that "it does not say it" (1983, 733, 737, 738, 744, 749).

The books—this is the substance of this testimony—"tell" what is registered in them by means of characters and figures. The "writers or learned men" among the natives, it must be kept in mind, are those "who understand them well."

The other testimony, also antedating Motolinía's epistle of 1541, is the so-called *History of the Mexicans Through Their Paintings*. Owing much, probably, to the research of Fray Andrés de Olmos during 1533–1536 (as in 1536 the manuscript was taken to Spain), it actually constitutes a "reading" of several indigenous books. Some copies of them are known to us and further reference will be made to them.

The testimony begins with these words:

By means of the characters and scriptures they employ, and through the accounts of elders who in the time of their paganism were priests and pontiffs, and according to what was declared by the lords and principals to whom their doctrines and law had been taught when they studied at their temples and there memorized them and who were assembled before me, presenting their books and figures that were old and many stained with human blood, it appears that they had a god whom they called *Tonacatecuhtl*, whose wife was *Tonacacihuatl* (*Historia de los mexicanos por sus pinturas* 1983, 691).

Following the sentence "it appears that . . .", the text is closely related to the contents of codices *Vatican A, Telleriano-Remensis* and others, which are probably partial copies of older manuscripts, those actually presented by "the priests and principals" who revealed their beliefs and history to the friar.

Even more explicit is a member of the Royal Audience, the chronicler Alonso de Zorita, who describes, around 1560, the procedure adopted by Fray Andrés de Olmos in obtaining the *Huehuehtlahtolli*, or testimonies of "The Ancient Word":

The principal Indians preserve them in their painted books and he [Olmos] asked them to commit them to writing, and they did so without his being present, and they took the texts from their paintings which are like their own script, and they understand themselves by means of them, and nothing was changed, but a division by paragraphs was introduced. . . . And he advised them that they should suppress the names of their gods and put instead that of the true God our Lord (Zorita, n.d., 112–13).

In this manner, as had happened with the *History of the Mexicans Through Their Paintings*, which starts with cosmic origins and ends with the days of Motecuhzoma, the *Huehuehtlatolli*, that is, the moral discourses of the elders, were taken from their books. The "principal Indians" who committed such discourses to alphabetic writing, did so "without introducing any changes except dividing them by paragraphs and suppressing the names of their gods."

Thus the *Huehuehtlahtolli* were committed in Nahuatl to linear alphabetic writing. External evidence supports the authenticity of the "texts" transcribed in this manner. Around 1545 Fray Bernardino de Sahagún, following a parallel procedure—"everything," he declares, "they gave me through their paintings"—independently obtained another ensemble of *Huehuehtlahtolli*, which includes discourses very similar to those collected by Olmos (*Florentine Codex* 1979, II, book VI). Among them the speeches of the father to his son stand out.

The same idea, that from the characters and figures, the pictoglyphic inscriptions of the books, one could obtain "texts," is repeated over and again by others, Spaniards and natives, who independently were concerned with this throughout the sixteenth century and into the first half of the following century. I will quote only from some of the most relevant testimonies.

The Dominican friar Diego Durán, who around 1560–1565 wrote the *Historia de las Indias de Nueva España*, based on oral indigenous testimonies and also, as he expressly states, on native documents, refers to them in this manner:

They [the Nahua young people] had their preceptors, teachers who taught and exercised them in all the military arts, religious knowledge and astrology through the observation of the stars. And on all these matters they had large and beautiful books with pictures and characters by means of which they taught these arts (Durán 1867–1880, II, 229).

Formal education required the use of the books with pictures and characters. Durán adds that there were also books of historical content: "They preserved the memory of happenings worthy of being preserved, their wars and victories . . . everything they had written therein . . . with the counts of the years, months and days in which they occurred" (Durán 1867–1880, II, 257). The previously quoted testimony provided by Sahagún's native informants concerning the ancient priestly schools explains how the books were used: *amoxotoca*, "following" their contents.

To the many references Sahagún makes to the indigenous books it will suffice to add another, in which he insists upon their importance as his primary sources:

All those things we discussed they gave me through their paintings which were the writings they used
from antiquity, and the grammarians [his former students] transcribed them in their language, writing
the declaration [i.e., the alphabetic text] at the bottom of the picture. I still have these originals (Sahagún
1956, I, prologue to book II).

Two other testimonies derived from as many indigenous compilations will help us better
appreciate the already adduced descriptions of the manner in which the books were employed. One comes from the *Annals of Cuauhtitlán*, a compilation in Nahuatl of "texts"
committed to the alphabet from the contents of the codices. Dealing with the life of
Huemac, lord of Tollan, it is stated, "More of what is said about him will be heard in
several books" (*Annals of Cuauhtitlán* 1975, fol. 8).

"What is said about him," *ihtolloca*, (his history), *cecni amoxpan*, "in several
books," *mocaquiz*, "will be heard." The books tell things; one has to follow their contents, recite what is therein, and thus it will be heard. The same idea, poetically expressed, resounds in this Nahuatl song, the other testimony to be recalled (*Cantares Mexicanos*, fol. 14 v.):

> I sing the pictures of the books,
> and see them widely known,
> I am a precious bird
> for I make the books speak,
> there in the house of the painted papers.

The importance of the indigenous books was so widely recognized that when
Philip II in 1578 ordered the preparation of the well known "Geographical Relations," in
many cases codices preserved in a number of villages were presented as reliable sources of
information. This took place, for instance, in the town of Coatepec—its *Relation* says:
"According to the old people, they knew through the paintings that were left to them"
(Acuña 1985, 144). And in a *Relation* of the province of Valladolid in Yucatán, it is declared that "they had paper from a bark of a tree, in which they wrote and represented the
days and months with great figures, and there they wrote. Unfolded, this book was about
six yards long, and there are others bigger or smaller" (Garza 1983, II, 40).

In the case of Yucatán, where a more complex and precise writing had been developed, the testimonies about books and inscriptions are particularly significant. Bishop
Diego de Landa says:

This people also used certain characters or letters with which they wrote in their books their ancient
happenings and sciences. And with these figures and some signs they understood their own things and
made others to understand and learn them. We found many books of these letters, and because there was
no one thing which did not contain superstitions and lies of the Demon, we put fire to all of them, which
they felt with great pain (Landa 1965, 105).

Recent research on Maya writing confirms Bishop Landa's statement. Maya inscriptions
on stone or ceramics, and in books are indeed examples of a writing system. By means of

"certain characters" representing syllables, complemented by other glyphic elements such as a rich set of affixes, this writing could convey sentences and a complete text. Today we know verbs, substantives, pronouns, names, and so on that have been recorded in it (Berlin 1977; Kelley 1976; Schele 1982; Mathews 1984; and Gockel 1988).

Concerning the Mixtec codices and their pictoglyphs, the Dominican friar Francisco de Burgoa provides a description which in its main traits coincides with those given by Motolinía, Olmos, Durán, and Sahagún. According to Burgoa, who lived in the first third of the seventeenth century:

There were found books in their own manner on sheets made of pieces of bark of trees which grow in the hot lands, and they tanned and prepared them as parchments of one third of a yard wide, more or less, and they sew or glue them to form a folding ensemble as long as needed. There they inscribed all their stories with characters so abbreviated that just one page conveyed the place, province, year, month and day, with all the other names of the gods, ceremonies and sacrifices, or victories they had. And in relation to this, they taught the sons of the lords they chose for their priesthood from their childhood, making them learn by heart those characters and stories, and I have had some of these books in my hands and heard with admiration some elders explain them. And they used to hang some of these papers extended as tables of cosmography in their main rooms as a sign of greatness and vanity, honoring themselves by dealing in their assemblies with such matters (Burgoa 1989, 210).

In close agreement with Burgoa's statements, Alfonso Caso, who devoted many years to the deciphering of the Mixtec codices (Caso 1960, 1964, 1966), describes their contents and writing in the following manner:

It is true that one finds at the beginning of the codices of this group references to the divine origin of the founders of the dynasties . . . but the contents of these codices is primarily historical. . . .

Dealing with pictorial manuscripts, we distinguish in these Mixtec codices some realistic representations, symbols or ideograms and combinations of glyphs which are phonetical elements.

Even if the codices should seem more like pictures than writing, since they represent scenes and human beings, these representations have a character more symbolic than realistic and are representations of ideas more than of things. . . . This combined system of writing, iconographic, ideographic or symbolic and phonetic, allows for rich possibilities of expression. For instance, I have found that it presents no difficulty in expressing substantives or verbs. . . . As to the latter I have a list of more than forty that can be represented iconographically or symbolically (Caso 1977, I, 18, 2–27).

In other words, according to Caso, the Mixtec codices can be actually "read" by following their pictoglyphic sequences. He recognizes that the written chronicles and the existence of a considerably large number of early colonial Mixtec manuscripts have aided him in fully understanding the contents of codices such as the *Bodley, Selden,* and *Colombino.* Nevertheless he affirms that those and other pre-Hispanic codices (e.g., *Vindobonensis, Nuttal*) could by themselves express the history of the various Mixtec chiefdoms. The Mixtecs, he tells us, called their books *Naandeye*, "*for the past's memory*" (Caso 1977, I, 11). Caso himself recognizes that the Mixtec writing system "has a special relationship with two others, the one which can be called *Pueblan-Tlaxcalan*, from which we think the Borgia Group comes, and the other from the Central region of Mexico, i.e., from cities such as Mexico, Tezcoco and Tacuba" (Caso 1977, I, 27).

The Borgia group of codices, as we have seen, are actually *tonalamatl*, books with several arrangements of the ritual 260-day count, and in some cases, pages with religious or even theological contents, as happens particularly in the *Codex Borgia* and in the *Fejérváry-Mayer*. Such books were conceived to be frequently consulted by the priests and sages as if they were the equivalent to a breviary of a Roman Catholic priest. Unfortunately, no pre-Hispanic Nahua book of historical contents has come down to us. This makes it difficult to judge their potentials of expression as the available materials are only extant in early colonial codices such as the *Tira de la Pergrinacion*, the *Azcatitlan, Mexicanus, Vaticano A* (the last few pages) and *Telleriano* (the last part) codices.

Edward E. Calnek, in "The Analysis of pre-Hispanic Central Mexican Historical Texts," recognizes that one can distinguish between the "annalistic texts" (historical codices) and the "administrative records" (census records and tribute lists). Concerning the administrative records, he asserts:

[they] were functionally specialized to accomplish specific tasks or objectives. . . . They were characterized especially by a constant repetition of the same information and required great flexibility only for the recording of proper names for persons, places and titles. This was achieved by means of the well-known "rebus" or glyphic information which, according to both Dibble and Nicholson, was used with increasing frequency in the last half century or so before the Spanish conquest (Calnek 1978, 245–46).

As to the historical books (from the only extant colonial materials) Calnek describes their expressive potentials as much less strong than those of the Mixtec codices. He takes as an example some parts of the *Tira de la Peregrinación*. In them he distinguishes the existence of "episodes" separated by "transitions." In his opinion, the informational content of any specific episode is limited by the pictorial scenes which, in some cases, include a few calendaric glyphs or others, which express personal, group, or place names. On the extant limited evidence of the few colonial manuscripts, Calnek believes an oral commentary, memorized in the schools, was required to really understand the meaning of each represented "episode" and of the various "transitions" in the codex. "The purpose of distinguishing "episodes" and "transitions" is an "attempt" to develop new and potentially more rigorous methods for the analysis of colonial period versions—pictorial and written—of pre-Hispanic historical traditions" (Calnek 1978, 261).

If we give credit to the testimonies I have quoted from people who studied how the sages "read" their books, one can add that (accepting the complementarity of the oral tradition formally memorized) the pre-Hispanic Nahua codices of historical content appear to be very similar to those of the Mixtecs. If such was the case, their expressive potentials were per se sufficient to convey a large and precise body of information. The word *amoxotoca*, "to follow" the contents of the book, seems eloquent enough in this context. By means of the *amoxotoca*, it is stated, the young people in the ancient schools learned the songs, discourses, annals, and other compositions. And also, as Olmos, Sahagún, and others expressly declared, by means of those pictoglyphic books, many of these compositions became, in the end, committed to linear alphabetic writing. If obscurities remain as to how such alphabetic renditions were made, it remains certain that formal oral tradition and the alphabetic renditions were directly linked, not to say anchored, in the contents of the books.

There is an available example of a "text" in Nahuatl committed to alphabetic writing, which, by internal evidence, appears to be the result of a "reading," that is, of *amoxotoca*, having "followed" the pictoglyphic contents of an indigenous codex. The description of the process of following such contents will illustrate in a living form the pictoglyphic potentials of Nahua and Mixtec codices as sources from which the alphabetically written texts derive.

The "Reading" of a Codex

An example of how the pictures and glyphs of an indigenous book could be sung or recited, and actually were, is provided by the Nahuatl text known as the *Legend of the Suns*, concerning the cosmogonic great happenings *(Codice Chimalpopoca* 1975). The written text encompasses several pieces of narrative—one could call them epic poems. The *Legend* was committed to alphabetic writing in Nahuatl (an introductory paragraph gives the exact date, May 22, 1558, in which an anonymous native scribe, working probably with a surviving old sage or priest, either completed or began his work).

Starting with the account of the successive foundations and destructions of the sun, earth, and man, the narrative depicts the rediscovery of fire, the formation of a new genre of man preceded by a journey of the god Quetzalcoatl to the Place of the Dead to recover the bones of past generations. Then one learns about the finding of maize at the Mountain of our Sustenance, the sacrifice of the gods in primeval Teotihuacan, followed by the epic stories of Mixcoatl, Xiuhnel, and Mimich. Quetzalcoatl, the culture hero and high priest of the Toltecs, is also present in the narrative. The epic account ends by describing the ruin of Tula, the ballgame between Huemac, its last ruler, and the Tlaloqueh, the gods of rain, with the victory of the former resulting in a great famine caused by the offended gods. The entrance of the Mexicas or Aztecs into the scene, to take the place of the Toltecs, closes the text which, in this manner, becomes for them a sort of epic national history.

The analysis of this narrative allows us to detect its stylistic features, parallel sentences, a certain rhythm in the expression, traits pertaining to a *Mexicacuicatl*, a song in the Mexican manner. In addition—and this is particularly important—the analysis permits us also to identify a good number of referential statements such as *in nican ca*, "here is"; *inin . . .* , "this . . ."; *iniqueh in*, "these . . ."; *inezca in nican can*, "of this, his appearance is here"; *izcatqui*, "here is . . ." Such referential statements, accompanied by the frequent use of the adverbial phrases *niman ic, niman ye, niman ye ic*, meaning "then, next, following on," reveal that the text is being "read," recited, and committed to linear alphabetic writing, following the pictoglyphic sequences of an indigenous book.

Two other manuscripts have been preserved, one clearly independent of the *Legend of the Suns*, and the other possibly related to it, which shed light on this process of "reading," or *amoxtoca*, and transcription. The first has been mentioned already. It is the

History of the Mexicans Through Their Paintings, also a "reading" of pictoglyphic books with cosmogonic and legendary contents. There it is stated explicitly that whatever is contained in it was taken from ancient pictoglyphic manuscripts. A close comparison of its contents with what is expressed in the *Legend of the Suns* shows striking coincidences. It is indeed interesting to discover that the two manuscripts independently committed to writing at a distance of more than twenty years coincide in so many respects.

The other manuscript, already mentioned, is a pictoglyphic book produced around the middle of the sixteenth century. It is known as *Codex Vaticanus A* because it is preserved in the Vatican Library. In it, several of the subjects of the narrative in the *Legend of the Suns* and in the *History of the Mexicans Through Their Paintings* are pictoglyphically represented. One could say that, if this codex was not the one "read" by the person or persons who committed the *Legend of the Suns* and the *History* to linear alphabetic writing, it is a partial copy of a pre-Hispanic book, perhaps the one actually consulted and "read."

The two texts mentioned above, "readings" of a codex, committed to linear alphabetic writing, illustrate what in simple words was noted and repeated by the missionary ethnographers Olmos, Sahagún, and others such as Motolinía, Durán, and Burgoa when discussing the narratives, discourses, and songs they claimed to have drawn from the contents of the painted books.

A third procedure can be adopted to deliberate on the authenticity of a "text" offered as being derived from a pre-Hispanic source. Such a procedure will now be considered.

One Cultural Weaving Throughout the Centuries

I intend to look for various kinds of external evidence which may support the pre-Hispanic authenticity of an alphabetically rendered indigenous text. Instead of considering particular cases of one or another text in Nahuatl, Maya, or another Native language, attention will be concentrated on several main themes which are referred to in a considerable number of independent testimonies, and found in various genres of sources, archaeological, documentary (as in the codices) and others, deriving from different areas and eras within Mesoamerica. The search for these sources of converging evidence is intended to discover if the written texts in which certain themes reappear can be taken as threads belonging to one and the same Mesoamerican culture weaving.

Let us begin with the spatial and temporal image of the universe, a theme essential to the Mesoamerican worldview. The conception of the horizontal surface of the universe has two extraordinary delineations, pictorial and glyphic, in Codex *Fejérváry-Mayer (Tonalamatl of the Pochtecas)*, page 1, and in the Maya *Tro-Cortesiano*, pages 75–76. Among the many symbols attached to these delineations one can refer to the cosmic colors, deities, trees, and birds, as well as to the orientation of time, that is, the days and the years whose glyphs are inserted therein. In the case of the Maya codex, the years' orientation is registered by means of the glyphs that denote the four cosmic directions.

The same glyphs appear in several archaeological findings, such as the Palenque inscription M and the recently unearthed tome 12 in Río Azul, in the Guatemalan Petén. Notable are the bas-reliefs on the Temple of the Panels in Chichén Itza, on which appear trees and birds arranged according to the regions of the universe.

A number of alphabetically written texts convey the same image, or important elements of it. The four quadrants of the universe are described, precisely related to the orientation of time, in a Nahuatl text collected by Sahagún (*Madrid Codex* 1906, VII, fol. 269 r.). Such a text sounds like a "reading" of what is delineated on page 1 of the *Fejérváry-Mayer* codex. The placement of *Xiuhtechuhtli*, Lord of Fire, at the center of the universe, seen in the codex, also has its counterpart in another Nahuatl text which describes him as "the one residing at the navel of the earth" (*Florentine Codex* 1979, II, book 6, fol. 71 v.). In addition, in the Maya text of the *Chilam Balam of Chumayel* (Roys 1933, 64), the cosmic trees and birds are referred to, and mention is made of the correspondent colors, and following the same scheme, east-north-west-south, as in *Codex Tro-Cortesiano*. Other texts committed to the alphabet, in Nahuatl, Maya, and Quiché, also provide coinciding reference to the image of the horizontal aspect of the universe. The list includes fol. 1 of the *Annals of Cuauhtitlán* (1975), the *Popol Vuh* (1944, 2), and *The Ritual of the Bacabs* (Roys 1965, 64).

As to the vertical aspect of the universe, plastic representations of it are found in the Mixtec, pre-Hispanic codices *Vindobonensis*, page 52, *Selden Roll* and in the early colonial codices *Gómez de Orozco* (Mixtec) and *Vaticano A*. A Nahuatl text included in the testimonies collected by Sahagún (*Florentine Codex* 1979, I, book III, fol. 25 r.–v.) appears to be a "reading" of page 1 of the *Vaticano A* as it describes the realities pertaining to each of the upper levels and of the underworld.

Frequent reference is made in the *Chilam Balam* books of the Mayas to the *Ox-lahun-ti-ku*, thirteen gods of the thirteen celestial levels or upper cosmic divisions, as well as of the *Bolon-ti-ku*, nine divine dwellers of the correspondent levels of the underworld (Barrera Vázquez 1948, 153–55). The same concept of vertical cosmic space has survived among several contemporary Mesoamerican goups. Such is the case with the Tzotzil of Larrainzar, Chiapas, as recorded by the ethnologist William R. Holland (1963, 69).

Concerning the concept of time and the cosmic ages, besides the archaeological evidences in monuments such as the Sunstone, where the glyphs of the successive "suns" or cosmic ages are carved, the pre-Hispanic codices which compose the Borgia Group and some pictures and glyphic texts in the Maya codices *Dresden* (Paris) and *Tro-Cortesiano*, give substantial information about the extremely complex concept of time in Mesoamerica.

The succession of the "suns" or ages, delineated in *Vaticano A* has, as we have seen, a written rendition in the Nahuatl text of the *Legend of the Suns*, and in a large list of other texts like the *Annals of Cuauhtitlán* (1938, 60–62), the *History of the Mexicans Through Their Paintings* (1983, 693–97), the *Historia* of Motolinía (1903, 346–47), Ixtlilxochitl's *Sumaria Relación* and *Historia de la Nación Chichimeca* (1891–1892, v I, 19–21, II, 25–26) *Popol Vuh* (Edmonson 1971, 3–31 and 145–60), and the *Chilam Balam* books (Barrera Vázquez 1948, 153–55).

"Readings" in Nahuatl and in Spanish (from a Nahuatl source) of the complex connotations of the 260 days count, with references to the destinies brought in by each day, are included in book IV of the *Florentine Codex* (1979, I, book IV) and in the *Historia de las Indias de Nueva España* of Diego Durán (1867–1880). A comparison of those two texts with the contents of the pre-Hispanic codices of the Borgia Group shows striking coincidences. Further evidence of the survival of that concept of the count of the days-destinies, is found in the Nahuatl texts collected by Hernando Ruiz de Alarcón during the first third of the seventeenth century (Ruiz de Alarcón 1984). Ethnological research shows that in modern times the same astrological calendar is alive among the Ixil of Guatemala (Lincoln 1942) and other groups in Guatemala (McArthur 1965, 33–38).

The concept of the divine as a dual entity is also an essential part of the ancient worldview and religious beliefs of the Mesoamericans, as is shown in several pages of pre-Hispanic codices, such as *Borgia, Fejérváry,* and *Vaticanus B,* as well as in the Mixtec *Vindobonensis, Selden Roll,* and the early colonial *Gómez de Orozco* and *Vaticano A.* Several *Huehuehtlahtolli* of three different original provenances (preserved in Florence and Mexico, as well as in Austin, Washington, and Berkeley, are replete with allusions to the Supreme Dual God and His/Her attributes. In various Nahuatl sacred hymns (in the *Florentine Codex*), in other songs (*Collection of Mexican Songs*), and the *Historia Tolteca-Chichimeca* (a manuscript that is a mixture of alphabetic and pictoglyphic renditions from the area of Cuauhtinchan, Puebla), invocations are found that shed light on the attributes and other titles of the same supreme Dual God. Parallel references can be identified in the *Popol Vuh* and the *Chilam Balam* books. Contemporary "texts" from the surviving oral tradition have been collected among several Nahuatl and Maya groups that convey coinciding ideas (Preuss 1976, 47–50).

The *Huehuehtlahtolli*, testimonies of the "Ancient Word," deserve special attention. Besides the remarkable coincidences that exist among several, transcribed in different times and places during the first half of the sixteenth century, there are others with parallel expressions committed to alphabetic writing in recent times (Ramírez 1980, 71–90). I have a tape recording of a *Huehuehtlahtolli* whose contents are the admonitions of a mother to her daughter similar to those expressed in texts transcribed in the sixteenth century. I refer to a *Huehuehtlahtolli* transmitted in 1989 by a native woman of the Nahuatl community of Santa Ana Tlacotenco (Milpa Alta, México, D.F.). Other contemporary *Huehuehtlahtolli*, committed to writing by several ethnologists, can be quoted as examples of the survival of this genre of compositions. The following texts preserve the ancient sylistic and moral patterns: "Textos de Xaltocan, Estado de México," collected around 1949 (Barrios and Barlow 1950, 1–25); "Tlahtolli tonameytzintli ipampa kampa ce kitokayotia xochitlachipantla" ("Words addressed to a child when it is named giver of flowers," from Los Reyes, Veracruz, 1981 (Ajactle 1982), and "Todos Santos y otras ceremonias," with texts registered in Chilacachapa, Guerrero, 1954 (Weitlaner 1955, 295–321).

It is indeed remarkable, not to say astonishing, to find that there are contemporary narratives in several Mesoamerican languages that closely follow themes of the "Ancient Word" and at times appear as "readings," done almost five hundred years later, of a page of a pre-Hispanic codex. As might be expected, variants are often introduced, including cases of Euro-Christian contamination. There are, for instance, texts which tell once again the story of the rediscovery of corn in the Mountain of our Sustenance, a narrative included in the sixteenth-century written *Legend of the Suns*. Among the Nahua-Pipil of El Salvador, the same story was recorded about 1930 (Schultze Jena 1935, 30–33). In Tzeltal, in Chiapas, a very similar narrative was transcribed by Marianna C. Slocum (1965, 1–7).

An unexpected Mixtec story was communicated in that language by two illiterate natives of Santa Cruz Mixtepec, Oaxaca, Serapio Ramírez and Basilio Gómez, to the ethnologist Thomas J. Ibach (1980, 243–47). This story is probably the best extant "reading" of page 37 of the Mixtec pre-Hispanic Codex *Vindobonensis* and of page 2 of the Codex *Selden* (also Mixtec). The story has to do with the Apoala tree from which the Mixtec nation originated. Can we doubt that this and the other quoted texts, whether committed to the alphabet in the sixteenth century or in recent times, are threads of one and the same Mesoamerican cultural weaving?

Coincidences between archaeological findings, contents of the codices, and "texts" committed to the alphabet in different native languages from various areas and times, encompass other themes also related to the Mesoamerican ancient worldview and religious beliefs. The following stand out: the deeds of Quetzalcoatl; the sacrifice of Nanahuatzin when the fifth Sun began to appear; the places to which the dead go in the beyond; the origins of man; the provenance of the ethnic groups from the Seven Caves; the concepts of what is good and what is evil, and so on.

I will give examples of the first three themes. The figure of Quetzalcoatl, god and culture hero, is represented in various attitudes in stone sculptures, in various pages of pre-Hispanic codices such as the *Borgia* and *Vindobonensis*, in the Nahuatl texts of the *Florentine Codex* and the *Annals of Cuauhtitlan*, in several chronicles in Spanish, and in modern texts, mainly from the region of the Gulf of Mexico, under the title "Stories of Tlamacazqui." Comparative critical studies are required which will shed light on the interrelation of some or all of these testimonies.

The sacrifice of Nanahuatzin, who burned himself to become transformed into the Sun, is described in the *Florentine Codex* (1979, II, book VII, fol. 2 v.–5v.) and in the *Legend of the Suns* (1975, fol. 77), as well as in modern texts that come from areas as far apart as Miahuatlan, Puebla (Ramírez 1950 1–4), and Piedra Gorda, Nayarit. This last version was transmitted in the Huichol language by the native Cruz de la Rosa (McIntosh 1949, 2, 19–21). Such distant and unexpected convergence, in which the variants do not obscure the central theme, indeed deserves attention.

On the subject of the places in the beyond to which the dead may go, it is remarkable to find striking coincidences between a Teotihuacan mural painting of the Tlalocan, or paradise of Tlaloc, in the ruins of the Tepantitlan palace, and a Nahuatl text in the *Florentine Codex* (1979, I, book II, fol. 27 v.–28 v.). Concerning the *Mictlan*, where Mitlantecuhtli, Lord of the Dead, reigns, as well as the celestial *Cihuatlan*, "place of the women," situated in the West, an ensemble of polychrome clay sculptures, some of large size, have been discovered in the interior of a late classic pyramid in El Zapotal, Veracruz. These sculptures represent Lord *Mictlantecuhtli* and the *Cihuateteoh*, or "deified women," who died in childbirth. Their effigies and attributes closely correspond to those depicted in codices of the Borgia Group and to their descriptions in Nahuatl texts of the *Florentine Codex* (1979, I, book 3, fol. 23 v.–27 v.).

Besides these genres of external evidence that give support to the authenticity of indigenous texts committed to the alphabet, there are also those of the independently done alphabetic renditions of the same composition, performed by persons living in distant places and times. Such is the case, to give an example, of a song of sorrow which, it is said, was intoned by the Mexica after their defeat at Chapultepec some time before they finally settled in the island of Tenochtitlan. The same song with slight variants appears in the 1528 manuscript of the *Annals of Tlatelolco* (1945, fol. 20), in the *Collection of Cantares Mexicanos* (fol. 37 r.), and in the *Annales of Cuauhtitlán* (fols. 16–17). On the other hand, the Mexica defeat at Chapultepec can be documented in several other independent sources such as codices *Azcatitlan, Mexicanus, Telleriano, Ramírez, Aubin*, and in the chronicles of Alvardo Tezozomoc, Chimalpahin, and Durán, all of whom assert that they wrote supported by the testimonies of ancient indigenous manuscripts, whose size and contents they sometimes describe (Chimalpahin 1983).

Conclusion

We have examined and compared various genres of extant Mesoamerican sources precisely to investigate whether any of the texts committed in Nahuatl, Maya, and other Native language to linear alphabetic writing can be accepted as testimonies from pre-Hispanic culture. Our search demonstrates the following:

1. The Mesoamericans had developed an orality which manifested itself in diverse circumstances in the form of song, discourse, and various recollections of important happenings, divine or human. Such orality was actually a verbal tradition formally learned in the schools and temples. To teach it, the priests and sages employed their books or codices. The Mayas in a strict sense *read* the logosyllabic sequences of their books. The Nahuas and Mixteca *amoxotoca*, "followed" the sequences of the pictures and glyphs included in their codices.

2. Mesoamericans, above all those living in the cities or large communities, did have deep appreciation for their books and inscriptions. The ideal image of their sages was that of the *amoxhua*, "the one to whom the books belong," *tlileh, tlapaleh*, "the one who had the black and red inks," to depict and write them. The comparison we have made with the case of the Incas is eloquent in this respect.

3. The testimonies provided by Indians, mestizos, and Spaniards who early in the sixteenth century contemplated how the Native books were employed, coincide in telling us that, even in the case of the Mixtec and Nahua books, their pictoglyphs had great potential of expression. They could convey not only information about the past in the form

of annals or as administrative records, but also more complex meaning-sequences, as those of the *Huehuehtlahtolli* and the songs. To what degree the complement of oral tradition was required is something about which we have to admit our ignorance. The chroniclers are not explicit about this, and besides we do not possess a single book of the sort mentioned by *Olmos* and *Sahagún*, who tell us that songs and *Huehuehtlahtolli* were obtained from the native books.

4. The example of how a Mesoamerican performed an *amoxotoca*, that is, "followed" the pictoglyphic sequences of a book to obtain the text called today *Legend of the Suns*, and commit it to alphabetic writing, deserves attention. It can also help us to see more clearly how other "texts" could have been rescued in the colonial period, compare the *Popol Vuh*, whose first sentences declare:

This is the beginning of the Ancient Word. . . . This we shall write already within the law of God, already within Christianity we shall save it, because the original Book of Counsel is no longer visible. There was the manuscript of it, and it was written long ago (*Popol Vuh* 1944, fol 1).

The ancient book, the one written long ago, could not be brought forth as the priests and sages who read it—so the text adds—"were hiding their faces," obviously in fear of being denounced as idolaters. Thus, already within Christianity, the Quiché scribe commits its contents, "the Ancient Word," to alphabetic writing. In such manner "the great account" will survive forever. And it did, since Father Francisco Ximénez, who found the scribe's old transcription in Chichicastenango, recopied it, commented on it, and preserved it.

5. Finally, the various forms of coinciding evidence adduced to see whether or not a written text has a pre-Hispanic provenance demonstrate that, in determined instances, a given composition is an authentic thread of the Mesoamerican cultural weaving. In some cases, as we saw, there exist several alphabetically written renditions of a text, obtained independently and with variants through oral tradition which, one can also demonstrate, is ultimately anchored in the contents of an ancient indigenous codex. This is particularly manifest in some Maya written texts, such as parts of several *Chilam Balam* books, which basically coincide as "transliterations" or direct morphosyntactic conversions of the ancient logosyllabic script to alphabetic writing. Recently, Victoria R. Bricker has brought this to the specialist's attention (Bricker 1989, 39–50). Oral tradition, surviving into modern times in many indigenous communities, provides another striking critical reinforcement concerning texts which have parallels in sixteenth-century transcriptions.

Using sound critical scholarship we can assert that in translating a number of texts written alphabetically in Nahuatl, Maya, Quiché, and other languages, we have indeed translated parts of the Mesoamerican "ancient word." Whether we have done it in an adequate form, with a solid linguistic, philological, and historical background, is a totally different question that poses other problems which people such as Sahagún have faced already and endeavored to answer.

References

Acuña, René. 1985. *Relaciones Geográficas de México*. National University. Mexico.

Ajactle, Margarito. 1982. "Tlajtoli Tonameyotzintli ipampa kampa se kitokayotia xochitla-chipanka," *Uejkavit Navavevejtlajtoli*, Conafe, Mexico.

Alva Ixtlilxochitl, Fernando. 1891–1892. *Obras Históricas*, 2 v., Mexico.

Anales de Tlatelolco. 1945. Edited by Ernst Mengin in *Codicum Americanorum Medii Evii*, Copenhagen.

Anghiera (Anglería), Peter Martyr of. 1953. *Epistolario*. Edited by José Lopez de Toro, Madrid.

———. 1964. *Décadas del Nuevo Mundo*, translated by Agustín Millares Carlos, 2 v., Mexico.

Baptista, Juan. 1988. *Huehuehtlahtolli, que contiene las pláticas que los padres y madres hicieron a sus hijos y los señores a sus vasallos, todas llenas de doctrina moral y politica*, facsimile reproduction of the 1600 edition, with an introduction by M. León-Portilla and a translation from the Nahuatl into Spanish by Librado Silva Galeana. National Commission of the V Centenary of the Encounter of Two Worlds, Mexico.

Barrera Vásquez, Alfredo. 1948. *El libro de los libros de Chilam Balam*, Fondo de Cultura Económica, México.

Barrios, Miguel, and Roberto Barlow. 1950. "Textos de Xaltocan, Estado de México," *Mesoamerican Notes*, Mexico City College, I, 1–25.

Bataillon, Marcel. 1959. "Les premières mexicains envoyés en Espagne par Cortés," *Journal de la Société des Americanistes de Paris*, Paris, V. XLVIII, 149.

Berlin, Heinrich. 1977. *Signos y Significaciones en las Inscripciones Mayas*, Ministerio de Educación, Guatemala.

Bricker, Victoria R. 1989. "The Last Gasp of Maya Hieroglyphic Writing in the Books of Chilam Balam of Chumayel and Chan Kan," in *Word and Image in Maya Culture: Explorations in Language, Writing and Representation*, edited by William F. Hanks and Don S. Rice, University of Utah Press, Salt Lake, 39–50.

Burckhart, Louise M. 1989. *The Slippery Earth: Nahua-Christian Moral Dialogue in Sixteenth-Century Mexico*, The University of Arizona Press, Tucson.

Burgoa, Francisco de. 1989. *Palestra Historial*, Editorial Porrúa, Mexico.

Calnek, Edward. 1976. "The Analysis of pre-Hispanic Central Mexican Historical Texts," *Estudios de Cultura Nahuatl*, National University, Mexico, v.13, 239–66.

Cantares Mexicanos. 1904. Facsimile reproduction by Antonio Peñafiel, Mexico.

Caso, Alfonso. 1977. *Reyes y Reinos de la Mixteca*, 2 v., Fondo de Cultura Económica, Mexico. See: *Codices Bodley, Colombino, Gómex de Orozco* and *Selden*.

Chimalpahin Cuauhtlehuanitzin, Domingo. 1983. *Octava Relación*, edited and translated into Spanish by José Romero Galván, National University, Mexico.

Codex Cospi. 1968. Introduction by Karl Anton Nowotny, Akademische Druck- und Verlaganstalt, Graz.

Codex Dresden. 1965. Commentary by Ferdinand Anders and H. Deckert, Akademische Druck- und Verlaganstalt, Graz.

Codex Fejérváry-Mayer (*Tonalamatl of the Pochtecas*). 1985. Commentary by Miguel León-Portilla, Celanese, Mexico.

Codex Land. 1966. Introduction by C.A. Burland, Akademische Druck- und Verlaganstalt, Graz.

Codex Mexicanus 23–24. 1952. Commentary by Ernst Mengin, 2 v., Societé des Americanistes, Paris.

Codex Nuttal. 1988. Commentary by Nancy Troike, Akademische Druck- und Verlaganstalt, Graz.

Codex Paris (Peresianus). 1968. Introduction by Ferdinand Anders, Akademische Druck- und Verlaganstalt, Graz.

Codex Tellerianus-Remensis. 1899. Introduction and paleography of the text by E. T. Hamy, Paris.

Codex Vaticanus A. 1979. Commentary by Ferdinand Anders, Akademische Druck- und Verlaganstalt, Graz.

Codex Vaticanus B, 3373. 1972. Introduction by Ferdinand Anders, Akademische Druck- und Verlaganstalt, Graz.

Codex Vindoborensis Mexicanus I. 1974. Introduction by O. Adelhofer, Akademische Druck- und Verlaganstalt, Graz.

Codice Azcatitlan. 1949. Commentary by Robert H. Barlow, 2 v., Societé des Americanistes, Paris.

Codice Bodley. 1960. Interpretation by Alfonso Caso, Sociedad Mexicana de Antropología, Mexico.

Codice Borgia. 1963. Commentary by Eduard Seler, 3 v., Fondo de Cultura Económica, Mexico.

Codice Chimalpopoca. 1975. Translated by Primo Feliciano Velázquez, National University, Mexico.

Codice Colombino. 1966. Interpretation by Alfonso Caso, Sociedad Mexicana de Antropología, Mexico.

Codice Gómez de Oroczo. 1954. Interpretation by Alfonso Caso, Talleres de Estampillas y Valores, Mexico.

Codice Selden 3135. 1964. Interpretation by Alfonso Caso, Sociedad Mexicana de Antropología, Mexico.

Codice Tro-Cortesiano. 1967. Introduction by Ferdinand Anders, Akademische Druck- und Verlaganstalt, Graz.

Codices Becker I-II. 1961. Commentary by Karl Anton Novotny, Akademische Druck- und Verlaganstalt, Graz.

Díaz del Castillo, Bernal. 1955. *Historia Verdadera de la Conquista de la Nueva España*, 2 v., Editorial Porrúa, Mexico.

Dibble, Charles E. 1971. "Writing in Central Mexico," *Handbook of Middle American Indians*, The University of Texas Press, Austin, v. 10, 322–32.

Durán, Diego. 1867–1880. *Historia de las Indias de Nueva España e Islas de Tierra Firme*, 2 v., Mexico.

Edmonson, Munro. 1971. *The Book of Counsel: The Popol Vuh of the Quiché Maya of Guatemala*, Tulane University, New Orleans.

———. 1982. *The Ancient Future of the Itza: The Book of Chilam Balam of Tizimin*, The University of Texas Press, Austin.

Fernández de Enciso, Martin. 1987. *Summa de Geografía*, edited by M. Cuesta Domingo, Museo Naval, Madrid.

Fernández de Oviedo, Gonzalo. 1945. *Historia General y Natural de las Indias*, 10 v., Editorial Guaranía, México.

Florentine Codex. 1950–1983. Edited and translated by J. O. Arthur Anderson and Charles E. Dibble, 12 v., University of Utah Press, Salt Lake City.

———. 1979. Facsimile, reproduction, published by the Archivo General de la Nación, 3 v., México.

Galarza, Joaquín. 1972. *Lienzos de Chiepetlan*, Mexico.

Garibay, K., Angel Ma. 1953–1954. *Historia de la Literatura Nahuatl*, 2 v., Editorial Porrúa, Mexico.

Garza, Mercedes de la. 1983. *Relaciones Geográficas de Yucatán*, 2 v., National University of Mexico.

Gockel, Wolfgang. 1988. *Die Geschichte einer Maya Dinastie. Entzifferung Klassischer Maya-Hieroglyphen am Beispel der Inschriften von Palenque*, Verlag Philip von Zabern, Mainz.

Goody, Jack. 1977. *The Domestication of the Savage Mind*, Cambridge University Press, Cambridge.

Grusinsky, Serge. 1988. *La Colonisation de l'imaginaire: Societés Indigenes et occidentalisation dans le Mexique espagnol XVI-XVIII siecles*, Gallimard, Paris.

Havelock, Eric, A. 1986. *The Muse Learns to Write: Reflections on Orality and Literacy from Antiquity to the Present*, Harvard University Press, Cambridge.

Historia de los Mexicanos por sus Pinturas. 1985. Attributed to fray Andrés de Olmos. In *Literaturas Indígenas*, edited by M. León-Portilla, Promexa, Mexico.

Historia Tolteca-Chichimeca. 1976. Edited and translated by Luis Reyes and Odena Güemes, National Institute of Anthropology, Mexico.

Holland, William R. 1963. *Medicina Maya en los Altos de Chiapas*, Instituto Nacional Indigenista, Mexico.

Ibach, Thomas J. 1980. "Mixtec Origin Myth," in *Tlalocan*, National University, Mexico, v. VIII, 243–47.

Kelley, David H. 1976. *Deciphering Maya Script*, University of Texas Press, Austin.

Klor de Alva, Jorge. 1988. "Sahagún and the Birth of Modern Ethnography," in *The Work of Bernardino de Sahagun*, edited by J. Klor de Alva et al., State University of New York at Albany.

Landa, Diego de. 1959. *Relación de las Cosas de Yucatán*. Edited by Angel Ma. Garibay K., Editorial Porrúa, Mexico.

León-Portilla, Miguel. 1963. *Aztec Thought and Culture*, Study of the *Ancient Nahuatl Mind*, University of Oklahoma Press, Norman.

———. 1983. "Cuicatl y Tlahtolli, las Formas de Expresión en Nahuatl," *Estudios de Cultura Nahuatl*, National University, Mexico, XVI, 13–108.

———, ed. 1985. *Literaturas indigenas*, Editorial Promexa, México.

———. 1988. *Time and Reality in the Thought of the Maya*. Second, enlarged edition, University of Oklahoma Press, Norman.

Libro de los Coloquios. 1986. The dialogues of 1524 according to the text by Bernardino de Sahagún, edited by M. León-Portilla, National University, Mexico.

Lincoln, J. Steward. 1942. *The Maya-Calendar of the Ixil of Guatemala*, Carnegie Institution of Washington, Contribution 528, Washington.

Madrid Codex. 1906. *Texts of the Indian Informants of Sahagun*, facsimile edition prepared by F. del Paso y Troncoso, Hauser y Menet, Madrid.

McArthur, Henry, and Lucille. 1965. *Notas sobre el calendario ceremonial de Aguacatán*, Huehuetenango, Instituto Lingüistico de Verano, Guatemala.

McIntosh, John. 1957. "Cosmogonía Huichol," *Tlalocan*, Mexico, v. 3, 14–21.

Mathews, Peter, and Justeson, John S. 1984. "Patterns of Sign Substitution in Maya Hieroglyphic Writing: The Affix Cluster," in *Phoneticism in Maya Hieroglyphic Writing*, edited by J. S. Justeson and Lyle L. Campbell, State University of New York at Albany, 185–234.

Motolinía, Toribio de Benavente. 1985. *Historia de los indios de Nueva España*, Historia 16, Madrid.

Novotny, Karl Anton. 1961. *Tlacuilolli, Die Mexikanischen Bilderhandschriften, Stil und Inhalt*, Verlag Gebr. MLNN, Berlin.

Popol Vuh, Das Heilige Buch der Quiche Indianer von Guatemala. 1944. Edited and translated into German by Leonhard Schultze-Jena, Iberoamericanischen Institut, Berlin.

Preuss, Konrad. 1976. *Nahua Texte aus San Pedo Jícora, Durango*, Dritter Teil: Gebete und Gesänge, Iberoamericanischen Institut, Berlin.

Ramírez, Cleofas and Karen Daken. 1985. "Huehuetlahtolli de Xalitla, Guerrero," *Tlalocan*, National University, Mexico, v. VIII, 71–90.

Roys, Ralph L., ed. 1965. *Ritual of the Bacabs*, University of Oklahoma Press, Norman.

Sahagún, Bernardino de. 1956. *Historia General de las Cosas de Nueva España*, edited by Angel Ma. Garibay K., Editorial Porrúa, Mexico.

Schele, Linda. 1982. *Maya Glyphs: The Verbs*. University of Texas Press, Austin.

Schultze-Jena, Leonhard. 1930. *Mythen in der Muttersprache der Pipil Von Izalco, El Salvador*, Verlag von G. Fischer, Jena.

Selden Roll. 1955. Commentary by C. A. Burland. *Monumenta Americana* von der Iberoamericanischen Bibliothek, Berlin.

Seler, Eduard. 1902–1923. *Gesammelte Abhandlungen zur Amerikanischen Sprach und Altertumskunde*, 5 v., A. Ascher und Co., Berlin.

———. 1964. *Comentarios al Códice Borgia*, 3 v., Fondo de Cultura Económica, Mexico.

Slocum, Mariane C. 1965. "The Origin of Corn and other Tzeltal Myths," *Tlalocan*, Mexico, IV, 1–27.

Smith, Mary Elizabeth. 1973. *Picture Writing from Southern Mexico, Mixtec Places, Signs and Maps*, University of Oklahoma Press, Norman.

Tedlock, Dennis, trans. 1985. *Popol Vuh: The Mayan Book of Creation*, Simon and Schuster, New York.

Thompson, J. Eric S. 1960. *Maya Hieroglyphic Writing: An Introduction*, University of Oklahma Press, Norman.

———. 1962. *A Catalog of Maya Hieroglyphs*, University of Oklahoma Press, Norman.

Tira de la Peregrinación. 1966. Facsimile edition published by the Secretaria de Hacienda, Mexico.

Torquemada, Juan de. 1975–1983. *Monarquía Indiana*, 7 v., edited by M. León-Portilla, National University, Mexico.

Villa Rojas, Alfonso. 1945. *The Maya of East Central Quintana Roo*, Carnegie Institution of Washington, Publication 559, Washington, D. C.

Weitlaner, Roberto J. 1955. "Todos Santos y otras ceremonias en Chilacalapa, Guerrero," *El México Antiguo*, Sociedad Alemana Mexicanista, Mexico, v. VIII, 295–322.

Whitaker, Gordon, and Michael Coe, eds. 1982. *Aztec Sorcerers in Seventeenth Century Mexico: The Treatise on Superstitions by Hernando Ruiz de Alarcón*, State University of New York at Albany.

Zorita, Alonso de. n.d. *Breve y Sumaria relación de los Señores de la Nueva España*, National University, Mexico.

The Amanuenses Have Appropriated the Text: Interpreting a Nahuatl Song of Santiago

Louise M. Burkhart

Christian devotional texts written in the indigenous languages of the Americas have received very little attention as works of Native American literature. This neglect arises from an assumption that such texts are nothing more than colonial propaganda, an appropriation of indigenous language for the purpose of cultural destruction. Dennis Tedlock has pointed out that catechistic texts written by priests familiar with local languages and cultures are important documents of intercultural dialogue.[1] In some cases, due to the heavy involvement of indigenous writers in their production, these texts take on significance not simply as records of culture contact but also as literary products of the colonized people themselves. Their translation reveals aspects of indigenous interpretations of Christianity not recoverable from other sources.

In early colonial Mexico, sons of the Nahua (Aztec) nobility studied Spanish and Latin, the liberal arts, and Christian theology under the guidance of Franciscan friars. Some of these men went on to assist the friars in the ethnographic study of Nahua culture; some became teachers themselves; some became the grammarians, translators, and editors on whom the priests depended for the production of linguistically accurate and rhetorically effective preaching materials in the Nahuatl language. These men belonged to the intellectual and political elite of indigenous society; without them the friars would have had very little impact on indigenous culture.

Thus, behind the friars whose names are printed on the title pages of Nahuatl books stand these Nahua interpreters, these cultural brokers, seldom named or even acknowledged. To the friars they were simply amanuenses, assistants whose help, though vital, was a passive, uncreative act. The friars saw translation as a direct and divinely inspired transmission of Christian signs into the words of the Nahuatl language. Woodcuts of Saint Francis receiving the stigmata from Christ appear on the title pages of several Franciscan grammars, vocabularies, and catechisms in Nahuatl, bearing the Latin caption "you signed, oh Lord, your servant Francis with the signs of our redemption." [2] This scene may be interpreted as a metaphor for the process of translation occurring upon the pages of the books: the imprint of Christ's signs upon the Nahuatl language. Rafael, discussing the translation of Christian doctrine into Tagalog in the colonial Philippines, makes an observation equally applicable to the Franciscans in Mexico: "The preaching of the Gospel in a foreign tongue is construed as a way of participating in the ritual of recalling the promise of salvation. Translation commemorates the perfect Word of the Father." [3]

In reality, the Nahuatl language encoded a vastly different perception of the world and human nature than did Spanish or Latin; translation from one language and cultural system to the other was a hazardous process in which meanings were lost, gained, and altered, and Christian teachings were adapted to indigenous structures of thought and indigenous concerns. I have discussed this process elsewhere; [4] at present I wish only to make the point that the indigenous interpreters were not simply vehicles for the direct transmission of the friars' words into Nahuatl. There was no single correct way to translate a Christian text into Nahuatl. By controlling word choice and discourse strategy, the Nahua interpreters had considerable control over how the Nahua populace understood and responded to the friars' teachings.

Many texts remain European in spirit and intent; often they have been translated nearly word for word from Spanish or Latin texts. They are characterized by homiletic and narrative styles of discourse that, though grammatically correct and often terminologically complex, show little conformity to indigenous literary aesthetics. Metaphors borrowed from Nahuatl rhetoric are common, and the texts are salted with couplets, but these devices are subordinated to the purposes of indoctrination. The friar's voice prevails: the texts are directed at prescribing belief and inducing conformity.

However, the Nahua interpreters did not always have priests dictating precisely what they should say, for some devotional texts are clearly of indigenous composition. The choice of subjects, the sophisticated literary style, the metaphorical language, and the extent to which Christian teachings are reformulated indicate that, within the bounds of what the priests who sponsored and preserved their work would tolerate, Nahua scholars are exercising their own creative genius. The amanuenses have become authors and have appropriated the discourses of Christian devotion to articulate their own view of the Christian order and their place within it. These texts are important records of colonial Nahua religion; they are also testaments of cultural survival and masterworks of Native American literature.

Because Nahuatl devotional literature treats subjects familiar to Western readers, it is all too easy to lose the Native voice in the Christian content. The presence of priestly censors meant that the writers sometimes had to veil their intent in understatement and double meaning, making their voices even less outspoken. Therefore, even more than with other genres of literature, the translator must be extremely attentive to nuances of meaning, metaphorical allusions, ambiguities and double meanings, references to self and audience, the use of different styles and stylistic devices, the treatment of loanwords, and, where possible, the text's relationship to Spanish or Latin sources. A literal translation of a Nahuatl word or phrase, even if clumsy, may be preferable to the use of its familiar—and emotionally loaded—Christian counterpart. One must make the text readable in English while conveying the features that make it the product not of some culturally universal Christian devotion but of a specifically Nahua Christianity.

A presentation of one text will do more to convey the character and interpretive potential of this literature than many pages of generalizations. I have selected a song about an imported saint, the apostle Saint James—a saint so closely associated with Spain and with conquest that his appropriation presented the Nahua interpreters with a considerable challenge.

The song is found in the *Psalmodia christiana*, a Nahuatl songbook written by four Nahua scholars under the direction of fray Bernardino de Sahagún, the great Franciscan ethnographer.[5] First composed in 1558–60, it circulated widely in manuscript form before it was finally published in 1583. It is the only Nahuatl songbook published in colonial Mexico. Intended to replace the songs from oral tradition that were being used in Church festivals (songs which friars found difficult to understand), the *Psalmodia* was an attempt to create a new Nahua-Christian song genre that would be acceptable to the indigenous communities.

The Nahua writers were graduates of the Franciscan college in Tlaltelolco, what was then the northern section of Mexico City. In his prologue to the *Psalmodia* Sahagún does not name the four men, but they may be the same four whom he names elsewhere as his ethnographic assistants at that time: Martín Jacobita, Antonio Valeriano, Alonso Vegerano, and Pedro de San Buenaventura.[6] Sahagún states that he "dictated" the songs and they "wrote" them; from the text it is obvious that the Nahua scholars may have followed the friar's outlines and suggestions but that they were largely responsible for the actual content. Though Sahagún would later become pessimistic about the success of the Franciscan mission and suspicious of Nahua Christianity, at the time of the *Psalmodia's* composition he was still an enthusiastic supporter of the Nahua Church. Had the *Psalmodia* been composed twenty years later, Sahagún might have been more critical of his students' work and supervised it more closely.[7]

In compiling their songbook, the collaborators made use of Latin breviaries, the Latin Bible, one or more books of saints' lives, drafts of the sahaguntine ethnographic corpus, and their own literary talents. They excerpted, recombined, condensed, and elaborated upon this material, mixing traditional styles of oral discourse with new styles originating from the translation of European texts. The result is a fascinating hybrid literary form and an outstanding work of Nahuatl literature.

Saint James the Apostle was the patron saint of Spain. As Santiago Matamoros ("Saint James Moor-slayer"), he was a warrior saint who led the reconquest of Spain from the Moors as well as the Spanish invasion of America. *Santiago y a ellos*, "Saint James and at them," was the Spanish soldier's battle cry at home and abroad. There were many stories of Santiago's apparitions, armed and resplendent on his white horse, alongside Spaniards in their battles with the Moors. It was part of the folklore of the conquest of Mexico that Santiago had been seen fighting on the side of Cortés's army; these stories followed Spanish armies throughout the Americas. Santiago was also the patron saint of Tlaltelolco, site of the Franciscan college and Martín Jacobita's hometown.

The *Psalmodia*'s chants are divided into "psalms" or cantos, each of which is subdivided into short stanzas arranged in the printed text as paragraphs. Throughout the Saint James song, these stanzas are quite brief and each has a period marked at the end. They can be considered discrete phrasal units of the text; because of their brevity they may be considered lines rather than stanzas. My subdivision of some of these lines into more than one sentence is arbitrary: they could all be translated as one or as several English sentences.[8] Each canto represents a grouping of five or six of these lines into a larger phrasal unit that in turn constitutes a discrete segment of the entire song.

In the following transcription I preserve the organization and orthography of the original text, though I have placed word divisions according to grammatical units.[9]

PRIMERO Psalmo.

(1) Ma onquiza, ma oncaoani, ma ueca actimoteca in itenio in imauizio, in itlaço in Dios, in Sanctiago Apostol.

(2) Ma iximacho, ma mocaqui, ma onmauiçolo in itlachiual, in inechicaual in vei tiacauh in toCapitan.

(3) Ma onmotta, ma teispan tlalilo, inic cuecueiuca in itlatqui iztac cauallo tlaçotlatquio, cenca mauiçauhqui.

(4) Ma iecteneoalo in itlaçoEspada, in cenca pepetlacatiuh, inic tlauitectiuh, in quīxaxamatztiuh in toiaoa.

(5) Vel mauiztli moteca in impan Morosme, in Turcosme motlapololtianime, inic ispampa eoa, pepechtli moteca.

(6) Cēca tlanestitiuh, tzitzilicatiuh in iteucuitlaeoauh, itepuzeoauh, maquiziotiuh, chalchiuhiotiuh.

SEGVNDO Psalmo.

(1) YN iehoatzi in toveitlatocauh in Iesus, oquimonochili, oquimopepenili inic yiauquizcauh in Sanctiago.

(2) In iquac ie quimopeoaltiliz in iauiotl, inic oiauchioaloc in vei tlacateculutl, yoan in isquichti in itlacateculupoa, niman quimonochili in vei tiacauh in Sanctiago, yoan in iteiccauh in sant Ioan.

(3) In iehoatzi in Sanctiago, yCapitan omuchiuh in toveitlatocatzi in Iesus, ca no yoan quimotecutlatocatitzino.

(4) Matlactli vmume in iautequioaque, oquinmopepenili in Iesus, auh in itecutlatocaoa, çan einti.

(5) Sant Pedro, Sanctiago, yoan sant Ioã, oquinmotecutlatocatitzino in iehoatzi in Iesus: çan no im eisti imispan oquimonestili in itlatocaiotzi in vmpa Thabor.

(6) çan no iehoanti imispã quimotlatlauhtili in itatzi Dios, yoan eztica omitonitzino, in vmpa suchitla Gethsemani.

TERCERO Psalmo.

(1) YN iquac oquinmoxexelhui in Iesus in iiautequioacaoa, inic nouian cemanaoac teuiutica iauiotl quichiuazque.

(2) Auh in iehoatl in toveiCapitan in Sãctiago, oitequiuh muchiuh in vmpa España, in quiniauchiuaz in tlatlacateculu.

(3) Vmpa oquimopeoaltili in itemachtil, itocaioca Galizia, miectlamantli tlamauiçolli oquimuchiuili.

(4) Cenca ic omauiçoloc in itemachtil, in ic otlaneltocac in vei ciuapilli Doña Loba.

(5) In vmpa Galicia, vmpa icac in iveiteupancaltzi, in cenca mauiztililo in nouian cemanaoac.

(6) Vmpa tlamauiçoto in vei teupisqui in sancto Padre: vmpa oquinoalisquetzteoac in Cardenales.

QVARTO Psalmo.

(1) YN tehoanti in nueua España titlaca, ma cenca ticmauiçoca in iveicaltzi in toCapitan, in vncan tlaçopialo in inacaiotzi, in itocaioca Galizia Sanctiago.

(2) çan no iehoatzi in quinmoiauchiuilico in nica nueua España in toiauoa tlatlacateculu, in iehoatzi in toveiCapitã in Sanctiago.

(3) IlhuicacaioCorona in iteucuitlaicpacsuchitl oquimocuili in ilhuicac, quimomaqli î Iesus totlaçotemaquisticatzi.

(4) Iecnemiliztica quimoteputztoquili, in toveitlatocatzi Iesus, in iehoatzi in toveiCapitan Sanctiago.

(5) çan no yoan imiquiztica oquimoteputztoquili, in ipampa tlaneltoquiliztli, oquimonoquili in itlapalteuilotlauhquecholezçotzi.[10]

First Psalm

(1) May it issue forth, may it resound forth, may it reach far and wide, the fame, the honor of God's precious one, Saint James the Apostle!

(2) May they be recognized, may they be heard, may they be marveled at, the deeds, the valor of the great warrior, our Captain!

(3) May it be seen, may it be placed before people, how they shimmer, the vestments of the white horse! It is covered with precious vestments, it is very wondrous!

(4) May his precious Sword be praised! It goes glimmering greatly! With it he goes thrashing things, he goes smashing our enemies!

(5) Truly, fear is cast down upon the Moors, the Turks, the confused ones! As they flee from his presence, saddles are cast down!

(6) Greatly it goes shining, it goes jingling, his skin of gold,[11] his skin of metal! It goes covered with bracelets, it goes covered with jades!

Second Psalm

(1) He, our great speaker, Jesus, he called him. He chose Saint James as his soldier!

(2) It was when he was about to begin the war, by which war was made on the great were-owl and all his fellow were-owls. Then he called him—the great warrior Saint James, and his younger brother Saint John!

(3) He, Saint James, he became our great speaker Jesus's Captain. And he also made him a magistrate!

(4) Twelve are the war commanders whom Jesus chose, but his magistrates are only three!

(5) Saint Peter, Saint James and Saint John—Jesus made them magistrates. Likewise, it was the three of them, it was in their presence that he revealed his realm, there at Tabor.

(6) Likewise, it was in their presence that he prayed to his father, God, and he sweated with blood, there at the garden, Gethsemane.

Third Psalm

(1) When Jesus divided up his war commanders, it was so that everywhere in the world in a sacred way they would make war.

(2) And our great Captain Saint James, it became his task to make war on the were-owls there in Spain.

(3) Where he began his teaching, it was in a place called Galicia. He did many wondrous things![12]

(4) Thus his teaching was greatly marveled at. Thus the great noblewoman Doña Loba considered the things to be true.[13]

(5) There in Galicia, there stands his great temple. It is greatly marveled at everywhere in the world.

(6) There the great priest, the Holy Father, went to marvel. There he left cardinals appointed.

Fourth Psalm

(1) We, we people of New Spain, let us marvel greatly at our Captain's great house, where his body is guarded as something precious, in the place called Galicia Saint James!

(2) Likewise he came to make war here in New Spain upon our enemies, the were-owls, he, our great Captain, Saint James!

(3) His heavenly Crown, his flowery chaplet of gold, he took it in heaven. He who gave him it was Jesus, our precious rescuer![14]

(4) With his good life[15] he followed behind our great speaker Jesus, he, our great Captain, Saint James!

(5) Likewise with his death he followed behind him. Because of belief he spilled the amethysts, the roseate spoonbills, of his blood!

I will proceed through the text according to its "psalms" or cantos, discussing some of the Nahuatl stylistic strategies the authors employ and the indigenous meanings they express or imply.[16]

The opening canto is written in an incantatory or invocatory style of discourse, as if to conjure forth the saint's presence for the celebration of his festival.[17] It begins by invoking the saint's fame, then his deeds and valor. The first two lines have the same structure: three optative clauses followed by a couplet of possessed nouns and then a couplet of titles for the saint. In the third line, what has merely been heard and known, perceived from a distance, begins to become visible and present. One does not yet see the saint, but his horse has materialized. Now there are only two optative clauses, followed by a series of visual images. In the fourth line the sword appears. The pace of the action increases even more: there is only one optative clause, followed by a visual image of the shining sword, then two verbs describing the saint's actions. The verbs for the sword's glimmering and for the saint's actions share the compounding verb -*tiuh*, which denotes that the subject is performing the action while "going." This creates a triplet; it also strengthens the sense of action: no sooner does the saint's sword materialize than he rides off to do battle with it.

In the fifth line optative clauses cease to be necessary, for the saint has now taken matters into his own hands. To create the desired effect one need merely report it: the enemies flee so rapidly that their saddles (*pepechtli*, "platform(s)") fall off. The verb *moteca*, "it lies down" or "it is cast down," describes both the fear that descends upon the triplet of enemies and the casting down of their saddles. The saint is associated with forward and outward movement; the enemies with movement downward, suggestive of defeat.

In its last line the canto finally provides a glimpse of the saint's person, but he is covered with shining armor. The saint himself is veiled by his attributes and is, in effect, identified with them, just as indigenous deity images and impersonators (*ixiptla*) took on a god's identity by wearing the appropriate regalia. The line consists of a couplet of *-tiuh* verbs, followed by a couplet of possessed nouns ending in the morpheme *-ehuauh* "skin," followed by another couplet in which the *-tiuh* verbal suffix is attached to nouns describing the saint's armor. The tight structure of this line reasserts order and stability after the violent action of the preceding lines. The enemies have been routed but the saint is still present, still moving outward, emanating light and sound, and covered with precious objects.

Rather than the fisherman's son of the Gospels or the pilgrim saint of medieval legend, the authors chose to invoke Santiago Matamoros. However, the saint of the *Reconquista* has been transformed into a numen of the Nahua sacred world. The saint's sword and the trappings of his horse shimmer with radiance. His armor is no longer a defensive weapon but a glistening treasure trove, which also creates music: the jingling bells represented by the onomatopoeic verb *tzitzilica*.

These reiterated references to radiance and preciousness are invocatory formulas for calling forth the sacred aspect of reality, perceived in terms of shimmering light, precious stones, brightly colored birds and flowers, fragrant scents, and pleasing music. This is the world of Nahua song, a paradisiacal otherworld which is also this world, ritually transformed to reveal the sacredness and preciousness immanent in created nature. Life itself is a bursting and blossoming of shimmering, radiant color. It is through the flower-filled poetry of song and the rhythm of dance that one achieves direct contact with this sacred world, which was, for Nahuas, the ultimate reality, the "really real." [18] The relationship between the immediately perceived world and this sacred transformation of it is metaphorical, in that elements from the flowery world can "stand for" things of the ordinary world, and yet it is more than metaphorical, for, in a sense, ordinary things "really are" their transformational selves, however fleeting and incomplete one's perception of those real selves may be.

Christian symbolism of paradise and beauty was oriented not toward the material, created world but toward the beyond: God and his favored ones, eternal life in glory of the resurrected and transfigured dead. The ultimate reality was spiritual and transcendant, bearing no direct tie to the earth and life upon it. Christian transcendentalism was meaningless to the Nahuas and was lost in translation. However, the existence within Christian symbolism of metaphors for holiness involving light, gardens, flowers, jewels, and the like provided a gateway through which the "flowery world" complex of Nahua belief slipped into colonial religion. Allusions to this symbolic complex abound in Nahua-Christian literature, particularly in texts directed at invoking and praising sacred beings.[19]

The first canto begins to develop double levels of meaning that will run through the rest of the song. The Spanish term *capitan*, "captain," is paired with the indigenous *huey tiacauh*, "great warrior." This creates ambiguity: is the man under the golden armor a Spanish soldier or a Nahua soldier? The possessive prefix *to-*, "our," attached to *capitan*, and not to *huey tiacauh*, suggests the direction in which this ambiguity is to be resolved: the text asserts indigenous possession. Santiago may be a *capitan*, but he is on our side. The golden armor, suggestive of Spanish soldiers and their greed, is, after all, overlain with bracelets and jades, which were more precious than gold in indigenous valuation.

In the fourth line Santiago routs "our enemies"; in the fifth his foes are Moors, Turks, and heretics ("confused ones"), foes of the Spanish Church who had little relevance to the indigenous community. This juxtaposition repeats the ambiguity between indigenous and Spanish referents. By equating these enemies with their own, the authors have again implied that Santiago is on their side, and theirs is the Christian community—on a par with any other—that he defends.

The saint's horse and sword are European imports,[20] but as ethnic markers they are ambiguous: high-ranking indigenous nobles were permitted to possess these items. The saint described may be a Spanish captain intent on conquest; he may also be an indigenous lord defending his community from dangerous outsiders. The text permits no unambiguous viewing of his face.

In the second canto, the scene shifts from the present to the past, and from incantatory to narrative discourse. This second canto is linked to the first through the continued use of military imagery, now combined with information from the Gospels. Christ, James, and the other apostles are categorized according to indigenous social rankings. Christ is the *huey tlatoani*, "great speaker," a title applied to the ruler of a city-state with many tributaries, like Tenochtitlan before the Spanish conquest. Christ selected James to be his *yaoquizqui*, "one who goes out as an enemy"; this is a general term for soldiers, denoting no particular rank or distinction. James also receives the titles *capitan* and *huey tiacauh* given him in the first canto. The loanword *capitan*, possessed by "us" in the first canto, is now possessed by Christ (line 3). "Our" *capitan* is also Christ's *capitan*; "we" and Christ are on the same side. The term has been removed from its ethnic Spanish context and used to link indigenous and Christian identity.

The twelve apostles are *yaotequihuaque*, "they whose work is the enemy"; this term denotes the commander of a rank of soldiers. Christ's closest companions saints Peter, James, and John are here designated his judges or magistrates. The office of *tecutlato*, "one who speaks as a lord," was, in preconquest times, granted to certain very successful warriors; they administered justice in the rulers' courts.[21]

The metaphor of spiritual warfare against the Devil and his minions is a common Christian figure; to describe the apostles as warriors required no particular inventiveness. But by describing these warriors in terms of the preconquest military hierarchy, referring to different rankings rather than simply using generic references to soldiers, the authors have associated the apostles with the social structure of preconquest Mexico. This narrative about the past describes a society similar to, or even identifiable with, that of the Mexican past. Events of the Christian scriptures are made meaningful through this association with preconquest society.

Since "devil" meant something somewhat different for Nahuas and European Christians, I have here translated *tlacatecolotl*, the Nahuatl term used for devils and demons, with the more literal but still malevolent-sounding "were-owl." *Tlacatecolotl* (plural *tlatlacatecolo*) literally means "human horned owl." This was the title given to a type of malevolent shaman who had the horned owl as his alter ego (*nahualli*); the friars appropriated this term, for lack of anything better, to refer to devils. Lucifer was then the "great *tlacatecolotl*." The term *tlacatecolotl* occurs in nearly all Nahuatl doctrinal texts, turning up also in indigenous chronicles. From its very specific original referent, it quickly expanded its meaning to encompass the hordes of malevolent non-human beings that populated the friars' world.

For Nahuas, especially for historically and culturally self-conscious Nahuas like Sahagún's students, the *tlatlacatecolo* were not simply creatures of the imported religion, for their ranks included the deities formerly worshipped in Mexico. From the very beginning the friars had argued for the rejection of these gods by identifying them as devils, an identification which the friars took quite literally. Nahuas learned to refer to their parents' gods as *tlatlacatecolo*. The "great *tlacatecolotl*" was sometimes associated with the deity Tezcatlipoca.[22]

Scattered throughout the *Psalmodia* there are stories of other apostles and martyrs of early Christianity who smashed idols, drove away *tlatlacatecolo* and brought people into Christianity. Nahuas of the first postconquest generation would have heard in such words the echoes of their own people's recent past. The beings on whom Christ and his warriors are to do battle are the deities of unconverted, unbaptized peoples.

Of all the New Testament events in which James participated, the authors mention only three. Christ chooses James and his brother John; no mention is made of their occupation as fishermen (Matthew 4:21–22), a role inconsistent with that of a Nahua warrior. As one of Christ's three "magistrates," Saint James witnessed events that the other apostles were not privileged to attend: Christ's transfiguration upon Mount Tabor and Christ's praying in Gethsemane, during which, according to Luke 22:44, his sweat was as drops of blood (*sicut guttae sanguinis*). Little is revealed about these events—least of all that the three men, in a swoon at the transfiguration and asleep at Gethsemane, could hardly be considered attentive participants. What is important is their attendance upon the deity; the authors honor Saint James by recounting his close relationship with Christ.

Like the preceding canto, this one has six lines; however, it is composed in a narrative style lacking the tight structure of the opening invocation. The discourse style of European written narrative, in which a chronological sequence of events is reported, competes with indigenous interest in formulas of oral recitation. The canto reads as a narrative; however, the events are recounted with minimal detail and are reduced to a series of images and assertions fitted into the six-line form.

Repetitive devices occur throughout the canto. The first line recounts Christ's calling of James; the same event is more elaborately told in the second line. The phrase "the great were-owl and all his fellow were-owls" is echoed in structure by "the great warrior Saint James and his younger brother Saint John"; one can imagine the apostles lined up against the demons for face-to-face combat.

The verbs *oquimonochili*, "he called him," and *oquimopepenili*, "he chose him," in the first line are repeated one by one in the *quimonochili*, "he called him," of line two and the *oquinmopepenili*, "he chose them," of line four; in the latter pair one sound has been altered in each word through the dropping of the *o-* past prefix in the first and the change to a plural object marker in the second (*qui-* to *quim-*). Other words also recur with slight variations that create echoes without creating monotony: line one's *tohueytlatocauh*, "our great speaker," is given a reverential suffix in line three, *tohueytlatocatzin*, "our (rev.) great speaker." The term *tecutlato* occurs in two verbalized and one possessed form: *quimotecutlatocatzino*, "he (rev.) made him a magistrate" (line three); *oquinmotecutlatocatzino*, "he (rev.) made them magistrates" (line five); *itecutlatocahuan*, "his magistrates" (line four).

The second part of line five forms a couplet with line six, *zan no imeixtin imixpan*, "just also they three before them," being nearly repeated in *zan no yehuantin imixpan*, "just also they before them." These introductory phrases are followed by descriptions of Christ's actions; both lines then close with a reference to place, "there at Tabor" and "there at the garden, Gethsemane."

The third canto recounts another phase of Christ's war against the devils. The first line refers to Christ sending his apostles to preach throughout the world. With this seemingly straightforward statement the authors are treading upon politically sensitive ground. According to Mark 16:15, the resurrected Christ told his followers: "Go ye into all the world, and preach the gospel to every creature." Christian lore distributed the apostles around the known world in such a way that all lands were at least nominally covered.

When Europe became aware of the Western Hemisphere, questions arose as to whether Christ had actually sent his apostles to "all the world." One popular solution was to follow Columbus's confusion and include the "Indies" with India. Saint Thomas had preached in India, and hence perhaps in the Indies as well. If one wished to find evidence of the saint's presence, one could do so; in Mexico the myth of Quetzalcoatl was so manipulated as to make him into Saint Thomas. The belief in previous evangelization became a feature of national consciousness among Mexicans of Spanish descent.[23]

Sahagún, like most Franciscans, chose not to believe in an earlier evangelization but to credit his own order with the original conversion of Mexico. In his Spanish prologue to the *Colloquios* he wrote: "we know for certain that our Lord God kept this land of diverse peoples and domains . . . concealed for his secret reasons until these our times."[24] Thus, Mexico was by special dispensation excluded from Christ's apostolate and reserved for the followers of Francis.

When Nahua writers refer to "everywhere in the world," one would expect that they would consider their own land as part of this expanse. By referring in a Nahuatl text to Christ's worldwide dispatch of his apostles, they imply that Christ did mean to include Mexico.

The rest of the third canto is a distillation into five lines of the medieval legend about Saint James's mission to Spain and the history of his shrine at Compostela in Galicia. Before beginning to discuss his activities in Spain, the authors reassert indigenous possession of the saint: he is *tohueycapitan*, "our great captain."

According to Spanish legend, Saint James, whose name means "fighter" (*luchador*), preaches in Spain but manages to convert only nine people. He then returns to Judea and is martyred. His disciples take his body and get into a boat, which an angel guides back to Galicia. The saint's body is swallowed up by a great rock. His disciples are persecuted by Queen Loba, the local ruler whom Saint James had been unable to convert. They enjoy a series of miraculous escapes, and Loba eventually converts. A church is built on the site of her palace to hold Saint James's remains. Many miracles occur there; it becomes a center for pilgrimages and is visited by many worthies. During the *Reconquista* the saint appears as a knight on horseback fighting on the Spanish side.[25]

The writers definitely had access to lengthy tellings of this legend, for in their songs about some of the other saints they include numerous hagiographic details that indicate the use of some edition of the *Flos sanctorum*. But they treat Saint James as a generic apostle. He enters Spain, his assigned territory; he fights non-Christian deities in the form of *tlatlacatecolo*; he performs miracles; he converts the local leader; an elaborate shrine is built for his remains. The last line, about an unnamed pope and his cardinals, hardly seems worthy of inclusion; it certainly does not bring the canto to a resounding close. The apostle most closely tied to Spanish national identity receives a summary treatment, while the tales of other apostles in other lands are recounted at length. This constitutes deliberate neglect of Spain.

Although the six-line form of the preceding cantos is maintained, this canto shows less stylistic development. The reiteration of *ompa*, "there," creates a sense of distant wonders being enumerated. The fourth line balances *ic omahuizoloc*, "thus it was marveled at," against *ic otlaneltocac*, "thus she believed." There is a reiteration of wonderment, with different forms of the verb *mahuizoa*, "to marvel at," presented in lines three through six. The authors are writing with care, but they are not putting forth their best effort.

The fourth canto shifts the scene from Spain to New Spain. The first line links the here and now to that distant place by continuing the series of "marveling" statements: we here in New Spain also participate in the worldwide wonderment at Saint James's shrine. The optative "let us marvel" is a call to action, marking a shift from the narration of past events back to the ongoing festival celebration.

The phrase "we people of New Spain" should be read as referring to the indigenous community, or specifically those who are at this moment reading or performing the text. It does not include people of Spanish descent. When the *Psalmodia* (and other Nahua-Christian texts) speaks of the Spaniards in Mexico it calls them *Castillan tlaca*, "people of Castile," and clearly distinguishes them from the "people here" (*nican tlaca*) or the "people of New Spain." There is a hint here of an incipient pan-Nahua or even pan-indigenous ethnic identity, at least among these Nahuatl speakers from different communities who have been raised and educated together under the Franciscans. Ethnic groupings such as Mexica, Acolhua, or Tepaneca were not meaningful to the Nahua Church; the *Psalmodia* is intended for use in all communities that understood its language. "We people of New Spain" is an appropriately inclusive term for the indigenous citizens of the colony; these are the faces behind the text's various first-person-plural statements.[26]

The second line of this canto is an understated utterance that speaks volumes. The opening "likewise" refers back to line two of the preceding canto, where Saint James was sent to make war on the demons in Spain. In the same way he came here to New Spain to make war on the "were-owls" who are "our" enemies. The authors have collapsed the conversion of Spain and the conversion of Mexico into a single continuous or repeating history. They have resolved the issue of Christ's universal apostolate by making New Spain an extension of Spain rather than of Saint Thomas's India. New Spain is included in that original apostolate without any intervening reversion to "paganism": the fifteen centuries between the life of Saint James and the conversion of Mexico are simply ignored.

The basis for this statement is the widely held belief that Saint James appeared and fought alongside the Spaniards in the conquest of Mexico. In that sense he did come to New Spain to make war. However, the song makes no mention of warfare between Spanish and indigenous armies. There is no indication that the Spaniards brought Saint James, that Saint James was on the Spaniards' side, or even that the Spaniards were involved. Instead, the people of New Spain are equated with the people of Spain as subjects of the saint's work, and the non-Christian deities of ancient Spain are equated with those of Mexico—"our enemies the were-owls." Saint James came to fight not the people of New Spain but only their former deities.

The radical nature of this statement is made even clearer by comparing it with a text that presents, in Nahuatl, a Spanish view of these events, and not that of a soldier or colonist but of a friar devoted to the Nahua Church. The Augustinian Fray Juan de la Anunciación wrote sermons for the festivals of the saints in a book published in 1577. His work, which was the *Psalmodia*'s only published rival in the field of hagiography, borrowed some of its material from a manuscript version of the *Psalmodia*; however, this friar tells a very different story about Saint James. He reminds his Nahua audience that only eight hundred to twelve hundred Spaniards were able to conquer them, even though they were "innumerable" and had many valiant rulers.

Auh macihui in amixachintin ancatca, vel oanpanahuiloq̄ ca çan quezquitoton in amechpehuaco, oquimpanahuiq̄ in amoculhuā, ca oquimmopaleuiliq̄ yxpātzinco in totecuiyo DIOS, in cihuapilli sancta Maria, yuā in Sāctiago, ca miecpa oquimmonextilitzinoq̄ oquimmotititzinoq̄.

And even though you were a great many, you were quite overcome. Just a very few came and conquered you; they overcame your grandfathers. Indeed, before our lord God, the noblewoman Saint Mary and Saint James helped them. Indeed, many times they appeared to them, they made themselves visible to them.[27]

Here, the saints helped the Spaniards to vanquish the grandfathers of the Nahua congregation. The friar goes on to explain that this is why "you Christians" should celebrate Saint James's festival.

In one line of a song, the *Psalmodia*'s authors have rewritten the history of the conquest and redrawn the political structure of colonial society. Saint James no longer validates the Spanish invasion. The Spaniards and the Nahuas are not pitched against one another but occupy the same status in relation to the saint and the demons/deities. The song tells a story not of invasion, warfare, and defeat but simply of conversion. In this revisionist history there is no justification for Spanish domination.[28]

The *Psalmodia* works similar magic upon the festival of the Roman martyr Saint Hippolytus. His festival was celebrated in Mexico because it happens to fall on August 13, the day that, in 1521, the Aztec ruler Cuauhtemoc was taken prisoner by Cortés; this event marked the effective beginning of Spanish colonial dominion. The song for this festival also celebrates "our" liberation from the "were-owls." The history of the conquest is left ambiguous and understated in the following lines:

Tintlacaoa ticatca in tlatlacateculu, auh in iehoantin in tetecuti, in tlatoque, quinpisticatca quintlaçotlaticatca in tlatlacateculu: auh in Dios quinoalmioali in iiaoquizcaoa, ic peoaloque in tlatlacateculu, yoan in intetlaçotlacaoa.

We were the slaves of the were-owls. And the lords and kings were keeping, were loving the were-owls. But God sent his soldiers. Thus the were-owls were conquered, and those who loved them.[29]

The speakers' "we" is dissociated from those who kept the old deities. God's soldiers are not ascribed any particular ethnic identity; they could even be saints, like James and his fellow "soldiers" of Christ. "Our grandfathers" are not directly implicated and the Spanish presence is not validated. Here again, the story of conquest is told as a story of conversion, and this story does not justify the continuing Spanish presence.

Having made their subtle political statement, the authors retreat to safer subject matter and close the canto with three lines about Saint James's martyrdom. He is crowned by Christ in heaven with the martyr's crown of flowers, the loanword *corona* being equated with the Nahuatl term for a chaplet made of flowers (literally, "on-his-head flowers"). This ornament suggests indigenous ritual accoutrements, to which flowers were as essential in colonial as in preconquest times, and which included wreaths worn on the head. Flowers were intrinsic to the Nahua view of the sacred, as described earlier. It is appropriate that saints in heaven should be adorned with flowers, but their wearing of them is an index of paradisiacal existence itself rather than a symbol of the moral rectitude for which, in Christian formulations, that existence is the reward.

The following line is the strongest moral statement in the entire text, and it is not a very strong moral statement. The *Psalmodia* as a whole is strikingly amoral, free of the intrusive, judgmental voice of the preaching friar. Like more traditional Nahuatl songs, it is concerned with the celebration and commemoration of the sacred rather than with human behavior. The line simply compares Saint James's lifestyle with that of Christ: the apostle followed Christ's good conduct. Priests told the lives of the saints to Nahua as to European audiences in order to inspire people to follow in the saints' footsteps. Fray Juan de la Anunciación makes this explicit in his hagiographic work: the ministers should preach to the natives (*naturales*) about the lives of the saints, *amonestandoles y animandoles à que las imiten y sigan*, "admonishing them and encouraging them to imitate and follow them."[30] Saint James imitated Christ; an endorsement of such behavior for ordinary humans would, in a priest's discourse, logically follow. But the writers are not interested in Saint James as a moral model, only in establishing his close relationship to the sacred.

This last canto is somewhat more stylized than the preceding one. In line three "his heavenly crown" and "his flowery chaplet of gold" form a couplet, and the first portion of this line (which I have translated as a sentence) forms a couplet with the second half, the verb *quimomaquili*, "he gave it," nearly repeating the structure of *oquimocuili*, "he took it," with a change of subject. The *zan no*, "likewise," introducing line two is repeated in line five. Lines two and four both end with "he, our great captain, Saint James"; line one also ends with the saint's name. The reference in line four to his life is followed by a parallel reference to his death, which as a martyrdom for faith was also an imitation of Christ. Thus, line four's *iyecnemiliztica quimotepotztoquili*, "with his good life he followed behind him," is echoed in line five's *imiquiztica oquimotepotztoquili*, "with his death he followed behind him"; once again, exact repetition is avoided by the selective inclusion of the *o-* prefix, which does not affect meaning in this context.

The very last word of the song, *itlapalteuilotlauhquecholezçotzi*, "his amethyst roseate spoonbill blood (reverential suffix)," is also its longest and most complex compound term. The flowers referred to two lines above are here joined by an allusion to precious stones and brilliantly colored birds, two other vital components of the sacred world. Martyrdom for faith has become a manifestation of Nahua sacred reality, as the saint's blood issues forth in the form of amethysts (or other reddish crystalline stones) and roseate spoonbills. This is metaphor, and more than metaphor: ultimately, it is of such things that this holy blood "really" consists. Like blood, amethysts and roseate spoonbills are reddish in color, and their Nahuatl names incorporate terms for redness. Amethyst is *tlapaltehuilotl*, "red crystal," *tlapalli* referring to red paint or dye. The roseate spoonbill is *tlauhquecholli, tlauh-* coming from *tlahuitl*, "red ochre," an element found also in terms referring to the light of torches and of the dawn, and *quecholli* referring to long-necked birds (from *quechtli* "neck" and *olli* "rubber" [31]).

The invention of this long (twelve-syllable), complex, and highly evocative compound word brings the song to a resounding finale, while alluding to traditional Nahua concerns with penitence and the life-giving powers of sacrificial blood. The canto is one line shorter than the preceding four; this shortening also marks a decisive ending to the text.

By describing the saint's travels to New Spain before discussing his death, the authors leave ambiguous the chronological sequence of the saint's actions. Perhaps he came here, as well as to Spain, before he died. Though his body is kept there in Spain, he is associated with symbols of the Nahua sacred world: shimmering light, jade and amethyst, flowers and tropical birds. He is a warrior, a magistrate, "our" captain, who can be invoked to ward off external dangers.

The Nahua authors have appropriated the patron saint of conquest and used him to legitimize indigenous society, to protect the indigenous community, to negate the significance of Spanish political domination, and to embody a distinctly non-Christian (though characteristically Nahua-Christian) perception of the sacred. This Santiago is not a precolumbian deity, but neither is he a Spanish captain or a fisherman of Galilee. He is a suitable patron for a colonial Nahua community.

The friars sought to silence indigenous voices and replace them with their own, with Christian word and text unaltered and eternal. Translation between two cultural worlds is never so straightforward a procedure. The friars' amanuenses saw translation as a transformative process through which they could construct texts with meanings appropriate to their own place and time and their own concerns as nobles and cultural brokers in a colonized society. By unmasking some features of the Nahua face behind Santiago's shining armor, I hope to have shown that texts of Christian devotion produced by indigenous writers, even under the direct supervision of priests, may record not the destruction of the authors' culture but their methods of coping and surviving, not the obliteration of native discourse styles but their creative adaptation to new outlets of expression. Translating their texts from a perspective of linguistic and cultural sensitivity not available to sixteenth-century priests, we may recover some lost aspects of colonial Native American experience.

Notes

1. *The Spoken Word and the Work of Interpretation* (Philadelphia: University of Pennsylvania Press, 1983), 333–34.

2. *Signasti domine servum tuum Franciscum signis redemptionis nostre.* Nahuatl works bearing this scene include Fray Alonso de Molina's vocabularies of 1555 and 1571, Molina's 1571 grammar, and the *Cartilla para enseñar a leer* of 1569. It also appears on Fray Maturino Gilberti's 1559 vocabulary of Tarascan.

3. Vicente L. Rafael, *Contracting Colonialism: Translation and Christian Conversion in Tagalog Society under Early Spanish Rule.* (Ithaca: Cornell University Press, 1988), 33.

4. See especially *The Slippery Earth: Nahua-Christian Moral Dialogue in Sixteenth-Century Mexico* (Tucson: University of Arizona Press, 1989).

5. Fray Bernardino de Sahagún, *Psalmodia christiana y sermonario de los sanctos del año en lengua mexicana* (Mexico: Pedro Ocharte, 1583), 120r–22r. I thank the John Carter Brown Library at Brown University for the reproduction of the *Psalmodia* that I have used for this study.

6. Sahagún, *Psalmodia*, prologue; Bernardino de Sahagún, *Florentine Codex*, trans. Arthur J. O. Anderson and Charles Dibble (Santa Fe: School of American Research and University of Utah Press, 1950–82) introductory volume, 54–55; Luis Nicolau D'Olwer, *Fray Bernardino de Sahagún (1499–1590)*, trans. Mauricio Mixco (Salt Lake City: University of Utah Press, 1987) 35, 84.

7. It is somewhat startling that the *Psalmodia* actually did get published. By 1583 Sahagún had become extremely critical of some of the earlier work by himself and his students. He (apparently) withdrew from the publication process the *Colloquios* of 1564, a text commemorating early Franciscan successes, which was going to be printed along with the *Psalmodia* (see J. Jorge Klor de Alva, "Sahagún's Misguided Introduction to Ethnography and the Failure of the *Colloquios* Project," *The Work of Bernardino de Sahagún: Pioneer Ethnographer of Sixteenth-Century Aztec*

Mexico, ed. J. Jorge Klor de Alva, H. B. Nicholson and Eloise Quiñones Keber (Albany: State University of New York, 1988).

8. All Nahuatl "nouns" and "verbs" are really "sentence-words" that can stand alone as sentences; nouns incorporate an understood copula and verbs incorporate a subject.

9. Elsewhere in this paper I employ a standardized orthography.

10. Sahagún, *Psalmodia*, 120r–22r.

11. *Teocuitlatl*, "sacred excrement," refers to both gold and silver, the two metals being distinguished by the modifiers *coztic*, "yellow," and *iztac*, "white," respectively. The term without modifiers appears to be more often associated with gold than with silver; hence my translation.

12. *Tlamahuizolli*, "something to be marveled at." This is the standard Nahuatl gloss for "miracle."

13. The verb form *tlaneltoca*, "to consider things as true," is used in Nahua-Christian writings in contexts where European texts speak of religious conversion or religious faith; both concepts were alien to indigenous culture.

14. *Temaquixtiani*, "one who takes (people) from the hands of others," was the standard Nahuatl term for Christ as savior.

15. I am reading the ambiguous *Iecnemiliztica* as the possessed form *iyecnemiliztica*, "with his good life," consistent wiht *imiquiztica*, "with his death."

16. My attention to the various forms of repetition and parallelism the authors employed in constructing this text was suggested by William F. Hanks's work with colonial Yucatec texts (e.g. "Elements of Maya Style," in *Word and Image in Maya Culture*, ed. William F. Hanks and Don S. Rice [Salt Lake City: University of Utah Press, 1989]; "Grammar, Style, and Meaning in a Maya Manuscript," rev. of *Heaven Born Mérida and its Destiny: The Book of Chilam Balam of Chumayel*, by Munro Edmonson, *International Journal of American Linguistics* 54 [1988]).

17. My use of exclamation points in this canto (as in the fourth canto) is obviously arbitrary. The invocatory tone set by the many optative constructions, as well as the gradual increase in activity from line to line, suggests an active, excited style of oral declamation.

18. For my knowledge of the characteristics and cultural distribution of this symbolic complex, I am indebted to Jane H. Hill and her paper entitled "The Flowery World of Old Uto-Aztecan," presented at the 86th Annual Meeting of the American Anthropological Association, Chicago, 1987. The relationship between the poetry of song and the Nahuas' deepest philosophical concerns was established by Miguel León-Portilla (*Aztec Thought and Cutlure* [Norman: University of Oklahoma Press, 1963]). Willard Gingerich has recently reevaluated and elaborated upon León-Portilla's ideas ("Heidegger and the Aztecs: The Poetics of Knowing in Pre-Hispanic Nahuatl Poetry," *Recovering the Word: Essays on Native American Literature*, ed. Brian Swann and Arnold Krupat [Berkeley: University of California Press, 1987]).

19. For a fuller description see Burkhart, "Flowery Heaven: The Aesthetic of Paradise in Nahuatl Devotional Literature," *Res* 20 (1991).

20. Indigenous weaponry included a swordlike weapon made of wood inset with obsidian blades, the *macuahuitl*. The use of the Spanish term *espada*, however, suggests that the authors are thinking of the European version.

21. The preconquest military hierarchy is described by Ross Hassig, *Aztec Warfare* (Norman: University of Oklahoma Press, 1988), Chapter 3. The *tecutlato*'s role as magistrate is discussed in Sahagún, *Florentine Codex*, IX, Chapters 14 and 21. This title was also applied to rulers of subject city-states (Hassig 28). *Tecutlato* is not used for Christ as judge at the Last Judgment. In that context terms based on the verb *tzontequi*, "to judge, sentence" (literally, "cut [someone's]

hair") are always used. Thus there would be no ambiguity between these preconquest-type judges or magistrates and Christ's role as judge.

22. For a fuller discussion of the term *tlacatecolotl* and its referents, see Burkhart, *The Slippery Earth*, 40–44. I owe to Michael D. Coe the term "were-owl" as a translation for *tlacatecolotl*.

23. For an excellent discussion of the issue of previous evangelization, see Jacques Lafaye, *Quetzalcoatl and Guadalupe: The Formation of Mexican National Consciousness, 1531–1813*, trans. Benjamin Keen (Chicago: University of Chicago Press, 1976).

24. Fray Bernardino de Sahagún, *Coloquios y Doctrina Cristiana*, trans. Miguel León-Portilla (Mexico; Universidad Nacional Autónoma de México, 1986), 72.

25. My discussion is based on two Spanish editions of the *Flos sanctorum*, one published in 1558 in Alcalá and the other in 1568 in Seville, in the collection of the Biblioteca Nacional, Madrid.

26. The term "Indians" (*indios*) very rarely appears in sixteenth-century Nahuatl texts.

27. Fray Juan de la Anunciación, *Sermonario en lengua mexicana* (México: Antonio Ricardo, 1577), 170r.

28. In this formulation there is a striking similarity to the Andean chronicler Guaman Poma de Ayala's revisionist history. According to him the Inca troops were so stunned by apparitions of Saint James and the Virgin Mary that they did not resist the Spanish forces. Since the Andeans peacefully accepted the Spanish presence and the Christian religion, the abusive colonial regime had no justification (see Rolena Adorno, *Guaman Poma: Writing and Resistance in Colonial Peru* [Austin: University of Texas Press, 1986]).

29. Sahagún, *Psalmodia*, 149r–v.

30. Anunciación, 130r.

31. I am following J. Richard Andrews's reading (*Introduction to Classical Nahuatl* [Austin: University of Texas Press, 1975], 465).

Suggested Reading

Arthur J. O. Anderson and John Keber are currently preparing for publication a translation of the entire *Psalmodia christiana*. See also my translation of the *Psalmodia's tlaocolcuicatl*, "sad song," in *Estudios de Cultura Náhuatl* 18:181–218 (1986) and Anderson's translation of the San Bernardino song in *Indiana* 9:107–14 (1984).

On the life and work of Sahagún, see Luis Nicolau D'Olwer, *Fray Bernardino de Sahagún 1499–1590* (Salt Lake City: University of Utah Press, 1987); J. Jorge Klor de Alva, H. B. Nicholson, and Eloise Quiñones Keber, eds., *The Work of Bernardino de Sahagún: Pioneer Ethnographer of Sixteenth-Century Aztec Mexico* (Albany: State University of New York, 1988); and Munro S. Edmonson, ed., *Sixteenth-Century Mexico: The Work of Sahagún* (Albuquerque: University of New Mexico Press, 1974).

I discuss other aspects of the indigenization of Christianity in *The Slippery Earth: Nahua-Christian Moral Dialogue in Sixteenth-Century Mexico* (Tucson: University of Arizona Press, 1989); "Flowery Heaven: The Aesthetic of Paradise in Nahuatl Devotional Literature," *Res* 20 (1991); and "The Solar Christ in Nahuatl Doctrinal Texts of Early Colonial Mexico," *Ethnohistory* 35:234–56 (1988).

Ten Types of Ambiguity in Nahuatl Poetry, or William Empson among the Aztecs

Willard Gingerich

The diabolical difficulty of translating the Nahuatl language poetry of the Aztec city-states has been notorious ever since Fr. Bernardino de Sahagún first compared its sacred texts to a jungle from which Satan launched his guerrilla sorties against the armies of Christ:

It is a very ancient practice of our adversary the Devil to seek out hiding places from which to conduct his business, as the Sacred Scripture says: "Those whose business is evil abhor the light." Accordingly, this Our Enemy has planted in this land a forest or badlands filled with many dense thickets out of which he can conduct his business and where he can hide so as not to be found out, just as do the savage beasts and venomous serpents. These forests or dense badlands are the songs which in this land he has devised that they use and perform in his service, as his divine cult and as psalms in his praise both within and without the temples—the which contain such artifice that they say whatever they like and broadcast whatever he commands, and only those he has instructed are capable of understanding them. It is a very confirmed fact that the cave, forest and badlands where even today this cursed adversary hides himself are the songs and psalms which have been composed and are sung to him, while none are capable of understanding what is mentioned in them save those who are native speakers and thoroughly familiar with this language, in such fashion that undoubtedly they chant in them everything he desires, whether peace or war, praises to him and affronts to Jesus Christ, without anyone else being able to understand (1979, 172).

Fr. Diego Durán, who grew up in New Spain, also found this oral poetry mysterious and opaque, while less demonic:

All the songs of these people are composed of such obscure metaphors that scarcely anyone understands them, if he has not very deliberately studied and discussed them in order to understand their meaning. I have set myself deliberately to listen very carefully to what they sing, among the words and terms of the metaphor, and, while they at first seem to me nonsense, after conferral and discussion they are admirable pronouncements (1967, I, 195).

But even Sahagún was unable finally to deny or banish its rhetorical power, and in 1583 he published in 236 folios a volume entitled *Psalmodia christiana y sermonario de los sanctos del año*, which adapted the old "demonic" poetics and language to biblical texts, hymns in praise of the Virgin and saints, antiphons and texts of the Latin mass, a volume still untranslated to either Spanish or English and the only work to see print in the lifetime of that indefatigable founder of modern ethnography.

We no longer attribute the complexity of Native American poetry to diabolical influence, but instead as a literary community do something equally unscientific and ill-informed: in our vast ignorance and historical forgetfulness of the diversity and resilience of Native American languages and their literatures, we have completely forgotten the complexity itself of those literatures, glimpsing them as we do only through snippets and fragments of often inadequately translated and totally decontextualized passages. Consequently, we tend to believe, if we give the work any attention at all, that Native American poets—such as they were—were all imagists of the Amy Lowell variety, and by and large childishly transparent. For those curious enough to dig for themselves, of course, there have been translated sources of major Native American texts, at least since Washington Matthews's late nineteenth-century work with the Navajo Night Chant in the United States and most notably in the pages of the reports of the Bureau of American Ethnology. Then in the past two decades, beginning with the monumental Anderson and Dibble translation of Sahagún's Florentine Codex, a new promise of rediscovery and general access to traditional Native American literatures has been made, following through the Edmonson translations of Quiché and Yucatec classics; Tedlock's work with Zuni texts and the Popol Vuh; the issuing of Kroeber's Yurok and Karok texts; the critical work of Hymes following Jacobs; Sullivan, Lockhart, Karttunen, and Bierhorst's translations of a range of Aztec texts; and now versions of more or less contemporary survivals of oral tradition from the Kuna of the Panamanian coast (Joel Sherzer) to the Cree of Manitoba (Howard Norman).

And now the complexity and ambiguity of the sixteenth-century Nahuatl texts, with which the transcribed record of Native American literature in North America begins, looks more like a challenge to our literary acumen than an affront to our religion. One scholar reported not long ago that he had spent two years working on a translation of the *Cantares Mexicanos* manuscript (Bierhorst 1985a)—which together with the *Romances de los Señores de la Nueva España* manuscript (Garibay 1964) is the primary record of mid to late sixteenth-century Nahuatl lyrical chant—but decided to give it up because the original was simply too confusing and ambiguous in many parts to ever sustain a clear and unequivocal translation.

To a literary scholar this sounds curiously reminiscent of the objections to the wrangling critical disputation over authoritative, correct, canonical interpretations of English poetry upon which William Empson founded his classic of New Criticism, *Seven Types of Ambiguity*, in 1930. By the time Empson published the first American edition of *Seven Types* in 1947, it had already come to stand for a perfection of critical acumen and sustained sensibility in the reading of poetry. In the years following, it did much to extract, enshrine, and privilege from readings of the canonical poets Shakespeare, Pope, Chaucer, Jonson, and Milton a poetic of grammatical ambiguity, figural tension, and paradox as the standard of literary judgment and helped confirm the reputations of Donne, Herrick, Marvell, and their champion, T. S. Eliot. It is a poetic much berated today for its formalist detachment from context, its failure to take sufficiently into account the historical forces of production which the New Historicism now ascendent insists must always set the terms of poetic creation and critical discussion alike. Empson, like Eliot, René Wellek, Robert P. Warren, Van Wyck Brooks, Ivor Winters, and their company of "close readers," is now exposed as insufficiently self-conscious about the determining historical forces of his own process of valuation—though it is unclear how this poetic would or could have been different if he or they had had the proper historical consciousness. There was, moreover, one aspect of analysis in which Empson was scrupulously historical: he spared no pains in historicizing a word (or phrase) in order to restore every possible breath of allusion or range of meaning it would have carried for the readers or listeners in Chaucer's, Shakespeare's or Donne's audiences. The historical life of the English language was a vital, working reality throughout *Seven Types*.

But whatever the current opinions of Empson's book, the mode of close rhetorical analysis he taught is still essential both to deconstructive formalism, which turned upon New Criticism's Romantic assumptions of organic unity with its own weapon of choice, the undulling razor of irony, and to the neo-Marxist readings and discourse analysis of the New Historicism. Empson's "trick" of discovering in ambiguity a constitutive poetic device of enormous complexity and range contributed substantially to the cultivation of an academic climate, at least in the United States, where the work of the "New Rhetoricians" (Krupat's phrase) from de Man to Hillis Miller would flourish, while his practice with that device underwent a variety of critiques and refinements.

Empson was able to plant his poetic of ambiguity on a deep subsoil of philological study which provided him the foundation, the etymologies and textual glosses, he needed to demonstrate readings of remarkable subtlety and effect. Further, he explicitly counted on the assumption of a canon as well as its familiarity and approval among his readers: "I can assume that my readers already understand and enjoy the examples I shall consider, and I am concerned only to conduct a sufficient analysis of their enjoyment to make it seem more understandable" (6). None of these assumptions can be made by critics or translators of Native American literatures, not even of Nahuatl poetry, which has a critical tradition reaching back as far as 1550 and enjoys a serious collection of full-length grammars (the first published in 1547 and the latest in 1988) and dictionaries (from 1571 to 1985). Only in 1976 (Karttunen and Lockhart) did we get a historical survey of the language. In fact, it remains to be demonstrated to indifferent, skeptical, or outright hostile audiences that there is a real native American, let alone Nahua, poetry at all, able to sustain serious critical scrutiny. "Are you still working on that naugahyde poetry?" one of my best graduate professors used to ask with some regularity.

Obviously, it would be a misapplication of both Empson's accomplishment and his types to attempt their transfer directly to a poetry as non-Western as the Aztec, an oral tradition inheriting by the time of Cortés's arrival (1519) centuries of independent stylistic and iconographic development, a tradition alien to most European genres and their expectations. But the Aztec lyrical performance mode, sung in precolumbian times and through the early colonial period to the accompaniment of hollow log drums (*teponaztli*), large standing drums (*huehuetl*), and gourd rattles of various types (*ayacachtli*), confronts any translator with such a host of ambiguous constructions and unusual agglutinative word formations that Empson's defense and analysis of this primal poetic trope comes easily to mind as model for discovering within an apparent textual chaos of indeterminacy a poetics of sophisticated and compressed emotional density—however distant from the Chaucerian and Shakespearean rhetoric on which Empson honed his critical instruments.

The ambiguities of Nahuatl poetry are of two classes: *textual* and *contextual*. The former are in some instances the consequence of the latter, which are further divided into *constitutive ambiguities*, characteristic of the interface at a given historical juncture between specific oral and literate traditions, conditions, and structural traces the oral performance mode imposes on a text when re-invented into a specific graphemic system (writing), and *historical ambiguities*, the uncertainties constraining (or liberating, if one chooses) Nahuatl poetry interpretation because of our fragmentary and imperfect knowledge of the performance contexts, the uses to which Nahua singers put their performances, or their modes of composition. These historical ambiguities have little to do with Empson's device, but they are unavoidable for the translating interpreter. All contextual ambiguities have repercussions for our ability to read the surviving texts of Nahuatl poetry, but not all textual or linguistic ambiguities have a contextual origin.

The first two types of ambiguity in Nahuatl poetry, then, are contextual historical uncertainties—unresolvable on the basis of known materials—concerning the literary sources of the performances redacted in the *Romances* and *Cantares* manuscripts and the actual circumstances of the accompanied singing, *huehuetitlan*, "beside the standing drum." I have elsewhere (1984) sketched the general picture we have of Nahua performance poetics; León-Portilla (1969, 1972) has discussed performance briefly and Bierhorst (1985a) includes a survey discussion in his Introduction to the *Cantares* Chapter 8. This performance ambiguity has textual repercussions. Bierhorst's controversial theory of the ghost song, a theory that the *Cantares* record the mystical texts of a secret nativist movement which sang down the spirits of the dead from another world, is essentially a theory of performance, drawn out of the ambiguities of the text itself: "The *Cantares Mexicanos* and its congeners comprise a closed system, unintelligible to those who have not been initiated, even if they are fluent speakers of Nahuatl. Neither the standard dictionaries of Molina and Siméon nor the voluminous Florentine Codex can provide the lexical information needed to comprehend this highly figurative and complex idiom" (16). The best defense of Bierhorst's theory is the "admirable pronouncements" he is sometimes able to extract from the figurative jungle of the text, but it remains to be seen if a strictly formalist analysis can successfully defend itself as an historical interpretation.

How Nahua singers composed their songs—or just who composed them—is an even more mysterious historical ambiguity. Study of the two lyric manuscripts, however, reveals several nearly literal repetitions between them, suggesting that singers worked to preserve the integrity of memorized song texts (Karttunen and Lockhart 1980). While numerous apparent attributions to compositors can be found in the *Cantares* texts and elsewhere (León-Portilla 1967) including a group supposedly composed by King Nezahualcoyotl, it is more likely that most songs were composed by professional court singers in the employ of city-state rulers, perhaps in the name of their patrons.

Constitutive contextual ambiguities are also of two types and have even closer textual ramifications on the one hand, while emerging from the implications of oral performance on the other; these two ambiguities are the use and meaning of vocables or nonsense syllables, and our lack of any clear knowledge of Nahuatl metrical canons. Apparently meaningless vocables, both freestanding and attached, are scattered liberally through every song of the *Cantares*; Bierhorst, in his concordance to the *Cantares* (1985b), lists some one hundred forty such untranslatable pure sound representations (729–36). Among the most common are *aya, ohuaya, ohuiya, ya, yao, yahue, ye,* and *yehua*. Whether or not any of these had a stanza marking function such as Hymes has suggested for initial vocables in Chinook narrative, or any other specific structural function is not clear from the redacted texts. The fact that they are repeated with exact regularity in those songs that appear in both manuscripts suggests that they may have been as important as words to the original singers. Bierhorst chose not to repeat them in his translation, which only suppresses their mysterious and certainly autochthonous beauty.

How Nahua singers measured their lines, stanzas, or structural prosodic units of any type is still quite unclear. While the *Cantares* manuscript displays clear paragraph-like units of redaction, it is not at all certain how those units releated to the musical units of a performance. The still undeciphered *teponaztle* (hand-held log drum) notations supplied at the head of several texts are made of four syllables and their combinations—*ti, to, qui,* and *co; tocotico tocoti, tocotico tiqui tiqui,* etc.—and if ever understood will certainly tell us more than we know now about how to measure out a line of Nahuatl poetry in English. The equally mysterious "explanation" of *huehuetl* (standing kettle drum) drumming technique on folio 7r of the *Cantares* manuscript would also help identify metrical structure if we knew 1) what it describes as actual hand technique, and 2) what its relationship is to the stanza paragraphs of the written text.

And the drum is beaten thus: when a stanza ends and another stanza is to follow, it's three-beat. And when it actually begins, it's one-beat. But as it comes back in, then the drum falls beneath it, and the hand just keeps on going. But when it is in the middle, again the voice of the drum emerges. This, however, must be seen from the hand of the singer who knows how it is beaten (Bierhorst, 152–53; I have given my own translation and impressions in 1984).

In the absence of any clear understanding of Nahuatl metrical/musical structure in song chant, Bierhorst has wisely chosen to simply reproduce in his translation the visual units as they appear in the Nahuatl text.

These four contextual ambiguities, however, have little or nothing to do with the complexities that inspired Sahagún's demonic-origins theory or drive the modern translator to distraction. Nor are they relevant to the formal ambiguities which Empson outlined in his tour of English tradition. Nahuatl poetry, however, is rife with the first of Empson's textual types of ambiguity:[1] "a word or a grammatical structure [that] is effective in several ways at once" (2) which emerges strongest where thickets of metaphor crowd closest. In Empson's still-echoing judgment, this type is "clearly . . . involved in . . . [poetic] richness and heightening of effect, and the machinations of ambiguity are among the very roots of poetry" (3). Empson affirms, with Shelly, Emerson, Herbert Read, and Heidegger, that "metaphor . . . more or less taken for granted (so as to be unconscious), is the normal mode of development of a language" (2), and that "all languages are composed of dead metaphors as the soil of corpses" (25). The "deliberate study and discussion" that Fr. Durán warns must be undertaken to understand Nahuatl metaphor is evident in lines such as *Xochinquahuitl malinticac huiconticac ya pixahuiinticcaco ye moquiapan a ycelteotl ymapan y tonnemi quetzalli coxcox ha toncuicatinemi hiyao hamao hama hohohiyaya* (Cantares, f. 67v, 16–18): "The flowering tree, twisted and entwined, already stands drizzling in your Place of Rains, O One God, and upon its branches you live, a quetzal pheasant, you live filled with a life of song, 'hiyao, hamao, hama, hohohiyaya.'" The flowering tree that "drizzles" (not "drips"), the Place of Rains, the One God who is a singing quetzal pheasant (itself a bird more mythic than actual) full of "hi's," "ha's" and "hohoya's" each occur repeatedly in the text of the *Cantares* and require more discussion than I have space for here to expose the "admirable pronouncements" masked in this heavily iconic imagery. Suffice it to say that the rain which certainly has a fertility component may also be a water of Christian salvation, but perhaps not, and is also a figure of poetic inspiration. This stanza appears in a *Xochicuicatl Cuecuechtli* or "Obscene Flower Song" in which the muse or the bird-god was probably represented by transvestites; it was a dance, Durán assures us, almost as bad as the Spanish zaraband, "and obviously a dance of dishonest women and lascivious men. . . . In it appear men dressed as women" (I, 193). It is not likely, therefore, that the "One God" could be thought of as Jehovah of the Israelites.

The second type of textual ambiguity (type six) follows close on the heels of the first and emerges from the theory of metaphor as a key to etymological consciousness, or, perhaps more accurately, to a poetic consciousness of etymology. The Nahuatl word for centipede is *petlazolcoatl* which combines *coatl*, "serpent," with *petlazolli*, "an old worn-out woven reed mat." Did the normal Nahuatl speaker "see" the obvious metaphorical construction "snake like a frayed-edge reed mat" whenever s/he said, "There goes a *petlazolcoatl*!"? Or was it part of a singer's extensive training to come to this consciousness and even compositional mastery of it? While there are numerous compound words like *petlazolcoatl* in Nahuatl, the urge to etymologize in Nahuatl linguistic analysis is now usually frowned upon, especially if it leads to the statements that the Nahuas thought this or that on the basis of such analysis alone. The fact is, there is no evidence to suggest the normal speaker thought anything but "centipede" when s/he said *petlazolcoatl*; we cannot tell, for the most part, where the Aristotelian tension between "ordinary usage" and "figurative swerving" begins. On the other hand, there are word constructions in the manuscripts which cannot represent anything other than the intentional work of poet-sing-ers. "Luxuriantly descriptive nouns of three or more terms are characteristic of the *Can-tares* but virtually nonexistent in other manuscripts" (Bierhorst 1985b, 720): *yxiuhque-cholcacahuaxochicalitec*, "within his house of green-swan cacao flowers," or *teocuit-laxochicoyolayacachuitzilin*, "golden flower-bell-rattle hummingbird" (both on f. 11). What figurative houses and birds are evoked or described by such one-of-a-kind word-phrases is a further ambiguity of extensive sublety and elegance—and obviously intended; such words could not be generated by anything but a conscious linguistic playfulness in the service of poetic license.

Type seven textual ambiguities arise in Nahuatl because "transitive sentences in-volving only third-person singular or third-person plural referents are ambiguous if the meaning of the verb stem permits an animate entity in both the subject role and the object role" (Andrews 195). Nahuatl does not make gender or human-animal distinctions corre-sponding to he/she/it; *-c-* or *-qui-* may mean any of these, so that *oquittac* may say "He saw her," "She saw him," "He saw him," "She saw her," "He saw it (a dog, or anything animate)," "She saw it," "It saw her," or "It saw him." Obviously, only context can tell. The textual consequences of this grammatical ambiguity, which may well have been eliminated in an oral context, are illustrated by the sequence of translations of a crucial Chichimec myth text in the *Leyenda de los soles* manuscript (Lehmann 358–62). The story tells how two brothers, Xiuhnel and Mimich, go into the desert hunting together. A were-deer woman with two heads appears and they pursue her; at night she calls them away from the fire with a seductive human voice, and Xiuhnel goes out into the darkness to meet her. What happens then is grammatically ambiguous if taken out of narrative con-text: *Auh in oquitecac niman ipan hualmixtlapachcuep niman ye quicua quelcoyonia*, "And when he/she laid him/her down, then he/she turned him/herself face down upon him/her, then he/she devoured him/her, tore open his/her breast." Only the context can determine whether she devours him or he devours her, obviously a question of some im-portance for any interpretive discussion of the narrative, not to mention an accurate rendi-tion of Chichimec mythology. The two original Spanish translations of this text (Veláz-quez 1975; Garibay 1964a) read the line similarly. Velázquez translates: *Después que se echó con ella, se volvió bocabajo sobre ella, la mordió y la agujeró*, "Then he threw himself down with her, turned face-down over her, bit her and opened her" (123). Garibay renders the line rather more interpretively: *Luego con ella se tiende, la oprime, la mordisquea, y al fin la desflora*, "Then he lies down with her, presses upon her, bites her, and finally deflowers her." In short, both Spanish versions read the original Nahuatl as an attack on the female were-deer by Xiuhnel. The subject-object pronoun ambiguity con-tinues through the narrative in such a way that both Velázquez and Garibay are able to follow this rendering through the passage, both interpreting the weeping survivor as the sister of the devoured or deflowered one. But such a translation leaves completely nonsensical two subsequent narrative facts: Mimich flees in apparent terror through his own campfire, and Xiuhnel disappears completely from the story. The correct translation had been supplied by the text's first editor, Walter Lehmann, in 1938: *Und nachdem sie ihn auf den Boden gelegt hat, da wandte sie sich mit dem Gesicht nach unten über ihn, Da frist sie ihn . . . macht sie ihm ein Loch in die Brust*, "And after she has laid him on the ground she turns herself face-down on him. Then she devours him, makes a hole in his breast." [2]

Type eight is the linguistic ambiguity of long and short vowels; there are four basic vowels in Nahuatl and each has a constrasting long and short form. This ambiguity is strictly an artifact of inadequate transcription—only Antonio de Rincón (1595) and Horacio Carochi (1645) of the early grammarians made consistent efforts to record and distinguish vowel length and glottal-stop phonemes in Nahuatl and vowel length is unmarked in any lyrical text. Therefore, while a Nahua poet may be rhyming *xihuitl*, "grass" or "turquoise," with *xīhuitl*, "comet," we may miss his meaning entirely and translate "turquoise" twice.

Type-nine textual ambiguities occur in combinations of sentences and are functions of the fact that order of sentence elements do not, as a rule, indicate syntactical function in Nahuatl (Andrews 197): *Yehhuatl notahtzin*, "He is my beloved father," or "My beloved father is that one." Which is the matrix, and which is the supplementary subject? This kind of choice can be common in poetic texts and may offer highly divergent readings. *Ach tleon aiuh quimati in tocnihuan y cocoya yiollo qualani* (Cantares, f.35, 29) might say "Perhaps our friends take it badly, his heart sickens, enraged" or maybe "Perhaps he takes it badly, our friends' hearts sicken, enraged" or even, as Bierhorst renders it, "Our friends are ill at ease? Sick, His hearts are vexed" (247).

The final, type-ten ambiguity is the ambiguity of the referent in honorific and reverential constructions with multiple objects: Is the honor directed to the actor, the agent, or the action itself (Andrews 115)? *Nechtlacelilia* is the non-honorific form saying "He/She receives something from me." *Nechmotlacelililia* is the honorific form which says literally (as Andrews explains it), "He receives something from me for his own benefit," which is construed as respectful formulation in Nahuatl. It is uncertain, however, if the object of respect is "he" (subject), the "something" (object), or the action of receiving itself. Translating is a trick in any case: "His Honor receives something from me"; "He receives an honored something from me"; "He receives honorably something from me"—none of which has a clean and clear English value.

It remains a dilemma of Nahuatl translation to English that no scholar has yet appeared who has both the requisite grasp of the full sophistication and subtlety of Nahuatl rhetorical style and at the same time a sufficient background in English stylistic usage to find the corresponding natural context for translation. The fact is that Nahuatl oratorical style, an elegantly evolved and polished example of the oral-formulaic style which characterizes pre- or semi-literate civilizations everywhere, favors a highly repetitious, often circular, incremental, and subtly varying mode of expression which is long out of vogue in contemporary English. Even the nineteenth-century record of the Bureau of Indian Affairs has numerous examples of American impatience with "the prolix and endless oratory of which the Indians are so fond." Anderson and Dibble were right in reaching back for a neo-King Jamesian biblical style in their translation of the Florentine Codex—"The first word is to enter near to, nigh unto our lord, the lord of the near, of the nigh, the master, the night, the wind. Give him all thy heart, thy body. Let not thy feet go astray." (Book VI, p. 91)—and for my taste these are still some of the most successful renditions of the dignity and rhythm of the original, which makes sense if we remember that large sections of the Old Testament derive from oral traditions. The final impression, however, is too much like sustained Quakerese than biblical stateliness and periodic rhythm—something to be expected, of course, since no one can write Jamesian English in 1965, and as John Barth has pointed out, it would only be embarrassing if someone did.

The idiom Bierhorst evolves for his bold translation is often too colloquial and occasionally too cheery to carry over the ritualized angst of the original: "I cry, I grieve, knowing we're to go away and leave these good flowers, these good songs. Let's be plea-sured, let's sing. We're off to our destruction" (Song 53, p. 247). In their recent transla-tion of the much shorter *Bancroft Dialogues* manuscript (*The Art of Nahuatl Speech: The Bancroft Dialogues*), a seventeenth-century transcription of a late sixteenth-century text, Karttunen and Lockhart have provided two versions, one fully translated into idiomatic English and a second which "sacrifices English idiom and ready intelligibility in favor of following the original more closely in original meaning." It is the latter, "intermediary" translation, in spite of its impossible clots of adverbs and adverbials and the translators' parenthetical asides marking untranslatable points of the original grammar, which comes closer to carrying off the extraordinarily belabored and figurative qualities of Nahuatl oral art (from the funeral oration for a dead ruler):

Perhaps still you will come back hither? Perhaps still five, still ten (days) your water, your mountain will await you? And your nails, your hair? No longer at all. (It is) already everything, (it is) already thus, already forever you have carried yourself (away), the pine torch, the light has already disappeared, has already been extinguished, already the water, the mountain of the Possessor of the close, Possessor of the near, spreads in silence, spreads in night. Let the tail, the wing weep, let it sorrow, and the hair of people, the nails of people, the children of people, let their tears sprinkle, scatter down. Let it call in sadness Him through whom there is life, the Possessor of the close, the Possessor of the near, let it say, "Alas, we have become unfortunate, we have been left orphans" (182).

Compare the pathos and imagery of that with:

Will you return? Are your city and your offspring to expect you in the future (to be awaiting you for a time)? No, never again. For that is all, that is enough; you have gone once and for all, the torch and light have gone out and been snuffed, the city of the All-pervasive lies silent and dark. Let the com-moners weep and sorrow, and let the tears of the well-born, the nobles, sprinkle and scatter down. Let them cry in sorrow to the Giver of life, the All-pervasive; let them say, "Alas, woe to us who have been left orphans" (131, 133).

One is tempted to say that the art of the original rescues the translators from their own language, but that is only to say that contemporary English is hardly adequate to the chal-lenge since it is unlikely that anyone now in the Nahuatl-translating business could do it much better.

No one, for example, has found a way to naturally and consistently translate the honorific and reverential inflections attached frequently to Nahuatl verbs, but that is certainly because no one now, if they ever did, naturally adopts in English the social relationships that these inflections require. Sullivan, for example, in the *Compendium* translates *In ye motlacatilitzinoa in ipiltzin tlatoani*, in which the verb *tlacati-*, "to be born," carries the reverential prefix and suffixes, as "The very revered son of the king is born." But in this case the verb is not transitive, it is the verb that unambiguously expresses the reverence, not the adjective, which doesn't exist in the original; the reverence is toward the action of the birth, and could only be translated by some ponderous circumlocution like "The noble son of the king is most reverently born." Andrews points out that since the honorific is generally formed from the causative form of the verb (someone causes himself or someone to do the action) it could be translated as an elaborate fiction in which the agent is represented as solely responsible for his action, so that the above sentence would be translated, "The noble son of the king causes himself to be born." But that, of course, carries no weight of honor or reverence whatever in English, and Andrews resorts to simply adding an untranslatable (H) or (R) after the verb. No English reader familiar with the current standard Nahuatl translations would have any idea how common the honorific form is in Nahuatl, nor how complex the sentence becomes when the verb is transitive and the honor or reverence may be invoked, ambiguously, by either or both the agent and the object.

In this, contemporary Spanish, with its still available wealth of florid and pettifogging (to American English tastes) rhetorical devices, is probably a superior vehicle for Nahuatl translation. Certainly, I would argue, Sahagún's sixteenth-century translations, however incomplete they might be, are better than anything since, not only because he was one of the most dedicated and gifted nahuatlatos ever, but because the viceregal Spanish idiom natural and available to him included a repertoire of forms closer to the Nahuatl usages. Consider, from Book VI of the *Historia General* (Garibay's 4th edition, 309), a passage very much parallel to the Bancroft passage above:

¿Por ventura fue a alguna parte de donde otra vez pueda volver acá, para que otra vez sus vasallos puedan ver su cara? ¿Por ventura vendrános a decir hágase esto, o aquello? ¿Vendrá por ventura otra vez a ver a los cónsules y regidores de la república? ¿Verle han por ventura más? ¿Conocerle han más? ¿Oirán por ventura más su mandamiento y decreto? ¿Vendrá algún tiempo a dar consuelo y refrigerio a sus principales y cónsules? ¡Ay dolor, que del todo se nos acabó su presencia y para siempre se nos fue! ¡Ay dolor, que ya se nos acabó nuestra candela y nuestra lumbre, el hacha que nos alumbraba del todo la perdimos!; dejó (en) perpetua orfandad y perpetuo desamparo a todos sus súditos e inferiores. . . . ¡Oh señor nuestro humanísimo! . . . Peligro es grande que este vuestro pueblo, señorío y reino, no corra gran riesgo si no se elige otro, con brevedad, que le ampare. Pues, ¿qué es lo que V(uestro) M(ajestad) determina de hacer? ¿es bien que esté a obscuras este vuestro pueblo, señorío y reino? ¿Es bien que esté sin cabeza y sin abrigo? ¿Queréisle por ventura asolar y destruir?

Thelma Sullivan was especially sensitive to these stylistic matters as a translator and her version of the "Prayer to Tlaloc" from Book VI of the Florentine Codex sets a standard for bringing the range of Nahuatl oral chant style into English.

Notes

1. I will not attempt here either to summarize or exemplify Empson's seven types, except those found directly in the Nahuatl texts. It is not assumed in the present discussion that the reader is familiar with Empson's book.

2. I have discussed this text elsewhere (1983).

References

Andrews, J. Richard. 1975. *Introduction to Classical Nahuatl*. Austin: University of Texas Press.

Bierhorst, John, ed. & trans. 1985a. *Cantares Mexicanos: Songs of the Aztecs*. Stanford: Stanford University Press.

———. 1985b. *A Nahuatl-English Dictionary and Concordance to the Cantares Mexicanos with Analytic Transcription and Grammatical Notes*. Stanford: Stanford University Press.

Durán, Fr. Diego. 1967. *Historia de las Indias de Nueva España e islas de la Tierra Firme*, Vol. I. A. M. Garibay, ed. Mexico: Editorial Porrúa.

Empson, William. 1947. *Seven Types of Ambiguity*. New York: New Directions.

Garibay, Fr. Angel M., ed. & trans. 1964a. *Épica Náhuatl*. Bib. Estudiante Universitario, no. 57. Mexico.

———. 1964b. *Poesía Nahuatl, I: Romances de los señores de Nueva España*. Mexico City: Universidad Nacional Autónoma de México.

———. 1965. *Poesía Nahuatl, II: Cantares mexicanos, primera parte*. Mexico City: Universidad Nacional Autónoma de México.

———. 1968. *Poesía Nahuatl, III: Cantares mexicanos, segunda parte*. Mexico City: Universidad Nacional Autónoma de México.

Gingerich, Willard. 1984. "An Aztec 'Song of Anguish': The Shape of Performance," *Southwest Review*, 69:2 (Spring): 201–9.

———, and Pat Carr. 1983. "The Vagina Dentata Motif in Nahua and Zuni Mythic Narrative: A Comparative Study" in B. Swann, ed., *Smoothing the Ground*. Berkeley: University of California Press.

Karttunen, Frances. 1983. *An Analytical Dictionary of Nahuatl*. Austin: University of Texas Press.

———, and James Lockhart. 1976. *Nahuatl in the Middle Years: Language Contact Phenomena in Texts of the Colonial Period*. University of California Publications in Linguistics, no. 85. Los Angeles: University of California Press.

———. 1980. "La estructura de la poesía náhuatl vista por sus variantes," *Estudios de cultura náhuatl*, vol. 14, 15–64.

Krupat, Arnold. 1989. *The Voice in the Margin: Native American Literature and the Canon*. Berkeley: University of California Press.

Lehmann, Walter, ed. & trans. 1938. *Die Geschichte der Königreiche von Colhuacan und México*, "Quellenwerke zur alten Geschichte Amerikas," vol. I. Stuttgart.

León-Portilla, Miguel. 1967. *Trece poetas del mundo azteca*. México: Universidad Nacional Autónoma de Mexico.

———. 1969. *Pre-Columbian Literatures of Mexico*. Norman: University of Oklahoma Press.

———. 1972. *Los antiguos mexicanos através de sus crónicas y cantares*. 2nd ed. México: Fondo de cultura económica.

Sahagún, Fr. Bernardino de. 1979. *Historia general de las cosas de Nueva España*. A. M. Garibay, ed., 4th ed. México: Editorial Porrúa.

Sullivan, Thelma D. 1988. *Thelma D. Sullivan's Compendium of Nahuatl Grammar*. W. R. Miller and K. Dakin, eds., T. D. Sullivan and N. Stiles, trans. Salt Lake City: University of Utah Press.

Velázquez, Primo F., trans. 1975. *Codice Chimalpopoca*. Instituto de Investigaciones Historicas. México: Universidad Nacional Autónoma.

Translating Poetic Features in the Sierra Popoluca Story of Homshuk

Kay Sammons

$\mathbf{F}$ollowing the work of Dell Hymes (1962, 1964), a functional view of language use has revealed the significance of taking sociocultural context into consideration in the analysis of communicative behavior.[1] In what has become known as the ethnography of speaking, functions of speech performance are examined within the context of naturally occurring speech events. This sociocultural information then helps to unveil important aspects of the communicative process that might otherwise go unnoticed.

Recently, a number of scholars working within the ethnography-of-speaking framework have turned their attention to analysis of Native American narratives, and particularly to ethnopoetic issues associated with transcribing, translating, and representing these texts on the printed page. Dell Hymes himself has also played a central role in the development of this research. Recently, two separate volumes, *Native South American Discourse* (Sherzer and Urban 1986) and *Native American Discourse* (Sherzer and Woodbury 1987), have given special attention to the problematic nature of that task, especially in relation to ethnopoetic features of performance. By combining the insights of the ethnography of speaking and ethnopoetics we can see discourse as the interface between language, culture, and society, created by actual instances of language use (Sherzer 1987:89). Essentially, the assumption is that much of what is often described as culture is actually constituted and transmitted by means of discourse (Sherzer and Urban 1986:2). In addition, it is especially in verbally artistic discourse that both grammatical and culturally symbolic resources are exploited most fully, revealing important aspects of the language–culture relationship (Sherzer 1987:89).

This essay provides a case study in translating poetic aspects of Sierra Popoluca oral literature, using as data one instance of a story about Homshuk, the maize spirit, recently recorded in the southern Mexican community of Soteapan, Veracruz. This type of empirical research on oral performance of verbal art is the first of its kind among the Sierra Popoluca, contributing much-needed data on oral literature in nonliterate societies. Where translation of the Homshuk story is concerned, presentation of the text in a way that reflects poetic structuring of performance is necessary if we are to understand the process through which these stories communicate more than a referential or literal message. This is especially true in relation to the interplay between formal and semantic patterning in the text, requiring increased attention to the representation of poetic features in a way that makes sense to an English-speaking audience. In this instance, formal patterning contributes significantly to the symbolic meaning of the text, replicating basic cosmological information that augments participants' understanding of events occurring within the course of the narrative. In addition, the emergent qualities of this type of discourse become especially salient in the translation that follows, since the storytelling genre allows individual narrators to combine poetic features in a variety of ways to achieve the rhetorical effect that best reflects their personal style and is most suitable to particular social situations.

The Community

In the southeastern part of the state of Veracruz, an estimated ten thousand Sierra Popoluca speakers live in about twenty-five communities between Lake Catemaco and the Tehuantepec Railway (Foster and Foster 1948:1; Elson 1967:270). This indigenous group forms by far the largest speech community in Soteapan, the municipal and ceremonial center that is home to more than nineteen hundred Sierra Popoluca speakers. Most members of this community also share a lifestyle organized around the subsistence production of maize. Other speech communities include more than four hundred monolingual Spanish speakers, twenty-eight bilingual Zapotec-Spanish speakers, and at the time of a recent census, six speakers of a Mayan language. The Sierra Popoluca are one of four groups of Veracruz Popoluca speakers. Their langauge is a member of the Zoquean branch of the Mixe-Zoquean family.

In recent times, artistic production of material objects such as woven fabrics and basketry has decreased substantially among Sierra Popoluca speakers residing in Soteapan, while performance of oral narratives such as the story of Homshuk has remained a vital force in their lives. It is likely that this social reality places special emphasis on oral performance as a means of reformulating and transmitting basic notions about ethnic identity and worldview from one generation to the next. Participation in performance of the Homshuk story is especially important in relation to concepts about the importance of subsistence maize production in the family maize field known locally as the milpa.

The Story of Homshuk

The story translated here is an account of the adventures of Homshuk, the maize spirit, who passes from childhood to old age each year during the life cycle of maize. This type of narrative usually contains various sets of episodes that can be left in or out as a means of foregrounding different aspects of the hero's character. Part of the reason for Homshuk's popularity as a hero is that the subsistence production of maize is such an important activity for milpa farmers. It is to Homshuk that agricultural ritual is directed at the familial level, since it is through his assistance that an abundant maize crop is assured for each family.[2]

The hero's supernatural identity is as a maize spirit who is most likely one of four aspects of an earth lord controlling all products used by mankind. In all three published variants of the Homshuk story, the hero gives metaphorical references to maize when asked to reveal his true identity. In Foster (1945:192), he tells the messenger of the storm deity, "I am he who sprouts at the knees. I am he who flowers." Later, he says, "My name is Homshuk. Tell him that I am the one who is shelled, and the one who is eaten." Reporting what he has learned to the storm deity, the messenger explains, "it is he who sprouts at the knees and gives fruit." The story in Elson (1947:209) has Homshuk referring to himself as ʔan-tsaany-tsits-a-paʔap, "one who becomes like a snake's teeth," since, according to informants, when maize first comes out of the ground it is small, sharp, and pointed like a snake's teeth. Also in Elson, he calls himself ʔay-kas-paʔap, "one who leafs out." In Munch (1983:167) Homshuk replies to the death deity's questions about his identity, "I am he who sprouts, I am new seeds, I am the reborn."

Every storyteller I have encountered in Soteapan and surrounding communities knows stories about Homshuk. That this culture hero is still alive in the minds of Sierra Popoluca-speaking residents of Soteapan is obvious in the comments of two individuals who said that failure to perform specific rituals honoring Homshuk in recent years has led to decreased maize production. Soteapanos also explain that the most common situation for performance of the Homshuk story is at the house of an important religious official during village festivals, particularly the festival honoring the patron saints, San Pedro and San Pablo. The central theme of this religious festival is the request for rain, abundant crops, and protection (Baez-Jorge 1973:134). According to reported evidence, the people most likely to participate in these storytelling sessions, including the narrator and his audience, are those who depend on subsistence production of maize.

Participants

In this performance of the Homshuk story, participants include the storyteller, a resident of Soteapan in his late seventies, his audience, a group of bilingual Spanish-Sierra Popoluca speakers, and myself as anthropologist. The narrator spent the first thirty years of his life as a milpa farmer in the nearby village of Ocotal Chico. He has become a respected member of the community over the years, actively participating in the civil-religious cycle in Soteapan, and providing legal advice to other Sierra Popoluca speakers from surrounding towns. He was deeply immersed in the performance, often lowering his head and almost closing his eyes, and using a variety of hand gestures and facial expressions, as well as impersonation of characters and verbal sound effects. This type of behavior is common among storytellers in Soteapan and surrounding communities, although each individual develops a particular style of performance.

Poetic Features of Performance

Concern with the presentation of Native American narratives on the printed page has led to formulation of the methodological principle that the function of any particular transcription or translation is to foreground some facet of discourse relevant to a specific set of analytical goals (Sherzer and Urban 1986:11). For work based within the discourse-centered approach, these goals often require presentation of text in a way that reflects poetic structuring of performance. According to Jakobson (1960:356) the poetic function of linguistic communication is at work when attention is focused on the message form for its own sake. This process "projects the principle of equivalence from the [paradigmatic] axis of selection into the [syntagmatic] axis of combination" through patterning of rhetorical elements (358). Aside from calling attention to message form, this rhetorical patterning can suggest how semantic content of the message is to be interpreted in particular sections of text (Urban 1986:39).

In the story of Homshuk, patterning in formal structure occurs in dynamic tension with thematic patterning in the referential content of the text. Combined, these features affect the cognitive structure of participants through the rhetorical function of speech. The resulting message helps to reformulate and transmit concepts about the central importance of maize production in the cosmic order, as well as provide the mythological justification for agricultural ritual practiced at the familial level.

Theoretically, all features of performance can function rhetorically, since this process includes any situation in which an individual or group receives messages that affect cognitive structure. In this performance, a number of formal devices occur throughout in unpredictable combinations to foreground different sections of narrative to varying degrees. Among these, parallelism (repetition with or without variation), pause phrasing, and intonational contour serve as line-marking devices, their dynamic tension functioning as an important aspect of the aesthetic appeal of performance (Urban 1986:21). Other types of foregrounding devices occurring in various combinations with these line markers include increased volume, pronunciation of words more slowly than usual, dialect variants from archaic Sierra Popoluca, Spanish loans, and emphatic use of personal pronouns. Often, a variety of processes work simultaneously to augment various aspects of a single message, as with the co-occurence of parallelism, increased volume, and ancient legitimization of narrative in lines two and three.

Some of the strongest rhetorical messages in the story of Homshuk are revealed through a systematic analysis of the relationship between formal and thematic patterning of the text. A comparison of formal and referential patterning reveals an important aspect of the process through which cognitive structure is influenced by participation in performance of this story. Often, repetition of important symbolic themes is accompanied by poetic features that foreground these highly significant sections of text. This occurs in lines 102–21, where two sets of quadruplet structures foreground the process through which the hero transforms the four colors of earth into the four colors of maize. The quadruplets are formed through paradigmatic substitution of color terms. In lines 102–5, the first three terms are metaphorically associated with the cardinal directions red/east, black/west, and white/north, but in place of the fourth directional color, that is, yellow/south, the storyteller uses the expression *chikiny,* "mottled, spotted." In lines 118–21, where the hero names the four color terms in succession as he performs the earth-to-maize transformation, the 'mottled' expression drops out and is replaced by *puʔuch,* "yellow," suggesting that an important relationship exists among these concepts of "mottled," "yellow," and (by extension from "yellow") "south." The association of color terms with cardinal directions, common among indigenous groups of Middle America in both ancient and modern times, varies in detail according to the historical legacy of specific regions. No one in Soteapan I spoke with actually agreed that these associations exist, although Munch (1983:369, 372) suggests that this belief is common in lowland Veracruz communities. For these groups, the color-directional scheme is the same as the one exhibited in this section of the Homshuk story. The formal replication of such cosmological concepts as the four-cornered universe is an important means through which participation in performance of the Homshuk story helps to pass such beliefs along from one generation to the next.

Thematic patterning is also present in this section of text, since the hero's transformation of earth into maize in episode three metaphorically replicates his own death and rebirth in episode two. In the earlier episode, Homshuk's mother places him on a metate and grinds him to death, while in the following section, Homshuk must beat the earth he intends to transform into maize. Next, Homshuk's mother tosses him into the water, just as he later places the earth into a washbowl. Finally, the hero is reborn, an event that has its parallel in the section where the various colors of maize emerge from the washbowl. The sequence in both episodes includes some form of destruction (grinding/beating), immersion in water, and transformation (death to life/earth to maize). This metaphorical association between the hero's death and rebirth and the transformation of earth into maize implies a connection between the two processes. This relationship is based on the central metaphor tying together the maize and human life cycles: where reproduction is concerned, mother is to son as earth is to maize. In addition, the congruence of formal and thematic patterning occurring in this section suggests that maize production is an especially important transformation process, a concept that parallels the reality of Sierra Popoluca worldview and social structure.

This part of the narrative also contains a particularly strong type of foregrounding that is based on the manipulation of various line-marking devices as a means of highlighting different sections of text to varying degrees. This strongest level of foregrounding is achieved through the use of downward intonation, pause, and parallelistic structure in congruence. Less intensive foregrounding is possible through the use of parallelism without downward intonation and pause. Anthony Woodbury (1987:179) suggests that several "rhetorical-structure" components such as pause phrasing and syntactic constituents can interact toward a single communicative end, with their alignments unpredictable, so that "each different allowable alignment would convey a different meaning." This is precisely the type of process employed in the tension among line-marking devices in this performance of the Homshuk story.

The question-and-answer session between Homshuk and Tsitsimat (lines 84–90) also exhibits this type of intense foregrounding. When Homshuk returns to life after being killed by his own mother earlier on, he approaches the old woman and places his hands over her eyes, asking, "Who am I?" (line 84) to which his mother replies, "Ah, you, you are my husband." Line 86 repeats the expression as Homshuk asks again, "Who am I?" This time, she guesses wrong again, saying "Ah, you, you are my brother." In line 88 the hero repeats the question, adding *pero,* "but," in the initial position. Homshuk's mother responds with another wrong guess, this time suggesting that the hero is her "brother from far away." In the next line (90) she finally guesses the hero's identity. This formal structure can be seen as two interrelated sets of triplets, the first consisting of Homshuk's three questions to his mother and the second of her responses. Line 85 also gives an example of how pronouns can be used emphatically, where Spanish loan *tu,* "you," is substituted for *mich,* "you," prior to prefix *man-,* "first person possessor/second person possessed in direct discourse." Separate pronouns also precede terms of reference for members of the old woman's family in lines 87 and 89. Each of these references has the *man-* prefix, referring to first person possessor (Tsitsimat) and second person possessed (her "husband," "brother," and "brother from far away," respectively). Together with repetitions of the question *ʔaʔiʔaʔich,* "Who am I?" in lines 84, 86, and 88, these expressions form a parallelistic sequence that calls attention to this section of text. The added emphasis provided by the use of redundant personal pronouns then goes beyond this first level of foregrounding and directs attention to the subject, Homshuk. The second set of parallel lines, where the hero asks three times in succession, "Who am I?" uses the pronoun *ʔich* as a highlighting device as well, forming a triplet based partially on pronominal reference to Homshuk in the first person. It is likely that this structure functions to foreground a central question with respect to the symbolic significance of this text: What is the hero's identity, especially in relation to his mother? A redundant pronoun also occurs in line 92, where

Tsitsimat correctly guesses the identity of her son. Redundant pronouns are used in this instance to emphasize the various relationships the old woman has with her family, then to reaffirm the central importance of the mother–son relationship as symbolically equivalent to the production of maize (since mother is to son as earth is to maize).

The Translation Process

Considering the important contribution poetic features make to the overall significance of performing the Homshuk story among Sierra Popoluca speakers in Soteapan, ignoring the poetic quality of the text in the translation process can obscure an important aspect of communication through storytelling. This type of information is a major component in a functional analysis designed to reveal the process through which language use communicates more than a referential or literal message. In addition, since the poetic function includes any aspect of performance that calls attention to the message form, the combination of various features into an aesthetically pleasing whole is as important as paying attention to the many components that go into creation of the verbally artistic *kwento* or "story" genre. With this in mind, I have attempted to structure the English translations in a way that approaches the poetic quality of the original Native American texts.[3] The resulting translation balances features of poetic structure and referential content to produce a general idea of how Sierra Popoluca speakers experience the text themselves. The discourse-centered approach arising within the field of linguistic anthropology contributes significantly to formulation of this translation methodology, providing an understanding of the dynamic tension among linemarking devices as well as among other signal-reflexive features of performance.

Line structure in the transcription and translation that follow is based mainly on the occurence of parallelistic features. However, pause phrasing and downward intonation help to determine line structure where parallellism does not occur. The contribution of these last two features to the line organization of Zuni and Quiche Mayan narratives has received attention from Dennis Tedlock (1982, 1987). On the other hand, Dell Hymes (1981, 1987) suggests that repetition of features other than pause will likely show alternate possibilities for line structure in Native American texts. Greg Urban (1986:21) explains that for both Western poetry and the Shokleng origin myth, "a skillful interweaving of lines defined by pause and those defined by other parallelistic means" creates a tension among line-marking devices that avoids the monotony resulting from perfect congruence between pause and parallelistic structure. This translation attempts to reflect this dynamic tension by using expressive features such as pause phrasing and intonation to determine line organization where parallelism does not occur.

The translation also strives to reflect the use of optional separate pronouns as a means of foregrounding referents in relation to the action under way in particular sections of text, allowing the storyteller to emphasize whatever actors and actions he sees fit in any particular setting. With regard to the instances of this process described above, although a literal translation of line 85, "Ah, you my husband," is true to referential content, repetition of "you" is required to emphasize the one who is possesssed, Wɨdyaaya, Tsitsimat's husband. The use of redundant personal pronouns is also reflected in lines 87 and 89, translated as, "Ah, you, you are my brother," and "Ah, you, you are my brother from far away," respectively.

Each of the ten episodes in this performance begins with the expression *bweno,* "well," spoken with downward intonation and followed by a long pause. Terms spoken with increased volume are highlighted with capital letters in the transcription, although this feature is not shown in the translation since poetic considerations often take precedence over precise literal interpretation, and morpheme-specific equivalents do not always occur. Letters separated by dashes indicate expressions spoken slowly and with clear pronunciation of individual sounds. The translation uses capital letters in sentence-initial positions, while the original text does not, since this feature is based on traditions in written English rather than indigenous concepts. The same is true for the use of quotation marks to indicate reported speech, as well as periods to separate sentences and commas to show grammatical separation of constituents within sentence boundaries. Spanish loans appear in bold type.[4]

Conclusions

As we have seen, one of the most important contributions a discourse-centered approach makes to the process of translating Native American narratives is an increased awareness of the poetic process and the necessity of representing signal-reflexive features of performance in a way that makes sense to an English-speaking audience. This attention-getting function not only foregrounds sections of text with particularly important symbolic meaning, but it also draws attention to the text as a whole through the aesthetically pleasing verbal performance. In addition, parallelistic structures within this particular performance of the Homshuk story go a step further to comment on the hero's actions in transforming earth to maize by replicating the notion of a four-cornered universe and reaffirming the cosmic significance of this transformational process. When analysis is directed toward any aspect of the symbolic meaning contributed through poetic structure, formal features of oral narratives must be taken into consideration during the processes of transcription and translation. Where the story of Homshuk is concerned, the functional view of language use as developed by Jakobson and Hymes contributes an understanding of the various signal-reflexive components that go into performance, including features such as pause phrasing, intonation, parallelistic structures, redundant personal pronouns, and the use of Spanish loans. Analysis of this particular performance reveals the emergent quality of the storytelling genre among Sierre Popoluca speakers in Soteapan, since these various rhetorical devices occur in unpredictable combinations based on the individual style of the storyteller and on the social context in which the narrative is performed. The translation that follows strives both to reflect the many rhetorical components that go into performance and to reproduce the overall aesthetic quality of the original text.

Heʔm Kwento de Homshuk

Episode 1

bweno
heʔm **kwento de** homshuk manaŋmataʔypa **porki**
yiʔp **kwento de** homshuk **ʔe-s** ts-a-m WINYUM
niʔmaytyaap heʔm wɨdyaaya nɨkpa maaki
kukɨtsa wɨdyaaya   5
pero heʔm ʔiwɨɨchoomo
ʔinyɨyi tsitsimat
niʔmaytyaap ʔAGI pɨʔnyum
nɨkpa ʔimaakiyah kuʔpu niʔkɨʔ kun ʔi**matayawl**
nɨmpa choomo nɨktam maaki   10
nɨkpa niʔkɨʔ
ʔimoh ʔimaakiyah
ʔimoh ʔimaakiyah
ʔimoh ʔinyɨkiyah
ʔipaʔt **kumo** KAʔNPU   15
kumo kaʔnpu
ʔimoh ʔimaakiyah ʔi dya ʔitsɨʔy
ʔimoh ʔimaakiyah ʔi dya ʔitsɨʔy
nɨmpa tsitsimat ʔatsakɨ
ʔɨCH ʔɨCH **SI**   20
ʔɨch **si**
ʔanɨkpa
ʔimaakpa
ʔimaakpa
ʔimaakpa   25
ʔi dya nunka ʔitsɨʔy
soʔpspa kutyiʔnyawum
niʔmaytyaap **kreo ki** tamɨgoʔypa **si** dya
heʔm niʔkɨ ʔaŋkiʔmpa yukmɨ ʔity
ʔa-a-a-a-h niʔmaytyaap **si**
heʔshɨk ʔity tanshiki tamponyi   30
HEʔSHɨK ʔity tanshiki tamponyi
NɨGɨ ʔaketɨ
nɨgum wɨdyaaya ket
tawiʔkpam
niʔmaytyaap dya yɨʔp tanakpoʔba   35
niʔmaytyaap **pero** dya tyiwɨɨ ʔiga tanakpoʔba
ʔɨch ʔapɨʔnyum ʔakuʔt niʔmaytyaap dya
kwaʔmaytyaap tuum **baul** hemum kukhomtaa
nɨk **siete dias**
hemum ʔAŊTOHON
ʔAŊHɨYUM   40

WEHUM
TSHshi haʔ dya maniʔmaytyum
NAYUM tanshiki tamponyi
nayum
niʔmaytyaap dya   45
niʔmaytyaap

Episode 2

bweno
ʔi **duro** ʔAŊWEHPA
ʔAŊWEHPA
ʔaktsutstaap   50
ʔi dya tyim
ʔi widyaʔipa heʔm heʔ kukɨtsa wɨdyaaya ʔitsak
tsitsimat choomo
niʔmaytyaap tsam miwehpa ʔiganam dya ʔiheʔum
ʔinyhaatuŋ wɨdyaaya
niʔmaytyaap sɨʔɨpum
niʔmaytyaap sɨʔɨpum   55
ʔinyishneʔbam
pɨgɨytyaa
tsayɨkhom hapkutsitstaap
kaʔum hapkutsitsTAAP
huty ʔaŋkukuhompa   60
nuku hoshom
nuku hoshom
poykukhom
nuku hoskukhom
ʔityop   65
ʔinynɨk niʔKʔɬ
niʔkɨ
ʔimoh ʔitsak
hemɨgam shutyu mɨhawum
ya heʔshɨk shutyu mɨhɨ   70
ʔiʔishum ʔihapkutsits
ʔihapkutsits
despwe de ki ʔihapkutsits
niʔmaytyaap sɨʔɨp ʔich ʔAMɨHAM
takpam choomo   75
tsitsimat choomo
tuum tsotso yukmɨ
tuum tsotso yukmɨ
sɨʔɨp ʔityak heʔm ʔipiʔityɨk
hemɨgam kiʔmneʔ   80
haʔityaap niʔmayTYAAP
yɨʔɨp nunta **letra** ʔakehaʔm ʔaŋwɨdyaaya
ʔiketpa heʔm ʔaŋmoʔgaʔityaap ʔiʔishkɨy
ʔaʔiʔaʔich
nɨmpa ʔah **tu** maŋwɨdyaaya   85

ʔaʔiʔaʔich
ʔah niʔmaytyaap **tu** maŋtɨɨwa
pero ʔaʔiʔaʔich
niʔmaytyaap **tu** heʔ maŋhuʔmtɨɨwa
dyaʔm ʔikutiʔɨyɨ ʔinyɨyimay ʔasta   90
nuk ʔihɨɨshi ʔiga niʔmaytyaap
ʔAAAAH **kreo** heʔm mamanɨk niʔmaytyaap
heʔm maŋhapkastsiniwɨ
hesɨgam ʔikɨtsɨgap
ʔaʔmtaawum
niʔmaytyaap siʔɨp ʔinyishpɨk ʔiŋmanɨk **verdad**   95
siʔɨp ʔiŋmanigap **pero** miʔiŋhapkastsin dya
ʔiŋmanigap
niʔmaʔytyaap SɨʔɨP ʔayuʔupa **mama**
kumo mich manaapa
mich **mi** tsitsimat choomo
pero dya tyi manɨk manɨnkiʔspa   100
tyi mop tyiʔiŋwatpa siʔɨp nɨkpa ʔinypɨk nas
tsabatsnas heʔm tsabatsmok
yɨknas yɨkmok
poopmoknas poopmok
chikinymok heʔm chikinypɨkmok   105

Episode 3

bweno
ya ʔoyum ʔipɨgɨytyaap
mohom
ʔiheʔytyaap
ʔiheʔytyaap   110
ʔiheʔyTYAAP
tɨgɨyum heʔm **palaŋana**hom
mohom
ʔikchiŋtyaap
naps ʔɨkshi put   115
naps ʔɨkshi put
put **diperente klas**
popopɨk
ʔi yɨkpɨk
tsabatspɨk   120
puʔuchpɨk
yɨʔmum ʔity niʔmaytyaap siʔɨp KUPIŊɨ
ya no mas ʔiga ʔiŋkiʔtketpa
ʔINYɨKPAK
siʔɨp ʔinyɨkpak **para semiya**   125
usaŋam ʔinshospa miwiʔkpak
siʔɨp nɨkpa ʔameʔts ʔaŋhatun niʔmaytyaap

bweno
porki heˀ kaˀ
ˀasta santa rumo   130
heˀ kaˀ
hemɨgam ˀikaˀ mahɨywiny
nuku wɨdya

Episode 5

bweno
ˀitsak heˀm ˀiˀɨkshi   135
pero nɨkpa ˀiˀish, ˀaga siˀɨp ˀimuts nuku
pero dya ˀiˀishpa huˀty ˀinyunpa
tuum tsaˀtehahoshom ˀityuk hemɨgam kukhomtaa
niˀmaytyaap huthut
hon
niˀmaytyaap nɨkpa ˀinkuish
tsuˀku hemɨgam ˀity monpa   140
ˀi hemum naaspa ˀityuˀts yukmɨ hemum
hemum nuku wɨdyaaya ˀityɨts
heˀm kɨlish kɨlish ˀITYɨTS heˀm nuku ˀihesum
pero heˀm hon ˀINYɨYI huthut

The Story of Homshuk

Episode 1

Well,
I will tell you the story of Homshuk because
this story of Homshuk is truly ancient.
They say that the old man went fishing.
Kukɨtsa Wɨdyaaya.   5
But his good old woman,
her name was Tsitsimat.
"I am very hungry now," she told him.
He went fishing for cuatopotes in the water with a net.
The old woman said, "Let's go fishing."   10
He went into the water.
He began fishing for them.
He began fishing for them.
He began going for them.
He found something like an egg.   15
Like an egg.
He began fishing for it and couldn't reach it.
He began fishing for it and couldn't reach it.
Tsitsimat said to him, "Leave it to me."
"I, I yes."   20

"I yes."
"I'll go."
She fished for it.
She fished for it.
She fished for it.   25
And never reached it.
She grew tired out of laziness.
"I think we have been deceived," she told him. "Yes, it is
not in the water, it is above."
"A-a-a-a-h," she said, "Yes."
"There is our laughter, our luck."   30
"There is our laughter, our luck."
"Go, take it down."
The old man went and took it down.
"We will eat it now."
She said to him, "No we will not split it open now."   35
She said to him, "But it is not good that we split it open."
"I am hungry now. I will eat it now." "No," she said.
They searched for a trunk and placed the egg in the center.
Seven days passed.
It broke open right there.
He spoke now.   40
He cried now.
"A child, ha! Didn't I tell you?"
"He was just born, our laughter, our luck."
"Just born."
"No," she said to him.   4
She said this to him.

Episode 2

Well,
he cried hard.
He cried.
She struck him.   50
But still, he was not calm.
And he went on crying because he knew that Kukɨtsa Wɨdyaaya
had left Tsitsimat Choomo.
"You cry a lot while your father, Kukɨtsa Wɨdyaaya,
is away," she said.
"Right now," she said.   55
"Right now," she said.
"You will see."
She grabbed him.
She ground him in the metate.
She crushed him to death.
"Where? In the center."   60
"In the cave of the army ant."
"In the cave of the army ant."
"In the center for a little while."

"In the center of the army ant cave."
She took him out.   65
"You go into the water."
"Into the water."
She began to leave him.
There small, he became big.
Now there a small thing became a big thing.   70
He saw the one who had ground him.
The one who had ground him.
After she had who ground him.
"Now I am big," he said.
The old woman wove,   75
Tsitsimat Choomo,
an orange tree above.
An orange tree above.
Now she wove her thread.
Right there she went up.   80
She found something written and said,
"This handwriting really looks like my husband's."
She came down. He covered her eyes for her.
"Who am I?"
She said, "Ah, you, you are my husband."   85
"Who am I?"
She said, "Ah, you, you are my brother."
"But who am I?"
She said, "You, you are my brother from far away."
Just now she understood. She said his name when   90
her thought arrived, she said,
"Aaaaah, I think he is my son."
"He is the one I have ground."
Just then he released her eyes.
He was seen.
He said to her, "Now do you recognize your son?"   95
"Now I am your son. But when you ground me I was not
your son."
"Now I am hungry, Mama," he said to her.
"Since you, you are my mother."
"You are my Tsitsimat Choomo."
"But now your son has nothing to eat."   100
"Surely you must do this." Now she went to get earth.
"Red earth, that is red maize."
"Black earth, black maize."
"White maize—earth, white maize."
"Mottled maize, that is mottled maize."   105

Episode 3

Well,
now after she went to get it,
he began.

He beat it.
He beat it.   110
He beat it.
He put it into the washbowl.
He began,
He washed it.
Pure maize kernels emerged.   115
Pure maize kernels emerged.
Different types emerged.
White ones,
and black ones,
red ones,   120
yellow ones.
"Here they are," he said to her, "Now hide them."
"Now take them down no more to eat."
"You plant them."
"Now you plant them for seed."   125
"Plant just a little, eat just a little seed."
"Now I will go looking for him, my father," he said to her.

Episode 4

Well,
because he died,
At Santa Roma,   130
he died.
Right there, he killed him, Mahɨywiny.
Army Ant Old Man.

Episode 5

Well,
he left his maize kernels.   135
But he went. He saw that now the army ant carried it.
But he did not see where he carried it.
Inside a cave in a hill of rock. Right there he placed it.
He spoke to roadrunner.
"Bird,"
he said to him, "You go investigate."
In the night, he was right there sleeping.   140
And there he passed over his tail.
There Army Ant Old Man cut it.
Cut his tail short, short. The ant, he did it.
But the bird's name is roadrunner.

Appendix
Event Structure in the Story of Homshuk

Episode 1

The story begins with an old couple finding an egg reflected in the waters of a stream. The old woman, Tsitsimat, has told her husband, Kukɨtsa, to go fishing for something she can eat to satisfy her craving. When he sees what looks like an egg in the water, Kukɨtsa repeatedly tries to fish it out but is unsuccessful. Now Tsitsimat goes through the same process, with a similar lack of success. When both have given up, the old woman realizes that the egg is perched above the stream, and sends Kukɨtsa to retrieve it. The old man suggests eating the egg immediately, but Tsitsimat insists that they take it home and wait. After seven days in the old woman's trunk, the egg breaks open, and a child is born.

Episode 2

The child begins to cry immediately after being born from the egg. His incessant crying irritates the old woman so much that she strikes him, then puts him into a metate and grinds him to death. She then decides to put Homshuk's remains into an ant "cave," a mound of earth constructed by army ants with a large hole at the top leading down into the cave below. Now she removes him from the ant cave and puts him into the water. It is through his immersion in both the cave and in water that Homshuk is reborn. He remains in the river until he is grown, then returns to his mother, who is identified in lines 71 and 72 as "the one who ground him." Next, Homshuk returns to his mother and announces that he has grown up in the waters of the river. She weaves an orange tree, and climbing up inside, finds handwriting resembling that of her husband. The hero covers her eyes and forces her to guess his identity. After three wrong guesses, including husband, brother, and brother from far away, she finally guesses correctly, identifying Homshuk as "the one I have ground" (line 92). When the hero releases her eyes, he asks his mother if she recognizes her son. He then tells her that since she is his mother and he is hungry, she must go and find for him the four colors of earth that he will then transform into the four colors of maize. In lines 102–5, falling intonation, pause, and syntactic parallelism are used in congruence to highlight the hero's reference to the transformation he is about to undertake.

Episode 3

Now Homshuk actually transforms the four colors of earth into corresponding colors of maize through the process of beating the earth, then placing it into a washbowl. After this, the hero admonishes the old woman to eat only a little of the maize he has given her and to plant the rest. He then announces that he is going in search of his father.

Episode 4

The storyteller explains in an aside that Homshuk's father has been killed earlier on by Mahɨywiny Nuku Wɨdyaaya, "Lightning Army Ant Old Man," at a place known as *santa rumo* ("Santa Roma" or "Holy Rome"). Discussions about this concept revealed that humans must wait until death to enter into *santa rumo*, although Homshuk and other deities are not subject to such restrictions.

Episode 5

As he begins his journey to find his father, the hero comes across an ant carrying a maize kernel into a cave and, curious to see where he hides the maize, he sends a roadrunner to investigate during the night. The bird enters the cave, falls asleep, and has this tail cut off short by "Army Ant Old Man," who is known in Spanish as *El Rayo Viejo del Sur,* or "Old Man Lightning Bolt of the South."

Notes

1. This essay benefits from a number of insightful suggestions from Joel Sherzer, Brian Stross, and Brian Swann. Special thanks to Brian Swann for his assistance with the aesthetic quality of the English translation of the original Sierra Popoluca text.

2. As early as 1942, George Foster suggests that the Virgin Carmen of Catemaco has come to be more powerful as a patroness of good crops, taking on a role similar in some respects to that of Homshuk. According to Foster (1942: 42), before breakfast on the day of sowing, prayers can be offered to either the Virgin Carmen or to Homshuk as *mok santu* ("maize spirit"). On Easter, those who have received good harvests often make the two-day trip to Catemaco to give thanks to the Virgin Carmen. Whatever the status of beliefs concerning this alternate source of productive potential, beliefs about Homshuk remain strong among many milpa farming families today.

3. It was in reading Brian Swann's commentary on the benefits of collaboration between poets and linguists/anthropologists (1987:247–54) that I became convinced that, at least where certain types of translations are concerned, anthropologists such as myself can play an important mediating role between Native American performers and English-speaking poets.

4. The transcription is phonemic, since this facilitates an understanding of the referential information contained in the text. This is essential in the analysis of thematic patterning of the text. Orthographic conventions are shown below.

This Transcription	Phonetic Alphabet
p	p
b	b
t	t
d	d
k	k
g	g
ʔ	ʔ
s	s

sh	š
h	h
ts	¢
ch	č
m	m
n	n
ny	ñ
ŋ	ŋ
l	l
r	r
w	w
y	y

References

Baez-Jorge, Feliz. 1973. *Los Zoque Popolucas: Estructura Social*. México: Instituto Nacional Indigenista, Secretaria Educación Pública.

Foster, George M. 1945. "Sierra Popoluca Folklore and Beliefs." In *University of California Publications in American Archeology and Ethnology,* vol. 42 (2), 177–250. Berkeley and Los Angeles.

———. 1967. "The Mixe, Zoque, Popoluca," in *Handbook of Middle American Indians,* vol. 7, 448–77. Austin: University of Texas Press.

Hymes, Dell. 1962. "The Ethnography of Speaking." In *Anthropology and Human Behavior,* Thomas Gladwin and William C. Sturtevant (eds.), 15–53. Washington, D.C.: Anthropological Society of Washington.

———. 1964. Introduction. In "The Ethnography of Communication," J. Gumperz and D. Hymes (eds.), *American Anthropologist,* vol 66 (6), Part II, 1–34.

———. 1981. *"In Vain I Tried to Tell You": Essays in Native American Ethnopoetics*. Philadelphia: University of Pennsylvania Press.

———. 1987. "Tonkawa Poetics: John Rush Buffalo's 'Coyote and Eagle's Daughter.'" In *Native American Discourse: Poetics and Rhetoric,* Joel Sherzer and Anthony C. Woodbury (eds.), 17–61. Cambridge: Cambridge University Press.

Jakobson, Roman. 1960. "Concluding Statement: Linguistics and Poetics." In *Style in Language,* T. A. Sebeok (ed.), 350–77. Cambridge: MIT Press.

Munch, Guido. 1983. "Cosmovisión y Medicina Tradicional entre los Popolucas y Nahuas del Sur de Veracruz." In Lorenzo Ochoa y Thomas A. Lee, Jr. (eds.), *Antropología y Historia de los Mixe-Zoques y Mayas,* 367–3,881. UNAM/BYU. Mexico D. F.

Sherzer, Joel, and Greg Urban. 1986. "Introduction." In *Native South American Discourse,* Joel Sherzer and Greg Urban (eds.), 1–13. Berlin: Mouton.

Swann, Brian. 1987. "A Note On Translation, and Remarks on Collaboration." In *Recovering the Word: Essays on Native American Literature*. Arnold Krupat and Brian Swann (eds.), Berkeley: University of California Press.

Tedlock, Dennis. 1983. *The Spoken Word and the Work of Interpretation*. Philadelphia: University of Pennsylvania Press.

———. 1987. "Hearing a Voice in an Ancient Text: Quiche Maya Poetics and Performance." In *Native American Discourse: Poetics and Rhetoric,* Joel Sherzer and Anthony C. Woodbury (eds.), 140–75. Cambridge: Cambridge University Press.

Urban, Greg. 1986. "The Semiotic Functions of Macro-parallelism in the Shokleng Origin Myth." In *Native South American Discourse,* Joel Sherzer and Greg Urban (eds.), 15–57. Berlin: Mouton.

Woodbury, Anthony C. 1987. "Rhetorical Structure in a Central Alaskan Yupic Eskimo Traditional Narrative." In *Native American Discourse: Poetics and Rhetoric,* Joel Sherzer and Anthony Woodbury (eds.), 176–239. Cambridge: Cambridge University Press.

Suggested Reading

Gumpertz, John J. 1982. *Discourse Strategies.* Cambridge: Cambridge University Press.

Hymes, Dell. 1974. "Ways of Speaking." In *Explorations in the Ethnography of Speaking.* Richard Bauman and Joel Sherzer (eds.), 433–51. Cambridge: Cambridge University Press.

Jakobson, Roman. 1968. "Poetry of Grammar and Grammar of Poetry." In *Lingua* 21:597–609.

Sherzer, Joel. 1987. "A Discourse-Centered Approach to Language and Culture," in *American Anthropologist,* vol. 89, 295–309.

———. 1987. "Poetic Structuring of Kuna Discourse: The Line," *Native American Discourse: Poetics and Rhetoric,* in Joel Sherzer and Anthony C. Woodbury (eds.), 103–39. Cambridge: Cambridge University Press.

———. 1987. "Strategies in Text and Context: Kuna Kaa Kwento." In *Recovering the Word: Essays on Native American Literature.* Arnold Krupat and Brian Swann (eds.), Berkeley: University of California Press.

———, and Anthony C. Woodbury. 1987. "Introduction." In *Native American Discourse: Poetics and Rhetoric,* 1–16. Cambridge: Cambridge University Press.

Modern Yucatec Maya Oral Literature

Allan F. Burns

The Yucatec Maya people of Mexico number over 500,000 in the states of Yucatán, Quintana Roo, and Campeche, as well as in the country of Belize. Other Maya, such as the Quiche, Mam, Tzeltal, and others living in southern Mexico and Guatemala, bring the total number of Maya people in the world today to over four million. While the Maya are often referred to as the "mysterious" civilization that left such monumental treasures as Uxmal or Tikal, the Maya today continue to live and work in their homeland, speaking Mayan and continuing with a tradition of poetry and narrative that is indigenous to the area. The Maya of architectural fame inhabited a relatively short period of time: the classic civilization and flowering of architectural splendor lasted only some four hundred years, while Maya people have lived in the area over three thousand years.

Listening to the Maya people today and translating their oral literature is an enjoyable task that provides a clear picture into the world of a people who have survived both their own and our civilization. In this exploration of how contemporary oral literature can be translated from Maya to English I begin with a discussion of the historical and situational features of the Maya today. Then a translation of a Maya Orpheus narrative is used to discuss the style and content of contemporary Maya verbal art.

Historical and Social Contexts of Mayan Narratives

The translation of the oral literature of the Yucatec Maya people of today is as much an ethnographic as it is a linguistic task. Translating contemporary Mayan texts begins with participating in and understanding the social situations in which they are performed. They are social situations that are informed by the history of Maya-European contact and conflict as they are informed by a conversational ethic of performance. As Paul Sullivan pointed out in his book about the attempts of the Maya to communicate with outsiders, *Unfinished Conversations,* the dialogues between the Maya and the non-Maya, including U.S. anthropologists, are highly charged events full of historic and contextual meanings that go beyond the message of individual words and phrases. Seemingly uncomplicated questions and responses are put forth with the weight of hundreds of years of historical memory implicit in them.

Yucatec Maya people have been engaged with Europeans for the past five hundred years, and so their own stories, poems, prayers, and other forms of verbal expression reflect this long encounter. Their poetic and mythic system is not separate from the Hispanic tradition. It is dualistic in that at times the oral literature is very indigenous and at times very European. It is a system that takes into account the encounter with Europeans at almost every level. An example of this articulation is found in the use of both Maya and Spanish in paired couplets. As many observers of Mayan verbal art have pointed out, including Tedlock, Sullivan, Edmonson, and Gossen, couplets are an ubiquitous feature in the formal genres of prayer, poetry, narrative, and prophecy among the Maya. But even the linguistic form of Yucatec Mayan couplets partakes in a bilingual and bicultural tradition. One story about Noah and the great flood that destroyed the generation of hunchbacks who lived on earth before our own generation (Burns 52) has a segment about how the land did not need water because it was naturally moist all of the time. The narrator uses couplets to say this:

> The land is constantly moist
> The land, the land gets water all of the time

In Mayan, the couplet is bilingual (Spanish words are italicized in the following example):

> Le lu'umo, *constante humedecer*naha'an
> Le lu'umo, tadz *ora* ukum ha, le lu'umo

The encounters between the Maya and others have been incorporated into the words and phrases of their language, but still, the encounters have been devastating. The civilization, architecture, population, and even history of the Maya have been overwhelmed by five hundred years of domination. A population once numbering perhaps up to ten million at contact has been reduced to a few hundred thousand in Yucatán. Poverty and relegation to an under class are everyday facts of life in the Yucatán, often reflected in narrative:

Who owns the land? Who? The People? The "*campesinos of the Maya zone*"? They get nothing. They aren't paid a good wage. They are in real poverty. All poor. Well, we are taking all of this into account. When will we be given respect, when will we be helped?

In this example, which I have translated from the original spoken Mayan, the narrator uses satire in his switch to Spanish for the phrase "*campesinos* (peasants) of the Maya zone." Such subtle satire is common in Yucatec Mayan performance. It is a way to comment on the injustices of living under the political and cultural authority of the Mexican government.

The engagement of the Maya and non-Maya worlds expressed through these bilingual couplets and phrases has a corollary in the social context of narrative performance in the Yucatán today. Narratives are expressed most often through conversational exchanges, instead of monologues, as is often the case with other oral literatures, Mayan stories, myths, and other forms of verbal art arise out of conversation. Often a myth is related only as an aside or anecdote during a conversation. When asked to tell a complete sacred narrative, few people can do so; instead they can and do refer to parts of the myth in everyday talk. Stories, myths, and other verbal art are in this way woven much thicker into the everyday lives of Maya people than in societies where storytelling is always seen as a special event.

Conversation and Participation in Stories

Recently I mentioned to an urban Maya person that I was taking a group of students to a famous cave in Yucatán. "You know that cave connects to a tunnel that comes out of the ground under the cathedral in Merida," he volunteered. I asked where else it went. "It goes through Teabo and Mani, too," he said. These short utterances referred to a rich mythic world of people who transformed themselves into invisible beings, who lived in the underworld in today's modern world, and whose roads and superhighways were under the limestone shelf that makes up the surface of Yucatán. In the context of this conversation we were creating a myth, one that began with the present-day use of Yucatán as a tourist zone and a place appropriate for student exchanges. The interlocutor quickly moved from this present day world to the world of myth by alluding to a series of stories and anecdotes about underground passages that connect several precontact ceremonial centers (one of which was his own birthplace) to the cathedral in Merida. The cathedral of Merida itself is on the site of a precolumbian center, and the stones from an earlier pyramid were used to build the church during the sixteenth century.

These kinds of conversational exchanges are at the heart of Maya performance of myth and poetry. Even highly ritual language, such as that to close off the storytelling events respect this dialogic exchange (Burns 18):

Don Pas: Let's Hunt.   *Don Felipe:* My rifle's broken.
Don Pas: Where are the parts?   *Don Felipe:* I burned them.
Don Pas: Where are the ashes?   *Don Felipe:* Eaten by a falcon.
Don Pas: Where's the falcon?   *Don Felipe:* Went to the sky.
Don Pas: Where in the sky?   *Don Felipe:* Fell.
Don Pas: Then where did it fall?   *Don Felipe:* Went in a well.
Don Pas: Where did it disappear?   *Don Felipe:* Into your belly.
Don Pas: True!

This use of dialogue as the center of Yucatec Maya verbal art is connected to the metaphysical bases of Maya thought as much as it is to the everyday world of talk. In the Quiche Mayan book of origins and history, the *Popol Vuh,* the world is created through the conversation of two founding deities. Conversation is a creative, productive force in Mayan cosmology as it is in everyday life. Translating Mayan texts involves becoming part of the conversations, because without participation in them, no stories can be heard.

My first attempts at learning Yucatec Mayan involved working with a brilliant traditionalist in a modern Maya town, Ticul. Alonzo sat patiently with me for five or six hours a day, repeating word lists, explaining verb declensions, and talking about his life. As I struggled to learn the pronunciation of the consonants and vowels of Mayan, Alonzo would press me into conversation. The first lesson I wrote down from our lessons was a text that focused on conversation (Burns 15):

Bix a beel? Bix tamaansic ti acabah? Contento'ech, wa?
How is your path? How did you pass the night? Are you happy?
Tech nuuctene than beyo, "Bix saasictech? Ma'alo?"
You answer the talk like that, "How did you wake up? Good?"
Cin wa'ic tun teche, "Ha'alibe, co'oxtun casic meyah."
I'll say then to you, "Well, let's start work."

Learning to speak Mayan this way is not difficult: the practice of writing the dialogues while simultaneously recording them on a tape recorder provided a series of lessons that I could recall even when my teacher was not there. After a few weeks Alono suggested that we break up the routine of linguistic elicitation with some walks through town and into the countryside. On the roads and paths we met friends and neighbors who stopped to tell political, social, or historical anecdotes. Some were about the bad luck of corn farming in a zone where rainfall was seldom predictable. Others were about jaguars with jade eyes that were found in the caves around town. Through all of this I learned that Yucatec Mayan narrative performance was a conversational art, something that arose out of these kinds of encounters and was sometimes elaborated into full-fledged stories or myths.

Later I moved to a more distant village of Maya who were followers of the Santa Cruz movement. Santa Cruz Maya were descendants of those Maya who first rose up during the Caste War rebellion between 1947 and today, the story of which is well told by historian Nelson Reed. I was told that I could not even record stories or prayers with my tape recorder if I did not enter into them as a respondent. I quickly learned that I could get by responding in a minimal way with Mayan utterances that translated as "Oh yes," and "Uhuh." But to go beyond superficial tales and anecdotes to more profound narratives, I had to learn to tell stories in Mayan and engage in the larger role of the respondent. This larger role included commenting on stories and adding appropriate follow-up narratives in performance. For several weeks I practiced a story about a magical snake, a boa constrictor, until I could tell parts of it in a coherent way. One context for stories of this type is during the rest stops in the jungle when corn farmers are walking to or from their fields. The story of the magical boa constrictor was reasonably well received, although I told it in a Mayan that had a strong English accent. As a result of this participation, I was allowed to tape-record many different narratives in the village. When a nearly blind friend and I chanced upon a boa in the fields one day, I had to kill it with a machete. Reports of my fear and wild flailing in the bush circulated in the community for months and added credence to the specialty I had developed as the teller of the magical snake tale.

The story about the little boa snake, or *X-tziciluulme,* was a narrative which Alonzo Gonzalez Mo' told at my request while I was learning Mayan. His title was a descriptive synopsis of the story, "A Corn Farmer and an Evil Thing, and a Priest and a Small Friend."

In the tale, a man brings his wife to the family corn garden, or, as it is called in both Mayan and non-Mayan Mexico, the *milpa.* There she falls in love with a feathered serpent in the guise of a white-haired gentleman. The serpent seduces her and then drags her down to the third level of the underworld. The farmer is told of his wife's plight by a friendly boa snake, called *xtziciluulme'* ("sh-tsikil oolme"). The farmer pursues his wife and finds her in the underworld. He rescues her and brings her back to the surface of the world. As the pair return up to the world of the living, her body becomes progressively thinner, until, at the mouth of a cave, her bones fall to the ground with the sound "be-nach be-nach be-nach."

I recorded two versions of this tale from the same narrator. In one version the farmer returns to his *milpa* and is never seen again. In the other, the farmer returns to town and confesses his sins to a priest. He is still in town, and, as a common ending in Maya oral literature, can be seen today in front of his house.

These two alternate tale endings are a short cut to the two complementary views of the world that make up Maya thought. The return of the farmer to the town and his subsequent confession to a priest represents a Maya-Spanish syncretic system where Catholic religious priests are equipped to handle sins and transgressions such as an encounter with the Devil. On the other hand, the ending that has the farmer going back to his corn garden and disappearing forever portrays a cosmological system where the corn garden or *milpa* is at the center rather than the town. Robert Redfield, in *The Folk Culture of the Yucatán,* describes the world of the Maya as encompassing both the town and the countryside. Although the disappearance of the farmer into his corn garden could be interpreted as death, a more likely interpretation is that the person left town life for the countryside. In the ending exchange presented earlier, the falcon disappears by transformations into a different system.

An Account of the Underworld

The oral literature of the Maya is best understood in its spoken form. In order to capture as much of the oral qualities as possible and make them available in English, I have translated the boa tale in a way that recreates the spoken nuances on paper. This ethnopoetic approach was developed by Dennis Tedlock, Jerome Rothenberg, Dell Hymes, and others who felt the traditional linguistic translation techniques of linguists to be too cumbersome and complicated to be useful to general readers. The aim of linguists in presenting detailed information was good, but the need to become trained in the international phonetic alphabet, syntactic theory, and other linguistic techniques made many texts unreadable. Likewise, anthropologists who paraphrased what native people said stripped the magnificence from the verbal art, often rendering them as folktales with little esthetic value. This led to a continued stereotyping of indigenous people by presenting them as childlike, listening to stories much as children might listen to bedtime tales read from collections of nursery lore.

One of the easiest ways to retain the oral qualities of a performance of a narrative like that of the boa is to pay attention to the rhythm of speech. Narrators in any society pause at points, sometimes to provide dramatic tension, other times to give the listener a chance to catch up with the action or think about a particularly complex issue. In addition to these artistic pauses, speakers of any language have regular pause rhythms in their speech. These shorter pauses last only a second or so, but are noticeable in that they structure the overall timing or cadence of speech. It is common to think that the punctuation of sentences in written langauge correspond to these pauses, but this is not the case. Punctuation has developed over the centuries so that now it has a tradition of its own. It does not reflect points in speech where people pause or take a breath, unless a written script is being read. A more effective means of capturing the pauses of natural speech is to transcribe each utterance between pauses as a *line,* such that the resulting transcription looks more like poetry than prose. When pauses last more than a second or so, they can be indicated by dots between the lines, with each dot signifying a second of silence. The dots have a visual appeal as they recall the use of bars and dots in the written system of numbers in classic Maya times.

The translation of these short and long silences in the spoken narratives of Maya people achieves a translation that can be put back into the oral world by reading, even by reading it in a language quite different from Mayan. Surprisingly, the syllable counts in both English and the original Mayan are very close for the utterances separated by pauses. In other words, a spoken Mayan original line of six or seven syllables can be carefully translated into English with the same number of syllables. Other oral features can be signaled through an ethnopoetic approach to translation, such as loudness through the use of capital letters and seriousness through italics.

The story of the boa snake was told by Alonzo Gonzalez Mo?. Notice that the story begins quite slowly with many pauses, but then moves more quickly as the narrator becomes enthusiastic about the story. There are episodes that are marked by changes in perspective and action in the story, but not necessarily marked by pauses. The pauses used in the oral rendition of the narrative are confined to heightening the dramatic quality of each line. More often than not, these pauses are anticipatory in that they are enacted before a particularly important line or word of the text rather than afterwards.

WELL
Afterwards, there was a man of the MILPA.
The milpa, then.
   .

He has a small milpa,
one he made.
  . . .

He goes to the MILPA every day.
  .

When he gets to the milpa,

  .

there is a FRIEND
called "Xtziciluulme."
  . .

Because the XTZICILUULME, the friend
guards
the corn bin of the milpa

  .

so that it won't be eaten by RATS.
  .

The thing is, XTZICILUULME is a real friend.
So when he is leaving the milpa
the man says to his friend,
  .

"Hey little SNAKE,
I think I'll go to my TOWN.
YOU STAY HERE to guard my BIN
so the corn won't be eaten by rats."
  .

Then he goes.
"TOMORROW
I'll come to see you again. I'll be going now."
Then he goes, that owner of the milpa.
He comes to his house.
  .

He says to
his wife just like this:
"If you want to SEE it TOMORROW, if you want,
we'll go to the milpa to walk AROUND
because there at the MILPA,
some "grace" [corn] has ripened.

THE CORN is getting fat.
You know, we can go there to eat a little roasted corn
in the milpa."

. . .

"O.K., we'll go."

So far in the narrative, the scene of the action has been set. The protagonist, a Maya corn farmer, talks to a little boa snake in the fields as if it were human. He is so proud that corn, the "sacred grace" of life, is growing well that he invites his wife out to see the garden. Women often work alongside of men in the milpa or corn garden, especially when the plants are growing and the first corn ceremony is at hand. In the narrative, an allusion is made to this when the farmer talks about eating some roast corn in the field. In the next episode, the scene shifts back to the milpa:

Then the next morning
he carried a little food.
Some good food to take to the milpa

.

[voice trails off] They went there . . .
They arrived at the milpa,

.

where there is a hut.
When he sees his friend there,
[in a higher voice] "Hello, friend, What's happening? You were left here alone.
Were there any rats to catch?"
"Well, THERE WERE."

.

"Uhuh, O.K."
Well, the man said to his wife,

.

"REST yourself a bit,
for a while.
I'm going to take a walk around the edge of the MILPA
to see if anything has happened to this corn."
"O.K."

Now the first transformation begins to be hinted at through the dialogue between the man and the snake. Transformations are a common device in Yucatec and other Maya literature, allowing for surprising and often humorous episodes. In this narrative, the transformation of the small snake into something with a human voice previews the next transformation of a large feathered serpent into a man. Earlier in the narrative, the snake is talked to "as if" it were human. In this section, the snake begins to answer him, and he is nonplused. He talks to it just as he talks with his wife.

"Well, I guess I'll be going.
Be careful not to go

into the corn;
already the sun, the sun has set.
Don't go out. Be careful not to be bitten by a *snake*.

.

You won't be left here alone.
There's a friend of mine here. He'll stay with you.

.

I'll be going now. I won't be long."
"O.K." "Fine, then, my wife."

.

[voice trails off] Again the man went on. The man goes . . .
He went with his rifle across his back.
He goes for a walk around the milpa.
He begins to walk AROUND the edge of the milpa
TO SEE if there is anything doing harm to the corn *in the milpa*.
Well, he went to the edge of the milpa.
The woman then,
just steps out of the door of the hut.

. .

By this time in the narrative, the admonition not to leave the hut has already given away
the next section. Obviously she is going to leave the hut and some harm will befall her.

She stands there; she stands there for a minute.
She sees

.

a MAN appear.
A RICH MAN.
He SAYS, "Come here, woman.
Come here.
I want to talk to YOU."
"No, I'm not coming

.

because *my husband isn't here*.
He is here, but he went to walk around the edge of the milpa.
It won't be long until he comes back. I'm not coming."
"Oh dear woman, come here. Let's talk here."
"What are you going to tell me.?"
"There are *things* . . . Come here."
"O.K., then, I'll be coming to hear what you want to tell me."
The woman goes to hear what he wants to say, that *rich man*.
The woman walks over.
[in a higher voice] "Well, here I am.
What are you going to tell me? What do you really want to say to me?"
"Well, this is what I want to tell you,
You LOOK GOOD TO ME. If you want,
I'll 'go' with you."
[in a suspicious voice] "NO. How you talk. I have my HUSBAND.

What will my husband say if I have

. .

accepted you."
[with great confidence] "What else is there to say?"
[hesitantly] "I don't know . . ." Well, what do you say?" "Well, O.K."
[again, with confidence] "He won't know anything. He had
to take a walk around the milpa. He won't come soon.
I'll tell you what, If you want, I'll give you A LOT
of money."
"O.K."

The seduction of the woman points to a theme that is elaborated in the next section and is at the very heart of the meaning of the narrative. She is seduced by a "rich" man, or *dzul* in Yucatec Mayan. The word *dzul* is used to refer not only to someone's wealth, but also their position. In today's world, *dzules* are outsiders, non-Maya, whereas the term originally meant someone of wealth. This points to the historical subjugation of the Maya in the Yucatán Peninsula and the disappearance of wealthy Maya since the time of the Conquest. Later in the account another "outsider" appears in the form of a Catholic priest. Before the priest appears, though, this "rich man" tricks the woman and drags her into the underworld.

The woman then

.

IS BEING TRICKED by the rich man, by the rich man.
Teeth of pure gold.
When he laughed,
his teeth were pure gold.
All of the hairs on his head were of pure gold.
He is really a rich man, a handsome rich man.
A PRINCE for the woman.
SHE LIKED HIM.
Well, he fooled the woman, he TRICKED HER.
"If you WANT,

.

bring yourself closer here. I will hug you."
"What are you saying?"
Bring yourself closer. I'll hug you, I'll kiss you.
    What do you think?
If you come with me,
I'll give you money."
"O.K., then." She came closer.
She was hugged by the rich man.

.

She began to be kissed by the rich man.
She kissed the rich man too.
When she realized that she

.

was hugged by the rich man,

when she realized it, the RICH MAN had already transformed himself
into a *large serpent*.
The woman fell to the GROUND with the serpent.
The woman changed her mind. She said, "Sweet Virgin Mary, what am I doing?
The man, by God, isn't human. It's an EVIL THING, by God.
Well, what more?
It is done.
I've been tricked."
She began to scream.

The seduction of the woman by the "rich man" is done with charm and money. The embrace of the "outsider," though, is an embrace of death. While this nightmarish scene is taking place, the small boa snake transforms himself into human form to tell the husband of the event. The form the snake takes is that of a small boy, akin to the traditional Maya *alux* or mischievous elflike creatures that guard cornfields and often trick people at night. In the following section, the narrator emphasizes this transformation by repeating the lines about it several times.

The little snake, Xtziciluulme, heard the woman scream.
He came running.
He transformed himself into a SMALL BOY.
When the small boy came, the Xtziciluulme, the thing, turned into a *small boy*.
Then the small boy came RUNNING.
The woman saw the boy in the milpa.
"HEY BOY, DO ME A FAVOR AND GO CALL MY HUSBAND,
because I'm being killed by a serpent.
I'm already wrapped up.
He's wound around me!
He's KILLING ME! Go find my husband!"
"O.K." The boy went running away to find the husband.
He came running to the edge of the milpa.
The man sees him at the edge of the milpa.
The man sees that a small boy is coming.
"HEY, BOY, WHERE ARE YOU GOING?"
"HEY, FRIEND, I came to talk to you.
Your wife is being rolled up by a large serpent."
"WHAT ARE YOU SAYING TO ME?"
"Just that. Come and see."
They went. The man arrives, "Where, boy?"
"THERE."
They went on.
The man sees that his wife is really wrapped up with the large serpent.
"My sweet Virgin Mary. My beautiful wife, *look how you're ending. With a snake!*"
Eh . . . There's no saving you." "What will you do?"
I'm going to run to town. In a minute, I'll tell the priest."
"O.K., then."
He left, running to tell the priest.

At this point in the narrative, the small boy or boa snake and the corn farmer share the trait of running to save the woman. The "large snake" or feathered serpent at first glance reminds Western readers of snakes in the Judeo-Christian tradition. But here the snake is not a devil in the same sense as the snake in the story of Genesis. This snake does seduce the woman, but does so in the guise of a rich foreigner, or, in modern Yucatecan thought, a rich American or European. The feathered serpent in the traditions of Middle America, including the Aztec and Maya, is a deity that is generally powerful but benevolent. The name of the feathered serpent is found in English in "Hurricane," a derivation of the Quiche Maya name for the feathered serpent. In Yucatec Maya tradition, the true feathered serpent or "Kukulcan" arrived in the peninsula in the guise of an actual Toltec leader from central Mexico in precontact times. Perhaps this is why even today the "large serpent" of this narrative is associated with outsiders. Since the "large snake" is associated with rich outsiders, the solution to the problem of the seduction and death of the woman is to contact representatives of other rich outsiders. In this case, the best representative is the local priest. While we might commonly think of priests as taking vows of relative poverty, in the Maya context of Yucatán, priests lived in enormous mansions next to immense churches that rivaled the cathedrals of Europe. Many of the colonial churches in Yucatán were built out of the stones of Maya temples, and so the association of richness and power with the priests is profound.

> He came running to the priest.
> "Hey, PADRE. If you can believe it, something happened to my wife.
> Come so that you can see how she became wrapped up with a serpent."
> "What are you saying?" "Let's go, Padre."
> Well, the priest went. The man brought the priest there to the MILPA.

The priest is taken out of his normal context of the town and brought to the milpa, a point emphasized by the narrator. The corn fields of the Maya are sacred places cut out of the surrounding forest each year and planted with ceremony and care. It is a world that few non-Maya people know about or even set foot in, even today.

> The man and the priest came to the milpa. He was brought to see
> the place of the snake and the woman.
> "There, Padre, look at my beautiful wife."
> "Is it possible? Look, son!
> Well, son what else is there?
> It's happened. The sin is already done
> with this,
> this thing.
> Finished, I guess.
> Let's make a prayer over her."
> They begin to pray. The priest began to pray.
> Then he said, "here's the prayer I'm going to make:
> Do you repent, son, for her?" "I repent for her, Padre.
> Because my wife is not of this world. She's gone to the underworld."
> Then the priest began to make a blessing.

Then the earth OPENED UP. AWAY they went, the woman and the snake.
The woman went away with the snake. *The earth closed up again.*
Then he blessed it, the place where they went,
that woman and the snake.
He blessed it.
"Well, son, take account of this.
Today you are without a WIFE. Your wife went to the UNDERWORLD."
"What?" "Let's go." "O.K., Padre."
They went. They returned. [voice trailing off] They went on, they went on to the town.
Well, the Padre came to the CHURCH.
Well, the man went to his HOUSE.
The small boy was left in the MILPA.

At the end of this episode, the narrator sums up the spatial arrangements of the Maya world: the corn garden or milpa, the house, and the town. The town is the provenance of the outsiders, ruled by non-Maya priests and politicians. The house, in this case devoid of the wife, is the realm of Maya culture. The corn field, abandoned for the moment by the humans, is left in the care of the small "helper," the boy-snake Xtziciluulme.

Well, LATER, the man came back.
He came and said, "Friend, listen, friend."
"You've returned." "I've returned, friend."
"What can I do, my small friend? My wife was CARRIED AWAY.
My eyes are sad since it happened."
"WOULD YOU LIKE TO GO AND SEE HER?"
"I'd like to go and see so I could find where she is."
"Good, fine. You'll have to go and see.
BUT there is a WAY to see. You are going to SEE, friend, THERE IS A
.
there is a
. . . . .
There is a skunk there on the ROAD.
A skunk on the ROAD.
That one is the KEY to the PLACE where you'll go.
It's also an 'Evil Thing.'"

The decision to descend into the underworld and see his wife puts the corn farmer into the realm of the boy-snake. The boy tells the man that skunks are "keys" to the underworld, and that they are part of the Maya pantheon of "evil things" like the feathered serpent that abducted his wife. The underworld is found through descending through the labyrinth of caves that make up the limestone shelf of the Yucatán. Caves are foreboding and rotten-smelling places; perhaps because of this, the terrible smelling skunk serves as a guide.

"Here's what you have TO DO:
You have to find, YOU HAVE TO MAKE about six SACKS OF GROUND, BURNT CHILI, you have to
    PREPARE IT to bring with you."
"Why will I need it?"
"Well, it's not for you.

When you get to the edge of town,
when you get to where you have to go,
you'll see a skunk COMING to BITE YOU.
GRAB the ground chili, THROW IT in its EYES.
While you are THROWING IT in its eyes, tie its throat, then go with him.
It will . . . It knows the road where you'll be taken."
"Oh. O.K."
"When it PAWS the ground to take you or to lose you, THROW MORE CHILI in its eyes.
MEANWHILE, tie it up.
You will go with it. You will be on the road.
The place that you go to will be where your wife is."
"O.K."
"But BE CAREFUL not to FALL there."
"O.K., friend."
Well, the man went to his town.

Some of the narrative is edited out of the following text for brevity. Maya narratives such as this one are normally performed in about an hour's time, with sufficient attention given to constructing details of the journey, of the other beings encountered in the underworld, and of the growing problems of the priest.

The rhythm of the performance continues. The man finds the priest and asks if he will accompany him on the journey. The priest brings a crucifix and a piece of rope and they set off. The skunk leads them through a cave into the first level of the underground.

Then they arrived at the FIRST PLACE.
It was over the spot. As they went they saw the

world had already disappeared.
Then they went underground. They went through a CAVE to go on
The first place they ARRIVED at was the house of the little PUTRID THINGS.
The house of the little Putrid Things was the first place.
The house of the LITTLE PUTRID THINGS.
Well, naturally the little Putrid Things went with the little SKUNK.
Well, they gave it some chili.
Then they began to be led along.
They went on.
They were close to the little Putrid Things.
The little Putrid things, not TRUE BAD THINGS.
Those ones were still very little.
They said to the skunk,
"Let's go to another place."

Well, *they went on.*
That little skunk is also a Putrid Thing, a key to the door of the house of the Evil Things.
Well, that little one wanted to stomp the ground to carry them away to the underworld,
so they use the chili formula.
It rubs and rubs its eyes,

and doesn't go.

Meanwhile he puts more on its eyes and that one CARRIES THEM AWAY.

As the group travels into the underworld, the evil beings become more and more frightening. As this happens, the priest becomes more and more afraid of them. Soon he is trembling and stuttering, unable to even use his prayers to ward off the danger around him. The narrative takes on a humorous vein as the priest becomes a liability in the underworld.

> Then they get to another little TOWN a town of PUTRID THINGS.
> Not very big Evil Things, LITTLE ONES.
> Well, they PASS THROUGH the entrance and go looking for the wife.
> [higher voice] She isn't found there!
> Those Evil Things come. A bunch of them come, grouped together like that.
> They come in a group.
> They come . . .
> They CLOSE IN on them.
> They are next to the HUMANS to do *evil*
> to those people.
> Well, the priest says then [higher voice], "Ave María Santísima—here come the Evil Things,
>   those pure Putrid Ones."
> "Pray, Padre, do a *Credo*." He begins to pray.
> The thing is, the padre is too frightened to pray.
> He says, [higher voice] "pa pa pa, ta ta ta ta ta, pa pa pa. ."
> He isn't able to start a prayer. HE'S SCARED.
> "Padre, pray! Don't be afraid!"
> [higher] 'Titititi, papapapapa." "Pray, padre!" "titititi." "PRAY!"
> The padre was scared.
> Well, the padre began to pray even though he was afraid.
> Well, true God looked down. The Evil Things left and they were once again among the little
>   Putrid Ones.
> "Well, then, I have to go to ONE MORE TOWN
> in the world to see if my wife is there."
> They start going there.
> Well, while they're going, the little Putrid One, the skunk,
> the one who DANCES on the earth,
> he begins to carry the people into the UNDERWORLD.
> He THROWS THE CHILI into its eyes. It SHAKES and pounds on the ground again.
> They go on.
> . .
> While they are going, they go on, they go on like that.
> Then they arrive
> at the edge of a town,
> the entrance to the Great Putrid Ones.
> Well, the old man says, the husband, that is, says,
> "Hey Padre, we've
> arrived where you told me, my friend."
> The Evil Things are so very large here, the Putrid Ones are so very large at this place here.
> "Well, let's go."

They go in, but the thing is, those Putrid Ones look frightening.
They grab that small Putrid One, that key, the key of the Evil Things.
Well, [voice trailing off] they go on.
They come to the center of the town,
so he says, "Well, we've come all the way."
A great group of Putrid Ones come toward them.
A great BUNCH of Putrid Ones.
A GREAT BUNCH of Putrid Ones come. The Putrid Ones COME all together.
They group together, they want to suffocate them.
Well, the PADRE IS SCARED.
The PRIEST IS SCARED.
"Padre, don't be afraid,
PRAY!"
[higher, in a frightened voice] "Titi . . papa . . titititi Ah . . . ah . . . a . . . Our Father,
tatatata Santa María . . ."
The prayer doesn't come out of the Padre.
"Pray! we'll be crushed to death."
[higher, in a frightened voice] "Tatatata . . . Here's the Crucifix!"
The Padre is FRIGHTENED.
Well, all of the things move away,
the EVIL THINGS.

This slapstick comedy with a trembling, frightened priest at a loss for words when confronted with the inhabitants of the Maya underworld continues. The husband and the priest walk around the town, looking for his wife, all the time with the priest tugging at his sleeve and asking him to leave. They do find the wife who pleads with them to take her out of the underworld. As they leave, the Putrid Things again surround them to the dismay of the frightened priest.

The Putrid Ones see the poor wife going away with her husband like that.
They ALL COME TOGETHER, ALL OF THE EVIL THINGS come together again.
The people are going away with the priest in the MIDDLE like that.
The man says,
"Hey Padre, pray! Here come the people."
"I will. sisisisi tatatata papapapap. But I . . . I . . . I'm scared!"
"Well, pray, Padre!"
[higher and frightened] "Titititi Ave Maria S . . . s . . . s . . . Santa María . . ca . . . ca . . .
ca . . . Credo."
The prayers won't come out of the padre.

The group is saved by showing the cross again. They return through the several layers of the underworld and notice that the woman, who was once quite heavy, is getting thinner.

"But wife, what's happening to you?"
"I don't know, my husband, how is it possible?
Look at me now!"
"Let's go. I have to get you out of here."
She is carried off.

When she is BROUGHT to the edge of the town where the little Putrid Ones are, she is left
 without much.
She is so very thin, just *bones*.
Well, they start to leave.
There, where she is about to be taken through the entrance
of the cave, where they entered,
the woman became a skeleton.
Almost all of her flesh had fallen off.
Then, as they LEFT the entrance of the cave, as they WENT OUT,
he says, "Well, my beautiful wife, we've made it! Let's go."
While he's saying "let's go," he HEARS A FALLING SOUND: BE-NACH, BE-NACH, BE-NACH.
The flesh had fallen off the woman.
She was left without anything.
She became an Evil Thing because of the Evil Things,
because of the Putrid Ones.

The man, now despondent, goes back to town for a while, visits his friend the small boa
snake in the milpa one last time. There in the milpa tall weeds have taken over the land.
The man goes home. In a traditional ending motif, the narrator at this time brings the story
back into the realm of the every day world by saying,

This all happened.
When I passed by there earlier, the man was QUIET.
He was in his house.
His wife had gone back to the *Putrid Ones*.

Discussion

The real surprise of the narrative is not the journey through the underworld or the irrevers-
ible path that the wife took, but the priest. The priest brings his crucifix and prayers with
him but is unable to use them effectively. He becomes a frightened, trembling liability to
the man who is searching for his wife. The priest in this sense is out of place. He cannot
function effectively, and so becomes a buffoon, a comic character who brings humorous
relief to the encounter with the underworld inhabitants, including the feathered serpent.

Mocking authority is a common topic in narratives of many subjugated peoples.
In the Maya world, however, the authority of the priest is not completely mocked. As the
priest travels farther and farther from the town, his authority, confidence, and utility diminish. He is still the guardian of the farmer, but is not an effective guardian. When the
priest is in the town, his authority and status is high. Even after the unsuccessful attempt
to bring his wife back from the underworld, the farmer goes back to the priest in town and
"confesses" and in so doing is released from the experience. In effect, this narrative
marks a division in the worldview of the Maya. The Maya indigenous system, here described in terms of the forest, the cornfields, the caves, and the underworld, is a place
where Spanish power and status are not effective. Indigenous ritual procedures are the

ones that work to win the favor of the skunk guardian, and the journey through the unknown levels of the underworld is made with the farmer as the leader. In contrast, the priest, associated with the Hispanic towns, regains control of the Maya farmer in that context. The two worldviews coexist in contemporary Maya cosmology. The Spanish influenced world of the cities and towns is not denied or ignored; by the same token, the indigenous system of the Maya in the world of growing corn is seen as vital and in many ways inaccessible to the representatives of Western culture, here represented by the priest.

Translation of Native American texts can be done through attention to the linguistic forms of the original performances, but to do so represents only half of the work of the translator. The other half is in the participation in the events where oral literature takes place. This participation has often been a passive one, with the translator behaving in a quiet, unobtrusive way so as not to influence the event. As this example from the Yucatán of Mexico suggests, such a pose is not necessarily the best. Narrators select stories, including Orpheus-like narratives like the boa story, with the audience in mind. The stories are entertaining and esthetically pleasing in their oral performance, but their meaning is also an important element in the events. In this case the narrative points to the division of the Maya worldview between an indigenous system and a Hispanic system. Both systems are recognized, but the story is careful to emphasize that syncretism, or the blending of Maya and non-Maya elements, is not a particularly critical feature of the Maya world. But neither is the denial of the Hispanic presence in the Maya cosmos. Both Maya and Spanish systems exist side by side, and sometimes there is an articulation between the two. The task of the translator is to participate in the oral literature events, recognize the historical and social meaning of the texts, and bring both the esthetics of the tale and the historic context into another language and culture.

References

Burns, Allan F. 1983. *An Epoch of Miracles: Oral Literature of the Yucatec Maya*. Austin: University of Texas Press.

Edmonson, Muro. 1986. *Heaven Born Merida and Its Destiny: The Book of Chilam Balam of Chumayel*. Norman: University of Oklahoma Press.

Gossen, Gary. 1974. *Chamulas in the World of the Sun: Time and Space in a Maya Oral Tradition*. Cambridge, Mass.: Harvard University Press.

Hymes, Dell. 1981. *"In Vain I Tried to Tell You:" Essays in Native American Ethnopoetics*. Philadelphia: University of Pennsylvania Press.

Redfield, Robert. 1941. *The Folk Culture of the Yucatán*. Chicago: University of Chicago Press.

Reed, Nelson. 1964. *The Caste War of the Yucatán*. Stanford: Stanford University Press.

Rothenberg, Jerome. 1985. *Technicians of the Sacred* (2nd edition). Berkeley: University of California Press.

Sullivan, Paul. 1989. *Unfinished Conversations*. New York: Knopf.

Suggested Reading

Bartolomé, Miguel Alberto. 1988. *La Dinamica Social de los Mayas de Yucatán: Pasado y presente de la situación colonial*. México, D. F.: Insituto Nacional Indigenista.

Diego de Landa, Fray. 1985. *Relación de las cosas de Yucatán* (edición de Miguel Rivera). Madrid: Historia 16.

Karasik, Carol. 1988. *The People of the Bat: Mayan Tales and Dreams from Zinacantan*. Washington, D.C.: Smithsonian Institution Press.

Souza Novelo, Narciso. 1970. *Leyendas Mayas*. Merida, Yucatan: Distribuidora de Libros Yucatecos.

Urban, Greg. 1986. Ceremonial Dialogues in Native South America. *American Anthropologist* 88: 371–86.

The
Story
of
Evenadam

Dennis Tedlock

Fieldwork, when it takes us any distance at all from home, from what is familiar, calls into question our own traditions of textualization, translation, and interpretation. The problems do not arise solely in the transition between the speech of others and our own inscription of that speech, but are always already there within the words of Others, in the transition between one act of speech and the quoting of that speech in a later act of speech, or in the multiple transitions between acts of narration and acts of interpretation that take place within any story.[1] The Others, when it comes to the processes by which their own discourse might be represented, edited, and expounded upon, have their own habits and notions before we get there. If this were not true, there could be no such thing as culture.

What concerns us here is the meeting, in the field and again at home, of Mayan practices in the representation and interpretation of discourse with our own. What makes this case particularly interesting is that writing, even in the strictest sense of the term, has been present in the Mayan world for better than two thousand years.[2] The characters of Mayan script were replaced by those of the roman alphabet in the sixteenth and seventeenth centuries, but the aftereffects of Mayan modes of textualization can be traced in alphabetic texts and in contemporary oral discourse.

Mayan hieroglyphic writing allowed the sowing, within the same visible field of discourse, of phonetic, iconic, and indexical signs, many of them calling for multiple interpretations. It is quite unlikely that two different reciters of the "same" hieroglyphic text, or even the same reader on two different occasions, said exactly the same thing—or at least what we mean by the same thing. Even when alphabetic writing came along, demanding a monocropping of the visible field of discourse, the sixteenth-century Quiché writers who undertook the transcription of the *Popol Vuh,* a hieroglyphic book, did not produce a glyph-by-glyph reading of the original but interwove their alphabetic version with their own explanations, speculations, and disclaimers, together with allusions to recent events (Tedlock 1983: chap. 12; 1985:32–33, 59).

Even when moving entirely within the alphabetic field, writers among the Quiché Maya of Guatemala did not (and do not) take advantage of the editorial opportunity to make repeated discourse match its source on a word-for-word basis. When they represent a character in a narrative as quoting what another character has already said, they routinely reword and rephrase the original statement, just as Quiché weavers modify motifs rather than repeat them exactly (Tedlock and Tedlock 1985). When scripts for centuries-old dramas are recopied, newly composed speeches are inserted and old ones are altered or left out (Bode 1961:220–26). Printed books are slowly revised with scissors and paste; they are given new covers in the form of collages, and cut-out texts from other sources are mounted with glue on their very pages.

When fieldworkers seek help in transcribing tapes of Quiché oral narratives, their informants, even when they have been instructed to repeat just what they hear from the machine, may rephrase what comes off the tape, insert lines that were not there at all, and, wherever there are words or phrases of obvious Spanish origin, replace them with Quiché ones wherever possible. Not only that, but the very people who allowed themselves to be recorded may not accept what is on a tape as an authoritative version of what they said in the first place. We seem to have entered a world where *every act of representation is also an act of interpretation.* (These days, of course, it has been dawning on a lot of us that we have been living in just such a world all along.)

In the Mayan world in general, a great value is placed on the ground from which all discourse arises and the ground to which it must return if it is to remain discourse, which is the ground of dialogue. The question of the authority of a "text" is not independent of the question as to whether and how that text might be viable in the ongoing world of dialogue, where the time and place and audience are never quite the same as on any prior occasion (Burns 1980; Tedlock 1983:chap. 10). A Mayan is unlikely to tell a story to a fieldworker in the first place unless the conversation already under way seems to suggest a particular story. Once the story is under way the fieldworker is expected to respond, even to the extent of commenting or asking questions, and thus becomes involved on both sides of the process of textualization.

A good many contemporary Mayan stories (like a good many Native North American stories) are of the kind in which Europeans or Americans see something familiar looking back at them—something from the Bible, for instance. Such stories once gladdened the hearts of diffusionists, but they have always distressed researchers who imagine there is such a thing as a transparent window on a pristine past. When we approach these stories on the ground of dialogue they take on a new interest, reflecting back on us and not only on the Other.

In retelling a Mayan story here at home, it seems to me, the only proper thing to do is to frame that story within the story of how it came to be told and see where it might arrive in the process of textualization.[3] But even when it comes to the story proper I will be drawn into the text, as you will see, and I will interrupt the already interpreted text in order to further interpret it.

The outlines of mounds can be traced on the peak named Thunderer, beneath the trees and in the clearing, and strewn about are slabs of gray basalt, quarried nearby, and silvery schist brought in from somewhere to the north. After the first of all dawns, when the god, the daimon known as Thunderer turned to stone, his arbor of bromeliads and hanging mosses was replaced by a temple, and a few houses were built for people who came up here on retreats.

When Thunderer first found his home here there were "masses of serpents and masses of jaguars, rattlesnakes, yellowbites" all around, so says the *Popol Vuh*. And today people say that if you come to a place like this, to any high place that has a hearth, a gaping mouth, for offerings, and if you have touched your woman or man on that day, or quarreled or fought on that day, or if you have let your gods go thirsty and hungry too long, then a puma will show his face here, or a jaguar, a rattler, or that viper with the yellow lower jaw, the fer-de-lance. The Holy World, Holy Earth, lord of this mountain, lord of this day, they all have mouths. In the valleys below live people who know how to feed them. A Quiché man, Mateo Uz Abaj, brought us up here today, don Mateo and his youngest daughter and youngest son. Three Quichés with the three of us. Here is doña Bárbara, my wife, and I am don Dionísio, and with us is don Mal-cum, our friend. Three gringos, all three of us ethnographers—and don Mateo has shown us all how to feed these mouths.

The first person ever to come up here was a *chuchkajaw,* a motherfather. Don Mateo is a motherfather, the living bearer of the visible face of whichever motherfather may have stood at the beginning of his line of descent, long before the birth of his father's father's father, past the point where the memory of the names of the men and their wives blacks out. He knows how to speak the right words on the right days, from among all the days with thirteen numbers and twenty names, two hundred and sixty in all, the days it takes from the time a child first makes its presence known in the womb till the time it sees the light. Today is the day *Wajxaqib' Tz'ikin,* Eight Bird, the day whose secret names are *oq'etalik, sik'italik, ri pwaq, ri pwaq,* Eight Call, Eight Cry, Eight Silver, Eight Money. A good day to climb this mountain, to call, to cry out to the lord of this mountain, to ask a favor. Today also happens to be Sunday, the second Sunday in Advent, but that is not why we are here.

Now, with our tall wax candles still making an offering of light, tallow candles soaking the earth, coals of copal incense smoking the sky, rocks anointed with liquor still wet, we settle down on the rubble that rims the shrine: an old dynamite crater, blasted by treasure hunters. Looters looking for a priceless idol would never know which of the stones at the back of the hearth might be the one haunted by the daimon of the place, the stone with a gape, with lips that like to be wet with strong liquor and sometimes get a taste of hot blood from a hen with her head cut off. But don Mateo, who looks at stones with the eye of a diviner, spotted the one with the mouth the moment we got here.

We unfold the squares of brocaded cloth that wrap the part of the picnic we brought for ourselves. Every now and then don Mateo stirs the coals with a stick, making sure every last puff of incense gets free. The three ethnographers are quite content not to be doing ethnography. We've joined him in asking every imaginable god to be present here on the day Eight Bird, to accept the sustenance we've offered on the hearth, we've been sniffing the smoke of that banquet ourselves, and now we're getting high on straight shots of the same liquor the stones got dizzy on, we're taking big bites from fresh tortillas. But don Mateo has something he wants to say. A story he wants to tell. We haven't asked any questions at all today, much less a question that would give him a reason to tell a story. So he'll ask a question himself if he has to. A big question. He says, to no one in particular:

Why? Why?

And who knows what we'd remember of his answer if we hadn't had a tape recorder with us, just in case ethnography started to happen in the middle of a picnic.

Now here I am, not on a mountaintop in Guatemala but back at the keyboard in my study, and I'm listening to his story again, but this time I can stop it, rewind, and repeat. So let's play the game now, let's take up the question after all this time and ask him, "Why?" (and "Why?"), and take down his answer:

Because, truly,
Eve and Adam
were crucified in the world, Eve and Adam.
He was the first man who married.

Crucified? Eve and Adam were "crucified"? Here's a word don Mateo got from Spanish, one of "our" languages, from "our" side of the Atlantic. Does he mean to be using *crear* here, "create," instead of *crucificar*, or is he folding the New Testament back over on top of the Old? He's not far off if we consider that Christ is sometimes called "the second Adam," and certainly what happened to Adam was cruel. What happened to Eve was cruel too, though it's doubly hard to think her onto a cross. But all right. "Truly," he says, he wants us to take him at his word, he's not just making this up.

So we're about to hear the story of Adam and Eve, as told by don Mateo on the day Eight Bird on top of the mountain called Thunderer. Or rather the story of "Eve and

Adam," he's reversed the order twice already, there's no mistake about it, and perhaps the twist in his version will involve more than folding the New back onto the Old—though people who speak his language nearly always put "her" first when talking about "him and her," or rather "her and him." But don Mateo is doing this to a pair of names that've always been spoken the other way around, all the way back to the Hebrew.

What, then, is the question before us? It would seem to have something to do with our condition as human beings. We're all descended from Eve and Adam, we are the way we are because they "were crucified in the world." And, don Mateo tells us, Adam "was the first man who married." So the question would also concern why we're still here today, after all this time. Here follows a lot of noise on the tape, but in the midst of the zaps and rumbles some words can be made out:

> ≈≈≈✳✳✳!! ◆◆≈≈!!!!
> ◆ano◆ther◆ th✳i✳ng that ≈de≈fea✳ted ≈us
> was a de≈vi≈l
> who was ✳ca✳lled the Ser◆pent.

Right here I hear myself on the tape, saying, "The Serpent?" Maybe I'm hoping it'll turn out to be a New World serpent, the Plumed Serpent even, and not just that wretched serpent in the Garden. Don Mateo simply says "Yes," it's a serpent, and the noise comes up again, we've only this hint to the turn of the plot that hasn't even got started yet, but no matter. People who live in these mountains are always folding stories back on themselves. Whatever it was we missed, we'll be able to pick up on it later. When the tape is clear again we're in the midst of the next scene:

> Well.
> Then, yes
> after that
> the Lord Jesus Christ said,

and now don Mateo gives the voice of the Lord Jesus Christ a magisterial tone,

> "So.
> Now—
> let their sin begin."
> Because they hadn't known how to sin,
> Eve and Adam.
> They were already adults, but they didn't know how to sin.
> So he said,
> "Let their sin begin."

Here He is, the Lord Jesus Christ, already on the scene way back when. It's beginning to sound as though Adam, or even Eve and Adam, will be in the role of the second Christ. And the Lord isn't saying, "Let there be light," or "Let the earth bring forth the living creature after his kind." He's saying, "Let their sin begin." Whatever the Serpent may have done under the cover of those zaps and rumbles, sin doesn't come into the world until the Lord gives his say-so. And it's the practice of sin that matters, not the concept. Eve and Adam don't even know *how* to sin until Jesus says, "Let their sin begin." The Word is made flesh.

At this point don Mateo expects to hear something from us, he's beginning to wonder about us, about whether we understand what "sin" is. He turns to us, speaks to us gringos in the same tone of voice he'd use if he were getting impatient with his children:

> You're still a little young.
> But not me.

Then he gets right back into his story, he asks a question about the beginning of sin and doesn't wait for us to volunteer an answer:

> But why?
> In order to make the world **abound.**
> ▶ ▶ ▶

Here he pauses longer than usual, about two seconds—that's a long time in the middle of a story—to let his answer sink in. In case we were still wondering what kind of sin it was the Lord Jesus was speaking into existence, it's the kind that makes the world **abound.** Now don Mateo repeats the same words (and the same pause), but shifts his emphasis:

> In order to make the **world** abound.
> ▶ ▶ ▶

Then he offers an interpretation, he opens the breach between text and interpretation in the midst of his own words:

> So there would be more people,
> there would be more
> Christians.

He uses the word *cristianos* in the same way Spaniards used it when they came here from out of the Middle Ages; it's synonymous with "people." And as far as that goes, he's been baptized and so have his wife and children and many previous generations, and the same goes for the three ethnographers who happen to be with him today. Except that he and his forebears have never seen any contradiction between sprinkling water on babies and giving drinks of strong liquor to stones. By this time the three ethnographers don't see any contradiction either, or at least not today they don't.

Now we're ready to get back to the story, to find out what happened between Eve and Adam. Don Mateo starts out on a long high pitch, as if he were just able to bear a pain from somewhere inside him, then comes back to words again:

Eeeeeeeee Eve
began to cry.
▶ ▶ ▶
Because for Eve
it was just a little difficult.
▶ ▶ ▶

So Eve's part in making the world abound is painful, just as it is in the Old World Book.
And why is it difficult for her?

Because females
are hard
and they are
somewhat physical,
I mean.

So it's not because she's being punished for something she did, but because it's in the very
being of women to be more of this world than men. Women know this through their pain,
the pain that makes Eve cry, but they are "hard" in the face of this pain. When don Mateo
says, "somewhat physical, I mean," the tape has the sound of my voice, I'm letting go of
a chuckle, perhaps a laugh of recognition at hearing a notion that sounds like one of our
own. But a laugh from his audience is not what he's looking for, he turns to me to affirm
what he just said, in a gentle tone but with a dip in his pitch that bears a hint of annoyance:

Ye$_{e_{eeees}}$—

and suddenly he narrows his eyes and sharpens his voice:

I'm telling you the **truth.**
It's because I'm older
that I'm speaking to you about this question.

At this point doña Bárbara concedes him the point with "Yes." He drops his sharp tone
but he's not through defending his authority against my chuckle:

And also
you've already seen my sacred book?
You've done that already.
All right, then.
Mm hm.

So we're not getting the story of Eve and Adam by word of mouth alone, he has a book.
He's made this move before, and the authors of the alphabetic version of the *Popol Vuh*
made a similar move four centuries ago, saying their work was based on a prior book in
"the ancient writing." Don Mateo keeps his book on his altar at home, hidden behind the

parapet of the tabernacle that holds an image of the most mystical of the Twelve Apostles, right next to the crystal that brings him dreams.

Somewhere, someone in these mountains probably has another manuscript of the *Popol Vuh* tucked away somewhere, or maybe even a version in hieroglyphs. Or better yet, a hieroglyphic book with alphabetic notes crammed into the white spaces, an inter-linear translation into Spanish, made long ago and lost from view until who knows when. Haven't we all been waiting for the weighty Book that could bear the name Rosetta?

The book don Mateo has at home is octavo, thin, stapled along the fold line, and battered. The color-lithograph illustrations are of Bible scenes and the text is a retelling of Bible stories, in Spanish—the sort of thing that's handed out in Sunday school. But a book it is, and it stands for The Book. Don Mateo never thinks of rereading it. It's there for the fact of it, there to have its existence revealed to those who need to know of its existence. And when he's away from home it's for citing, and now that he's cited it he takes a good bite from a tortilla and gets back to his story:

> Then
> Adam said to her,

and here he speaks as if to someone farther away than any of us,

> "You, Eve:
> ▶ ▶ ▶
> you have to make a shirt.
> You have to make some
> pants, you have to make everything.
> And
> with cotton."
> "And you, Adam:
> you have to work."

As Eve continues her speech don Mateo picks up the stick he's been using to stir the in-cense and begins to whack a stone with it. Life is going to get just as hard in his story as it got outside the gates of the Old World Eden:

> "With a pWHACKickaxe,
> withWHACK a machete," WHACK
> wWHACKith evWHACKerythWHACKing that
> thWHACKat WHACK WHACK
> that we have here in the world. WHACK WHACK

So Eve and Adam tell each other what their respective lots will be, they're making a con-tract, it's not just coming down from on high. And come to think of it, in "our" version of the story Eve isn't even given work to do, unless it's in that line that goes, "In sorrow thou shalt bring forth children," or hidden in the line about Adam that goes, "He shall rule over thee."

Now don Mateo gets in one last whack:

For this reason we're here
in the world
physically
working. **WHACK**
And **why?**
Because God
told us.

Here is physicality again, as with Eve's "Eeeeeeeee," and work is one of the things that comes along with it. And it seems that God is behind this matter of work after all, despite that conversation between Eve and Adam. But at least they did have a conversation and they both have their work.

The next six lines, up there on the mountain that day, went by very fast. We can't ask the tape machine to answer questions, but this time around we can at least catch the words:

Because Evenadam
were a god
equal to Jesus Christ.
They are the first
humans who
are in the world.
► ► ►

So "they *are* the first humans" and "*are* in the world," but they "*were* a god." They (and we) are now working, but weren't before. And why are we working? "Because God told us." Why did he do this to us? "Because Evenadam were a god."

Let's try this one a little slower. "Eve and Adam" sound like "Evenadam," *Evayadán,* don Mateo runs the words together as one. But then he says they "were," making them plural again, and next he says they were "a god," making them one again. It's like those pairs of gods in the *Popol Vuh,* the New World Book, where we're never quite sure whether we're dealing with two gods or one, unless the two halves of a pair start talking to one another. And it's like Jaguar Many Trees, the first of all human beings, who's a "motherfather" all by ^{her}himself before White Sea Turtle becomes his wife. Of course there's something androgynous about the Adam of the Old World Book too, whose name simply means "human" in Hebrew, and part of the very substance of this human became the substance of Eve—a "rib" or (as it could've been translated) a "side." Eve as the "other side" of a not-yet-divided human.

The way don Mateo tells the story, Eve and Adam were, or the god Evenadam was, "equal to Jesus Christ," but when Jesus Christ said, "Let their sin begin," and when they went to work in the world, they became mere humans, and that's why we're all here. If we ever had any potential for rivaling the gods, Jesus Christ took care of that by weighing down our very existence with physicality and by making sure there would be any number of us. We were a problem to the gods of the New World Book, too, when one of them warned the others about us by saying, "They'll become as great as gods, unless they procreate, unless they proliferate." And the Lord God of the Old World Book said, "Behold, the man is become as one of us," whatever he may have meant by "us" (and whoever he may have been talking to), just before he gave Adam and Eve the news about giving birth and tilling the ground.

Now, with the former Evenadam firmly established as the Eve and Adam of this world, with all their physicality, don Mateo is ready to move on, right past the next nine months at least:

> And then
> later
> then, after this,
> they had a son
> who was c a l l e d
> who was called
> Pastor.
> ► ► ►
> And then they had another son who was called
> who was called—
> I have it in a book there,
> I'm going to show you there,

and here doña Bárbara and don Dionísio both say "Yes," we're humoring him, here he goes with his book again,

> I'll show you.

And doña Bárabara adds, "At home," yes, his book is at home. No one offers him any help with names, even though all three of us gringos know Cain and Abel. We let it go when he says Pastor instead of Cain, and never mind that the firstborn son of Adam and Eve was not a pastor. We keep Abel to ourselves as well, even when he comes right out and asks us for the name of the second son:

> Then
> who was c a l l e d
> ► ► ►
> what was this son called?

After all, we're ethnographers, not missionaries. We want to hear what don Mateo might say, what a Quiché Indian might say, without any prompting from us. What he might say if we weren't even here, never mind that plenty of other people from the Old World got here before us. So he gives up on naming the second son of Eve and Adam and goes on:

> Then—
> this Pastor
> ► ► ►

is more, is more—
I don't know
why
but what I'm trying to say is that
he's physical.

So Pastor is more "physical" than his younger brother, just as Eve is more "physical" than Adam. Eve's physicality is evidenced in her hardness, her endurance of the pain that comes with childbirth. How, then, do we know that Pastor is "physical"?

Because he killed his brother.

Is don Mateo merely saying that giving birth to a child and killing a man are both grossly physical acts, or could there be something more to it than that? For the glimmer of an answer we have to look over to the west in Mexico and back to the time before Europeans arrived, where women who died in childbirth and men who died in battle were sent off to share the same celestial paradise, while people who died from other causes were sent off to earthly worlds beneath the land of the living. Don Mateo's story seems in harmony with this scheme of things, but it concerns a woman who gives birth *without* dying and a man who kills without *being* killed. Instead of going off to a celestial paradise, these two survivors have an even greater burden of physicality than other earthly beings.

When doña Bárbara heard that Pastor "killed his brother" she said "Oh," perhaps startled at the way don Mateo was giving away the main event in a story whose characters he'd barely introduced. Now, having heard her "Oh," he goes back and repeats his previous words, but with emphasis added:

He killed his **brother.**

Now don Mal-cum interjects, "Wasn't it in the milpa?" which is to say in a garden of maize, squash, and beans. For the first time, one of the three ethnographers reveals that he might already know something about the story. After all, don Mateo has already given the killing away, and didn't Cain kill Abel in a field of grain? And wouldn't don Mateo interpret that field as a milpa? Or mightn't missionaries have told him it was a milpa, devising a small lie in the service of their Big Truth? Don Mateo answers aside with a quick "Yes," seeming to accept what don Mal-cum has ventured, but he doesn't let it change his course—he goes right on describing Pastor, the man who will kill his brother once the story gets told:

It seems
he had a lot of livestock.
Those of a single color
are his brother's.
And those of two colors

> belong to Pastor,
> he was a pastor.

So we're not dealing with Cain the gardener and Abel the herder. Rather, both brothers own livestock. But where does don Mateo get this division of livestock by color? To find that we'll have to read ahead, twenty-six chapters and twenty generations beyond the story of Cain and Abel: "And he removed that day the he goats that were ringstraked and spotted, and all the she goats that were specked and spotted." It was Jacob who did that, separating his own animals from Laban's according to a bargain they had struck, and Jacob did indeed end up, as don Mateo has it, with "a lot of livestock." But Laban was Jacob's maternal uncle and father-in-law, not his brother. Jacob had a brother all right, the twin who was born from Rebekah just ahead of him: Esau, the hunter. But it was Esau who thought of killing Jacob, not the other way around. So it would seem that don Mateo has put a prosperous Abel into the body of a homicidal Cain and a prosperous Jacob into the body of a homicidal Esau, and then called them all Pastor. No wonder he can't seem to find a name for the other brother.

> And then—
> after that—
> they talked.
> And since young were born from those of two colors, only from
> those of two colors,
> then
> only the
> only Pastor had
> animals,
> cows and bulls and however many things.
> And
> this what's-his-name
> he didn't have anything, because

now don Mal-cum interrupts, he's trying to be helpful again but his timing is bad. In saying "what's-his-name" here, don Mateo wasn't really asking for an answer, nor did he leave a big enough pause for one. But between "because" and whatever he meant to say after it, don Mal-cum inserts "Abel," which may or may not be a logical name for Pastor's brother. No matter; don Mateo doesn't pick up on it anyway. He says "Eh?" aside and then, without waiting for don Mal-cum to repeat the name (and without finishing whatever was hanging on "because"), he reasserts his claim to be telling a story. He makes the most basic of all narrative moves, saying,

> Then

and again don Mal-cum interrupts. Having once decided to intervene, he wants his intervention to make a difference. Now he offers information about Abel, translated the way a missionary might translate it, saying, "He was a milpero," a gardener who planted maize, squash, and beans. He's so caught up in don Mateo's story he's forgotten that if anybody was a milpero in the Old World Book, it was Cain and not Abel. As for don Mateo, he goes ahead with the new sentence whose space he staked out with "Then":

>   he said,

and here follows a conversation between Pastor's younger brother what's-his-name and someone else. It's a secret conversation, and don Mateo goes into it so deeply that he almost keeps it secret from the rest of us. He partly whispers, partly mutters with a tight-mouthed meanness. This could almost be an internal dialogue on the part of what's-his-name, or even an internal dialogue on the part of don Mateo. It's almost as hard to follow as that earlier part of the tape where nothing but the words "devil" and "serpent" came through, and the next thing we knew the Lord Jesus Christ was saying, "Let their sin begin." The only intelligible words are these, in which someone is trying to turn what's-his-name against Pastor:

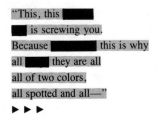

Once again we miss out on what the "because" might be, why it is that Pastor, who has the right to all the animals of two colors, ends up with a lot of livestock and what's-his-name doesn't have anything. If Pastor was like Joseph of the Old World Book, he must've used sorcery.

At this point don Mateo leaves off quoting and switches to the double voice of indirect discourse, speaking as narrator and yet staying with what's-his-names's point of view:

>   Then none of them came out black, none of them came out
>   none
>   dark, none came out—
>   these—
>   ► ► ►

he breaks off as his children move in close and want something to nibble on, then shifts from the narrative to the interpretive mode long enough to tell us that even this part of the story is an origin story:

>   Because of this
>   cows remain distinct,

yes, in distinct classes.
There are
white, there are black, there a r e
roan, and there a r e all of them
because of this
this matter.

▶ ▶ ▶

Twice he stretches the sound of the verb "are," as if to include all the colors he doesn't mention by name.

Now what's-his-name ends his secret dialogue with whoever-it-is has been telling him he's been getting screwed. He's made a decision:

"Well,
by Jesus,
I'm going,"
he went to, to Pastor,
he was thinking of fighting
with his brother.

Yes, the younger brother is thinking of fighting with the elder, _{Esau} ^{Jacob} Abel is on the move against Cain. But one thing hasn't changed: the prosperous brother is the one who's in danger, in which case Cain _{Esau} is on the move against Abel ^{Jacob}. Either way, Pastor is in physical danger, so he is like a woman in labor or a man in battle. But before don Mateo gets around to letting what's-his-name confront Pastor, he feels the need to claim authority for his story again—only this time, instead of citing a book, the book he has at home, he cites something older and deeper than that:

This is the Ancient Word.
Because
the Ancient Word is, is about Pastor and the
other son of Adam.

Back in the time when the New World Book had its first confrontation with the Old World Book, don Mateo's ancestors called the speech that came out of reading their own book the *Ojer Tzij,* the "Ancient" or "Prior Word," and they called the speech that came out of the invaders' book *uch'ab'al Dios,* or "God talk." After four hundred years of preaching, the story of Pastor and the other son of Adam, if not quite the story of Cain and Abel, nor quite the story of Esau (or Laban) and Jacob, has come to qualify as part of the Ancient Word. Or else the Ancient Word has taken those stories unto itself. Either way, two brothers are about to have it out:

Then—
they went off
since they always went to round up the
the animals.

Now Pastor's nameless brother begins to make trouble, saying,

> "What is this?
> I'm going
> ▶ ▶ ▶
> I'm going to count the animals.
> I'm going to count the **animals.**
> And I don't have any more than before.
> Only one, two, three.
> Well, one
> is pure black.
> Another is pure, pure
> pure—"
> what's it called?
> Another color that's not pure black, it's not pure
> white, it's pure—
> mm.

Again the three ethnographers refuse to come to the rescue; they won't even risk putting the name of a color in don Mateo's mouth. He closes the matter with "mm" and moves back to the angry words of Pastor's brother:

> Then,
> ▶ ▶ ▶
> you have more," he says.

This last line is hard to make out from the tape, and the problem is about to get worse. Again don Mateo goes too far inside his story for the rest of us to follow. He's thinking his characters through rather than acting them out. For Pastor's reply he uses such a tense, low, close-mouthed voice that only the fact of denial comes through:

> "No.
> No, ▬▬▬▬▬."

Whatever may have happened beyond an exchange of words, don Mateo is content to tell us, in a single line we've already heard anyway, what prosperous Pastor did to end the argument started by his jealous brother—and then we're off on a new episode:

> He killed his brother.
> Then, after that—

the next thing we know, we're hearing (or trying to hear) what will turn out to be the words of Adam, as he breaks the news of Pastor's deed to Jesus Christ:

> "My Lord,
> 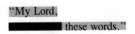 these words."

Then, after that he said—
"He killed his brother."
► ► ►

After that pause, don Mateo goes back to filling in something he should have told us before he got to the words of Adam:

And when he killed his brother
the blood
of the brother
wasn't
wasn't accepted by the Holy World.
The Holy World didn't accept it.
Because
he hadn't talked with the World.

The three ethnographers prick up their ears, they're always listening for twists that would move a story like this one a little farther from the Old World and closer to the New. On the tape doña Bárbara can be heard saying "Aha." *Aha,* it begins to sound as though Pastor *sacrificed* his brother. But when he did, the blood wasn't accepted by the Holy World, Holy Earth. Pastor didn't talk with the earth, he didn't have the words to make the sacrifice acceptable. Except for his name and his cattle, he could be a character out of the New World Book. The gods of that book would have wanted him to be their "provider, nurturer," but there was something even more important for them than sacrifice. As they put it, "Our recompense is in words."

Even in the Old World Book, the problem with the spilling of Abel's blood isn't limited to the fact of the fratricide. God says to Cain, "The voice of thy brother's blood crieth out from the ground. And now art thou cursed from the earth, which hath opened her mouth to receive thy brother's blood from thy hand." So the earth is almost a character is the story, at least for this brief moment. She "opened her mouth" to receive Abel's blood, but she didn't accept it as a proper offering—or else it was God who didn't accept it, that jealous God who wanted to cut off any possibility of offerings to the earth.

Now we're ready to hear what Adam has to say about Pastor, whose blood offering wasn't accepted by the Holy World:

Then
he said,
Adam did,
"Jesus Christ,"
he said,
"Now then:

and here Adam speaks with sharp pain:

What am I going to **do** with my **son?**
Because for me

it hurts me a lot, because
because my son
is burning
the blood
only for the Holy World.
He's burning it only for the Holy World
who doesn't accept
the cursèd World doesn't accept it."
▶ ▶ ▶

So Pastor has been *burning* the blood. Don Mateo has combined the spilling of the blood with the idea of a burnt offering. Shades of Abraham, only this Abraham has gone up on the mountain to sacrifice not his son but his brother, and he's gone through with it. But the fact that Pastor's burnt offering consists of blood makes sense right here on this mountain where the story is being told, on the day Eight Bird. The copal that still smolders on the hearth before us was made from the sap of trees, and sap is *kik'* in the Quiché language, the *kik'* means "blood." We are burning blood right here. Not only that, but the New World Book tells us that the first piece of incense *ever* burned was a substitute for the heart and blood of a sacrifice.

But Adam thinks Pastor shouldn't be burning blood for the World, since "the cursèd World doesn't accept it." But he's about to be told he's wrong:

After that he said to him,
Jesus Christ did, "No.
The World
is not cursed:
what it is, is sacred."

Jesus, of all people (or gods), comes to the defense of the World, becomes the Saviour of the World in a new sense, declaring the World itself, the earth in all its materiality, to be sacred. Again the three ethnographers pay close attention; they are members of a generation of gringos who worry about the way their society seems bent on the destruction of the earth, the biosphere itself. The problem seems to go back at least as far as the Old World Book, where God tells man to "subdue" the earth and gives him "dominion" over it, which spells disaster for the earth—and then, in no time at all, the disaster becomes mutual. Adam is told, "Cursed is the ground for thy sake," and just one chapter later Cain is told, "Now art thou cursed from the earth." But don Mateo's Ancient Word has Jesus calling the earth "sacred," and the moment she hears it doña Bárbara says "Yes." Don Mateo acknowledges her response by repeating the words of Jesus:

"The World
is not **cursed.**
What it is, is **sacred,**"
▶ ▶ ▶
says Jesus Christ.

This time he gives "cursed" and "sacred" more punch, emphasizing the difference between them, but he makes no change in the words themselves, nor in their timing. Here's a bit of fixed text in the midst of improvisation. Indeed, the original words constitute a rhymed Spanish couplet: *El Mundo no es condenado; lo que es, es sagrado.* This is the kind of statement motherfathers like to make when they argue with members of the Catholic Action movement, which aims to remove the stains of paganism from people like don Mateo and make them into *real* Catholics. Converts to the movement memorize their arguments in catechism classes; meanwhile, people who burn copal to the Holy World have been developing a countercatechism. Catechists question the worship of the World, just as Adam is doing here, and counter-catechists try to straighten them out with pro-World statements liked the catchy couplet used by Jesus, *El Mundo no es condenado; lo que es, es sagrado.* But Adam resists:

> "Mm hm.
> That's all very well," he said.
> "But what I say is,
> it is cursed.
> What's to be done?" he said.
> ▶ ▶ ▶
> "You have only to clean it, and then it isn't cursed,
> this World."

So Adam and Pastor have some cleaning to do before the World will accept Pastor's offering. The kind of cleaning Jesus is talking about is partly done by prayer. When burning offerings one should always say, even before striking a match, "Make my guilt vanish." If it weren't possible for one's guilt to disappear, at least for as long as it took to present offerings down by a spring or up on a mountain, then it wouldn't be possible to set foot in a holy place without profaning it. But there is another kind of cleaning, "the washing of the plate and cup," the sweeping out of ashes from the earth and stones of the shrine itself. What vanishes then are the wrongs that may have been done during the very act of making prayers and offerings. Perhaps someone asked that illness enter the body of a neighbor, or perhaps the perfectly good words someone spoke aloud in prayer were mingled with the words of an inner voice that couldn't let go of some resentment. Pastor's own brother might've been thinking about the uneven division of livestock while he prayed at the very shrine where his own blood was destined to be burned. If so, that could be the root of the curse that prevents the World from accepting the blood.

In any case, having told Adam that a cleaning will set things right, Jesus goes on talking about the Holy World:

> "Because
> **you must go with him,**" he said.
> ▶ ▶ ▶
> "Walk with him,
> talk with him—"

and with these words, don Mateo has made his pro-World Jesus stand the cryptocatechist Adam on his head. "Go with him," or "*Vaya con Él*"—"Him" with a capital H—these are the words used by Catholic catechists and Protestant evangelists only with reference to the Lord Jesus, and here Jesus Himself goes right ahead and uses them with reference to the Holy World. And as if that weren't enough, He goes on to paraphrase a hymn about Himself, the one whose English version goes, "He walks with me / and He talks with me." Don Mateo has accomplished a conversion, the conversion of the archconverter Himself, who, in His turn sets Adam back on the right track, here on the face of the Holy World.

Now there's lots more tape to play—it's a l o n g story—but there's no more time. So I'll fast-forward to the last sounds of the day Eight Bird, recorded while the three Quichés and the three ethnographers were getting up to leave. Someone is whistling, it's one of the ethnographers, and—what's this? It's a Bach recessional.

Notes

Portions or earlier versions of this text were presented to the Department of Religion at McMaster University, the Department of English at the University of Wisconsin at Madison, and the Latin American Studies programs at Brown University and Emory University. The narrative portion is from a larger work in progress, *Breath on the Mirror.*

1. For a fuller development of these arguments, see Tedlock (1990).

2. By writing "in the strictest sense" I mean a graphic system with signs that correspond to the sounds of a language, independently of the words those sounds may occur in. It is now well established that the ancient Maya script included not only logographs (signs for particular words) but a complete inventory of signs for syllables as well; for a concise and up-to-date introduction to the script, see Lounsbury (1989).

3. In the story, short pauses (one second or a little less) are indicated by line changes and longer pauses (a second and a half to two seconds) by arrows. A complete intonational contour, ended by a steep drop in pitch, is marked by a period, and a shallower drop by a comma. At the end of a line a lack of punctuation indicates that a contour is broken off, while a dash indicates an emphatic incompleteness, marked by a deliberate rise. Boldface type calls for a relatively loud voice, and small type calls for a soft voice. Spaced-out words should be pronounced slowly and precisely.

References

Bode, Barbara. 1961. The Dance of the Conquest of Guatemala. In *The Native Theatre in Middle America,* ed. Margaret A. L. Harrison and Robert Wauchope, 204–97. Publications of the Middle American Research Institute 27.

Burns, Allan F. 1980. Interactive Features in Yucatec Mayan Narratives. *Language in Society* 9:307–39.

Lounsbury, Floyd. 1989. The Ancient Writing of Middle America. In *The Origins of Writing,* ed. Wayne M. Senner, 203–37. Lincoln: University of Nebraska Press.

Tedlock, Barbara, and Dennis Tedlock. 1985. Text and Textile: Language and Technology in the Arts of the Quiché Maya. *Journal of Anthropological Research* 41:121–46.

Tedlock, Dennis. 1983. *The Spoken Word and the Work of Interpretation.* Philadelphia: University of Pennsylvania Press.

———. 1985. *Popol Vuh: The Mayan Book of the Dawn of Life.* New York: Simon & Schuster.

———. From Voice and Ear to Hand and Eye. *Journal of American Folklore* 103 (1990):133–56.

Modes of Representation and Translation of Native American Discourse: Examples from the San Blas Kuna

Joel Sherzer

This essay is intended as a contribution to an ongoing experimentation in the transcription, written representation, translation, and analysis of Native American verbal art that began with a pioneering article by Dell Hymes (1965), and continued with the insistence of both Hymes and Dennis Tedlock on the importance of the matter through extensive exploration of models, the founding of the journal *Alcheringa: Ethnopoetics* (1970) which focused on the representation and translation of Native American as well as other oral verbal art traditions, and the ongoing work of both Hymes and Tedlock, as well as a growing number of others, including Ellen Basso, Victoria Bricker, William Bright, Alan Burns, Gary Gossen, Bruce Mannheim, Sally McLendon, Greg Urban, Anthony Woodbury, and myself. It is now widely recognized that questions which emerge in transcribing oral discourse, representing it in printed form, and translating it are not marginal to analytical and indeed theoretical concerns, but to the contrary, central to them.

Breaking with an earlier generation, these researchers, myself included, believe that Native American oral discourse and especially verbal art is best analyzed and represented as linear poetry rather than block prose. In particular, we pay considerable attention to such features of poetic organization as grammatical and semantic parallelism, intonation, pause patterning, and other oral features of the dramatization of the voice so characteristic of and so essential to verbal performances. The determination of line and verse structure is central to the enterprise.

One important aspect of our cultural and linguistic competence as members of the contemporary Western world is to be able to listen to or read instances of discourse, whether a story, a political speech, or a newspaper article, and understand and interpret it. This means comprehending a totality of elements, from sound patterns, through tense and aspect, to narrative logic. The same is true for the San Blas Kuna, whose verbal art is my focus here. I consider my task, in transcribing, representing, and translating Kuna discourse is twofold—first to capture the Kuna ways of experiencing this discourse, and second to render the Kuna experience meaningful for a non-Kuna audience, in particular for an English-reading audience. This twofold task is the essence of ethnopoetics.

Recent research has demonstrated that there are many different organizing principles involved in the structuring of Native American discourse. These include the patterned use of various features, including vocabulary; grammatical units of various kinds, such as particles, prefixes, and suffixes; pitch, intonation, and musical shape; volume of speech; pausing; and participant interaction (various speakers, speaker and audience, etc.). The discovery of each new element of patterning raises the possibility of a different way of transcribing a text, or representing it on a printed page. One solution is to choose one type of patterning and make it the governing principle for the transcription and representation of the text. Dell Hymes, working from texts taken down in dictation by previous generations of scholars and without the availability of tape recordings, uses grammatical, semantic, and content analysis as the basis for his transcription and representation of discourse from Chinookan and other languages of western North America (Hymes 1981). Dennis Tedlock, using tape recordings, pays attention to expressive features of the voice, especially pause and pitch patterns, in his representation of Zuni narratives (Tedlock 1978, 1983). In his work with Quiché discourse, while he continues to focus on expressive features of the voice, his segmentation derives as well from consideration of all aspects of discourse I have discussed here (Tedlock 1987). William Bright and Sally McLendon, investigating Karok and Eastern Pomo, have noted a fair degree of convergence between discourse units determined by grammatical and lexical features and discourse units determined by pauses and intonation. In their emphasis on convergence, they tend to be more concerned with normative behavior (characteristic of a particular genre) than the non-convergences that emerge as moments of individual artistry (Bright 1979, McLendon 1981). Anthony Woodbury studies the interplay of convergences and non-convergences in the emergent structure of Central Yupik Eskimo discourse (Woodbury 1985, 1987). It is important to recognize in all this work that grammatical and lexical features, like pause and pitch, can be expressive and esthetic, just as pause and pitch, like grammar and lexicon, can at times not serve expressive and esthetic ends. A significant part of the linguistic and stylistic analysis of verbal art I propose and engage in here is precisely to figure this all out. And paying serious attention to modes of representation and translation is crucial to the task.

My investigation of Kuna discourse has revealed that each of the line and verse-marking devices, grammatical, intonational, musical (in the case of chanting), and social interactional, is highly elaborated and developed in and of itself, and enters into different types of relationships with the others, sometimes congruent, synchronic, and isomorphic, sometimes creating contrasts, tensions, and counterpoint. Given this situation, it might then seem appropriate to provide several written representations of the same performance, according to each of the different organizational criteria. In my work to this date, I have not done this, but rather have opted for a single transcription and representation of each performance which aims at capturing as much as possible of what members of a Kuna audience actually feel in listening to a performance. Here, however, I propose a different approach, namely to experiment with different modes of representation and translation, precisely to unpack the different structuring principles involved in performance and to highlight each of them, hopefully at the same time demonstrating that the Kuna performers themselves are manipulating, playing, and creatively experimenting with modes of representing their own discourse.

The Kuna Indians are probably best known for their molas, colorful appliqué and reverse-appliqué blouses made and worn by Kuna women and sold all over the world. They are one of the largest indigenous groups in the South American tropics, numbering more than thirty thousand individuals, the majority of whom inhabit San Blas, a string of island villages stretching from near the Canal Zone to the Panama–Colombia border, quite close to the jungle mainland where they farm. Living on the edge of modern, urban civilization, the Kuna have managed to maintain their cultural uniqueness through a creative integration of old and new, constantly adapting and manipulating traditional patterns to make them fit new situations.

The Kuna have a rich and dynamic verbal life. Like most tropical forest and lowland South American Indian societies, the Kuna's world is permeated by and in fact organized by means of their discourse—the mythical chants of chiefs; the histories, legends, and stories of traditional leaders; the magical chants and secret charms of curing specialists; the speeches and reports of personal experience of all men and women; and the greetings, leave-takings, conversations, and joking of everyday life. All of this is oral—spoken, chanted, sung, shouted, and listened to.

While to a certain degree all Kuna discourse, including everyday conversations and joking, is verbally artistic, it is especially in formal and ritual contexts that the Kuna most consider themselves to be verbally "on stage" and "on display," attempt to heighten the quality of their own verbal artistry, and critically evaluate the artistry of others. One major ritual context is the centrally located gathering house, in which chiefs chant about myths, legends, local history, and personal experiences; political leaders counsel, debate, and report in long and eloquent speeches; and expert storytellers unfold their serious and humorous tales. The other major type of ritual verbal performance involves communication with representatives of the spirit world. This communication, whose purpose is magical and curative, is in the form of long chants, usually performed in the home of the performer or his or her patient.

Kuna verbal art, because of its ongoing diversity and vitality, provides a virtual laboratory for the study of Native American verbal art in particular and for an exploration of the complex nature of oral discourse more generally. The structuring principles and processes involved in the performance of Kuna verbal art are complex; they constitute the poetics of performance. Attention to details of transcription and representation enable us to appreciate this poetics in action. Presenting an oral performance in written form reveals the native conception and perception of the performance, as well as performance strategies. Providing different transcriptions and representations of the same performance brings out the very different aspects of its structuring and poetics.

My first example is *pisep ikar* (*The way of the basil plant*), performed by Pranki Pilos from the San Blas island of Mulatuppu. This magical chant, addressed to the spirit of the basil plant (named *inapiseptili* in Kuna magical, ritual language), is used to insure success in the hunting of wild animals in the jungle. The hunter bathes in a potion made from the fragrant basil plant and has this chant performed for him by a specialist. The opening portion of the chant, which is my focus here, deals with the birth (symbolically described) of the basil plant.

In my first representation of the performance, lines are determined by a parallelism of melodic shape, as well as grammatical and semantic parallelism. Pairs of lines constitute verses. There is a short pause after the first line of a verse, a laryngeal tightening followed by a long pause after the second line of a verse. Here is a transcription and representation which highlights the extreme repetition and parallelism of words and grammatical affixes, by lining them up, stacking them under one another.

> inapiseptili olouluti tulalemaiye
>   olouluti tulallemaiye
> inapiseptili olouluti sikkirmakkemaiye
>   olouluti sikkirmakmamaiye
> inapiseptili olouluti wawanmakkemaiye
>   olouluti wawanmakmainaye
> inapiseptili olouluti aktutumakkemaiye
>   olouluti aktutulemainaye
> inapiseptili olouluti kollomakkemaiye
>   olouluti kollomakmainaye
> inapiseptili olouluti mummurmakkemaiye
>   olouluti mummurmakmainaye

Notice a crucial feature of this representation, namely that in order to highlight the parallelism so strikingly characteristic of this text, I have left blank spaces at the beginning of the second line of each verse, even though there is no long pause in the oral performance, which is what blank spaces conventionally represent. In the translation of this passage, I propose another representation, namely one in which the short pauses are not represented by blank spaces:

> Inapiseptili in the golden box is moving
> In the golden box is moving

Inapiseptili in the golden box is swinging from side to side
In the golden box is swinging from side to side

Inapiseptili in the golden box is trembling
In the golden box is trembling

Inapiseptili in the golden box is palpitating
In the golden box is palpitating

Inapiseptili in the golden box is making a noise
In the golden box is making a noise

Inapiseptili in the golden box is shooting out
In the golden box is shooting out

Notice that this representation captures the flow of the voice, but no longer highlights the striking parallelism, which was so well demonstrated in my first representation. Both of these representations aim at capturing aspects of the poetics of performance and are therefore oriented toward verbal art.

Another representation was made on Sound Edit, a computer program which displays sound in terms of amplitude and pause pattern. Here are the first two verses, labeled as follows: 1a (first line of first verse), 1b (second line of first verse), 2a (first line of second verse), 2b (second line of second verse).

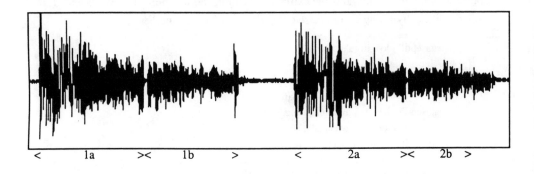

1a	inapiseptili olouluti tulalemaiye
1b	olouluti tulallemaiye
2a	inapiseptili olouluti sikkirmakkemaiye
1b	olouluti sikkirmakmamaiye

This representation/display shows the parallelism of the two verses in terms of amplitude, from high to low. The sharp burst of amplitude at the end of the first verse is a loud laryngeal tightening which sounds very much like a cough. Notice the long pause between verses, the very short pause between lines within a verse.

Still another transcription is a more conventional linguistic representation and specifies the grammatical divisions of the text as well as its most literal meaning. Words are divided into morphemes (minimal meaningful and grammatical units) by means of dashes. This representation is multilinear.

inapiseptili	olouluti	tulalemaiye
ina-pisep-tili	olo-ulu-ti	tula-le(k(e))-ma(i)-ye
RP-NOUN-RS	RP-NOUN-RS	ADJ-PAS-POS-OPT
medicinal-basil-nominal	golden-box-nominal	alive-is-horiz-hopefully
Inapiseptili	in the golden box	is moving

	olouluti	tulal(l)emaiye
	olo-ulu-ti	tula-le(k(e))-ma(i)-ye
	RP-NOUN-RS	ADJ-PAS-POS-OPT
	golden-box-nominal	alive-is-horiz-hopefully
	In the golden box	is moving

inapiseptili	olouluti	sikkirmakkemaiye
ina-pisep-tili	olo-ulu-ti	sikkir-makk(e)-ma(i)-ye
RP-NOUN-RS	RP-NOUN-RS	VERB-V FORM-POS-OPT
medicinal-basil-nominal	golden-box-nominal	swing-verbal-horiz-hopefully
Inapiseptili	in the golden box	is swinging from side to side

	olouluti	sikkirmakmamaiye
	olo-ulu-ti	sikkir-makk(e)-ma(i)-ma(i)-ye
	RP-NOUN-RS	VERB-V FORM-POS-POS-OPT
	golden-box-nominal	swing-verbal-horiz-horiz-hopefully
	In the golden box	is swinging from side to side

inapiseptili	olouluti	wawanmakkemaiye
ina-pisep-tili	olo-ulu-ti	wawan-makk(e)-ma(i)-ye
RP-NOUN-RS	RP-NOUN-RS	VERB-V FORM-POS-OPT
medicinal-basil-nominal	golden-box-nominal	tremble-verbal-horiz-hopefully
Inapiseptili	in the golden box	is trembling

	olouluti	wawanmakmainaye
	olo-ulu-ti	wawan-makk(e)-ma(i)-na(e)-ye
	RP-NOUN-RS	VERB-V FORM-POS-DIR-OPT
	golden-box-nominal	tremble-verbal-horiz-go-hopefully
	In the golden box	is trembling

inapiseptili	olouluti	aktutumakkemaiye
ina-pisep-tili	olo-ulu-ti	aktutu-makk(e)-ma(i)-ye
RP-NOUN-RS	RP-NOUN-RS	VERB-V FORM-POS-OPT
medicinal-basil-nominal	golden-box-nominal	palpitate-verbal-horiz-hopefully
Inapiseptili	in the golden box	is palpitating

	olouluti	aktutulemainaye
	olo-ulu-ti	aktutu-le(k(e))-ma(i)-na(e)-ye
	RP-NOUN-RS	VERB-PAS-POS-DIR-OPT
	golden-box-nominal	palpitate-verbal-horiz-go-hopefully
	In the golden box	is palpitating

inapiseptili	olouluti	kollomakkemaiye

ina-pisep-tili	olo-ulu-ti	kollo-makk(e)-ma(i)-ye
RP-NOUN-RS	RP-NOUN-RS	VERB-V FORM-POS-OPT
medicinal-basil-nominal	golden-box-nominal	make noise-verbal-horiz-hopefully
Inapiseptili	in the golden box	is making a noise
	olouluti	kollomakmainaye
	olo-ulu-ti	kollo-makk(e)-ma(i)-na(e)-ye
	RP-NOUN-RS	VERB-V FORM-POS-DIR-OPT
	golden-box-nominal	make noise-verbal-horiz-go-hopefully
	In the golden box	is making a noise
inapiseptili	olouluti	mummurmakkemaiye
ina-pisep-tili	olo-ulu-ti	mummur-makk(e)-ma(i)-ye
RP-NOUN-RS	RP-NOUN-RS	VERB-V FORM-POS-OPT
medicinal-basil-nominal	golden-box-nominal	shoot out-verbal-horiz-hopefully
Inapiseptili	in the golden box	is shooting out
	olouluti	mummurmakmainaye
	olo-ulu-ti	mummur-makk(e)-ma(i)-na(e)-ye
	RP-NOUN-RS	VERB-V FORM-POS-DIR-OPT
	golden-box-nominal	shoot out-verbal-horiz-go-hopefully
	In the golden box	is shooting out

Line 1 of each row in the representation is a transcription of the tape recording of the performance. In line 2 morpheme boundaries are indicated by dashes. The morphemes are presented in their fullest, most underlying, and abstract form. Parentheses () surround vowels which are potentially deletable according to Kuna rules of phonology and morphology. In line 3 the grammatical categories of morphemes are labelled. RP = ritual prefix, a nominal prefix used in magical chants. NOUN = noun stem. RS = ritual suffix, a nominal suffix used in magical chants. ADJ = adjectival stem. PAS = passive suffix. POS = one of four verbal suffixes which indicate the position of the subject of a sentence in ongoing movement. OPT = optative mood. VERB = verb stem. V FORM = verb formative suffix. DIR = one of verbal suffixes which indicate the direction of the subject of a sentence. Line 4 provides a literal translation of morphemes. Line 5 is a freer translation.

A close examination of the multilinear representation reveals a certain degree of play, manipulation, and, apparently, experimentation on the part of the performer, Pranki Pilos, with the basic structure of this memorized chant. One of the invariables of the text is the syntactic structure of the lines and verses, the first line of each verse consisting of two nominals followed by the verb and the second line of each verse paralleling the first without the initial nominal. Another invariable is the inclusion of the positional verbal suffix and the final verbal suffix, the modal *ye*.

The variable aspects of the text draw on the potential provided by the polysynthetic structure of this language, in which many suffixes are potentially strung along, especially after verb stems. Here are some examples. The most abstract, underlying form of the verb formative suffix is *makke,* represented as *makk(e)* on line 2 of the multilinear representation. This is also the usual ritual form this morpheme takes, its more everyday variant being *mak*. Interestingly, Pranki Pilos alternates *makke* and *mak,* the ritual and everyday forms, in lines 1 and 2 of verses 2, 3, 5, and 6 of this performance.

A related manipulation involves an alternation between the verb formative suffix and the passive suffix. The passive suffix is used in both lines of verse 1 and in this sense contrasts with all other verses. The two lines of verse 4 exploit this contrast as well. Line 1 of this verse has the verb formative suffix; line 2 has the passive suffix. Both of these examples involve breaking with an overall pattern of repetition and parallelism and creating another within it. The *makke/mak* alternation is particularly striking in that it inserts an everyday, colloquial form into a ritual performance, a possibly dangerous move, but one that provides one more level of poetic tension and that in itself provides still another pattern of repetition and parallelism.

Another performance manipulation is the reduplication of the positional suffix *mai,* which occurs only in line 2 of verse 2. In lines 2 of verses 3 through 6 *mai* is followed by the directional suffix *nae,* thus creating another pattern of parallelism. From the point of view of ordinary Kuna grammar, this sequence is ungrammatical and illogical. In addition, since *nae* appears in its short, everyday form *na,* it is perhaps ambiguous with *nai,* a positional suffix with the meaning "hanging" or "perched," thereby providing even more tension in the text.

What this seemingly and at first glance purely linguistic representation captures is individual creativity, play, and manipulation against the backdrop of a highly ritual, repetitive, parallelistic, memorized chant. In all of this, grammatical, semantic, sociolinguistic and logical rules and structures are played down and poeticized, in the service of Pranki Pilos's performance in which formal patterning competes with referential meaning.

This leads to still another representation of this performance, a most abstract one, which highlights the formal patterning of repetition and parallelism, of variants and invariants. In this representation, a and b stand for the nominals *inapiseptili* (the name of the basil plant) and golden box; c, d, e, f, g, and h stand for the various verb stems; p stands for the passive suffix; W and w stand for the verb formative suffix, W in its ritual form and w in its everyday form; x stands for the positional suffix; y stands for the directional suffix; and z stands for the optative suffix.

a	b	c	p	x		z
a	b	c	p	x		z
	b	c	p	x		z
a	b	d	W	x		z
	b	d	w	x	x	z
a	b	e	W	x		z
	b	e	w	x	y	z
a	b	f	W	x		z
	b	f	p	x	y	z
a	b	g	W	x		z
	b	g	w	x	y	z
a	b	h	W	x		z
	b	h	w	x	y	z

Each of the representations of Pranki Pilos's performance of *The way of the basil plant* that I have presented here reveals different aspects of the poetic structuring of the actual performance. A comparison of all of them brings out the dynamic intersection of all of the resources that Kuna performers draw on—grammatical, lexical, intonational, paralinguistic, and musical—and demonstrates quite clearly the interplay of congruences, isomorphisms, repetitions, and parallelisms, as well as the tensions, contrasts, and counterpoints so characteristic of the dynamics of Kuna verbal art. In this particular performance we have an excellent illustration as well of the interplay of memorization and creative improvisation, which is also clearly evident in a comparison of the different representations.

The next example is the opening portion of *kurkin ikar* (*The way of the hat*), performed by Olowitinappi of Mulatuppu. *Kurkin* means "hat" and, metaphorically, "brain." This is a magical, curing chant, used for headaches. In the first representation each line is followed by an English translation. As in *The way of the basil plant*, lines are paired into verses. This representation, which is a segmental transcription of sounds, morphemes, and words in which line and verse structure is based on musical and pause pattern, reveals the grammatical and semantic parallelism characteristic of this chant and this performance.

kurkin ipekantinaye.
Owners of kurkin.
olopillise pupawalakan akkuekwiciye.
Your roots reach to the level of gold.

kurkin ipekantinaye.
Owners of kurkin.
olopillise pe maliwaskakan upoekwiciye.
Your small roots are placed into the level of gold.

kurkin ipekantinaye.
Owners of kurkin.
olopillise pe maliwaskakana pioklekekwiciye.
Your small roots are nailed into the level of gold.

kurkin ipekantinaye.
Owners of kurkin.
olopillipiiye   apikaekwiciye kurkin ipekantinaye.
You are resisting within the very level of gold owners of kurkin.

olopilli aytikkimakkekwici kurkin ipekantinaye.
You weigh a great deal in the level of gold owners of kurkin.

olopilli kwamakkekwici kurkin ipekantinaye.
You are firmly placed in the level of gold owners of kurkin.

olopilli aytitimakkekwakwiciye kurkin ipekantinaye.
You are moving in the level of gold owners of kurkin.

A second representation is a musical transcription devised by Sammie Ann Wicks (see Sherzer and Wicks 1982) and captures pitch and tempo. Here are the first two verses.

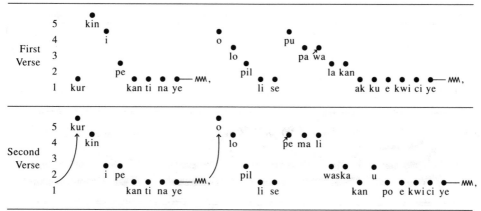

Here is the Sound Edit display of the amplitude and pause pattern of the first two verses, followed by a pitch tracking, also done on Sound Edit. Notice that the pitch tracking has the amplitude and pause pattern display beneath it, for comparison.

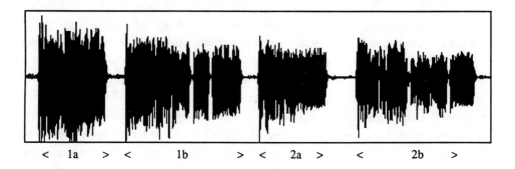

1a kurkin ipekantinaye.
     Owners of kurkin.
1b olopillise pupawalakan akkuekwiciye.
     Your roots reach to the level of gold.

2a kurkin ipekantinaye.
     Owners of kurkin.
2b olopillise pe maliwaskakan upoekwiciye.
     Your small roots are placed into the level of gold.

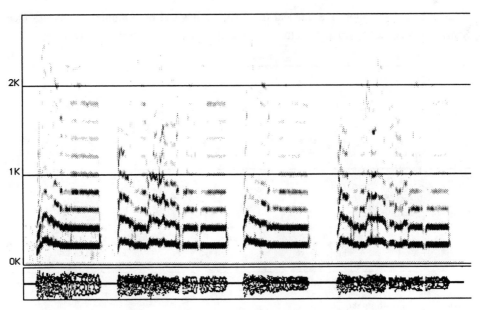

The Sound Edit display clearly shows the falling pitch and volume characteristic of lines and verses in this genre, as well as the long pauses between lines.

A comparison of the different representations of *The way of the hat* reveals Olowitinappi's creativity in this performance. In the first three verses, there is an isomorphic congruence in the use of grammatical affixes and words, musical and grammatical parallelism, and pauses. Each verse begins with a vocative line and ends in the optative suffix *-ye*. The second line of each verse begins with *olopillise* and ends with a verb with the following sequence of suffixes: *-kwici*, "in a vertical position," *-ye*. Final vowels are lengthened. In the fourth verse, while continuing to use the same musical and pausal structure, except for a pause after the first word of the second line, Olowitinappi introduces a new model, creating a moment of nonparallelistic contrast. In this new model, *kurkin ipekantinaye*, which was in the first position of lines and verses, is now in final position in lines and verses, and *-kwici-ye* now no longer marks the end of lines. The new model is used to create a new system of parallelism in which each verse consists of only a single line. Thus Olowitinappi, in this contrastive interplay between grammatical and musical parallelism, like Pranki Pilos in his performance of *The way of the basil plant,* demonstrates individual creativity in the performance of a chant that he has memorized word for word. All of this is revealed and indeed highlighted by means of the comparison between different forms of representation.

The next example is of gathering-house chanting, which is performed in the form of a ritual dialogue between two chiefs. The second chief, called the responder, chants *teki*, "indeed," after each verse, thus quite clearly marking verse endings. The responder begins to chant during the lengthened final vowel of the principal chanting chief, who in turn begins his next verse during the lengthened *i* of *teki*. In gathering-house chanting there is thus never silence, since each chanter begins his turn by overlapping the long, held vowel of the previous voice. This central esthetic feature of the event is clearly shown in this Sound Edit display of two verses from a chant by Muristo Pérez of Mulatuppu.

Muristo's verses are labeled CC (for chanting chief), those of the responder RC (for responding chief). Two verses are represented here. Each verse consists of two lines. The lines and verses are represented as 1a, 1b, 2a, and 2b. The Sound Edit display is followed by a segmented transcription of sounds, words, and morphemes, together with a translation, and then by a pitch tracking.

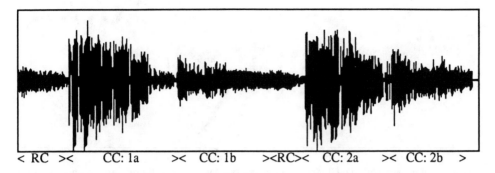

< RC ><   CC: 1a   ><   CC: 1b   ><RC><   CC: 2a   ><   CC: 2b   >

CC: 1a   sunna sukkun kaluse tayle soke l ittoe kirmar patto l an apintakkekwici ipiti.
           Indeed I got to Sukkunya I say and the brothers were already waiting for me.

    1b   sunna tar ku tayleye.
           Indeed it is thus see.

RC: teki
    Indeed.

CC: 2a   kirmare l anka soymarku "muistaraki pe itu natmarmo" tayle sok itto.
           "The brothers said to me "a little while before you they left" it is said it is heard.

    2b   "pitto tiwar mos epinso" soyye.
           They have already arrived at the river I think" it is said.

Here is the pitch tracking of this chant:

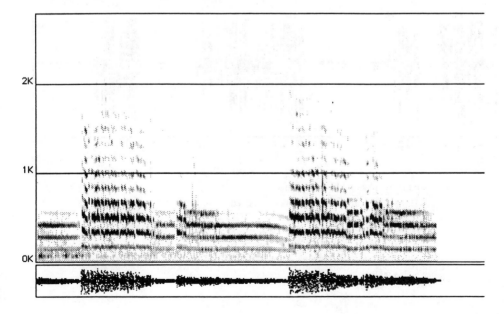

Here is a representation of the first verse of this portion of the chant, now displayed in terms of pitch and tempo.

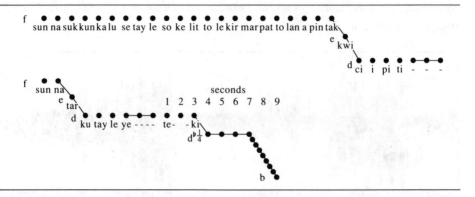

Chief's chants are followed by a spoken reformulation, translation, and recasting by a chief's spokesman. There is a clear delimitation of lines and verses by means of a pause pattern, which involves long rhetorical/poetic pauses between lines and especially verses. The spokesman's monologic performance constitutes a quite different esthetic from the overlapping voices of the dialogic performance of chanting chiefs. Here is a Sound Edit display of three verses from one such interpretation, performed by Spokesman Armando of Mulatuppu. The Sound Edit display is followed by a segmental transcription of sounds, morphemes, and words. The first verse consists of two lines, labeled 1a and 1b. The second verse consists of one line, with three phrases marked by short pauses, which are represented here by commas. The phrases are labeled 2x, 2y, and 2z. The third verse consists of one line, with two phrases, labeled 3x and 3y.

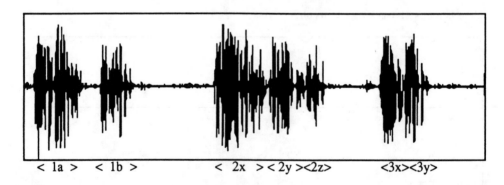

< 1a >   < 1b >   < 2x > < 2y ><2z>   <3x><3y>

1a. "tule nuy nikka nikka taylekutina.
    "The people with names with names indeed.
1b. we neyse upononi" takken soke.
    Have come to enter this house" see it is said.

2x. "tule saylakanakwar tayle nase nonimala, 2y. tule arkarkanakwar takkenye," 2z. sayla anmar owiso takken.

"The people who are chiefs indeed have come together, the people who are spokesmen see," the chief informs us see.

3x. "tule taylekuti polisiakanakwar," 3y. takken soke.
"The people indeed who are policemen," see it is said.

Sound Edit clearly shows the remarkably long pauses between verses.

The challenge of studying and especially of representing the other has recently received considerable attention from social and cultural anthropologists. What I have proposed here, by looking rather intensely at a series of examples, which I have transcribed, represented, translated, and thus analyzed in a variety of ways, is a discourse- and performance-centered approach to this challenge. Discourse is at the heart of language-culture-society relations. For this reason we must take seriously the study of discourse, in all of its aspects. In this, transcription, representation, and translation are essential and constantly revealing.

Native speakers and performers interpret their language and culture and the intersection of their language and their culture through their verbal interactions and performances. They create, play with, and experiment with the structuring of, representation of, and translation of their own discourse. We as analysts, in our own experimenting with the transcription, representation, and translation of this same discourse, in the kinds of ways I have been doing here, can interact with and in this sense contribute to an understanding of the dynamism of the native creative and interpretive process, which involves linguistic and cultural as well as literary imagination.[1]

Note

1. In addition to the works of Hymes and Tedlock cited above, an overview of the issues discussed in this paper can be found in Sherzer and Urban 1986 and Sherzer and Woodbury 1987. My research on the Kuna is presented in Sherzer 1983 and Sherzer 1990.

References

Bright, William. 1979. A Karok myth in "measured verse": The translation of a performance. *Journal of California and Great Basin Anthropology* 1:117–23.

Hymes, Dell. 1965. Some North Pacific Coast poems: A problem in anthropological philology. *American Anthropologist* 67:316–41.

———. 1981. *"In Vain I Tried to Tell You": Essays in Native American Ethnopoetics.* Philadelphia: University of Pennsylvania Press.

McLendon, Sally. 1981. Meaning, rhetorical structure, and discourse organization in myth. In Deborah Tannen (ed.), *Analyzing Discourse: Text and Talk.* Georgetown University

Roundtable on Language and Linguistics 1981, 284–305. Washington, D.C.: Georgetown University Press.

Sherzer, Joel. 1983. *Kuna Ways of Speaking: An Ethnographic Perspective*. Austin: University of Texas Press.

———. 1990. *Verbal Art in San Blas: Kuna Culture Through its Discourse*. Cambridge: Cambridge University Press.

———, and Greg Urban (eds.). 1986. *Native South American Discourse*. Berlin: Mouton Publishers.

———, and Sammie Ann Wicks. 1982. The intersection of music and language in Kuna discourse. *Latin American Music Review* 3:147–64.

———, and Anthony Woodbury (eds.). 1987. *Native American Discourse: Poetics and Rhetoric*. Cambridge: Cambridge University Press.

Tedlock, Dennis. 1978. *Finding the center: Narrative Poetry of the Zuni Indians*. Lincoln: University of Nebraska Press.

———. 1983. *The Spoken Word and the Work of Interpretation*. Philadelphia: University of Pennsylvania Press.

———. 1987. Hearing a voice in an ancient text: Quiché Maya poetics in performance. In Joel Sherzer and Anthony Woodbury (eds.), *Native American Discourse: Poetics and Rhetoric*, 140–75. Cambridge: Cambridge University Press.

Woodbury, Anthony C. 1985. The functions of rhetorical structure: a study of Central Alaskan Yupik Eskimo discourse. *Language in Society* 14:153–90.

———. 1987. Rhetorical structure in a Central Alaskan Yupik Eskimo traditional narrative. In Joel Sherzer and Anthony Woodbury (eds.), *Native American Discourse: Poetics and Rhetoric*, 176–239. Cambridge: Cambridge University Press.

Verse Analysis of "The Condor and the Shepherdess"

Nancy H. Hornberger

The approach to analysis of narrative which Hymes calls verse analysis and which he and others have developed over the last dozen years or so (cf. Hymes, *"In Vain"*) is based on the discovery that narratives have poetic organization. This approach falls under the general approach to verbal art increasingly known as ethnopoetics, a term that embraces "both the native conceptions and performances of verbal art and the analysts' attempts to represent, analyze, and translate it" (Sherzer and Woodbury 2).

In ethnopoetics, as in sociolinguistics in general, the relationship between language function and language form is seen as fundamental: one must understand the one in order to understand the other. In verse analysis, "the mind of the narrator is seen to be working along two tracks at once" (Hymes, "Verse Analysis," 954); "not only a track of what, but also a track of how, organizing performance through the synchronization of incident with measure" (Hymes, "A Note on Ethnopoetics," ii). When we analyze a narrative in terms of its poetic organization, we gain insight into the story told; at the same time, it is the story itself which provides the overall organization of the narrative.

In this essay I will analyze and compare two Peruvian versions of the Quechua story, "The Condor and the Shepherdess," in terms of both tracks: the "track of incident, speech act, and image" and the track of the patterning of the texts in terms of "lines and groups of lines." The paper asks, first of all, whether Quechua oral narratives use the same kinds of organizational devices that Hymes and others have found in other Native American oral narratives; and, second, what that poetic organization reveals about the narratives. Additional questions as to what verse analysis of Quechua texts reveals about verse analysis itself and about Quechua narrative as a whole are only broached here; their full consideration awaits further analysis of a larger body of Quechua texts.

The analysis follows the principles of verse analysis summarized by Hymes as follows:

(1) Performed oral narratives are organized in terms of lines, and groups of lines (not in terms of sentences and paragraphs).

(2) The relations between lines and groups of lines are based on the general principle of poetic organization called equivalence (Jakobson 1960).

(3) Sequences of equivalent units commonly constitute sets in terms of a few pattern numbers. Sets of two and four are commonly found together, as are sets of three and five.

(4) Texts are not ordinarily constituted according to a fixed length or fixed sequence of units. Rather, each performance of a narrative may differ from another, responsive to context and varying intention.

(5) Variations and transformations in narratives appear to involve a small number of dimensions, corresponding to the components of the ethnography of speaking (Hymes, "A Note on Ethnopoetics," ii).

In the sections that follow, these five principles will serve as organizing themes for the comparison and discussion of the two narratives in terms of both form and meaning. First, however, I will introduce the two versions of the story and discuss some of their limitations.

Two Versions

The two stories presented here were chosen at random from various Quechua narratives in my library. My only criteria were that they be narratives representing genuine oral performances, that they provide some basis for comparison, and that at least one of them be from the unpublished collection of Father Jorge Lira which, in my opinion, represents gems in need of publication.

After consideration of a number of possibilities, including a comparison among various of the stories collected by Lira, I decided on a comparison of two versions of the same story, since such a comparison offers the most opportunity for consideration of both incident and line organization. The two versions differ in length and in origin and should provide fruitful ground for comparison. Furthermore, such a choice enabled me to focus on one of the better-known and "typical" Quechua stories, "The Condor and the Shepherdess," known and recorded in Bolivia and Ecuador as well as in Peru.

Both versions come to me as written prose transcriptions of orally performed narratives; I do not have access in either case to tape recordings of the performances, nor was I present at them. This limits my analysis in two ways. First, working from written transcriptions means that patterns and recurrences in sound are not available for my analysis (see Sherzer "Poetic Structuring," Sherzer and Woodbury, and Tedlock on the value of attention to sound as well as syntactic form and content in verse analysis, and V. Hymes, 65, on the possibility of doing without).

The second limitation is that I do not have detailed contextual and situational information about the performances the narratives represent. A fundamental premise of the work of Hymes, Tedlock, Sherzer, Bauman, and others is that "performance is crucial in the study of verbal artistry" (Sherzer and Woodbury 5). The term performance, in both conventional and ethnopoeticists' usage, conveys a dual sense of both artistic action and artistic event. That is, not only does the performance mean the thing that is performed, but also the situation of its performance—the performer, the artform, the audience, and the setting (Bauman 4).

In the present case, I lack precise information on the identity of the performer, the members of the audience, and the characteristics of the setting. Nevertheless, I can draw on both the ethnographic literature and my own knowledge of contemporary Andean language and culture in interpreting these two texts of the present century (cf. Hymes on a Tonkawa text and Tedlock on the *Popol Vuh,* both in Sherzer and Woodbury). Furthermore, I do know something of the origins of the two texts.

The first version analyzed here, "Kunturpa munasqan sipasmanta" ("The Shepherdess who was loved by a Condor," hereafter, Sipas), 454 lines long, is an unpublished version as collected and written down by Jorge Lira. Father Lira served as parish priest for much of this century in the Department of Cusco, in the Urubamba valley and in Marangani, among other places.

Lira devoted much of his life to the study and recording of Quechua language and literature. His best known work is probably his *Diccionario kkechuwa-español,* published in Argentina in 1941 (second edition published in Colombia in 1982). He has also published a book of Quechua poetry in Quechua and Spanish (*Canto de amor*); a drama in Quechua and Spanish (*Issicha Puytu*); and a story in Spanish only (*Tutupaka*), all of them collected firsthand from Quechua oral tradition, many during a three-year period in the early 1940s from performances by Carmen Taripha Mamani of Wayllapunku (Marangani district, Canchis province). José María Arguedas describes the circumstances of Lira's collection of more than sixty narratives and lauds its fidelity to oral Quechua tradition (Arguedas 178–83).

Regrettably, at the time of Lira's death in 1984, far more of his collection of Quechua oral literature remained unpublished than published. The story presented here is from among those unpublished works, although it has appeared in English translation (Arguedas 126–38). It is unfortunately not identified by date or place of collection, but it certainly comes from the Department of Cusco and most likely dates from the 1930s or 1940s.

This story and others in his collection are Lira's written representations of narratives he heard told on repeated occasions. Although we cannot know the exact circumstances of his collection, we know from his own account that he gathered them *"integramente, palabra a palabra, frase a frase,"* "as a complete whole, word for word and phrase by phrase" (*Issicha Puytu,* 10).

The second version analyzed here, "Kunturmantawan p'asñamantawan" ("Of the Condor and the Shepherdess" hereafter, P'asña), 222 lines long, was published in 1983 in *Unay pachas,* volume 1, by the Experimental Bilingual Education Project of Puno. The stories in this volume were collected and transcribed by Rufino Chuquimamani and Kurt Komarek, as performed by "community members, farmers, shepherds, teachers, and schoolchildren" (*Unay pachas,* 6) in communities of the Department of Puno in the early 1980s. In this case, the performances of the narratives were tape-recorded for subsequent transcription by Chuquimamani. So far as I know, the stories are presented in written form exactly as they were told, without editing.

This brings us to the final limitation of the written prose transcriptions I am working from: both versions represent performances of the narratives before an audience that was, at least in part, non-native. Sherzer and Woodbury note that the specifics of text performance include not only the features of the voice and the social and cultural context of the performance which were mentioned above, but also the norms of interpretation and interaction shared between performers and audiences (5). The presence of non-native audience members (or the absence of a native audience) may have had an effect on the performance of these narratives. There is some evidence that a widespread pattern in Native American narrative is one of "coparticipant dialogic interaction" (Sherzer, "Poetic Structuring," 373; Sherzer and Woodbury 7); a non-native audience might not know enough to participate in this way.

It should be noted, however, that such a situation does not necessarily imply significant differences in the performance. Comparisons made by V. Hymes between recorded narratives told with and without a native-speaking audience among the Warm Springs Sahaptin revealed little difference in the performances (64).

Furthermore, for the two versions considered here, the audience was not altogether non-native. Chuquimamani is a native of Puno and a speaker of Quechua as a mother tongue; and Lira was, at the time of his collection of narratives, a fluent (if not native) Quechua speaker and a fully integrated member of the community, albeit in the special role of priest. We will return briefly to these matters of the context of the performance in discussion of the fifth principle.

Form and Meaning of the Narratives

Verse analysis focuses, of necessity, on the native-language original of the narrative, rather than on the translation (cf. Sherzer and Woodbury 10). Implicit in the approach, however, is the notion that a translation which presents the narrative in a way that represents the poetic organization revealed through verse analysis of the original comes closer to conveying the narrative's meaning and artistry than one that does not. Accordingly, the translations presented here are faithful to the poetic organization of the originals, although I by no means claim to have achieved a poetic equivalent to the originals in terms of nuances of grammar and lexicon.[1]

Here is the story in brief (episodes occurring only in the Sipas version are enclosed in parentheses):

One day, a beautiful young shepherdess, out pasturing her family's animals, meets a handsome, well-dressed young man and talks with him. They continue to meet in the same way day after day, and she never tells her parents. (After some time, when she tells the young man she is pregnant, they agree to go away to his house without telling her parents.) She willingly gets on his back at his request, but as he takes off in flight and carries her to his clifftop nest, his true identity as Condor is revealed. He keeps her captive there (and in time the child is born).

As her parents sit lamenting at home, Hummingbird flies by, hinting that he knows something about their daughter. (At first they are angry that Hummingbird makes light of their sorrow, and they throw a stone at him, breaking his leg; but then they become interested and eventually ask for Hummingbird's help, after first mending his leg.) They ask Hummingbird to bring their daughter back, and Hummingbird does so. (He instructs the parents to keep their daughter and her child hidden, as Condor will surely come after them; then he returns to Condor's home to be there and set the stage, with the help of Frog, for Condor's return.) Condor returns home and discovers that his wife and child are gone.

(While Condor sits watching and waiting for his wife and child to come back, Hummingbird reveals himself and tells Condor that she's back in her parents' home.) Condor accuses Hummingbird of taking his wife and chases after him, but Hummingbird escapes. (Condor goes, as a handsome young man, to the shepherdess's home, but her parents tell him no one has come. Hummingbird, too, visits the parents and tells them to prepare a big pot of boiling water; he also asks them for some hot pepper.) Hummingbird and Condor meet up again and Condor once again chases after Hummingbird. This time, Hummingbird flies into a small hole and tells Condor he'll be right out but Condor must open his mouth and his other end too. Condor opens his mouth, and Hummingbird flies right into his mouth and out the other end, and escapes. (Condor sets out after Hummingbird again and eventually finds him. Hummingbird flies into another hole, and this time tells Condor to wait just a minute and then open his eyes wide. Hummingbird flies out, slaps the hot pepper he has just ground up onto Condor's eyes, and escapes.) Hummingbird arrives at the shepherdess's home, and tells the parents that Condor will come again; and that they must tell him they have not seen their daughter, invite him in anyway, seat him on the pot of boiling water covered with a cloth to look like a place to sit, and when he falls in, push him in completely with a stick. They do as Hummingbird instructs, and the handsome young man is revealed to be nothing more than an old condor.

In both versions, the basic contours of the story are: (Rapture) the shepherdess falls in love with a handsome young man who persuades her to come away with him, but he turns out to be a Condor and she is miserable in her life at Condor's nest on top of a cliff; (Refuge) through the intervention of Hummingbird, the shepherdess is returned to her parents' home and Condor is left with an empty nest; and (Revenge) the family has its revenge on Condor, largely through the resourcefulness and efforts of Hummingbird. The basic contours of the two versions may be compared by consulting the outlines. The profiles, texts, and translations of Act II are in the Appendixes.

Outline of *Kunturpa Munasqan Sipasmanta* (Sipas)

Act	Scene		Stanza	
I (RAPTURE)	i	(Courtship)	A	Frame
			B	Meetings
			C	Pregnancy
	ii	(The Flight)	A	Preparation
			B	Meeting
			C	Release llamas
			D	Onto his back
			E	In flight
	iii	(The Clifftop)	A	Cliff
			B	Alone
			C	Meat and water
			D	Condor leaves
			E	Birth of child
II (REFUGE)	i	(Hummingbird)	A	Encounters mother
			B	Leg broken
			C	Information
	ii	(The Return Home)	A	Mother's request
			B	Shep'dess' request
			C	Return home
			D	Instructions
			E	Shepherdess
	iii	(The Empty Nest)	A	Frog
			B	Condor arrives
			C	Child gone
			D	Condor anxious
			E	Frog disappears
III (REVENGE)	i	(Hummingbird and Condor: Encounter)		
			A	H'bird escapes
			B	Condor's visit
			C	H'bird instructs
	ii	(The Trick)	A	Hummingbird hides
			B	Flies thru
			C	Hides again
			D	Throws pepper
			E	Instructs family
	iii	(Condor's Death)	A	Condor arrives
			B	Mother invites
			C	Condor sits

Outline of *Kunturmantawan P'asñamantawan* (P'asña)

Act	Scene		Stanza	
I (RAPTURE)	i	(Courtship)	A	Frame
			B	Meetings
			C	Carry each other
	ii	(The Flight)	A	Onto his back
			B	In flight
			C	Condor revealed

	iii	(The Clifftop)	A	Meat
			B	Pot
			C	Fire
II (REFUGE)	i	(Hummingbird)	A	Shepherdess
			B	Her family
			C	The request
	ii	(The Return Home)		
	iii	(The Empty Nest)		
III (REVENGE)	i	(Hummingbird and Condor: Encounter)		
	ii	(The Trick)	A	Hummingbird hides
			B	Condor calls
			C	H'bird flies thru
	iii	(Condor's Death)	A	Preparation
			B	Condor arrives
			C	Condor sits

In the presentation of the outlines, profiles, text, and translation, I have followed Hymes's conventions in using upper case roman numerals for acts (II), lower case roman numerals for scenes (ii), upper case roman letters for stanzas (B), and lower case roman letters for verses (b). Successive lines within a verse are successively indented two spaces at a time (a poetic line that runs over to a subsequent line on the page is not indented).

The stories are quite long, 454 and 222 lines respectively, and for reasons of space, I present here only the second act, entitled "Refuge," in full profile, text, and translation (see the Appendixes). In this act Hummingbird first presents himself to the shepherdess and her family, offering himself as rescuer in return for some sweets (Hummingbird); he then carries the shepherdess home on his back (The Return Home); and Condor, finding the shepherdess gone, becomes very angry (The Empty Nest).

First Principle: Lines and Groups of Lines

In the absence of access to evidence on patterns in terms of sound, and cognizant of possible distortions because of it (cf. Tedlock 57–61), I have followed Hymes in assigning one line to each predication (cf. V. Hymes 68). In doing so, I have usually not assigned separate lines to subordinated verbs (as in P'asña iAe, Sipas iiBa),[2] except when they are part of a list or a parallel structure (as in Sipas iiEa). Nor have I assigned a separate line to the simple closing frame of quotation frames around direct quoted speech (a simple quotation frame consists of the words *Nin,* "he/she said," *nispas nin* "thus saying, he/she said," or a close variant thereof (e.g., *nin(si), nisqa),* appearing at the beginning and end of the speech, e.g., P'asña iBe).

In addition to these instances where two predications appear in one line, there are also instances where a line occurs with no predication at all. A verse-initial particle that occurs immediately before a direct quoted speech is assigned its own line; and when there is a parallel structure of two or more nouns, each is assigned its own line (Sipas iAb includes both kinds of exceptions).

The two versions differ in the type of subordinate clause construction used: P'asña makes more use of the subordinator *chayqa,* "if," or a variant thereof (e.g., *chaypachaqa* in iAe);[3] while Sipas uses the subordinating verbal suffixes (*-qti* conditional; *-spa* adverbial; *-sqa* past tense relativizer; and *-na* future tense relativizer). The versions also differ in that Sipas makes greater use of alliteration and rhyme in establishing lines of verse. The recurring refrain, *Piqpa, maypa wawanchá qaqapi waqashan?,* "Whose child, which child, is weeping on the cliff?" (Sipas iAd, iBe), has both internal rhyme and alliteration. Although Mannheim points out that neither alliteration nor rhyme carries great esthetic weight in Southern Peruvian Quechua, given the frequency of their occurrence in everyday speech ("Popular Song" 55), their relative absence in P'asña as compared to Sipas is nevertheless noticeable.

After I broke the narrative into lines, I began the process of grouping the lines into verses, verses into stanzas, and so on, by moving back and forth between a bottom-up and a top-down analysis. In the bottom-up analysis, I sought to establish equivalence by identifying markers signaling a new unit (verse, stanza, scene, or act) and looking for patterns among lines to form a verse. In the top-down analysis, I sought to identify the major plot units of the story being told.

Second Principle: Equivalence

One of the more interesting comparisons of form between the two versions is that of the diversity of devices employed to establish poetic equivalence. We will take up first the devices for signaling or marking a new unit, and then those providing cohesion within units.

In both versions, new verses are marked in terms of content by such devices as a change of actor, a change of location, a turn at talk, or a time word (see the profiles for examples). In terms of syntactic form, new verses are signaled by the reportive validator, the verse-initial particles, and shifts in tense or aspect.[4]

The reportive validator (*-si* on a consonant-final word and *-s* on a vowel-final word) indicates that the information being reported is not personally attested by the speaker (the counterpart is the witness validator, *-mi* or *-m, -n*). In both versions, the reportive validator appears as near to the beginning of the verse as possible; usually on the first word.

However, there is a vast difference in the two versions' use of the reportive. P'asña attaches it almost exclusively to the word *hina;* eighteen of the twenty-three verses begin with *hinas* "then," and *hinas* appears in other positions only twice (in verses iAa and iiib). In contrast, in Sipas, the range of words to which the reportive validator is attached includes not only *hina[s]* and *hinaspa[s],* "and [so]," but also such words as *warmitaq[si],* "now the woman" (iBa), *chaytaq[si],* "now with that" (iBb), *pasarqun-taq[si]* "now again he flew past" (iiBc), and so on.

Furthermore, Sipas frequently omits the opening reportive validator when the beginning of the verse coincides with the opening of a quotation frame (e.g., iCb, iCc, iiAa, iiAb, iiAc, etc.). Such a device seems to make the speech more immediate to the listener.

Sipas also uses a sequence of reportive validators in consecutive lines to mark the beginning of a new stanza (at iiB, iiC, iiD, iiE, iiiA, iiiB, and iiiE). This device reinforces the boundary of the new larger unit.

The verse-initial particle also signals a new verse. For this, both versions make extensive use of the word *hina*. Indeed, when the narrative P'asña is presented according to its poetic organization, what had appeared in prose transcription as boring and erratic repetition of *hinas* turns out to be a significant cue to the structure of the text.

Nevertheless, while P'asña uses almost exclusively the form *hinas* (*hina* + *-s*), "then," as verse-initial particle, Sipas takes advantage of morphological variation to use other forms of *hina* as well: *hinaqa*, "so"; *hinata*, "thus"; *hinaspa*, "and"; *hinaspaqa*, "and then"; and especially *hinaspas*, "and so." Furthermore, Sipas regularly uses other verse-initial particles: *aknas*, "in this way"; *aknaspas*, "now then"; *chaykamas*, "meanwhile"; and *-taqsi*, "now."

Cohesion within units is achieved through syntactic parallelism in both versions. Patterned verb morphology establishing equivalence between lines within verses includes consistency or repetition of tense or aspect; of person and number inflection (e.g., *-wanki* in Sipas iCb); of conditional inflection (e.g., *-man* in Sipas iCb); of imperative inflection (e.g., *-ay* in P'asña iAd); of the subordinating suffixes noted above; and of a range of derivational verbal suffixes, such as *-pu* benefactive or permanence marker (e.g., Sipas iAa; cf. Cusihuamán, "Gramática" 215), *-yku* courtesy marker (e.g., Sipas iCb), *-rqu* marker of thoroughness, and *-ri* inceptive. Patterning is also achieved through repetition of independent suffixes, such as *-chá* conjectural (e.g., P'asña iib, iiia).

Sipas makes use of a greater variety of syntactic patterns to provide cohesion within verses and stanzas than does P'asña. Sipas makes extensive use of the repeated narrative tense marker *-sqa* (e.g., iAc, iBc, iCd, iiiEa), while P'asña has no instance of this and in fact rarely uses *-sqa*, relying instead on the validator *-si* or *-s* and an occasional *kasqa* (iAb, iBb, iib) to establish the reported quality of the narrative. Sipas also uses patterned noun morphology, achieved by repetition of noun suffixes for person, number, and case inflection (e.g., accusative marker *-ta* and independent additive suffix *-pis* in iCc, genitive *-[q]pa* in iAd and iiBb, third-person possessive marker *-n* and independent topic marking suffix *-qa* in iAb, and second-person plural possessive marker *-ykichis* iiDa).

In addition to syntactic patterning, Sipas also binds verses and stanzas together through semantic patterns, achieved by sequences of verbatim repeated or semantically parallel content. The repetition of *pasarqun*, "he flew past," in iAd, *usqhay*, "hurry up," in iiiAc and iiiAd, *kutimunqachá*, "maybe she'll come back," in iiiEb, and *ñachu*, "ready yet?" in iiiDa builds tension. Lines in stanza iiB are linked not only to one another within the stanza by the repeated onomatopeic words *riyuw q'inti*, "whirr hummingbird whirr," but also across stanzas to iA, iB, and iiC. The first three times *riyuw q'inti* occurs it is immediately followed by the formulaic refrain: *piqpa, maypa wawanchá* (or *mamataytanchá*), "whose?, which? child" (or "parents") (iAd, iBe, iiBb). Such repeated patterns add unity and expectation to the telling of the story.

In addition to exact verbatim repetition, Sipas achieves semantic parallelism by use of triplets of statements with parallel content accompanied by patterned verb tense and other markers (cf. the triplets identified in Aymara narrative by Briggs (1988) and Huanca (1987, cited in Briggs 1988). There is definite semantic symmetry here: in iCb, the progression is from breaking Hummingbird's leg to healing his leg with sweets and then to giving him sweets; in iiiBa, Condor is coming, Hummingbird is waiting, Frog is washing; the scene is set.

These are not a triplet form of the semantic couplets found in Quechua popular song by Mannheim, where "two otherwise morphologically and syntactically identical lines are bound together by the alternation of two semantically related word stems [which] . . . are a semantic minimal pair" (Mannheim, "Popular Song," 56; cf. also "Poetic Form" and "Couplets"; and see Lengyel, "On the Structure," for a discussion of the occurrence of semantic couplets in Mayan discourse). However, there are suggestions of such semantic couplets in sequences of semantic minimal pairs, such as *hamusqa, rikhurimusqa,* "[he] came there, showed up there," in iAc; *waqasqa, llakisqa,* "weeping, sorrowing," in iBa; and *waqaspalla, llakispallas,* "weeping and sorrowing," in iBd. Verse iAb comes close to a couplet in alternating the subject and verb of the first line with the "empty" subject and verb of the second.

Thus, while both versions establish equivalence by marking new units and providing cohesion within units, Sipas uses a greater variety of markers in a greater range of ways, as compared to P'asña. Both versions use the reportive validator, the verse-initial particle *hina,* and tense/aspect shifts to mark new units; and patterned use of independent suffixes and verb morphology to establish cohesion within units. In Sipas, however, examples of the greater variety of markers include various forms of *hina,* the narrative tense marker *-sqa,* patterned noun morphology, and semantic as well as syntactic parallelism. The use of the reportive validator in Sipas exemplifies the greater range of ways markers are used there: it is attached to a variety of words, used in sequence to mark a new stanza, and omitted occasionally at the opening frame of reported speech, all uses which do not occur in P'asña.

Third Principle: Sets and Patterns

The outlines and profiles reveal the built-in proportion and symmetry in both narratives: three acts of three scenes each, each scene made up of three or five stanzas, and each stanza in turn made up of three or five verses (note, however, that not every verse is made up of three or five lines). Hymes notes that "when texts come from a culture grounded in oral tradition and a narrative view of life, it is not surprising to find text after text [of performed oral narrative] that shows rewarding artistry" ("A Note on Ethnopoetics," iii); these Peruvian Quechua texts surely bear out his point.

Furthermore, the clear showing of relationships of three and five in this major South American language is of theoretical significance to the verse-analysis approach to narratives, in that it confirms patterns which have already been identified in other oral narrative traditions. The sets of three and five fit other characteristics suggested by Hymes as well: the threes depict "an onset, ongoing (or continuation), and outcome," while the fives consist of two overlapping sets of three, in which "the outcome of the first set is the onset of the second, simultaneously" (Hymes, "Verse Analysis," 954). The three acts (Rapture, Refuge, Revenge), the three scenes within the acts (e.g., Hummingbird, Return Home, Empty Nest), and the sets of three stanzas within a scene (e.g., scene i: encounters mother, leg broken, information) correspond well to the onset, ongoing, outcome sequence; while, for example, the five stanzas of Sipas scene iii "The Empty Nest" consist of:

(onset)	Hummingbird arrives at Condor's home and instructs Frog;
(ongoing)	Condor arrives and speaks to Frog;
(outcome/onset)	Condor notices missing child and urges Frog to finish;
(ongoing)	Condor becomes impatient with Frog and tries to kick;
(outcome)	Frog and the diapers disappear.

Fourth Principle: Content, Length and Sequence

Sipas is more than twice as long as P'asña, and yet they tell the same story, clear evidence that texts are not constituted according to a fixed length. At the level of acts and scenes, the two versions share the same profile, but at the level of stanzas and verses, they differ considerably in both content and sequence, clear evidence that texts are not constituted according to a fixed sequence of units.

In Act II, scenes ii and iii consist of five stanzas each in Sipas, but only one in P'asña. The sequence of the stanzas is reversed between the two versions of Act II, scene i: in Sipas Hummingbird goes first to the shepherdess's family and in P'asña to the shepherdess herself.

The content of the verses and stanzas of Act II differ as well. Sipas incorporates a number of elements that do not appear in P'asña at all: Hummingbird's broken leg, the giving of sweets to Hummingbird, Hummingbird's instructions to the family to hide the shepherdess, Frog pretending to be the shepherdess, Condor looking for his child. Sipas often has extended speeches by all the characters, while the speeches in P'asña are fewer and shorter.

These differences, Hymes tells us, reflect a responsiveness to context and varying intention of the narrator. This brings us to the fifth principle.

Fifth Principle: Variations and the Ethnography of Speaking

In answer to the first question I posed, it seems clear that the presentation of the narratives in lines and the diversity of devices used to establish poetic equivalence reveal an underlying poetic organization to these narratives. It remains to consider what verse analysis reveals about the narratives.

First, the analysis provides a basis for comparing the poetry of the two versions.

As we have seen, both narratives make use of poetic devices such as syntactic patterning; but Sipas makes greater use of these and also employs a number of other poetic devices, including semantic patterning, alliteration, and the use of a grammatical marker to make a sharp contrast between narrative text and direct speech.

Second, the analysis makes clear that the two narratives share a similar overall structure, one that not only provides symmetry and proportion to the narrative but also brings out the essential elements of the story. For that reason, P'asña is still a well-told story despite some of the lacks suggested above. The variations between the two narratives only serve to underline the essentials of the story. For example, in P'asña the shepherdess cooks raw meat while on the clifftop, but in Sipas she bears a child and washes its diapers. It seems that what is significant for the story is the domesticity of these activities in such incongruous surroundings, and not the specific activity itself. Similarly, it is the essential unity of the shepherdess and her family in requesting Hummingbird's help, and not the order of those requests, that is significant in Hummingbird's sequential visits to each.

Third, the analysis may tell us something about the speech situation and culture in which the narratives were performed. Here we move from the domain of the narrated event to the speech event in which the narrative was performed (cf. Hymes, *Foundations*, 23, following Jakobson "Shifters"). I noted in the first part of this essay that the term performance conveys both the thing performed and the situation of its performance, what Hymes has distinguished as the underlying "score" of the text and its actual performance (Sherzer and Woodbury 5). Bauman argues that the "emergent quality of performance resides in the interplay between communicative resources, individual competence, and the goals of the participants, within the context of particular situations" (38).

I noted above Hymes's suggestion that the differences in length and sequence of the performed narratives reflect a responsiveness to context and varying intention of the performer. Differences in the use of poetic devices may also reflect such responsiveness. That is, differences in the two narratives may correspond to differences in the components that made up the speech situation in which each was performed: setting, participants, ends, norms, and the like. Conversely, it is also true that similarities between the two narratives may correspond to similarities in the components that made up the speech situation. Such similarities might point to a generalized Quechua culture (cf. Sherzer, "A Discourse-Centered Approach," 305–6).

As noted earlier, I lack specific information on the particular performance situations for these two texts. Nevertheless, based on my knowledge of the origins of the texts and of contemporary Andean language and culture, it is possible to suggest some dimensions of contrast between the two situations that may have a bearing on the differences between the texts. The scene of the one performance (P'asña) was probably a tape-recorded short visit and of the other (Sipas) a long-term reciprocal relationship. The narrator in the one might have been a schoolchild and in the other a community adult well practiced in oral tradition. The ends for the one group of participants might have been a task to be performed and for the others the sharing of a cultural tradition. In each case, given the value placed in Andean indigenous communities on long-term reciprocal relationships (cf. Allen, Chapter 2) and on the knowledge of elders (cf. Allen, Chapter 3), the former characteristic suggests the likelihood of a brief performance and the latter an extended one, complete with cultural and linguistic detail.

Similarities between the narratives may correspond to cultural values documented in the ethnographic literature on contemporary Quechua speaking communities. Certainly the characters of Condor, Hummingbird, and Frog, which appear not only in these two narratives but also recurringly in Quechua oral literature, require cultural translation. Harrison describes how, in the Quechua myth of Quni Raya (recorded in the seventeenth-century Huarochiri manuscripts), condor, puma, and falcon, the three animals that the hero Quni Raya praises, are associated with highland environments and light; while the others (including skunk, fox, and parrot) are associated with the lowlands and darkness (103). Condor is a frequent hero in Quechua stories, while Fox is frequently the butt of tricks. Interestingly, although Hummingbird is not a frequent main character in Quechua narratives, in the myth of Quni Raya, falcon is given the right to eat hummingbirds (Harrison 102). Frog (*k'ayra*) may be associated with the toad (*hamp'atu*) which, Harrison reports, has "long been associated with bad luck [and] is seen as a bad omen," while at the same time it is often used in ritual processes for curing (108). In the story I have analyzed here, the cultural values represented by Condor, Hummingbird, and Frog seem less clear. Frog is certainly a bad omen for Condor, while at the same time part of the cure effected for the shepherdess; yet Condor, far from being a hero, is not only an evildoer but a defeated one, and Hummingbird plays a trickster role more often filled by the mouse (*huk'ucha*) in Quechua narratives.

As for the story itself, the warning against going off with strange men, the refuge and safety represented by family, and the close association between humans and the natural world are cultural values reflected in the narratives (cf. Arguedas 180; Stephan 13); one could also suggest that the narratives reflect values of defending oneself in the face of deception and imposition by outsiders (cf. Isbell); or a recognition of the resources and resistance of women in the face of abuse by men (cf. Harrison, Chapter 5). Perhaps the truth is that the stories reflect all of these values.

It is to be hoped that more verse analyses such as those attempted here will be carried out on a wide variety of oral Quechua narratives collected from performances in a wide variety of documented settings. Then we may find answers to some of these questions, and to others we have not even thought to ask.

Appendixes

Kunturpa Munasqan Sipasmanta (Sipas) - Profile, Text, Translation

Profile of Kunturpa Munasqan Sipasmanta *(Sipas) - Act II*

Act	Scene	Stanza	Verse	Incident	Markers
					(reportive validator throughout)
II				(REFUGE)	
	i			(Hummingbird)	
		A	a	"What happened?"	location, actor change
			b	"swallowed her up"	hinas
			c	Hummingbird comes	time word, hinaspas
			d	"who's crying?"	turn at talk, hinaspas
			e	Hummingbird says	hinatas
		B	a	"how could you!"	turn, -taqsi
			b	throws stone	-taqsi
			c	leg broken	hinaspas
			d	mother crying	actor change
			e	"who's crying?"	actor change, hinaspas
		C	a	"do you know?"	turn
			b	"I know"	turn
			c	"Yes, I'll give you"	turn
			d	Hummingbird eats	actor change, hina
			e	"She's on the cliff"	turn, hinaspas
	ii			(The Rèturn Home)	
		A	a	"Bring her to me"	turn, hinaspa
			b	"Give me sweets"	turn
			c	"I will"	turn
			d	"ok"	turn
			e	H. flew away	hinata
		B	a	H. waits at cliff	loc., hinaspas
			b	"Who's crying?"	turn, hinaspas
			c	and again	turn, -taqsi
			d	"Take me home"	turn, hinas
			e	"I'll take you"	turn

Text of *Kunturpa Munasqan Sipasmanta* (Sipas) - Act II

II			(REFUGE)
	i		(Hummingbird)

A a Taytamamantaqsi waqayushaq wasinpi:

     —Imanapunchá waway.

       Maytachá ripun!—nispa.

    b Hinas:

     —Pachachá millp'un wawayta.

Act	Scene	Stanza	Verse	Incident	Markers
		C	a	He takes her	hinaspas, aknas, chayaspas
			b	"Thank you"	turn
			c	sweets	hinaspas
		D	a	"Hide her"	turn, hinaspas
			b	"I'll come tomorrow"	time word
			c	"ok"	turn
		E	a	they hide her & ask	hinaspas
			b	"He took me"	turn
			c	"Condor took me"	tense change
	iii			(The Empty Nest)	
		A	a	H. instructs Frog	time word, loc., turn
			b	"ok"	turn
			c	"He'll ask"	turn, -taqsi
			d	"You hide"	time word
			e	H. hopped up	-taqsi, aspect change
		B	a	Condor arriving	-taqsi
			b	"What are you doing?"	turn, hinaspas
			c	"I'm washing"	turn
			d	"hurry up"	turn
			e	"ok"	turn
		C	a	Condor goes in	actor change, hinaspas
			b	no child	manas
			c	"it's there"	turn
			d	"hurry up!"	turn
			e	"in a minute"	turn
		D	a	"ready yet?"	turn
			b	"almost"	turn
			c	"I'll kick you!"	turn
		E	a	Frog disappears	act. ch.
			b	Condor waits	act. ch., aknaspas
			c	He doesn't reappear.	act. ch., manas

Translation of *Kunturpa Munasqan Sipasmanta* (Sipas) — Act II

II

   i

      (REFUGE)

      (Hummingbird)

A a   Now her father and mother were crying in their home:

        —What could have happened to our child!

          Where could she have disappeared to!—they said.

    b   Then:

        —The earth must have swallowed up our child.

Imachá imanan wawayta!—
    nispas waqashaq taytanqa,
        mamanqa.

c   Hinaspas, huk p'unchay mamanqa waqakushasqa kancha qhipachapi,
    hinaspa chayman q'inti hamusqa,
        rikhurimusqa.

d   Hinaspas nisqa q'intiqa muyupayaspa, *riyuw q'inti, riyuw q'inti:*
    —Piqpa, maypa wawanchá qaqapi waqashan?—
        nispas pasarqun,
            pasarqun.

e   Hinatas q'inti phawakusqanpi nimushaq.

B   a   Chay warmitaqsi nisqa:
        —Q'inti, imaynachá waqasqa, llakisqa kakushani wawaymanta,
        hinaspa chaywanraq hamushanki.—nispa.

    b   Chaytaqsi, rumita huqarirquspa ch'aqirqusqa rumiwan q'intita.

    c   Hinaspas chakinta p'akirqusqa.
        Hina chakinta p'akirquqtinqa
        q'intiqa phawarikapusqa wasi patanta.

    d   Waqaspalla,
        llakispallas
            kashasqa sipaspa mamanqa.

    e   Hinaspas yapamanta kutimusqa,
        muyumullasqataq q'inti, *riyuw q'inti, riyuw q'inti:*
        —Piqpa wawanchá qaqa patapi waqashan?—nispa.

C   a   Chay warmiqa nisqas:
        —Icha yachashanmanpaschá wawaypa maypi kasqanta.—nispa.
            Hinaqa:
            —Yachashankipaschá wawaypa maypi kasqanta q'inti, siwar q'inti.—
                nispa tapuykukusqa.

    b   Tapuykukuqtinqa:
        —Yachashaniyá maypis kasqanta.
            Chakichallayta ama p'akiwankimanchu karqan.
                Chankakawan chakiyta hampiykuwankiman chayqa,
                    misk'ita quykuwankiman wakta,
                        willaykusqaykiyá.—nispas nin.

    c   —Riki. Kutichipusqaykiyá misk'itapis chankakatapis watakunaykipaq.—nispas nin.
        Hina warmiqa rantisqa chankakata, misk'itapis,
            hinaspa rumi pataman churaykusqa.

    d   Hinaspas siwar q'inti chimpaykuspa
        mikhurakapusqa misk'ita,
            chakintapis watayukusqa chankakawan.

    e   Hinaspas willaykusqa warmimanqa:
        —Qaqapi waqashan wawaykiqa.—nispa.

ii   (The Return Home)

A   a   Hinaspa:
        —Q'ipirampuway, ári.—
            nispas warmiqa mañakun.

What could have happened to our child!—
  so saying, they wept, her father
   and her mother.

c And so one day her mother was weeping just behind the outside wall
   and Hummingbird came there,
    showed up there.

d And so, as Hummingbird flew around, he spoke, whirr hummingbird whirr:
   —Whose child, which child is weeping on the clifftop?—
   so saying, he flew past,
    and flew past again.

e Thus Hummingbird spoke to her as he flew by.

B a Now the woman also spoke:
   —Hummingbird, here I am weeping, sorrowing over my child,
   and you come to me with that!—she said.

b Now with that, she took up a stone and hit Hummingbird with it.

c And so she broke his leg.
   As soon as she broke his leg,
    Hummingbird flew up to the top of the house.

d The shepherdess's mother was there
   weeping
    and sorrowing.

e And so, again he came back,
   Hummingbird came around again, whirr hummingbird whirr:
   —Whose child is weeping on the clifftop?—he said.

C a That woman said:
   —Maybe he knows where my child is.—she said.
    So:
   —Maybe you know where my child is, Hummingbird, beautiful turquoise
   Hummingbird.
    —she asked.

b And when she asked:
   —Yes, I do know where she is.
   You shouldn't have broken my leg.
    If you fix my leg with some brown molasses,
     if you give me some sweets too,
      then I will tell you where she is.—he said.

c —Of course. I will thank you by giving you sweets and molasses to tie up your leg.
  —she said.
   Then the woman bought molasses and sweets
    and she put them on top of a rock.

d And so Hummingbird, drawing near,
   ate the sweets,
    and tied up his leg with the molasses.

e And so he told the woman:
   —Your child is weeping on the clifftop.—he said.

ii (The Return Home)

A a And:
   —Bring her to me, please.—
    thus saying, the woman pleaded for a favor.

b   —Misk'ita quykapuwanki chayqa, q'ipirampusqaykiyá paqarin.—nispas nin.

c   —Qupullasqaykin.—

     nispas warmiqa nin.

d   —Chay.—

     nispaqa ninsi q'inti.

e   Hinata nispas pasapun phawaylla wasi patanta q'intiqa.

B a   Hinaspas chay p'asñaq tiyasqan qaqa pataman chayaspa qhawasqa kunturpa pasananta.

     Kunturqa pasansi.

       Phawayllas chinkaripun.

  b   Hinaspas, kuntur chinkariqtin hinas q'inti p'asñamanqa rin, *riyuw q'inti, riyuw q'inti:*

     —Piqpa, maypa mamataytanchá waqashan wasinpi?—nispa.

     Pasarqun.

  c   Pasarquntaqsi q'inti:

     —Piqpa mamataytanchá 'q'ipirampuway wawayta' nispa waqashan?—nispa.

     —Munaqtiykiqa q'ipiruykimanyá.—

       riyuw q'inti, riyuw q'inti nispasyá p'asñataqa muyupayashan.

  d   Hinas p'asñaqa nisqa:

     —Siwar q'inti, q'ipiqarqapuwayári.—nispa.

     —Manapunichu q'ipirapuwankiman mamataytayman?—nispas nin.

  e   —Q'ipirqapusqaykiyári.

     Wawantintachá apasqayki.

     Chaypaq allinta kamarirqukuy.—nispas nin.

C a   Hinaspas, wawantin q'ipicharikun chay sipasqa.

     Aknas q'intiqa q'ipirikamun wawantinta taytamamanpa wasinman.

     Chayaspas taytamamanta nisqa *riyuw q'inti, riyuw q'inti:*

     —Kayqa ususiykita chayachinpushani.—nispa.

  b   —Kusa, q'inti, q'ipinpuwanki wawayta.—

     nispa taytamamanqa nisqa.

  c   Hinaspas misk'ita quykapusqa q'ipimusqanmanta.

D a   Hinaspas q'intiqa:

     —Wisq'aychis ususiykichista.

     Hamunqa qatayniykichis,

       ama rikuchinkichischu.—nispas nisqa.

       —Wawantinta wisq'ankichis.—

         nispas kamachisqa.

  b   —Paqarinña hamusaq qatayniyki hamuqtin willaqniyki.—

  c   —Chay.—

     nispas qhipakunku.

E a   Hinaspas wisq'allanku ususintaqa.

     Chaypis tapunku sipasta,

       maypi kamusqanta,

         piwan purikusqanta,

           imaynapi wawayuq rikukusqanmanta imas.

  b   Payqa willasqas:

     —Huk mistin pusawan hañawaspa.

     Q'ipiwanmi wasinman.

b   —If you give me sweets, I will bring her to you tomorrow.—he said.

c   —I'll give them to you.—
     thus saying, the woman said.

d   —Good.—
     thus saying, Hummingbird said.

e   Thus saying, Hummingbird flew up over the top of the house.

B a   And so, arriving at that clifftop where the shepherdess was sitting,
        he waited for Condor to leave.
            Condor left.
                He disappeared quickly.

   b   And so, as soon as Condor had disappeared Hummingbird went to the
        shepherdess, whirr hummingbird whirr:
            —Whose parents, which parents are weeping in their home?—he said.
            He flew past.

   c   Now again Hummingbird flew past:
            —Whose parents are weeping, saying "bring back our child"?—he said.
            —If you want me to, I'll take you back.—
                saying whirr hummingbird whirr, he flew around and around the shepherdess.

   d   Then the shepherdess said:
            —Beautiful turquoise Hummingbird, please carry me back.—she said.
            —But perhaps you won't really take me to my parents?—she said.

   e   —Yes, I will take you.
        I'll take you and your child too.
            Get yourself all ready.—he said.

C a   And so he bundled both her and her child on to his back.
        In this way, Hummingbird carried her, with her child, back to her parents' home.
            When they arrived, he spoke to the parents, whirr hummingbird whirr:
                —Here I have brought you your daughter.—he said.

   b   —Thank you, Hummingbird, for bringing our child.—
        so saying, her parents spoke.

   c   And so they gave him sweets for having brought their daughter.

D a   And so, Hummingbird:
            —Hide your daughter.
                Your son-in-law will come,
                    don't show her to him.—so saying, he spoke.
                        —Hide her child too.—
                            so saying, he instructed them.

   b   —Tomorrow I will come to warn you when your son-in-law comes.—

   c   —Good.—
        so saying, they stayed behind.

E a   And so they hid their daughter.
        And in there, they asked her,
            where she had gone,
                who she had gone with,
                    and how she came to have a child.

   b   And she told them:
            —A misti who attracted me took me away.
            He carried me to his home.

Chaypin hap'imuwan.

Kay wawatapis wachakamunin chaypin.—nispas.

c —Kunturmi runaq rikch'ayninpi taripamuwarqan,

hinaspas pusawarqan wasinta.

Paypa wawanyá kay wawa.—

nispas willakun.

iii (The Empty Nest)

A a Chaykamas q'intiqa chayasqa chay kunturpa wasinta.

K'ayratas yacharqachisqa, qaqa pukyupi k'ayrata:

—Qanmi kaypi mallkuq chayamunanpaq t'aqsakuq tukunki warminman tukuspa.

Wawanpa p'achallanta t'aqsakuq tukunki.—nispas nin.

b —Aw.—

nispas k'ayraqa nin.

c Hina niqtintaqsi, q'inti nin:

—Chayarqamunqa chayqa,

'Imata ruwashanki?' niqtinqa 'T'aqsakushanin' nispan ninki.

Hinaspaqa 'Usqhayá, usqhay t'aqsakuy' nispan nisunki.

d Ñachu t'aqsarunkiña' niqtinqa 'Manaraqmi, manaraqmi' ninki.

'Usqhayta, usqhayta hamuy' nisuqtiykitaq pasayaqapunki unuman.

Pakarakapunki.

Ama lluqsimunkiñachu huktawanpis.—ninsi.

e Chayta niykuspataqsi qaqa pataman p'itarqun q'inti.

K'ayrataqsi warmi tukurqun.

Hinaspas t'aqsakun warmi.

B a Kunturtaqsi hamushanña.

Q'intitaqsi qaqa patamanta qhawashan pakachallamanta.

K'ayrataqsi t'aqsaykushan pukyupi.

b Kunturqa hinaspas chayan k'ayraq t'aqsakusqan chay pataman.

—Imatan ruwashanki?—nispas nin.

c —T'aqsakushaniraqmi, wiraqucháy.—nispas nin.

d —Usqhayá, usqhayá t'aqsakuy.—nispas nin.

e —Ari.—

nispas nin k'ayra warmiqa.

C a Hinaspas pasaykun kunturqa wasinta.

Kunturqa chaypiqa wawanta waturikun.

b Manas kapusqachu wawanqa.

"Maytataq aparqunri wawatari?"

nispas nin kunturqa.

—Maytaq wawari?—

nispas nin kunturqa warminta wawata waturikuspari.

c —Chaypichá kashan riki.—nispas nin.

d —Usqhay, usqhaylla hamuy!

Aychatan apamushani.

Chayta wayk'unki.—ninsi.

e —Kunallan, kunallan.—nispas nin.

D a —Ñachu, ñachu?—

nispas yapa qhawarillantaq.

—Ñachu, ñachu?—

nispas mat'in.

There he took me

and this baby was born there too.—she said.

c   —A condor with the appearance of a man got hold of me,

and so he took me to his home.

This child is his child.—

thus she told them.

iii   (The Empty Nest)

A   a   Meanwhile, Hummingbird arrived at Condor's home.

He instructed Frog, Frog who was playing in the spring:

—When Condor arrives you will be his wife washing clothes here.

You will be washing his child's clothes.—he said.

      b   —Ah.—

thus saying, Frog spoke.

      c   As soon as he spoke thus, Hummingbird said:

—When he arrives,

and when he says, "What are you doing?" you say, "I'm just washing clothes."

And then he will say, "Hurry up, hurry up with the washing."

      d   And when he says, "Are you finished washing yet?" you say, "Not quite yet."

And when he says, "Hurry, hurry up and come," you disappear into the water.

Hide.

Don't come out again.—he said.

      e   Now having said that, Hummingbird hopped up to the top of the cliff.

Now Frog turned into a woman.

And so, the woman was washing clothes.

B   a   Now Condor is coming.

Now Hummingbird is watching, hidden, from the clifftop.

Now Frog is washing at the spring.

      b   And so Condor arrived at the spot where Frog was washing.

—What are you doing?—he said.

      c   I'm still just washing clothes, my dear.—she said.

      d   —Hurry up, hurry up with the washing.—he said.

      e   —Yes.—

the Frog, woman, said.

C   a   And so Condor went into his home.

Condor looked for his child in there.

      b   But his child was not there.

"Where did she take the child?"—

Condor said.

—Where is the child?"—

so saying, Condor asked his wife, looking for the child.

      c   —It must be there, of course.—she said.

      d   —Hurry, hurry up and come!

I brought some meat.

You can cook it.—he said.

      e   —In a minute, in a minute.—she said.

D   a   —Are you ready yet? Are you ready yet?—

so saying, he looked again.

—Are you ready yet? Are you ready yet?—

so saying, he demanded.

b   —Chayraqmi, chayraqmi t'aqsashani.—
    nispas nin warmiqa.

c   Hina niqtinqa, phawarispa:
    —Hayt'asayki má!—
    nispas nin kunturqa.

E   a   Hinas unuman, *p'ultín!* nispa pasayarakapusqa k'ayraqa.
        Manas wawa warapis kasqachu.
            Rumichallas chaypi kasqa.
                Kunturpa ñawillanpaqsi hina rikhurisqa.

    b   Aknaspas tiyaspa qhawashasqa pukyuta kunturqa:
        —Kutimunqachá,
            kutimunqachá.—nispa.

    c   Manas kutimunchu.

Kunturmantawan P'asñamantawan (P'asña) — Profile, Text, Translation

Profile of *Kunturmantawan P'asñamantawan* (P'asña) — Act II

Act	Scene	Stanza	Verse	Incident	Markers (reportive validator throughout)
II				(REFUGE)	
	i			(Hummingbird)	
		A	a	Condor leaves	time word
			b	Hummingbird comes	hinas, time word
			c	Hummingbird sees her	hinas
			d	She laments	turn at talk, hinas
			e	H. bargains	turn, hinas
		B	a	H. goes to her home	location, hinas
			b	flowers	hinas
			c	H. enjoying	hinas
			d	man chases H.	hinas
			e	"you hit me!"	turn, hinas

	b	—Almost, I'm still washing.—
		so saying, the woman spoke.
	c	As soon as she said this, Condor flew out:
		—I'll kick you!—
		so Condor spoke.
E	a	Then into the water, splash!, the Frog disappeared.
		And there were no diapers.
		There were only stones there.
		It had only been for Condor's eyes.
	b	Now then, Condor sat down and waited, watching at the spring:
		—Maybe she'll come back.
		maybe she'll come back.—he said.
	c	But she did not come back.

Act	Scene	Stanza	Verse	Incident	Markers
II				(REFUGE)	
		C	a	"you know where?"	turn, hinas
			b	"I've seen"	turn, hinas
			c	"Bring her home"	turn, hinas
	ii			(The Return Home)	
			a	H. goes	loc., hinas
			b	Condor gone	actor change
			c	Shepherdess only	actor change
			d	H. takes her	act. ch., hinas
			e	H. leaves her safe	loc.
	iii			(The Empty Nest)	
			a	Condor comes home	act. ch., hinas
			b	Condor angry	turn, hinas
			c	Condor asks	act. ch., hinas
			d	no one knows	act. ch., manas
			e	someone suggests	act. ch., hinas

II			(REFUGE)
	i		(Hummingbird)
	A	a	Kunturqa sapa kuti hinas wasinmanta uraqashallanpuni,

                        tatakuqa aycha maskhaqchá purishan.

       b   Hinas huk p'unchay kuntur aychaman purishanankamas,

                  huk luli waqaqta uyarispas kunturpaq wasinta waykurquq kasqa.

       c   Hinas luliqa chaypi huk sipasta tupachin.

       d   Hinas sipasqa khuyayta waqaspas luliman willakun:

            —Llamayta michikusharqani hinan huk wayna taripamuwarqan

            hinaspataq ñawiyta ch'irmiykuchispa kayman kuntur

            q'ipiykarqamuwan.

               Chaymantapachan kaypi llakikuymanta wañurqushaniña.

               Tatamamaypas manan kaypi kasqayta yachanchu.

                Khuyapayariway!

                 Ama hinachu kay!

                  Tatamamayman willarinpuway.

                   Nuqaña, imatan mañakunki chayta

                   churaykapusqayki!—

                    nispas sipasqa lulita nin.

       e   Hinas luliqa:

            —Misk'ita churaykapuwankiman chaypachaqa puriyman ari.—

            nispas willakuq pasan.

     B   a   Hinas luliqa chay sipaspaq wasinta purin.

            Chay wasita chayan.

       b   Hinas chaypiqa huk t'ika kancha kasqa.

       c   Hinas luliqa t'ikakunataq chaypi ch'unqashan.

       d   Hinas huk qhari lulitaqa hayurparin.

       e   Hinas luliqa chay runata nin:

            —Nuqata hark'ashawankiraqtaq!

            Manachu nuqaqa ususiyki maypi kasqanta yachashani?—nispas nin.

     C   a   Hinas kay runaqa chayta uyarispa lulita tapuykun:

            —Qan yachashankichu ususiy maypi kasqanta?—

            nispas tapurikun.

       b   Hinas luliqa nillantaq:

            —Arí, nuqa rikushani ari.

            T'ika kanchaykimanta mana hark'awankimanchu hina,

             nuqa ususiykita chayarquchimuykiman ari.—

             nispas luliqa nin.

       c   Hinas chay runaqa kusirikuspa lulita nin:

            —Ususillayta maymantapas chayarquchimpuwayqa!

            Hinaspaqa t'ika kanchaypi tuta p'unchaypas kakushay,

             manan pipas hark'asunkichu.—

             nispas runaqa nin.

   ii   (The Return Home)

       a   Hinas luliqa kunturpaq wasinta pasan.

Translation of *Kunturmantawan P'Asnamantawan* (P'asña)—Act II

II			(REFUGE)
	i		(Hummingbird)
	A	a	Frequently, Condor flew away from his home,

        perhaps he was going to look for meat.

      b   Then one day while Condor was gone looking for meat,

           Hummingbird, hearing weeping, came into Condor's home.

      c   Then Hummingbird found the shepherdess there.

      d   Then the shepherdess, weeping piteously, told Hummingbird:

           —As I was watching my llamas, a young man came up to me

           and a condor brought me here with my eyes tightly closed.

             Since then I am here dying of sorrow.

              My parents don't know I'm here.

                Take pity on me!

                  Please!

                    Go tell my parents!

                      Whatever you ask for, I will give to you!—

                        so saying, the shepherdess spoke to Hummingbird.

      e   Then Hummingbird said:

           —If you would give me sweets, I would go tell them.—

           so saying, he went off to tell them.

    B a   Then Hummingbird went to her home.

           He arrived at that home.

      b   Then there was a flower garden there.

      c   Then Hummingbird went in there to suck the flowers.

      d   Then a man shooed Hummingbird off.

      e   Then Hummingbird said to that man:

           —So, you want to keep me away!

           But aren't I the one who knows where you daughter is?—so saying,

             he spoke.

    C a   Then, when he heard that, the man asked Hummingbird:

           —Do you know where my daughter is?—

           so saying, he asked him.

      b   Then, Hummingbird spoke again:

           —Yes, I have seen her.

           If you don't try to keep me out of your flower garden,

             I will bring your daughter here to you.—

             so saying, Hummingbird spoke.

      c   Then, full of joy, that man said to Hummingbird:

           —Bring my daughter here to us from wherever she may be!

           And then stay in the flower garden whenever you want, day or night,

             no one will stop you.—

             so saying, the man spoke.

    ii   (The Return Home)

      a   Then Hummingbird went back to Condor's home.

b   Kunturqa manas wasinpichu kasqa,
      maypichá kunturqa,
        llama uña suwakuqchá purin.

c   Sipasllas khuyay waqasqa chaypi kashasqa.

d   Hinas luliqa sipasta q'ipirikun,
      hinaspas wasin chayay pasan.

e   Sipastaqa tatamamanpaq makinmansa saqiykampun,
      hinaspas luliqa t'ikata ch'unqarikuspa wasinta kutipun.

iii   (The Empty Nest)

a   Hinas kunturqa llama aycha aparisqa wasinta chayan.
      Warmintachá waturikun.
        Tukuy chhikatachá maskhan.

b   Hinas kunturqa pasaq phiñas kashan, hinas:
      —Mayqin supaypaq wawantaq warmiytari aparqun?
      Tariylla tarisaqqa
        mikhurqusaqpuni.—
          nispas kunturqa wasinmanta lluqsirqamun.

c   Hinas kunturqa tupachisqanpi hina tukuyllatas tapukun.

d   Manas pipas rikuq kanchu.

e   Hinas pichá willarqun:
      —Luli warmiykitaqa q'ipirqun!—nispa.

Acknowledgments

This paper is dedicated to the memory of Padre Jorge A. Lira and to the Quechua Community Ministry Project and its director, Stephan H. Hornberger, for their unflagging devotion to the Quechua people, their language, and their culture. It was under the auspices of the Quechua Community Ministry Project that I was able to learn Quechua and become acquainted with Padre Lira and his work.

Acquaintance with the work of the Proyecto Experimental de Educación Bilingüe—Puno (PEEB), including its publication, *Unay Pachas,* came through research carried out in 1982–1983 with the permission and support of the PEEB, the Dirección Departamental de Educación in Puno, Peru, and the Instituto Nacional de Investigación y Desarrollo de la Educación (INIDE) in Lima. The Inter-American Foundation and the U.S. Department of Education (Fulbright-Hays) provided financial support. Their assistance is gratefully acknowledged.

A version of this paper was presented at the Conference on American Indian Languages at the annual meeting of the American Anthropological Association in November 1988 in Phoenix. I am grateful for comments by those at the session and for subsequent comments from Dell Hymes and Brian Swann.

b	Condor was not at home,
	he might be anywhere,
	perhaps he was out to steal a baby llama.
c	The shepherdess was in the house, weeping piteously.
d	Then Hummingbird put the shepherdess on his back,
	and so left to take her home.
e	He left the shepherdess safely in the hands of her parents,
	and so, having sucked on a few flowers, he returned to Condor's home.

iii   (The Empty Nest)

a   Then Condor arrived at his home, carrying llama meat.
        He looked for his wife.
        He looked everywhere.

b   Then Condor was very angry, then:
        —What child of the devil has taken my wife?
        When I find him,
           I will eat him.—
              so saying, Condor left his home.

c   Then Condor asked everyone he met.

d   No one had seen.

e   Then someone suggested:
        —Hummingbird took your wife away!—they said.

Notes

1. A few notes on the translations. First, in these stories, the gender of the Condor and the Shepherdess is clearly identified, while that of Frog (appearing only in Sipas) and Hummingbird is not. The shepherdess is clearly female, not by virtue of being a *llama michiq*, "one who shepherds the llamas," but by virtue of being a *sipas*, "young woman." Condor is clearly male, identified as *wayna*, "young man," in "P'asña and *wiraqucha*, "gentleman," in Sipas. Frog and Hummingbird, on the other hand, are never identified in such a way, and because personal pronouns and possessive markings in Quechua are gender-neutral, such ambiguity can be preserved. Unfortunately, in the translation into English, I have found it impossible to preserve this gender-neutral use of pronouns for Hummingbird without making an exceedingly awkward text. I have chosen to use the masculine personal pronoun for Hummingbird, primarily for reasons of ease in following Hummingbird's conversations with the shepherdess and with her mother.

Second, the reportive validator (*-si* or *-s;* see discussion above) and the narrative tense marker (*-sqa;* see discussion above and note 3), used to establish the reported (rather than witnessed) nature of the narrative, are not overtly translated in the English version; again in the interests of avoiding an awkward and confusing text.

Third, P'asña uses the word *luli*, rather than *q'inti*, for hummingbird. *Q'inti* appears in the Cusihuamán, Lira, and Hornberger and Hornberger dictionaries, with the meaning "hummingbird." *Luli* appears only in the Cusihuamán dictionary, with the meaning "mute." I do not know the origin or extent of the use of *luli* to mean hummingbird.

2. In citing from the narratives, I will refer to them by shortened title followed by the verse number. All citations in this paper are from Act II of the respective narratives. Thus, the citation Sipas iiBc refers to: "Kunturpa munasqan sipasmanta," Act II, scene ii, stanza B, verse c.

3. For explanations of Quechua grammar referred to here and throughout the paper, see Cerrón-Palomino, especially 278–88 and 310–15.

4. The tense/aspect shifts do not show up well in the translation, but may be seen in the original (e.g. at Sipas iBc to iBd, iiEb to iiEc, iiiAe to iiiBa; and at P'asña iiia to iiib). In general, southern Peruvian Quechua distinguishes three basic tenses (past, marked with *-rqa;* present or non-future; and future), the progressive aspect (marked with *-sha*), and the narrative tense (marked with *-sqa*). Narrative tense, so called because it is used primarily in narratives, indicates that the speaker was not a direct participant in the action described. It may indicate that the speaker was not present (e.g., as in the remote past), or not in control (as in dreams or in drunkenness); or it may express an attitude of surprise on the part of the speaker (cf. Cerrón-Palomino 212, 273; Cusihuamán 170).

References

Allen, Catherine J. *The Hold Life Has: Coca and Cultural Identity in an Andean Community.* Washington: Smithsonian Institution Press, 1988.

Arguedas, José María. *The Singing Mountaineers: Songs and Tales of the Quechua People.* Edited and with an introduction by Ruth Stephan. Austin: University of Texas Press, 1957.

Bauman, Richard. *Verbal Art as Performance.* Rowley, Massachusetts: Newbury House, 1984.

Briggs, Lucy T. "Talking Foxes or Dog that Speaks Latin: Two Expressions of Andean Myth." Paper presented at the 46th International Congress of Americanists. Amsterdam, July 1988.

Cerrón-Palomino, Rodolfo. *Lingüística Quechua.* Cusco, Peru: Centro de Estudios Rurales Andinos "Bartolomé de Las Casas," 1987.

Cusihuamán G., Antonio. *Diccionario Quechua: Cuzco-Collao.* Lima, Peru: Ministerio de Educación, 1976.

———. *Gramática Quechua: Cuzco-Collao.* Lima, Peru: Ministerio de Educación, 1976.

Harrison, Regina. *Signs, Songs, and Memory in the Andes: Translating Quechua Language and Culture.* Austin: University of Texas Press, 1989.

Hornberger, Esteban, and Nancy Hornberger. *Diccionario Tri-lingüe Quechua de Cusco: Quechua, English, Castellano.* 1978. La Paz, Bolivia: Wiraqocha Biblioteca, 1983.

Hymes, Dell H. *Foundations in Sociolinguistics: An Ethnographic Approach.* Philadelphia: University of Pennsylvania Press, 1974.

———. *"In Vain I Tried to Tell You": Essays in Native American Ethnopoetics.* Philadelphia: University of Pennsylvania Press, 1981.

———. "Language, Memory, and Selective Performance: Cultee's 'Salmon's Myth' as Twice Told to Boas." *Journal of American Folklore* 98(1985): 391–434.

———. "Verse Analysis of a Kathlamet Chinook Text Preserved by Franz Boas: Charles Cultee's 'Southwest Wind's Myth.'" *Exigences et perspectives de la sémiotique: Recueil d'hommages pour A. J. Greimas/Aims and Prospects of Semiotics: Essays in honor of A. J.*

Greimas. Ed. H. Parret and H. G. Ruprecht. Amsterdam/Philadelphia: John Benjamins Publishing Co., 1985. 953–72.

——. "A Note on Ethnopoetics and Sociolinguistics." *Working Papers in Educational Linguistics* [Philadelphia: University of Pennsylvania, Graduate School of Education] 3.2 (1987): i–xxi.

Hymes, Virginia. "Warm Springs Sahaptin Narrative Analysis." *Native American Discourse: Poetics and Rhetoric*. Ed. Joel Sherzer and Anthony Woodbury. Cambridge: Cambridge University Press, 1987. 62–102.

Isbell, Billie Jean. *To Defend Ourselves: Ecology and Ritual in an Andean Village*. Austin, Texas: Institute of Latin American Studies, 1978.

Jakobson, Roman. "Shifters, Verbal Categories and the Russian Verb." Cambridge, Massachusetts: Harvard University, Russian Language Project, 1957. (Reprinted in his *Selected Writings*, 2:130–47. The Hague: Mouton, 1971).

——. "Concluding Statement: Linguistics and Poetics." *Style in Language*. Ed. Thomas Sebeok. Cambridge, Massachusetts: MIT Press, 1960. 350–73.

Lengyel, Thomas E. "On the Structure and Discourse Functions of Semantic Couplets in Mayan Languages." *Anthropological Linguistics*, 30.1 (1988): 94–127.

Lira, Jorge A. *Canto de amor*. Lima, Peru: Talleres Gráficos P. L. Villanueva S. A., 1956.

——. *Diccionario kkechuwa-español*. 1941. Bogotá, Colombia: Secretaria Ejecutiva Permanente del Convenio "Andres Bello," 1982.

——. *Issicha Puytu: Drama Quechua anónimo (edición bilingüe)*. Lima, Peru: Milla Batres Editorial, 1974.

——. *Tutupaka llakta o el mancebo que venció al diablo*. Lima, Peru: Milla Batres Editorial, 1974.

Mannheim, Bruce. "Poetic Form in Guaman Poma's Wariqsa Arawi." *Amerindia: revue d'ethnolinguistique amérindienne* 11 (1986): 41–57, 64–67.

——. "Popular Song and Popular Grammar, Poetry and Metalanguage." *Word* 37.1–2 (1986): 45–75.

——. "Couplets and Oblique Contexts: The Social Organization of a Folksong." *Text* 7.3 (1987): 265–88.

Sherzer, Joel. "Poetic Structuring of Kuna Discourse: The Line." *Language in Society* 11 (1982): 371–90.

——. "A Discourse-Centered Approach to Language and Culture." *American Anthropologist* 89.2 (1987): 295–309.

Sherzer, Joel, and Anthony Woodbury, eds. *Native American Discourse: Poetics and Rhetoric*. Cambridge: Cambridge University Press, 1987.

Stephan, Ruth. "Introduction." *The Singing Mountaineers: Songs and Tales of the Quechua People*. Ed. José María Arguedas. Austin: University of Texas Press, 1957. 3–21.

Tedlock, Dennis. *The Spoken Word and the Work of Interpretation*. Philadelphia: University of Pennsylvania Press, 1983.

Unay pachas: Qheshwa simipi qollasuyu aranwaykuna. Lima, Peru: Proyecto Experimental de Educación Bilingüe, 1983.

Index

Benjamin, Walter, 64
Beowulf, 250
Berman, D., 145
Bevis, William, 15
Bierhorst, John, 12, 359–60, 361, 363, 364
Big Elk (Omaha orator), 43
Big Jewish Book, A (Rothenberg), 66
Bilingualism, 115
Bird imagery, 44–45
Bird, Larry, 195
Black Buffalo (Teton leader), 43
Black Elk, Nicholas, 44
Blake, William, 68
Blanchot, Maurice, 64
Blankets, rabbit-fur, 216
Blessingway, 250
"Blood Clot Boy," 286–88
Boa myths, 393–98
Boas, Franz: Deloria and, 276; "Der Donnervogel" and, 165–73; *Indianische Sagen,* 164, 165; Kathlamet Salmon myth and, 97; *Kootenai Tales,* 12–13; *Kwakiutl Tales,* 129; Kwakw'ala texts and, 125–62; Pentlatch and, 163–66; scientific literality and, 11–13, 46
"Boil Story," 187–88
Books. *See* Manuscripts
Borgia codices, 327, 331, 333. *See also Codex Borgia; Codex Fejérváry-Mayer*
Bourdieu, Pierre, 230, 233, 234
Bradbury, John, 43
Breton, André, 67, 68, 70
Bright, William, 98, 427
Brinton, Daniel Garrison, 7, 46
Brotchie, William, 130
Brulé texts, 39, 40–42, 44
Buechel, Eugene, 295
Buenaventura, Pedro de San. *See* San Buenaventura, Pedro de
Buffalo, John Rush, 95, 98, 106–12, 113, 114
Burgoa, Francisco de, 326
Burke, Kenneth, 83, 84, 85, 94
Burlin, Natalie Curtis, 9–10, 11
"Butterfly" songs and dances, 19, 232–38

Cadastrial records, 318
Caedmon's Hymn, xiv
Cain (Old Testament character), 415–16, 417–18, 419, 421
Calendars, Mesoamerican, 331
Calligrammatic owl-songs, 73
Calnek, Edward E., 327
Cano, Juan, 322, 323

Cantares Mexicanos, 331, 333; authorship of, 360; imagery in, 361, 362; on Mesoamerican books, 325; *Romances de los Señores de la Nueva España* and, 357–58, 359; trustworthiness of, 315
Canto de amor (Lira), 443
"Caps" (narrative devices), 198
Cardenal, Ernesto, 56–58
Carochi, Horacio, 363
Carpenter, Edmund, 77
Carrasco, Pedro, 57
Cashinawa myths, 53
Caso, Alfonso, 319–20, 326
Cass, Lewis, 35–36, 38, 43–44, 45
Castillo, Bernal Díaz del. *See* Díaz del Castillo, Bernal
Castro, Michael, 11
Catechistic texts, 339–41
"Categorical abstraction," xvii
Catholic Action movement, 423
Centipede imagery, 361–62
Central American texts, 46, 313–440
Central Yupik Eskimo discourse, 427
Ceremony (Silko), 55, 56
Change of Skin, A (Fuentes), 59
Channing, Walter, 37
Chanson de Roland, 250
Chants: Chippewa, 6–7; Kuna, 429–39; Mazatec, 59–60; Navaho, 7–8, 59; Seneca, 68. *See also* Melodies; Songs
"Chant to the Fire-Fly," 6–7
Chantway ceremonies, 243
Chantway novels, 55–56
Charles V, Holy Roman emperor, 322
Cherokee war songs, xv–xvi, 6, 15, 34
Chiasmus, 193, 197
Chichimec myths, 362
Chiefs, 116, 214, 436–39
Chilam Balam of Chumayel, 330, 331
Children, 94–95
"Children of the Forest of Word-Souls" (Cardenal), 57
Chimalpahin (Mesoamerican chronicler), 333
Chinook Jargon, 164–65
Chinook texts, 84, 85, 93, 105–6, 114–15, 427. *See also* Clackamas narratives; Wishram Chinook narratives
Chippewa chants, 6–7
Choctaw texts, 34, 47

Chona, Maria, 213
Christian devotional texts, 339–53
Chuquimamani, Rufino, 444
"Circular figures" (narrative devices), 197–98, 199, 201
Clackamas narratives, 12, 16–17, 90, 99, 100, 115, 288
Clans, Hopi, 212, 214. *See also* Kinship, Desert Indian
Clark, Ella E., 115
Clavigero, Francisco Javier, xiii
Clifford, James, 4
Codex Borgia, 321, 331, 332
Codex Fejérváry-Mayer, 321, 329, 330, 331
Codex Selden, 332. *See also* Selden Roll
Codex Tro-Cortesiano, 321, 329, 330
Codex Vaticanus A, 323, 327, 329, 330, 331
Codex Vaticanus B, 331
Codex Vindobonensis, 321, 330, 331, 332
Codice Chimalpopoca, 328
Colby, L. W., 304–5
Collection of Mexican Songs. See Cantares Mexicanos
Coloquios y Doctrina Cristiana (Sahagún), 348
Color terms, 372. *See also* Redness metaphors
Comox people, 163, 166, 167
Compendium of Nahuatl Grammar (Sullivan), 365
"Condor and the Shepherdess, The," 441–69
Constitutive ambiguities, 359, 360
Contextual ambiguities, 359, 360, 361
"Corn Farmer and an Evil Thing, and a Priest and a Small Friend, A," 391–404
Corn myths, 332, 368–86, 394
Corrales (Spanish colonial administrator), 316–17, 322
Cortés, Hernán, 322, 351
Cosmology, Mesoamerican, 321, 329–31, 372, 404
Couplets, 388, 450
"Coyote and Deer," 89–90
"Coyote and Eagle's Daughter," 95, 98, 99, 106–12, 113, 114, 117–19
"Coyote and Junco," 86
"Coyote and Tree Chief," 12–13
Coyote lore, Navajo, 246, 251
"Coyote Releases Water Dammed up by the Frogs," 96–97

Pueblan-Tlaxcalan script, 326
Pueblo song-poems, 231–32, 234
Puget Sound Basin languages, 180–81
Pulsifer, Louisa, 177–79, 182, 186, 187, 188
Purdy, Liza, 183, 185
Puritans, 34
Puyallup narratives, 181

"Qaniè qaò yaè," 7–8
"Q̓ániqiɫaẁ and Ćáću," 131–57
Quechua narratives, 441–69
Quechua people, 316
Quetzalcoatl (Cardenal), 57, 58
Quetzalcoatl narratives, 58, 59
Quetzalcóatl no era del PRI (del Río), 58
Quiché Maya narratives, 374, 406–25, 427
Quileute narratives, 115
Quipus, 316
Q̓umgiləs (Kwagul informant), 156
Quni Raya myth, 453
Quotatives, 284–89

"Rabbit Dance Song," 307
Rabbit-fur blankets, 216
Rafael, Vicente L., 340
Ragas, 308
Ramírez, Serapio, 332
Ramsey, Jarold, 114, 116
Rank, social, 155, 166, 346
Rasmussen, Knud, 77
Rath, John, 145
Raw and the Cooked, The (Lévi-Strauss), 54
Reade, John, 46
Rebuses, 320
Red English language, 18–19, 196
Redfield, Robert, 391
Red Moustache (Navajo storyteller), 250
Redness metaphors, 352
Redundant personal pronouns, 373–74, 375
Reed, Nelson, 391
Reichard, Gladys, 249, 250
Reincarnation, 154, 155
Reportive validators, 448–49
Reservations, Navajo, 244
"Restitution," translational, 51–52
Reuben, Nettie, 98
Rexroth, Kenneth, 301
Rhyme, 448
Rhythm, 39, 392
Ribeiro, Darcy, 54, 56

Rincón, Antonio de, 363
Río, Eduardo del, 58
Ritual of the Bacabs, The, 330
Rituals, Hopi, 214, 216
Rius (Eduardo del Río), 58
River Junction Curly (Navajo storyteller), 250–51
Romances de los Señores de la Nueva España, 357, 359
Romanticism, 44
Rosa, Cruz de la, 332
Ross, Charlotte, 93
Rothenberg, Jerome, 13–14, 59, 60, 69
Rude, Noel, 87–88
Ruffo de Forli, Juan, 322
Ruiz de Alarcón, Hernando, 331

Saanich Salish narratives, 98, 114
Sabina, María, 59
"Sacred Pipe Recordings" (Cardenal), 57
Sacred symbolism, 345–46, 352
Sacred, The, 195
Sage, Rufus B., 39, 40–42, 43, 44, 46
Sahagún, Bernardino de, xiv, 324, 330, 341, 348, 356–57, 365
Sahaptin narratives, 180, 444
Salamander myths, 53
Salish language, 181. *See also* Pentlatch language; Saanich Salish narratives; Twana nursery tales
Salmon myths: in Columbia River narratives, 115–16; Kathlamet, 97; Kwagul, 150; Lushootseed, 197, 200, 201
Sam, Casimir, 195
San Blas Kuna discourse, 426–40
San Buenaventura, Pedro de, 341
Santa Cruz Maya, 390–91
Sapir, Edward, 87, 90, 92, 114, 213, 260
Satire, 389
Sautel, Mary Madeline de. *See* De Sautel, Mary Madeline
"Scene-agent ratio," 85
Schoolcraft, Henry Rowe: *Algic Researches,* 33; Burlin and, 10; "Chant to the Fire-Fly" and, 6–7; editorial practices of, 42–43, 44–45, 46; Evers/Molina and, 23; Longfellow and, 38, 51–52; *Oneóta,* 42, 43, 44–45; Simms and, 38
Schwitter, Kurt, 65
Scientific literality, 11–14, 46

Scripts. *See* Hieroglyphic writing system; Logosyllabic writing system; Pictoglyphic writing system
"Seal and Her Younger Brother Lived There," 16–17
Sechelt people, 163, 167
"Second Order" religious societies, 211
Seduction theme, 396–97
Sekaquaptewa, Emory, 232
Selden Roll, 330, 331. *See also Codex Selden*
Seneca texts, 68, 71, 72
Senghor, Leopold S., 67
"Sentence straighteners," Desert Indian, 261
Serpent myths, 393–98, 410–11
"17 Horse-Songs of Frank Mitchell," 70, 71, 73–76
Seven Types of Ambiguity (Empson), 358
Sexuality: in "A Corn Farmer and an Evil Thing," 396–97; fish and, 153–54; in Kwagul housestories, 155–56; in "Q̓ániqiɫaẁ and Ćáću," 138–39, 145, 156; in "White Plume," 283
Seymour, Peter, 18
Shah-co-pee (orator), 36–37
Shaking the Pumpkin (Rothenberg), 14, 69
Shape-gender system, Kwakw'ala, 150–51
"Shepherdess Who Was Loved by a Condor, The," 443, 446–52, 454–63
Sherzer, Joel, 368, 371, 444
"She Who Dwells in the Rocks," 289
Shokleng origin myth, 374
Shootingway, 250
Sickness, 272
Siebert, Frank T., xv
Sierra Popoluca narratives, 368–86
Silko, Leslie Marmon, 55, 56, 196
"Silver E" (Waldman), 59
Simms, William Gilmore, 37, 40
Simpson, Louis, 84–85, 87, 89–90, 92
Sin, 410–11
Sioux texts, 11
"Sipas," 443, 446–52, 454–63
Skagit people, 186
Skokomish Twana nursery tales, 176–90
Skunk myths, 399–400
Slocum, Marianna C., 332

Argument realization ... c2000.   (Card 2)

ISBN 1-57586-265-4 (alk. paper). — ISBN 1-57586-266-2 (pbk. : alk. paper)

1. Grammar, Comparative and general—Verb phrase.   2. Lexical-functional grammar.   3. Grammar, Comparative and general—Case.   I. Butt, Miriam, 1966-   .   II. King, Tracy Holloway, 1966-   .   III. Title.   IV. Series.

P281.B88   2000   415—dc21   0-41344
                                                                                                            MARC